Fodor's 2009

S0-BRB-326

COSTA RICA

Where to Stay and Eat
for All Budgets

Must-See Sights
and Local Secrets

Ratings You Can Trust

Fodor's Travel Publications   New York, Toronto, London, Sydney, Auckland
www.fodors.com

FODOR'S COSTA RICA 2009

Editors: Joanna G. Cantor, Adam Taplin
Editorial Contributors: David Dudenhoefer, Dorothy MacKinnon, Suzanna Starcevic, Jeffrey Van Fleet

Editorial Production: Tom Holton
Maps & Illustrations: David Lindroth, Mark Stroud, *cartographers*; Bob Blake, Rebecca Baer, *map editors;* William Wu, *information graphics*
Design: Fabrizio La Rocca, *creative director*; Guido Caroti, Siobhan O'Hare, *art directors*; Tina Malaney, Chie Ushio, Ann McBride, Jessica Walsh, *designers*; Melanie Marin, *senior picture editor*
Cover Photo (Playa Tamarindo): Heeb Christian/age fotostock
Production/Manufacturing: Angela L. McLean

ISBN 978–1–4000–1956–4

ISSN 1522–6131

SPECIAL SALES

This book is available at special discounts for bulk purchases for sales promotions or premiums. Special editions, including personalized covers, excerpts of existing books, and corporate imprints, can be created in large quantities for special needs. For more information, write to Special Markets/Premium Sales, 1745 Broadway, MD 6-2, New York, New York 10019, or e-mail specialmarkets@randomhouse.com.

AN IMPORTANT TIP & AN INVITATION

Although all prices, opening times, and other details in this book are based on information supplied to us at press time, changes occur all the time in the travel world, and Fodor's cannot accept responsibility for facts that become outdated or for inadvertent errors or omissions. So **always confirm information when it matters,** especially if you're making a detour to visit a specific place. Your experiences—positive and negative—matter to us. If we have missed or misstated something, **please write to us.** We follow up on all suggestions. Contact the Costa Rica editor at editors@fodors.com or c/o Fodor's at 1745 Broadway, New York, NY 10019.

PRINTED IN THE UNITED STATES OF AMERICA

10 9 8 7 6 5 4 3 2 1

Be a Fodor's Correspondent

Your opinion matters. It matters to us. It matters to your fellow Fodor's travelers, too. And we'd like to hear it. In fact, we need to hear it.

When you share your experiences and opinions, you become an active member of the Fodor's community. That means we'll not only use your feedback to make our books better, but we'll publish your names and comments whenever possible. Throughout our guides, look for "Word of Mouth," excerpts of your unvarnished feedback.

Here's how you can help improve Fodor's for all of us.

Tell us when we're right. We rely on local writers to give you an insider's perspective. But our writers and staff editors—who are the best in the business—depend on you. Your positive feedback is a vote to renew our recommendations for the next edition.

Tell us when we're wrong. We're proud that we update most of our guides every year. But we're not perfect. Things change. Hotels cut services. Museums change hours. Charming cafés lose charm. If our writer didn't quite capture the essence of a place, tell us how you'd do it differently. If any of our descriptions are inaccurate or inadequate, we'll incorporate your changes in the next edition and will correct factual errors at fodors.com immediately.

Tell us what to include. You probably have had fantastic travel experiences that aren't yet in Fodor's. Why not share them with a community of like-minded travelers? Maybe you chanced upon a beach or bistro or B&B that you don't want to keep to yourself. Tell us why we should include it. And share your discoveries and experiences with everyone directly at fodors.com. Your input may lead us to add a new listing or highlight a place we cover with a "Highly Recommended" star or with our highest rating, "Fodor's Choice."

Give us your opinion instantly at our feedback center at www.fodors.com/feedback. You may also e-mail editors@fodors.com with the subject line "Costa Rica Editor." Or send your nominations, comments, and complaints by mail to Costa Rica Editor, Fodor's, 1745 Broadway, New York, NY 10019.

You and travelers like you are the heart of the Fodor's community. Make our community richer by sharing your experiences. Be a Fodor's correspondent.

Happy traveling!

Tim Jarrell, Publisher

CONTENTS

MAPS

COSTA RICA IN FOCUS

ABOUT THIS BOOK

Our Ratings

Sometimes you find terrific travel experiences and sometimes they just find you. But usually the burden is on you to select the right combination of experiences. That's where our ratings come in.

As travelers we've all discovered a place so wonderful that its worthiness is obvious. And sometimes that place is so experiential that superlatives don't do it justice: you just have to be there to know. These sights, properties, and experiences get our highest rating, **Fodor's Choice,** indicated by orange stars throughout this book.

Black stars highlight sights and properties we deem **Highly Recommended,** places that our writers, editors, and readers praise again and again for consistency and excellence.

By default, there's another category: any place we include in this book is by definition worth your time, unless we say otherwise. And we will.

Disagree with any of our choices? Care to nominate a place or suggest that we rate one more highly? Visit our feedback center at www.fodors.com/feedback.

Budget Well

Hotel and restaurant price categories from ¢ to $$$$ are defined in the opening pages of each chapter. For attractions, we always give standard adult admission fees; reductions are usually available for children, students, and senior citizens. Want to pay with plastic? **AE, D, DC, MC, V** following restaurant and hotel listings indicate whether American Express, Discover, Diners Club, MasterCard, and Visa are accepted.

Restaurants

Unless we state otherwise, restaurants are open for lunch and dinner daily. We mention dress only when there's a specific requirement and reservations only when they're essential or not accepted—it's always best to book ahead.

Hotels

Hotels have private bath, phone, TV, and air-conditioning and operate on the European Plan (aka EP, meaning without meals), unless we specify that they use the Continental Plan (CP, with a continental breakfast), Breakfast Plan (BP, with a full breakfast), or Modified American Plan (MAP, with breakfast and dinner), or are all-inclusive (AI, including all meals and most activities). We always

list facilities but not whether you'll be charged an extra fee to use them, so when pricing accommodations, find out what's included.

Many Listings	
★	Fodor's Choice
★	Highly recommended
✉	Physical address
✛	Directions
⌂	Mailing address
☎	Telephone
🖶	Fax
⊕	On the Web
✍	E-mail
✒	Admission fee
☉	Open/closed times
Ⓜ	Metro stations
▭	Credit cards

Hotels & Restaurants	
🏨	Hotel
⤴	Number of rooms
☐	Facilities
⦿	Meal plans
✕	Restaurant
⌔	Reservations
⌁	Smoking
🕮	BYOB
✕🏨	Hotel with restaurant that warrants a visit

Outdoors	
⛳	Golf
⛺	Camping

Other	
☕	Family-friendly
⇨	See also
✉	Branch address
☞	Take note

**SAN JOSÉ**	This is not the Costa Rica of the postcards and travel brochures, and you should not sacrifice precious rain-forest and beach days for time in the sprawling, congested capital of San José. It is the political, economic, and cultural center of the country, the font from which all things emanate and hub to which all roads lead. To liken the city to New York or London is grossly unfair; it can't compare. But to the Costa Rican out in the provinces, it is the Big Apple … well, maybe "Big Pineapple." San José is also an amazingly friendly city, and though you should keep your wits about you, it is safer than many other Latin American capitals. No place in Costa Rica can top the city for restaurants, culture, and nightlife, and after a week of slogging through the rain forest, your body may crave a dose of civilization.
**THE CENTRAL VALLEY**	San José is smack dab in the center of this tidy, prosperous mountain valley with numerous day-trip possibilities. The valley's many beautiful inns are alternatives to staying in the capital on your first and last nights in Costa Rica. And in fact, the international airport is not in San José, but in the Central Valley, in Alajuela. The metro area's urban sprawl is spreading to the Central Valley in some spots, as is evidenced by the shopping-malled, office-towered, fast-food-ed highway entrances to Escazú and Santa Ana, but a few kilometers away, oxcarts bearing sugarcane bound for the local mill or coffee beans destined for the local processor trundle down gravel roads. Three provincial capitals—Alajuela, Cartago, and Heredia—pinpoint the valley; all are quieter versions of what San José once was and never will be again. Farther afield lie the country's two most accessible active volcanoes (Poás and Irazú), the historic Orosi Valley, and the agricultural community of Turrialba, fast becoming Costa Rica's white-water capital.
**THE NORTHERN PLAINS**	It's tough to pigeonhole the vast region that Costa Ricans call the *Zona Norte* (Northern Zone). Suffice it to say, if you can't find something in the Northern Plains that interests you, you should consider turning in your passport. Monteverde Cloud Forest, a cooler tropical forest, is the place to fly through the forest on a canopy tour—this is the region that gave birth to the concept of zipping along cables (while securely harnessed) between treetop platforms. Nearby, Lake Arenal beckons windsurfers, and Arenal Volcano, one of the world's 10 most active, spits fire and warms the waters of

WHAT'S WHERE

	the Tabacón Hot Springs. Two overlooked and underrated destinations with eco-appeal are the Sarapiquí region, whose many eco-lodges deserve more popularity, and the wetland Caño Negro Reserve near the Nicaraguan border.
THE NORTH PACIFIC	Guanacaste Province, the country's most touristed region, manages to combine beaches and bovines without missing a beat. The dry, grassland interior of the Nicoya Peninsula remains the domain of cowboys and cattle, the folkloric image most associated with Costa Rica, although the rest of the country has happily embraced it as its own. A chain of enormously popular beaches lines the coast, and this is the North Pacific of the tourist brochures. Each beach has traits that confer on it a unique personality: Flamingo's quiet refinement is a respite for the well-to-do; Tamarindo's nightlife is legendary; Avellanas's strong swells draw the surfers; Ostional's nesting sea turtles continue a millennia-old cycle of life; and the Papagayo Peninsula's all-inclusive resorts envelop you in creature comforts. And here's a region with its own small-but-growing international airport, in Liberia. So if your travels are concentrated here, there's no reason to fly in and out of San José at all.
THE CENTRAL PACIFIC	Costa Rica's Central Pacific coast mixes sophistication and funkiness, sometimes right down the street from each other. The port city of Puntarenas, once the country's favorite beach destination (but no longer), anchors the region. The beaches south of here are some of the nearest to San José, hours closer than those on the North Pacific coast, and undeniably popular because of their easy access. This is Costa Rica's "party hearty" region, with funky surf towns Jacó and Malpaís and somewhat more refined, but still lively, twin communities Quepos and Manuel Antonio. You need not be a 19-year-old spring-breaker to enjoy the Central Pacific. Plenty of grown-up and family-friendly activities are available between the dens of revelry, and we've found the best selection of restaurants outside San José on this section of the coast. Some of the strands of beach get downright isolated—just you, the macaws, and the monkeys. And calmer beach towns like New Agey Montezuma are just a ferry ride away, across the gulf on Nicoya Peninsula's southern tip.

The South rarely sees first-time visitors. In fact, many second- and third-timers have never ventured south of Cartago. But inevitably, once they do, they kick themselves for waiting so long. Terms get bandied about to describe the region: "the Amazon of Costa Rica" or "the most biodiverse place on the planet." Clichéd though they sound, they're true. Corcovado National Park conjures up the Tarzan-movie jungle images you've seen. Lodges in its Osa Peninsula accommodate those who wish to bond with nature but don't wish to sleep *directly* in it. But not all is jungle down here: the region takes in Chirripó, Costa Rica's highest peak, a long hike of moderate difficulty. And Dominical, Zancudo, and Pavones, three of our favorite beach towns—ones rarely mentioned in the fun-in-the-sun pantheon—are here in the South Pacific. Access (or lack thereof) means everything here, and roads can be atrocious even by Costa Rican standards, making it essential to travel by 4WD vehicle or fly.

Despite its name, Costa Rica's Caribbean is no St. Lucia. It doesn't have miles of white-sand beaches or crystal-blue waters. There is a similar English-speaking, Afro-Caribbean population here, but mixed with indigenous, Asian, and the dominant Latino culture. What this version of the Caribbean (also called "the Atlantics") *does* have is nature galore, with dense forests, coral reefs, and lumbering turtles engaging in age-old nesting rituals. Long the province of European backpackers, the region is less known in North American circles. Many Costa Ricans write it off as all reggae, rain, and robbery. Yes to the first. Mostly yes to the second: it does rain more here than elsewhere in the country, which is why it's so green. But no to the third: crime is no more prevalent here than anywhere else in the country. If you seek luxury resorts, look elsewhere. Instead, the Caribbean has a wide price range in everything from backpackers' digs to trendy bed-and-breakfasts at a fraction of Pacific-coast prices.

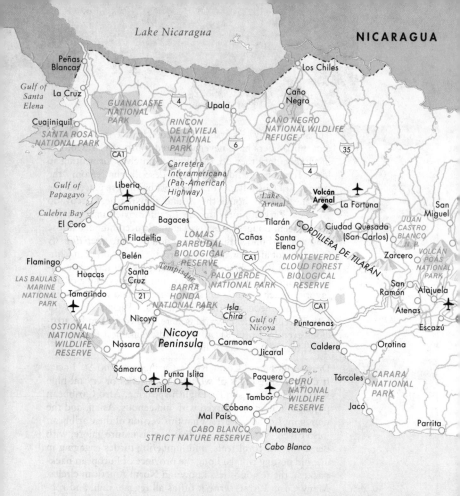

Lake Nicaragua

NICARAGUA

Peñas Blancas

Gulf of Santa Elena

La Cruz

Los Chiles

Caño Negro

Upala

4

Cuajiniquil

GUANACASTE NATIONAL PARK

RINCON DE LA VIEJA NATIONAL PARK

CAÑO NEGRO NATIONAL WILDLIFE REFUGE

SANTA ROSA NATIONAL PARK

6

35

CA1

Carretera Interamericana (Pan-American Highway)

4

✈ Liberia

Gulf of Papagayo

Comunidad

Volcán Arenal ◆ ✈ La Fortuna

San Miguel

JUAN CASTRO BLANCO N.P.

Culebra Bay

El Coro

Bagaces

Tilarán

Ciudad Quesada (San Carlos)

VOLCÁN POAS NATIONAL PARK

Filadelfia

Cañas

Santa Elena

CORDILLERA DE TILARÁN

Zarcero

Lake Arenal

Belén

LOMAS BARBUDAL BIOLOGICAL RESERVE

CA1

MONTEVERDE CLOUD FOREST BIOLOGICAL RESERVE

Flamingo

Huacas

Santa Cruz

Tempisque

PALO VERDE NATIONAL PARK

San Ramón

Alajuela

LAS BAULAS MARINE NATIONAL PARK

✈ Tamarindo

21

BARRA HONDA NATIONAL PARK

Isla Chira

Gulf of Nicoya

CA1

Atenas

Escazú

Nicoya

Puntarenas

Orotina

OSTIONAL NATIONAL WILDLIFE RESERVE

Nosara

Nicoya Peninsula

Carmona

Jicaral

Caldera

Sámara ✈ Punta Islita

Paquera

Tárcoles

CARARA NATIONAL PARK

Carrillo

✈ Tambor

CURÚ NATIONAL WILDLIFE RESERVE

Jacó

Cobano

Mal País

Montezuma

Parrita

CABO BLANCO STRICT NATURE RESERVE

Cabo Blanco

PACIFIC OCEAN

TO ISLA DEL COCO
↓

0 _____ 30 miles

0 _____ 45 km

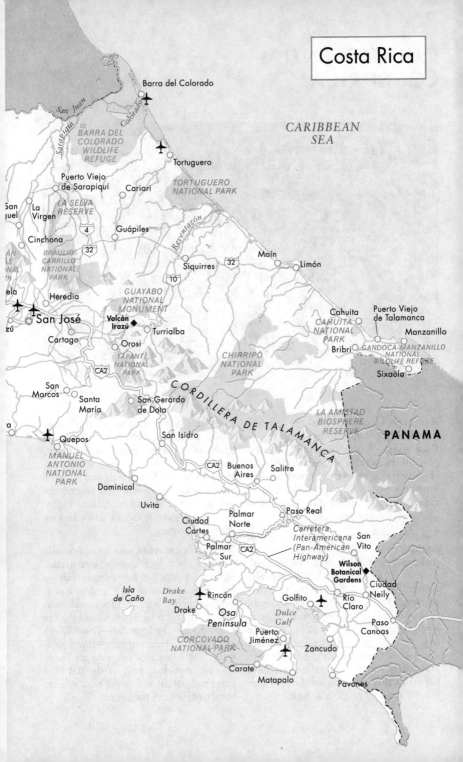

Costa Rica

QUINTESSENTIAL COSTA RICA

Coffee

If nearby Honduras was the original "Banana Republic," 19th-century Costa Rica was a "Coffee Republic." Coffee remains inexorably entwined with the country, with economists paying close attention to world prices and kids in rural areas still taking class time off to help with the harvest.

The irony is that it's hard to get a decent cup of the stuff here. True to economic realities of developing countries, the quality product gets exported, with the inferior coffee staying behind for the local market. (The same is true of bananas, Costa Rica's other signature agricultural product.) The best places to get a cup of high-quality Costa Rican coffee are upscale restaurants and hotels. Owners understand foreign tastes and have export-quality coffee on hand. Gift shops sell the superior product as well.

Festivals

Every day is a patron saint's day somewhere in Costa Rica, and unless you spend all your time ensconced in a resort, you'll probably see a sign for some community's annual *festejo patronal* (patron-saint festival), in homage to its namesake and protector. A loud firecracker explosion rouses participants at dawn to kick off the festivities.

The festivals mirror Costa Rica: devoutly Catholic but increasingly secularized, with bingo games, rickety carnival rides—a certain amount of luck and prayer is in order here—horse parades, and amateurish bullfights (the bull is not killed in Costa Rica). The Imperial—Costa Rica's most popular brand of beer—flows copiously. But it is still a religious tradition, and an important part of the day is a mass and parade where the saint's figure is carried through the streets.

Futbol

Like everyone else on this soccer-mad isthmus, Costa Ricans take their game seriously and can get nasty when it comes to their national team; U.S. players reported being pelted with batteries and bags of urine during one game. When the national team returned after three consecutive losses in the 2006 World Cup, an angry crowd met them at the airport chanting "dog" at the coach.

Costa Rica's most esteemed player is Paulo Wanchope, who scored 45 times in 78 matches and has starred for teams like Manchester United in England. The big local rivalry ("derby" in soccer parlance) is between LD Alajuelense and Deportivo Saprissa (La Monstruo Morado, or "The Purple Monster"), who have each won the Costa Rican championship 24 times.

Celebrating Smallness

In a bigger-is-better world it's refreshing to find a country that revels in its smallness. The monuments glittering with gold common elsewhere in Latin America are nowhere to be found here. Streets and sidewalks seem a little narrower in Costa Rica, and beds and doorways are a little shorter, too. Even the name Costa Ricans give to themselves, Ticos, comes from their peculiar way of forming the diminutive of nouns. Other Spanish speakers add the suffix -*ito* to denote something small (*un momentito*), but Costa Ricans say *un momentico*.

QUINTESSENTIAL COSTA RICA

Oxcarts

The oxcart is the folkloric symbol of Costa Rica and a common subject for local artisans. The western Central Valley town of Sarchí is the best place to buy these souvenirs, which can take the form of objects as small as paper-clip holders, ashtrays, and earrings; larger items like salad bowls and planters; or full-size oxcarts–turned–coffee tables. (The larger works can be disassembled and shipped home.)

Oxcarts do still lumber along rural roads ferrying coffee and sugarcane (and sometimes passengers) to and fro. But in the 21st century they are more likely to do parade duty; San José holds a large oxcart festival the last weekend in November. The brightly painted carts look anything but utilitarian, with wheels rotating in kaleidoscopic colors.

Mom & Pop Places

Some 75% of the properties in Costa Rica are small, independently owned lodgings with fewer than 30 rooms, even in San José. An individual style imprints each of those lodgings, from scruffy hostels to fashionable inns. What these places lack in a concierge and business center they more than make up for in individuality.

The chain hotels are beginning to take hold in Costa Rica, especially on the North Pacific coast. But the fly-'em-in, fly-'em-out mass tourism, fine-tuned in Mexico and the Caribbean Islands, remains in its infancy here. That can make a visit to Costa Rica a bit pricier, since you are usually purchasing your lodging, airfare, transportation, and tours à la carte. But it also keeps tourism here more small-scale and exclusive.

WHEN TO GO

Costa Rica has an astounding number of microclimates, dictated by its many forests and changes in altitude, so the weather varies dramatically for such a small country. *For information about specific regions, see "When to Go" at the front of each chapter.*

The sunniest, driest season in most of the country occurs from roughly mid-December through April, which is the busiest tourist season. For you, that means more advance planning, some flexibility in choosing a hotel, and higher prices. Afternoon showers kick in by May and last through November most everywhere, with a brief dry season in June and July. The Caribbean coast flies in the face of these norms with rains spread out fairly evenly throughout the year, with brief *drier* seasons February through April and September through October. Costa Rica promotes the rainy season as the "green season," touting lush vegetation, smaller crowds, and lower prices. Showers interrupt your afternoon beach time, and remote roads can be washed out during the worst of the rains.

Temperatures generally range between 70°F (20°C) and 85°F (30°C). It's the humidity, not the heat, that causes you discomfort, especially in the dense forest of the Caribbean coast, the northern lowlands, and the Osa Peninsula. The arid North Pacific is Costa Rica's hottest region, with temperatures frequently exceeding 90°F (33°C) in the dry season.

One final point: we typically hear, "I didn't realize the rain forest would be so … *rainy.*" Well, you heard it here: it rains often and heartily in the rain forest. The dense foliage and elaborate root systems rely on frequent showers year-round.

Climate

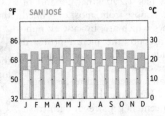

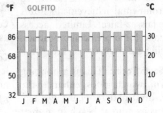

IF YOU LIKE

Beaches

Costa Rica has 1,290 km (799 mi) of coastline to choose from, most of it lined with beaches which are, by law, all public. Most are not the picture-postcard white strands of the Caribbean Islands or Mexico; the dark sand here is of volcanic origin and waters tend to be rough, not crystal blue. Note that beaches near population centers get strewn with trash quite quickly. It's one of the great ironies of Costa Rica that a country renowned for its environmental achievements litters with such laissez-faire. Limited access tends to make for more scenic beaches. The following are some of our favorites.

Dominical, South Pacific. This is a hopping surfer town, which does enhance the experience, and in that regard we recommend this as a great beach in a great beach town.

Malpaís, Central Pacific. Accessed via a steep gravel road, Malpaís is a quiet strand ripe for beachcombing and sunning.

Playa Flamingo, North Pacific. Though not very isolated, Flamingo is an example of how environmentally conscious communities can make their beaches sparkle.

Playa Grande, North Pacific. Conservationists have kept this beach pristine for nesting leatherback turtles.

Playa Pavones, South Pacific. The surfing is good at remote Pavones, a stunning combination of black sand, tropical forest, and glistening waters.

Punta Uva, Caribbean. This beach is the farthest from town of the Puerto Viejo de Talamanca beaches, and the most pristine.

Tortuguero, Caribbean. The turtle population here makes this isolated beach one of the world's top naturalist draws.

Bird-Watching

As part of the narrow isthmus connecting the Americas, Costa Rica is a natural biological melting pot. With less than 0.03% of the planet's surface, it is home to some 875 bird species, more than the United States and Canada combined. Some stay year-round; others come and go with winter migration.

Caño Negro, Northern Plains. Waterfowl, such as jabiru and snail kites, are abundant.

Carara National Park, Central Pacific. Scarlet macaws are reliable sightings, as are great egrets, boat-billed herons, anhingas, and trogons.

Cerro de La Muerte, South Pacific. This is probably the best place in the country to spot a resplendent quetzal.

Corcovado National Park, South Pacific. The largest population of (endangered) scarlet macaws in the country lives here.

Monteverde Cloud Forest, Northern Plains. The resplendent quetzal, the blue-crowned motmot, the orange-bellied trogon, and the emerald toucanet are just some of the 400 species that have been logged here.

La Selva Biological Station, Northern Plains. If you're interested in (but totally clueless about) bird-watching, sign up in advance for the Birdwatching 101 course. Scientists have tallied nearly 500 species here.

Tortuguero National Park, Caribbean. The bare-throated tiger heron, the American sun grebe, and the agami heron are some of Tortuguero's many waterfowl species.

Rain Forests

Costa Rica has set aside some 15% of its territory for national parks and reserves. Yet deforestation takes place at an alarming rate. The country's old-growth forests have been falling victim to illegal logging. This is aided by a scarcity of resources to enforce environmental laws and the pressures of development. That said, Costa Rica's existing rain forests thrive. A typical hectare (2½ acres) of forest might be home to nearly 100 species of trees. (Contrast that with a mere 30 in the richest forests of North America.) Go with a guide, both for your safety and for the information they can provide. We forever marvel at their ability to spot a sloth at a hundred paces.

Braulio Carrillo National Park, Northern Plains. Though it's the closest rain forest to San José, this primary swath of jungle is difficult to access, with dense flora and tough trails. But determination yields impressive mammals, birds, and plants.

Corcovado National Park, South Pacific. If you don't mind the mud, you'll love the wild and woolly primary forests here.

Manuel Antonio National Park, Central Pacific. Even a quick jaunt along the trails lets you see squirrel monkeys, white-faced coatis, and iguanas.

Monteverde Cloud Forest Reserve, Northern Plains. This forest is the most famous of Costa Rica's cloud-forest reserves.

Surfing

Deliciously warm water, year-round waves, and two coasts add up to one of the world's best-known surfing destinations. There's even better news: that popularity hasn't yet translated into overcrowding. Most surfers bring their own boards, as evidenced by the crowds that get off the plane and make a beeline for the oversize luggage carousel, but you'll find plenty of places to rent equipment if you're not quite that hard-core.

Jacó, Central Pacific. Easily accessible Jacó draws the many surfers who come here as much for the partying as the waves.

Pavones, South Pacific. It's a long trip to get here, but your reward is one of the world's longest left-breaking waves.

Puerto Viejo de Talamanca, Caribbean. One of the world's best (and toughest) waves, Salsa Brava, laps right offshore in town.

La Selva Biological Station, Northern Plains. This provides one of the best opportunities to see lots of wildlife without roughing it.

Tamarindo, North Pacific. The north coast's consummate surfing town and a good place for beginners; the stretch of shoreline north to Playa Grande and south to Playa Negra satisfies experts.

Volcanoes

Of Costa Rica's 300 or so volcanoes, some 230 are underwater and extinct. Of the 70 on dry land, 5 are active (listed below), 15 have been labeled "dormant"—projected to spring back to life at some undetermined future date—and the rest are extinct. Volcán Irazú got its second wind in 1963 after 30 years of inactivity. No one was more surprised than John F. Kennedy, who was here on a visit at the time and was sprinkled with ash like everyone else. Over four decades later, prediction is still an imprecise science.

Arenal, Northern Plains. The most famous volcano in Costa Rica, Arenal has a classic cone that forms an iconic backdrop

IF YOU LIKE

to the town of La Fortuna. On clear nights you can see red-hot lava spitting from its summit.

Irazú, Central Valley. A cinch to visit as a day trip from San José, here you can walk right up to the edge of steaming craters.

Poás, Northern Plains. Like Irazú, at Poás you can get close to the crater, and it is also close to San José. We find Poás, with its beautiful crater lake, a bit more impressive.

Rincón de la Vieja, North Pacific. This moonlike landscape of steaming craters and fizzing fumaroles is worth the rugged drive and rough hike.

Turrialba, Central Valley. The least-visited of the active volcanoes, Turrialba rises 3,330 meters (10,910 feet) above sea level. You can see the Pacific on a clear day.

White-Water Adventures

Insanely steep hills and heavy rainfall make the country a mecca for white-water sports, and there's a level of ease or difficulty to match anyone's expertise (or lack thereof). Have fun, but be brutally frank with yourself about your abilities and fears before setting out on any rafting or kayaking excursion. *(See CloseUp box "White-Water Thrills" in Chapter 2 for more guidelines.)* Base yourself in these places to find white-water outfitters.

La Fortuna, Northern Plains. Trips on the Toro, Balsa, San Carlos, and Sarapiquí rivers are offered out of La Fortuna.

Puerto Viejo de Sarapiquí, Northern Plains. Outfitters based here can take you on excursions similar to those offered from La Fortuna.

Quepos, Central Pacific. Head here for action on the Savegre and Naranjo rivers.

San José. You might not guess it, but San José is a major rafting center; the Reventazón and Pacuare rivers are close enough that you can be back in time for dinner. The Pacuare, El General, and Corobicí rivers lend themselves to overnight or multiday trips.

Turrialba, Central Valley. Many outfitters congregate in Turrialba, arguably the country's white-water capital, and close to the action.

GREAT ITINERARIES

BEACHES, RAIN FORESTS, AND VOLCANOES

Day 1: Arrival

Arrive in San José (most arrivals are in the evening) and head straight to one of the small luxury hotels north of the city in the Central Valley. A favorite of ours is Finca Rosa Blanca, a fairy-tale retreat overlooking miles of coffee farms.

Logistics: Brace yourself for long lines at immigration if you arrive in the evening along with all the other large flights from North America. Try to get a seat near the front of the plane and don't dawdle when disembarking.

Day 2: Poás Volcano & Tabacón Hot Springs

Volcán Poás, where you can peer over the edge of a crater, lies nearby. Fortify yourself with the fruits, jellies, and chocolates sold by vendors on the road up to the summit. A scenic drive takes you to the La Fortuna/Arenal Volcano area. Drop your luggage at one of many fantastic hotels (Montaña de Fuego is our pick for fabulous volcano views), and go directly to Tabacón Hot Springs & Resort. Take a zip line or hanging bridges tour through the forest canopy and then pamper yourself with a spa treatment. Finish the day by sinking into a volcanically heated mineral bath with a cocktail at your side as the sun sets behind fiery Arenal.

Logistics: Get an early start to get the best views of Poás. Shuttle vans (⇨ Bus Travel in Essentials) can get you to Arenal and have hotel-to-hotel service.

Day 3: Caño Negro Wildlife Refuge

Spend your entire day in the Caño Negro Wildlife Refuge, a lowland forest reserve replete with waterfowl near the Nicaraguan border.

Logistics: Book your trip the night before; tour operators in La Fortuna keep evening hours for exactly that reason. All transport will be included.

Day 4: Scenic Drive to the Central Pacific

Today's a traveling day—a chance to really see the country's famous landscape and infamous roads. (Believe us, they get a lot worse than this route.) A few hours' drive from Arenal takes you to fabled Manuel Antonio on the Central Pacific coast. Beyond-beautiful hotels are the norm here, and you have your choice of seaside villas or tree-shrouded jungle lodges. We like the hillside La Mariposa, which has commanding views.

Logistics: Hotel-to-hotel shuttle-van services (⇨ Bus Travel in Essentials) can get you to Manuel Antonio. If you drive instead, start out as early as possible. You'll pass through two mountainous stretches (between La Fortuna and San Ramón, and between Atenas and the coast) that fog over by midafternoon.

Day 5: Manuel Antonio National Park

Manuel Antonio is Costa Rica's most famous national park for a reason: it has beaches, lush rain forest, mangrove swamps, and rocky coves with abundant marine life. You can—and should—spend an entire day exploring the park, home to capuchin monkeys, sloths, agoutis, and 200 species of birds. It's also one of two locales in the country where you'll see squirrel monkeys.

Logistics: Almost all Manuel Antonio hotels have transport to the park. If yours doesn't, taxis are plentiful and cheap.

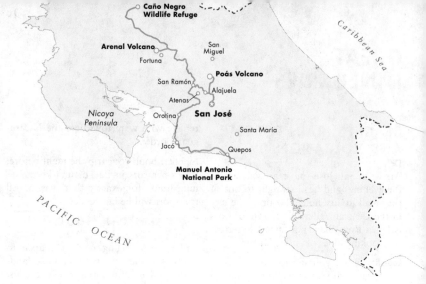

Day 6: Beach Yourself

Days 1 through 5 were "on the go" days. Reward yourself today with lots of relaxation. Manuel Antonio means beaches, and there are several to choose from. Manuel Antonio and neighboring Quepos mean restaurants, too, the best selection of any beach community in the country.

Logistics: Most everything you need here strings along the 5-km (3-mi) road between Quepos and Manuel Antonio National Park. It's practically impossible to get lost.

Day 7: San José

A morning drive back to San José gives you time to spend the afternoon in the city. We like the cozy, classy Hotel Le Bergerac. Visit the Teatro Nacional, the capital's must-see sight, and save time for late-afternoon shopping. An evening dinner caps off your trip before you turn in early to get ready for tomorrow morning's departure.

Logistics: As the number of visitors to Costa Rica grows, so does the number of passengers using Juan Santamaría Airport. We recommend you check in three hours before your flight. Better safe than sorry.

TIPS

■ Aside from Day 2, it's entirely possible to do this route without a car.

■ Hotels in the Central Valley and San José are used to booking visitors for their first and last nights in the country, and may allow you to leave items so you don't have to lug them around.

■ Arenal lies equidistant between Liberia and San José, but we suggest flying into San José for this itinerary because road access to Arenal and from Manuel Antonio is better.

■ Cloud cover makes volcano viewing the luck of the draw, and no one can negotiate with Mother Nature. Early mornings and dry season give you the best chances for seeing Arenal and Poás in action.

■ Get as early a start as possible if you're driving. The mountain roads between San José and La Fortuna and between Manuel Antonio and San José can fog over by midafternoon.

GREAT ITINERARIES

MORE BEACHES, RAIN FORESTS, AND VOLCANOES

Day 1: Arrival

Most arrivals to Liberia, Costa Rica's second international airport, are in early afternoon. You can't go wrong with any North Pacific beach, but we like Playa Hermosa for its pivotal location, one that lets you use it as a base for visiting area attractions. Check out small, personal, breezy Hotel Playa Hermosa/Bosque del Mar, the perfect antidote to the megaresorts that lie not too far away.

Logistics: The big all-inclusives up here have their own minivans to whisk you in air-conditioned comfort from airport to resort. Smaller lodgings such as Hotel Playa Hermosa/Bosque del Mar can arrange to have transport waiting, with advance notice.

Day 2: Playa Hermosa

Morning is a great time to laze on the beach in this part of Costa Rica. The breezes are refreshingly cool and the sun hasn't started to beat down. After lunch, explore Playa Hermosa's metropolis, the small town of Playas del Coco. Quite frankly Coco is our least favorite beach up here. But we like the town for its little souvenir shops, restaurants, and local color.

Logistics: Taxis are the easiest way to travel between Playa Hermosa and Coco, about 10 minutes away. Have your hotel call one, and flag one down on the street in town when it's time to return.

Day 3: Rincón de la Vieja Volcano

The top of Rincón de la Vieja Volcano with its steaming, bubbling, oozing fumaroles lies about 90 minutes from Hermosa. Lather on the sunscreen and head for the Hacienda Guachipelín and its volcano-viewing hikes, canopy tours, rappelling, horse riding, mountain biking, and river tubing. Cap off the day with a spa treatment, complete with thermal mud bath.

Logistics: If you don't have a rental car, book a private driver for the day, which can usually be arranged through your hotel.

Day 4: Golf or Diving

Golf is big up here. The 18-hole Garra de León course at the Paradisus Playa Conchal resort is about 45 minutes from Hermosa. The other popular, slightly pricey, sport here is scuba diving. Dive operators are based in nearby Playas del Coco or Playa Panamá. A daylong course gives you a taste of the deep.

Logistics: The resort will arrange transport to and from the golf course, and dive operators will pick you up from and return you to your hotel.

Day 5: Palo Verde National Park

We like the morning guided tours at Palo Verde National Park, one of the last remaining dry tropical forests in Central America. The Organization for Tropical Studies, which operates the biological station here, has terrific guides. Spend the afternoon observing nature in a more relaxed fashion with a float down the nearby Río Corobicí. (These are not the screaming rapids so famed in whitewater circles.)

Logistics: This excursion is a bit roundabout, so this is the day your own vehicle would come in handiest. But you can also hire a private driver (arranged through your hotel). Bring water to drink: it gets hot here.

Day 6: Sailing

Make your final day a relaxing one with a few hours on the waves. Many sailboats operate from this section of coast. Our choice is the 52-foot *Samonique III* (⇨ *Chapter 4*), which sails out of Playa Flamingo most afternoons at 2. A four-hour excursion includes sandwiches, appetizers, and an open bar. Legendary Pacific sunsets are tossed in at no extra charge.

Logistics: The *Samonique III* folks can arrange transport from hotel to boat and back again.

Day 7: Departure

Grab a last dip in the ocean this morning, because your flight departs from Liberia in the early afternoon.

Logistics: The advent of international flights to Liberia has fueled this region's meteoric rise to fame, but the airport's size has not kept pace with the number of passengers. Expansion is eventually on the way, but presently, lines can be long. Allow yourself plenty of time for check-in.

TIPS

■ Fly into Liberia. Although it's logical to think "San José" when planning flights to Costa Rica, it makes no sense if you plan to spend your entire time in the North Pacific.

■ A car is ideal for this itinerary, yet many area attractions and tour operators provide transport to and from area lodging if you aren't too far afield. (One of the reasons we like Playa Hermosa.)

■ All-inclusive resorts do a good job of organizing local excursions with local operators, so if you're staying at one, take advantage of them.

■ Getting from beach to beach often requires travel back inland. There is no real (i.e., navigable) coastal road.

■ If ever there were a case for an off-season vacation, this is it. This driest, hottest part of the country gets very dry and hot from January through April. The rains green everything up, and frankly, we prefer the region during the low season.

San José

Post Office, San José

WORD OF MOUTH

"We wish we had stayed an extra day to hang out in San Jose. I know it's not the highlight of Costa Rica, but we're city people and enjoyed feeling like we weren't surrounded by Americans all the time. . . . we tooled around shopping (cheap shoes for my wife!) and stopped for dessert and coffee. Latin America has great parks, plazas, and public art, which we enjoyed."

–tompak

WELCOME TO SAN JOSÉ

TOP REASONS TO GO

★ **Historic Barrios Amón and Otoya:** Enjoy the quiet tree-lined streets and century-old houses turned trendy hotels and restaurants.

★ **Gold and Jade museums:** They're not the Louvre or the Smithsonian, but still fascinating and worth a visit.

★ **Eating out:** The only place in Costa Rica with such a variety of cuisines.

★ **Nightlife:** The hottest scene in the country for dance clubs, bars, and chilled-out late-night cafés.

★ **Location, location, location:** From the capital's pivotal position you can be on a coffee tour, at the base of a giant volcano, or riding river rapids in just 30 minutes.

GETTING ORIENTED

In a high valley, 3,809 feet above sea level, San José lies just 9° north of the equator, but the altitude keeps things refreshingly temperate year-round. The metropolitan area holds more than 1 million residents, but the city proper is small, with some 300,000 people living in its 44 square km (17 square mi). Most of the sights are concentrated in three downtown neighborhoods, La Soledad, La Merced, and El Carmen, named for their anchor churches. The borders of the city are fuzzy: San José melts into its suburbs with nary a sign to denote where one community ends and another begins.

Parque Central

1 West of Downtown. The primarily residential neighborhoods West of Downtown are anchored by large La Sabana Park. Here you'll find the Museum of Costa Rican Art.

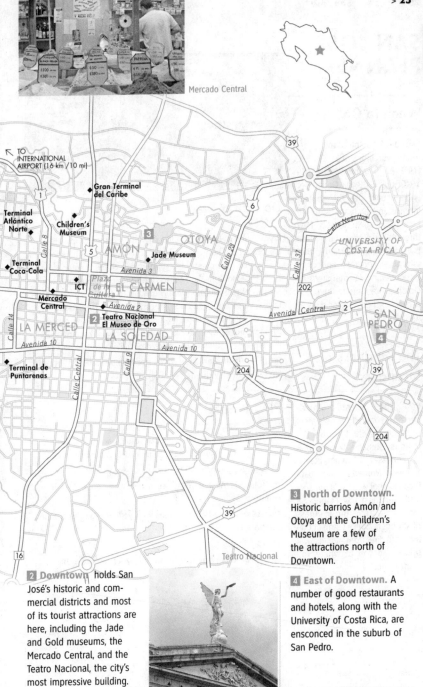

Mercado Central

TO
INTERNATIONAL
AIRPORT (16 km / 10 mi)

Gran Terminal
del Caribe

Terminal
Atlántico
Norte

Children's
Museum

OTOYA

Calle Negritos

UNIVERSITY OF
COSTA RICA

AMÓN

Terminal
Coca-Cola

Jade Museum

Calle 8

Calle 5

Avenida 3

EL CARMEN

Calle 20

Calle 37

ICT

Plaza
de la
Cultura

202

Mercado
Central

Avenida 2

Avenidal Central

2

SAN
PEDRO

LA MERCED

Teatro Nacional
El Museo de Oro

LA SOLEDAD

4

Avenida 10

Avenida 10

Calle 14

Calle Central

Calle 9

204

Terminal de
Puntarenas

39

16

204

3 North of Downtown.
Historic barrios Amón and
Otoya and the Children's
Museum are a few of
the attractions north of
Downtown.

39

Teatro Nacional

Teatro Nacional

2 Downtown holds San
José's historic and com-
mercial districts and most
of its tourist attractions are
here, including the Jade
and Gold museums, the
Mercado Central, and the
Teatro Nacional, the city's
most impressive building.

4 East of Downtown. A
number of good restaurants
and hotels, along with the
University of Costa Rica, are
ensconced in the suburb of
San Pedro.

SAN JOSE PLANNER

When to Go

San José is pleasant year-round, with highs of 26°C–28°C (79°F–83°F) and lows of 17°C–19°C (65°F–68°F). December and January are the coolest months. In March and April the heat picks up noticeably. May through November, the pattern is usually sunny mornings, brief afternoon showers, and clear brisk evenings. September and October are waterlogged, and it can rain nonstop for days at a time.

The Kindness of Strangers

In a 2003 *Scientific American* study called "Simple Acts of Kindness" (a take on the famous Blanche DuBois line in Tennessee Williams's play *A Streetcar Named Desire*), Costa Rica's capital was rated the second-friendliest city among 58 worldwide. Here the kindness of strangers doesn't stop at giving you directions; locals will often lead you to where you want to go.

Do It in a Day

If you have only a day in the city, the must-see stops are the National Theater and the Gold Museum, on the same block. We recommend the guided tour of the theater. If you have time, take in the Museo del Jade (Jade Museum) and Museo Nacional (National Museum) as well. Or pay a visit to the Museo para la Paz (Peace Museum). The Museo de Niños (Children's Museum), north of downtown, is a popular kid-pleaser. Our Good Walk (⇨below) takes you past the top sights, giving you a taste of the city in just an hour.

■TIP→ **Within San José, taxis are inexpensive and much faster than city buses.**

Play It Safe

San José is safer than most other Latin American capitals; the biggest problem is theft. Standard precautions apply:

- Exchange money only at banks.
- Select ATMs in well-lighted areas, and conceal cash immediately.
- Use only licensed red taxis with yellow triangles on the front doors.
- Park in guarded, well-lighted lots.
- Never leave anything in sight in your parked vehicle.

Day Trips from the Capital

Some of these attractions provide pickup service in San José. Alternatively, tour operators include many of these attractions on their itineraries. (⇨ See *Central Valley Planner* in Chapter 2 and *Northern Plains Planner* in Chapter 3 for tour-operator contacts.)

DESTINATION	FROM SAN JOSÉ (BY CAR)	
Butterfly Farm	45 min. west	⇨ p. 84
Café Britt	30 min. north	⇨ p. 94
Carara National Park	2 hrs. southwest	⇨ p. 291
Doka Estate	1 hr. west	⇨ p. 86
Guayabo National Monument	2 hrs. southeast. 4WD necessary	⇨ p. 109
INBioparque	10 min. north	⇨ p. 91
Irazú Volcano	60 min. east	⇨ p. 96
La Paz Waterfall Gardens	2 hrs. north	⇨ p. 84
Orosi Valley	60 min. southeast	⇨ p. 97
Poás Volcano	60 min. northwest	⇨ p. 108
Rain Forest Aerial Tram	45 min. north	⇨ p. 412
River Rafting	2–2½ hrs. southeast or north	⇨ p. 107
Sarchí	60 min. northwest	⇨ p. 121
Tortuga Island	3 hrs west	⇨ p. 280

■ TIP→ When you head back to town, browse the shops around Parque Morazán or in the suburb of Moravia.

WHAT IT COSTS IN DOLLARS				
¢	$	$$	$$$	$$$$
Restaurants				
under $5	$5–$10	$10–$15	$15–$25	over $25
Hotels				
under $50	$50–$75	$75–$150	$150–$250	over $250

Restaurant prices are per person for a main course at dinner. Hotel prices are for two people in a standard double room in high season, excluding service and tax (16.4%).

City Tours

Grayline Tours Costa Rica (☎2220–2126 ⊕www.graylinecostarica.com) operates an afternoon sightseeing-and-shopping tour.

The **Instituto Costarricense de Turismo** (⇨ *San José Essentials, below*) gives out a brochure outlining a self-guided historical walk through downtown.

Tico Walks (☎2283–8281 ⊕www.ticowalks.com) gives two-and-one-half-hour guided walking tours of downtown. Show up in front of the Teatro Nacional at 10 AM, Tuesday, Thursday, Saturday, or Sunday.

EXPLORING SAN JOSÉ

DOWNTOWN

By Jeffrey Van
Fleet

It's a trend seen the world over: businesses and residents flee city center for the ample space, blissful quiet, and lower-priced real estate of the suburbs. Costa Rica's burgeoning capital is no exception to that rule but downtown San José still remains the historic and vibrant (if noisy and congested) heart of the city. Government offices have largely stayed put downtown—actually, the presidency is the only public institution to have moved its headquarters to the 'burbs, but it's slated to come back to the *Centro* in the next few years—as have the majority of tourist attractions. If you spend any time here sightseeing, you'll find yourself in the center of San José.

Make no mistake: the city's traffic is overwhelming, and the narrow downtown streets, laid out in the days of the oxcart, barely handle the daily influx of vehicles. Pedestrians have the right of way here, but no driver seems to know or care about that little annoyance. You can take refuge along the several blocks of Avenidas Central and 4 and Calles 2 and 17 that have been converted into pedestrian malls, and take heart that more of those traffic-free streets—they call them *bulevares* here—are on city planners' drawing boards.

WHAT TO SEE

⑬ Catedral Metropolitana *(Metropolitan Cathedral)*. Built in 1871, and completely refurbished in the late 1990s to repair earthquake damage this neoclassical structure with a corrugated tin dome is not terribly interesting outside, but inside are patterned floor tiles, stained-glass windows depicting various saints and apostles, and framed polychrome bas-reliefs illustrating the 14 Stations of the Cross. The renovation did away with one small time-honored tradition: rather than purchase and light a votive candle, the faithful now deposit a 50-colón coin illuminating a bulb in a row of tiny electric candles. The interior of the small Capilla del Santísimo (Chapel of the Host) on the cathedral's north side evokes ornate old Catholicism, much more so than the main sanctuary itself, and is a place for quiet reflection and prayer. A marble statue of Pope John Paul II, created by Costa Rican sculptor Jorge Jiménez and unveiled in 2006, graces the garden on the building's north side. Masses are held throughout the day on Sunday starting at 7 AM, with one in English each Saturday at 4 PM, except the first Saturday of the month when it starts at 3 PM. ⊠ *C. Central, Avdas. 2–4, Barrio La Merced* ☎ 2221–3820 ☾ *Weekdays 6–6, Sun. 6 AM–9 PM.*

⑦ Centro Nacional de la Cultura *(National Cultural Center)*. Costa Rica cherishes its state enterprises. Here the government is your light and water utility, your phone company, your Internet service provider, your bank, your insurance agent, and your hospital. It is also your distillery and this complex served as the headquarters of the Fábrica Nacional de Licores (FANAL, or National Liquor Factory) until 1981, when it moved to a modern facility west of Alajuela. In a heartwarming exception to the usual "tear it down" mentality so prevalent in San José the Ministry of Culture converted the sloped-surface, double-block 1853 factory into a 14,000-square-meter center for its own offices, two theaters, and a museum. The metal **Teatro FANAL** (☎2222–2974), once the fermentation area, now hosts frequent theater and music performances. The clay-brick **Teatro 1887** (☎2222–2974) served as the factory's personnel office, and today dedicates itself to performances by the National Dance Company. What is now the theater's lobby was once the chemical testing lab. The stone-block storage depot next to the water towers at the southeast side of the complex became the **Museo de Arte y Diseño Contemporáneo** (⇨ *below*). A stone gate and sundial grace the entrance nearest the museum. ⊠ *C. 13, Avdas. 3–5, Barrio Otoya* ☎ *2257–5524* ⊙ *Weekdays 8–5, Sat. 10–5.*

⑯ **Correos de Costa Rica** *(Central Post Office).* The handsome, carved sea-green exterior of the post office, dating from 1917, is hard to miss among the bland buildings surrounding it. Stamp collectors should stop at the **Museo Filatélico** (*Philatelic Museum* ☎2223–6918), to the left as you face the stamp windows, for its display of first-day stamp issues. Early-20th-century telegraphs and telephones are also on display. The museum is open weekdays 8–5; admission is free. From the second-floor balcony you can see the loading of *apartados* (post-office boxes) going on below: Ticos (which is what Costa Ricans call themselves) covet these hard-to-get boxes, as the city's lack of street addresses makes mail delivery a challenge. ⊠ *C. 2, Avdas. 1–3, Barrio La Merced* ☎ *2202–2900* ⊙ *Weekdays 8–5:30, Sat. 8–noon.*

⑱ **Mercado Central** *(Central Market).* This block-long melting pot is a warren of dark, narrow passages flanked by stalls packed with spices (some purported to have medicinal value), fish, fruit, flowers, pets, and wood and leather crafts. But the 1880 structure is a kinder, gentler introduction to a Central American market; there are no pigs or chickens or their accompanying smells to be found here. A few stands selling tourist souvenirs congregate near the entrances, but this is primarily a place where the average Costa Rican comes to shop. There are also dozens of cheap restaurants and snack stalls, including the country's first ice-cream vendor. Be warned: the concentration of shoppers makes this a hot spot for pickpockets, purse snatchers, and backpack slitters. Enter and exit at the southeast corner of the building (Avda. Central at C. 6). The green-and-white SALIDA signs direct you to other exits, but they spill onto slightly less–safe streets. Use the image of the Sacred Heart of Jesus, the market's patron and protector, near the center of the building, as your guide; it faces that safer corner by which you should exit. (Things probably weren't planned that way.) ⊠ *Bordered by Avdas. Central–1 and Cs. 6–8, Barrio La Merced* ⊙ *Mon.–Sat. 6–6.*

NEED A BREAK?

Pop's. Here's the place to get the crème de la crème of locally made Costa Rican ice cream. Mango is a favorite flavor. After a long walk on crowded sidewalks, it may be just what the doctor ordered. This prolific chain is everywhere, and you'll find three outlets downtown. ⊠ C. 3, Avdas. Central–1 ⊠ Avda. 2, Cs. 2–4 ⊠ C. 4, Avdas. Central–1.

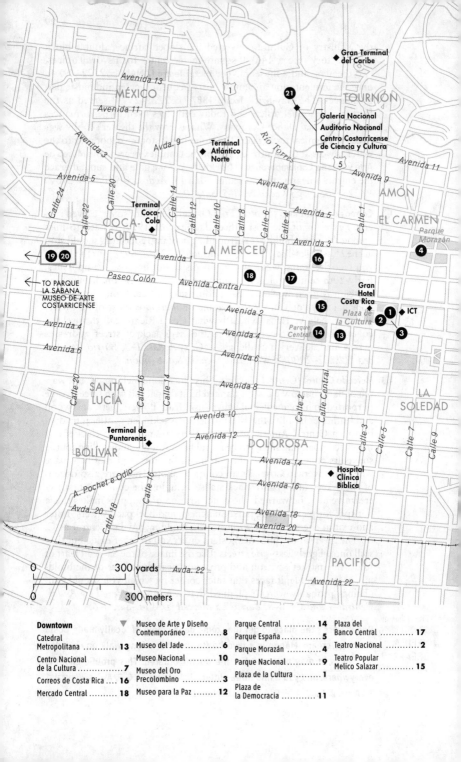

Avenida 13

MÉXICO

Avenida 11

Avenida 13

Avda. 9

Avenida 3

Avenida 5

Calle 24

Calle 22

Calle 20

COCA-COLA

Terminal Coca-Cola

Terminal Atlántico Norte

Río Torres

Calle 14

Calle 12

Calle 10

Calle 8

Calle 6

Calle 4

Avenida 7

Avenida 5

Avenida 3

Avenida 1

LA MERCED

21

Galería Nacional
Auditorio Nacional
Centro Costarricense
de Ciencia y Cultura

TOURNÓN

Gran Terminal
del Caribe

Avenida 11

Avenida 9

AMÓN

EL CARMEN

Parque Morazán

4

Calle 1

16

Paseo Colón

TO PARQUE
LA SABANA,
MUSEO DE ARTE
COSTARRICENSE

19 **20**

Avenida Central

18

17

Gran Hotel
Costa Rica

Plaza de
la Cultura

15

1 **2** ICT

3

Avenida 2

Parque
Central

14

13

Avenida 4

Avenida 6

Calle 20

Calle 16

Calle 14

SANTA
LUCÍA

Avenida 8

Avenida 10

Terminal de
Puntarenas

Avenida 12

BOLÍVAR

A. Pochet e Odio

Avda. 20

Calle 18

Calle 16

DOLOROSA

Avenida 14

Avenida 16

Calle 2

Calle Central

Hospital
Clínica
Bíblica

Avenida 18

Avenida 20

Calle 3

Calle 5

Calle 7

Calle 9

LA
SOLEDAD

PACÍFICO

Avda. 22

Avenida 22

0   300 yards

0   300 meters

Downtown

Catedral
Metropolitana **13**

Centro Nacional
de la Cultura **7**

Correos de Costa Rica **16**

Mercado Central **18**

▼ Museo de Arte y Diseño
Contemporáneo **8**

Museo del Jade **6**

Museo Nacional **10**

Museo del Oro
Precolombino **3**

Museo para la Paz **12**

Parque Central **14**

Parque España **5**

Parque Morazán **4**

Parque Nacional **9**

Plaza de la Cultura **1**

Plaza de
la Democracia **11**

Plaza del
Banco Central **17**

Teatro Nacional **2**

Teatro Popular
Melico Salazar **15**

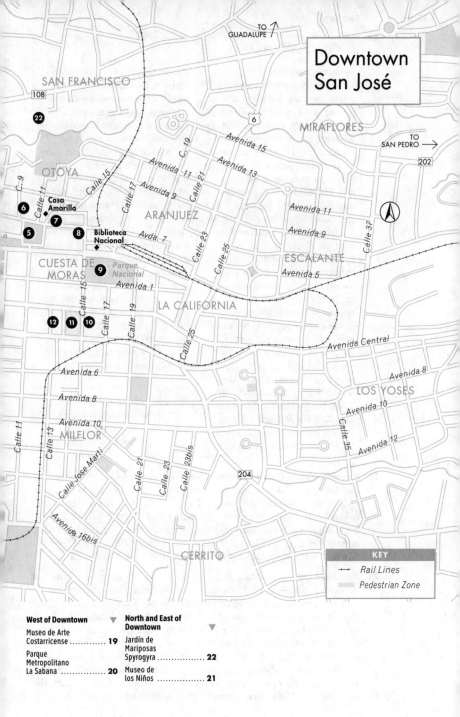

Downtown
San José

TO
GUADALUPE

SAN FRANCISCO

108

22

MIRAFLORES

6

TO
SAN PEDRO

202

OTOYA

C. 9

Calle 11

6

Casa
Amarilla

7

5

8

Biblioteca
Nacional

Calle 15

Calle 17

Avenida 15

C. 19

Avenida 11

Calle 21

Avenida 13

Avenida 9

ARANJUEZ

Avda. 7

Avenida 11

Calle 37

Avenida 9

ESCALANTE

CUESTA DE
MORAS

9

Parque
Nacional

Calle 23

Calle 25

Avenida 5

Avenida 1

LA CALIFORNIA

Calle 15

Calle 17

Calle 19

12

11

10

Calle 25

Avenida Central

Avenida 6

Avenida 8

LOS YOSES

Avenida 8

Avenida 10

Avenida 10

Calle 35

Avenida 12

Calle 11

Calle 13

MILFLOR

Calle José Martí

Calle 21

Calle 23

Calle 23bis

204

Avenida 16bis

CERRITO

KEY
Rail Lines
Pedestrian Zone

A GOOD WALK

All visitors manage to find their way to the **Plaza de la Cultura**, a favorite meeting spot in the heart of the city, and it makes a good kick-off point for a walk. The ornate **Teatro Nacional** sits on the south side of the plaza. Pop in and buy a ticket for an evening performance, and/or grab a cup of coffee at the lobby café. The **Museo del Oro Precolombino** lies under the plaza. The gold collection could easily captivate you for an hour or two. From here, head two blocks north on Calle 5 to **Parque Morazán**, whose centerpiece Templo de Música is the symbol of the city. Traffic is particularly dangerous here, so take heed. The Edificio Metálico, a metal building that serves as a school, fronts the park's north side. Continue just east of the park on Avenida 3 to the small **Parque España**, one of the city's most pleasant green spaces. The ornate building on the park's north side is the Andrew Carnegie–funded Casa Amarilla. At Avenida 7 is the modern Instituto Nacional Segoros (INS) building, whose ground-floor

Museo del Jade has an extensive American jade collection. The Ministry of Culture complex, the **Centro Nacional de la Cultura** fronts the park's east side. From Parque España, walk one long block east to the **Parque Nacional**. Two blocks south on Calle 17 is a pleasant pedestrian mall. Pass the Asamblea Legislativa, where Costa Rica's congress meets, and come to the **Museo Nacional**. Loop around to the museum's west side to one of the higher levels on the Plaza de la Democracia, a great vantage point for sunsets—but otherwise just an expanse of concrete. Avenida Central fronts the plaza's north side. Head back downhill, into the hustle and bustle of the city center. The avenue becomes a lively pedestrian mall at Calle 9, and two blocks later you return to the Plaza de la Cultura.

TIMING TIPS

The walk takes about an hour at a stroll. If you take a more leisurely approach, lingering at the parks or museums, the walk could take hours.

8 Museo de Arte y Diseño Contemporáneo *(Museum of Contemporary Art and Design).* This wonderfully minimalist space is perfect as the country's premier modern-art venue. The MADC, as it is known around town, hosts changing exhibits by artists and designers from all over Latin America. You can arrange for a guided visit with a couple of days' advance notice. ⊠ *C. 15, Avdas. 3–5, Barrio Otoya* ☎ *2257–7202* ⊕ *www.madc.ac.cr* ✑ *$2, free Mon.* ☉ *Mon.–Sat. 10:30–5:30.*

6 Museo del Jade *(Jade Museum).* This is the world's largest collection of
★ American jade—that's "American" in the hemispheric sense. Nearly all the items on display were produced in pre-Columbian times, and most of the jade (pronounced *hah*-day in Spanish) dates from 300 BC to AD 700. In the spectacular Jade Room, pieces are illuminated from behind so you can appreciate their translucency. A series of drawings explains how this extremely hard stone was cut using string saws with quartz-and-sand abrasive. Jade was sometimes used in jewelry designs, but it was most often carved into oblong pendants. The museum also has other pre-Columbian artifacts, such as polychrome vases and three-

Where the Streets Have No Name

The Irish group U-2 could have written one of its signature songs about Costa Rica's capital. Admittedly, some of the streets in San José do have names, but no one seems to know or use them. Streets in the center of the capital are laid out in a grid, with *avenidas* (avenues) running east and west, and *calles* (streets), north and south. Odd-number avenues increase in number north of Avenida Central; even-number avenues, south. Streets east of Calle Central have odd numbers; those to the west are even. The farther you get from downtown, the scarcer street signs become. Costa Ricans rely instead on a charming and exasperating system of designating addresses by the distance from well-known landmarks, as in "100 meters

north and 50 meters west of the school." Another quirk: "100 meters" always refers to one city block, regardless of how long it actually is. Likewise, "200 meters" is two blocks, and so on. Historically, the reference point was the church, but these days it might be anything from a bar to a Burger King, or even a landmark that no longer exists: the eastern suburb of San Pedro uses the *higuerón*, a fig tree that was felled long ago, but lives on in the hearts of Costa Ricans. It's no wonder that those who can afford it opt to have their mail delivered to a post-office box. (Getting a pizza delivered is quite another challenge.) Your best bet is to follow the time-honored practice and *ir y preguntar*: keep walking and keep asking.

legged *metates* (small stone tables for grinding corn), and a gallery of modern art. The final room on the tour has a startling display of ceramic fertility symbols. A photo-filled, glossy guide to the museum in English sells for $15; the Spanish version is only $3. The museum is looking for a new home at this writing, with tentative plans to transfer the collection to an as-yet-unconstructed facility somewhere near the Plaza de la Democracia. Look for a change in venue in 2010 at the earliest. ⊠*INS building, Avda. 7, Cs. 9–11, Barrio El Carmen* ☎*2287–6034* ⊕*portal.ins-cr.com/Social/MuseoJade/* ☞*$7* ⊙*Weekdays 8:30–3:30, Sat. 9–1.*

⓾ Museo Nacional (*National Museum*). In the whitewashed Bellavista Fortress, which dates from 1870, the National Museum gives you a quick and insightful lesson in English and Spanish on Costa Rican culture from pre-Columbian times to the present. Glass cases display pre-Columbian artifacts, period dress, colonial furniture, religious art, and photographs. Some of the country's foremost ethnographers and anthropologists are on the museum's staff. Outside are a veranda and a pleasant, manicured courtyard garden. A former army headquarters, this now-tranquil building saw fierce fighting during a 1931 army mutiny and during the 1948 revolution, as the bullet holes pocking its turrets attest. But it was also here that three-time president José "Don Pepe" Figueres abolished the country's military in 1949. ⊠*C. 17, between Avdas. Central and 2, Barrio La Soledad* ☎*2257–1433* ⊕*www.museocostarica.go.cr* ☞*$4, $2 students* ⊙*Tues.–Sat. 8:30–4:30, Sun. 9–4:30.*

③ ★ Museo del Oro Precolombino *(Pre-Columbian Gold Museum).* The dazzling, modern museum of gold, in a three-story underground structure beneath the Plaza de la Cultura, contains the largest collection of pre-Columbian gold jewelry in Central America—20,000 troy ounces in more than 1,600 individual pieces—all owned by the Banco Central, and displayed attractively

> **CAUTION**
>
> Don't drive in the city if you can avoid it. The streets are narrow and congested, and many drivers treat traffic regulations as suggestions rather than laws.

in low-lit, bilingual exhibits. Many pieces are in the form of frogs and eagles, two animals perceived by the region's pre-Columbian cultures to have great spiritual significance. All that glitters here is not gold: most spectacular are the varied shaman figurines, which represent the human connection to animal deities. One of the halls houses the **Museo Numismática** (Coin Museum; admission included with Gold Museum), a repository of historic coins and bills and other objects used as legal tender throughout the country's history. Rotating art exhibitions live on another level of the complex. ⊠ *Eastern end of Plaza de la Cultura, C. 5, Avdas. Central–2, Barrio La Soledad* ☎ *2243–4202* ⊕ *www. museosdelbancocentral.org* 🎟 *$7, $4 students* ☉ *Daily 9:30–5.*

⑫ Museo para la Paz *(Peace Museum).* Former president Oscar Arias won the 1987 Nobel peace prize for his tireless efforts to bring reconciliation to a war-torn Central America, and today he remains a vocal force for international peace and social justice. His Arias Foundation operates this museum, with bilingual exhibits documenting the isthmus's turbulent history and promoting the cause for peace. Messages from other Nobel laureates—the Dalai Lama, Lech Walesa, Rigoberta Menchú, Jimmy Carter, and Henry Kissinger among them—adorn one room. Begin your visit in the auditorium watching a 12-minute video in English, *The Dividends of Peace*. There's also an hour-long video that delves into the topic. The museum usually does not appear to be open when you walk by. Call and let the attendant know you're coming. ⊠ *Avda. 2 and C. 13, Barrio La Soledad* ☎ *2223–4664* ⊕ *www. arias.or.cr* 🎟 *Free* ☉ *Weekdays 8–noon and 1–5.*

⑭ Parque Central *(Central Park).* At the city's nucleus, this simple tree-planted square—it's more a plaza than a park—has a gurgling fountain and concrete benches, and a life-size bronze statue of a street sweeper cleaning up some bronze litter. In the center of the park is a spiderlike, ochre-color gazebo donated by former Nicaraguan dictator Anastasio Somoza. Several years ago a referendum was held to decide whether to demolish the despot's gift, but Ticos voted to preserve the bandstand for posterity. ⊠ *Bordered by Avdas. 2–4 and Cs. 2–Central, Barrio La Merced.*

⑤ Parque España. One of our favorite spots in the capital is this shady little park. A bronze statue of Costa Rica's Spanish founder, Juan Vásquez de Coronado, overlooks an elevated fountain on its southwest corner; the opposite corner has a lovely tiled guardhouse. A bust of Queen Isabella of Castile stares at the yellow compound to the east of the park, the Centro Nacional de la Cultura (National Center of Culture). Just west of the park is a two-story, metal-sided school made in Belgium and shipped to Costa Rica in pieces more than a century ago. Local lore holds that the intended destination for the appropriately named Edificio Metálico (Metal Building) was really Chile, but that Costa Rica decided to keep the mistakenly shipped building components. The yellow colonial-style building to the east of the modern INS building is the 1912 **Casa Amarilla,** home of Costa Rica's Foreign Ministry. (The building is not open to the public.) The massive ceiba tree in front, planted by John F. Kennedy and the presidents of all the Central American nations in 1963, gives you an idea of how quickly things grow in the tropics. A garden around the corner on Calle 13 contains a 2-meter-wide section of the Berlin Wall donated by Germany's foreign ministry after reunification. Ask the guard to let you into the garden if you want a closer look. ⊠*Bordered by Avdas. 7–3 and Cs. 11–17, Barrio El Carmen* ☎2257-7202.

RAINY DAY TIPS

■ Do outdoor sightseeing in the morning, before the afternoon rains arrive.

■ Duck into museums—our top choices are the Gold and Jade museums.

■ Do as Costa Ricans do and *tomar café* (take a coffee break).

■ Don't wait until the evening rush hour (5–7 PM) to get a cab—empty ones are nearly nonexistent when it rains.

❹ **Parque Morazán.** Anchored by the 1920 Templo de Música (Temple of Music), a neoclassic bandstand that has become the symbol of the city, the largest park in downtown San José is somewhat barren, though the pink and golden trumpet trees on its northwest corner brighten things up when they bloom in the dry months. The park is named for Honduran general Francisco Morazán, whose dream for a united Central America failed in the 1830s. Avoid the park late at night, when a rough crowd and occasional muggers appear. ⊠*Avda. 3, Cs. 5–9, Barrio El Carmen.*

❾ **Parque Nacional** *(National Park).* A bronze monument commemorating Central America's battles against American invader William Walker in 1856 forms the centerpiece of this large and leafy park. Five Amazons, representing the five nations of the isthmus, attack Walker, who shields his face from the onslaught. Costa Rica maintains the lead and shelters a veiled Nicaragua, the country most devastated by the war. Guatemala, Honduras, and El Salvador might dispute this version of events, but this is how Costa Rica chose to commission the work by French sculptor Louis Carrier Belleuse, a student of Rodin, in 1895. Bas-relief murals on the monument's pedestal depict key battles in the war against the Americans. ⊠*Bordered by Avdas. 1–3 and Cs. 15–19, Barrio La Soledad.*

❶ **Plaza de la Cultura.** The crowds of people, vendors, and street entertainers at the Plaza de la Cultura—it's a favored spot for local marimba bands, clowns, jugglers, and colorfully dressed South Americans playing Andean music—hide the fact that the expanse is really just a mass of concrete. The ornate Teatro Nacional, one of San José's signature buildings, dominates the plaza's southern half. Pop in and buy a ticket for an evening performance—the prices are amazingly reasonable. The Museo del Oro Precolombino, with its highly visited exhibits of gold, lies under the plaza. The plaza's western edge is defined by the Gran Hotel Costa Rica, with its 24-hour Café 1930. ⊠*Bordered by Avdas. Central–2 and Cs. 3–5, Barrio La Soledad.*

⓫ **Plaza de la Democracia.** President Oscar Arias built this terraced open space west of the Museo Nacional to mark 100 years of democracy and to receive dignitaries during the 1989 hemispheric summit. The view west toward the dark-green Cerros de Escazú is nice in the morning and fabulous at sunset. The plaza is dominated by a statue of José "Don Pepe" Figueres, three-time president and leader of the 1948 revolution. Sadly, the plaza sits in a state of dilapidation at this writing, victim of swarms of graffiti artists who protested a free-trade agreement with the United States throughout 2007. Remodeling and sprucing-up is slated for the near future. Until then, use the site as a landmark if not a destination in its own right. Jewelry, T-shirts, and crafts from Costa Rica, Guatemala, and South America are sold in a string of stalls along the western edge. They are worth a stop. ⊠*Bordered by Avdas. Central–2 and Cs. 13–15, Barrio La Soledad.*

Duck into the **Café del Teatro Nacional** (⊠Plaza de la Cultura, Barrio La Soledad ☎2221–3262), off the theater lobby, to sit at a marble table and sip a hazelnut mocha beneath frescoed ceilings. The frescoes are part of an allegory of seminude figures celebrating the 1897 opening of the theater. Coffees run from $2 to $4, depending on how much alcohol or ice cream is added. Sandwiches and cakes are $3 to $5. The café keeps the same hours as the theater, but is open only until curtain time on performance nights, and during intermission.

⓱ **Plaza del Banco Central** *(Central Bank Plaza).* An extension of Avenida Central, the plaza is popular with hawkers, money changers, and retired men, and can be a good place to get a shoe shine and listen to street musicians. Outside the western end of Costa Rica's modern federal-reserve bank building, don't miss Fernando Calvo's *Presentes,* 10 sculpted, smaller-than-life figures of bedraggled *campesinos* (peasants). *La Chola,* a bronze 500-kg (1,100-lb) statue by Manuel Vargas of a buxom rural woman resides at sidewalk level on the small, shady plaza south of the bank. It's public art at its best. Beware: the money changers here are notorious for circulating counterfeit bills and using doctored calculators to shortchange unwitting tourists. Instead, change money at banks or through cash machines, where you get the best rate. ⊠*Bordered by Avdas. Central–1 and Cs. 2–4, Barrio La Merced.*

⓯ **Teatro Popular Melico Salazar** *(Melico Salazar Theater).* Across Avenida 2 on the north side of Parque Central stands San José's second major performance hall (after the Teatro Nacional). The 1928 building is on the site of a former 19th-century military barracks felled by an earthquake.

Teatro Nacional

The **National Theater** is easily the most enchanting building in Costa Rica, and San José's don't-miss sight. Chagrined that touring prima donna Adelina Patti bypassed San José in 1890, wealthy coffee merchants raised import taxes to hire Belgian architects to design this building, lavish with cast iron and Italian marble. The theater was inaugurated in 1897 with a performance of Gounod's *Faust*, featuring an international cast. The sandstone exterior is marked by Italianate arched windows, marble columns with bronze capitals, and statues of strange bedfellows Ludwig van Beethoven (1770–1827) and 17th-century Spanish golden-age playwright Pedro Calderón de la Barca (1600–81). The Muses of Dance, Music, and Fame are silhouetted in front of an iron cupola. The sumptuous neo-Baroque interior sparkles, too. Given the provenance of the building funds, it's not surprising that frescoes on the stairway inside depict coffee and banana production. Note Italian painter Aleardo Villa's famous ceiling mural *Alegoría del Café y Banano* (*Allegory of Coffee and Bananas*), a joyful harvest scene that appeared on Costa Rica's old five-colón note. (The now-defunct bill is prized by collectors and by tourists as a souvenir, and is often sold by vendors in the plaza between the theater and the Gran Hotel Costa Rica next door.) And what's an old theater

without its resident ghost? Patrons have claimed to see moving figures in the second-floor paintings in the Teatro Nacional, although no sightings have been reported in years. French designer Alain Guilhot created the nighttime external illumination system for the building. (He did the same for the Eiffel Tower.) The soft coppers, golds, and whites highlight the theater's exterior nightly from 6 PM–5 AM.

The best way to see the theater's interior is to attend one of the performances, which take place several nights a week; intermission gives you a chance to nose around. The theater prizes punctuality, one of the few institutions in this country to do so. Performances start on time. Stop at the *bolitería* (box office) in the lobby and see what strikes your fancy. (Don't worry if you left your tuxedo or evening gown back home; as long as you don't show up for a performance wearing shorts, jeans, or a T-shirt, no one will care.) Alternatively, a nominal admission fee gets you in beyond the lobby for an informative guided daytime visit. Thirty-minute tours in English, Spanish, or French are given on an as-needed basis throughout the day. The theater is sometimes closed for rehearsals, so call before you go. ✉ *Plaza de la Cultura, Barrio La Soledad* ☎ *2221-1329* ⊕ *www.teatronacional.go.cr* 🎟 *$5* ⊙ *Mon.–Sat. 9–4.*

The venue was later named for Costa Rican operatic tenor Manuel "Melico" Salazar (1887–1950). It was constructed specifically to provide a less highbrow alternative to the Teatro Nacional. But these days the Melico is plenty cultured, and provides the capital with a steady diet of music and dance performances. ✉ *Avda. 2 and C. 2, Barrio La Merced* ☎ *2233-5424* ⊕ *www.teatromelico.go.cr/teatro_popular_cr.html.*

WEST OF DOWNTOWN

Paseo Colón, one of San José's major boulevards, heads due west from downtown and leads to the vast La Sabana park, the largest parcel of green space in the city. La Sabana anchors the even vaster west side of the city. A block or two off its exhaust-ridden avenues are quiet residential streets, and you'll find the U.S., Canadian, and British embassies here.

WHAT TO SEE

⓳ **Museo de Arte Costarricense** *(Museum of Costa Rican Art)*. A splendid collection of 19th- and 20th-century Costa Rican art, labeled in Spanish and English, is housed in 12 exhibition halls here. Be sure to visit the top-floor Salón Dorado to see the stucco, bronze-plate bas-relief mural depicting Costa Rican history, created by French sculptor Louis Feron. Guided tours are offered Tuesday–Friday 10–3. Wander into the sculpture garden in back and take in Jorge Jiménez's 7-meter-tall *Imagen Cósmica,* which depicts pre-Columbian traditions. ✉ *C. 42 and Paseo Colón, Paseo Colón* ☎ *2222–7155* ⊕ *www.musarco.go.cr* ✇ *$5, free Sun.* ⊙ *Tues.–Fri. 10–6, weekends 10–4.*

> **NEED A BREAK?**
>
> Costa Rica gave the world the so-called canopy tour, and you used to have to go pretty far afield to zip via cables through the treetops Tarzan style. The metro area now counts two outlets of the **Urban Canopy** (✉ Parque Metropolitano La Sabana, La Sabana ☎ 2215–2544 ✉ Parque del Este, near the Christ statue on the Sabanilla Highway, Sabanilla ✇ $20 ⊙ 9–5). The west-side branch in La Sabana park takes you over a series of eight cables, four bridges, and a rappel climb. On the far east side, the outlet in the Parque del Este contains a series of seven cables, with hiking trails for before or after offering ample birding opportunities.

⓴ **Parque Metropolitano La Sabana.** Though it isn't centrally located, La Sabana (The Savannah) comes the closest of San José's green spaces to achieving the same function and spirit as New York's Central Park. A statue of 1930s president León Cortes greets you at the park's principal entrance at the west end of Paseo Colón. Behind the statue a 5-meter-tall menorah serves as a gathering place for San José's small Jewish community during Hanukkah. La Sabana was once San José's airport, and the whitewashed Museo de Arte Costarricense, just south of the Cortes statue, served as terminal and control tower. The round Gimnasio Nacional (National Gymnasium) sits at the southeast corner of the park and hosts sporting events and the occasional concert. The Estadio Nacional (National Stadium) near the park's northwest corner is the site of occasional soccer matches, and is one of the country's major outdoor concert venues. In between are acres of space for soccer, basketball, tennis, swimming, jogging, picnicking, and kite flying. The park hums with activity on weekend days. You're welcome to join in the early-morning outdoor aerobics classes on Saturday and Sunday. A small building boom is taking place these days, with condos and office buildings going up around the perimeter of the park, another resemblance to New York's Central Park. (Because of building codes, "skyscraper" means a maximum of about 10 floors in earthquake-prone Costa Rica.) Like most of San José's green spaces, La Sabana should be avoided at night. ⊠ *Bordered by C. 42, Avda. de las Américas, and Autopista Próspero Fernández, Paseo Colón.*

NORTH AND EAST OF DOWNTOWN

Immediately northeast of downtown lie the splendid historic neighborhoods of Barrio Amón and Barrio Otoya. Both are repositories of historic houses that have escaped the wrecking ball, and many now serve as hotels, restaurants, and offices. (And a few actually are private residences as well.) Barrio Escalante, to the east, is not quite as gentrified, but fast becoming a fashionable address.

CAUTION

The ubiquitous TOURIST INFORMATION signs you see around downtown are really private travel agencies looking to sell you tours rather than provide unbiased information. The ICT (⇨ *San José Essentials, below)* is the official tourist office.

The sprawling suburb of San Pedro begins several blocks east of downtown San José. The town is home to the University of Costa Rica and all the intellect and cheap eats and nightlife that a student or student-wannabe could desire. But away from the heart of the university, San Pedro is also awash in the consumerism of shopping malls, fast-food restaurants, and car dealerships, although it manages to mix in stately districts such as the stylish Los Yoses for good measure. To get to San Pedro, take a $2 taxi ride from downtown and get off in front of Banco Nacional, just beyond the rotunda with the fountain at its center.

WHAT TO SEE

㉒ ★ ☪ Jardín de Mariposas Spyrogyra *(Spyrogyra Butterfly Garden).* Spending an hour or two at this magical garden is entertaining and educational for nature lovers of all ages. Self-guided tours enlighten you on butterfly ecology and give you a chance to see the winged creatures close up. After an 18-minute video introduction, you're free to wander screened-in gardens along a numbered trail. Some 30 species of colorful butterflies flutter about, accompanied by six types of hummingbirds. Try to come when it's sunny, as butterflies are most active then. A small, moderately priced café borders the garden and serves sandwiches and Tico fare. Spyrogyra abuts the northern edge of Parque Zoológico Simón Bolívar, but you enter on the outskirts of Barrio Tournón, near El Pueblo Shopping Center. ⊠ *50 m east and 150 m south of main entrance to El Pueblo, Barrio Tournón* ☎ *2222–2937* ⊕ *www.butterfly gardencr.com* ⊠ *$6, $3 children under 12* ☉ *Daily 8–5.*

㉑ ☪ Museo de los Niños. San José's Children's Museum is housed in a former prison, and big kids may want to check it out just to marvel at the castlelike architecture and the old cells that have been preserved in an exhibit about life behind bars. Three halls in the complex are filled with eye-catching seasonal exhibits for kids, ranging in subject from local ecology to outer space. The exhibits are annotated in Spanish, but most are interactive, so language shouldn't be much of a problem. The

Missing History

Blame it on the earthquakes. Costa Ricans are quick to attribute the scarcity of historic architecture in San José and around the country to a history of earth tremors. Indeed, major earthquakes have struck various locales around Costa Rica 10 times since the mid-18th century (6 times in the 20th century), felling untold numbers of historical structures.

But blame it on the wrecking ball, too, says architect Gabriela Sáenz, who works with the Ministry of Culture's Center for Research and Conservation of Cultural Patrimony. The tear-it-down approach really began to take its toll in the 1970s, an era when boxy, concrete buildings were in vogue around the world, Sáenz says. Costa Rica didn't establish its first school of architecture until 1972, staffed by faculty from Mexico, England, and Brazil. "It was hard for a real Costa Rican tradition to take hold," she explains. Mix that with a lack of government regulation and what Sáenz calls a typical Tico do-your-own-thing penchant, and the result is the San José, chock-full of squat buildings, you see today.

The tide began to turn in 1995 with the passage of the Law of Historic and Architectural Patrimony. Over 300 historic structures in the country are presently protected under the legislation, and new buildings are added to the registry each year. But legal protection is no guarantee of funding necessary to actually restore a historic landmark.

You need to look hard, but San José really does have several diamonds in the rough. The National Theater and Central Post Office remain the two most visited examples of historic architecture in the capital. But the National Museum; the Museum of Forms, Spaces and Sounds; the National Center of Culture; and several small hostelries and restaurants around town—especially in Barrios Amón and Otoya—all are modern transformations and restorations of structures with past histories.

museum's most popular resident is the Egyptian exhibit's sarcophagus; the mummy draws the "oohs" and "eews." Officially, the complex is called the Centro Costarricense de Ciencia y Cultura (Costa Rican Center of Science and Culture), and that will be the sign that greets you on the front of the building. The **Galería Nacional,** adjoining the main building, is more popular with adults; it usually shows fine art by Costa Rican artists free of charge. Also adjoining the museum is the classical music venue **Auditorio Nacional.** Though just a short distance from downtown, the walk here takes you through a dodgy neighborhood. Take a taxi to and from. ⊠*North end of C. 4, Barrio El Carmen* ☎*2258–4929* ⊕*www.museocr.com* ✉*$2* ⊘*Tues.–Fri. 8–4:30, weekends 9:30–5.*

NEED A BREAK?

We have to admit that Costa Rican baked goods tend toward the dry-as-dust end of the spectrum. But Italian-style bakery Giacomín (⊠Next to Automercado, Los Yoses, San Pedro ☎2234-2551 ⊠C. 2, Avdas. 3–5, Barrio La Merced ☎2221–5652)**, near the University of Costa Rica, is an exception—it seems that a touch of liqueur added to the batter makes all the difference. Stand,**

European-style, at the downstairs espresso bar, or take your goodies to the tables and chairs on the upstairs balcony. Both branches close from noon to 2.

WHERE TO EAT

Wherever you eat in San José, be it a small *soda* (informal eatery) or a sophisticated restaurant, dress is casual. Meals tend to be taken earlier than in other Latin American countries; few restaurants serve past 10 PM. Local cafés usually open for breakfast at 7 AM and remain open until 7 or 9 in the evening. Restaurants serving international cuisine are usually open from 11 AM to 9 PM. Some cafés that serve mainly San José office workers are closed Sunday. Restaurants that do open on Sunday do a brisk business: it's the traditional family day out (and the maid's day off). Casino restaurants in downtown San José are open 24 hours.

SAN JOSÉ

AMERICAN

$–$$

✕**News Café.** Pounce on one of the street-side tables if they're free when you enter. (They probably won't be available: a regular expat crowd holds court here.) The passing parade on Avenida Central is yours for the price of a cup of coffee. Breakfast and dinner fare is hearty, but the café is most popular at lunchtime and cocktail hour. You can get a Caesar salad and other American dishes here. A 2007 remodeling took away some of the old-town tavern feel, but the good food—burgers, sandwiches, and salads—remains. The café is on the first floor of the 1960s landmark Hotel Presidente. ✉*Avda. Central and C. 7, Barrio La Soledad* ☎2222–3022 ▤*AE, D, DC, MC, V* .

ASIAN

$$

Fodor'sChoice

★

✕**Tin Jo.** The colorful dining rooms of this converted house just southeast of downtown evoke Japan, India, China, Indonesia, or Thailand. In the Thai room a 39-foot mural depicts a Buddhist temple. You can select from all of the above cuisines, with menus to match the varied dining areas. Start with a powerful Singapore sling (brandy and fruit juices) before trying such treats as *kaeng* (Thai shrimp and pineapple curry in coconut milk), *mu shu* (a beef, chicken, or veggie stir-fry with crepes), samosas (stuffed Indian pastries), and sushi rolls. The vegetarian menu is extensive. Tin Jo stands out with always exceptional food, attention to detail, and attentive service that make it, hands down, the country's top Asian restaurant. ✉*C. 11, Avdas. 6–8, Barrio La Soledad* ☎2257–3622 *or* 2221–7605 ▤*AE, D, DC, MC, V.*

CAFÉS

$$–$$$

Fodor'sChoice

★

✕**Café Mundo.** You could easily walk by this corner restaurant without noticing its tiny sign behind the foliage. The upstairs café serves meals on the porch, on a garden patio, or in two dining rooms. The soup of the day and fresh-baked bread start you out; main courses include shrimp in a vegetable cream sauce or *lomito en salsa de vino tinto* (tenderloin in a red-wine sauce). Save room for the best chocolate cake in town, drizzled with homemade blackberry sauce. Café Mundo is a popular, low-key gay hangout that draws a mixed gay-straight clientele. This is one of the few center-city restaurants with its own parking lot. ✉C. 15 and Avda. 9, Barrio Otoya ☎2222-6190 ▭AE, D, DC, MC, V ✆Closed Sun. No lunch Sat.

$ ✗**Café de la Posada.** The lack of alfresco dining in this tropical city is disappointing, but this café's terrace with tables fronting the Calle 17 pedestrian mall is a pleasant exception. The owners of this small café come from Argentina, and they know how to make a great cappuccino. Salads, quiches, and empanadas are the food specialties. The best bargains are the four rotating *platos del día* (daily specials), with entrée, salad, beverage, and dessert for $4. If you opt for dinner, make it an early one: the place closes at 7 on weeknights. ✉C. 17, Avdas. 2–4, Barrio La Soledad ☎2258-1027 ▭AE, D, DC, MC, V ✆Closed Sun. No dinner Sat.

CHINESE ✗**Don Wang.** In a country where "Chinese cuisine" often means rice
$$ and vegetables bearing a suspicious resemblance to *gallo pinto* ("spotted rooster," a typical Costa Rican dish of black beans and rice), Don Wang's authenticity comes as a real treat. Cantonese cuisine is the mainstay here—the owner comes from that region of China—but these folks will Szechuan it up a bit if you ask. Mornings give way to the immensely popular dim sum, called *desayuno chino*, literally "Chinese breakfast." You can order dim sum all day, but the $5 specials last only until 11 AM. The dining area is built around a stone garden and small waterfall. There's no television blaring here, a refreshing change from many Costa Rican restaurants. ✉C. 11, Avdas. 6–8, Barrio La Soledad ☎2233-6484 ▭AE, D, DC, MC, V.

COSTA RICAN ✗**La Cocina de Leña.** The name translates literally as "firewood kitchen,"
$$ and it evokes the age-old Tico style of cooking. Indeed, you'll see bun-
★ dles of wood as well as old tools and straw bags hung on the walls to make you feel like you're down on the farm, but rustic this place is not. Popular Tico dishes such as black-bean soup, ceviche, tamales, oxtail with cassava, and plantains are served, and the restaurant has live marimba music several nights a week during high season. Although the kitchen closes at 11 PM, you're welcome to stay as long as the band keeps playing. It is one of the few places that doesn't close during Holy Week. ✉Centro Comercial El Pueblo, Avda. 0, Barrio Tournón ☎2223-3704 ▭AE, D, DC, MC, V.

$ ✗**La Criollita.** Kick off your day with breakfast at this emerald-green restaurant. Mornings are the perfect time to snag one of the precious tables in the back garden, an unexpected refuge from the noise and traffic of the city. Choose from the *americano*, with pancakes and toast; the *tico*, with bread, fried bananas, and *natilla* (sour cream); or the huge *criollita*, with ham or pork chops; all have eggs on the side. Workers from nearby government office buildings begin to pour in late in the morning, and the lunchtime decibel level increases appreciably. (This is the one time of day we recommend avoiding the place.) They filter out about 2 PM and once again you have a quiet place for coffee and dessert. ✉Avda. 7, Cs. 7–9, Barrio Amón ☎2256-6511 ▭AE, D, DC, MC, V ✆Closed Sun. No dinner Sat.

$ ✗**Mama's Place.** Mama's is a Costa Rican restaurant with a difference: the owners are Italian, so in addition to *corvina al ajillo* (sea bass sautéed with garlic) and other staple Tico fare, they serve homemade seafood chowder, traditional Italian pastas, and meat dishes with delicate wine sauces. The brightly decorated coffee shop opens onto busy Avenida 1; the more subdued dining room upstairs accommodates the overflow crowd. (You'll see former Chicago Bears football coach Mike Ditka's autographed picture up there.) At lunchtime it's usually packed with business types drawn to the delicious and inexpensive daily specials—choose from the rotating *platos del día* (daily specials) with pasta, meat, fish, or poultry—all to the accompaniment of ample focaccia. Mama's closes at 7 PM on weeknights. ✉ *Avda. 1, Cs. Central–2, Barrio El Carmen* ☎ 2223–2270 *or* 2256–5601 ▤ *AE, D, DC, MC, V* ⊘ *Closed Sun. No dinner Sat.*

$ ✕ **Manolo's.** For any San José dweller, a mention of Manolo's brings their signature menu item *churros con chocolate* (fried dough with hot fudge sauce) to mind. But this 24-hour eatery is also known for its great sandwiches and espressos. Its location on the bustling Avenida Central pedestrian thoroughfare and its outdoor tables allow for some of the city's best people-watching. Inside, however, the place feels more like a diner than a café, down to its plastic-coated menu and its promise of breakfast food at any hour. The owner always prepares a few Spanish favorites in addition to the typical Tico fare, such as *tortilla española* (a thick potato-and-onion omelet). ✉ *Avda. Central, Cs. Central–2, Barrio La Merced* ☎ 2221–2041 ▤ *AE, D, DC, MC, V.*

$ ✕ **Nuestra Tierra.** But for the traffic zipping by on one of San José's busiest thoroughfares—and on that note, opt for a table on the side facing less busy Calle 15—you might think you're out in rural Santa Ana. Bunches of onions and peppers dangle from the ceiling, recalling a provincial Tico ranch. The generous homemade meals are delicious, and the incredibly friendly waitstaff, who epitomize Costa Rican hospitality and dress in traditional folkloric clothing, prepare your coffee filtered through the traditional cloth *chorreador.* The place is open 24 hours, just in case *gallo pinto* (Costa Rican-style rice and beans) pangs hit at 3 AM. Some disparage the place as "too touristy." Perhaps it is, but it's also fun. ✉ *Avda. 2 and C. 15, Barrio La Soledad* ☎ 2258–6500 ▤ *No credit cards.*

¢ ✕ **Soda Argey.** It's really a bit too upscale to qualify as a typical soda, but you'll find standard Costa Rican fare and a rotating selection of *casados* (rice and beans with fried plantains, meat, chicken, or fish, and assorted add-ons). These folks even deliver. ✉ *200 m south and 100 m west of Automercado, Los Yoses, San Pedro* ☎ 2280–1183 ▤ *No credit cards* ⊘ *Closed Sun. No dinner Sat.*

¢ ✕ **Soda La Vasconia.** Hundreds of sports photos plaster the wall in what the owner calls his *museo futbolístico* (soccer museum), and the place draws crowds for that reason as well as for the hearty food. It's one of the few downtown San José sodas to keep late-night hours. ✉ *Avda. 1, Cs. 3–5, Barrio El Carmen* ☎ 2223–4857 ▤ *No credit cards.*

ECLECTIC ✕ **Jürgen's.** Jürgen's is a common haunt for *politicos,* and San José's
$$–$$$ elites meet to eat here. Decorated in gold and terra-cotta with leather and wood accents, the dining room of this contemporary restaurant feels more like a lounge than a fine restaurant. In fact, the classy bar, with a large selection of good wine and good cigars, is a prominent

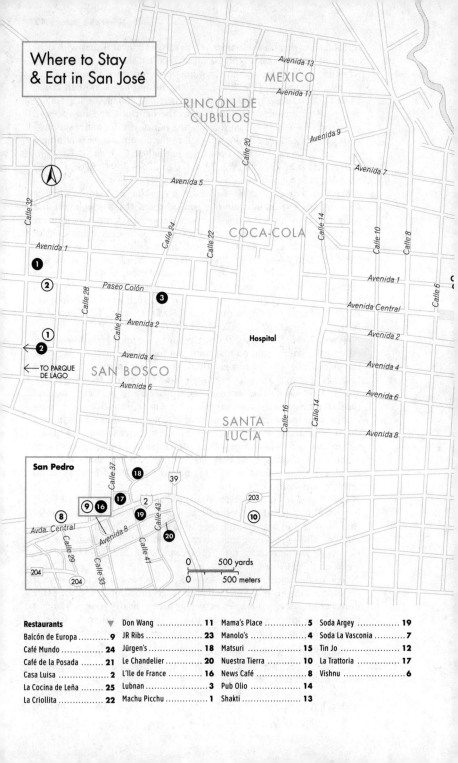

Where to Stay & Eat in San José

Avenida 13

MEXICO

Avenida 11

RINCÓN DE CUBILLOS

Avenida 9

Avenida 7

Avenida 5

Calle 32

Calle 20

Avenida 1

① ②

Calle 24

Calle 22

COCA-COLA

Calle 14

Calle 10

Calle 8

Avenida 1

Calle 28

Paseo Colón

③

Avenida Central

Calle 6

Calle 26

Avenida 2

Hospital

Avenida 2

① ②

Avenida 4

Avenida 4

← TO PARQUE DE LAGO

SAN BOSCO

Avenida 6

Avenida 6

SANTA LUCÍA

Calle 16

Calle 14

Avenida 8

San Pedro

Calle 37

⑱

39

⑰

2

203

⑨ ⑯

⑲

Calle 43

⑩

⑧

Avda. Central

Avenida 8

⑳

Calle 29

Calle 41

204

Calle 33

204

0   500 yards

0   500 meters

Restaurants

Balcón de Europa **9**
Café Mundo **24**
Café de la Posada **21**
Casa Luisa **2**
La Cocina de Leña **25**
La Criollita **22**

Don Wang **11**
JR Ribs **23**
Jürgen's **18**
Le Chandelier **20**
L'Ile de France **16**
Lubnan **3**
Machu Picchu **1**

Mama's Place **5**
Manolo's **4**
Matsuri **15**
Nuestra Tierra **10**
News Café **8**
Pub Olio **14**
Shakti **13**

Soda Argey **19**
Soda La Vasconia **7**
Tin Jo **12**
La Trattoria **17**
Vishnu **6**

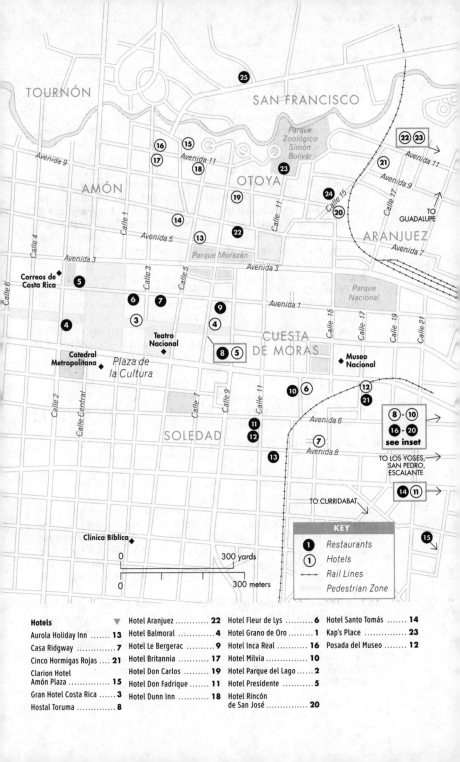

Hotels

feature. The inventive menu, with such delicacies as medallions of roast duck and tuna fillet encrusted with sesame seeds, sets this place apart from the city's more traditional venues. ⊠ *250 m north of the Subaru dealership, on Blvd. Barrio Dent, Barrio Dent* ☎*2283–2239* ▭*AE, D, DC, MC, V* ☯*Closed Sun. No lunch Sat.*

FRENCH
$$$$

✕**Le Chandelier.** San José does not get classier than this restaurant, where formal service and traditional sauce-heavy French dishes are part of the experience. The dining room is elegant, with wicker chairs, a tile floor, and original paintings. The Swiss chef, Claude Dubuis, might start you off with saffron ravioli stuffed with ricotta cheese and walnuts. His main courses include such unique dishes as corvina in a *pejibaye* (peach palm) sauce, hearts of palm and veal chops glazed in a sweet port-wine sauce, and the more familiar *pato a la naranja* (duck à l'orange), or for a tropical twist on that classic dish, try Dubuis's *pato a la maracuyá* (duck in passion fruit). ⊠ *50 m west and 100 m south of ICE building, San Pedro* ☎*2225–3980* ▭*AE, D, DC, MC, V* ☯*Closed Sun. No lunch Sat.*

$$$
Fodor'sChoice
★

✕**L'Ile de France.** Long one of San José's most popular restaurants, L'Ile de France, in the Hotel Le Bergerac—it's technically a separate business—has dining in a tropical garden courtyard. The fairly traditional French menu has some interesting innovations. Start with the classic onion soup or with *pâté de lapin* (rabbit liver pâté); then sink your teeth into a pepper steak, broiled lamb with seasoned potatoes, or corvina in a spinach sauce. Save room for the profiteroles filled with vanilla ice cream and smothered in chocolate sauce. L'Ile de France blends exactly the right level of intimacy, grace, and style, giving it a slight edge over the sophisticated Chandelier. ⊠*Hotel Le Bergerac; C. 35, Avdas. Central–2, first Los Yoses entrance, San Pedro* ☎*2283–5812* ⌲*Reservations essential* ▭*AE, D, DC, MC, V* ☯*Closed Sun. No lunch.*

ITALIAN
$$

✕**Balcón de Europa.** With old sepia photos and a strolling guitarist who seems to have been working the room forever, Balcón de Europa transports you to the year of its inception, 1909. Pasta specialties such as the *plato mixto* (mixed plate with lasagne, tortellini, and ravioli) are so popular that they haven't changed much either. (Why tamper with success?) For something lighter, try the scrumptious hearts-of-palm salad or sautéed corvina. Grab a table away from the door (i.e., from the noise of the bus stop across the street). FYI, old-timers refer to the place as Balcón de Franco; the late, legendary chef Franco Piatti was the restaurant's guiding light for years. ⊠*Avda. Central and C. 9, Barrio La Soledad* ☎*2221–4841* ▭*AE, D, DC, MC, V* ☯*Closed Mon. Mar.–Nov.*

$

✕**La Trattoria.** The green and gold here might make a Green Bay Packers fan feel right at home, but it's the excellent, reasonably priced homemade pasta dishes that make this popular lunch spot worth the stop. Begin your meal with fresh bread and any number of excellent antipasti, continuing on with your favorite pasta dish. And for dessert, who can resist tiramisu? ⊠*Behind Automercado, Barrio Dent, San Pedro* ☎*2224–7065* ▭*AE, D, DC, MC, V* ☯*No dinner Sun.*

JAPANESE
$–$$

✗ **Matsuri.** It's a bit off the beaten tourist path and it's in a shopping center, but this is one of the capital's best sushi joints. The chefs here have created 48 recipes for original rolls, sushi, and sashimi, using high-quality imported ingredients. Bento boxes serve as the weekday lunch specials. The oohing and aahing you hear upstairs is for the chefs performing at the teppanyaki grills to the delight and applause of patrons. ⊠ *Plaza Cristal, 600 m south of Pop's ice-cream shop, Curridabat* ☎ *2280–5522* ▬ *AE, D, DC, MC, V.*

MEDITERRANEAN
$–$$

✗ **Pub Olio.** Although this combination pub and restaurant serves the full contingent of Mediterranean cuisine, we like to visit the place for drinks and Spanish-style *tapas* (appetizers). The century-old redbrick house with stained-glass windows draws everybody from tie-clad businessmen to university students who have money to spend on something more upscale than run-of-the-mill campus-area bars. Groups liven up the large front room—the quieter, smaller back rooms maintain a bit more romance—and the staff hauls umbrella-covered tables out to the sidewalk on warm evenings. Olio is extremely proud that it offers a copy of its menu in Braille. ⊠ *200 m north of Bagelmen's, Barrio Escalante* ☎ *2281–0541* ▬ *AE, D, DC, MC, V* ۞ *Closed Sun. No lunch Sat.*

MIDDLE EASTERN
$–$$

✗ **Lubnan.** Negotiate the quirky wrought-iron-and-burlap revolving door at the entrance, and you've made it into one of San José's few Middle Eastern restaurants. The Lebanese owners serve a wide variety of dishes from their native region, so if you can't decide, the *mezza* serves two people and gives you a little bit of everything. For your own individual dish, try the juicy shish kebab *de cordero* (of lamb), or if you're feeling especially adventurous, the raw ground-meat *kebbe naye* (with wheat meal) and *kafta naye* (without wheat meal). A hip bar in the back serves the same menu, but definitely eat out in the front restaurant Thursday night for the 9 PM belly-dancing show. ⊠ *Paseo Colón, Cs. 22–24, Paseo Colón* ☎ *2257–6071* ▬ *AE, D, DC, MC, V* ۞ *Closed Mon. No dinner Sun.*

PERUVIAN
$$
★

✗ **Machu Picchu.** A few travel posters and a fishnet holding crab and lobster shells are the only props used to evoke Peru, but no matter: the food is anything but plain, and the seafood is excellent at both the east- and west-side branches of this mainstay. The *pique especial de mariscos* (special seafood platter), big enough for two, presents you with shrimp, conch, and squid cooked four ways. The ceviche here is quite different from and better than that served in the rest of the country. A blazing Peruvian hot sauce served on the side adds zip to any dish, but be careful—apply it by the drop. Oh, and one more warning: the pisco sours go down very easily. ⊠ *C. 32, 130 m north of KFC, Paseo Colón* ☎ *2222–7384* ⊠ *150 m south of Ferretería El Mar, San Pedro* ☎ *2283–3679* ▬ *AE, D, DC, MC, V* ۞ *Paseo Colón location closed Sun.*

SOUTHWESTERN
$

✗ **JR Ribs.** Frederic Remington meets Barrio Amón in this restaurant made to look like an Old West saloon. Texas-style ribs are still enough of a novelty cuisine in Costa Rica that the diners have fun here, even if they haven't mastered the art of not getting the tangy barbecue sauce on their ties, blouses, or the plastic faux-rawhide tablecloths. For the less adventurous, an upstairs dining room serves Costa Rican food buffet-style weekdays for lunch. Stay downstairs; it's much more entertaining. ⊠*Avda. 11 and C. 11, Barrio Amón* ☎*2223–0523* ▤*AE, D, DC, MC, V* ⊗*No dinner Sun.*

SPANISH ✕**Casa Luisa.** A big open window looking into the kitchen—where chef
$$$ María Luisa Esparducer and her staff proudly show off their trade—is
Fodor'sChoice the first thing you encounter as you're shown to your table in this
★ homey, upscale Catalan restaurant. The place is eclectic, with wood floors, arresting artwork, soft lighting, and flamenco music in the background. Start the meal with gazpacho or eggplant pâté, accompanied by a glass of top Spanish wine. The excellent main dishes include rosemary lamb chops, suckling pig, and rabbit in white wine sauce with truffles. Finish with a platter of nuts, dates, and figs drizzled with a wine sauce or the decadent *crema catalana* with a *brûlée* glaze. We give Casa Luisa the nod as the city's best Spanish restaurant for its combination of style and coziness. ⊠*400 m south and 40 m east of the Contraloría, Sabana Sur* ☎*2296–1917* ▤*AE, D, DC, MC, V* ⊗*Closed Sun.*

VEGETARIAN ✕**Shakti.** The baskets of fruit and vegetables at the entrance and the
¢ wall of herbal teas, health-food books, and fresh herbs for sale by the register tell you you're in a vegetarian-friendly joint. The bright and airy macrobiotic restaurant—much homier than Vishnu, its major veggie competition—serves breakfast, lunch, and an early dinner, closing at 7 PM weekdays and 6 PM Saturday. Homemade bread, soy burgers, pita sandwiches (veggie or, for carnivorous dining companions, chicken), macrobiotic fruit shakes, and a hearty plato del día that comes with soup, green salad, and a fruit beverage fill out the menu. The *ensalada mixta* is a meal in itself, packed with root vegetables native to Costa Rica. ⊠*Avda. 8 and C. 13, Barrio La Soledad* ☎*2222–4475* ⌦*Reservations not accepted* ▤*MC, V* ⊗*Closed Sun.*

¢ ✕**Vishnu.** HACIENDO UN NUEVO MUNDO proudly proclaims the sign at the door. "Making a new world" might be a bit ambitious for a restaurant goal, but Vishnu takes its vegetarian offerings seriously. The dining area looks institutional—you'll sit at a sterile booth with Formica tables and gaze at posters of fruit on the walls—but the attraction is the inexpensive macrobiotic food. A yummy, good-value bet is usually the plato del día, which includes soup, beverage, and dessert, but the menu also includes soy burgers, salads, fresh fruit juices, and a yogurt smoothie called *morir soñando* (literally, "to die dreaming"). ⊠*Avda. 1, west of C. 3, Barrio El Carmen* ☎*2233–9976* ⌦*Reservations not accepted* ▤*AE, D, DC, MC, V* .

WHERE TO STAY

DOWNTOWN

Staying in the downtown area allows you to travel around the city as most Ticos do: on foot. Stroll the city's parks, museums, and shops, and then retire to one of the many small or historic hotels with plenty of character to offer.

$$$ 🏨**Aurola Holiday Inn.** The upper floors of this veritable skyscraper in a city of low-lying buildings give you commanding vistas of the surrounding mountains—day views are the best, since San José doesn't glitter quite like New York at night. The good restaurant and casino are also on the top floor, making full use of their vantage points. Inside, however, you could just as well be in Ohio, as the interior decoration betrays no local influence. The high-ceiling lobby is modern and airy, with lots of shiny marble, and the place has all the facilities a business traveler's heart could desire. ■TIP➔You'll get the hotel's best rates by reserving in advance via the local Costa Rican number or the hotel's own Web site, rather than the international Holiday Inn site. **Pros:** Business facilities, central location.**Con:** Sameness of chain hotel. ✉ *Avda. 5 and C. 5, Barrio El Carmen* ✆ *Apdo. 7802–1000* ☎*2523–1170, 866/857–0647 in North America* 🖷*2255–1171* ⊕*www.aurola-holidayinn. com* 🛏*188 rooms, 12 suites* &*In-room: safe, refrigerator, Ethernet, Wi-Fi. In-hotel: 2 restaurants, room service, bar, pool, gym, spa, laundry service, concierge, public Internet, airport shuttle, parking (no fee), no-smoking rooms* ▭*AE, D, DC, MC, V* ⦿*BP.*

$$ 🏨**Gran Hotel Costa Rica.** You cannot get more centrally located than the long-time grande dame of San José lodgings. This center-city landmark is a good deal for the money and a first choice of travelers who want to be where the action is, or want an in-house casino. A formal dining room and grand piano just off the lobby evoke the hotel's 1930s heyday. Rooms are large and bright, with small windows and tubs in the tiled baths. Even if you don't stay here, the arcaded Café 1930 that fronts the hotel is a pleasant stop for a bite any time of the day or night—it's open 24 hours. ■TIP➔Check the hotel's Internet site for frequent Web-only special rates. **Pro:**Central location.**Con:**Some street noise. ✉ *Avda. 2 and C. 3, Barrio La Soledad* ✆ *Apdo. 527–1000* ☎*2221–4000, 800/949–0592 in U.S.* 🖷*2255–0139* ⊕*www.grandhotel costarica.com* 🛏*104 rooms, 5 suites* &*In-room: safe, refrigerator, Wi-Fi. In-hotel: 3 restaurants, room service, bar, gym, laundry service, concierge, public Internet, parking (no fee), no-smoking rooms* ▭*AE, D, DC, MC, V* ⦿*BP.*

$$ 🏨**Hotel Balmoral.** You're just as likely to hear Japanese spoken in the Balmoral's lobby as you are Spanish and English; the place is quite popular with Asian visitors. As with the Presidente across the street, you'll find all the standard amenities of a medium-price business-class hotel here, and like the Presidente, the Balmoral draws a huge number of leisure travelers, too. But we prefer the Balmoral's dark wood and plush, older feel, as well as the bright, airy, recently remodeled restaurant El Patio, which dishes up Costa Rican specialties amid two floors of greenery. **Pro:** Central location. **Con:** Some street noise. ✉ *Avda. Central and C. 7, Barrio La Soledad* ☎*2222–5022, 800/691–4865 in North America* 🖷*2221–1919* ⊕*www.balmoral.co.cr* 🛏*112 rooms, 8 suites* &*In-room: safe, Wi-Fi. In-hotel: restaurant, bar, gym, laundry service, concierge, public Internet, parking (no fee)* ▭*AE, D, DC, MC, V* ⦿*BP.*

$$
★ 🏨**Hotel Fleur de Lys.** Can a three-floor Victorian house with a brassy hot-pink-and-lavender exterior offer anything of interest beyond its

front doors? Peek inside. The answer is a resounding yes. A quiet elegance that you'd never imagine lies inside this 80-year-old home, with garden restaurant and art gallery, on a block-long street that gets little traffic. Unsurprisingly, given the name of the place, rooms are tagged with names of flowers rather than numbers. We like the suites, which have raised bathtubs—two of them have whirlpool tubs as well—and dramatic glassed-in balcony entrances. Smoking is permitted in the hotel's common areas only. **Pro:** Cozy rooms. **Con:** Some noise from downstairs bar. ⊠ *C. 13 and Avdas. 2–6, Barrio La Soledad* ⅏ *Apdo. 10736–1000* ☎ *2223–1206 or 2257–2621* ⎙ *2221–6310* ⊕ *www. hotelfleurdelys.com* ⇨ *30 rooms, 6 suites* ⚲ *In-room: no a/c, safe, Wi-Fi. In-hotel: restaurant, bar, no elevator, laundry service, public Internet, parking (no fee), no-smoking rooms* ⊟ *AE, MC, V* ⎟⊙⎟ *EP.*

$$ **Hotel Presidente.** The *presidente* referred to here is John F. Kennedy, who walked by during his 1963 visit as the hotel was under construction. You're looking at standard, medium-price, business-class accommodation here. Each of the comfortable rooms has one double and one single bed. The hotel draws a large contingent of business and leisure-travel guests. The rooftop terrace with hot tub has one of those secret great views of the city that no one knows about. **Pro:** Central location. **Con:** Some street noise. ⊠ *Avda. Central and C. 7, Barrio La Soledad* ⅏ *Apdo. 2922–1000* ☎ *2256–1165* ⎙ *2221–1205* ⊕ *www. hotel-presidente.com* ⇨ *88 rooms, 12 suites* ⚲ *In room: safe, Wi-Fi. In-hotel: restaurant, room service, bar, gym, laundry service, public Internet, parking (no fee)* ⊟ *AE, D, DC, MC, V* ⎟⊙⎟ *BP.*

¢–$$ **Posada del Museo.** This green Victorian wooden 1928 house is a great place to stay if you're bound for San José's museums; hence the name. It sits diagonally across the street from the Museo Nacional. Each room is different. In the restoration, the friendly Argentine owners have maintained the original tiles, wooden double doors, and artfully painted ceilings. The hallway on the second floor overlooks the two-story lobby from what the owners call their "Romeo and Juliet balcony." The Internet-ready data ports in each room are a rarity in a lodging of this size. **Pros:** Cozy rooms, near museums. **Con:** Rush-hour train passes by. ⊠ *Avda. 2 and C. 17, Barrio La Soledad* ☎ *2258–1027* ⎙ *2257–9414* ⊕ *www.hotelposadadelmuseo.com* ⇨ *11 rooms, 3 suites* ⚲ *In-room: no a/c. In-hotel: restaurant, no elevator, laundry service, public Internet, parking (no fee)* ⊟ *AE, D, DC, MC, V* ⎟⊙⎟ *BP.*

¢–$ **Kap's Place.** This lodging literally sprawls around the neighborhood:
★   one of the three annexes is almost two blocks away from the main building. (And if you drive by too quickly, you'll likely miss that main building with its unassuming sign and white metal door.) Inside are bright, tropical rooms with lots of tile and wood; coffee and tea are brewing all the time in the reception area, and you can use the shared kitchen. You'll be asked to sign a two-page agreement when you register attesting that you'll keep the noise down and won't bring unregistered guests to your room. The owners are anxious to maintain a family atmosphere here. **Pros:** Good budget value, quiet. **Con:** Far from sights. ⊠ *C. 19 and Avdas. 11–13, 200 m west, 50 m north of Shell station, Barrio Aranjuez* ☎ *2221–1169 or 2257–0432* ⎙ *2256–4850* ⊕ *www.*

kapsplace.com ⟞*22 rooms, 17 with bath* ⟐*In-room: no a/c, no TV, Wi-Fi. In-hotel: public Internet, parking (fee), no-smoking rooms* ▤*AE, D, DC, MC, V* ❶❶*EP.*

¢ ⬚**Casa Ridgway.** If you prefer lodgings with a social conscience, this is the place for you. (And even if you don't, it's a great budget find.) Affiliated with the Quaker Peace Center next door, Casa Ridgway draws travelers concerned about peace, the environment, and social

DONDE ESTA EL HO-JO?

Don't play it safe at a chain hotel, other than the few we recommend. They're all here in the city, but most provide you with the exact sameness you'd find in Cleveland. Smaller hotels and their Tico hospitality (although many are owned by foreigners) are quintessentially Costa Rica.

issues, and the knowledgeable staff can give you the scoop on what's going on in those areas. In an old house on a quiet street, the bright premises include a planted terrace, a lending reference library, and a kitchen where you can cook your own food. Rooms are pretty basic and offer the option of bunk, single, or double beds. The dorm-style rooms sleep four, six, or eight. **Pros:** Rock-bottom prices, socially conscious management. **Cons:** Shared rooms, small rooms. ✉*Avda. 6 Bis and C. 15, Barrio La Soledad* ✆*Apdo. 1507–1000* ☎☎*2233–6168* ⊕*www.amigosparalapaz.org* ⟞*8 dorm-style rooms with shared bath, 1 double room* ⟐*In-room: no a/c, no phone, no TV. In-hotel: laundry service, public Internet, parking (no fee)* ▤*No credit cards* ❶❶*BP.*

¢ ⬚**Hotel Aranjuez.** Several 1940s-era houses with extensive gardens and lively common areas with visitors swapping travel advice constitute this family-run bed-and-breakfast. Each room is different; some have private gardens or small sitting rooms. The Aranjuez is a short walk from most San José attractions and has discount tour services. The complimentary breakfast buffet is an amazing spread of eggs, pastries, tropical fruit, good Costa Rican coffee, and more, served on a marvelous, palm-shaded garden patio. And, a rarity in the heart of the city, this place walks the eco-walk, too, with solar-heating panels for hot water, composted gardens, and recycling. Smoking is not permitted in the hotel. Luxurious it is not, but this is deservedly one of San José's most popular budget lodgings; reserve well in advance during the high season. ▪**TIP→Be sure to confirm your reservation 48 hours before you arrive and, if possible, on the day of your arrival, giving an estimated arrival time. If you don't, you might find yourself without a room when you arrive, despite your reservation.** You'll get a small discount if you pay in cash. **Pro:** Good budget value. **Cons:** Cumbersome reservations system, far from sights. ✉*C. 19, Avdas. 11–13, Barrio Aranjuez* ☎*2256–1825, 877/898–8663 in U.S.* ⧠*2223–3528* ⊕*www.hotelaranjuez.com* ⟞*35 rooms, 30 with bath* ⟐*In-room: no a/c, safe, Wi-Fi (some). In-hotel: restaurant, no elevator, laundry service, public Internet, parking (no fee), no-smoking rooms* ▤*MC, V* ❶❶*BP.*

BARRIOS AMÓN AND OTOYA

Just north of downtown, old homes converted into small lodgings populate Barrios Amón and Otoya, two of the capital's most historic neighborhoods. Though we generally eschew the big hotel franchises, our favorite San José chain lodging is here.

$$–$$$$

Fodor'sChoice

★

Clarion Hotel Amón Plaza. The pink Amón Plaza achieves everything we like in a business-class hotel. It transcends its chain status and provides you with all the services and amenities you need without being a cookie-cutter high-rise. Though large for a Barrio Amón lodging, the low-rise hotel doesn't overpower the surrounding neighborhood, and takes pride in the fact that each of its 80-plus rooms is slightly different. (One common feature: there's nothing mini about the minibars.) The price of the suites (but not the double rooms) includes all international calls and shuttle transport to anywhere in the metro area. Friday night sees cocktails and a buffet dinner at the hotel's open-air Cafetal de la Luz to the accompaniment of light music, but the café makes for a pleasant stop any time, any day, whether you stay here or not. **Pro:** Business facilities. **Con:** Lacks the more personal hospitality of a smaller hotel. ⊠ *Avda. 11 and C. 3 Bis, Barrio Amón* ☎ *2523–4600, 877/424–6423 in North America* 🖷 *2523–4614* ⊕ *www.choicehotels. com* 🛏 *60 rooms, 27 suites* ⌂ *In-room: safe, refrigerator, Ethernet, Wi-Fi. In-hotel: 2 restaurants, room service, bar, gym, spa, laundry service, public Internet, airport shuttle, parking (no fee), no-smoking rooms* ⊟ *AE, D, DC, MC, V* ⫿◎⫿ *BP.*

$$

Hotel Britannia. This mango-color home is the largest and most luxurious of the old Barrio Amón houses that now serve as lodgings. Technically, the Britannia is two houses in one: a stately old building with tile porch that has changed little since its construction in 1910, except for the conversion of the old wine cellar into an intimate international restaurant; and a newer addition with slightly smaller, carpeted rooms. We like the deluxe rooms and junior suites in the original house: they're spacious, with high ceilings and windows on the street side, and are worth the extra money but are close enough to the street that noise might be a problem if you're a light sleeper. All rooms are no-smoking. **Pros:** Good value, cozy rooms. **Con:** Borders on sketchy neighborhood. ⊠ *C. 3 and Avda. 11, Barrio Amón* 🖃 *Apdo. 3742–1000, San José* ☎ *2223–6667, 800/263–2618 in North America* 🖷 *2223–6411* ⊕ *www.hotelbritanniacostarica.com* 🛏 *19 rooms, 5 suites* ⌂ *In-room: no a/c (some), safe. In-hotel: restaurant, room service, bar, no elevator, laundry service, concierge, public Internet, public Wi-Fi, parking (no fee), no-smoking rooms* ⊟ *AE, MC, V* ⫿◎⫿ *BP.*

$$

★

Hotel Santo Tomás. Don't be put off by the fact that the front of this century-old former coffee-plantation house butts up against the sidewalk on a busy street; close the front door behind you and you'll find the lobby and rooms are set back away from the traffic noise. On the fringe of Barrio Amón, the hotel has spacious rooms with wood or tile floors and lots of deep, varnished-wood furnishings. Some of the tiled bathrooms have skylights. A bright breakfast room adjoins an interior patio, and if you keep traveling back into the interior of the building, you'll find a small outdoor pool, a rarity in a hotel of this size in the capital. The especially friendly, helpful staff makes this a real find. **Pros:** Good value, central location. **Cons:** Difficult parking, borders on sketchy neighborhood. ✉*Avda. 7, Cs. 3–5, Barrio Amón* ☎*2255–0448* 📠*2222–3950* ⊕*www.hotelsantotomas.com* ⬅*19 rooms* ⚘*In-room: no a/c, Wi-Fi. In-hotel: restaurant, bar, pool, gym, public Internet, parking (fee)* ▤*AE, MC, V* ❍*BP.*

$–$$ 🏨**Hotel Don Carlos.** One of the city's first guesthouses (technically it's ★ three different houses), the Don Carlos has been in the same family for four generations. But the spirit of Carlos Bálser, the hotel's Liechtenstein-born founder—painter, geologist, archaeologist, and general jack-of-all-trades—lives on. Most rooms in the rambling old coffee-baron house have ceiling fans and big windows. Those in the Colonial Wing have a bit more personality, and several newer rooms on the third floor have views of the Irazú and Barva volcanoes. Orchids and pre-Columbian statues adorn the abundant public areas, and the 272-tile mural in the lobby depicts the history of San José. Even if you don't stay here— and this is an old favorite among fodors.com forums users—the Don Carlos has arguably the best hotel gift shop in the country, well worth a stop. **Pros:** Good value, good place to meet fellow travelers. **Con:** Some noise in interior rooms. ✉*C. 9 and Avda. 9, Barrio Amón* ✉*Box 025216, Dept. 1686, Miami, FL33102-5216* ☎*2221–6707, 866/675– 9259 in North America* 📠*2258–1152* ⊕*www.doncarloshotel. com* ⬅*33 rooms* ⚘*In-room: no a/c (some), safe, Wi-Fi. In-hotel: restaurant, room service, no elevator, laundry service, public Internet, airport shuttle, parking (no fee)* ▤*AE, D, DC, MC, V* ❍*BP.*

$–$$ 🏨**Hotel Dunn Inn.** Adjoining 1926 and 1933 houses fuse to create the cozy Barrio Amón experience at bargain prices, so the Dunn Inn is justifiably immensely popular. (Reserve well in advance.) Pinewood dominates in one section; brick in the other. Sun-filled rooms bear indigenous Bribri names. One room has a balcony, and a few do not have street-facing windows but look onto an interior courtyard. All have terra-cotta floors and little touches such as fresh flowers. The delightful, skylight-covered central patio serves as a bar and breakfast room. **Pros:** good value, friendly staff. **Cons:** difficult to get reservations, interior rooms catch noise from lobby and bar. ✉*Avda. 11 at C. 5, Barrio Amón* ☎*2222–3232 or 2222–3426* 📠*2221–4596* ⊕*www. hoteldunninn.com* ⬅*25 rooms* ⚘*In-room: no a/c (some), safe, refrigerator, Wi-Fi. In-hotel: restaurant, bar, no elevator, public Internet, parking (fee)* ▤*AE, MC, V* ❍*EP.*

$ 🏨**Hotel Inca Real.** The Ecuadorian owners have constructed a modern Spanish colonial–style hotel that evokes South, rather than Central, America. Rooms congregate around a bright, skylight-covered, plant-filled central patio with wrought-iron gates around the second- and third-floor passageways. All rooms are ample in size. Those on the first floor are tiled; those on the second and third floors are carpeted. Some rooms have three beds, and all have back-friendly orthopedic mattresses. **Pro:** Good value. **Con:** Borders on sketchy neighborhood. ✉*Avda. 11, Cs. 3–5, Barrio Amón* ☎*2223–8883* 📠*2223–5318* ⊕*www.hotelincareal.com* ⬅*31 rooms* ⚘*In-room: safe, Wi-Fi. In-*

hotel: restaurant, bar, laundry service, public Internet, parking (no fee) ☰ *V* ☖*CP.*

$ ☖ **Hotel Rincón de San José.** Never mind that the interior looks more European than Latin American. (It was once called the Hotel Edelweiss, and everyone still refers to it by its old name.) This elegant little inn has comfortable rooms in a charming area near the Parque España. Rooms have carved doors, custom-made furniture, and small bathrooms. Most have hardwood window frames and floors; several have bathtubs. Complimentary breakfast is served in the garden courtyard, which doubles as a bar. The owners speak German and Dutch, in addition to the requisite English and Spanish. **Pros:** Good value, friendly management. **Con:** Small rooms. ☒ *Avda. 9 and C. 15, Barrio Otoya* ☎*2221–9702* 🖷*2222–2145* ⊕*www.hotelrincondesanjose.com* ⟿*38 rooms* ⌂*In-room: no a/c, safe, no TV (some), Wi-Fi. In-hotel: bar, no elevator, laundry service, public Internet, parking (fee)* ☰*AE, D, DC, MC, V* ☖*CP.*

¢–$ ☖ **Cinco Hormigas Rojas.** The name of this whimsical little lodge trans-
★ lates as "five red ants." Behind the wall of vines that obscures it from the street is a wild garden—it's an unexpected urban bird-watching venue, and you'll get a guide to what you can see—leading to an interior space filled with original artwork. The largest, newest room (the Hoja Dansante, or Dancing Leaf) overlooks the mini-jungle that is the front entrance. Color abounds, from the bright hues on the walls right down to the toilet seats. Sure enough, the resident owner is an artist—Mayra Güell turned the 80-year-old house she inherited from her grandmother into San José's most original B&B–cum–art gallery. She tosses in thoughtful touches such as a healthy boxed breakfast if you're heading out on an early-morning excursion, and coffee and tea 24/7. If you need everything just so and cherish the sameness and predictability of a chain hotel, look elsewhere, but if there's an artistic, Bohemian bent to your personality, this is your place. **Pros:** Friendly owner, artistic decor, bird-filled patio. **Cons:** Small rooms, dark rooms. ☒ *C. 15, between Avdas. 9–11, Barrio Otoya* ☎*2255–3412* 🖷 *2257–8581* ⊕*www.cincohormigasrojas.com* ⟿*4 rooms, 2 with bath* ⌂*In-room: no a/c (some), no phone, no TV (some). In-hotel: no elevator, laundry service, public Internet, parking (fee)* ☰ *AE, MC, V* ☖*BP.*

WEST OF DOWNTOWN

San José's vast west side contains only a smattering of lodgings, but you'll find one of the city's best here.

$$$ ☖ **Hotel Parque del Lago.** The management that brought you the South Pacific's Lapa Ríos (⇨ See Cabo Matapalo in Chapter 6), also runs things at this eco-conscious, west-side lodging, away from the hubbub of downtown. But business travelers—they make up the bulk of the clientele—are looking for business services as much as they are for more than the recycling and environmentally friendly soap, and they're here, too. Rooms are a mix of sizes, but all have big windows, polished furniture, and armoires, in addition to ample closet space. **Pro:** Good business facilities. **Con:** Far from sights. ☒*C. 40, Avda. 2, Paseo Colón* ☎*2257–8787* 🖷*2223–1617* ⊕*www.parquedellago.com* ⟿*30* *rooms, 10 suites △In room: refrigerator, Wi-Fi. In hotel: restaurant, bar, gym, laundry service, public Internet, airport shuttle, parking (no fee) ☰AE, D, DC, MC, V ⦿|BP.*

$$ 🖼 **Hotel Grano de Oro.** Two wooden houses on San José's west side—
Fodor'sChoice one dates from the turn of the 20th century, and the other from the
★ 1950s—have been melded together and converted into one of the city's most charming inns, decorated throughout with old photos of the capital and paintings by local artists. A 2007 remodeling has turned the public areas into glitz and elegance, but head up to your room for the old coffee plantation feel for which the hotel is still known. Each room in the place is different, and although you can't go wrong with any of them, the older house's rooms are the nicest, especially the Garden Suite, with hardwood floors, high ceilings, and private garden. The sumptuous restaurant ($$$$), run by a French-trained chef, wraps around a lovely indoor patio and bromeliad-filled gardens, and has become one of the capital's premier dining venues. The hotel's sundeck has a view of both the city and the far-off volcanoes. The Grano de Oro is a consistent favorite with posters to fodors.com forums. **Pros:** Friendly management, top-notch service. **Con:** Far from sights. ✉*C. 30, Avdas. 2–4, Paseo Colón* ☎*1701 N.W. 97th Ave., SJO 36, Box 025216, Miami, FL33102-5216* ☎*2255–3322* 🖷*2221–2782* ⊕*www. hotelgranodeoro.com* ⟿*40 rooms, 3 suites △In-room: no a/c, safe, refrigerator, dial-up. In-hotel: restaurant, room service, no elevator, laundry service, public Internet, public Wi-Fi, parking (no fee), no-smoking rooms ☰AE, D, DC, MC, V ⦿|EP.*

EAST OF DOWNTOWN

The small properties beyond downtown, toward the university, offer personalized service and lots of peace and quiet. Plenty of restaurants and bars are within easy reach, and downtown San José is just a 10-minute cab ride away.

$$–$$$ 🖼 **Hotel Le Bergerac.** Any other lodging of this caliber would be content
Fodor'sChoice to live off its reputation, and we'd never begrudge Le Bergerac if it did
★ rest on its well-established laurels as one of San José's great hotels. But these folks are always tweaking and remodeling, and each time you return you'll likely discover something new. (What *doesn't* change much is the rates; they've kept pretty constant over time.) The hotel occupies two former private homes and is furnished with antiques. All rooms have custom-made wood-and-stone dressers and writing tables; deluxe rooms have two beds, private garden terraces or balconies, and large bathrooms. The location on a steep hill might disorient you; you could walk upstairs to your room, fling open the terrace doors, expecting to walk out onto a balcony, and find instead a ground-level patio and mountain view. The in-hotel restaurant, L'Ile de France *(⇨ Where to Eat)*, is one of the city's best, so dinner reservations are essential, even for guests. Breakfast is served on a garden patio. As befits the name, on parle français. Le Bergerac remains the cream of a crop of small, upscale San José hotels. There are many of them, but the service, attention to detail, and ample gardens set this place apart. Hands down, this is our favorite lodging in the city. **Pros:** Top-notch

service, cozy rooms, terrific restaurant. **Con:** Rooms on the smaller side. ⊠ *C. 35, Avdas. Central–2, first entrance to Los Yoses, San Pedro* ✉*Apdo. 1107–1002, San José* ☎*2234–7850* 🖷*2225–9103* ⊕*www. bergerachotel.com* ✍*26 rooms* ⚅*In-room: no a/c, safe, Ethernet. In-hotel: restaurant, bar, no elevator, laundry service, public Internet, air-port shuttle, parking (no fee), no-smoking rooms* ▤*AE, D, DC, MC, V* ⵏⵔⵍ*BP.*

$ ☷ **Hotel Don Fadrique.** This tranquil, family-run B&B on the outskirts of San José was named after Fadrique Gutiérrez, an illustrious great-uncle of the owners who constructed the Fortín in Heredia. A collection of original Costa Rican art decorates the lobby and rooms, most of which have hardwood floors, peach walls, and pastel bedspreads. Several car-peted rooms downstairs open onto lots of lush garden space. There are also an enclosed garden patio and an adjoining small art gallery where meals are served. Parking is free, but on the street, with a guard present 24/7. **Pro:** Good value. **Cons:** Difficult parking, far from sights. ⊠*C. 37 at Avda. 8, Los Yoses, San Pedro* ✉*Apdo. 1754–2050, San Pedro* ☎*2225–8186 or 2225–7050* 🖷*2224–9746* ⊕*www.hoteldonfadrique. com* ✍*20 rooms* ⚅*In-room: no a/c, safe, Wi-Fi. In-hotel: restaurant, room service, no elevator, laundry service, public Internet, airport shut-tle* ▤*AE, MC, V* ⵏⵔⵍ*BP.*

$ ☷ **Hotel Milvia.** Apply the principles of feng shui to an old militia arms depository, and you get a charming B&B on a San Pedro backstreet. Manager Florencia Urbina belongs to a local art consortium called Bocaracá, whose motto is "Art in Society." She takes that maxim seri-ously: the group's lush tropical paintings adorn the lobby, breakfast salon, small bar, and common areas. Your room will be decorated with lovely hand-painted tiles and classic Tico furniture, and you pass through a Zen meditation garden each time you enter and exit the building. The Milvia is a great value, and makes for a charming, artsy respite from the noise of the city. Julia Roberts and Susan Sarandon are a couple of celebrities who have stayed here. **Pros:** Good value, artistic decor. **Con:** Far from sights. ⊠*100 m north and 100 m east of Cen-tro Comercial Muñoz y Nanne, San Pedro* ✉*Apdo. 1660–2050, San Pedro* ☎*2225–4543 or 2283–9548* 🖷*2225–7801* ⊕*www.hotelmilvia. com* ✍*9 rooms* ⚅*In-room: no a/c, safe, Wi-Fi. In-hotel: bar, no ele-vator, laundry service, public Internet, parking (no fee), no-smoking rooms* ▤*AE, D, DC, MC, V* ⵏⵔⵍ*BP.*

¢   ☷ **Hostal Toruma.** The headquarters of RECAJ, Costa Rica's active Hostelling International network, is housed in a colonial-style bunga-low, built around 1900, several blocks east of downtown. Backpack-ers from around the world hang out and exchange travel tales in the bright tiled lobby and veranda. The on-site information center offers discounted tours. Beds on the ground floor are in small compartments with doors; rooms on the second floor have standard bunks. There are also three private rooms for couples. HI cardholders receive a 20% discount. **Pro:** Rock-bottom budget value. **Cons:** Shared rooms, small rooms. ⊠*Avda. Central, Cs. 29–31, Barrio La California* ✉*Apdo. 1355–1002, San José* ☎*2234–8186* 🖷🖷*2224–4085* ⊕*www.hicr.org* ✍*80 beds in 17 dormitory rooms with shared baths, 3 private rooms* *without bath* ⚡*In-room: no a/c, no phone, no TV. In-hotel: public Internet, parking (no fee)* ⊟*MC, V* ⊧ⓞ|*CP.*

NIGHTLIFE & THE ARTS

THE ARTS

The best source for theater, dance, film, and arts information is the "Viva" entertainment section of the Spanish-language daily *La Nación*. The paper also publishes the "Tiempo Libre" section each Friday, highlighting what's going on over the weekend. *San José Volando* is a free monthly magazine found in many upscale hotels and restaurants, and publishes features about what's going on around town. Listings in both publications are in Spanish, but are easy to decipher. The "Weekend" section of the English-language weekly *Tico Times* lists information about arts and culture, much of it events of interest to the expatriate community. The paper comes out each Friday.

ART GALLERIES

San José's art galleries, public or private, museum or bohemian, keep daytime hours only, but all kick off a new show with an evening exhibit opening. They're free and open to the public, and offer a chance to rub elbows with Costa Rica's art community (and to sip wine and munch on appetizers). Listings appear in *La Nación*'s "Viva" section. Your time in the capital might coincide with one of these by happenstance. (They're rarely announced in the paper more than a day or two in advance.) Look for the term *inauguración* (opening).

THEATER & MUSIC

Broadway or the West End it isn't, but San José has an active theater scene. More than a dozen theater groups (many of which perform slapstick comedies) hold forth in smaller theaters around town. If your Spanish is up to it, call for a reservation. The curtain rises at 8 PM, Friday through Sunday, with some companies staging performances on Thursday night, too.

The **Eugene O'Neill Theater** (⊠ *Centro Cultural Costarricense–Norteamericano, Avda. 1 and C. 37, Barrio Dent, San Pedro* ☎*2207–7554*) has chamber concerts and plays most weekend evenings. The cultural center is a great place to meet expatriate North Americans.

For six decades, the **Little Theatre Group** (☎*8355–1623* W*www.little theatregroup.org*) has presented English-language community-theater productions several times a year at various venues around town. The "Weekend" section of the English-language *Tico Times* has listings.

The **Teatro La Aduana** (⊠ *C. 25, Avda. 3, Barrio La California* ☎*2257–8305*) holds frequent dance and stage performances, and is home to the Compañía Nacional de Teatro (National Theater Company). The baroque **Teatro Nacional** (⊠ *Plaza de la Cultura, Barrio La Soledad* ☎*2221–1329*) is the home of the excellent National Symphony Orchestra, which performs on Friday evenings and Sunday mornings between April and November. The theater also hosts visiting musical groups and dance companies. Tickets are $4–$40. San José's second-most popular theater, the **Teatro Popular Melico Salazar** (⊠ *Avda. 2, Cs. Central–2, Barrio La Merced* ☎*2233–5424*) has a full calendar of music and dance, as well as a few offbeat productions. Something goes on nearly every night of the week; tickets are $2–$20.

> **BE AWARE**
>
> A few gems really do populate the downtown area, but several bars there double as prostitute pickup joints or are just boozy places where patrons go to pick fights. (If you're in the center city at night, stick to a drink in your hotel or to the places we recommend, and don't wander directly south or west of Parque Central on foot.)

NIGHTLIFE

The metro area's hottest nightlife has migrated to the Central Valley suburbs of Escazú and Heredia these days. (⇨ See Chapter 2.) Both are about 20-minute taxi rides from downtown San José. The capital isn't devoid of places to go in the evening, however. It still contains plenty of bars, dance places, and restaurants and cafés where you can spend the evening. Take taxis to and from when you go. Most places you might go will be happy to call you a cab when you're ready to call it a night.

BARS

No one could accuse San José of having too few watering holes, but aside from the hotels there aren't many places to have a quiet drink, especially downtown—Tico bars tend to be on the lively side.

El Observatorio (⊠ *C. 23, across from Cine Magaly Barrio La California* ☎*2223–0725*) strikes an unusual balance between casual and formal: it's the kind of place where an over-30 crowd goes to watch a soccer game on TV, but wears a tie or dress to do so. The capital's best live-music venue, hands-down, is the New York–style

★ **Jazz Café San Pedro** (⊠ *Avda. Central next to Banco Popular, San Pedro* ☎*2253–8933* ⊕*www.jazzcafecostarica.com*) draws big crowds, especially for live jazz on Tuesday and Wednesday nights. The moniker "Jazz Café" used to suffice, but with the 2008 opening of a branch in the Central Valley suburb of Escazú, the location was added to the name.

Costa Rica's only microbrewery, **K & S Brewery** (⊠ *Centro Comercial Cristal, 600 m south of Pop's ice-cream shop, Curridabat* ☎*2280–5468*), serves its own pilsners and lagers—they're a refreshing change from the ubiquitous Imperial brand drunk by the masses. The bar and restaurant frequently host '60s and '70s nights.

An older expat crowd hangs out at **Mac's American Bar** (⊠ *South side of La Sabana Park, next to the Tennis Club, Sabana Sur* ☎*2234–3145*), which gets our nod for serving the city's best burgers and usually has a sporting event playing on the television.

Fill up on Spanish-style tapas at Mediterranean bar and restaurant **Pub Olio** (⊠*200 m north of Bagelmen's, Barrio Escalante* ☎*2281–0541*). It draws a mix of professionals and older college students.

A refreshing change from the ubiquitous Imperial beer is what you'll find at **Stan's Irish Pub** (⊠*125 m west of Casa Presidencial, Zapote* ☎*2253–4360*),which has Guinness on tap as well as an around-the-world selection of brews.

CAFÉS AND RESTAURANTS

For a country so economically dependent on coffee, there's little evidence of a café culture à la Starbucks here. Costa Ricans do observe coffee breaks religiously at home and at work, but outside a few places we list below, making a special trip to converse somewhere with friends over coffee isn't too common.

Near the university, **Fezcafé** (⊠*C. de la Amargura, San Pedro* ☎*2280– 6982*) is a quiet alternative to the rowdy nightlife nearby, at least until 8 PM on weeknights.

CASINOS

Ask about casino rules before you dive in and play: there are a few Costa Rican variations—for example, you don't get a bonus for blackjack, but you do for three of a kind or straights under local rules—and yet some places proudly boast that they play exactly like they do in Las Vegas.

The term "casino" gets tossed around loosely in Costa Rica: a hotel can put a couple of video poker machines in its lobby and claim it operates a casino. The casino at the pink Hotel del Rey in Barrio El Carmen—arguably the city's most famous and definitely its most notorious gambling establishment—swarms with prostitutes. Avoid it.

A few of the city's larger hotels have legitimate casinos, including the Clarion Amón Plaza, the Aurola Holiday Inn (the view from the casino is breathtaking), and the Gran Hotel Costa Rica.

The 24-hour **Casino Colonial** (⊠*Avda. 1, Cs. 9–11, Barrio El Carmen* ☎*2258–2807*) has a complete casino, bar, restaurant, and cable TV.

DANCE CLUBS

San José's discos attract a *very* young crowd. Quite frankly, you'll feel ancient if you've passed 25. Live-music halls draw dancers of all ages, but most of these populate rougher neighborhoods on the city's south side and are best avoided.

Ebony 56 (⊠*Centro Comercial El Pueblo, Avda. 0, Barrio Tournón* ☎*2223–2195*) does triple duty as disco, sports bar, and café and draws an under-25 crowd. **Friends** (⊠*Centro Comercial El Pueblo, Avda. 0, Barrio Tournón* ☎*2233–5283*) plays mostly pop and Latin music and draws a still young clientele, but slightly older than that of Ebony 56 next door. For a dance-hall experience in a good neighborhood, we recommend the enormous **El Tobogán** (⊠*200 m north and 100 m east of La República, Barrio Tournón* ☎*2223–8920*), an alternative to the postage stamp–size floors of most discos. Live Latin bands get everyone on their feet Friday and Saturday nights, and Sunday afternoon.

FOLKLORE

Noches Costarricenses (Costa Rican Nights) performances take place at **Pueblo Antiguo** (✛ *3 km (2 mi) west of Hospital México, La Uruca* ☎2257–4171), a Tico version of Colonial Williamsburg west of the city depicting Costa Rica between 1880 and 1930. The spectacle gets under way on Friday and Saturday nights from 6:30 to 9:30, with dinner and music and dance performances. The $50 tour price includes transportation to and from San José hotels and English-speaking guides. Arrange through your hotel's front desk.

GAY & LESBIAN

San José has a few bars, restaurants, and dance places patronized primarily by a gay and lesbian clientele, although all are welcome. Another tier of businesses, exemplified by the venerable Café Mundo, draws a mixed gay-straight crowd. Many more establishments dot the city than the tried-and-true places we mention below. A couple we visited preferred not to be listed in a guidebook. Others cater to tastes not quite so conventional. The popularity of still others waxes and wanes with changing fashions, but the few we list below have drawn crowds for years.

Al Despiste (✉*Across from Mudanzas Mundiales, Zapote* ☎2234–5956) is a gay bar that serves light bocas (appetizers), and has dance nights Wednesday–Sunday. A gay and lesbian crowd frequents **La Avispa** (✉*C. 1, Avdas. 8–10, Barrio La Soledad* ☎2223–5343), which has two dance floors with videos and karaoke, and a quieter upstairs bar with pool tables. The last Wednesday of each month is ladies' night. **El Bochinche** (✉*C. 11, Avdas. 10–12, Barrio La Soledad* ☎2221–0500) is a gay bar and dance club that doubles as a Mexican restaurant. **Club Oh!** (✉*C. 2, Avdas. 14–16A, Barrio El Pacífico* ☎2248–1500) is a mostly gay, techno-heavy disco with two dance floors and weekly drag shows. Take a taxi to and from here; the neighborhood's sketchy.

> ### DANCE FEVER
>
> Step into a San José nightclub and you might think Costa Ricans are born dancing. They aren't, but most learn to merengue, rumba (*bolero* here), mambo, cha-cha, and *swing* (called *cumbia* elsewhere) as children. Play catch-up at dance school **Merecumbé** (☎*2224–3531* ✉ *merecumbe@racsa.co.cr*), which has 10 branches around the metro area. With a few days' notice you can arrange a private lesson with an English-speaking instructor and get the fundamentals of merengue and bolero, both of which are easy to master and work well with a variety of music.

SHOPPING

Although it might seem more "authentic" to buy your souvenirs at their out-country source, you can find everything in the city, a real bonus if you're pressed for time. If the capital has any real tourist shopping district, it's found loosely in the cluster of streets around Parque Morazán, just north of downtown, an area bounded roughly by Avenidas 1 and 7 and Calles 5 and 9. Stroll and search, because many other businesses congregate in the area as well. The northeastern suburb of Moravia contains a cluster of high-quality crafts and artisan shops, for good reason very popular with tour groups, in the three blocks heading north from the Colegio María Inmaculada. The street is two blocks behind the city's church.

SPECIALTY STORES

BOOKS & MAPS

The New York Times, the Wall Street Journal, the Miami Herald, and *USA Today* arrive in San José the morning of publication, printed here and bound on bond paper. Find them at a select few outlets and shops in large hotels or at the airport.

With several locations around the metro area, **Casa de las Revistas** (⊠ *C. 5, Avdas. 3–5, Barrio El Carmen* ☎ *2256–5092* ⊠ *Plaza del Sol, Curridabat* ☎ *2283–0822* ⊠ *Plaza Mayor, Blvd. de Rohrmoser, Rohr-*

TALKING SHOP

Shopping in Costa Rica will seem blissfully low-key, especially if you've earned your stripes in places with high-pressure sales pestering, such as Mexico and Jamaica. Vendors will ask, *"¿En qué puedo servirle?"* ("How can I help you?"), as you walk by their stands, but if you're just looking, a simple *"No gracias"* ("No, thank you") reply suffices to be left alone. Prices are fixed, but fair. There's no haggling here.

moser ☎ *2296–7943* ⊠ *C. Central, Avdas. 2–4* ☎ *2222–0987*) has San José's best selection of magazines in English. **Librería Internacional** (⊠ *300 m west of Taco Bell, Barrio Dent* ☎ *2253–9553*) is San José's largest bookstore and the closest it has to a place with a Borders or Barnes & Noble feel, although on a much smaller scale. It stocks English translations of Latin American literature and myriad coffee-table books on Costa Rica. The affable owners of **7th Street Books** (⊠ *C. 7, Avdas. Central–1, Barrio La Soledad* ☎ *2256–8251*) make this store *the* place to stop in and see what's going on in the expat community. It has the city's best selection of books in English and is also strong on Latin America and tropical ecology. You can pick up *the Tico Times* here.

CRAFTS

The arts-and-crafts tradition in Costa Rica is not as strong as in, say, Guatemala or Peru, and at first glance you might be disenchanted with what you see in the run-of-the-mill souvenir shops around town. Keep your disappointment in check until you visit two of San José's outstanding purveyors of fine artisan work.

Fodor'sChoice
★
Downtown San José's must-stop shop is **Galería Namu** (⊠ *Avda. 7, Cs. 5–7, behind Aurola Holiday Inn, Barrio Amón* ☎ *2256–3412* ⊕ *www. galerianamu.com*), which sells Costa Rican folkloric art and the best indigenous crafts in town. Its inventory brims with colorful creations by the Guaymí, Boruca, Bribri, Chorotega, Huetar, and Maleku peoples—all Costa Rican indigenous groups. You can also find exquisitely carved ivory-nut Tagua figurines and baskets made by Wounan Indians from Panama's Darién region. Take note of carved balsa masks, woven cotton blankets, and hand-painted ceramics. The store looks expensive

when you first walk in—and indeed, the sky is the limit in prices—but if your budget is not so flush, say so: the good folks here can help you find something in the $10–$20 range that will make a more cherished souvenir of your trip than a *Pura Vida* T-shirt. And as an added bonus you'll get an information sheet describing your work's creator and art style. Namu has a reputation for fair prices for customers, and for fair pay to artists or artisans.

★ The staff and selection at **Kaltak Artesanías** (✉ *50 m north of Colegio María Inmaculada, Moravia* ☎ *2297–2736*) make it a real standout from all the Moravia shops. Walk in with some unformulated "I'm not sure what I want" notions, and the folks here will help you find that perfect souvenir or gift from among the selection of ceramics (Pefi and Osenbach designs, trademarks of two well-known artisans in the capital, are well represented), wood-and-leather rocking chairs, oxcarts of all sizes, orchids, and carvings from native *cocobolo* and *guápinol* woods and ash wood.

SOUVENIRS

Hotel gift shop **Boutique Annemarie** (✉ *Hotel Don Carlos, C. 9 and Avda. 9, Barrio Amón* ☎ *2233–5343*) has a huge selection of popular souvenirs and CDs of Costa Rican musicians. Stop by souvenir shops **Casa Tica, El Cafetal, Morpho,** and **Terra Verde** in the **Aeropuerto Internacional Juan Santamaría** (✛ *16 km (10 mi) northwest of downtown San José, just outside Alajuela*) for those last-minute purchases. Choose from various blends of coffee ($5 per pound) and a terrific selection of good-quality merchandise, such as hand-carved bowls and jewelry, aromatherapy candles, banana-paper stationery, and Costa Rica travel books, Fodor's included. (Merchandise selection is slightly different in each.) There's nary another store in the country carrying such a variety all in one place. The catch is that the airport shops charge U.S. prices for this luxury.

Some 100 souvenir vendors congregate in the block-long covered walkway known as the **Calle Nacional de Artesanía y Pintura** (✉ *C. 13, Avdas. Central–2, western side of Plaza de la Democracia*), and offer some real bargains in hammocks, wood carvings, and clothing. Dozens of souvenir vendors set up shop on the two floors of **La Casona** (✉ *C. 2, Avdas. Central–1, Barrio El Carmen* ☎ *2222–7999*), in a rickety old downtown mansion. It's much like a flea market, and it's a fun place to browse.

If you can't find it at **Mundo de Recuerdos** (✉ *Across from Colegio María Inmaculada, Moravia* ☎ *2240–8990*), it probably doesn't exist. Here's the largest of the Moravia shops with simply everything—at least of standard souvenir fare—you could ask for under one roof.

The museum-shop concept barely exists here, but the **Museo del Oro Precolombino** (✉ *C. 5, Avdas. Central–2, Barrio La Soledad* ☎ *2243–4217*), at the Gold Museum entrance, is the exception, with its terrific selection of pre-Columbian-theme jewelry, art, exclusively designed T-shirts, coin- and bill-theme key chains, notebooks, and mouse pads.

EDIBLE SOUVENIRS

Costa Rica's foremost product is its foremost souvenir: Café Rey, Café Volio, and the ubiquitous Café Britt are superior brands of arabica coffee, and you'll find their foil-wrapped export-quality packages in supermarkets—which have the best prices—or souvenir shops. Their labels read *grano entero* (whole bean) or *molido* (ground); and *tostado claro* (light roast) or *tostado oscuro* (dark roast). The good ground stuff will also say *puro* (pure), and will not be mixed with sugar the way that Costa Ricans drink it. Britt is the only one that offers you the more sedate *descafeinado* (decaffeinated) option. And while you're at it, pick up a *chorreador*, too. Most gift shops sell the small stands with a cloth through which you can brew coffee the time-honored Tico way. (It's more tedious than Mr. Coffee, but is guaranteed to generate more conversation among your guests back home.)

Costa Rica's best **rum** is the aged Centenario—pick up a bottle for about $10. In addition to *añejo* (aged), it also comes *blanco* (white), and *conmemorativo* (commemorative), a premium aged, limited-production edition. There are several brands of **coffee liqueurs** (*licor de café*), including Café Rica and Golden Cream, but Britt makes the best one (although the Don Braulio–brand hand-painted bottles add visual pizzazz to your home bar). Buy these at any of San José's abundant supermarkets and liquor stores. FANAL, the government distillery, bottles Cacique-brand **guaro**, a 60-proof sugarcane liquor. "Firewater" might be a better description for it; try it only if you dare.

Any self-respecting Tico home or restaurant keeps a bottle of **Salsa Lizano,** one of the country's signature food products, on hand. Its tang brightens up meat, vegetable, and rice dishes.

One major caveat applies these days: Costa Rican airports enforce passenger liquid-transport restrictions similar to those of North America and Europe. You must pack liquor or hot sauce in your checked luggage—not an easy proposition, to be sure—or purchase such items in the airport shops beyond security. (They will be delivered to the plane when you board.) Coffee is easier to tuck into your carry-on.

All these edibles can be found at **Más x Menos** (pronounced "Más por Menos") supermarkets throughout the country. It beats souvenir stores' prices for coffee, food, liquor, and other beverages. The main San José branch is at Avenida Central, between Calles 11 and 13.

SAN JOSÉ ESSENTIALS

TRANSPORTATION

BY AIR

ARRIVING & DEPARTING Two airports serve San José. Aeropuerto Internacional Juan Santamaría is the destination for all international flights as well as those of domestic airline SANSA in a terminal a couple of blocks away. Domestic Nature Air flights depart from Aeropuerto Internacional Tobías Bolaños. Arrival and departure at the tiny Tobías Bolaños Airport is very informal. *For in-depth information about arriving at Juan Santamaría Airport, getting to and from the airport, and airlines, see By Air in Costa Rica Essentials.*

Airports **Aeropuerto Internacional Juan Santamaría** (*SJO* ✈ *16 km [10 mi] northwest of downtown San José, just outside Alajuela* ☎ *2437–2400*). **Aeropuerto Internacional Tobías Bolaños** (*SYQ* ✈ *3 km [2 mi] west of the city center, Pavas* ☎ *2232–2820*).

BY BUS

ARRIVING &
DEPARTING

San José has no central bus terminal, and buses to many destinations depart from street corners. The four largest bus stations—the Gran Terminal del Caribe, the Terminal Atlántico Norte, the Terminal de Puntarenas, and the so-called Terminal Coca-Cola (the former Coke bottling plant)—are all in dicey neighborhoods. Always take a taxi to and from the bus station, and at the Coca-Cola *never* take your eyes off your belongings. Call your individual bus line for information about schedules rather than the terminal itself. Consider the comfort of a shuttle-van service in an air-conditioned minivan for travel out of the capital. *For bus and shuttle-van information and departure points from San José to other areas of the country, see By Bus in Costa Rica Essentials.*

Bus Terminals **Gran Terminal del Caribe** (⊠ *C. Central and Avda. 13, Barrio Tournón*). **Terminal Coca-Cola** (⊠ *C. 16, Avdas. 1–3, Barrio México*). **Terminal Atlántico Norte** (⊠ *C. 12 and Avda. 9, Barrio México*). **Terminal de Puntarenas** (⊠ *C. 16, Avdas. 10–12, Barrio Cuba*).

GETTING
AROUND

City bus service is absurdly cheap (30¢–50¢) and easy to use. For Paseo Colón and La Sabana, take buses marked SABANA–CEMENTERIO from stops at Avenida 2 between Calles 5 and 7, or on Avenida 3 next to the *correos* (post office). For the suburbs of Los Yoses and San Pedro near the university, take ones marked SAN PEDRO from Avenida Central, between Calles 9 and 11.

BY CAR

ARRIVING &
DEPARTING

San José is the hub of the national road system. Paved roads fan out from Paseo Colón west to Escazú and northwest to the airport and Heredia. For the Pacific coast, Guanacaste, and Nicaragua, take the Carretera Interamericana (Pan-American Highway) north (CA1), which continues beyond the airport. Calle 3 runs north into the highway to Guápiles, Limón, and the Atlantic coast through Braulio Carrillo National Park, with a turnoff to the Sarapiquí region. If you follow Avenida Central or 2 east through San Pedro, you'll enter the Pan-American Highway south (CA2), which has a turnoff for Cartago, Volcán Irazú, and Turrialba before it heads southeast over the mountains toward Panama.

Weekday driving restrictions apply in central San José to all vehicles, including your rental car, in a zone bounded by Avenidas 9 and 16, and Calles 11 and 22. Vehicles may not operate in the area from 7–8:30 AM and 4–5:30 PM on Monday (for license plates ending in 1 and 2),

Tuesday (3 and 4), Wednesday (5 and 6), Thursday (7 and 8), and Friday (9 and 0).

GETTING AROUND   Almost every street in downtown San José is one-way. Try to avoid driving at peak hours (7–9 AM and 5–6:30 PM), as traffic gets horribly congested. Parking lots, scattered throughout the city, charge around $1 an hour. Outside the city center you can park on the street, where *guachimen* ("watchmen" or car guards) usually offer to watch your car for a 500-colón tip, more if you're going to be away from the car for a few hours. Even so, never leave shopping bags or valuables inside your parked car. *For car-rental information, see Car Rental in Costa Rica Essentials.*

BY TAXI

GETTING AROUND   Taxis are a good deal within the city. You can hail one on the street (all licensed taxis are red with a gold triangle on the front doors) or have your hotel or restaurant call one for you, as cabbies tend to speak only Spanish and addresses are complicated. (A good way to avoid getting lost is to have someone write down the address to show to the driver.) A 3-km (2-mi) ride costs around $2, and tipping is not the custom. Taxis parked in front of expensive hotels charge about twice the normal rate. By law, all cabbies must use their meters—called *marías*—when operating within the metropolitan area; if one refuses, negotiate a price before setting off, or hail another. ■ TIP→**The surest way to antagonize a driver is to slam the door; be gentle.** Cab companies include Alfaro, San Jorge, Coopetaxi, and if you need to go to the airport, the orange Taxis Unidos. Many unofficial taxis (*piratas*) ply the streets as well. They might be red cars with a margarine container on the dashboard painted to resemble a taxi sign. Some locals use them, but they have no meters, are illegal and often unsafe, and carry no insurance in the event of an accident.

Taxi Companies **Alfaro** (☎ *2221–8466*). **Coopetaxi** (☎ *2235–9966*). **San Jorge** (☎ *2221-3434*). **Taxis Unidos** (☎ *2221-6865*).

CONTACTS & RESOURCES

BANKS & EXCHANGING SERVICES

Get all the cash you need before you head out of San José. Outside the capital there are fewer banks and ATMs, making it more difficult to change money (although the situation is improving). It is virtually impossible to change currency other than U.S. dollars or traveler's checks outside of San José. Euros and Canadian dollars are becoming easier to exchange at banks in San José, but we recommend playing it safe and bringing U.S. dollars. Lines at the state banks—Banco Nacional, Banco de Costa Rica (BCR), Bancrédito (BCAC), and Banco Popular—move *very* slowly, but you can change dollars and cash traveler's checks. The private Scotiabank, BAC San José, and HSBC perform the same services with more palatable lines, but they have many fewer outlets. (Though branches of international banks of the same name, Scotiabank and HSBC here provide no access to your accounts back home, other than with your ATM card.) You can get local currency using your MasterCard or Visa at the Juan Santamaría Airport: there are machines in the check-in area, near Gate 4 of the boarding area, and near the baggage-claim carousels. You'll find a branch of BAC San José in the check-in area for currency exchange. Do *not* use the airport's Global Exchange currency windows in the boarding and baggage-claim areas if you can help it; they give a markedly lower rate. The ATH (A Toda Hora) and Red Total (look for the lion's head symbol) networks accept Plus- and Cirrus-affiliated cards. A few—very few—Red Total machines give cash against American Express and Diners Club cards as well. Ask at your hotel for the location of the nearest bank or *cajero automático* (ATM), and specify whether you need a MasterCard- or Visa-friendly machine.

Banks **BAC San José** (⊠ *Avda. 2, Cs. Central–1, Barrio El Carmen* ☎ *2295–9797*). **Banco de Costa Rica** (⊠ *Avda. Central, Cs. 4–6, Barrio La Merced* ☎ *2287–9008*). **Banco Nacional** (⊠ *Avda. 1, Cs. 2–4, Barrio La Merced* ☎ *2212–2000*). **Bancrédito** (⊠ *Avda. 4, Cs. Central–2, Barrio La Merced* ☎ *2212–7000*). **HSBC** (⊠ *C. Central, Avda. 1, Barrio La Merced* ☎ *2287–1000*). **Scotiabank** (⊠ *Behind Teatro Nacional, Barrio La Soledad* ☎ *2521–5680*).

EMERGENCIES

Hospitals The private Clínica Bíblica and Clínica Católica hospitals are superior (if more expensive) alternatives to San José's state hospitals. Both have English-speaking staff. **Clínica Bíblica** (⊠ *Avda. 14, Cs. Central–1, Barrio El Pacífico* ☎ *2522–1000* ⊕ *www.clinicabiblica.com*). **Clínica Católica** (⊠ *Attached to San Antonio Church on C. Esquivel Bonilla, Guadalupe* ☎ *2246–3000* www.clinicacatolica.com).

Late-Night Pharmacies **Fischel Pharmacy** (⊠ *Clínica Católica, attached to San Antonio Church on C. Esquivel Bonilla, Guadalupe* ☎ *2283–6616* ⊠ *Across from Banco Popular, San Pedro* ☎ *2295–7694*).

INTERNET

There are Internet cafés on almost every block in downtown San José. Many of those just south of the Universidad de Costa Rica in San Pedro are open 24 hours. Competition keeps prices at $1 or less per hour. A few restaurants and cafés in the city offer wireless Internet service to their customers, but we've read reports of robberies. You can use your laptop at your hotel, in an office, or at the airport, but be wary of doing it anywhere else. All gates at Juan Santamaría Airport are Wi-Fi-equipped for free last-minute logging-on.

VISITOR INFORMATION

The Instituto Costarricense de Turismo (ICT) staffs a tourist information office beneath the Plaza de la Cultura, next to the Museo del Oro Precolombino. Pick up free maps, bus schedules, and brochures weekdays 9–5.

Contacts **Instituto Costarricense de Turismo** *(ICT)* (⊠ *C. 5, Avdas. Central–2, Barrio La Soledad* ☎ *2222–1090*).

The Central Valley

Pacuare River

WORD OF MOUTH

". . . I would add an extra day to the Orosi Valley to truly enjoy it at your leisure. It's a nice part of the country—fewer tourists, etc., which spells Perfect for me!"

—shillmac

WELCOME TO CENTRAL VALLEY

View from Irazú Volcano

TOP REASONS TO GO

★ **Coffee:** Get up close and personal with harvesting and processing on coffee tours at two of the valley's many plantations: Café Britt and Doka Estate.

★ **The Orosi Valley:** Spectacular views and quiet, bucolic towns make this area a great day trip or overnight from San José.

★ **Rafting the Pacuare River:** Brave the rapids as you descend through tropical forest on one of the best rivers in Central America.

★ **The views:** Ascend the volcanic slopes that border the valley, meeting superb views almost anywhere you go.

★ **Avian adventures:** Flock to Tapantí National Park to see emerald toucanets, resplendent quetzals (if you're lucky), and nearly every species of Costa Rican hummingbird. Rancho Naturalista is the bird-lovers' hotel of choice.

1 **North & West of San José.** The areas north and west of San José are dominated by coffee farms and small valley towns whose beautiful hotels attract lots of tourists on their first and last nights in the country. Café Britt and Doka Estate are both here, as is the international airport, near Alajuela.

2 **Cartago & Irazú Volcano.** In the eastern Central Valley are Cartago and Irazú Volcano. Cartago is an older city than San José, with some significant historic attractions. Irazú is Costa Rica's tallest volcano. On a clear day you can see both the Atlantic and Pacific oceans from its peak.

3 **The Turrialba Region.** Rafting trips on the Pacuare and Reventazón are based in Turrialba, a bustling little town. The nearby Guayabo Ruins, of a city deserted in AD 1400, is Costa Rica's only significant archaeological site.

4 **The Orosi Valley.** An often overlooked beauty is the Orosi Valley. The drive into the valley is simply gorgeous, and a tranquil way to spend a day. Birding destination Tapantí National Park is at the southern edge of the valley.

Guayabo National Monument

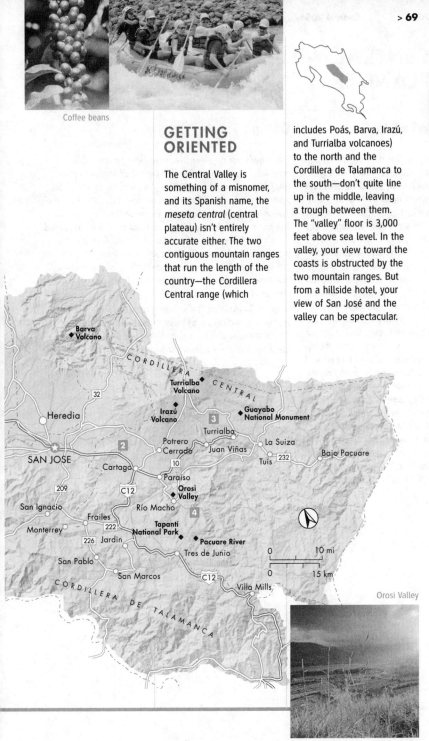

2

Coffee beans

GETTING ORIENTED

The Central Valley is something of a misnomer, and its Spanish name, the *meseta central* (central plateau) isn't entirely accurate either. The two contiguous mountain ranges that run the length of the country—the Cordillera Central range (which includes Poás, Barva, Irazú, and Turrialba volcanoes) to the north and the Cordillera de Talamanca to the south—don't quite line up in the middle, leaving a trough between them. The "valley" floor is 3,000 feet above sea level. In the valley, your view toward the coasts is obstructed by the two mountain ranges. But from a hillside hotel, your view of San José and the valley can be spectacular.

Barva Volcano

CORDILLERA CENTRAL

Turrialba Volcano

32

Heredia

Irazú Volcano

3

Guayabo National Monument

Turrialba

Potrero Cerrado

Juan Viñas

La Suiza

2

232

Bajo Pacuare

SAN JOSE

Cartago

Tuis

10

209

Paraiso

C12

Orosi Valley

San Ignacio

Río Macho

4

Frailes

222

Monterrey

Tapantí National Park

226

Jardín

Pacuare River

San Pablo

Tres de Junio

0   10 mi

0   15 km

San Marcos

C12

Villa Mills

CORDILLERA DE TALAMANCA

Orosi Valley

CENTRAL VALLEY PLANNER

When to Go

Known for its "eternal spring," the Central Valley lacks the oppressive seasonal heat and rain of other parts of the country and is almost always suitable for a visit. Average highs are 24°C–27°C (75°F–80°F). Afternoon downpours are common from mid-May to December (with a slight drop-off around July), but the amount of rain is modest compared to the Caribbean coast and the southern Pacific. Don't rule out the rainy season—fewer travelers mean you won't need reservations, rain is usually during afternoon siesta hours, and the valley is swathed in green after a few months of moisture. Holy Week (the week before Easter) and the last two weeks of the year are prime vacation times for Ticos, so reserve cars and hotel rooms in advance.

Getting There

The region has an extensive network of paved roads in relatively good shape. The Pan-American Highway runs roughly east–west through the valley and the center of San José. Mountains ring the valley, so most trips to or from the lowlands require a drive up in elevation then back down. The bus network is good, but since sights tend to be spread out it's less time-consuming to travel by car. Consider taking taxis. They're plentiful, they know the roads (most of the time), and the prices are reasonable. Even several $10 taxi rides per day—and $10 gets you quite a ways—are cheaper than a rental car.

■TIP→ **Navigating the winding roads around the Central Valley is difficult at best, and absurd at its worst. Call ahead for directions, and don't hesitate to ask a local for assistance along the way.**

How Much Time?

You could spend an entire week in the Central Valley without getting bored, but if you have only a week or two in Costa Rica, we recommend a maximum of two days before heading to rain forests and beaches in other parts of the country. Spending a day after you arrive, then another day or two before you fly out gives you a taste of the region, breaks up the travel time, and makes your last day interesting, rather than spent in transit back to San José. The drive between just about any two points in the Central Valley is two hours or less, so it's ideal for short trips. In a day you can explore the Orosi Valley and Cartago, raft the Pacuare River, or hop from the Butterfly Farm to a coffee plantation.

■TIP→ **Bring a jacket—it can get chilly at night in any of the Central Valley towns, and downright cold at higher elevations.**

Recommended Tour Operators

These San José–based tour operators arrange transport from some hotels (generally those in San José and around the airport) and have myriad tour options:

Costa Rica Sun Tours (☎2296–7757 ⊕www.crsuntours.com).

Costa Rica's Temptations (☎2508–5000 ⊕www.crtinfo.com).

Gray Line Tours Costa Rica (☎2220–2126 ⊕www.graylinecostarica.com).

Horizontes (☎2222–2022 ⊕www.horizontes.com) has countrywide natural-history and adventure trips.

Swiss Travel (☎2282–4898 ⊕www.swisstravelcr.com).

WHITE-WATER OUTFITTERS

Most outfitters are based in San José. Tico's River Adventures, Costa Rica Ríos (multiday packages only), and Rainforest World are in Turrialba. Many have both rafting and kayaking.

Costa Rica Expeditions (☎2257–0766 ⊕www.costaricaexpeditions.com).

Costa Rica Nature Adventures (☎2225–3939 or 2224–0505, 800/283–5032 in North America ⊕www.costaricanatureadventures.com).

Costa Rica Ríos (☎2556–9617 or 888/434–0776 ⊕www.costaricarios.com).

Exploradores Outdoors (☎2222–6262 or 646/205–0828 toll-free ⊕www.exploradoresoutdoors.com).

Rainforest World (☎2556–0014 or 8357–7250 ⊕www.rforestw.com).

Ríos Tropicales (☎2233–6455 or 866/722–8273 ⊕www.riostropicales.com).

Choosing a Place to Stay

For getting away from it all and still being close to the country's primary transportation hub, the lodges around San José are ideal. Rustic *cabinas* (cottages), sprawling coffee plantations, nature lodges, and hilltop villas with expansive views are some of your options. The large chains are here as well, but the real gems are the so-called boutique hotels, many of which have unique designs that take advantage of exceptional countryside locations. Tropical gardens are the norm, rather than the exception, and air-conditioning is usually not necessary.

WHAT IT COSTS IN DOLLARS				
¢	$	$$	$$$	$$$$
Restaurants				
under $5	$5–$10	$10–$15	$15–$25	over $25
Hotels				
under $50	$50–$75	$75–$150	$150–$250	over $250

Restaurant prices are per person for a main course at dinner. Hotel prices are for two people in a standard double room in high season, excluding service and tax (16.4%).

WEST OF SAN JOSÉ

Updated
by Suzanna
Starcevic

As you drive north or west out of San José, the city's suburbs and industrial zones quickly give way to arable land, much of which is occupied by coffee farms. Within Costa Rica's coffee heartland are plenty of tranquil agricultural towns and two provincial capitals, Alajuela and Heredia. Both cities owe their relative prosperity to the coffee beans cultivated on the fertile lower slopes of the Poás and Barva volcanoes. The upper slopes, too cold for coffee crops, are dedicated to dairy cattle, strawberries, ferns, and flowers, making for markedly different and thoroughly enchanting landscapes along the periphery of the national parks. Since the hills above these quaint valley towns have some excellent restaurants and lodgings, rural overnights are an excellent alternative to staying in San José.

ESCAZÚ

5 km (3 mi) southwest of San José.

Once a traditional coffee-farming town at the foot of a small mountain range (the Cordillera de Escazú), Escazú is now primarily a bedroom community for San José. As you exit the highway and crest the first gentle hill, you might think you made a wrong turn and ended up in southern California, but farther up you return to small-town Central America. Narrow roads wind their way up the steep slopes, past postage-stamp coffee fields and lengths of shoulder-to-shoulder, modest houses with tidy gardens and the occasional oxcart parked in the yard. Unfortunately, the area's stream of new developments and high-rises has steadily chipped away at the rural landscape—each year you have to climb higher to find the kind of scene that captured the attention of many a Costa Rican painter in the early 20th century. In their place are plenty of fancy homes and condos, especially in the San Antonio and San Rafael neighborhoods. Escazú's historic church faces a small plaza, surrounded in part by weathered adobe homes. The town center is several blocks north of the busy road to Santa Ana, which is lined with a growing selection of restaurants, bars, and shops.

GETTING HERE & AROUND

To drive to Escazú from San José, turn left at the western end of Paseo Colón, which ends at the Parque La Sabana. Take the first right, and get off the highway at the second exit. The off-ramp curves sharply left; follow it about 1 km (½ mi), sticking to the main road, to El Cruce at the bottom of the hill (marked by a large Scotiabank). Continue through the traffic light for San Rafael addresses; turn right for the old road to Santa Ana. The trip takes about 15 minutes. A steady stream of buses for Escazú runs from several stops around the Coca-Cola terminal in San José (Avdas. 1–3, Cs. 14–16), with service from 5 AM to 11 PM.

ESCAZÚ ESSENTIALS

Bank/ATM **Banco Nacional** (⊠ *Southwest side of Parque Central* ☎ *2228–0009*). **Banco de Costa Rica ATM** (⊠ *North side of church*).

Hospital **Hospital CIMA** (⊠ *Next to PriceSmart, just off the highway to Santa Ana* ⊹ *12 km [7½ mi] west of downtown San José* ☎ *2208–1000*).

Pharmacy **Farmacia San Miguel** (⊠ *North side of Parque Central* ☎ *2228– 2339*).

Internet **Bagelmen's** (⊠ *San Rafael de Escazú, 500 m southwest of the Trejos Montealegre shopping center* ☎ *2228–4460*). **Internet CF** (⊠ *Northwest corner of Parque Central, upstairs in Plaza Escazú mall* ☎ *2289–5706*).

Post Office **Correos** (⊠ *100 m north of church*).

Taxis **Coopetico** (☎ *2224–7979*).

EXPLORING

High in the hills above Escazú is the tiny community of **San Antonio de Escazú,** famous for its annual oxcart festival held the second Sunday of March. The view from here—of nearby San José and distant vol-canoes—is impressive by both day and night. If you head higher than San Antonio de Escazú, brace yourself for virtually vertical roads that wind up into the mountains toward **Pico Blanco,** the highest point in the Escazú Cordillera, which is a half-day hike to ascend. Our preference is **San Miguel,** one peak east. You can often park at the Mirador Valle Azul restaurant 2 km (1 mi) north of San Antonio de Escazú. Call for directions the evening before (☎ *2254–6281*). The latter takes you past three large crosses and spectacular scenery, and there's less risk of getting lost.

WHERE TO EAT

$$$–$$$$ ✕ **Restaurante Cerutti.** The diva of San José's Italian eateries, this lit-tle restaurant promises minimalist elegance in a lovely adobe house built in 1817. The extensive menu, focusing on modern Italian cuisine, ranges from roasted scallops with Spanish chorizo to ravioli stuffed with duck and Italian ham. Core dishes are complemented by a variety of selections that change every month or so. No one disputes that the quality of the food is high—with prices to match. ⊠ *Southeast corner of El Cruce de San Rafael de Escazú* ☎ *2228–4511* ⊕ *www.cerutti restaurante.com* ⊟ *AE, DC, MC, V* ⊘ *Closed Sun.*

$$$ ✕ **Taj Mahal.** This burst of northern Indian flavor is such a rarity in Cen-tral America that we can overlook the slightly less-than-factual claim that the restaurant is the isthmus's only such option. Richly swathed in warm fuchsias, red ochres, and golds, the mansion's dining area sprawls through a handful of small, intimate rooms and out to a gazebo in the tree-covered backyard. The price-to-portion ratio is a little high, particularly for North Americans used to good, cheap Indian food, but the sharp tandoori dishes, curries, and *biryanis* (seasoned rice dishes) are a welcome vacation from ubiquitous European and American fare. Vegetarians may swoon at the options. Helpful waiters, in black or maroon traditional Punjabi dress, are frank about recommendations. ⊹ *1 km (¾ mi) west of Paco mall on old road to Santa Ana* ☎ *2228– 0980* ⊟ *AE, DC, MC, V* ⊘ *Closed Mon.*

$–$$$ ✕ **Barbecue Los Anonos.** Since 1960, Costa Ricans have flocked to Los Anonos to enjoy its family-friendly grill fest. The original dining room,

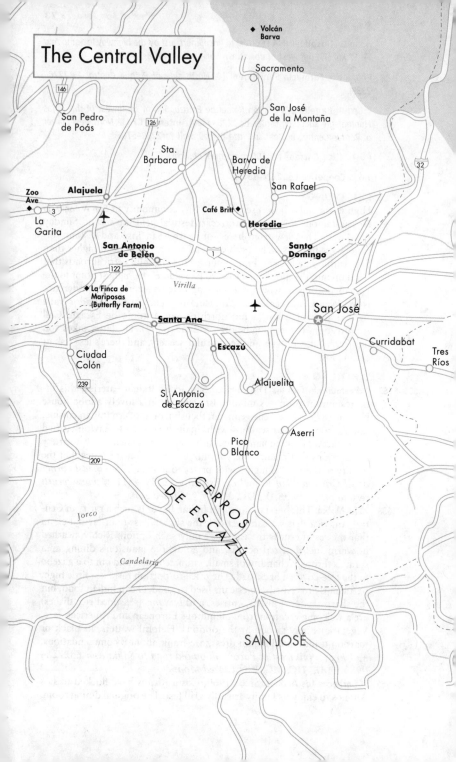

The Central Valley

Volcán Barva

Sacramento

San José de la Montaña

San Pedro de Poás

Sta. Barbara

Barva de Heredia

San Rafael

Café Britt

Heredia

Zoo Ave

Alajuela

La Garita

San Antonio de Belén

Santo Domingo

La Finca de Mariposas (Butterfly Farm)

Virilla

San José

Santa Ana

Escazú

Curridabat

Ciudad Colón

Tres Ríos

Alajuelita

S. Antonio de Escazú

Aserri

Pico Blanco

Jorco

CERROS DE ESCAZÚ

Candelaria

SAN JOSÉ

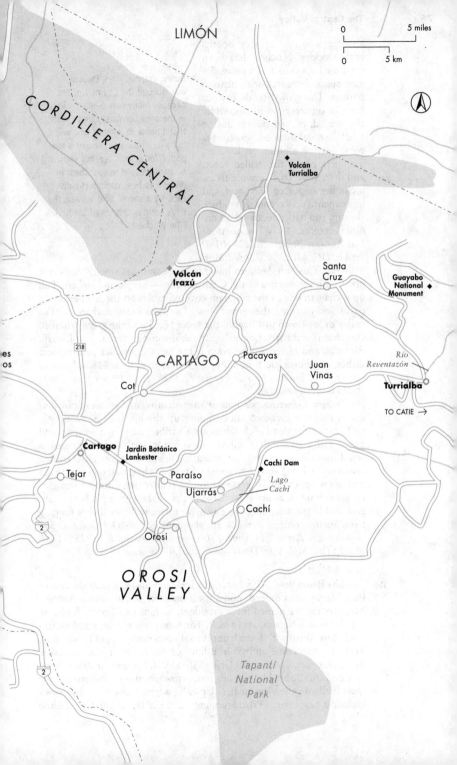

a rustic collection of deep booths with wooden benches, has been expanded upon to add a more elegant space decorated with historic photos. The crowd tends toward families on weekend nights, while the weekdays are busier during lunch, when business executives come for the economical lunches. The best bet is the grilled meat, and there is plenty to choose from, including imported U.S. beef and less expensive Tico cuts. Fresh fish, shrimp, and half a dozen salads are other choices. ⊠ *400 m west of Los Anonos Bridge* ☎ *2228–0180* ▱ *AE, DC, MC, V* ⊘ *Closed Mon.*

> **HOCUS POCUS**
>
> During colonial days, Escazú was dubbed the City of Witches because many native healers lived in the area. Locals say that Escazú is still home to witches who will tell your fortune or concoct a love potion for a small fee, but you'd be hard-pressed to spot them in the town's busy commercial district. Try a soccer field instead; the city's team is christened Las Brujas (The Witches).

$ ✕ **Cerros.** This San Antonio hills favorite combines smoky thin-crust pizza with the essence of the Central Valley—simple and sincere. Pull up a chair to one of the gingham-covered tables on the semi-enclosed patio, and you have the perfect view of a Costa Rican microcosm. The valley drops down just behind the soccer field and the green-trimmed church across the street, revealing the shimmering panorama of Escazú, Alajuela, and Heredia. The pizza is the main draw, but pastas, meat dishes, and Costa Rican standbys are well represented. ⊠ *South side of soccer field, San Antonio de Escazú* ☎ *2228–1831* ▱ *No credit cards* ⊘ *No lunch weekdays.*

$ ✕ **El Gaitero.** Generous portions of Spanish tapas and entrées draw diners to this whitewashed adobe house up the hill near San Antonio de Escazú. Wooden-bench tables are distributed along a wraparound porch with views of the Central Valley; inside, settings are arranged in small-to-medium rooms. Antonio and Olga, the passionate Asturian owners, will bring you up to speed with what's best that night and even pull out recipes to share. Presentation isn't the strong suit here: straight-up good food is, as are reasonable prices. Start with a pitcher of sangria and begin sampling; the extensive menu includes dishes ranging from Spanish omelet to mock angula (baby eel). ⊠ *Del Cruce de San Antonio and Barrio El Carmen, 100 m east, 50 m south* ☎ *2228–1850* ▱ *AE, DC, MC, V* ⊘ *Thurs.–Sun. until 6*

WHERE TO STAY

$$$ ⛫ **White House Hotel.** This luxurious little inn and spa near the top of Pico Blanco does indeed model itself on 1600 Pennsylvania Avenue. Most rooms are named for a president, so fans of Clinton, Bush, or, say, Thomas Jefferson, are in luck. The rooms are spacious and expensively furnished, with French doors that open onto the public veranda. You can even come and go in a limo or helicopter if you so desire. The restaurant, The Capitol Grill ($$$–$$$$), features American-style surf-and-turf dishes like filet mignon, prime rib, and swordfish, and the glass walls do the view justice. Upscale, adrenaline-fueled diversions include a new casino. **Pros:** Stunning view, VIP treatment. **Cons:** Little

room for anything but a U.S. vibe, some say restaurant can be pricey for what you get. ✛ *½ km (¼ mi) south of the cemetery of San Antonio de Escazú* ☎*2288–6362 in Costa Rica, toll-free 954/302–2144 (hotel), 954/272–8566 (reservations) in U.S.* 🖷*2288–6365* ⊕*www. whitehousecostarica.com* ➮*5 rooms, 6 suites, 2 apartments, 1 bungalow* ⚘*In-room: no a/c, safe, fireplace (some), Jacuzzi (some). In-hotel: restaurant, room service, bar, pool, spa, laundry service, public Wi-Fi, airport shuttle, no kids under 12* ☰*AE, DC, MC, V* ⦿*CP.*

$$ 🏠**Posada El Quijote.** Perched on a hill in the Bello Horizonte neighborhood, with a great view of the city, this bed-and-breakfast strikes the right balance between a small inn and a private residence. Being here feels like visiting a friend—albeit a friend with great taste. The quiet, homey feel draws low-key, mature travelers. The best view is from the sundeck, just off a spacious living room with a couch, a fireplace, and lots of modern art. The apartments and the two "deluxe" rooms have comparable views. Smaller "standard" rooms overlook the surrounding gardens, and aren't nearly as nice. The staff is extremely helpful. It's a bit hard to find, so you may want to take a taxi, or call for directions. **Pros:** Peaceful, friendly place to spend first or last night; staff provides excellent support; pet-friendly. **Con:** Location makes car or taxi outings necessary and a little tricky. ⊠*Bello Horizonte de Escazú, first street west of Anonos Bridge* ✛*1 km (½ mi) up hill* ☎*2289–8401* 🖷*2289–8729* ⊕*www.quijote.co.cr* ➮*8 rooms, 2 apartments* ⚘*In-room: a/c (some). In-hotel: no elevator, laundry service, public Wi-Fi, airport shuttle, some pets allowed.* ☰*AE, DC, MC, V* ⦿*BP.*

$ 🏠**Casa de las Tías.** The gamut of city services is at your doorstep, but you're blissfully apart from them at this tranquil B&B in San Rafael de Escazú. The name means "The Aunts' House," which is appropriate for this yellow house with a front porch and picket fence at the end of a short road. A few old photos of the ladies themselves complete the effect. The rooms and furnishings feel slightly aged, but make up for it in charm, and the large backyard and gardens give the illusion of being far from a major commercial street. **Pros:** Tranquillity without sacrificing convenience, service that goes the extra mile, excellent breakfast. **Cons:** Some say walls could be a little thicker, slightly aged feeling. ⊠*100 m south and 150 m east of El Cruce; turn east just south of Restaurante Cerutti* ☎*2289–5517* 🖷*2289–7353* ⊕*www.hotels.co.cr/ casatias.html* ➮*4 rooms, 1 junior suite* ⚘*In-room: no a/c, no TV. In-hotel: laundry service, public Wi-Fi, airport shuttle, no kids under 12, no-smoking rooms* ☰*AE, MC, V* ⦿*BP.*

$ 🏠**Costa Verde Inn.** When they need to make a city run, many beach-living expats head straight for this quiet B&B on the outskirts of Escazú. Rooms make nice use of local hardwoods and traditional South American art, and the main building serves as a gathering place with a large sitting area, comfortable chairs, and a fireplace. The inn is surrounded by gardens, and at night you can see the lights of San José twinkling to the east, though just three of the rooms take advantage of the view. The inn is at the end of a narrow driveway with an unassuming gate, but you'll see a sign if you've found the right place, so ring the bell. **Pros:** Inviting public areas, excellent value. **Cons:** July–September often brings large student groups (check when booking); pool is for plungers, not swimmers. ✉*From southeast corner of second cemetery (the farthest west), 300 m south* ☎*2228–4080* 🖷*2289–8591* ⊕*www. costaverdeinn.com* ➴*12 rooms, 3 apartments, 3 studios* ⚭*In-room: no a/c, phone (some), refrigerator. In-hotel: plunge pool, no elevator, airport shuttle* ⊟*AE, MC, V* ❯◉|*BP.*

NIGHTLIFE

Escazú is the Central Valley's hot spot for nightlife—many Josefinos head here for the restaurants, bars, and dance clubs that cater to a young, cell phone–toting crowd. The highest concentration of nightspots is in the shopping center called **Trejos Montealegre** (✉*On your left as you enter Escazú, just off the highway between San José and Ciudad Colón*). One of the more popular watering holes with the under-30 set is **Henry's Beach Cafe** (✉*500 m west of El Cruce, Plaza San Rafael, 2nd fl.* ☎*2289–6250*), which features televised sports by day, varied music by night, and an islands decor of beach paintings and surfboards. Costa Ricans refer to this style of bar as an "American Bar," which is fairly accurate. A young, sophisticated crowd keeps **Il Panino** (✉*Centro Comercial Paco* ☎*2228–3126* ⊕ *www.jazzcafecostarica. com* 🍽*$6–$8* ⊘*Closed Sundays*) buzzing. A great place to start or end an evening.Music fans on the west side cheered the 2008 opening of **Jazz Café Escazú** (✉*Next to Comfort Suizo, across the highway from Hospital Cima; first exit after the toll booths* ☎*2288–4740* ⊕*www. jazzcafecostarica.com* 🍽*$6–$8* ⊘*Closed Sundays*). The boxy club hosts an eclectic live-music lineup similar to that of its popular sister venue in San Pedro and has double the capacity. The high-end **Itskatzú** complex, 1 km (½ mi) east of Multiplaza, has a number of restaurants and bars ranging from the low-brow (Hooters) to sophisticated sushi and live Cuban music.

SHOPPING

★ If you get the shopping bug and absolutely must visit a mall while on vacation, Escazú is the place to do it. **Multiplaza,** on the south side of the Autopista Próspero Fernández, approximately 5 km (3 mi) west of San José, is a big one. Malls and complexes have also sprung up in Heredia and San Antonio, in addition to the long-standing **Mall Internacional** in Alajuela. **Biesanz Woodworks** (✉*Bello Horizonte, 800 m south of Escuela Bello Horizonte* ☎*2289–4337* ⊕*www.biesanz.com*) is where local craftsmen ply their trade and expat artist Barry Biesanz creates unique, world-class items from Costa Rican hardwoods, which are turned (a form of woodworking) on-site. It's difficult to find, so take a taxi or call for directions from your hotel.

SANTA ANA

17 km (10 mi) southwest of San José.

This once-tranquil agricultural community on the opposite side of the *cordillera* (mountain range) from Escazú is in the midst of a boom, and shopping malls and housing developments are popping up along its periphery. But the town center, with its rugged stone church sur-

CLOSE UP

Speaking Costa Rican

Spanish in Costa Rica tends to be localized. This is a land where eloquent speech and creative verbal expression are highly valued. For example, here the response to a "thank you" is the gracious, uniquely Tico *"Con mucho gusto"* ("With much pleasure") instead of *"De nada"* ("It's nothing"), which is used in much of Latin America. In other cases, informality is preferred: the conventional *Señor* and *Señora*, for example, are eschewed in favor of the more egalitarian *Don* and *Doña*, used preceding a first name. Even President Abel Pacheco is called Don Abel. Exercise caution when selecting from the list below, however. Although young Costa Rican men address everyone as *maje* (dude), you might get a withering look if you, a visitor, follow suit.

adios good-bye; but also used as "hello" in rural areas
agarrar de maje to pull someone's leg
birra beer
brete work
cachos shoes
chunche any thingamajig
clavar el pico to fall asleep
estar de chicha to be angry

estar de goma to have a hangover
harina money
jupa head
macho, macha a person with blonde hair
maje buddy, dude, mate
mamá de Tarzán know-it-all
maría a woman's name; also a taxi meter
matar la culebra to waste time
montón a lot
paño towel
pelo de gato cat hair; or fine, misty rain that falls during December
peso colón
pinche a tight-fisted person
ponerse hasta la mecha to get drunk
porfa please
pura vida fantastic, great
rojo red; also a 1,000-colón note
soda an inexpensive local restaurant
torta a big mistake or error
tuanis cool
tucán toucan; also a 5,000-colón note
upe anyone home?
Con mucho gusto used in response to "thank you" instead of "de nada"
Muy bien, gracias a Dios very well, thank goodness
Muy bien, por dicha very well, luckily
Si Dios quiere God willing

rounded by homes and businesses, has changed little in the past decade. The church, which was built between 1870 and 1880, has a Spanish-tile roof, carved wooden doors, and two pre-Columbian stone spheres flanking its entrance. Its rustic interior—bare wooden pillars and beams and black iron lamps—seems appropriate for an area with a tradition of ranching. Because it is warmer and drier than the towns to the east, Santa Ana is one of the few Central Valley towns that doesn't have a good climate for coffee, and is instead surrounded by pastures and patches of forest—it isn't unusual to see men on horseback here.

GETTING HERE & AROUND

From San José, turn left at the western end of Paseo Colón, which ends at the Parque La Sabana. Take the first right, and get on the highway. Get off at the sixth exit; bear left at the flashing red lights, winding past roadside ceramics and vegetable stands before hitting the town center, about 2 km (1 mi) from the highway. The trip takes about 25 minutes. Green-and-white buses to Santa Ana leave from 200 meters north of San Juan de Dios hospital every eight minutes, leaving for places along the Autopista Próspero Fernández or Piedades; take buses marked "Pista" or "Multiplaza." Those marked "Calle Vieja" leave every 15 minutes from the Coca-Cola terminal itself and pass through Escazú on the old road. Buses run from 5 AM to 11 PM.

SANTA ANA ESSENTIALS

Bank/ATM Banco de Costa Rica (⊠ *100 m west of church* ☎ *2203–4281*). **Banco Popular** (⊠ *Southwest corner of church* ☎ *2203–7979*). **Banco Nacional** (⊠ *Northwest corner of church* ☎ *2282–2479*).

Pharmacy Farmacia Sucre (⊠ *25 m south of church* ☎ *2282–1296*).

Internet Internet Café El Sol (⊠ *Southwest corner of church, across from Banco Popular* ☎ *2282–8059*).

Post Office Correos (⊠ *Northwest corner of church*).

WHERE TO STAY & EAT

$$$ ✕ **Bacchus.** Take a Peruvian chef trained in France and an Italian owner, and you get Bacchus, a welcome addition to the local dining scene. The cuisine is a mix of French and Italian dishes such as duck breast in a port sauce, baked mushroom-and-polenta ragout, and a variety of pizzas. Modern art decorates the simple but elegant interior, and outdoor seating is available. An extensive wine list and reasonable prices make it a great pick for dinner. ⊠ *200 m east and 100 m north of church* ☎ *2282–5441* ▤ *AE, DC, MC, V* ⊗ *Closed Mon.*

$ ✕ **Tex Mex.** This Gringo favorite serves a fairly standard Mexican menu—tacos, burritos, quesadillas, and so on—plus a few grilled meat items, such as the Argentinean *churrasco* (a thick tenderloin cut), complete with *chimichurri* (diced garlic and parsley in olive oil). There are about two dozen *bocas* (appetizers), which are mostly smaller versions of entrée items. The enchiladas may not be as good as what you find in San Antonio, but the setting is pleasant, with a yard shaded by massive trees. Seating is on a covered brick patio or in an adjacent dining area enclosed by windows, for cool nights. ⊠ *50 m northeast of Catholic church* ☎ *2282–6342* ▤ *AE, DC, MC, V* ⊗ *Closed Mon.*

$$$ ▥ **Alta.** The view from this colonial-style hotel perched on a hillside
★   above Santa Ana is impressive, but then, so is the hotel. The sloping stairway entrance lined with tall columns and greenery is reminiscent of a narrow street in southern Spain, an effect reinforced by the barrel-tile roof and ocher-stucco walls; the narrow hallways feel like an old castle. Guest rooms are spacious, with colonial-style furniture and bathrooms with hand-painted tiles; ask for one on the fourth or fifth floor to take advantage of the view. The restaurant, La Luz ($$$), has a hardwood floor, a beamed ceiling, and plenty of windows for admiring the distant hills and the pool and gardens below. The eclectic and unusual menu includes baked goat cheese salad, macadamia-encrusted fish, and Moroccan chicken. **Pros:** Classy service, panoramic views, excellent value for price. **Cons:** Lower-floor rooms lose out on the view, little to do within walking distance. ⊹ *2½ km (1½ mi) west of Paco*

shopping center, on old road between Santa Ana and Escazú, Alto de las Palomas ☎2282–4160, 888/388–2582 in U.S. 🖷2282–4162 ⊕www.thealtahotel.com ⇆18 rooms, 5 suites ♿In-room: safe, Ethernet, Wi-Fi. In-hotel: restaurant, pool, gym, laundry service, airport shuttle ▤AE, MC, V ⦿CP.

$$ 🏨**Hotel Posada Canal Grande.** This small Italian-owned hotel tucked into the hills to the west of Santa Ana is a great value. Each room is different, and most have wicker beds. Second-floor rooms, each with a balcony over the pool, have excellent views, but the first-floor rooms aren't bad either. Two four-poster beds are placed in the shade by the pool, just to lounge on. On a clear day you can see the Gulf of Nicoya to the west. Poolside chatter is in French, Spanish, and German as much as it is in English. **Pros:** Great value, international feel. **Cons:** Spartan bathrooms feel worn, dining options limited. ✉*On the Próspero Fernández highway to Ciudad Colón, 500 m north of Piedades de Santa Ana bus terminal* ☎2282–4089 or 2282–4101 🖷2282–5733 ⊕www.hotelcanalgrande.com ⇆12 rooms ♿In-room: no a/c, safe, Wi-Fi. In-hotel: bar, pool, no elevator, laundry service, airport shuttle ▤AE, DC, MC, V ⦿BP.

SHOPPING

★ Large glazed pots with ornate decorations that range from traditional patterns to modern motifs are the specialties at **Cerámica Las Palomas** (✉*Old road to Santa Ana, opposite Alta Hotel* ☎2282–7001). Flowerpots and lamps are also common works, and the staff will eagerly show you the production process, from raw clay to art.

NORTH OF SAN JOSÉ

As you set out from San José to explore the towns to the north, you first encounter nothing but asphalt, hotels, and malls—not especially scenic. Santo Domingo and San Antonio de Belén blend into the outskirts of San José, and it's only when you get to the heart of these small towns that you feel you've arrived in Central America. Farther north, Alajuela and Heredia are bustling provincial capitals with charismatic central parks. Throughout this area, tucked into the urban scenery and lining volcanic slopes, are fields of that great Costa Rican staple, coffee.

SAN ANTONIO DE BELÉN

17 km (10 mi) northwest of San José.

San Antonio de Belén has little to offer visitors but its rural charm and proximity to the international airport. The latter led developers to build several of the San José area's biggest hotels here. The town also lies on the route of entry for Alajuela's Butterfly Garden, and it's a convenient departure point for trips to the western Central Valley, Pacific coast, and northern region. If you stay at the Marriott, you likely won't even see the town, just the busy highway between San José and Alajuela.

GETTING HERE & AROUND

From San José, turn right at the west end of Paseo Colón onto the Pan-American Highway (Carretera General Cañas). The San Antonio de Belén exit is at an overpass 6 km (4 mi) west of the Heredia exit, by the Real Cariari Mall. Turn left at the first intersection, cross over the highway, and continue 1 km (¾ mi) to the forced right turn, driving 1½ km (1 mi) to the center of town. San Antonio is only 10 minutes from the airport.

SAN ANTONIO DE BELÉN ESSENTIALS

Bank/ATM Banco de Costa Rica (⊠ *50 m north of rear of church* ☎ *2239–1149*). **BAC San José ATM** (⊠ *200 m west of soccer field*).

Pharmacy Farmacia Sucre (⊠ *North side of church* ☎ *2239–3485*).

Internet Belén Web Café (⊠ *West end of soccer field* ☎ *2239–4181*).

Post Office Correos (⊠ *3 blocks west and 25 m north of church*).

Taxis Asotaxis Belén (☎ *2293–4712*).

WHERE TO STAY

$$ **El Rodeo.** This quiet hotel bills itself as a "country hotel," though this is more in image than fact—El Rodeo's proximity to the airport and major business parks is the real draw. Spacious rooms, most with polished hardwood floors, high ceilings, and narrow balconies, overlook small gardens and rooms in the adjacent building. An open-air lounge on the second floor has a pool table and wicker furniture. The new Grand Café serves breakfast each morning. The large wooden El Rodeo Steakhouse Restaurant ($$) in front of the hotel is quite popular with Ticos, who pack it on weekends. Decorated with saddles, steer skulls, and other ranching paraphernalia, the restaurant serves an array of grilled meats, from the Argentinean churrascos to T-bones, as well as several fish and shrimp dishes. **Pros:** Proximity to airport, newly renovated facilities, spacious rooms. **Con:** Generic ambience. ⊠ *Road to Santa Ana* ✛ *2 km (1 mi) east of Parque Central* ☎ *2293–3909* 🖷 *2239–3464* ⊕ *www.elrodeohotel.com* ⬬ *26 rooms, 3 suites* ⚿ *In-room: safe, refrigerator, Wi-Fi. In-hotel: restaurant, tennis court, pool, no elevator laundry service* ▤ *AE, DC, MC, V* ⓞ*BP.*

$$$ **Marriott Costa Rica Hotel.** Newly renovated and expanded, the stately
★   Marriott offers comprehensive luxury close to the airport. Towering
☾   over a coffee plantation west of San José, the thick columns, wide arches, and central courtyard are re-creations straight out of the 16th century, and hand-painted tiles and abundant antiques complete the historic appearance. Guest rooms are more contemporary, but they're elegant enough, with hardwood furniture. Some have sliding glass doors that open onto tiny balconies; new rooms feature flat-screen TVs. The place is always abuzz with upscale tourists, business travelers, and participants in the many events that take place at the facilities. **Pros:** Excellent service, lavish grounds, close to airport. **Cons:** Tendency to nickel-and-dime (Internet access costs $12.95), size precludes a more personal experience. ✛ *¾ km (½ mi) west of Firestone, off Autopista General Cañas* ☎ *2298–0000, 800/228–9290 in U.S.* 🖷 *2298–0011*

2

⊕*www.marriott.com* ↩*291 rooms, 8 suites, 1 villa* ⌂*In-room: safe, Ethernet. In-hotel: 2 restaurants, bar, tennis courts, pools, gym, laundry service, concierge, public Wi-Fi, airport shuttle, parking (no fee)* ▤*AE, DC, MC, V* ⎯◉⎯*EP.*

ALAJUELA

20 km (13 mi) northwest of San José.

Because of its proximity to the international airport (5–10 minutes away) many travelers spend their first or last night in Alajuela, but the beauty of the surrounding countryside persuades some to stay longer. Alajuela is Costa Rica's second–most populated canton (250,000 people, with 50,000 in the city), and a mere 30-minute bus ride from the capital, but it has a decidedly provincial air. Architecturally, it differs little from the bulk of Costa Rican towns: it's a grid of low-rise structures painted in dull pastel colors.

GETTING HERE & AROUND

To reach Alajuela, follow directions to San Antonio de Belén *(⇨above).* Continue west on the highway past the San Antonio turnoff and turn right at the airport. Buses travel between San José (⊠ Avda. 2, Cs. 12–14, ✛opposite the north side of Parque La Merced*),* the airport, and Alajuela, and run every five minutes from 4:40 AM to 10:30 PM. The bus stop in Alajuela is 400 meters west, 25 meters north of the central park (⊠ *C. 3 and Avda. 1).* Buses leave San José for Zoo Ave from La Merced church (C. 14 and Avda. 4) daily at 8, 9, 10, 11 AM, and noon, returning on the hour from 10 AM to 3 PM.

ALAJUELA ESSENTIALS

Bank/ATM Banco de Costa Rica (⊠*Southwest corner of Parque Central* ☎*2440–9039*). **Banco Nacional** (⊠*West side of Parque Central* ☎*2441–0373*).

Hospital Hospital San Rafael (✛*1 km (½ mi) northeast of airport, on main road to Alajuela* ☎*2436–1001, 2436–1342 for emergencies*).

Pharmacy Farmacia Chavarría (⊠*Southwest corner of Parque Central* ☎*2441–1231*). **Farmacia Catedral** (⊠*Northeast corner of Parque Central* ☎*2441–3555*).

Internet Internet Inter@ctivo (⊠*In front of BAC San José bank, 100 m north of Parque Central* ☎*2431–1984*).

Post Office Correos (⊠*200 m north and 100 m east of Parque Central*).

Taxis Cootaxa (☎*2443–3030 or 2442–3030*).

EXPLORING

Royal palms and massive mango trees fill the **Parque Central** (⊠*C. Central, Avdas. 1–Central*), which also has a lovely fountain imported from Glasgow and concrete benches where locals gather to chat. Surrounding the plaza is an odd mix of charming old buildings and sterile concrete boxes, including a somewhat incongruous McDonald's.

The large, neoclassical **Alajuela Cathedral** (⊠ *C. Central, Avdas. 1–Central* ☎ *2443–2928*) has columns topped by interesting capitals decorated with local agricultural motifs, and a striking red metal dome. The interior is spacious but rather plain, except for the ornate cupola above the altar. It's open daily 5 AM–6 PM.

Alajuela was the birthplace of Juan Santamaría, the national hero who lost his life in a battle against the mercenary army of U.S. adventurer William Walker when the latter invaded Costa Rica in 1856. The **Parque Juan Santamaría** (⊠ *C. Central and Avda. 2*) has a statue of the young Santamaría. After a restoration in early 2005, Juan should keep his youthful good looks for years to come—which, sadly, is more than can be said for the abandoned-looking, weedy concrete lot he stands on.

Juan Santamaría's heroic deeds are celebrated in the **Juan Santamaría Museum** (Museo Juan Santamaría) housed in the old jail, one block north of Parque Central. It's worth a look, but not a linger, which is too bad because Santamaría's story is an interesting one. At this writing, a remodeling project to connect the jail with the adjoining cuartel was in progress and the museum was due to reopen in December 2008. ⊠ *Avda. 3, Cs. Central–2* ☎ *2441–4775* ☞ *Free* ☉ *Tues.–Sun. 10–5:30.*

☾ Spread over the lush grounds of **Zoo Ave** is a collection of large cages holding toucans, hawks, and parrots (the macaws range free), not to mention crocodiles, caimans, a boa constrictor, turtles, monkeys, wild cats, and other interesting critters. The zoo, the best in Costa Rica, runs a breeding project for rare and endangered birds, all of which are destined for eventual release. It has 115 bird species, including such rare ones as the quetzal, fiery-billed aracari, several types of eagles, and even ostriches. An impressive mural at the back of the facility shows Costa Rica's 850 bird species painted to scale. ⊠ *La Garita de Alajuela,* ✛ *head west from Alajuela center past cemetery, turn left after stone church in Barrio San José, continue on 2 km (1 mi); or head west of Pan-American Hwy. to Atenas exit, then turn right* ☎ *2433–8989* ⊕ *www.zooave.com* ☞ *$15* ☉ *Daily 9–5.*

★ Observe and photograph butterflies up close at **The Butterfly Farm** (La
☾ *Finca de Mariposas*). The farm's several microclimates keep comfortable some 40 species of tropical butterflies. Come when it's sunny if you can—they don't flutter around when it rains. This is the original butterfly farm, but there are other butterfly gardens near Volcán Poás at La Paz Waterfall Gardens and in Monteverde. In 2004 the museum launched an annual mural contest, turning not only its own buildings but surrounding corner stores and houses into canvases for talented Costa Rican artists. You can get here via tours from San José that depart from the capital at 7:20, 10, and 2. ✛ *From San José, turn south (left) at the intersection just past Real Cariari Mall, follow the road to the north side of church of San Antonio de Belén, take a left at the corner, then follow the butterfly signs* ☎ *2438–0400* ⊕ *www. butterflyfarm.co.cr* ☞ *$15, $30 with transportation from San José* ☉ *Daily 8:30–5.*

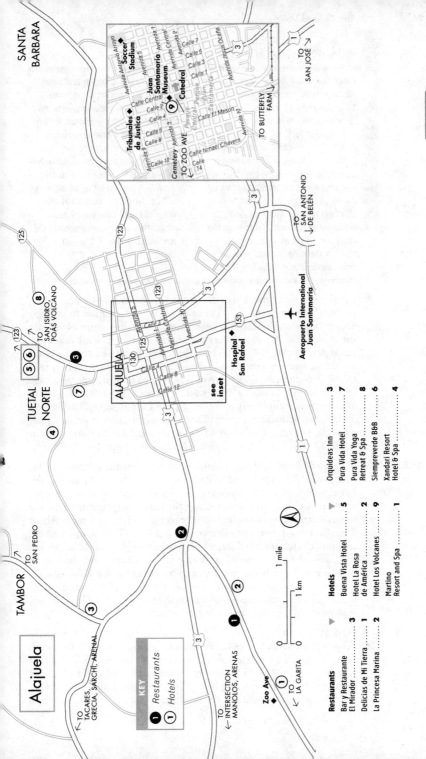

Alajuela

KEY
- **1** *Restaurants*
- ① *Hotels*

Restaurants
Bar y Restaurante
El Mirador **3**
Delicias de Mi Tierra **1**
La Princesa Marina **2**

Hotels
Buena Vista Hotel **5**
Hotel La Rosa
de América **2**
Hotel Los Volcanes **9**
Martino
Resort and Spa **1**
Orquideas Inn **3**
Pura Vida Hotel **7**
Pura Vida Yoga
Retreat & Spa **8**
Siempreverde B&B **6**
Xandari Resort
Hotel & Spa **4**

SANTA BARBARA

TAMBOR

TUETAL NORTE

ALAJUELA

see inset

Hospital San Rafael

Aeropuerto Internacional Juan Santamaria

TO SAN ANTONIO DE BELÉN

TO SAN ISIDRO POÁS VOLCANO

TO TACARES, SARCHÍ, ARENAL
TO GRECIA
TO SAN PEDRO

TO INTERSECTION MANOLOS, ARENAS

TO LA GARITA

Zoo Ave

TO ZOO AVE

1 mile
1 km

Inset:
Soccer Stadium
Avenida Antonio Arroyo
Juan Santamaria Museum
Tribunales de Justicia
Catedral
Parque Central
Cemetery
TO BUTTERFLY FARM
TO SAN JOSÉ

Calle Central, Calle 1, Calle 3, Calle 5, Calle 7
Calle 2, Calle 4, Calle 6, Calle 8, Calle 10
Calle El Meson
Calle Ismael Chavern
Calle 14

Avenida 1, Avenida 2, Avenida 3, Avenida 5
Avenida Central
Avenida 10
Avenida 9, Avenida 11
Avenida Jesús Ocaña

2

A National Hero

When the Costa Ricans drove invader Walker's army from their country, in 1856, they chased his troops to Rivas, Nicaragua. The filibusters took refuge in a wooden fort. Juan Santamaría, a poor, 24-year-old drummer with a militia from Alajuela, volunteered to burn it down to drive them out. Legend says that Santamaría ran toward the fort carrying a torch, and that although he was shot repeatedly, he managed to throw it and to burn the fort down. His bravery wasn't recognized at the time, probably because of his modest origins, but in 1891 a statue depicting a strong and handsome soldier carrying a torch was placed in Alajuela, thus immortalizing Santamaría. For this occasion, Ruben Darío, the great Nicaraguan writer, dedicated a poem to him. The entire account may be apocryphal; some historians doubt there ever *was* such a person. But don't tell that to the average Tico. April 11 is now a national holiday in Costa Rica, called Juan Santamaría Day, which celebrates the Costa Rican victory at the Battle of Rivas.

★ Considering the amount of coffee you'll drive past in the Central Valley, you might want to devote an hour or so of your vacation to learning about the crop's production. **Doka Estate,** a working coffee plantation for more than 70 years, offers a comprehensive tour that takes you through the fields, shows you how the fruit is processed and the beans are dried, and lets you sample the local brew. The best time to take this tour is during the October-to-February picking season. ✛ *10 km (6 mi) north of Alajuela's Tribunales de Justicia; turn left at San Isidro and continue 6 km (4 mi), follow signs, San Luis de Sabanilla* ☎ *2449– 5152* ⊕ *www.dokaestate.com* ✉ *$16; transportation from San José, Alajuela, Heredia, Escazú, or San Antonio available* ☉ *Tours: daily at 9, 10, 11, 1:30, 2:30, and 3:30; weekends last tour at 2:30.*

EN ROUTE

If you head straight through Alajuela, with the Parque Central on your right, you'll be on the road to Poás Volcano; you should pass the Tribunales de Justicia (the county courthouse) on your right as you leave town. If you turn left upon reaching the Parque Central, and pass the town cemetery on your right, you'll be on the old road to Grecia. About 3 km (2 mi) northwest of town on that road, you'll come upon an old concrete church on the right, which marks your arrival in Barrio San José, a satellite community of Alajuela. A left turn after the church will take you to a lovely rural area called **La Garita** (the Guardhouse), from which the road continues west to Atenas and the Central Pacific beaches. La Garita is a popular weekend destination for Tico families, who head here for the abundant restaurants.

WHERE TO EAT

$$ ✗ **Bar y Restaurante El Mirador.** Perched on a ridge several miles north of town, El Mirador has a sweeping view of the Central Valley that is impressive by day but more beautiful at dusk and night when the basin is filled with twinkling lights. Get a window table in the dining room, or one on the adjacent porch if it isn't too cool. The menu, which

includes *lomito* (tenderloin) and *corvina* (sea bass) served with various sauces, and several shrimp or chicken dishes, plays second fiddle to the view. You could just stop in around sunset for drinks and appetizers. Free transportation from most Alajuela hotels is sometimes available. There are at least two other restaurants nearby with similar names and views—this one is on the main road, close to the Buena Vista Hotel. ⊠*Road to Poás* ✛*5 km (3 mi) north of Tribunales de Justicia* ☎*2441–9347* ⌑*Reservations essential weekends* ▭*MC, V.*

$ ✕**La Princesa Marina.** This large open-air eatery (part of a chain) at the intersection of the old Alajuela–Grecia road and the road to La Garita is popular with Ticos, who pack it on weekends to feast on inexpensive seafood. The selection is vast, with 10 types of fish, shrimp, or octopus ceviche, fish fillets served with various sauces, three sizes of shrimp prepared a dozen ways, whole fried fish, lobster tails, and several *mariscadas* (mixed seafood plates). Pastas, rice dishes, beef, and chicken are some other choices, but the seafood is your best bet. The decor is utilitarian—bare tables, ceiling fans, and dividers of potted plants separating the sections, but you avoid that feeling of being in a contrived tourist venue. ⊠*Barrio San José, north of church* ☎*2433–7117* ▭*AE, DC, MC, V.*

¢ ✕**Delicias de Mi Tierra.** The name translates as "Delights of my Land," and tasty and traditional Tico favorites are in fact served here: *pozol* (corn and pork soup), *casado campesino* (stewed beef with rice, beans, corn, potatoes, and plantains), and *chorreada con natilla* (a corn-bread pancake with sour cream). Long wooden tables and benches are surrounded by cane walls, decorative oxcart wheels, dried gourds, and tropical plants—the kind of decor trying so hard to be traditional that it's anything but. Ordering a few *entraditas* (appetizers) is a good way to sample dishes, as is the *parrillada de campo* (country barbecue), a platter with grilled chicken, beef, pork, rice, beans, fried plantains, and salad, or the larger *fiesta de gallos,* a mixed platter of corn tortillas with various fillings. There are also cheap but hearty breakfasts. Get here early for dinner, as closing time is 8 PM. ✛*1½ km (1 mi) west of the Barrio San José church* ☎*2433–8536* ▭*AE, DC, MC, V.*

WHERE TO STAY

$$$–$$$$ ▣**Xandari Resort Hotel & Spa.** The tranquil and colorful Xandari is a
FodorsChoice strikingly original inn and spa, tailor-made for honeymooners and
★ romantic getaways. Its bold design is the brainchild of a talented couple—he's an architect, she's an artist. Contemporary pueblo-esque villas along a ridge overlooking Alajuela and San José are spacious, with plenty of windows, colorful paintings, large terraces, and secluded lanais (sunbathing patios). It's the kind of place that makes you want to take pictures of your hotel room. Some villas stand alone and some share a building, but nearly all of them have spectacular views. So does the restaurant ($$), which serves tasty, often organic, low-fat food. A 4-km (3-mi) trail through the hotel's forest reserve winds past five waterfalls. **Pros:** Amazing service, ideal setting for romance, guilt-free gourmet delights. **Con:** Some guests have complained about noise and thin walls; newly reinforced walls and lowered maximum occupancy rates have significantly addressed this. ✛*5 km (3 mi) north of Tribu-*

nales de Justicia; turn left after small bridge, follow signs ☎2443–2020, *866/363–3212 in U.S.* 🖷2442–4847 ⊕*www.xandari.com* ☚*21 villas* ♨*In-room: no a/c, safe, refrigerator, no TV, Wi-Fi. In-hotel: restaurant, bar, pools, spa, laundry service, public Internet, airport shuttle, no-smoking rooms* ☰*AE, MC, V* ⑩*CP.*

$$$ 🏨 **Pura Vida Yoga Retreat & Spa.** Yoga workshops are an integral part of your stay here, and you should have at least some interest in the discipline to fully enjoy your stay. The spa has the full range of traditional offerings, as well as cutting-edge treatments like *watsu* (water shiatsu) and hot-stone massage. The variety of rooms ranges from large suites to carpeted and furnished tents; all are quite nice, if not super-luxurious. Most of the bamboo-filled rooms have large windows and look out over the valley or tropical gardens, where more than 40 bird species have been sighted. The weekly rate includes yoga classes, full-day rafting, and two half-day ecotours, airport transfers, three healthful meals per day, and one massage. You can drop in for any number of days, but the experience is structured around the five- to seven-day "Mind, Body & Spirit" package. **Pros:** International team of yoga and massage professionals, beautiful view. **Cons:** Not much around the property, only appropriate for yoga vacations. ⊕*7 km (4 mi) northeast of stadium; make a sharp left at the Nuevo Apolo 15 Bar, continue ½ km (¼ mi) to cream-color gate, Pavas de Carrizal* ☎2483–0033, *888/515–4580 in U.S.* 🖷2483–0041 ⊕*www.puravidaspa.com* ☚*34 rooms, 3 suites, 14 tent bungalows, 1 house* ♨*In-room: no a/c, no phone, no TV. In-hotel: restaurant, spa, airport shuttle* ☰*MC, V* ⑩*FAP.*

$$ 🏨 **Buena Vista Hotel.** Perched high above Alajuela, this hotel's superb staff makes up for the somewhat dated, uninspired decor. It does have the "good view" it is named for, but few of its rooms share in that vista, which is best appreciated from the back lawn. Three balcony rooms on the second floor in back have decent views of the Central Valley, but even better are the views of Poás Volcano from the three rooms above the lobby. Most rooms, however, overlook the lawns or pool area. They are fairly standard—carpeted and sparsely decorated, with small baths and TVs—with none of the pizzazz of similarly priced options. The restaurant behind the lobby serves international dishes and grilled items. **Pros:** Excellent service, family friendly. **Cons:** Uninspired ambience, some say the restaurant could do better, farther away from the airport than other Alajuela options. ⊕*6 km (4 mi) north of Alajuela's Tribunales de Justicia on road to Poás* ☎2442–8595, *800/506–2304 in U.S.* 🖷2442–8701 ⊕*www.hotelbuenavistacr.com* ☚*11 rooms, 4 junior suites, 9 deluxe suites, 1 master suite* ♨*In-room: no a/c, no phone, Wi-Fi. In-hotel: restaurant, bar, pool, airport shuttle, no-smoking rooms* ☰*AE, MC, V* ⑩*CP.*

$$ 🏨 **Martino Resort and Spa.** This relatively small Italian-style resort hotel is a small step below the international luxury chains in both quality and price, but still a good value. Amenities include a casino, spa, and spacious grounds, with the occasional classical sculpture to catch your eye. The ample facilities and value attract longer-term guests along with travelers splurging for their first or last night. The rear of the main building is gorgeous, with a restaurant balcony that looks over the

2

pool. The rooms have terraces, wood furnishings, and carved wooden doors, and the restaurant, which is well regarded locally, serves pastas and Italian-style meat and seafood dishes. **Pros:** Excellent restaurant, affordable frills, proximity to attractions such as Zoo Ave. **Con:** Too distant for quick pops into San José. ⊠*Diagonally across from Zoo Ave on the road to La Garita* ☎*2433–8382, 888/886–5042 in the U.S.* ⊞*2433–9052* ⊕*www.hotelmartino.com* ⊅*35 junior suites, 4 deluxe suites, 2 master suites, 3 villas* ⚑*In-room: Wi-Fi. In-hotel: restaurant, room service, bar, pool, gym, spa, no elevator, laundry service, no-smoking rooms* ⊟*AE, DC, MC, V* ⦿*BP.*

$$ 🏨**Pura Vida Hotel.** Extremely well-informed, helpful owners and prox-
★ imity to the airport (15 minutes) make this a good place to begin and end a trip. Thanks to its location on a ridge north of town, several of this hotel's rooms have views of Poás Volcano, and all of them offer tranquillity and abundant birdsong. The two rooms in the main house have the best views, but *casitas* (little houses) scattered around the large garden offer more privacy. Bright and cheery bungalows have small terraces with chairs where guests, typically well traveled, lounge. Continental breakfasts and delicious dinners (by reservation) are served on a covered terrace behind the house. Ask about their books-for-schools program. **Pros:** Helpful, informed owners active in the local community; stellar breakfast. **Cons:** Well-trained, quiet but large dogs may turn off those with less-than-fuzzy feelings for animals; not ideal for visitors who have trouble with stairs. ⊠*Tuetal* ⚑*2 km (1 mi) north of Tribunales de Justicia; veer left at Y* ☎*2430–2929* ⊞*2430–2630* ⊕*www.puravidahotel.com* ⊅*2 rooms, 4 bungalows* ⚑*In-room: no a/c, no phone, no TV. In-hotel: restaurant, no elevator, laundry service, public Internet, airport shuttle, no-smoking rooms* ⊟*AE, DC, MC, V* ⦿*CP.*

$–$$ 🏨**Orquideas Inn.** A favorite with young couples and families, the friendly Orquideas proves that affordable does not have to equal generic. From a classy Spanish-style main building to a bar dedicated to Marilyn Monroe, this place has style. Deluxe rooms, on a hill with a view of three volcanoes, are spacious, with bamboo furniture, but can smell a bit musty. Smaller rooms have terra-cotta tile floors and Guatemalan fabrics that have seen better days; those on the garden side are quieter, and worth the extra $10. A sumptuous breakfast buffet is served on the bar's patio. The restaurant's ($$) eclectic selection ranges from straightforward Costa Rican *cuisine* to over-the-top presentations (ceviche served in a half-coconut, for one) that have to be seen (and tasted) to be believed. **Pros:** Spirited environment, great for first or last night, excellent service. **Cons:** Bedding and rooms are ready for a face-lift, roadside rooms noisy. ⚑*2½ km (1½ mi) northwest of the Princesa Marina* ☎*2433–9346* ⊞*2433–9740* ⊕*www.orquideasinn.com* ⊅*20 rooms, 6 suites* ⚑*In-room: safe, Wi-Fi (some). In-hotel: restaurant, bar, pool, laundry service, airport shuttle* ⊟*AE, DC, MC, V* ⦿*BP.*

$ 🏨**Hotel La Rosa de América.** This small hotel tucked off the road to La Garita is a simple and relaxed place to unwind. New owners add a welcoming energy and a personalized touch to a place that would otherwise be simply serviceable. There are six buildings, most divided into two units, arranged around the pool and gardens. The white-wall rooms are simple, but it's a quiet place to sleep. Calling ahead for directions is a good idea, but once you're here, you'll have easy access to nearby restaurants and Zoo Ave. **Pros:** Great for families, helpful owners, close to a number of restaurants celebrating Costa Rican cuisine. **Con:** Lacks flair of other options in this price range. ✛*2½ km (1½ mi) from La Princesa Marina* 🏠2433–2741 *or* 2433–2455 ⊕*www. larosadeamerica.com* ☎*12 rooms* ⌂*In-room: no a/c, no phone, safe. In-hotel: pool, no elevator, laundry service, public Internet, no-smoking rooms* ⊟*AE, DC, MC, V* ⎮⊙⎮*BP.*

$ 🏨 **Siempreverde B&B.** A night at this isolated B&B in the heart of a coffee plantation might be as close as you'll ever come to being a coffee farmer, or to truly getting away from it all. The attractive wooden house has seven sparsely decorated rooms upstairs, with hardwood floors and small windows; ask for the Cuarto Azul (the Blue Room). There are also a living room, kitchen, lounge, and terrace in back where breakfast is served. Photos of the coffee harvest decorate the walls, and just beyond the yard and manicured gardens that surround the house, neat rows of coffee plants stretch off into the distance. **Pros:** A sense of being dropped into an emblematic Costa Rican vignette, tranquillity. **Cons:** Isolated location, tour groups pass by for breakfast most mornings. ✛*12 km (5 mi) northwest of Tribunales de Justicia de Alajuela; turn left at high school* ☎2449–5562 🏠2239–4539 ⊕*www.siempreverde bandb.com* ☎*7 rooms with bath* ⌂*In-room: no a/c, no phone, no TV. In-hotel: no elevator* ⊟*AE, DC, MC, V* ⎮⊙⎮*BP.*

¢   🏨 **Hotel Los Volcanes.** Budget travelers looking for airport proximity will find this urban oasis an excellent value. Descendants of the Catalan family that thrived in this heritage house in 1920 still live next door, and historic photos of the mansion in its heyday line the earth-tone walls inside. The spacious rooms have low-slung, wide beds that make the ceilings seem sky-high—but avoid the room next to the washer and dryer. Breakfast is served in a courtyard shaded by a fig tree. Plenty of restaurants are within walking distance, the airport is a 10-minute taxi ride away, and just a few blocks away is the bus stop for La Garita, Poás, and most destinations in central and northwest Costa Rica. **Pros:** Airport proximity, good value, historic ambience. **Con:** City location is convenient, but lacks the fresh air and views of slightly more expensive, outlying options. ⊠*Avda. 3, Cs. 2–Central, or 100 m north, 25 m east of the northwest corner of Parque Central, across from the Juan Santamaría Museum* ☎2441–0525 🏠2440–8006 ⊕*www.hotel losvolcanes.com* ☎*11 rooms, 7 with bath* ⌂*In-room: no a/c, Ethernet, Wi-Fi. In-hotel: no elevator, laundry service, no-smoking rooms (some)* ⊟*MC, V* ⎮⊙⎮*BP.*

SANTO DOMINGO

18 km (11 mi) northeast of Escazú, 7 km (4 mi) northwest of San José.

Between Heredia and San José, the town of Santo Domingo de Heredia has plenty of traditional architecture and a level of tranquillity that

belies its proximity to the capital, a
mere 20-minute drive away. Established in the early 19th century,
Santo Domingo is surrounded by
coffee farms and several smaller,
even quieter communities. It has
two Catholic churches, including
one of the country's two basilicas.
The Iglesia del Rosario, which faces

> **COFFEE'S MELTING POT**
>
> Coffee is touted as a quintes-
> sential part of Costa Rica's history
> and culture; paradoxically, most
> coffee-plantation workers in the
> country today are Nicaraguan.

the town's sparsely planted Parque Central, was built in the 1840s and
is open for mass every morning from 7 to 10. The larger Basílica de
Santo Domingo, which stands across from a soccer field in the northeast end of town, is open for evening mass from 5 to 7, and is a venue
for classical music concerts throughout the year, including the July-to-
August International Music Festival.

GETTING HERE & AROUND

For the 30-minute trip from downtown San José, head north on C. Central 4 km (2½ mi) to the central park in Tibás; continue 100 meters and
turn left. Follow this road another 2½ km (1¼ mi) to Santo Domingo.
From the west end of Paseo Colón, turn right onto the Pan-American
Highway (aka the Carretera General Cañas), then right off the highway just before it heads onto an overpass, after the Hotel Irazú (on the
right). Keep to this road for about 2 km (1 mi) to the first intersection
after it becomes one-way. Turn right at the lights, continue 3 km (1½
mi), passing INBioparque, until the road Ts; a left here brings you into
town. *See Heredia, below, for bus information.*

EXPLORING

Santo Domingo's main attraction is **INBioparque,** which does a good job
of explaining the country's various ecosystems. It's a useful, if slightly
expensive, primer before you head out to the hinterlands. Wander trails
through climate-controlled wetlands and out to tropical dry forest. The
forests may not look much different, but your English-speaking guide
will explain the subtleties. Along the way, stop at the butterfly farm,
snake and insect exhibits, and bromeliad garden. The tour is packed
with information—perhaps too much—but if you're visiting Costa
Rica for its ecology, it's a worthwhile lesson. Kids love the virtual aerial
flyover of Central America introduced by astronaut Franklin Chang. A
restaurant serves typical Costa Rican fare, and the gift shop has souvenirs and books on natural history. Reservations are required for tours.
✉ *Road between Santo Domingo and Heredia, 400 m north and 200 m
west of Shell gas station* ☎ *2507–8107* ⊕ *www.inbio.ac.cr/inbioparque*
🗩 *$23* ⏱ *Tues.–Sun. 8–6 (last admission at 4). Tours at 9, 11, and 1.*

WHERE TO STAY

$$ 🏨 **Hotel Bougainvillea.** This hotel is a top choice for business travelers
and small-scale conferences, but its extensive grounds, which bump up
against coffee farms, are ideal for lazy strolls or families with energetic
kids. You might even forget that you're only 20 minutes from San
José. The spacious and carpeted but otherwise unremarkable rooms
are furnished with local hardwoods. Rooms on the second and third

floors have large balconies; get one with a view of the gardens behind the hotel. The 8-acre garden, shaded by large trees, holds an extensive bromeliad collection. Pre-Columbian pottery and paintings by Costa Rican artists decorate the lobby and restaurant ($$), which serves a small but excellent selection of continental cuisine. An hourly shuttle takes you to the Hotel Villa Tournón in San José. **Pros:** Lush and open spaces; of the urban hotels, one of the better bird-watching sites. **Con:** Slightly institutional smell and feel in the hallways. *⊹2 km (1 mi) east of Santo Domingo de Heredia, Santo Tomas* ☎2244–1414 ⎙2244–1313 ⊕www.hb.co.cr ⇴77 rooms, 4 suites ⎇In-room: no a/c, Wi-Fi. In-hotel: restaurant, bar, tennis courts, pool, laundry service, public Internet, no-smoking rooms ⊟AE, DC, MC, V ⎮⊙⎮EP.*

HEREDIA

4 km (3 mi) north of Santo Domingo, 11 km (6 mi) northwest of San José.

With a canton population of around 117,000, Heredia is the capital of one of Costa Rica's most important coffee provinces, with some of the country's best-preserved colonial towns. Founded in 1706, the city bears witness to how difficult preservation can be in an earthquake-prone country; most of its colonial structures have been destroyed by the tremors and tropical climate—not to mention modernization. Still, the city and neighboring towns retain a certain historic feel, with old adobe buildings scattered amid the concrete structures. The nearby villages of Barva and Santo Domingo de Heredia have more colonial and adobe buildings, and the roads that wind through the hills above those towns pass through charming scenery and rural enclaves, making them excellent routes for exploration.

GETTING HERE & AROUND

The narrow routes to Heredia are notoriously clogged at almost all times; avoid them during rush hours if possible. Turn right at the west end of Paseo Colón. Follow Pan-American Highway 2 km (1¼ mi); take the second exit, just before the highway heads onto an overpass, and just after the Hotel Irazú (on the right). To get to the center of Heredia, follow that road for 5½ km (3½ mi), then turn left at the Universidad Nacional; continue north past the university instead of turning to reach the Britt Coffee Tour, Museo de Cultura Popular, Sacramento, Barva, and points beyond. Buses run between San José (300 m east of Hospital San Juan de Dios) and Heredia every 5 to 10 minutes daily (between 5 AM and 10 PM), following the above car route. The steady stream of buses leaving from C. 1, Avdas. 7–9 every three to five minutes passing through Santo Domingo are sometimes a better bet during rush hour, particularly the *directo* buses that start after 3:30 PM; these buses also run from midnight to 3:30 AM on the hour. If you're without a car, a taxi is the best way to get to Café Britt or Barva.

HEREDIA ESSENTIALS

Bank/ATM **Banco Popular** (⊠ *200 m east of northeast corner of Parque Central* ☎ *2260–9407*). **Banco Nacional** (⊠ *Southwest corner of Parque Central* ☎ *2277–6900*).

Pharmacy **Farmacia Chavarria** (⊠ *Southwest corner of Parque Central* ☎ *2263–4670*).

Internet **Internet Cosmos** (⊠ *300 m east of Parque Central* ☎ *2262–4775*).

Post Office **Correos** (⊠ *Northwest corner of Parque Central*).

EXPLORING

Heredia proper is centered around tree-studded **Parque Central,** which is surrounded by a few historic buildings. The park has a cast-iron fountain imported from England in 1879 and a simple kiosk where the municipal band plays Sunday-morning and Thursday-night concerts. ⊠ *C. Central and Avda. Central.*

The impressive **Church of the Immaculate Conception** (Iglesia de la Inmaculada Concepción) is a whitewashed stone church built between 1797 and 1804 to replace an adobe temple dating from the early 1700s. Its thick stone walls, small windows, and squat buttresses have kept it intact through two centuries of quakes and tremors. It has a pale interior with marble floors and stained-glass windows, and is flanked by tidy gardens. There are Sunday services at 6 AM, 9 AM, 11 AM, and 6 PM. ⊠ *Eastern end of Parque Central* ☎ *2237–0779* ⊙ *Daily 6–6.*

To the north of the Parque Central stands a strange, decorative tower called the **Fortín** *(Little Fort),* which was built as a military post in the 1870s by the local oligarch Fadrique Gutiérrez. It never did see action and now serves as a symbol of the province. It's worth a walk by, but is closed to the public. The old brick building next to the Fortín is the Palacio Municipal (Town Hall). ⊠ *C. Central and Avda. Central.*

Two blocks south of the Parque Central is Heredia's **Mercado Viejo** (Old Market), which has fewer souvenirs for sale than San José's Mercado Central but is less cramped and safer. On the next block to the southeast is the **Mercado Nuevo** (New Market), which holds dozens of *sodas* (simple restaurants). ⊠ *C. Central and Avda. 6* ⊙ *Mon.–Sat. 7–6.*

At the edge of a middle-class neighborhood between Heredia and Barva is the **Museo de Cultura Popular** (Museum of Popular Culture), which preserves a farmhouse built in 1885 with an adobe-like technique called *bahareque.* Run by the National University, the museum is furnished with antiques and surrounded by a garden. An adjacent open-air restaurant serves inexpensive Costa Rican lunches on weekends. Just walking around the museum is instructive, but calling ahead to reserve a hands-on cultural tour (such as tortilla making) really makes it worth the trip. ⊠ *Between Heredia and Barva; from the Musmanni in Santa Lucia de Barva, 100 m north ✛1 km (½ mi) east; follow signs* ☎ *2260–1619* ⊕ *www.ilam.org/cr/museoculturapopular* ▦ *$2* ⊙ *Weekdays 8–4, Sun. 10–4; closed Sat.*

Coffee, the Golden Bean

When Costa Rica's first elected head of state, Juan Mora Fernández, began encouraging his compatriots to cultivate coffee back in 1830, he could hardly have imagined how profound an impact the crop would have on his country. Over the last 100 years coffee has transformed Costa Rica from a colonial backwater into a relatively affluent and cosmopolitan republic.

It was the "golden bean" that financed the construction of most of the nation's landmarks. Lured by plantation jobs, tens of thousands of immigrant families from Europe and elsewhere in the Americas moved to Costa Rica in the 1800s and early 1900s, and were given land in exchange for cutting down the forest and planting coffee. They formed the backbone of a middle-class majority that has long distinguished Costa Rica from most of the rest of Latin America.

Thanks to its altitude and mineral-rich volcanic soil, the Central Valley is ideal for growing coffee, and the crop once covered nearly every arable acre of this region; now it accounts only for the use of approximately 1% of all land. Coffee is not actually native to Costa Rica: plants first arrived in Costa Rica from the Caribbean in 1791.

The coffee-growing cycle begins in April/May, when rains make the dark-green bushes explode into a flurry of white blossoms. By November the fruit starts to ripen, turning from green to red, and the busy harvest begins as farmers race to get picked "cherries" to *beneficios* (processing plants or mills), where the beans—two per fruit—are removed, washed, dried by machine, and packed in burlap sacks for export. Costa Rica's crop is consistently among the world's best, and most of the high-grade exports wind up in Europe and the United States.

Traditionally, coffee bushes are grown in the shade of trees. Recently, however, many farmers have switched to sun-resistant varieties, cutting down shade trees to pack in more coffee bushes, and destroying habitats for migratory birds in the process. Environmentalists and many farmers are promoting a return to the old system by labeling shade coffee ECO-OK. (And shade coffee *does* actually taste better.) Though coffee prices have risen significantly since 2002, a major slump up until then drove a number of Costa Rican producers out of business. However, innovative marketing has ensured that the crop still remains king in the Central Valley.

Ticos are fueled by lots of coffee, and generally make it in a *chorreador*, a wooden stand with a cloth filter—which makes a strong cup of java. Reliable brands are Café Rey's Tarrazú, Café Britt, Volio, and Montaña.

★ The producer of Costa Rica's most popular export-quality coffee, **Café Britt,** gives a lively tour that highlights Costa Rica's history of coffee cultivation through a theatrical presentation that is admittedly a bit hokey. Your "tour guides" are professional actors, and pretty good ones at that, so if you don't mind the song and dance, it's fun. Take a short walk through the coffee farm and processing plant, and learn how professional coffee tasters distinguish a fine cup of java. One major difference between this tour and that of Doka Estate in Alajuela is that Doka takes you through the mill. Britt, ever the innovator, provides a similar tour add-on by request. ⊠*From Heredia, take road to Barva; follow signs* ☎*2277–1500, 800/462–7488 in North America* ⊕*www.cafebritt.com* ✉*$20 tour only, $27 with transportation, $35 with transportation and lunch* ⊙*Tours: Dec.–May, daily at 11 and 3; June–Nov., daily at 11.*

WHERE TO EAT

$–$$ ✕**L'Antica Roma.** The food here more than makes up for the less-than-tasteful red curtains, gold walls, and faded images of the Colosseum. The ample menu offers more than 40 pizza varieties, all baked in a wood-burning oven, and homemade fresh pasta, such as three-mushroom ravioli. Two TVs with sports are suspended indoors; the tables out on the wrought-iron–enclosed patio lend themselves better to conversation. ⊠*C. 7 and Avda. 7, across from the Hotel Valladolid* ☎*2262–9073* ☰*AE, DC, MC, V.*

$ ✕**Oky Grill & Cafe.** Barva's main draw is strong Costa Rican flavor, so you may be inclined to pass by Oky Café on the way to or from the Museum of Culture. But if you're hungry, that would be a shame. The large wall canvases and dark-wood tables and chairs suggest Europe— as does the food, overseen by the café's namesake and owner, Oky María Numez. If you're not up for the German-style steak or anything in a heavy sauce, asparagus crepes and an assortment of light sandwiches are delicious alternatives. There's a generous German dessert selection and an extensive list of shakes and iced coffees, too. ⊠*From the Automercado in Barva de Heredia, 500 m north, 200 m east* ☎*2263–6632* ☰*AE, DC, MC, V.*

WHERE TO STAY

$$$$ ▦**Finca Rosa Blanca Country Inn.** There's nothing common about this
Fodor'sChoice exclusive B&B overlooking coffee farms; new additions update the
★ Gaudí-esque hideaway's reputation as one of the country's top sumptuous splurges. The main building retains its soaring ceiling and white-stucco arches, set among tropical flowers and shaded by massive fig trees. All rooms—each with its own style—have been spruced up, from the addition of Jacuzzi bathtubs to new 100% bamboo sheets. The spacious two-story suite is out of a fairy tale, with a spiral staircase leading up to a window-lined tower bedroom. The owners work hard to make the hotel as eco-friendly as possible, using composting, solar panels, and other methods. The hotel is one of only four in the country to receive a top rating for sustainable tourism. Prix-fixe gourmet dinners are available at the new El Tigre Vestido restaurant ($$$), and guests can relax in the new bar or full-service spa. **Pros:** Top-of-the-line eco-consciousness, indulgence with style, service par excellence. **Con:** Some may find a few touches over the top. ⊠*800 m north of Café Britt Distribution Center in Santa Barbara de Heredia, Barrio Jesus* ☎*2269–9392* 📠*2269–9555* ⊕*www.fincarosablanca.com* ⇥*11 junior suites, 2 master suites* ♨*In-room: no a/c, safe, no TV, Ethernet, Wi-Fi. In-hotel: restaurant, bar, pool, spa, no elevator, laundry service, airport shuttle* ☰*AE, MC, V* ⦿*BP.*

$$ 🖼 **Hotel Valladolid.** This is hands down the best hotel in downtown Heredia. The tall (for Heredia) and narrow building has just 11 modern rooms, designed for business travelers and visiting professors at the nearby National University, although the typical guests are now just as likely to be vacationers. The tile floors and white walls aren't exactly inspired, but are just fine for a night's sleep. **Pro:** Best lodging in town. **Con:** Heredia's charms lie in the outskirts, not in town. ⊠ C. 7 and Avda. 7, 400 m north and 100 m west of the main entrance of La Universidad Nacional ☎2260–2905 🖨2260–2912 ⊕www.hotel valladolid.net 🛏11 rooms ⬥In-room: safe, refrigerator, Wi-Fi. In-hotel: bar, laundry service ☰AE, DC, MC, V ⦿CP.

¢ 🖼 **Hotel Ceos.** Occupying an old wooden home a block north of the Parque Central, the Hotel Ceos has basic accommodations for travelers on a tight budget. Historic photos decorate the ground floor, and the rooms are painted in pastels, but are small and timeworn. The large balcony on the second floor, furnished with a sofa and chairs, is perfect for shooting the breeze with a beer. The downstairs *soda* serves inexpensive breakfasts and light meals. **Pro:** Wallet-friendly crash pad. **Con:** Even for a budget place, service could be better. ⊠ Avda. 1 and C. 4, 100 m north and 100 m west of the Parque Central ☎2262–2628 🖨2260–9293 ⊕www.hotelamericacr.com 🛏10 rooms ⬥In-room: no a/c. In-hotel: restaurant, no elevator ☰AE, MC, V ⦿EP.

EN ROUTE

At the center of **Barva de Heredia,** a small community about 3 km (2 mi) north of Heredia proper, is the **Parque Central,** surrounded by old adobe shops with Spanish-tile roofs on three sides and a white-stucco church to the east. The stout, handsome church dates from the late 18th century; behind it is a lovely little garden shrine to the Virgin Mary. On a clear day you can see verdant Volcán Barva (⇨ Chapter 3) towering to the north, and if you follow the road that runs in front of the church and veer left at the Y, you will wind your way up the slopes of that volcano to Vara Blanca, where you can either drive north to the La Paz Waterfall Gardens, or continue straight to Poás Volcano National Park (⇨ Chapter 3). If instead you veer right at the Y and drive up the steep, narrow road, you'll pass through San José de la Montaña and Paso Llano to reach Sacramento, where the road turns into a rough dirt track leading to the Barva sector of Braulio Carrillo National Park (⇨ Chapter 3). If you turn left when you reach Barva's central plaza, you'll head to San Pedro and Santa Barbara, where roads head south to Alajuela and north to Vara Blanca.

CARTAGO AND IRAZÚ VOLCANO

Cartago, due east of San José, was the country's first capital, and thus has scattered historical structures and the remarkable Basílica de Los Angeles. To the north of Cartago towers massive Irazú Volcano, which is covered with farmland and topped by an impressive crater.

View of Arenal Volcano on a clear day.

(above) Manuel Antonio National Park coastline. *(opposite page, top)* Tica dancer performs at a cultural festival in San José. *(opposite page, bottom)* White-faced capuchins are the most commonly seen monkeys in Costa Rica.

(top) Digging into Class-IV rapids on the Pacuáre River. *(bottom)* Sky Walk's hanging-bridge hike in Monteverde Cloud Forest. *(opposite page)* A scarlet macaw and blue-and-gold macaw get chummy.

(top) Sun-seekers at Espadilla Beach, in Manuel Antonio National Park. *(bottom)* Black river turtles hang out in Tortuguero, Costa Rica's slowpoke central.

(top) Coffee beans must be hand-picked, because they don't all ripen at the same time. *(bottom)* Painted oxcarts are one of Costa Rica's signature crafts.

(top) The clear-blue crater lake at Poás Volcano. *(bottom left)* All that glitters is gold at San José's Pre-Columbian Gold Museum. *(bottom right)* The heliconia is found in abundance throughout Costa Rica.

CARTAGO

22 km (14 mi) southeast of San José.

Cartago is much older than San José, but earthquakes have destroyed most of its colonial structures, leaving just a few interesting buildings among the concrete boxes. Cartago became Costa Rica's second–most prominent city in 1823, when the seat of government was moved to the emerging economic center of San José. You'll see some attractive old buildings as you move through town, most of them erected after the 1910 quake. Most visitors see Cartago on their way to or from the Orosi Valley or Turrialba, and there is little reason to stay the night. The Orosi Valley, a short drive away, has better choices.

GETTING HERE & AROUND

For the 25-minute drive from San José, drive east on Avenida 2 through San Pedro and Curridabat to the highway entrance, where you have three road options—take the middle one marked Cartago. Shortly before Cartago, a Y intersection marks the beginning of the route up Irazú, with traffic to Cartago veering right. Buses between San José and Cartago leave every 10 minutes daily (25 m north of the Hotel Balmoral or 300 m south of the Teatro Nacional) from 5 AM to midnight; buses to Paraíso leave weekdays from the same terminal every half hour. Cartago buses to San José pick up 200 meters north of the Parque Central. Buses to Orosi leave Cartago every 15–30 minutes from 5:30 AM to 10 PM, 100 meters east, 25 meters south of the southwest corner of Las Ruinas.

CARTAGO ESSENTIALS

Bank/ATM Banco de Costa Rica (⊠*Avda. 4, Cs. 5–7* ☎*2552–9006*).**BAC San José** (⊠*100 m south of Las Ruinas* ☎*2295–9797*). **Scotiabank ATM** (⊠*Northwest corner of Las Ruinas*).

Hospital Hospital Max Peralta (⊠*200 m south, 150 m east of Las Ruinas* ☎*2550–1999 or 2551–2806* ⊕*www.hmp.sa.cr*).

Pharmacy Farmacia Central (⊠*Just south of Las Ruinas* ☎*2551–0698*).

Post Office Correos (⊠*Avda. 2, Cs. 15–17*).

Taxis Taxis El Carmen (☎*2551–0836*).

EXPLORING

Churches in some form or another have stood at the site of the present-day Parque Central since 1575, and have been knocked down by earthquakes and reconstructed many times. Undeterred by complete destruction in 1841, the citizens of Cartago began work on a Romanesque cathedral some years later, but the devastating earthquake of 1910 halted work and put an end to the last attempt at building a structure on the site. **Las Ruinas** (⊠*Avda. 2, Cs. 1–2*), or "the Ruins," of this unfinished house of worship, now stand in a pleasant park planted with tall pines and bright impatiens. You won't be able to go inside, but the site is spectacular from outside as well. Among the many legends attributed to the ruins is the gruesome story of the priest of one of the

La Negrita

On the night of August 1 and well into the early morning hours of August 2, the road to Cartago from San José clogs with worshippers, some of whom have traveled from as far away as Nicaragua to celebrate the 1635 appearance of Costa Rica's patron saint, La Negrita (the Black Virgin). At a spring behind the church, people fill bottles with water believed to have curative properties. Miraculous healing powers are attributed to the saint, and devotees have placed thousands of tiny symbolic crutches, ears, eyes, and legs next to her diminutive statue. Tour buses and school groups, along with shops selling the saint's likeness, make the scene a bit of a circus. The statue has twice been stolen, most recently in 1950 by José León Sánchez, now one of Costa Rica's best-known novelists, who spent 20 years on the prison island of San Lucas for having purloined the Madonna, always maintaining he was wrongfully imprisoned. It was another 20 years (1999) before the Supreme Criminal Court officially declared that he was, indeed, innocent.

earlier churches at the site, who after falling in love with his sister-in-law, was murdered by his brother. His ghost, dressed as a priest but headless, still haunts the grounds.

Our Lady of the Angels Basilica (*Basílica de Nuestra Señora de los Angeles*) (⊠ *C. 16, Avdas. 2–4, 7 blocks east of central square* ☎ *2551–0465*) is a hodgepodge of architectural styles from Byzantine to Baroque, with a dash of Gothic. The interior is even more striking, with a colorful tile floor, intricately decorated wood columns, and lots of stained glass. The church is open daily 6 AM to 7 PM. The basilica is also the focus of an annual pilgrimage to celebrate the appearance of La Negrita, or the Black Virgin, Costa Rica's patron saint.

WHERE TO EAT

While you can find decent pasta and pizza, haute cuisine just doesn't exist here. Instead, Cartago gives you a fine opportunity to eat some *comida típica*. On just about any street downtown you'll find a *soda* (simple café), and the women in the kitchen will serve you the same style food they cook at home for their own families. There are literally dozens of places of comparable quality. One rule of thumb: the busier the better—the locals know where to eat well.

VOLCÁN IRAZÚ

31 km (19 mi) northeast of Cartago, 50 km (31 mi) east of San José.

Volcán Irazú is Costa Rica's highest volcano, at 11,260 feet, and its summit has long been protected as a national park. The mountain looms to the north of Cartago, and its eruptions have dumped considerable ash on the city over the centuries. The most recent eruptive period lasted from 1963 to 1965, beginning the day John F. Kennedy arrived in Costa Rica for a presidential visit. Boulders and mud rained down on the countryside, damming rivers and causing serious floods.

Continued on page 105

DRIVING THE OROSI VALLEY LOOP

Gardens, Churches, and Landscapes. This classic day trip—popular with locals but still off the beaten tourist path—is not something you find in most guide books. But if you've got a day to spend near San José, we highly recommend this route past coffee plantations, small towns, and verdant landscapes, with countless breathtaking views.

The region is unique because it is one of the few areas in Costa Rica that still has remnants (ruins and churches) of 17th-century Spanish colonialism. But the highlight of the tour is spending at least a couple of hours in Tapantí National Park tracking the resplendent quetzal or marveling at the many orchid species.

■TIP➔Traffic jams are rarely a problem, but expect company on weekends from fellow motorists—and mountain bikes. (Costa Rica's Olympic cycling team trains here.)

The Drive

Start from Cartago, 22 km (14 mi) southeast of San José. At the basílica in the center of town turn right, and then left onto the busy road to Paraíso and Orosi. After 6 km (4 mi), a blue sign on the right marks the short road to the lush gardens of the **Jardín Botánico Lankester** (☎ 2552–3247 ✉ $5 ☉ Daily 8:30–4:30), one of the world's foremost orchid collections, with more than 1,100 native and introduced species of orchids. Bromeliads, heliconias, and aroids also abound, along with 80 species of trees, including rare palms. The best time to come is February through April, when the most orchids are in bloom. The garden's gift shop is one of the few places in Costa Rica to buy orchids that you can take home legally.

(They come in small bottles and don't flower for four years, so you'll need some serious patience.)

Head east toward Paraíso and then into the town itself. Hang a right at the central park. Some 2 km (1 mi) beyond is the **Sanchiri Mirador,** one of the valley's best *miradores* (lookout points). But our favorite vantage point is at a point on the road just beyond Sanchiri where the earth appears to drop away, and the valley comes into view as you make the steep descent to the town of Orosi. Here's a case for letting someone else do the driving.

Many a visitor has wondered, upon first seeing dreary Paraíso, with its concrete-block buildings and crowded roads, how it ended up with so prodi-

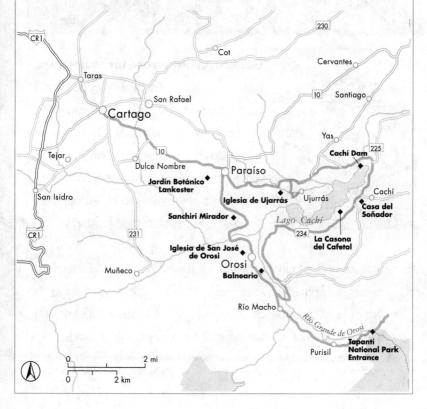

Orosi church

gious a name as "Paradise." But you need merely drive a couple of kilometers south from the central park and gaze down at the vast Orosi Valley to understand what inspired the town's founders. For travelers, Paraíso is on the map for only two reasons: it is the gateway to Orosi, and it has one of the country's best botanical gardens.

The town of Orosi, in the heart of the valley, has but one major attraction: the beautifully restored 1743 **Iglesia de San José de Orosi** (✉ Across from soccer field, center of town ☎ 2533–3051). It's the country's oldest church still in use, and one of the only structures still remaining from the colonial era. It has a low-slung whitewashed facade; the roof is made of cane overlaid with terracotta barrel tiles. Inside are an antique wooden altar and ancient paintings of the stations of the cross and the Virgin

of Guadalupe, all brought to Costa Rica from Guatemala. If you can find someone to open it for you, also take a look inside the religious-art museum next door. Admission to the museum is 75¢ and hours vary. The church is open Tuesday–Sunday 9–noon and 1–5.

It's not a must-do stop, but if you're craving relaxation, the **Los Patios Balneario** (Thermal Baths; ✉ South of Orosi on road to Orosi Lodge ☎ 2533–3009), fed by a hot spring, are open to the public for a nominal fee (less than $3) Tuesday through Sunday, 8:30–4.

South from Orosi, the road becomes a rugged track following the Río Grande de Orosi past coffee plantations, elegant *fincas* (farmhouses), and seasonal barracks for coffee pickers before it's hemmed in by the steep slopes of thick jungle. At the bottom of the loop road, deviate (follow signs) to enter **Tapantí**

Resplendent quetzal

National Park (⊠ 14 km/8 mi south of Orosi ☎ 2200–0090). Though it's worth the trip for just an hour or two of exploring, you could easily fill a day in the park. Stretching from the southern corner of the Orosi Valley up into the Talamanca Mountains, Parque Nacional Tapantí encompasses 47 square km (18 square mi) of largely pristine, remote cloud forest. It provides refuge for more than 400 bird species, including the emerald toucanet, violaceous trogon, and most of the country's hummingbirds.

The rangers' office and visitor center are on the right just after the park entrance. You can leave your vehicle at a parking area 1½ km (1 mi) up the road. From here loop trails head off into the woods on both sides. One trail passes a picnic area and several swimming holes with (cold) emerald waters. The other trail is along a forested hillside. About 1½ km (1 mi) up from the parking area is an entrance to the La Pava Trail on the right, leading down a steep hill to the riverbank. If you continue

¼ mi past the trailhead you arrive at a 300-foot stair trail leading to a lookout. Since the park clouds up in the afternoon, it's best to get an early start. Admission to the park is $6; it's open daily 7–5.

Amid coffee farms on the eastern end of the Orosi Valley, the village of Cachí survives on two industries: coffee and electricity. In the 1960s the national power company, ICE, dammed the Reventazón River near Cachí to create a reservoir for what was once the country's biggest hydroelectric project. The Represa de Cachí (Cachí Dam) is the closest thing the town has to a tourist attraction, and is worth stopping at for the view of the reservoir and narrow Reventazón Valley, but most people stop here to eat at the Casona del Cafetal, just south of the dam, and to shop for crafts at the Casa del Soñador.

Head back to the loop road and drive 15 km (9 mi) north, past the town of Cachí. Just before the Cachí Dam lies the immensely popular restaurant **La Casona del Cafetal** (⇨ Where to Eat *in* Cachí). It is touristy, but great fun, and well worth a stop for a late lunch. You'll have lots of company on a Sunday, the traditional maid's day off in Tico homes. Stop in at the unique artisan shop **Casa del Soñador** (House of the Dreamer; ⊠ 2 km/1¼ mi south of the Cachí Dam ☎ 2577–1186 or 2577–1983), established by local wood sculptor Macedonio Quesada. Though Macedonio died years ago, his sons Miguel and Hermes and a former apprentice are still here, carving interesting, often comical little statues out of coffee roots. You can learn about the carving process through a day-long apprenticeship, free of charge. The shop is open daily 8–6.

Continue past the dam into the small hamlet of Ujarrás, then follow the signs to the site of the ruins of Costa Rica's first church, **Iglesia de Ujarrás** (✉ In a small park, 1 km/½ mi from Restaurante Típico Ujarrás, Ujarrás ☎ 2574–8366). Built between 1681 and 1693 in honor of the Virgin of Ujarrás, the church, together with the surrounding village, was abandoned in 1833 after a series of earthquakes and floods wreaked havoc here, at the lowest point of the Orosi Valley. An unlikely Spanish victory in 1666 over a superior force of invading British pirates was attributed to a prayer stop here. The site is open daily 6–6. A final 6-km (3½-mi) drive to Paraíso from Ujarrás completes the loop.

Coffee Fields

Logistics

Renting a car in San José is the best way to go. Public transportation is a partial option only; buses run clockwise from Paraíso to Cachí or counterclockwise to Orosi, but neither route completes the loop. Several San José tour operators offer this excursion as a guided day trip from the capital. One such company is **Lava Tours** (☎ 2281–2458, 888/862–2424 in the U.S. ☎ 888/862–2424 in U.S. ⊕ www.lava-tours.com), whose bike tour between Orosi and Tapantí is $100.

WHERE TO STAY AND EAT

PARAÍSO

$$ ✕ ⦿ **Sanchirí Mirador.** The greatest asset of this rustic place is its amazing view, from a hillside high above the valley. The large open-air restaurant ($–$$), partially enclosed by windows, has simple wooden chairs and a menu dominated by Costa Rican standards such as *arroz con pollo* (rice with chicken). Twelve modern rooms were built in early 2005 to go with 6 older wooden cabins. All of the new rooms have the view, but only 3 of the cabins do. The rooms themselves are nothing spectacular, but waking up to the view is well worth the modest price. ✉ *2 km/1 mi south of Parque Central* ☎ *2574–5454* ⧉ *2574–8586* ⊕ *www.*

sanchiri.com ⇗ *20 rooms* ⧉ *Restaurant, bar, playground, laundry services, Internet; no elevator* ▤ *AE, DC, MC, V, BP.*

CACHÍ

★ **$** ✕ **La Casona del Cafetal.** The valley's best lunch stop is on a coffee plantation overlooking the Cachí Reservoir. It's firmly on the beaten path, which means frequent visits from tour groups. The spacious brick building has a high barrel-tile roof, with tables indoors and on a tiled portico on the lake side. Casados and other Costa Rican staples accompany inventive dishes such as corvina *guarumos* (bass stuffed with mushrooms). After lunch, take a stroll down to the lake or check at the gift shop. ⊠ *2 km/1 mi south of Cachí Dam* ☎ 2577-1414 ➟ *AE, DC, MC, V* ☺ *No dinner.*

¢ ✕ **Soda El Chilito Mexicano.** A great alternative to the touristy La Casona is this little café with some vaguely Mexican choices on the menu, but prepared Tico-style. This is where the locals eat, and it's good. ⊠ *Northwest side of the soccer field* ☎ 2577-1664.

OROSI

$ ✕ **Bar y Restaurante Coto.** This place has good food and a location right on the plaza. Options range from sandwiches to seafood dishes, and tenderloin in a "secret" *Orosi* sauce. Works by local artists are for sale. ⊠ *North side of Plaza de Deportes (soccer field)* ☎ 2533-3032 ➟ *AE, DC, MC, V.*

¢–$ ✕ **Gecko's.** This textbook backpacker hangout is the latest venture of Dutch and Canadian partners Toine and Sara Verkuijlen, who also run a Spanish school and hostel in Orosi. The café, located in the Optiac building, is bright and open, with groovy music and free-spirited clothes for sale. The creative menu ranges from traditional Costa Rican food to Kroket (deep-fried meat roll on a bun) and shish kebab. Helpful staff run a tourist-information desk inside. ⊠ *400 yds south of church* ☎ 2533-3640 ➟ *No credit cards.*

$$ ▦ **Hotel Río Perlas Spa & Resort.** Thermal springs fill one of the pools at this hotel squeezed into a small valley. The place has a condo community feeling, with a driveway running the length of the property and the rooms divided among many smaller buildings. Rooms are nice, but not especially luxurious; they have tile floors and wood furniture. Ask for one of the wooden cabins at the back of the property. There is a replica of the Orosi church here too. ⊠ *6 km/3 mi south of Paraíso, turn right at bridge, then 2 ½ km/1½ mi; look for large sign* ☎ 2533-3341 *or 2533-3085* ➟ *2533-3085* ⊕ *www.rioperlasspaandresort.com.*

$ ▦ **Orosi Lodge.** Run by a German couple who have built a warm rapport with the community, the little lodge blends in with Orosi's pretty, old-town architecture: whitewashed walls are trimmed in blue, ceilings are high, and natural wood is used throughout. Some furnishings, such as the clay lamps in the rooms, are done by local artisans. Common areas are colorful, with paintings and sculpture by local artists. Double beds have two twin-size comforters. Second-floor rooms have views of the Orosi Valley and Irazú Volcano. The hip coffee shop brews a great cup of joe, and Latin music usually plays from a 1960s' jukebox in the foyer. ⊠ *350 meters south, 100 meters west of the soccer field* ☎☎ 2533-3578 ⊕ *www.orosilodge.com.*

NEAR TAPANTÍ NATIONAL PARK

$ ▦ **Kiri Mountain Lodge.** This small, family-run hotel has easy access to the park and its own 70-hectare private reserve close to waterfalls and most of the same wildlife seen at Tapantí. The number of bird species in the lodge's gardens alone is impressive, especially hummingbirds. Rooms are small and simple, with tile floors and tiny bathrooms, but their porches have views of a jungle-laden hillside. The restaurant serves a small selection of Costa Rican food; fresh trout, raised in nearby ponds, is the best option. You can also catch your own trout and have them cook it for you. ⊠ *Turnoff 2 km/1¼ mi before Tapantí park entrance* ☎ 2533-2272 ⊕ *www.kirilodge.net.*

Although farmers who cultivate Irazú's slopes live in fear of the next eruption, they're also grateful for the soil's richness, a result of the volcanic deposits.

The road to the summit climbs past vegetable fields, pastures, and native oak forests. You pass through the villages of Potrero Cerrado and San Juan de Chicuá before reaching the summit's bleak but beautiful **crater**. Irazú is considered active, but the gases and steam that billow from fumaroles on the northwestern slope are rarely visible from the peak above the crater lookouts. ■ TIP→Set out as early in the morning as possible—before the summit is enveloped in clouds—and wear warm, waterproof clothing. When conditions are clear, you can see the chartreuse crater lake and, if you're lucky, views of nearby mountains and either the Pacific or Caribbean in the distance. There are no trails at the summit, but a paved road leads all the way to the top, where a small coffee shop sells hot beverages. Before reaching the park's main entrance, about 1 km (½ mi) from the village of Potrero Cerrado, Volcán Irazú's **Prusia Recreation Area** (Area Recreativa de Prusia) has hiking trails through oak and pine forest. It also has picnic areas. ☎2551–9398, 8200–5025 for ranger station ☞$7 ☉Daily 8–3:30.

GETTING HERE & AROUND

Follow directions to Cartago (⇨above), but shortly before the city a Y intersection marks the beginning of the road up Irazú; traffic to Cartago veers right, then left immediately past the first lights. From downtown Cartago, a 45-minute trip, take the road to Irazú at the northeast corner of the Basilica. Signs from Cartago lead you to the park. Buses head to Volcán Irazú from San José (Avda. 2, Cs. 1–3) daily at 8 AM and return at 12:30 PM.

WHERE TO EAT

$ ✕**Restaurant 1910.** Decorated with vintage photos of early-20th-century buildings and landscapes, this restaurant documents the disastrous 1910 earthquake that rocked this area and all but destroyed the colonial capital of Cartago. The menu is predominantly Costa Rican, with such traditional specialties as *trucha* (trout), and rice with chicken. One of the less common dishes is *corvina* (sea bass) fillet with béarnaise sauce. The *típico* buffet is a great introduction to Costa Rican cooking. ⊠*Road to Parque Nacional Volcán Irazú; 300 m north of Cot–Pacayas turnoff* ☎2536–6063 ▤AE, MC, V.

$ ✕**Restaurante Noche Buena.** If you've raced up Irazú to catch the clear
FodorśChoice early-morning views, a late breakfast or early lunch at this bright road-
★ side stop is a great excuse to linger in the area. Sample stick-to-your-
♺ ribs *gallo pinto* (a traditional dish made with rice and beans), *tres leches* (literally "three milks," a light and airy cake), and—not to be missed—the best fried yuca around. The pale wood floors and walls inside have a studied rustic charm, but the ample patio is a fresher option; neither has particularly impressive views. The Costa Rican owner, Federico Gutiérrez, has added a 3-km (2-mi) trail to waterfalls and a high-tech, interactive volcano museum ($4) that shouldn't be missed. Get here early, as the restaurant closes at 5. ⊠*At Km 24.5,*

road to Parque Nacional Volcán Irazú ☎2530–8013 ⊕*www.noche buena.org* ⊟*AE, DC, MC, V.*

THE TURRIALBA REGION

The agricultural center of Turrialba and the nearby Guayabo ruins lie considerably lower than the Central Valley, so they enjoy a more tropical climate. There are two ways to reach this area from San José, both of which pass spectacular scenery. The more direct route, accessible by heading east through both Cartago and Paraíso, winds through coffee and sugar plantations before descending abruptly into Turrialba. For the second route, turn off the road between Cartago and the summit of Irazú near the town of Cot, heading toward Pacayas. That narrow route twists along the slopes of Irazú and Turrialba volcanoes past some stunning scenery—stately pollarded trees lining the road, riotous patches of tropical flowers, and metal-girder bridges across crashing streams. As you begin the descent to Turrialba town, the temperature rises and sugarcane alternates with fields of neat rows of coffee bushes. Roberto Barahona at La Feria restaurant has written a book on the area; if you speak some Spanish, he's the go-to guy for all things Turrialba.

TURRIALBA

58 km (36 mi) east of San José.

The relatively well-to-do agricultural center of Turrialba (canton population 70,000) suffered when the main San José–Puerto Limón route was diverted through Guápiles in the late 1970s. The demise of the famous Jungle Train that connected these two cities was an additional blow. But today, because of the beautiful scenery and a handful of upscale nature lodges, ecotourism is increasingly the focus of the town's efforts. The damming of the Reventazón River has cut down on the number of tourists, but significant numbers of kayakers and rafters flock here to run the Pacuare. Turrialba has two major factories: Conair, which you'll see on the road to Siquirres, and a Rawlings factory, which makes all the baseballs used in the Major Leagues. Though pleasant enough and with a youthful vibe from the nearby university and the white-water folk, Turrialba doesn't have much to offer, but the surrounding countryside hides some spectacular scenery and patches of rain forest. Finally, there's Volcán Turrialba, which you can ascend on foot or horseback, and it's well worth the effort.

GETTING HERE & AROUND

The road through Cartago continues east through Paraíso, where you turn left at the northeast corner of the central park to pick up the road to Turrialba. Marked by signs, this road leads north to Guayabo National Monument. Buses between San José and Turrialba leave hourly (5:15 AM to 10:30 PM) from C. 13, Avda. 6, just northeast of the downtown court buildings. Direct buses depart from the new Turrialba terminal (at the entrance to Turrialba) for San José on the hour; on the half hour to Cartago, and every two hours to Siquirres.

White-Water Thrills

You're struggling to hang on and paddle, you can't hear a thing over the roar, and you were just slammed with a mighty wall of water. Sound like fun? Then you're in the right place. The **Río Pacuare** and the **Río Reventazón** draw rafters and kayakers from all over the world to Turrialba. Right next to Turrialba, the Reventazón has Class II, III, and IV rapids. The Pacuare, farther from Turrialba, has a spectacular 29-km (18-mi) run with a series of Class III and IV rapids. The scenery includes lush canyons where waterfalls plummet into the river and expanses of rain forest.

Nearly every outfitter has day trips, but some also have multiday trips that include jungle hikes. Costa Rica Nature Adventures and Ríos Tropicales (⇨ Central Valley Planner, above) even have their own lodges on the river. Age requirements for children vary by outfitter; Costa Rica Expeditions runs a family trip on the gentler Pejibaye River that kids as young as five can enjoy. The typical trip starts with a van ride to the put-in; including a breakfast stop, it usually takes about 2½ hours from hotel to river. After the first half of the run, guides flip one of the rafts over to form a crude lunch table. Then you continue up the river to Siquirres, and pile back in the van for the ride home.

It would be unwise to choose your company based merely on price: those with bargain rates are probably skimping somewhere. Good outfitters require you to wear life vests and helmets, have CPR-certified river guides with near-fluent English skills, and have kayakers accompany the rafts in case of emergencies. A 5:1 guest-to-guide ratio is good, 10:1 is not. Local Turrialba companies have better prices and allow you to book a trip at the last minute. Hotels and travel agencies book trips with larger outfitters, who can pick you up from nearly anywhere in the Central Valley. Prices range from about $75 to $100.

People fall out of the raft all the time, and it is no big deal. The worst-case scenario is getting caught underwater or under the raft, but surprisingly, most fatalities are heart-attack victims, so don't participate if you're high-risk. You should also be able to swim. Almost every long-standing company has had a death—it is simply the reality of the business. Don't hesitate to ask about safety records. The vast majority of trips, however, are pure exhilarating fun.

In 2006 the government decided to keep long-stalled plans to dam the Pacuare on ice for the time being, but reserves the right to revive them in the future. This would be the last nail in the coffin for the rafting industry (the Reventazón was dammed in the 1960s) and would destroy one of nature's real gems. Locals will surely put up a fight, but run it now while you can.

TURRIALBA ESSENTIALS

Bank/ATM **Banco Nacional** (✉ C. 1 at Avda. Central ☎ 2556–1211). **Banco de Costa Rica** (✉ Avda. 0, C. 1 ☎ 2556–0472).

Hospital **Hospital Dr. William Allen** (✉ Avda. 2, 100 m west of C. 4 ☎ 2558–1300).

Pharmacy **Farmacia San Buen Aventura** (✉ 50 m south of west side of central park ☎ 2556–0379).

Internet **Dimensión Internet** (✉ *East side of central park* ☎ *2556–1586*).

Post Office **Correos** (✉ *Avda. 6 at C. Central 50 m north of central park*).

Taxis **Transgalo** (☎ *2556–9393*).

EXPLORING

Although you can't easily drive up to its summit as you can at Poás and Irazú, **Volcán Turrialba** is still worth visiting. The easiest way to arrange the excursion is to call the **Volcán Turrialba Lodge** (☎ *2273–4335*) and request a guide. You can ascend the 6 km (4 mi) from the lodge on foot or horseback in one to two hours (allow up to 4 hours for the round-trip, plus exploring time), and at 3,340 m (10,958 feet) with luck you'll see clear down to the Caribbean coast. Normally you can linger, but at this writing visits

CORRUPTION CRACKDOWN

Long a proponent of do-as-I-say, not-as-I-do anticorruption policies, Costa Rica got tough on bigwigs in 2004. Three former presidents were taken into custody for allegedly accepting bribes in a telecommunications deal. One—Miguel Ángel Rodríguez—was forced to step down two weeks after taking over the presidency of the Organization of American States. The sight of former leaders being led away in handcuffs has shaken many Costa Ricans' faith in their democracy, but others see it as a positive sign that no one is above the law.

were limited to a 20-minute max—a protective measure implemented in response to heightened volcanic rumbling. On the road that runs from Pacayas to Turrialba through Santa Cruz there is a signed turnoff at La Pastora, west of Santa Cruz, that leads up the mountain. The drive up is 15 km (9 mi) and starts paved, but the road gets worse the higher you go. In most cases you'll need a 4WD to make the last section before the trailhead, which is in a very small community called La Central de Turrialba. The road veers left toward the Volcán Turrialba Lodge, while a very washed-out road leads right, toward the summit. If you want to take the latter route, you can park on the left just after the school; usually someone is around to charge you a few dollars for the privilege, but as elsewhere in the country, this in no way guarantees your car's safety. We recommend parking at Volcán Turrialba Lodge—they don't charge, will point out the way, and you can rest up with some snacks and hot chocolate at the restaurant when you're done. Get an early start and dress for the weather—it can get chilly up here even during the day. A park employee sometimes hangs out at the top to collect the $1 entrance fee and hand out maps.

OFF THE BEATEN PATH

A good place for bird-watching, the **Tropical Agricultural Research and Higher Education Center** (Centro Agronómico Tropical de Investigación y Enseñanza), better known by its acronym, CATIE, is one of the leading tropical research centers in Latin America. You might catch sight of the yellow-winged northern jacana or the purple gallinule in the lagoon near the main building. The 10-square-km (4-square-mi) property includes landscaped grounds, seed-conservation chambers, greenhouses, orchards, experimental agricultural projects, a large swath of rain forest, labs and offices, and lodging for students and teachers.

Behind the administration building lies the lake that once was rapids on the Reventazón River. The CATIE staff is working to improve visitor access; two-hour guided tours (call ahead to reserve) of the impressive Botanical Garden have been added, and forest trails are planned for the future. Groups of 10 or more now may add on lunch at the new café (Costa Rican and Spanish plates) and/or a fruitful tasting session of bounty from the garden ($4 per person extra). ✛ *3 km (2 mi) outside Turrialba, on road to Siquirres* ☎ *2558–2000* ⊕ *www.catie.ac.cr* ✍ *$5; $15 with guide; $25 for full facility tour, $10 per person for groups of more than 5* ⊙ *Daily 7–4.*

On the slopes of Turrialba Volcano is **Guayabo National Monument,** Costa Rica's most significant archaeological site. It's interesting, but definitely no Chichén Itzá. Records mentioning the ruins go back to the mid-1800s, but systematic investigations didn't begin until 1968, when a local landowner out walking her dogs discovered what she thought was a tomb. A friend, archaeologist Carlos Piedra, began excavating the site and unearthed the base wall of a chief's house in what eventually turned out to be the ruins of a large community (around 10,000 inhabitants) covering 49 acres, 10 of which have been excavated. The city was abandoned in AD 1400, probably because of disease or war. Guided tours (about 2 hours) in Spanish or English are provided by freelance guides that wait at the entrance. They'll take you through the rain forest to a *mirador* (lookout) from which you can see the layout of the excavated circular buildings. Only the raised foundations survive, since the conical houses themselves were built of wood. As you descend into the ruins, notice the well-engineered surface and covered aqueducts leading to a trough of drinking water that still functions today. Next you'll pass the end of an 8-km (5-mi) paved walkway used to transport the massive building stones; the abstract patterns carved on the stones continue to baffle archaeologists, but some clearly depict jaguars, which were revered as deities. The hillside jungle is captivating, and the trip is further enhanced by bird-watching possibilities: 200 species have been recorded. If you arrive from the east via the Santa Teresita (Lajas) route, you can make it in any car; but via the alternative Santa Cruz route you'll need a 4WD vehicle to get here. ✛ *Drive through the center of Turrialba to a girdered bridge; take road northeast 16 km (10 mi, about 20 minutes driving); take a left at the well-marked turnoff, continue another 3 km (2 mi) to the monument. If you've taken the scenic Irazú foothills route to Turrialba and have a 4WD, the Santa Cruz route—11 km (7 mi, about 35 minutes driving)—is an option. Turn left on rough road from Santa Cruz; climb 5 km (3 mi), past the Escuela de Guayabo; turn right at the sign for the monument; the road descends 6 km (4 mi) to the site* ☎ *2559–1220* ✍ *$4* ⊙ *Daily 8–3:30.*

OUTDOOR ACTIVITIES

The two best ways to reach the summit of Turrialba Volcano are on foot or on horseback. **Volcán Turrialba Lodge** (☎ *2273–4335*) arranges guided horseback and hiking trips.

WHERE TO EAT

$ ✕**Restaurante La Feria.** A permanent exhibition of national art and the Turrialba expertise of owner Don Roberto (if you speak Spanish) make this a worthwhile stop. This family-style restaurant has the usual mid-scale Costa Rican fare, ranging from fast food to filet mignon. Casados and gallo pinto compete with more familiar chicken and seafood dishes. Even paella is on the menu (with three hours' notice). ⊠ *Just west of Hotel Wagelia, at entrance to town* ☎2556–0386 ☐AE, DC, MC, V ⊘*No dinner Tues.*

¢–$ ✕**La Garza Bar y Restaurante.** Similar to La Feria in scope but slightly more atmospheric and with a bar, La Garza also runs the gamut from hamburgers to chicken, but has a better seafood selection. (Sorry vegetarians, "beetsteak" is a misprint.) This is a good place for a late dinner, as it's open until 11. ⊠*Northwest corner of park* ☎2556–1073 ☐AE, DC, MC, V.

WHERE TO STAY

$$$$ ▦**Rancho Naturalista.** Customized guided bird-watching within a 160-acre private nature reserve is the reason to stay here. The ranch is a birder's paradise, and the narrow focus may be too much for those not interested in our feathered friends. More than 400 species of birds and thousands of different kinds of moths and butterflies live on the reserve and nearby sites, and a resident ornithologist helps you see and learn as much as you want. The two-story lodge is upscale modern with rustic touches, as are the separate cabins. Good home cooking is served in the indoor and outdoor dining rooms, both of which have beautiful views of Volcán Irazú and the Turrialba Valley. Guided tours, meals, horseback riding, and your birding guide are all included in the price. **Pros:** Birder's paradise, 11 km of trails for guests, warm atmosphere. **Cons:** Rooms can be musty, faded bird pictures give common spaces a dated feel, not a great base for adventure day trips. ✛*20 km (12 mi) southeast of Turrialba, 1½ km (1 mi) south of Tuís, then up a rough road* ☎2433–8278 *for reservations, 2554–8100 for directions* ☐2433–4925 ⊕*www.ranchonaturalista.net* ⬅*15 rooms, 13 with bath* ⌂*In-room: no a/c, no phone, no TV, dial-up. In-hotel: restaurant, no elevator, laundry service, airport shuttle, no-smoking rooms* ☐*No credit cards* ⦿*FAP.*

$$ ▦**Casa Turire.** Set near sugar plantations and overlooking an artificial
★ lake, this timeless hotel is an elegant base for nearby adventure day trips. The building looks like a manor house that has survived mysteriously intact from the turn of the 20th century. In fact, it's the product of more recent imaginations. From the royal palms that line the driveway to the tall columns and tile floors, Casa Turire is an exercise in attention to detail. High-ceiling guest rooms have hardwood floors and furniture,

small balconies, and bright bathrooms with tubs. The central courtyard is a civilized spot in which to relax after a day's adventure, and the restaurant serves reasonably priced international cuisine. The master suite is exceptional, built on two floors with a huge wraparound balcony. A model farm on the property gives kids hands-on time with animals. **Pros:** Excellent value, beautiful grounds, good base for adventure trips. **Con:** Some say restaurant could be more consistent with quality. ✛*8 km (5 mi) south on Carretera a la Suiza from Turrialba* ☎*2531–1111* 🖷*2531–1075* ⊕*www.hotelcasaturire.com* 🛏*12 rooms, 4 suites* ⚓*In-room: a/c (some), safe. In-hotel: restaurant, room service, bar, pool, bicycles, no elevator, laundry service, public Internet, public Wi-Fi* ▤*AE, MC, V* ¶⦾*BP.*

$$ 🏨**Volcán Turrialba Lodge.** On the slope of the volcano, usually accessible only by 4WD vehicle (which the lodge will arrange for a fee), the lodge has simple but comfortable rooms, most with a wood-burning stove. Rates include three meals. You'll eat well: the proprietors serve healthful Costa Rican food. Even more compelling are the tours. Mountain-biking and horseback-riding trips can be arranged, as well as a 10-hour trek from the Volcán Turrialba to Guápiles via Braulio Carrillo National Park. This place is not for everyone—it gets chilly at over 10,000 feet, but it's a unique mountain escape and a great value. **Pros:** Good value, proximity to volcano. **Cons:** Gets chilly, options limited on bad-weather days. ■**TIP**➔**Day-trippers are welcome.** ✛*20 km (12 mi) east of Cot, turn right at Pacayas on road to Volcán Turrialba, 4 km (2½ mi) on dirt road* ☎☎*2273–4335* 🖷*2273–0703* ⊕*www.volcanturrialbalodge.com* 🛏*28 rooms* ⚓*In-room: no a/c, no phone, no TV. In-hotel: restaurant, bar, pool, no elevator* ▤*AE, MC, V* ¶⦾*FAP.*

$ 🏨**Turrialtico.** Dramatically positioned on a hill overlooking the valley east of Turrialba, this hotel has impressive views of the surrounding countryside; it's the best budget option in the area. An open-sided restaurant occupies the ground floor, above which are handsome rooms with hardwood floors. Ask for one on the west side—these have dazzling views of Turrialba and, if there are no clouds, Volcán Irazú. The restaurant serves a small selection of authentic Costa Rican and international dishes. The only problem is that the rustic wooden construction makes the rooms anything but soundproof. **Pros:** Rich views at budget prices, good opportunity to mingle with Ticos. **Cons:** Thin walls, less service oriented than other more international options. ✛*8 km (5 mi) east of Turrialba on road to Siquirres* ☎*2538–1111 or 2538–1415* 🖷*2538–1575* ⊕*www.turrialtico.com* 🛏*12 rooms, 6 cabins* ⚓*In-room: no a/c, no phone, TV (some). In-hotel: restaurant, bar, no elevator, laundry service, public Wi-Fi* ▤*AE, DC, MC, V* ¶⦾*BP.*

CENTRAL VALLEY ESSENTIALS

TRANSPORTATION

BY AIR
There is no regional air travel within the Central Valley.

ARRIVING & The Juan Santamaría International Airport is only 10 km (6 mi) from
DEPARTING   Alajuela. You can get taxis from the airport to any point in the Central
Valley for $8 to $50. On your left, just before exiting the terminal,
you'll see a counter where you can hire a taxi. Some hotels arrange
pickup. *For more information, see By Air in Costa Rica Essentials.*

BY BUS
ARRIVING & Buses leave the international airport for Alajuela several times an hour;
DEPARTING   from Alajuela you can catch buses to Grecia, Sarchí, and San Ramón.
Less frequent buses (1 to 3 per hour) serve Heredia. For travel between
the airports and Escazú, Cartago, or Turrialba, you have to change
buses in San José, which usually means taking a taxi between bus terminals. All buses heading toward San José from Alajuela can drop you
off at the airport, but you need to ask the driver when you board, and
then remind him again as you draw near to the stop, *"Aeropuerto, por
favor"* ("Airport, please"). *For more detailed information, see By Bus
in Costa Rica Essentials.*

GETTING   Many visitors never consider taking a local bus to get around, but
AROUND   doing so puts you in close contact with locals—an experience you miss
out on if you travel by taxi or tour bus. It's also cheap. If your Spanish
and sense of direction are up to snuff and you have the time, give it a
shot. Your hotel can help you get to the correct bus stop and get you
a current schedule. Always opt for the taxi at night or when you're in
a hurry.

BY CAR
ARRIVING & All points in the western Central Valley can be reached by car. For San
DEPARTING   Antonio de Belén, Heredia, Alajuela, and points north of San José, turn
right at the west end of Paseo Colón onto the Pan-American High-
way (Carretera General Cañas). All the attractions in the eastern Central Valley are accessible from San José by driving east on Avenida 2
through San Pedro, then following signs from the intersection to Cartago. To get to the Orosi Valley, head straight through Cartago, turn
right at the Basílica de Los Angeles, and follow the signs to Paraíso. The
road through Cartago and Paraíso continues east to Turrialba.

GETTING   The best way to get around the Central Valley is by car. Most of the
AROUND   car-rental agencies in San José have offices at the airport in Alajuela.
They will deliver vehicles and contracts to any of the hotels listed in this
chapter, except those in Turrialba and the Orosi Valley. *For car-rental
information, see Rental Cars in Costa Rica Essentials.*

BY TAXI

All Central Valley towns have taxis, which usually wait for fares along the central parks. Taxis in Alajuela, Cartago, and Heredia can take you up to Poás, Irazú, and Barva volcanoes, but the trips are quite expensive (about $50). If you don't have a car, the only way to get to Tapantí National Park is to take a cab from Orosi (about $15 each way).

CONTACTS & RESOURCES

Banks, Internet cafés, post offices, and emergency contacts follow each town listed in the chapter.

BANKS & EXCHANGING SERVICES

There are ATMs in just about every Central Valley town, and most of them accept both Visa and MasterCard, but some accept only one of the two. Shopping centers and some gas stations have ATMs. Bank branches in all but the tiniest Central Valley towns exchange U.S. dollars, though it's quicker to get colones from an ATM. Most hotels, restaurants, tour operators, taxi drivers, and gift shops accept or change U.S. dollars, though at slightly less than the bank rate. Don't try to pay for things with $100 bills; banks will change them, but many retail establishments won't take them.

INTERNET

Internet cafés are common in Central Valley towns, and tend to charge the equivalent of $1 per hour. In most towns you can find one or more within easy walking distance of the central park. Many hotels offer Internet access, but some of them charge as much as $3–$6 per hour. Free wireless options at places like Bagelmen's can be convenient, but be alert—they've also become draws for thieves, who hang around outside and watch who saunters in with a laptop.

The Northern Plains

Guanacaste cowboy

WORD OF MOUTH

"Much of Costa Rica is covered with forest that receives enough annual rainfall to be considered rain forest. The Arenal area (and many other areas) will expose you to that. Perhaps you would be more interested in one of the cloud forests such as Monteverde. Really stunning and exotic. Be prepared for mud. A car for day trips to Carara [Biological Reserve], the crocodile bridge, and restaurants in Jaco might be in order."

—Kinkazote

www.fodors.com/forums

WELCOME TO NORTHERN PLAINS

TOP REASONS TO GO

★ **Walk in a cloud (forest):** Explore Monteverde's misty world on treetop walkways up to 138 feet off the ground.

★ **Windsurfing:** Lake Arenal is one of the top windsurfing spots on earth; winds can reach 50–60 mph December through April.

★ **Arenal Volcano:** You can hear the rumblings of the world's thirdmost active volcano for miles around, and, on clear nights, watch crimson lava ooze down its flanks.

★ **Watching wildlife:** Water birds, monkeys, turtles, crocodiles, jaguars, and sloths abound in the 25,000-acre Caño Negro National Wildlife Refuge.

Arenal Volcano

1 Northwest of San José. are one of the country's best crafts communities, Sarchí, and some luxurious country-side lodges.

2 The Arenal Volcano area. is one of the hottest tourist destinations in Costa Rica. La Fortuna is the closest town to the volcano; among many nearby diversions are the Tabacón Hot Springs. Tilarán, west of Lake Arenal, is the place to be if you're a windsurfer.

3 Monteverde Cloud Forest Area. Home to the rainiest of cloud forests, the Monteverde Cloud Forest Area is also the canopy-tour capital of Costa Rica. Hanging bridges, treetop tram tours, and zip lines: it's got it all. As if that's not enough, there are horseback riding, rappelling, and nature hikes.

4 Caño Negro National Wildlife Refuge. in the Far North, is great for fishing, bird-watching, and communing with nature.

5 The Sarapiquí Loop. circles Braulio Carrillo National Park, rare for its easy-to-access primary rain forest. The loop's highlight is Poás Volcano; its turquoise crater lake and steaming main crater make it the favorite volcano of many visitors.

Sky Walk, Monteverde

San Jose · Upala · El Ampao · Colonia Puntarenas · San Rafael · Tronadora · Cataratas de la Fortuna · Tilarán · Arenal Volcano · Cañas · Lake Arenal · Monteverde Cloud Forest · Gotera · CR1

4 Caño Negro National Wildlife Refuge

Sky Trek, Monteverde

GETTING ORIENTED

Geographically, the Zona Norte (Northern Zone), as it is known locally, separates neatly into two alluvial plains. The rich, lush terrain runs from the base of the Cordillera Central in the south to the Río San Juan, on the border with Nicaragua in the north. Most visitors begin their visit to Costa Rica in San José, many then heading north to La Fortuna, using it as a base for exploring the volcano, waterfall, and Caño Negro, and participating in activities like sportfishing, windsurfing and kitesurfing at Lake Arenal, and rafting on the Sarapiquí River.

NICARAGUA

Río San Juan

Río Sarapiquí

35

Acapulco

Pangola

Puerto Viejo

4

Boca Arenal

Braulio Carrillo National Park

La Fortuna

35

Chiles

5

Puerto Viejo Loop

San Isidro

Quesada

San Miguel Angeles

1

Poás Volcano ◆

15 mi

Naranjo

20 km

Sarchí

Grecia

Hiking down to La Fortuna Waterfalls

NORTHERN PLAINS PLANNER

When to Go

Late November to April is considered high season. The rainy season is July–December, but the region is always hot and humid, and rainy. Expect highs of 26°C–32°C (80°F–90°F) and lows of 15°C–20°C (60°F–70°F). Nights are cool and comfortable. At almost 5,000 feet, Monteverde has a significantly different climate: it's cool, damp, and breezy much of the time, with average highs around 20°C (70°F) and lows around 13°C (55°F). Visibility changes daily (and hourly), so your chances of seeing the Arenal and Poás craters are more or less the same year-round, though you may have more luck from February to April, the hottest and driest time of the year.

Getting There

The cheapest and slowest way to get here is via public bus. The fastest and priciest is flying to La Fortuna (via NatureAir or SANSA), driving yourself, or hiring a driver. A mid-range option is taking a private shuttle-bus service. Many San José–based tour companies arrange transportation and tours in the area. But Arenal and Monteverde are also full of tour companies that will arrange same-day or next-day transportation and tours for you.

Rain Forests Are . . . Rainy

There's a reason they call it the rain forest! During the rainy season it's not unusual for it to rain for several days straight. But don't curse the wet weather—it's what keeps the forests green and gorgeous. Just bring a poncho or rain jacket and waterproof footwear so you don't end up cursing yourself.

The Early Bird Catches the Sun

In the rainy season it's almost a given that you'll get a bit damp on your canopy tour, hike, or horseback ride, and most tour operators provide ponchos. But to avoid a thorough soaking, plan activities for the morning. Rains usually begin at around 2 PM, like clockwork, from July through December. The clearest time of day is normally before 8 AM.

What to Do

ACTIVITY	WHERE TO DO IT
Bungee Jumping	Colorado River (Grecia), La Fortuna
Canopy Tours	La Fortuna, Monteverde
Fishing	Lake Arenal
Hiking	Lake Arenal, Tilarán, La Fortuna
Horseback Riding	La Fortuna, Monteverde
Rafting	La Fortuna, Puerto Viejo de Sarapiquí
Rappelling	La Fortuna
Wildlife-viewing	La Fortuna, Caño Negro, Monteverde
Windsurfing	Lake Arenal

How Much Time?

If your visit is limited to two or three days, make La Fortuna your base. Don't miss the volcano, the Tabacón Hot Springs, or Caño Negro Wildlife Reserve. Most tour operators who have volcano hikes end the day at the hot springs. "Half-day" tours to Caño Negro actually take most of a day, from around 7:30 AM to 4 PM. A week in the Northern Plains is more than enough time to experience a great deal of this area—especially if you're longing to get out and get moving. Give yourself four days in La Fortuna/Arenal for rafting trips on area rivers, horseback rides, and kitesurfing or windsurfing on Lake Arenal. Devote the rest of your week to Monteverde Cloud Forest.

Recommended Tour Operators

Aventuras Naturales (☎2225–3939 ⊕ www.adventure costarica.com) has five-day biking tours that combine Monteverde and Lake Arenal with the Central Valley.

Costa Rica Expeditions (☎2257–0766 ⊕ www.costarica expeditions.com) customizes almost limitless vacations.

Costa Rica Study Tours (☎2645–7090 ⊕ www.crstudy tours.com) can fix you up with all manner of excursions around Monteverde.

If you don't have much time, **Ecoscape Nature Tours** (☎2297–0664 ⊕ www.ecoscapetours.com) has the best daylong Sarapiquí Loop tour, as well as a more leisurely extended itinerary that lasts two days. It also has nighttime jungle tours in the Selva Verde reserve.

Horizontes Nature Tours (☎2222–2022 ⊕ www. horizontes.com) customizes tours to Monteverde and Arenal, as well as to anywhere else in Costa Rica.

WHAT IT COSTS IN DOLLARS				
¢	$	$$	$$$	$$$$
Restaurants				
under $5	$5–$10	$10–$15	$15–$25	over $25
Hotels				
under $50	$50–$75	$75–$150	$150–$250	over $250

Restaurant prices are per person for a main course at dinner. Hotel prices are for two people in a standard double room in high season, excluding service and tax (16.4%).

Pack Right

It's warm and wet here much of the year—but think chilly and wet for Monteverde—so don't think fashion, think comfort and utility. Must-haves include walking shoes (sneakers are fine unless you're planning on serious hiking), water sandals, and clothing made of quick-drying materials. Don't forget a good hat to shield your face from the sun and rain, and sunglasses. A light rain jacket or poncho, and mini umbrella, are worth the space as well.

Choosing a Place to Stay

The La Fortuna/Arenal area has luxury resorts, mid-price hotels, budget places, and campsites. Though no longer as cheap as it once was, hotel rates are low compared to U.S. prices. If you plan to raft, hike, and go to the hot springs, a simple and comfortable cabina ($20–$40) in or around La Fortuna allows easy access to tours, restaurants, and buses—a good choice if you don't have a car. For privacy, quiet, luxury, and a volcano view, try the resorts west of La Fortuna ($75–$185), closer to the volcano.

NORTHWEST OF SAN JOSÉ

By Jeffrey Van Fleet

The rolling countryside northwest of San José and west of Alajuela holds a mix of coffee, sugarcane, and pasture, with tropical forest filling steep river valleys and ravines. The Pan-American Highway makes a steady descent to the Pacific coast through this region, which is also traversed by older roads that wind their way between simple agricultural towns and past small farms and pastoral scenery. West of San Ramón the valley becomes narrow and precipitous as the topography slopes down to the Pacific lowlands. An even narrower valley snakes northward from San Ramón to the northern lowlands beyond.

GRECIA

26 km/16 mi (45 mins) northwest of Alajuela, 46 km/29 mi (1 hr) northwest of San José.

Founded in 1838, the quiet farming community of Grecia is reputed to be Costa Rica's cleanest town—some enthusiastic civic boosters extend that superlative to all Latin America—but the reason most people stop here is to admire its unusual church.

GETTING HERE & AROUND

From San José continue west on the highway past the airport—the turnoff is on the right—or head into Alajuela and turn left just before the Alajuela cemetery. Buses traveling between San José and Ciudad Quesada make stops in Grecia. From Alajuela, buses to Grecia/Ciudad Quesada pick up on the southern edge of town (C. 4 at Avda. 10).

GRECIA ESSENTIALS

Bank/ATM **Banco Nacional** (⊠ *Northwest corner of Central Plaza* ☎ *2494–3600).* **BAC San José** (⊠ *100 m north of Central Park).*

EXPLORING

The brick-red, prefabricated iron **Church of Our Lady of Mercy** (Iglesia de las Mercedes) was one of two buildings in the country made from steel frames imported from Belgium in the 1890s (the other is the metal schoolhouse next to San José's Parque Morazán), when some prominent Costa Ricans decided that metal structures would better withstand the periodic earthquakes that had taken their toll on so much of the country's architecture. The frames were shipped from Antwerp to Limón, then transported by train to Alajuela—from which point the church was carried by oxcarts. ⊠ *Avda. 1, Cs. 1–3* ☎ *2494–1616* ☼ *Daily 8–4.*

☾ On a small farm outside Grecia, the **World of Snakes** (Mundo de las Serpientes) is a good place to see some of the snakes that you are unlikely—and probably don't want—to spot in the wild. Sequestered in the safety of cages here are some 50 varieties of serpents, as well as crocodiles, iguanas, poison dart frogs, and various other cold-blooded creatures. Admission includes a 90-minute tour. ⊠ *Poro ✛ 2 km (1 mi) east of Grecia, on road to Alajuela* ☎ *2494–3700* ⊕ *www.theworldof snakes.com* ☑ *$11, $6 ages 7–15, free under 7* ☼ *Daily 8–4.*

OUTDOOR ACTIVITIES

BUNGEE
JUMPING

A 265-foot-tall bridge that spans a forested gorge over the Río Colorado is the perfect place to get a rush of adrenaline in a tranquil, tropical setting. Even if you aren't up for the plunge, it's worth stopping to watch a few mad souls do it. **Tropical Bungee** (⊠ *Pan-American Hwy.* ✚ *2 km (1 mi) west of turnoff for Grecia, down a dirt road on the right* ☎2248–2212 *or* 8398–8134 ⊕*www.bungee.co.cr* ☉*Daily 8– 11:30 and 1–4*) organizes trips to the bridge. The first jump is $65 and the second is $30. Transportation is free if you jump; $10 if you don't. Reservations are essential. If it's your last hurrah in Costa Rica, a van can take you straight to the San José airport after your jump.

PAINTED OXCARTS

Coffee has come to symbolize the prosperity of the Central Valley and the nation. Nineteenth-century coffee farmers needed a way to transport this all-important cash crop to the port of Puntarenas on the Pacific coast. Enter the oxcart. Artisans began painting the carts in the early 1900s. Debate continues as to why: the kaleidoscopic designs may have symbolized the points of the compass, or may have echoed the landscape's tropical colors. In any case, the oxcart has become the national symbol. Give way when you see one out on a country road and marvel at the sight.

WHERE TO STAY

$$–$$$
Fodor'sChoice
★

🏨**Vista del Valle Plantation Inn.** Honeymooners (and many posters to fodors.com) frequent this bed-and-breakfast on an orange and coffee plantation outside Grecia overlooking the canyon of the Río Grande. Cottages are decorated in minimalist style with simple wooden furniture and sliding doors that open onto small porches. Each has its own personality; the Nido, removed from the rest and with the nicest decor, is the most romantic. The hotel's forest reserve has an hour-long trail leading down to a waterfall. Breakfast is served by the pool or in the main house, where you can relax in a spacious living room. The food is quite good, and special dietary requests are accommodated with advance notice. It's a mere 20-minute drive from the airport. **Pros:** Attentive staff, secluded cabins, healthy food served. **Con:** Car is necessary for staying here. ⊠ *On highway* ✚ *1 km (½ mi) west of Rafael Iglesia Bridge; follow signs* ✉*c/o M. Bresnan, SJO–1994, Box 025216, Miami, FL33102-5216* ☎2450–0800 🖷2451–1165 ⊕*www. vistadelvalle.com* ⇨*12 cottages* ⏚*In-room: no a/c, no phone, no TV. In-hotel: restaurant, pool, airport shuttle* ▤*AE, MC, V* ⚹*BP.*

SARCHÍ

8 km/5 mi west of Grecia, 53 km/33 mi (1½ hrs) northwest of San José.

Tranquil Sarchí is spread over a collection of hills surrounded by coffee plantations. Though many of its inhabitants are farmers, Sarchí is also Costa Rica's premier center for crafts and carpentry. People drive here from all over central Costa Rica to shop for furniture, and tour buses regularly descend upon the souvenir shops outside town. The area's most famous products are its brightly painted oxcarts—replicas of those traditionally used to transport coffee.

GETTING HERE & AROUND

To get to Sarchí from San José, take the highway well past the airport to the turnoff for Naranjo; then veer right just as you enter Naranjo. Direct buses to Sarchí depart from Alajuela (C. 8, between Avdas. 1 and 3) every 30 minutes 6 AM–9 PM; the ride takes 90 minutes.

SARCHÍ ESSENTIALS

Bank/ATM **Banco Nacional** (⊠ *South side of soccer field* ☎ *2454–3044*).

Post Office **Correos** (⊠ *50 m west of central plaza*).

EXPLORING

Sarchí's **Parque Central** resembles the central park of any other Costa Rican small town—a fairly nondescript church fronts the open space and it serves as a gathering place for townspeople to talk and gossip—but it is home to the world's largest oxcart, constructed and brightly painted by longtime local factory Taller Eloy Alfaro e Hijos, installed in 2006, and enshrined in the Guinness Book of World Records. The work logs in at 18 meters (45 feet) and weighs two tons. Since no other country is attached to oxcarts quite the way Costa Rica is, we don't look for that record to be broken any time soon. ⊠ *Center of Sarchí.*

The town's only real oxcart factory, **Taller Eloy Alfaro e Hijos** (*Eloy Alfaro and Sons Workshop*), was founded in 1925, and its carpentry methods have changed little since then, although the "e Hijos" portion of the family (the sons) runs the operation these days. The two-story wooden building housing the wood shop is surrounded by trees and flowers—mostly orchids—and all the machinery on the ground floor is powered by a waterwheel at the back of the shop. Carts are painted in the back, and although the factory's main product is a genuine oxcart—which sells for about $2,000—there are also some smaller mementos that can easily be shipped home. ⊠ *200 m north of soccer field* ☎ *No phone* 🖭 *By donation* ☉ *Weekdays 8–4.*

If you enjoy plants, the **Jardín Botánico Else Kientzler** (*Else Kientzler Botanical Garden*) is well worth a break from your shopping. The site exhibits some 2,000 plant species, tropical and subtropical, over its sprawling 17 acres. The German owner named the facility, affiliated with an ornamental-plant exporter, after his plant-loving mother. About half of the garden's pathways are wheelchair accessible. ⊠ *800 m north of soccer field* ☎ *2454–2070* ⊕ *www.elsegarden.com* 🖭 *$12, $6 children 5–12, free under 5* ☉ *Daily 8–4.*

SHOPPING

Sarchí is the best place in Costa Rica to buy miniature oxcarts, the larger of which are designed to serve as patio bars and can be broken down for easy transport or shipped to your home. Another popular item is a locally produced rocking chair with a leather seat and back.

FodorsChoice
★   There's one store just north of town, and several larger complexes to the south. The nicest is the **Fábrica de Carretas Chaverri** (*Chaverri Oxcart*

Factory ⊠*Main road* ✛*2 km (1 mi) south of Sarchí* ☏*2454–4411*),
and you can wander through the workshops in back to see the artisans
in action. (Despite the name, much more is for sale here than oxcarts.)
Chaverri is a good place to buy wooden crafts; nonwood products are
cheaper in San José. Chaverri also runs a restaurant next door, **Las Carretas** (☏*2454–1633*), which serves international meals all day until 6
PM and has a good lunch buffet.

SAN RAMÓN

*23 km/14 mi west of Sarchí, 59 km/37 mi (1½ hrs) northwest of San
José.*

Having produced a number of minor bards, San Ramón is known
locally as the City of Poets. San Ramón hides its real attractions in the
countryside to the north, on the road to La Fortuna, where comfortable
lodges offer access to private nature preserves. There's not much to see
in San Ramón other than its church.

GETTING HERE & AROUND
San Ramón is on the Pan-American Highway west of Grecia. To reach
the hotel we list north of town, head straight through San Ramón and
follow the signs. Buses leave hourly for San Ramón from San José's
Terminal de Puntarenas. From Alajuela, buses to San Ramón/Ciudad
Quesada pick up on the southern edge of town (C. 4 at Avda. 10).

SAN RAMÓN ESSENTIALS
Bank/ATM **HSBC** (⊠*150 m north of Palí supermarket* ☏*2445–3602*). **Scotiabank**
(⊠*Pan-American Highway, entrance to San Ramón* ☏*2447–9190*).

Internet **Cybercafé San Ramón** (⊠*100 m east of Banco Central* ☏*2447–
9007*).

EXPLORING
Aside from its poets, the massive **Church of San Ramón** (Iglesia de San
Ramón), built in a mixture of the Romanesque and Gothic styles, is
the city's claim to fame. In 1924 an earthquake destroyed the smaller
adobe church that once stood here, and the city lost no time in creating a replacement—this great gray concrete structure took a quarter
of a century to complete, from 1925 to 1954. To ensure that the second church would be earthquake-proof, workers poured the concrete
around a steel frame that was designed and forged in Germany (by
Krupp). Step past the formidable facade and you'll discover a bright,
elegant interior. ⊠*Across from Parque Central* ☏*2445–5592* ☉*Daily
6–11:30* AM *and 1:30–7* PM.

WHERE TO STAY & EAT
$–$$ ✕**La Colina.** Here's the only Costa Rican restaurant whose food has
been transported into outer space: Astronaut Franklin Chang, a fan of
La Colina's *cajetas especiales,* a sweet orange-coconut dish, took some
with him on one of his NASA missions. This roadside diner, with its
requisite plastic chairs, has an eclectic menu. Start your meal with a
delicious ceviche, moving on to the famous rice and chicken or, for the

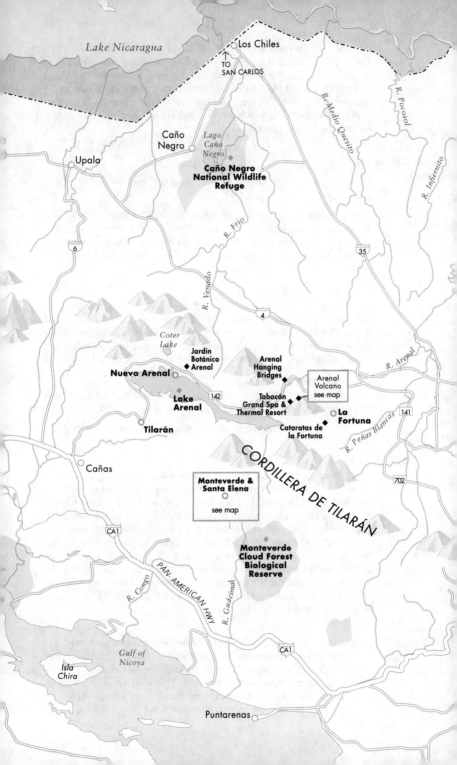

The Northern Plains

NICARAGUA

San Juan

R. San Juan

R. Sarapiquí

R. Toro

R. San Carlos

Boca Tapada

R. Pital

R. Tres Amigos

R. Aguas Zarcas

4

Puerto Viejo de Sarapiquí

La Selva Biological Station

R. Sardinal

La Virgen

LA SELVA RESERVE

Cariari

140

Aguas Zarcas

R. Sardinal

San Miguel

Magsasay Ranger Station

Las Horquetas

Rara Avis

R. Puerto Viejo

JUAN CASTRO BLANCO N.P.

Ciudad Quesada (San Carlos)

126

Cinchona

4

Guápiles

Volcán Poás

La Paz Waterfall Gardens

Braulio Carrillo National Park

32

Zarcero

702

VOLCÁN POÁS NATIONAL PARK

Vara Blanca

Carrillo Ranger Station

Quebrada González Ranger Station

141

Fráijanes

Barva Volcano

Sarchí

Grecia

Barva Ranger Station

Zurquí Ranger Station

San Ramón

Mundo de las Serpientes

Sacramento

Barva

Atenas

Alajuela

CA1

San Rafael

Heredia

San José

30 miles

45 km

more adventurous, *lengua en salsa* (tongue in tomato sauce). Meals begin with complimentary chips and pickled vegetables. ⊠*Highway to Puntarenas* ⚐*2 km (1 mi) west of San Ramón* ☎*2445–4956* ⊟*AE, D, DC, MC, V.*

$$$ ★ 🏨 **Villablanca.** This charming hotel is on a working dairy and coffee farm constructed and once owned by former Costa Rican president Rodrigo Carazo. The farmhouse contains the reception desk, bar, and restaurant; down the hill are lovely casitas, each a replica of a traditional adobe farmhouse complete with whitewashed walls, tile floors, cane ceilings, and fireplaces. Resident guides lead nature walks through the adjacent cloud-forest reserve, which is excellent bird-watching territory. Horses are available for exploring the rest of the farm. **Pros:** Attentive service, secluded location. **Con:** Far from sights. ⚐*20 km (12 mi) north of San Ramón on road to La Fortuna* ⌂*Apdo. 247–1250, Escazú* ☎*2461–0300* 🖷*2461–0302* ⊕*www.villablancacr.com* ⇆*34 casitas* ⚐*In-room: no a/c, no phone, refrigerator, no TV. In-hotel: restaurant, bar, spa* ⊟*AE, D, DC, MC, V* ⊚*BP.*

> **FINDING YOUR WAY**
>
> No sun to help you get your bearings? Just remember that the entrance to most Catholic churches in Costa Rica faces west, so that the congregation can face east toward Rome. Churches in La Fortuna, Orosi, and Turrialba are notable exceptions.

EN ROUTE The small town of **Zarcero**, 15 km (9 mi) north of Sarchí on the road to Ciudad Quesada, looks like it was designed by Dr. Seuss. Evangelisto Blanco, a local landscape artist, modeled cypress topiaries in fanciful animal shapes—motorcycle-riding monkeys, a lightbulb-eyed elephant—that enliven the park in front of the town church. The church interior is covered with elaborate pastel stencil work and detailed religious paintings by the late Misael Solís, a well-known local artist. Sample some cheese if you're in town, too; Zarcero-made cheese is one of Costa Rica's favorites.

THE ARENAL VOLCANO AREA

Whether you come here from San José or Liberia, prepare yourself for some spectacular scenery—and a bumpy ride. As you bounce along on your way to Arenal, you may discover that "paved" means different things in different places, and that potholes are numerous. Any discomfort you experience is more than made up for by the swaths of misty rain forest and dramatic expanses of the Cordillera Central. Schedule at least 3½ hours for the trip.

CIUDAD QUESADA (SAN CARLOS)

55 km/33 mi (60 mins) northwest of Zarcero.

Highway signs point you to CIUDAD QUESADA, but it's simply "San Carlos" in local parlance. Like so many other places in Costa Rica, the landscape is splendid, but what passes for architecture varies from ordinary to downright hideous. San Carlos is where everyone in the region comes to shop, take in a movie, get medical care, and generally take care of the necessities. There's also an enormous bus terminal (with shopping center and multiplex movie theater) where you can make connections to almost anywhere in the northern half of the country. If you're traveling from San José to points north, your bus will stop here even if it's a so-called express. This lively mountain market town–provincial capital serves a fertile dairy region and is worth a stop for a soak in the soothing thermal waters in the area.

GETTING HERE & AROUND

Ciudad Quesada lies 55 km (33 mi) off the Pan-American Highway north of Zarcero. Buses from San José leave Terminal Atlántico Norte on the hour, from 5 AM to 7 PM. The trip takes around three hours. The Ciudad Quesada bus terminal is a couple of kilometers from the center of town; taxis wait at the terminal to take you into town. Driving is straightforward in this part of the country, as long as you don't get stuck behind a slow-moving truck transporting sugarcane to the Central Valley. Try to get an early start if you're driving yourself; the road between Zarcero and Ciudad Quesada begins to fog over by early afternoon.

> ### VOLCANIC BEGINNINGS
>
> Many people who settled the Northern Plains came to the then-isolated region in the 1940s and 50s from other parts of the country to take part in government-sponsored homesteading programs. Thanks to rich volcanic soil, the agricultural region became one of the most productive in Central America. More recently, since the 1968 Arenal eruption (the first eruption in nearly 500 years), Ticos have been drawn by jobs in the ever-expanding tourism industry. In the far northern section of the region, close to the border, a great number of residents are Nicaraguan.

CIUDAD QUESADA ESSENTIALS

Bank/ATM **Banco Nacional** (⊠ *Across from north side of cathedral* ☎ *2401–2000*). **BAC San José** (⊠ *100 m north and 125 m west of cathedral*).

Scotiabank (⊠ *Across from Mercado de Artesanías* ☎ *2461–9660*).

Hospital **Hospital de San Carlos** (⊹ *2 km [1 mi] north of park* ☎ *2460–1176*).

Internet **Internet Café** (⊠ *150 m north of park* ☎ *2460–3653*).

Post Office **Correos** (⊠ *Across from Escuela Chávez*).

EXPLORING

Termales del Bosque lets you soak those tired muscles, as you watch the birds, for a more reasonable price than most of the other hot springs in the region. ⊠ *Hwy. 140* ⊹ *7 km (4½ mi) east of Ciudad Quesada* ☎ *2460–4740* ⊕ *www.termalesdelbosque.com* 🎟 *Day pass $10, $5 children under 12* ⊙ *Daily 8 AM–10 PM*.

WHERE TO STAY

$ ⭐ Laguna del Lagarto Lodge. One of Costa Rica's smaller eco-lodges, this hideaway in a 1,250-acre rain forest near the Nicaraguan border gives shelter to 380 bird species and counting. Rustic cabins come with single beds. Buffet-style meals are served on a patio with river and forest views. Rates include one guided walk on the 10 km (6 mi) of forest trails, a tour of the butterfly garden, and use of canoes. Recommended extras include horseback riding and a boat trip up to the border on the San Carlos River. (Bring your passport, since Río San Carlos is officially Nicaraguan territory.) Ask about transfers available (at extra cost) from various points, including San José. The knowledgeable personnel here speak German, in addition to the requisite English and Spanish. **Pros:** Small size, attentive service, great excursions. **Con:** Rough road to get here. ⊕ *7 km (4 mi) north of Boca Tapada, 135 km (78 mi) northeast of Ciudad Quesada* ☎ *2289–8163* 📠 *2289–5295* ⊕ *www.lagarto-lodge-costa-rica. com* ⬦ *20 rooms, 18 with bath* ⚇ *In-room: no a/c, no phone, no TV. In-hotel: restaurant, bar, laundry service* ▣ *MC, V* ❑⊠▦.

> **CAUTION**
>
> The ubiquitous OFFICIAL TOURIST INFORMATION signs around La Fortuna and Monteverde aren't "official" at all, but are merely storefront travel agencies and tour operators hoping to sell you tours.

LA FORTUNA

50 km/30 mi (45 mins) northwest of Ciudad Quesada, 75 km/45 km (90 mins) north of San Ramón, 17 km/11 mi east of Arenal Volcano, 190 km/118 mi (3 hrs by car; 25 mins by plane) northwest of San José.

At the foot of massive Volcán Arenal, the small community of La Fortuna attracts visitors from around the world. Nobody comes to La Fortuna—an ever-expanding mass of hotels, tour operators, souvenir shops, and *sodas (small, family-run restaurants)*—to see the town itself. Instead, thousands of tourists flock here each year to use it as a hub for visiting the natural wonders that surround it. The volcano, as well as waterfalls, vast nature preserves, great rafting rivers, and an astonishing array of birds, are to be found within an hour or less of your hotel. La Fortuna is also the best place to arrange trips to the Caño Negro National Wildlife Refuge *(⇨below)*.

After the 1968 eruption of Arenal Volcano, La Fortuna was transformed from a tiny, dusty farm town to one of Costa Rica's tourism powerhouses, where tourists converge to see the volcano in action. Volcano viewing can be hit or miss, though, especially during the rainy season (May–November). One minute Arenal looms menacingly over the village; the next minute clouds shroud its cone. Early morning is always the best time to catch a longer gaze.

NAVIGATING LA FORTUNA | Taxis in and around La Fortuna are relatively cheap, and will take you anywhere; a taxi to the Tabacón resort should run about $8. Get a cab at the stand on the east side of Parque Central.

3

GETTING HERE & AROUND

Choose from two routes from San José: for a slightly longer, but better road, leave the Pan-American Highway at Naranjo, continuing north to Zarcero and Ciudad Quesada. Head northwest at Ciudad Quesada to La Fortuna; or for a curvier, but shorter route, continue beyond Naranjo on the Pan-American Highway, turning north at San Ramón, arriving at La Fortuna about 90 minutes after the turnoff. Either route passes through a mountainous section that begins to fog over by afternoon. Get as early a start as possible. NatureAir and SANSA fly daily to La Fortuna (FTN); flights land at an airstrip at the hamlet of El Tanque, 7 km (4 mi) east of town. **Sunset Tours** (⊠*South side of church, La Fortuna* ☎*2479–9800*) serves as the local agent for NatureAir and provides transportation to and from the airstrip for $5 each way. Shuttle-van service *(⇨The Northern Plains Essentials, below)* is a cheaper way to get to La Fortuna, and the vans will pick you up from various San José–area hotels, traveling as far west as Tabacón. Buses head to La Fortuna from San José three times daily, departing in the morning. Buses make multiple stops and can take much longer than driving yourself; for example, the trip from Ciudad Quesada can take 1½ hours by bus, but is only 45 minutes by car. **Desafío Adventures** (⊠*Behind church, La Fortuna* ☎*2479–9464* ⊕*www.desafiocostarica.com*) provides a fast, popular three-hour transfer between Monteverde and La Fortuna via taxi, boat, then another taxi, for $21 each way.

LA FORTUNA ESSENTIALS

Bank/ATM BAC San José (⊠*75 m north of gas station*). **Banco de Costa Rica** (⊠*Money exchange booth; across from south side of church*). **Banco Nacional** (⊠*Central Plaza* ☎*2479–9355*). **Banco Popular** (⊠*50 m east of Central Plaza* ☎*2479–9422*).

Medical Clinic Seguro Social (⊠*300 m east of Parque Central* ☎*2479–9643*).

Pharmacy FarmaTodo (⊠*50 m north of La Fortuna's gas station* ☎*2479–8155*).

Internet Destiny Internet (⊠*50 m north of Banco Nacional* ☎*2479–9850*). **Expediciones Fortuna** (⊠*Across the street from Central Plaza* ☎*2479–9104*).

Post Office Correos (⊠*Across from north side of church*).

EXPLORING

The town's squat, pale, concrete **Church of San Juan Bosco,** unremarkable on its own, wins Costa Rica's most-photographed-house-of-worship award. The view of the church from across the central park, with the volcano in the background, makes a great photo of the sacred and the menacing. ⊠*West side of Parque Central.*

The **Danaus Ecocenter** *(Ecocentro Danaus),* a small ecotourism project outside of town, exhibits 300 species of tropical plants, abundant animal life—including sloths and caimans—and butterfly and orchid gardens. It's also a great place to see Costa Rica's famed red poison dart frogs up close. ⊹*4 km (2½ mi) east of La Fortuna* ☎*2479–7019* w

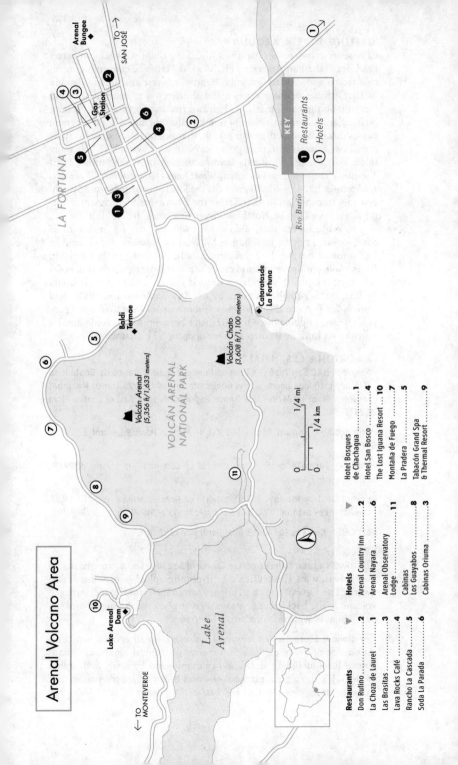

Arenal Volcano Area

TO MONTEVERDE →

Lake Arenal
Lake Arenal Dam ◆ ⑩

VOLCÁN ARENAL NATIONAL PARK

Volcán Arenal
(5,356 ft/1,633 meters) ▲

Volcán Chato
(3,608 ft/1,100 meters) ▲

Baldi Termae ◆

Cataratas de La Fortuna ◆

⑥ ⑤ ⑦ ⑧ ⑨ ⑪

Rio Burio

LA FORTUNA

Arenal Bungee ◆

TO SAN JOSÉ →

Gas Station

① ②

0   1/4 mi
0   1/4 km

KEY
① *Restaurants*
① Hotels

Restaurants ▶
Don Rufino 2
La Choza de Laurel 1
Las Brasitas 3
Lava Rocks Café 4
Rancho La Cascada 5
Soda La Parada 6

Hotels ▶
Arenal Country Inn 2
Arenal Nayara 6
Arenal Observatory Lodge 11
Cabinas Los Guayabos 8
Cabinas Oriuma 3
Hotel Bosques de Chachagua 1
Hotel San Bosco 4
The Lost Iguana Resort ... 10
Montaña de Fuego 7
La Pradera 5
Tabacón Grand Spa & Thermal Resort 9

≅$6 ⊙ *Mon.–Sat. 8–4, Sun. 9–3. A two-hour guided evening tour ($30) should be reserved in advance.*

Getting to **Fortuna Waterfall** (*Cataratas de la Fortuna*), requires a strenuous walk down ¼ mi of precipitous steps, but is worth the effort. Allow
25 to 50 minutes to reach the falls. Swimming in the pool under the
waterfall is usually safe. Wear sturdy shoes or water sandals with trac-
tion, and bring snacks and water. You can get to the trailhead from
La Fortuna by walking or taking an inexpensive taxi ride. Arranging
a tour with an agency in La Fortuna is the easiest option. ⊠ *Yellow
entrance sign off main road toward volcano* ✛ *7 km (4 mi) south of
La Fortuna* ≅$6 ⊙ *Daily 8–4.*

Fodor'sChoice
★

**OFF THE
BEATEN
PATH**

In 1945 a farmer in the mountain hamlet of Venado fell in a hole, and
thus were discovered the **Venado Caverns** (*Cavernas de Venado*). The
limestone caves contain eight chambers extending about 1½ mi. Sunset
Tours (⇨ *Outdoor Activities, below*) runs trips. If you're nonclaustro-
phobic, willing to get wet, and don't mind bats—think carefully—this
could be the ticket for you. ⊠ *45 mins north of La Fortuna and 20 mins
southeast of San Rafael* ☎ 2479–9415 ≅$35 ⊙ *Daily 7–8.*

BUNGEE
JUMPING

You don't even need to leave town to plummet from a 130-ft tower these
days. **Arenal Bungee** (⊠ *500 m east of church* ☎ 2479–7440 ⊕ *www.
arenalbungee.com* ⊙ *Daily 9:30–8:30*), on the east edge of La Fortuna,
offers a bungee jump (into a pool if you like) for $39. For another $39,
the facility's Rocket Launcher catapults you into the air, with bungee-
like recoils to follow. The Big Swing ($29), the third activity here, takes
you on an 85-ft-high, 180-degree arc through the air. You can mix and
match activities, too, or do all three for $100. The site is open after
dark, but remember that La Fortuna does not face the lava-flow side
of Arenal. Twilight is an especially beautiful time to ascend to the top
of the tower to catch the sun setting behind the volcano.

Fodor'sChoice
★

Desafío Adventures (⊠ *Behind church* ☎ 2479–9464 ⊕ *www.desafio
costarica.com*) can take you rafting, horseback riding, hiking, canyoning, and rappelling. **Sunset Tours** (⊠ *Across from south side of church*
☎ 2479–9800, 866/417–7352 in North America ⊕ *www.sunsettourcr.
com*) pioneered excursions to the Caño Negro Wildlife Refuge and
Venado Caverns and is one of the country's best tour operators. **Jacamar Naturalist Tours** (⊠ *Across from Parque Central* ☎ 2479–9767
⊕ *www.arenaltours.com*) launches a variety of tours.

FISHING

Lake Arenal is enormous and stocked with game fish, including tilapia, *guapote* (Central American rainbow bass), and *machaca* (Central American shad). Most tour operators and hotels can set you up
with guides. Rates begin at $150. **Jacamar Naturalist Tours** (⇨ *above*) has
morning and afternoon sport-fishing trips to Lake Arenal.

HORSEBACK
RIDING

If you're interested in getting up to Monteverde from the Arenal–La
Fortuna area without taking the grinding four-hour drive, there's an
alternative:

★ **Desafío Adventures** (⊠ *Behind church* ☎ 2479–9464 ⊕ *www.desafio
costarica.com*) has a 4½-hour guided horseback trip ($65). The trip

Continued on page 134

ARENAL VOLCANO

Costa Rica's most active volcano dominates the landscape here. Night is the best time to see it in action: on a clear evening you can see rocks spewing skyward and molten lava rolling down its sides.

Volcán Arenal, at 1,624 meters (5,328 feet), looms over the Northern Plains.

Volcanologists estimate Arenal's age at around 4,000 years. It lay dormant for at least 400 years until 1968. It may be local folklore, but Ticos that homesteaded this area in the 1930s and '40s referred to Arenal as "the mountain" and apparently, despite its conical shape, did not realize it was a volcano. On July 29, 1968, an earthquake shook the area, and 12 hours later Arenal blew. The village of Arenal, to the west, bore the brunt of the shock waves, poisonous gases, and falling rocks. Some 100 people were killed in three days. Since then, Arenal has been in a constant state of activity—eruptions, accompanied by thunderous rumbling sounds, are sometimes as frequent as one per hour. An enormous eruption in 1998 put the fear back into the local community, though there were no casualties, and led to the

NOW YOU SEE IT, NOW YOU DON'T

The volcano is often hidden in cloud cover, so you may have to stay more than one day to get in a good viewing session. Your chances are best during the dry season (February–April), and dawn hours are the best for seeing the cone. The lava flow is most visible between midnight and pre-dawn, one reason to book a hotel on the lava side of the volcano. Tip: Wait until around 2 PM or so to see if the weather is clear, then book your afternoon volcano hike.

closure of Route 42 and the evacuation of several nearby hotels. Another eruption two years later did kill a guide and a tourist, who may have been hiking too close. These earthshaking events reminded everyone what it really means to coexist with the world's third most active volcano.

The volcano is within 30,000-acre Arenal Volcano National Park, one of Costa Rica's largest parks and most popular destinations. Also in the park are Lake Arenal, the country's most important source of hydroelectric power, and Cerro Chato, an extinct volcano. Cerro Chato's collapsed crater, now an aquamarine lake, can be reached if you're up to a vigorous and steep four-hour hike. ⊠ *Turnoff to ranger station 3½ km/2 mi east of Lake Arenal, and 2 ½ km/1 ½ mi west of Tabacón* ☎ *695–5180* 🎫 *$10*

⊘ *Daily 8 AM–4 PM and at night with authorized guides and groups.*

Volcano Hikes

Desafío and Jacamar get you close to the action, but still a safe distance away.

Desafío Adventures. ⊠ *Behind the church, La Fortuna* ☎ *2479–9464* ⊕ *www.desafiocostarica.com* 🎫 *$20* ⊘ *Tours at 3:30 PM.*

Jacamar Naturalist Tours ⊠ *Across from Parque Central, La Fortuna* ☎ *2479–9767 www.arenaltours.com* 🎫 *$30* ⊘ *Tours at 8 AM and 3 PM.*

⚠️Never hike beyond the warning signs, even if the volcano appears to be calm. Toxic hot gases are released by even small eruptions (which are frequent), and they move faster than you can.

HOT SPRINGS

Tabacón Grand Spa & Thermal Resort

Where else can you lounge in a natural hot-springs waterfall with a volcano spitting fireballs overhead? Tabacón Resort's Tabacón Hot Springs is a busy day spa and hotel with gardens, waterfalls, hot mineral-water soaking streams, swimming pools, swim-up bars, and restaurants, all in a florid Latin interpretation of grand European baths. Make spa-treatment appointments at least one day in advance. A shuttle can bring you from central La Fortuna. ⊠ *Highway toward Nuevo Arenal, 13 km/8 mi northwest of La Fortuna* ☎ *2460–2020 or 2519–1900* ⊕ *www.tabacon.com* 🎫 *Day pass with lunch $60, with dinner $85, 60-min massage $100–150* ⊘ *Daily noon–10.*

A little more economical and less crowded, Baldi Termae has 10 hot-springs-fed pools that vary in temperature and share views of Volcán Arenal. It has a swim-up bar, too. ⊠ *4 km/2½ mi west of La Fortuna* ☎ *2479–9651* ⊕ *www.baldihotsprings.com* 🎫 *$28* ⊘ *Daily 10–10.*

ROOMS WITH A VIEW

Some or all rooms at the following La Fortuna area hotels have views of the volcano's lava-flow side.

- Tabacón Grand Spa & Thermal Resort
- Arenal Observatory Lodge
- Lost Iguana Resort
- Cabinas Los Guayabos
- Montaña de Fuego
- Arenal Nayara

From the La Fortuna side, you can still see the volcano, if not the lava.

- Hotel San Bosco
- Arenal Country Inn
- La Pradera
- Cabinas Oriuma

involves taxi or van service from La Fortuna to the southern shore of Lake Arenal, and from that trail's end you ride to Monteverde, circumventing poorly maintained trails. A boat ride across Laguna de Arenal is included. You leave La Fortuna at 7:30 AM and arrive in Monteverde around 2:30 PM. You can also take the trip in reverse. ■TIP→**Many other agencies, many of them nothing more than a guy and a horse, lead riding tours between La Fortuna and Monteverde, but along treacherous trails, and some riders have returned with stories of terrified horses barely able to navigate the way. Stick with Desafío.**

> **CAUTION**
>
> What's the newest craze in Monteverde and Arenal? Four-wheel all-terrain vehicles. Seemingly everybody rents them out these days, but we've heard too many reports of rollover accidents and don't recommend them. (They're also very noisy, and we object to them on that principle.)

The ride from La Fortuna to the Fortuna Waterfall is appropriate for both novice and experienced riders. **Chaves Horse Tours** (☎8354–9159 or 2479–9023) has guided horseback tours to the waterfall.

RAFTING &
KAYAKING

Several La Fortuna operators offer Class III and IV white-water trips on the Río Toro. The narrow river requires the use of special, streamlined boats that seat just four and go very fast. The easier Balsa, Peñas Blancas, Arenal, and San Carlos rivers have Class II and III rapids and are close enough to town that they can be worked into half-day excursions. **Canoa Aventura** (☎2479–8200 ⊕www.canoa-aventura.com) can design a canoeing trip with ample wildlife viewing on the Río Peñas Blancas and also has daylong canoe tours of the Caño Blanco Wildlife Refuge. Tours are appropriate for beginners, with a selection of easy floats if you're not feeling too adventurous, and instruction is provided, but the folks here can tailor excursions if you're more experienced.

★ **Desafío Adventures** (⊠Behind church ☎2479–9464 ⊕www.desafio costarica.com) pioneered rafting trips in this region, and has day trips on the Río Toro for experienced rafters ($85), half-day rafting and kayaking outings on the nearby Arenal and Balsa rivers ($65) ideal for beginners, as well as a leisurely wildlife-viewing float on the Peñas Blancas ($45). **Ríos Tropicales** (⊕1 km (½ mi) west of La Fortuna ☎2479–0075 ⊕www.flowtrips.com) does the standard trips on the Toro, Peñas Blancas, and Arenal rivers.

RAPPELLING

Rappel down four waterfalls and one rock wall ranging in height from 60 to 150 feet with **Pure Trek Canyoning** (☎461–2110, 866/569–5723 in North America ⊕www.puretrekcostarica.com). Two guides lead small groups—10 is the maximum size—on a four-hour tour ($90) that departs at 7 AM or noon to a private farm near La Fortuna, with plenty of wildlife-watching opportunities along the way. The excursion includes transportation, all gear, breakfast (for the morning tour), and a light lunch.

EN
ROUTE

Increased development on the highway between La Fortuna and the Tabacón resort has led to a noticeable increase in traffic. It is hardly the proverbial urban jungle, and it is one of the country's prettiest stretches of road, but you should drive with caution. Cars dart in and out of driveways. Visitors congregate along the side of the road (likely a sloth-spotting). Drivers gaze up at the volcano that looms over the highway. Keep your eyes on the road.

WHERE TO EAT

$$–$$$ ✕**Don Rufino.** The town's most elegant-looking restaurant is really quite informal. The L-shape bar fronting the main street has become a popular expat and tourist hangout and lends a relaxed air to the place. No need to dress up here: this is La Fortuna, after all. The friendly waitstaff might suggest tilapia in bacon and tomato sauce or spinach ricotta to the accompaniment of coconut rice. ⊠*Across from gas station* ☎2479–9997 ⊟*AE, D, DC, MC, V.*

$$ ✕**Lava Rocks Café.** A couple of trendy steps above the average *soda* in food and atmosphere (and a bit higher in price), this open-air café has tasty *casados* (plates with rice, beans, fried plantains, and fish, chicken, or meat) and sandwiches, and we love their rich fruit *batidos* (milk shakes). ⊠*Across from south side of church* ☎2479–8039 ⊟*AE, D, DC, MC, V.*

$ ✕**Las Brasitas.** Chicken turns over wood on a rotisserie in a brick oven at this pleasant restaurant on the road heading out of town toward the volcano. Try the succulent chicken when it ends up in the tasty fajitas or any of the other ample-size Mexican dishes. Service is good, and you have your choice of three open-air dining areas arranged around a garden. Two are secluded and intimate; the third less so, being closer to the road. ⊠*200 m west of church* ☎2479–9819 ⊟*AE, D, DC, MC, V.*

$ ✕**La Choza de Laurel.** Tantalizing rotisserie chicken, and pretty cloves of garlic and bunches of onions dangling from the roof draw in passersby to this old favorite, open-air Costa Rican–style restaurant a short walk from the center of town. The place opens early, perfect for a hearty breakfast on your way to the volcano. ⊠*300 m northwest of church* ☎2479–7063 ⊟*AE, D, DC, MC, V.*

$ ✕**Rancho la Cascada.** You can't miss its tall, palm-thatch roof in the center of town. The festive upstairs contains a bar, with large TV, neon signs, and flashing lights. Downstairs the spacious dining room—decorated with foreign flags—serves basic, mid-price Costa Rican fare. Its location right in the center of town makes it a favorite for tour groups. ⊠*Across from northeast corner of Parque Central* ☎2479–9145 ⊟*AE, D, DC, MC, V.*

¢ ✕**Soda La Parada.** Here's a case study in what tourism does to a place: La Fortuna's only 24-hour eatery was once a hole-in-the-wall joint across from the bus stop. It has now expanded greatly and even has sit-down dining. It is still a convenient place to grab a quick and cheap meal, and

---

ADVENTURE ALTERNATIVE

If you're feeling more community-minded than adventurous, Desafío Adventures (⊠*Behind church* ☎2479–9464 ⊕*www.desafiocostarica.com*) has a day-long tour ($75) that takes you to an area animal-rescue center, women's arts-and-crafts cooperative, organic medicinal-plant farm, and recycling center. Lunch is included.

3

to stock up on snacks for long bus rides. ⊠*Across from Parque Central and regional bus stop* ☎2479–9547 ⊟*No credit cards.*

WHERE TO STAY

$$$$ ⚏**Tabacón Grand Spa & Thermal**
★ **Resort.** Without question, Tabacón, with its impeccably landscaped gardens and hot-spring rivers at the base of Volcán Arenal, is one of Central America's most famous and compelling resorts. The hot springs and small but lovely spa customarily draw visitors inland from the ocean with no regrets. All rooms have tile floors, a terrace or patio, and big bathrooms. Some have volcano views; others overlook the manicured gardens. The suites are some of the country's fin-

est lodgings, with tile floors, plants, beautiful mahogany armoires and beds, and two-person whirlpool baths. The hotel's intimacy is compromised by its scale and its popularity with day-trippers—a reservations system for day passes is limiting the intrusion and improving that situation somewhat—but it has some private areas for overnight guests only, including a dining room and pool. ▪TIP➔**Tabacón offers frequent Internet-only discounts if you book directly through its Web site.** **Pros:** Luxurious hot springs, great volcano views, good restaurant. **Con:** Popular with tour groups. ✛*13 km (8 mi) northwest of La Fortuna on highway toward Nuevo Arenal* ☎2460–2020, 2519–1900 in San José, 877/277–8291 in North America ☎2460–5724, 2519–1940 in San José, 877/277–8292 in North America ✉Apdo. 181–1007, San José ⊕www.tabacon.com ➾114 rooms, 11 suites ⌂In-hotel: 2 restaurants, bars, pools, gym, spa, public Wi-Fi, airport shuttle, no-smoking rooms ⊟AE, D, DC, MC, V ⊙BP.

$$$ ⚏**Arenal Nayara.** Opened in early 2008 just off the road between La Fortuna and Tabacón, this newest entry into the upscale Arenal sweepstakes has expansive grounds scattered with cabins, all strategically aligned to provide balcony views of the volcano. Each is decorated in bright tropical colors and comes with dark-wood furnishings, four-post canopy beds, plasma TVs, DVD players, whirlpool tubs, and two showers, one indoors and one outdoors. Those are amenities rarely seen up here, and rarely seen in Costa Rica at all, for that matter. **Pros:** Luxurious rooms, great volcano views, good restaurant. **Con:** Massive grounds navigable only by golf cart shuttles. ⊠*5 km/3 mi west of La Fortuna* ☎2479–1600 B– ⊕www.arenalnayara.com ➾24 rooms ⌂In-room: safe, refrigerator, DVD. In hotel: restaurant, room service, bar, tennis court, pool, spa, laundry service, public Wi-Fi ⊟AE, D, DC, MC, V ⊙EP

$$$ ☒ **Arenal Observatory Lodge.** You're as close as anyone should be to an active volcano at the end of the winding road leading to the lodge—a mere 1¾ km (1 mi) away. The isolated lodge was founded by Smithsonian researchers in 1987. It's fairly rustic, emphasizing that outdoor activities are what it's all about. Rooms are comfortable and simply furnished (comforters on beds are a cozy touch), and most have stellar views. After a hike, take a dip in the infinity-edge pool or 12-person hot tub, which face tall pines on one side and the volcano on the other. The dining room, which serves tasty and hearty food, has great views of the volcano and lake. **Pro:** Best volcano views. **Cons:** Rough road, isolated location. ⊹*3 km (2 mi) east of dam on Laguna de Arenal; from La Fortuna, drive to Tabacón resort and continue 4 km (2½ mi) past resort to turnoff at base of volcano; turn and continue for 9 km (5½ mi)* ☎*Apdo. 13411–1000, San José* ☎*2479–1070, 2290–7011 in San José* ☎*2479–1074, 2290–1000 in San José* ⊕*www.arenal observatorylodge.com* ☞*42 rooms, 37 with bath; 2 suites* ☽*In-room: no a/c, no phone, no TV. In-hotel: restaurant, bar, pool, laundry service* ▭*AE, D, DC, MC, V* ⦿*BP.*

$$$ ☒ **The Lost Iguana Resort.** Despite its relative isolation—you're several kilometers beyond Tabacón—the Lost Iguana hums with activity, and is a favorite among fodors.com posters. Buildings here scale a hillside a short drive up a rugged road above the Arenal Dam. Each unit comes with a huge picture window that leads out onto an individual balcony with stupendous volcano views. Rooms are decorated with locally made art and bamboo-frame beds. Suites come with vaulted ceilings, private garden showers, and private whirlpools. A few cottages tuck away on the grounds and make ideal getaways for families. The location makes this a good bet if you have your own vehicle, but taxis can ferry you to and from area attractions, too. **Pros:** Secluded location, great volcano views, many activities. **Con:** Removed from sights. ⊹*31 km (19 mi) west of La Fortuna on highway toward Nuevo Arenal* ☎*2479–1555, 2267–6148 in San José* ☎*2267–7672 in San José* ⊕*www.lostiguana resort.com* ☞*41 rooms* ☽*In-room: safe, refrigerator, Wi-Fi. In-hotel: restaurant, room service, bar, pools, spa, no elevator, laundry service, no kids under 6 except in houses* ▭*AE, MC, V* ⦿*EP.*

$$–$$$ ☒ **Montaña de Fuego.** On a manicured grassy roadside knoll, this highly
FodorsChoice   recommended collection of cabins affords utterly spectacular views of
★   Volcán Arenal. (If you don't stay here, Montaña de Fuego's Acuarela Restaurant dishes up tasty Costa Rican cuisine and throws in the same stupendous views.) The spacious, well-made hardwood structures have large porches, and rooms have rustic decor. The friendly management can arrange tours of the area. ■**TIP→Montaña de Fuego offers periodic Internet-only discounts when you book via its Web site.** **Pros:** Great volcano views, many activities for guests only, good restaurant. **Con:** Some cabins face highway noise. ⊹*8 km (5 mi) west of La Fortuna* ☎*2479–1220* ☎*2479–1221* ⊕*www.montanadefuego.com* ☞*68 cabinas* ☽*In-room: safe, refrigerator. In-hotel: restaurant, bars, pools, spa, laundry service, public Internet, public Wi-Fi* ▭*AE, DC, MC, V* ⦿*BP.*

$$ ☒ **Arenal Country Inn.** It doesn't quite approximate an English country inn, although it is charming. Each brightly furnished modern room

has two queen-size beds and a private patio. The lush grounds have great views of the Arenal volcano. A big breakfast is served in the restaurant, an open-air converted cattle corral. You can take lunch and dinner there as well. **Pro:** Good value. **Con:** Several blocks from center of town. ✛*1 km (½ mi) south of church of La Fortuna, south end of town* ☎*2479–9670, 2283–0101 in San José* 🖷*2479–9433, 2280–7340 in San José* ⊕*www.arenalcountryinn.com* ⌨*20 rooms* ♿*In-room: safe, refrigerator. In-hotel: restaurant, bar, pool, laundry service* ▤*AE, DC, MC, V* ⦿*BP.*

$$ 🏨**Hotel Bosques de Chachagua.** At this working ranch, intersected by a brook, you can see *caballeros* (cowboys) at work, take a horseback ride into the rain forest, and look for toucans from the open-air restaurant, which serves local meat and dairy products. Each cabina has a pair of double beds and a deck with a picnic table. Large, reflective windows enclosing each cabina's shower serve a marvelous purpose: birds gather outside your window to watch their own reflections while you bathe and watch them. The lodge is 3 km (2 mi) up a rough track—4WD is a must in rainy season—on the road headed south from La Fortuna to La Tigra. **Pro:** Secluded location. **Cons:** Rustic rooms, far from sights. ✛*12 km (7 mi) south of La Fortuna* ✉*Apdo. 476–4005, Ciudad Cariari* ☎*2468–1010* 🖷*2468–1020* ⊕*www.chachaguarainforest hotel.com* ⌨*32 cabinas* ♿*In-room: no a/c, no TV. In-hotel: restaurant, bar, pool* ▤*AE, D, DC, MC, V* ⦿*BP.*

$–$$ 🏨**Hotel San Bosco.** Covered in blue-tile mosaics, this two-story hotel is certainly the most attractive and comfortable in the main part of town. Two kitchen-equipped cabinas (which sleep 8 or 14 people) are a good deal for families. The spotlessly clean, white rooms have polished wood furniture and firm beds and are linked by a long veranda lined with benches and potted plants. **Pros:** Good value, close to center of town. **Con:** Some rooms get street noise. ✉*220 m north of La Fortuna's gas station* ☎*2479–9050* 🖷*2479–9109* ⊕*www.arenal-volcano. com* ⌨*34 rooms* ♿*In-room: no phone, refrigerator (some), Wi-Fi. In-hotel: pool, no elevator, public Internet* ▤*AE, D, DC, MC, V* ⦿*BP.*

$ 🏨**Cabinas Los Guayabos.** A great budget alternative to the more expensive lodgings lining the road to the volcano is this group of basic but spotlessly clean cabins managed by a friendly family. The units have all the standard budget-lodging furnishings, but each comes with its own porch facing Arenal—ideal for viewing the evening spectacle. **Pros:** Good budget value, great volcano views. **Con:** Rustic rooms. ✛*9 km (5½ mi) west of La Fortuna* ☎🖷*2479–1444* ⊕*www.cabinaslosguayabos. com* ⌨*8 cabins* ♿*In room: no phone, refrigerator* ▤*V* ⦿*EP.*

$ 🏨**La Pradera.** "The Prairie" is a simple roadside hotel with comfortable guest rooms that have high ceilings, spacious bathrooms, and verandas. Two rooms have whirlpool tubs. Beef eaters should try the thatch-roof restaurant next door. The steak with jalapeño sauce is a fine, spicy dish. **Pros:** Good value, good restaurant. **Con:** Spartan rooms. ✛*2 km (1 mi) west of La Fortuna* ☎*2479–9597* 🖷*2479–9167* ⊕*www.lapradera delarenal.com* ⌨*28 rooms* ♿*In-room: no a/c (some), no phone. In-hotel: restaurant, bar, pool* ▤*MC, V* ⦿*BP.*

¢ ⬚**Cabinas Oriuma.** Right in the center of town, Oriuma is a popular choice for budget travelers and tour groups. The modern rooms are sparkling clean. The second-floor balcony is a pleasant spot to relax and read, watch the happenings in the Parque Central across the street, or plan your next adventure. **Pros:** Good budget value, close to center of town. **Con:** Some rooms get street noise. ⊠*15 m north of Parque Central* ☎*2479–9111* ✎*oriuma@ice.co.cr* ⇄*25 rooms* ⚒*In-room: no a/c (some), no phone* ⊟*No credit cards* ⫶OⵏEP.

SHOPPING

Lunática (⊠*350 m east of town church* ☎*2479–8255* ✎*lunaticarte2@ ice.co.cr*) sells vibrant, colorful works by artists both known and unknown from around the country, some of them local. Charming owner Francesa Marchi knows the area's arts, from the works of the nearby indigenous Maleku groups to those from a cooperative made up of women from local villages. The shop closes on Sunday.

★ **Toad Hall** (⊠*Road between Nuevo Arenal and La Fortuna* ☎*2692– 8001*), open daily from 8 to 6, sells everything from indigenous art to maps to recycled paper and used books. The owners can give you the lowdown on every tour and tour operator in the area; they also run a deli-café with light snacks and views of the lake and volcano.

NIGHTLIFE

People in La Fortuna tend to turn in early, though there are a few clubs and discos for the night owls. **Volcán Look Disco** (⊹*5 km (3 mi) west of La Fortuna* ☎*2479–9616*), which bills itself as the largest Costa Rican disco outside San José, erupts with dancing and music on weekends. Pizzeria **Vagabundo** (⊹*3 km (2 mi) west of La Fortuna* ☎*2479–9565*) turns into a lively bar in the evening with foosball and billiards in the back room.

LAKE ARENAL

Shimmering Lake Arenal, all 125 square km (48 square mi) of it, lies between green hills and a rumbling volcano. It's Costa Rica's largest inland body of water. Many visitors are surprised to learn it's a man-made lake, created in 1973 when a giant dam was built. A natural depression was flooded, and a 20-mi-long by 9-mi-wide lake was born. The almost constant winds from the Caribbean make this area a wind-surfing mecca. Outfitters in La Fortuna, Nuevo Arenal, and Tilarán run fishing, windsurfing, and kitesurfing trips on the lake. Desafío, an operator based in La Fortuna and Monteverde, has a half-day horse-back trip between the two towns, with great views of the lake (*see Exploring in La Fortuna, above*).

NUEVO ARENAL

40 km/25 mi (1 hr) west of La Fortuna.

Much of the original town of Arenal, at one of the lowest points near Lake Arenal, was destroyed by the volcano's 1968 eruption, and the rest was destroyed in 1973, when Lake Arenal flooded the region. The *nuevo* (new) town was created about 30 km (19 mi) away from the site of the old. It doesn't have much to interest tourists, but is about halfway between La Fortuna and Tilarán, making it a good stop for a break, and an even better base with a couple of truly lovely lodgings nearby.

> ### IN MEMORIAM
>
> Those yellow hearts with halos painted on the pavement mark spots where people have died in car accidents or vehicles have struck and killed pedestrians. An alarming number of them dot streets and roads around the country. Drive (and walk) with utmost caution.

GETTING HERE & AROUND
The route from La Fortuna to Nuevo Arenal around the north shore of Lake Arenal is in better shape than it has been in years, with only a couple of short atrocious sections to negotiate. Expect smooth sailing west of the Tabacón resort as far as the Arenal Dam, beyond which you should stick to daylight travel only. Watch out for the raccoonlike coatimundis (*pizotes* in Spanish) that scurry along the road. Longtime human feeding has diminished their ability to search for food on their own, and the cookies and potato chips they frequently get make matters worse.

Public buses run twice daily from La Fortuna to Nuevo Arenal and beyond to Tilarán.

NUEVO ARENAL ESSENTIALS
Bank/ATM Banco Nacional (⊠ *West side of church* ☎ *2694–4122*).

Internet Tom's Pan (⊠ *300 m south of gas station* ☎ *2694–4547*).

Post Office Correos (⊠ *Next to Guardia Rural*).

WHERE TO STAY
$$$ 🏨 **La Mansión Inn Arenal.** Halfway between La Fortuna and Nuevo Arenal, the elegant La Mansión Inn sits at the point where the volcano begins to disappear from sight, but the lake views (and the sunsets) remain as spectacular as ever. Individual cottages scatter around the 25-acre grounds on Arenal's north shore. Brightly colored wrought-iron furnishings decorate every split-level unit. As befits such a secluded place, bird-watching opportunities abound. **Pro:** Luxurious furnishings. **Con:** Far from sights. ⊠ *Road between Nuevo Arenal and La Fortuna* ☎ *2692–8018* 🖷 *2692–8019* ⊕ *www.lamansionarenal.com* 🗨 *17 cottages, 4 suites* 🔑 *In-room: no a/c (some), no phone, refrigerator, DVD (some), no TV (some). In-hotel: restaurant, bar, pools, spa, laundry service, public Wi-Fi* 🖃 *AE, D, DC, MC, V* ¶⊙¶*BP.*

$$ 🏨 **Villa Decary.** There's everything to recommend at this hillside lodging overlooking Lake Arenal, but it all goes back to owners Jeff and Bill and their attentive service. Rooms have large picture windows and private balconies—great places to take in the ample bird-watching opportunities—and bright yellow-and-blue spreads and drapes. Higher up the hill, spacious bungalows afford an even better view. The hotel accepts payment in American Express traveler's checks, too.

Fodor's Choice
★

Pros: Attentive owners, great breakfasts, good value. **Con:** Need car to stay here. ⊹*2 km (1½ mi) east of Nuevo Arenal* ☎*8383–3012* ☎☎*2694–4330* ⊕*www.villadecary.com* ⟿*5 rooms, 3 bungalows* ⟐*In-room: no a/c, no phone, no TV. In-hotel: restaurant, no elevator* ▤*MC, V* ⟐*BP.*

$ ⊞**Chalet Nicholas.** John and Cathy Nicholas (and their resident Great
*Fodor's*Choice   Danes) have converted their hillside home into a charming B&B with
★   stunning views of the lake and volcano. The two rosewood rooms downstairs have tile floors. Up a spiral staircase lies the L-shape, all-wood double loft with three beds and a back porch that overlooks the large garden. All rooms have volcano views. Birds abound: 100 species have been catalogued on the grounds. The entire property is no-smoking. **Pros:** Attentive owners, great breakfasts, good value. **Con:** Best for dog lovers. ⊹*3 km (2 mi) west of Nuevo Arenal* ☎*2694–4041* ⊕*www.chaletnicholas.com* ⟿*3 rooms* ⟐*In-room: no a/c, no phone, no TV. In-hotel: restaurant, no elevator, no-smoking rooms* ▤*No credit cards* ⟐*BP.*

TILARÁN

Heading west around Laguna de Arenal, you pass a couple of small villages and arrive at the quiet whitewashed town of Tilarán, on the southwest side of the lake. A windmill farm in the hills high above the town attests to its being the windiest place in the country, and it's used as a base by bronzed windsurfers. For those days when you get "skunked" (the wind fails to blow), horseback riding and mountain biking can keep you busy. A lakeside stroll is a pleasant way to while away a few hours.

GETTING HERE & AROUND
22 km/14 mi (45 mins) southwest of Nuevo Arenal, 62 km/38 mi (1½ hrs) west of La Fortuna.

The road from La Fortuna via Nuevo Arenal is in reasonable shape these days with a few short potholed stretches. Give yourself sufficient time—say, two hours—for the trip, and make the trip during daylight hours. Public buses travel to and from La Fortuna twice daily, and from a small terminal at Calle 20 and Avenida 3 in San José five times daily.

TILARÁN ESSENTIALS
Bank/ATM Banco Nacional (⊠*Central Plaza* ☎*$$695–5610*). **CooTilarán** (⊠*150 m north of church* ☎*$$695–6155*).

Hospital Clínica Tilarán (⊠*200 m west of Banco Nacional* ☎*$$695–5093*).

Post Office Correos (⊠*115 m west of municipal stadium*).

OUTDOOR ACTIVITIES
WINDSURFING   The best selection of wind- and kitesurfing equipment for rent or pur-
& KITESURFING   chase can be found at **Tilawa Wind Surf** (⊠*Hotel Tilawa* ⊹*8 km (5 mi) north of Tilarán* ☎*2695–5050* ⊕*www.windsurfcostarica.com*).

It's the only outfitter here open year-round. Beginner's lessons start at $65.

Rent wind- and kitesurfing equipment at **Tico Wind** (⊕ *30 km (18 mi) west of Nuevo Arenal* ☎2692–2002 w*www.ticowind.com*) during the December–April season. It offers beginner's lessons starting at $45, or enroll in a multiday course for $200.

WHERE TO STAY

$$ 　🏨**Hotel Tilawa.** This Costa Rican homage to the Palace of Knossos on Crete has neoclassical murals, columns, and plant-draped arches that somehow don't seem dramatically out of place. The large rooms have two queen-size beds with Guatemalan bedspreads and natural wood ceilings; the bathrooms are especially spacious. Sailing tours in a 39-foot catamaran, the windsurfing and kitesurfing school and shop, and the skateboarding park make this a practical place to base yourself if you want an active vacation. Packages include the use of windsurfing gear. The open-air patio restaurant dishes up steaks and seafood. **Pro:** Many activities. **Cons:** Isolated location, some reports of lackluster staff. ⊕*8 km (5 mi) north of Tilarán* ☎2695–5050 🖷2695–5766 ⊕*www.hotel-tilawa.com* ✆*Apdo. 92–5710, Tilarán* ⬏*23 rooms* ♿*In-room: no a/c, no TV. In-hotel: restaurant, bar, pool, spa, water sports, bicycles, no elevator, laundry service* ▤*MC, V* ¶◎ ⊠🖷.

MONTEVERDE CLOUD FOREST AREA

Monteverde is a rain forest, but you won't be in the tropics, rather in the cool, gray, misty world of the cloud forest. Almost 900 species of epiphytes, including 450 orchids, are found here; most tree trunks are covered with mosses, bromeliads, ferns, and other plants. Monteverde spans the Continental Divide, extending from about 1,500 meters (4,920 feet) on the Pacific slope and 1,350 meters (4,430 feet) on the Atlantic slope up to the highest peaks of the Tilarán Mountains at around 1,850 meters (6,070 feet).

MONTEVERDE CLOUD FOREST BIOLOGICAL RESERVE

★ *10 km/6 mi (30 mins) south of Santa Elena, 35 km/22 mi (2 hrs) southeast of Tilarán, 167 km/104 mi (5 hrs) northwest of San José.*

In close proximity to several fine hotels, the private Reserva Biológica Bosque Nuboso Monteverde is one of Costa Rica's best-kept reserves, with well-marked trails, lush vegetation, and a cool, damp climate. The collision of moist winds with the Continental Divide here creates a constant mist whose particles provide nutrients for plants growing at the upper layers of the forest. Giant trees are enshrouded in a cascade of orchids, bromeliads, mosses, and ferns, and in those patches where sunlight penetrates, brilliantly colored flowers flourish. The sheer size of everything, especially the leaves of the trees, is striking. No less astounding is the variety: 2,500 plant species, 400 species of birds, 500 types of butterflies, and more than 100 different mammals have so far been catalogued at Monteverde. A damp and exotic mixture of shades, smells, and sounds, the cloud forest is also famous for its population of quetzals, which can be spotted feeding on the *aguacatillo* (similar to avocado) trees; best viewing times are early mornings from January until September, and especially during the mating season of April and May. Other forest-dwelling inhabitants include hummingbirds and multicolor frogs.

For those who don't have a lucky eye, a short-stay aquarium is in the field station; captive amphibians stay here just a week before being released back into the wild. Although the reserve limits visitors to 160 people at a time, Monteverde is one of the country's most popular destinations. We do hear complaints (and agree with them) that the reserve gets too crowded with visitors at times. As they say, the early bird catches the worm, and the early visitor has the best chance at spotting wildlife. Allow a generous slice of time for leisurely hiking to see the forest's flora and fauna; longer hikes are made possible by some strategically placed overnight refuges along the way. At the reserve entrance you can buy self-guide pamphlets and rent rubber boots; a map is provided when you pay the entrance fee. You can navigate the reserve on your own, but a guided tour (7:30 and 11:30 AM and 1 PM) is invaluable for getting the most out of your visit. There's also another option: take advantage of their two-hour guided night tours starting each evening at 7:15 (reservations required), and the reserve provides transport from area hotels for an extra $2. ✉ *10 km/6 mi south of Santa Elena* ☎ *2645–5122* ⊕ *www.cct.or.cr* ☜ *$15 ($7.50 for students with International Student Identity Card) plus $15 with guide services; $15 night tour* ⊙ *Daily 7–4.*

GETTING HERE & AROUND
Buses from Santa Elena leave at 6 AM and 1 PM daily. Taxis from Santa Elena are $7. Buses from Tilarán leave once a day, at 1 PM. Buses from San José leave twice daily from the Terminal Atlántico Norte (C. 12 at Avda. 9), at 6:30 AM and 1:30 PM. The roads to the area are some of the worst in the country.

MONTEVERDE & SANTA ELENA

Monteverde is 167 km/104 mi (5 hrs) northwest of San José. Santa Elena is 6 km/4 mi (30 mins) north of Monteverde and 35 km/22 mi (2 hrs) southeast of Tilarán.

The area's first residents were a handful of Costa Rican families fleeing the rough-and-ready life of nearby gold-mining fields during the 1940s. They were joined in the early 1950s by Quakers, conscientious objectors from Alabama fleeing conscription into the Korean War. A number of things drew them to Costa Rica: just a few years earlier it had abolished its military, and the Monteverde area offered good grazing. But it was the cloud forest that lay above their dairy farms that soon attracted the attention of ecologists. Educators and artisans followed, giving Monteverde and its "metropolis," the village of Santa Elena, a mystique all their own. Monteverde's Quakers, or more officially, the

Continued on page 148

CANOPY TOURS

Why should monkeys have all the fun? Biologists have long known that much of the action in the rain forest happens off the ground, near the tops of trees. This is where the most eye-catching animals—birds and monkeys—make their homes.

What Is a Canopy Tour?

There are two basic types of canopy tours: one that gives you a chance to see treetop animals up close; and one that lets you behave like them. The former are canopy tours in the literal sense, where you walk along suspension bridges, ride along in a tram, or are hoisted up to a platform to get a closer look at birds, monkeys, and sloths. They may also be called hanging-bridges tours, sky walks, or platform tours.

The latter, and much more popular, type of canopy tour has less to do with learning about nature. Instead, it is a fast-paced and fun experience where you are attached to a zip line with a safety harness and then "fly" from one tree platform to the next. When most people say "canopy tour" they are generally referring to a zip-line tour. These tours are great fun, but don't plan on seeing the resplendent quetzal as you zip from platform to plat-form. (Your shouts of exhilaration will probably scare them all away.)

Tree-to-tree zip lines date back to the 19th century, and were introduced as a means for rain-forest study in Costa

Rica in the 1970s by U.S. biologist Donald Perry. Darren Hreniuk, a Dutch-turned-Tico entrepreneur, opened the country's first commercial canopy tour in Monteverde in the mid-1990s. It was an almost immediate success. Within a decade, there were close to 100 canopy tours operated by various companies and individuals. Canopy tours now generate some $120 million annually, and attract a reported 200,000 tourists each year. They have also sprouted up in several Western Hemisphere countries.

■**TIP→** If the day is overcast, save your money. All you'll see are clouds, and you can do that for free back on the ground.

Is It Safe?

Flying through the air, while undeniably cool, is also inherently dangerous. So before you strap into a harness, be certain that the safety standards are first rate. Like so much in Costa Rica, there is little government oversight of canopy tours, so you are dependent on the representations of the operators.

Since 1997 two zip-line tour deaths have been attributed to faulty equipment; one in 2000 on a San Lorenzo Canopy Tour in San Ramón, the other in 1997, at a canopy tour near La Fortuna. Both women plummeted to earth after their harnesses came apart. Considering that thousands of tourists enjoy the canopy tours each year, the safety record is quite good. Nevertheless, don't fall for sales pitches, and take your time to choose wisely. If anything seems "off" or makes you uncomfortable, walk away. Remember: Once you start out, there's no turning back.

Just as importantly: Listen closely to the guides and follow their instructions. Don't attempt to take photos in flight and never argue with the guide when s/he is making a decision to preserve your safety. A good operator will refund your money or reschedule your tour if it's cancelled due to weather.

3

IN FOCUS CANOPY TOURS

ZIP-LINE TOURS IN MONTEVERDE & ARENAL

Reservations are required for all zip-line tours.

The Arenal Rain Forest Reserve (⇨ *Hanging Bridges and Trams*) is a suspension-bridge and gondola tour with a zip-line option.

Aventura Canopy takes you over 16 cables—some extending 2,000 feet—one rappel, and one Tarzan swing on a 2½-hour tour. ⊠ *Office across from Super Compro, Santa Elena* ☏ *2645–6959* ⊕ *www.aventuracanopy.com* ✉ *$40.*

The Original Canopy Tour near Santa Elena was the first zip-line tour in Costa Rica, with 10 platforms in the canopy, and lasting 2½ hours. You arrive at most of the platforms using a cable-and-harness traversing system and climb 42 feet inside a strangler fig tree to reach one. ☏ *2291–4465 in San José for reservations* ⊕ *www.canopytour.com* ✉ *$45.*

★Fodor's Choice **Selvatura** is the only zip-line tour built entirely inside the cloud forest. It has 15 lines and 18 platforms. Mix and match packages to include the complex's hanging bridges, hummingbird and butterfly gardens, and reptile exhibition. ⊠ *Office across from church, Santa Elena* ☏ *2645–5929* ⊕ *www.selvatura.com* ✉ *$40.*

Sky Trek has 11 cables that are longer than those of the Original Canopy Tour—the longest more than 2,500 feet. The zip lines here extend between towers above the canopy, rather than between trees, and you'll more likely notice the effects of the wind on this one. ⊠ *Office across from Banco Nacional, Santa Elena* ☏ *2645–5238* ⊕ *www.skytrek.com* ✉ *$44, shuttle $1.*

CAN I DO IT?
You don't need any particular skills or athleticism to participate in a zip-line tour, but you do need some degree of fearlessness to allow yourself to be suspended hundreds of feet in the air. You'll also be asked to "brake" for yourself by squeezing the zip line before you get to the tree, so those with hand injuries or arthritis may have problems. Talk with the tour operator before you book. Tour operators usually have (and should have) weight and age restrictions; ask about these beforehand.

ASK BEFORE YOU BOOK:

■ How long has the company been in business, and are they insured?

■ Is the company a member of the Association of Adventure Tour Operators, and/or does it abide by the association's safety guidelines?

■ Are cables, harnesses, and other equipment manufacturer-certified?

■ Is there a second safety line that connects you to the zip line in case the main pulley gives way?

■ Are participants clipped to the zip line while on the platform? (They should be.)

■ What sort of training do the guides receive?

■ Does the tour operator give a thorough pre-tour safety briefing—in English—that addresses such issues as how much climbing and walking are involved?

■ What's the price? Costs vary from around $20 to $75. An extremely low price may indicate a second-rate operation.

HANGING BRIDGES AND TRAMS

Natural Wonders Tram is an hour-long ride through the rain-forest canopy in a two-person carriage on an elevated track. You control the speed of your carriage. Alternatively, a 1½-km (1-mi) walk gives you a ground-level perspective. The site opens for night visits with advance reservations. ⊠ *Off main road between Santa Elena and Monteverde, on turnoff to Jardín de Mariposas* ☎ *2645–5960* ✉ *$15* ⊘ *Daily 8 AM–6 PM.*

Tree Top Walkways, at Selvatura, takes you to heights of 500 feet on a 3-km (2-mi) walk along very stable bridges, ranging from 36 to 150 feet, through the same canopy terrain as the zip-line tour. ⊠ *Office across from church, Santa Elena* ☎ *2645–5929* ⊕ *www.selvatura.com* ✉ *$20.*

Sky Walk allows you to walk along five hanging bridges, at heights of up to 138 feet, connected from tree to tree. Imposing towers, used as support, mar the landscape somewhat. Reservations are required for guided tours. A tram, similar to that found at the Arenal Rain Forest reserve, is under construction at this writing. ⊠ *Across from Banco Nacional, Santa Elena* ☎ *2645–*

5238 ⊕ *www.skytrek.com* ✉ *$17* ⊘ *Daily 7–4.*

Arenal Hanging Bridges is actually a series of trails and bridges that form a loop through the primary rain forest of a 250-acre private reserve, with great bird-watching and volcano-viewing. Fixed and hanging bridges allow you to see the forest at different levels. It's open rain or shine, and there are things to do in both climates. Shuttle service from La Fortuna can be arranged. ⊠ *Arenal Dam, 4 km/2½ mi west of Tabacón* ☎ *2479–9686 or 2290–0469* ⊕ *www.hangingbridges.com* ✉ *$34; $45 bird tour, shuttle $12* ⊘ *Daily 7–4:30; evening tour at 5:30.*

Arenal Rain Forest Reserve, a canopy tour–bridge walk complex near La Fortuna, is operated by the Sky Trek–Sky Walk folks in Monteverde. Alpine-style gondolas transport you to the site, from which you can descend via a zip-line canopy tour or hike through the cloud forest along a series of suspended bridges. ⊠ *12 km/7 mi west of La Fortuna, El Castillo* ☎ *2479–9944* ⊕ *www.skytrek.com* ✉ *$60, $50 tram only, shuttle $8* ⊘ *Daily 7–4.*

CLOSE UP

What Is a Cloud Forest?

Cloud forests are a type of rain forest, but are very different from the hot, humid lowland forests with which most people are familiar. First of all, they're cooler. Temperatures in Monteverde Cloud Forest, for example, are in the 65°F range year-round, and feel colder due to the near-constant cool rain. Cloud forests—also known as montane forests—occur at elevations of around 6,500 to 11,500 feet. At this altitude, clouds accumulate around mountains and volcanoes, providing regular precipitation as well as shade, which in turn slows evaporation. Moisture is deposited directly onto vegetation, keeping it lush and green. The trees here, on top of high ridges and near the summits of volcanoes, are transformed by strong, steady winds that sometimes topple them and regularly break off branches. The resulting collection of small, twisted trees and bushes is known as an elfin forest. The conditions in cloud forests create unique habitats that shelter an unusually high proportion of rare species, making conservation vital. Monteverde is Costa Rica's most touristed cloud forest, but not its only one. Other cloud forests are in nearby Santa Elena Reserve, the Los Angeles Cloud Forest Reserve near San Ramón (⇨ *above*), and around San Gerardo de Dota (⇨ *Chapter 6*).

Society of Friends, no longer constitute the majority these days, but their imprint on the community remains strong.

In any case, Monteverde looks quite a bit different than it did when the first wave of Quakers arrived. New hotels have sprouted up everywhere, while traffic grips the center of town. A glut of rented all-terrain vehicles contributes to the incessant din that disrupts Monteverde's legendary peace and quiet. Some define this as progress. Others lament the gradual chipping-away at what makes one of Costa Rica's most special areas so, well, special. Locals have taken to posting signs that exclaim "¡PARQUEO, NO! ¡PARQUE SÍ!" ("PARKING LOT, NO! PARK, YES!") We side with them. You can still get away from it all up here, but you'll have to work harder at it than you used to. In any case, you'll not lack for things to do if seeing nature is a primary reason for your visit.

Note that a casual reference to "Monteverde" generally refers to this entire area, but officially the term only applies to the original Quaker settlement, which is located by the dairy-processing plant just down the mountain from the reserve entrance. If you follow road signs exclusively, you'll end up a bit outside of town.

CAUTION

The San José–Monteverde public bus route is notorious for theft; watch your bags, and never let your passport and money out of your sight—or off your person.

Never take advice from the street "guides" who meet incoming buses in Monteverde and La Fortuna. They claim to want to help you find accommodations and tours, when in reality they receive kickbacks for sending tourists to less-than-desirable hotels or to unqualified "tour guides."

The only way to see the area's reserves, including the Monteverde Cloud Forest, is to hike them *(⇨ Hiking in Outdoor Activities, below).*

There will be times you wish you had your own vehicle, but it's surprisingly easy to get around the Monteverde area without a car. Given the state of the roads, you'll be happy to let someone else do the driving. However, if you do arrive by rental car, the road up the mountain from Santa Elena is paved as far as the gas station near the entrance to the Hotel Belmar. Taxis are plentiful; it's easy to call one from your hotel, and restaurants are happy to summon a cab to take you back to your hotel after dinner. Taxis also congregate in front of the church on the main street in Santa Elena. Many tour companies will pick you up from your hotel and bring you back at the end of the day, either free or for a small fee.

GETTING HERE & AROUND

Getting here means negotiating some of the country's legendarily rough roads, but don't let that deter you from a visit. Years of promises to pave the way up here have collided with politics and scarce funds, but many residents remain just as happy to keep Monteverde out of the reach of tour buses and day-trippers. ("Do we really want this to be shore excursion for cruise ships?" some residents ask.) Your own vehicle gives you the greatest flexibility, but a burgeoning number of shuttle-van services connect Monteverde with San José and other tourist destinations throughout the country. And once you're here, if you're without wheels the community's rugged taxis can get you from hotel to restaurant to reserve. **Desafío Adventures** (⊠ *Across from Supermercado Super compro* ☎ *2645–5874* ⊕ *www.desafiocostarica.com*) provides a fast, popular three-hour transfer between Monteverde and La Fortuna. The taxi-boat-taxi service costs $21 one-way.

If your bones can take it, a very rough track leads from Tilarán via Cabeceras to Santa Elena, near the Monteverde Cloud Forest Biological Reserve, doing away with the need to cut across to the Pan-American Highway. You need a 4WD vehicle, and you should inquire locally about the current condition of the road. The views of Nicoya Peninsula, Lake Arenal, and Volcán Arenal reward those willing to bump around a bit. Note, too, that you don't really save much time—on a good day it takes about 2½ hours as opposed to the 3 required via Cañas and Río Lagarto on the highway.

MONTEVERDE & SANTA ELENA ESSENTIALS Bank/ATM **Banco Nacional** (⊠ *50 m north and 50 m west of bus station, Santa Elena* ☎ *2645–5027*).

Medical Clinic **Seguro Social** (⊠ *150 m south of soccer field, Santa Elena* ☎ *2645–5076*).

Pharmacy **Farmacia Vitosi** (⊠ *Across from Super compro supermarket, Santa Elena* ☎ *2645–5004*).

Internet **Historias Internet Café** (⊠ *Road to Jardín de Mariposas, 75 m down from Pizzería de Johnny, Cerro Plano* ☎ *2645–6914*).

Post Office **Correos** (⊠ *Center of Santa Elena*).

Tourist Information **Centro de Visitantes Monteverde** (⊠ *Across from Super compro supermarket, Santa Elena* ☎ 2645-6565).

EXPLORING

Several conservation areas that have sprung up near Monteverde make attractive day trips, particularly if the Monteverde Reserve is too busy. The **Santa Elena Reserve** just west of Monteverde is a project of the Santa Elena high school, and has a series of trails of varying lengths and difficulties that can be walked alone or with a guide. The 1.4-km Youth Challenge Trail takes about 45 minutes to negotiate and contains an observation platform with views as far away as the Arenal Volcano— that is, if the clouds clear. If you're feeling hardy, try the 5-km (3-mi) Caño Negro Trail, clocking in at around four hours.

The **Camino Verde Information Center** (⊠ *Main street in town*) operates a shuttle service to the reserve with fixed departures and returns. Reservations are required, and the cost is $2 each way. ✛ *6 km (4 mi) north of Santa Elena* ☎ 2645-5390 ⊕ *www.reservasantaelena.org* ☎ *$12, plus $15 with guide services* ☉ *Daily 7-4.*

☾ If your time in Monteverde is limited, consider spending it at **Selvatura,** a kind of nature theme park—complete with canopy tour and bridge walks—just outside the Santa Elena Reserve. A 100-bird hummingbird garden, an enormous enclosed 50-species *mariposario* (butterfly garden), and a *herpetario* (frog and reptile house) sit near the visitor center. Transportation from area hotels is included in the price. You can choose from numerous mix-and-match packages, depending on which activities interest you, or take it all in, with lunch and guide included, for $109. Most visitors get by for much less given that you couldn't take in all there is to do here in one day. ⊠ *Office across from church, Santa Elena* ☎ 2645-5929 ⊕ *www.selvatura.com* ☎ *Prices vary, depending on package* ☉ *Daily 8:30-4:30.*

Only in Monteverde would visitors groove to the nightlife at an exhibition of 20 species of frogs, toads, and other amphibians. Bilingual biologist-guides take you through a 45-minute tour of the terrariums in
☾ the **Ranario de Monteverde** (Frog Pond of Monteverde), just outside Santa Elena. For the best show, come around dusk and stay well into the evening, when the critters become more active and much more vocal. (Your ticket entitles you to a second visit the same day.) There's a small frog-and-toad-theme gift shop. ✛ *½ km (¼ mi) southeast of Supermercado Super compro, Santa Elena* ☎ 2645-6320 ⊕ *www.ranario.com* ☎ *$10, $8 for students, free for kids under 6* ☉ *Daily 9-8:30.*

☾ At the **Serpentario Monteverde** (Serpentarium of Monteverde), greet 40 species of live Costa Rican reptiles and amphibians with glass safely between you and them. Guided tours in English or Spanish are included in your admission price. ⊠ *Just outside Santa Elena on road to Monteverde* ☎ 2645-6002 ⊕ *www.snaketour.com* ☎ *$8* ☉ *Daily 9-8.*

The 200-acre **Sendero Tranquilo Reserve** is managed by the Hotel Sapo Dorado and bordered by the Monteverde Cloud Forest Biological

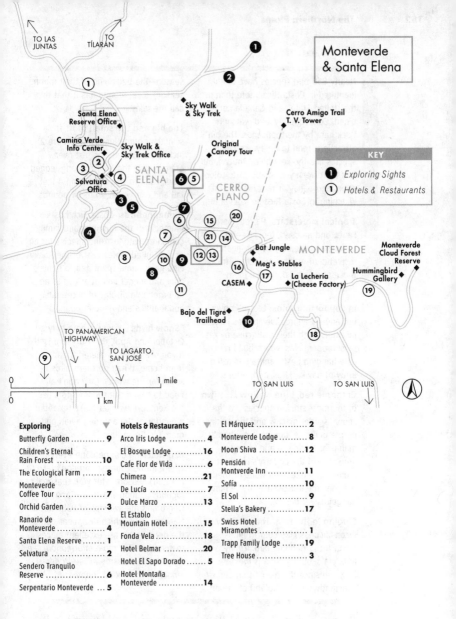

Monteverde
& Santa Elena

TO LAS JUNTAS

TO TÍLARAN

Sky Walk & Sky Trek

Cerro Amigo Trail
T. V. Tower

Santa Elena
Reserve Office

Camino Verde
Info Center

Sky Walk &
Sky Trek Office

Original
Canopy Tour

SANTA
ELENA

CERRO
PLANO

Selvatura
Office

MONTEVERDE

Bat Jungle

Meg's Stables

Monteverde
Cloud Forest
Reserve

Hummingbird
Gallery

CASEM

La Lechería
(Cheese Factory)

Bajo del Tigre
Trailhead

TO PANAMERICAN
HIGHWAY

TO LAGARTO,
SAN JOSÉ

0   1 mile
0   1 km

TO SAN LUIS

TO SAN LUIS

Bird Country

Nearly 850 bird species have been identified in Costa Rica, more than in the United States and Canada combined. Consequently, bird-watchers flock here by the thousands. The big attractions tend to be eye-catching species like the keel-billed toucan, but it is the diversity of shape, size, coloration, and behavior that makes bird-watching in Costa Rica so fascinating.

Tropical superstars: Parrots, parakeets, and macaws; toucans and toucanets; and the elusive but legendary resplendent quetzal are a thrill for those of us who don't see them every day.

In supporting roles: Lesser known but equally impressive species include motmots, with their distinctive racket tails; oropéndolas, which build remarkable hanging nests; and an amazing array of hawks, kites, and falcons.

Color me red, blue, yellow . . . : Two of the most striking species are the showy scarlet macaw and the quirky purple gallinule; tanagers, euphonias, manakins, cotingas, and trogons are some of the country's loveliest plumed creatures, but none of them matches the iridescence of the hummingbirds ($\Rightarrow$ *below*).

Singing in the rain: The relatively inconspicuous clay-color robin is Costa Rica's national bird. It may look plain, but its song is melodious, and since the males sing almost constantly toward the end of the dry season—the beginning of their mating season—local legend has it that they call the rains.

The big and the small of it: The scintillant hummingbird is a mere 2½ inches tall and weighs just over 2 grams, while the jabiru, a long-legged stork, can grow to more than 4 feet tall and can weigh up to 14 pounds.

Hummingbirds: Costa Rica hosts 51 members of the hummingbird family, compared with just one species for all of the United States east of the Rocky Mountains. Time spent near a hummingbird feeder will treat you to an unforgettable display of accelerated aerial antics and general pugnacity.

"Snow birds": If you're here between October and April, don't be surprised if you see some feathered friends from home. When northern birds fly south for the winter, they don't all head to Miami. Seasonal visitors like the Kentucky warbler make up about a quarter of the amazing avian panorama in Costa Rica.

Bird-watching can be done everywhere in the country. And don't let the rainy season deter you: seasonal *lagunas* (lagoons) such as Caño Negro and the swamps of Palo Verde National Park, which disappear during the dry months, are excellent places to see birds. *For more information, see the Wildlife Glossary in the Understanding Costa Rica chapter.*

Reserve and the Guacimal River. Narrow trails are designed to have as little impact on the forest as possible (only groups of two to six are allowed). A guide leads you through primary and secondary forest and an area that illustrates the effects of deforestation. Because of the emphasis on minimal environmental impact, animals here tend to be more timid than at some other reserves. ⊹ *3 km (2 mi) north of Monte-*

verde Reserve entrance, Cerro Plano ☎2645–5010 w 🖼$22 ⊘*Tours depart daily at 7:30* AM *and 1* PM; *reservations required.*

Bite your tongue before requesting Costa Rica's ubiquitous Café Britt up here. Export-quality Café Monteverde is the locally grown product.

★ The **Monteverde Coffee Tour** lets you see the process up close from start to finish, from shade growing on the area's Turín plantation, 7 km (4 mi) north of Santa Elena; transport to the *beneficio,* the processing mill where the beans are washed and dried; and finally to the roaster. Reservations are required, and pickup is from area hotels. ☎2645–7090 ⊕*www.crstudytours.com* 🖼$25 ⊘*Tours at 8* AM *and 1* PM.

The **Ecological Farm** (Finca Ecológica) is a private wildlife refuge with four trails on its 75 acres, plus birds, sloths, agoutis, coatimundis, two waterfalls, and a coffee plantation. If you can't make it all the way up to the Monteverde Reserve for the evening hike, there's a top-notch guided, two-hour twilight walk that begins each evening at 5:30. Reservations are required. ⊠*Turnoff to Jardín de Mariposas, off main road between Santa Elena and Monteverde* ☎2645–5869 🖼$9, *twilight walk $15* ⊘*Daily 7–5.*

☾ Forty species of butterflies flit about in four enclosed botanical gardens at the **Butterfly Garden** (Jardín de Mariposas). Morning visits are best, since the butterflies are most active early in the day. Your entrance ticket includes an hour-long guided tour. ⊠*Near Pensión Monteverde Inn; take right-hand turnoff 4 km (2½ mi) past Santa Elena on road to Monteverde, continue for 2 km (1 mi)* ☎2645–5512 ⊕*www.monteverdebutterflygarden.com* 🖼$9, $3 for kids under 12 ⊘*Daily 9:30–4.*

☾ Butterflies, frogs, and snakes already have their own Monteverde-area exhibits. The **Bat Jungle** gives its namesake animal equal time with guided tours into the life of one of the planet's most misunderstood mammals. An adjoining museum documents the history of the region, in particular, its early settlement by the Quakers. ⊠*Across from Casem Monteverde* ☎2645–6566 🖼$10 ⊘ *Daily 9:30—8:30*

The **Orchid Garden** (Jardín de Orquídeas) showcases more than 400 species of orchids, one of which is the world's smallest. The Monteverde Orchid Investigation Project manages the gardens. ⊠*150 m south of Banco Nacional* ☎2645–5308 w 🖼$7 ⊘*Daily 8–5.*

☾ The 54,000-acre **Children's Eternal Rain Forest** (Bosque Eterno de los Niños) dwarfs the Monteverde and Santa Elena reserves. It began life as a school project in Sweden among children interested in saving a piece of the rain forest, and blossomed into a fundraising effort among students from 44 countries. The reserve's **Bajo del Tigre trail** makes for a gentle, self-guided 1½-km (1-mi) hike through secondary forest. Along the trail are 27 stations at which to stop and learn about the reserve, many with lessons geared toward kids. A separate guided twilight walk ($15) begins at 5:30 PM and lasts two hours, affording the chance to see the nocturnal side of the cloud forest; reservations are required. Much of the rest of the reserve is not open to the public, but the Monteverde Conservation League offers stays at San Gerardo and Poco Sol, two remote field stations within the forest. The $34 packages include dormitory accommodation and meals. ✉*100 m south of CASEM* ☎*2645–5003* ⊕*www.acmcr.org* ✦*Forest $7; transportation from area hotels $2* ⊙*Daily 8–4:30.*

> **I LOVE A PARADE**
>
> Tread carefully when you see a tiny green parade on the ground before you. It's a troop of leaf-cutter ants carrying compost material to an underground nest.

NEED A BREAK?

Long before tourists flocked up here, dairy farming was the foundation of Monteverde's economy. Quakers still operate what is locally referred to as the Cheese Factory, or La Lechería (✛ ½ km (¼ mi) south of CASEM, halfway between Santa Elena and Monteverde Reserve ☎2645–2850, 2645–7090 tours). The factory store sells local cheeses and ice cream. Stop in for a cone. It's open Monday–Saturday 7:30–5 and Sunday 7:30–4. If you have more time, take a two-hour tour of the operation Monday–Saturday at 9 or 2. Tours are $8 and wind up with a cheese-sampling session. Reserve in advance. If you're not heading up the mountain, these folks also operate a stand across from the Treehouse restaurant on the main street in Santa Elena.

HORSEBACK RIDING
★

Long-established **Desafío Adventures** (✉*Across from Super compro supermarket, Santa Elena* ☎*2645–5874* ⊕*www.monteverdetours. com*) leads four-hour horseback tours to the San Luis Waterfall, an area not often taken in by Monteverde visitors, and also has shorter excursions on farms around Santa Elena. For the Monteverde–La Fortuna trip ($65), you travel by car and boat, with a three-hour horseback ride on a flat trail along Lake Arenal. Farms for resting the animals are at each end. It's infinitely more humane for the horses (and you) than the muddy, treacherous mountain trails used by dozens of other individuals who'll offer to take you to Arenal. Tour prices range from $25 to $48.

■TIP→ The ride from Monteverde to La Fortuna can be dangerous with outfitters that take inexperienced riders along steep trails. Desafío should be your only choice for getting from Monteverde to La Fortuna on horseback.

Escorted half-day horseback-riding tours ($40) with **Caballeriza El Rodeo** (✉*West entrance of town of Santa Elena, at tollbooth* ☎*2645–5764* ✐*rodeo@racsa.co.cr*) are on a private farm. Excursions are for everyone from beginner to experienced rider. A two-hour sunset tour ($25) begins at 4 PM. Family-operated **El Palomino** (✉*Just outside of Santa Elena* ☎*2645–5479*) gives escorted afternoon half-day horseback-riding tours on farm areas around Santa Elena. Transportation from your hotel is included.

On a horseback tour with **Gold Tours** (✉*Monteverde Homestay, 150 m northeast of school, Cerro Plano* ☎*2645–6914*) you visit a 1920s gold mine. The excursion ($40) includes a demonstration of the panning methods used during those heady days, and on the trip back a visit to a *trapiche*, a traditional sugarcane mill. Everyone from small children to seasoned experts can participate on these guided horseback-riding trips ($15–$50) with **Meg's Stables** (✉ *Main road, across from CASEM* ☎*2645-5419*). Reservations are a good idea in high season, and essential if you want an English-speaking guide. A tour to the San Luis waterfalls is geared toward experienced riders.

■**TIP**➡Book horseback trips in the morning during rainy season (July–December). Rains usually begin at around 2 PM.

WHERE TO EAT

$$$ ✕**De Lucía.** Cordial Chilean owner José Belmar is the walking, talking (in five languages) menu at this elegant restaurant, always on hand to chat with guests. All entrées are served with grilled vegetables and fried plantains, and include sea bass with garlic sauce and orange chicken. The handsome wooden restaurant with red mahogany tables is given a distinct South American flavor by an array of Andean tapestries and ceramics. An excellent dessert choice is *tres leches* (three milks), a richer-than-rich cake made with condensed, whole, and evaporated milk. ✉*Turnoff to Jardín de Mariposas, off main road between Santa Elena and Monteverde, Cerro Plano* ☎*2645-5337* ▭*AE, MC, V.*

$$ ✕**Sofía.** Here's one of the area's most stylish restaurants, but this is still Monteverde, so you can leave your eveningwear at home. Waiters in crisp black aprons scurry attentively around the three dining rooms with ample window space. We like Sofía for its variety of about a dozen main courses: a mix of chicken, beef, pork, seafood, and vegetarian entrées. Try the chimichanga with corvina and shrimp and a side of coconut rice. There's an extensive wine and cocktail selection, too. ✉*Turnoff to Jardín de Mariposas, off main road between Santa Elena and Monteverde, Cerro Plano* ☎*2645-7017* ▭*AE, D, DC, MC, V.*

$ ✕**Cafe Flor de Vida.** This popular vegetarian restaurant has a menu that includes chili, a huge veggie burger, sandwiches, soups, salads, bagels, and plenty of desserts. Filling, but nothing fancy here. ✉*Road to Monteverde Reserve* ⚓*1½ km (1 mi) southeast of Santa Elena* ☎*2645-6328* ▭*AE, DC, MC, V.*

$ ✕**Chimera.** Karen Nielsen, owner of nearby Sofía, recently opened this all-tapas (appetizers) offering, where you can mix and match small plates from the à la carte menu. Prices do add up quickly, but two or three menu items will make a filling meal out of such diverse mini-dishes as sea bass with passion-fruit cream, or coconut shrimp in mango-ginger sauce. Excellent dessert choices include a chocolate mousse or vanilla ice cream with pineapple-ginger-rum syrup, and a terrific selection of tropical-style cocktails and European and South American wines. A scant nine tables dot the place. Arrive before 7 if you want a guaranteed table, although the wait is never too long. ✉*Cerro Plano* ☎*2645-6081* ▭*AE, D, DC, MC, V.*

$ ✕**Dulce Marzo.** It's a tiny place with a small menu, but what this place does, it does well. The ever-changing blackboard menu might offer skewered chicken with cilantro or mixed greens with passion-fruit dressing. Dulce Marzo—with its orange walls, white-tile floors, and wood ceiling—makes a good afternoon break from your nature trekking, a good place to warm up with one of the café's gourmet coffee drinks. Be sure to grab a pastry on your way out. ⊠*100 m north of Cerro Plano school, Cerro Plano* 🕿*2645–6568* ▭*No credit cards.*

$ ✕ **El Márquez.** Seafood is an unexpected treat up here in the mountains, and it's fresh: the owner gets shipments from Puntarenas several times weekly. The place is nothing fancy—expect plastic tables and chairs, with lots of local flavor—but when area residents want a special restaurant meal, this is where they come. Portions are big, but prices aren't. You could have trouble finishing the generous mixed seafood platter with shrimp, crab, and octopus in a white-wine sauce, or the jumbo shrimp with a sauce of mushrooms and hearts of palm. ⊠*Next to Suárez veterinary clinic, Santa Elena* 🕿*2645–5918* ▭*MC, V* ☉*Closed Sun.*

$ ✕ **Moon Shiva.** Costa Rica meets the Middle East at this casual place. Falafel, pita, tahini, and baba ghanoush figure prominently on the menu, but fillings for the *gallos* (build-your-own tortilla-wrapped "burritos") include standard Tico black-bean paste as well as hummus. The house sauce of pineapple, curry, and coconut garnishes many a dish. Ice cream with fried bananas in rum and cinnamon is a sweet finale. The place has live music most evenings at 8. ⊠*100 m north of Cerro Plano school, Cerro Plano* 🕿*2645–6270* ▭*AE, MC, V* ☉*No lunch Sun.*

$ ✕ **Stella's Bakery.** This local institution is one of the few spots that open at 6 AM. It's a good place to get an early-morning fix before heading to the Monteverde Reserve. Pastries, rolls, muffins, natural juices, and coffee are standard breakfast fare. Take them with you if you're running short of time. Lunch consists of light sandwiches, soups, and pastas. Make it a very early dinner here; the place closes at 6 PM. ⊠*Across from CASEM, Monteverde* 🕿*2645–5560* ▭*AE, D, DC, MC, V.*

$ ✕ **Tree House.** The name describes the place: this two-story restaurant on Santa Elena's main street is built around a 60-year-old fig tree. Tree branches shelter first-floor tables from the afternoon mist, but not entirely. If that's a problem, grab a table on the covered upper floor. The menu mixes pastas and seafood with Costa Rican cuisine. For a taste of everything, try the *típico* platter. The service here is "leisurely" or "slow," depending on your perspective. Spending at least $6 here gets you 30 minutes of free Internet use at the bank of computers downstairs. ⊠*Across from AyA, Santa Elena* 🕿*2645–5751* ▭*AE, D, DC, MC, V.*

WHERE TO STAY

$$$ 🏨 **Hotel Montaña Monteverde.** The area's first lodging—it dates from 1979—underwent a 2007 makeover worthy of a reality TV show. The few of the original cabins that still remain are being phased out in favor of new rooms all in a main building. Some of the hotel's seclusion has been lost as a result, but the sparkle of the updated furnishings makes up for it. Each comes with shower and tub, flat-screen TV, brightly colored drapes and spreads, and large windows with super views. On the topic of views, the terrace restaurant also offers superb vistas of the far-off Gulf of Nicoya. **Pros:** Luxurious furnishings, new remodeling. **Con:** A little farther outside Santa Elena than some might want. ⊠*Cerro Plano* 🕿*2645–5046* B– ⊕*www.monteverdemountainhotel.*

com 🛏*38 rooms* &*In-room: refrigerator. In-hotel: restaurant, room service, bar, sauna, public Internet* ☐*AE, D, DC, MC, V* ❑*EP.*

$$$
Fodor'sChoice
★
🏨**Monteverde Lodge.** The well-established Costa Rica Expeditions operates this longtime favorite close to Santa Elena. Rooms have vaulted ceilings, bathtubs—an amenity rarely seen here—and great views. A table abuts the angled bay window overlooking the 15 acres of grounds, a perfect place to have a cup of coffee and bird-watch from indoors. The restaurant and bar congregate around an enormous but cozy lobby fireplace. Relax in the whirlpool tub in the enormous solarium, a perfect place to unwind after a day of tromping through the reserves. Or take in the evening slide presentation, showcasing cloud-forest life. These folks also offer packages that include meals, guided walks, and round-trip transportation from San José. **Pros:** Rustic luxury, attentive service, many activities. **Con:** Ground-floor rooms can be noisy. ✉*200 m south of Ranario de Monteverde, Santa Elena* ⌂*Apdo. 6941–1000, San José* ☎*2645–5057, 2257–0766 in San José* 🖷*2257–1165 in San José, 800/886–2609 in North America* ⊕*www.costaricaexpeditions. com* 🛏*27 rooms* &*In-room: no a/c, no TV. In-hotel: restaurant, bar, no elevator, public Internet* ☐*AE, D, DC, MC, V* ❑*EP, FAP, MAP.*

$$–$$$
🏨**El Establo Mountain Hotel.** "The Stable" began life as just that, a stable near the road, remodeled and apportioned into comfortable rooms with basic furnishings. Over the years, ever-upward expansion has turned this place into a sprawling operation. A newer pink building perches on the hill with large suites with wood-and-stone walls. Some contain lofts; all come with amenities rarely seen up here, such as bathtubs, phones, and enormous windows with views of the Gulf of Nicoya. The two newest buildings, higher on the hill, have rooms with hot tubs, private balconies, and even more commanding views. This is, by far, the area's largest hotel complex—you'll need the minivan shuttle to transport you up and down the hill. In that regard, El Establo is somewhat "un-Monteverde," but its guests undeniably have fun with its many facilities, including the 2008 addition of a private canopy tour. Oh, and those original stable rooms? They're not in use anymore. **Pros:** Luxurious furnishings, many activities. **Con:** Massive grounds. ⊹*3½ km (2 mi) northwest of Monteverde* ☎*2645–5110* 🖷*2645–5041* ⊕*www. hotelelestablo.com* 🛏*160 rooms* &*In-room: no a/c, safe, refrigerator, no TV (some). In-hotel: 2 restaurants, bar, pool, spa, no elevator* ☐*AE, D, DC, MC, V* ❑*BP.*

$–$$$
★
🏨**Arco Iris Lodge.** You're almost right in the center of town, but you'd never know it. This tranquil spot has cozy cabins set on 4 acres of birding trails. Cabin decor ranges from rustic to plush, but all lodgings come with porches. Start your day with a delicious breakfast buffet, including homemade bread and granola. You need not be a honeymooner to stay in the sumptuous three-level honeymoon cabin, secluded off on a corner of the property, with private patio, whirlpool tub, and DVD player. The laid-back German management can provide good advice about how to spend your time in the area. **Pros:** Attentive owner and staff, terrific breakfasts, ecology-minded place. **Con:** New bank blocks views. ✉*50 m south of Banco Nacional, Santa Elena* ☎*2645–5067* 🖷*2645–5022* ⊕*www.arcoirislodge.com* 🛏*20 cabins,*

1 suite ⚙In-room: no a/c, no phone, safe (some), DVD (some), no TV (some). In-hotel: laundry service, public Internet ⊟MC, V ⏐O⏐EP.

$$ ▦ **El Sol.** A charming German family tends to guests at one of those
Fodor'sChoice quintessential get-away-from-it-all places just 10 minutes down the
★ mountain from—and a noticeable few degrees warmer than—Santa Elena. Two fully furnished *ojoche*-wood cabins perch on the mountainside on the 25-acre farm. Every vantage point in the cabins—the living area, the bed, the desk, the shower, and even the toilet—has stupendous views. The property has 3 km (2 mi) of trails, a stone-wall pool, and a Finnish sauna. Meals can be arranged and taken in the main house or brought to your cabin. **Pros:** Great views, whimsically decorated cabins. **Con:** Need car to get here. ⊹4 km (2½ mi) southwest of Santa Elena ☎2645–5838 ⬚2645–5042 ⊕www.elsolnuestro.com ⏎2 cabins ⚙In-room: no a/c, no phone, no TV. In-hotel: restaurant, pool ⊟No credit cards ⏐O⏐EP.

$$ ▦ **Fonda Vela.** Owned by the Smith brothers, whose family was among
Fodor'sChoice the first American arrivals in the 1950s, these steep-roof chalets have
★ large bedrooms with white-stucco walls, wood floors, and huge windows. Some have views of the wooded grounds; others, of the far-off Gulf of Nicoya. The most innovatively designed of Monteverde's hotels is also one of the closest to the reserve entrance. Both restaurants ($$$) prepare local and international recipes with flair, served indoors or on the veranda. The place is a longtime favorite of those who post to fodors.com Latin America discussion board. **Pros:** Rustic luxury, secluded location, terrific restaurant. **Cons:** Far from town, rough road to get here. ⊹1½ km (1 mi) northwest of Monteverde Reserve entrance, Monteverde ☎2645–5125, 2257–1413 in San José ⬚2645–5119, 2257–1416 in San José ⊕www.fondavela.com ⌓Apdo. 12–5655, Santa Elena, Monteverde ⏎40 rooms ⚙In-room: no a/c, refrigerator. In-hotel: 2 restaurants, bar, no elevator, laundry service, public Internet ⊟AE, D, DC, MC, V ⏐O⏐EP.

$$ ▦ **Hotel Belmar.** Built into the hillside, Hotel Belmar resembles two tall Swiss chalets and commands extensive views of the Golfo de Nicoya and the hilly peninsula. The amiable Chilean owners have designed both elegant and rustic rooms, paneled with polished wood; half the rooms have balconies. In the restaurant ($$–$$$) you can count on adventurous and delicious *platos del día* (daily specials) of Costa Rican and international fare. **Pro:** Good value. **Con:** Far from town. ⊹4 km (2½ mi) north of Monteverde ☎2645–5201 ⬚2645–5135 ⊕www.belmarmonteverde.com ⌓Apdo. 17–5655, Monteverde ⏎28 rooms ⚙In-room: no a/c, no phone (some), no TV. In-hotel: restaurant, bar, laundry service, public Internet ⊟AE, MC, V ⏐O⏐EP.

$$ ▦ **Hotel El Sapo Dorado.** After beginning its life as a nightclub, the "Golden Toad" became a popular restaurant and then graduated into a very pleasant hotel. Geovanny Arguedas's family arrived here to farm 10 years before the Quakers did, and he and his wife, Hannah Lowther, have built secluded hillside cabins with polished paneling, tables, fireplaces, and rocking chairs. The restaurant ($$) is well known for its pastas, pizza, vegetarian dishes, and sailfish from Puntarenas. **Pro:** Rustic luxury. **Cons:** Trails between cabins get muddy in rainy season, no

screens on some windows. ⊕*6 km (4 mi) northwest of Monteverde Reserve entrance, Monteverde* ☎*2645–5010* 🖷*2645–5180* ⊕*www. sapodorado.com* 🖃*Apdo. 9–5655, Monteverde* ⬕*30 rooms* ⌂*In-room: no a/c, no phone, refrigerator, no TV. In-hotel: restaurant, bar, no elevator, public Internet* ⊟*AE, D, DC, MC, V* ⍩|*BP.*

$$ 🖳**Trapp Family Lodge.** The enormous rooms, with wood paneling and ceilings, have lovely furniture marvelously crafted from—you guessed it—wood. The architectural style is appropriate, as the lodge is surrounded by trees, just a 10-minute walk from the park entrance, making it the closest lodge to the reserve. (This means, though, that the trip into town is longer.) The friendly Chilean owners are always around to provide personalized service. Other than a small hutlike enclosure near the entrance, the entire property is no-smoking. **Pros:** Rustic luxury, good value, close to reserve entrance. **Cons:** Far from town, rough road to get here. ⊠*Main road from Monteverde Reserve, Monteverde* 🖃*Apdo. 70–5655, Monteverde* ☎*2645–5858* 🖷*2645–5990* ⊕*www. trappfam.com* ⬕*26 rooms* ⌂*In-room: no a/c, no TV (some). In-hotel: restaurant, bar, laundry service, public Internet, no-smoking rooms* ⊟*AE, D, DC, MC, V* ⍩|*EP.*

$ 🖳**El Bosque Lodge.** Convenient to the Bajo del Tigre nature trail and Meg's Stables, El Bosque's quiet, simple rooms are grouped around a central camping area. A bridge crosses a stream and leads to the hotel. Brick-oven pizzas are served on the veranda. **Pro:** Good budget value. **Con:** Basic rooms. ⊕*2½ km (1½ mi) southeast of Santa Elena on road to Monteverde Reserve, Monteverde* 🖃*Apdo. 5655, Santa Elena* ☎*2645–5221* 🖷*2645–5129* ⬕*28 rooms* ⌂*In-room: no a/c, no TV. In-hotel: restaurant, bar, laundry service, public Internet* ⊟*AE, DC, MC, V* ⍩|*EP.*

$ 🖳**Swiss Hotel Miramontes.** Switzerland meets the cloud forest at this Swiss-owned and -operated small inn. Each room has a private porch. Guests have access to a private orchid garden with over 300 varieties. If you're tired of rice and beans, the restaurant serves a variety of Swiss, Austrian, Italian, and French dishes. **Pro:** Pleasant, small operation. **Con:** Not many frills. ⊕*1 km (½ mi) south of Santa Elena* ☎*2645– 5152* 🖷*2645–5297* ⊕*www.swisshotelmiramontes.com* ⬕*8 rooms* ⌂*In-room: no a/c. In-hotel: restaurant* ⊟*MC, V* ⍩|*BP.*

¢ 🖳**Pensión Monteverde Inn.** One of the cheapest inns in the area is quite far from the Monteverde Reserve entrance, on a 28-acre private preserve. The bedrooms are basic, but they have stunning views of the Gulf of Nicoya as well as hardwood floors, firm beds, and powerful, hot showers. Home cooking is served by the chatty David and María Savage and family. **Pro:** Good rock-bottom budget value. **Con:** Spartan rooms. ⊠*50 m past Butterfly Garden on turnoff road, Cerro Plano* 🖷🖷*2645–5156* ⬕*13 rooms* ⌂*In-room: no a/c, no phone, no TV. In-hotel: restaurant* ⊟*No credit cards* ⍩|*BP.*

SHOPPING

ARTS & CRAFTS   **Atmosphera** (⊠*Turnoff to Jardín de Mariposas, Cerro Plano* ☎*2645– 6555*) specializes in locally made primitivist wood carvings. **Bromelia's** (⊠*100 m east of CASEM, Monteverde* ☎*2645–6272*) bills itself as a bookstore, but sells colorful batiks, masks, and jewelry, too. The

Cooperativa de Artesanía de Santa Elena y Monteverde (*CASEM* ✉*Next to El Bosque Lodge, Monteverde* ☎*2645–5190*) , an artisans' cooperative made up of 89 women and three men, sells locally made crafts. The prices are higher than at most other places. **Coopesanta Elena** (✉*Next to CASEM* ☎*2645–5901*) is the distributor for packages of the area's gourmet Café Monteverde coffee and accoutrements. The **Hummingbird Gallery** (✉*Just outside entrance to Monteverde Reserve* ☎*2645–5030*) sells books, gifts, T-shirts, great Costa Rican coffee, prints, and slides by nature specialists Michael and Patricia Fogden, as well as watercolors by nature artist Sarah Dowell.

> ## THE UBIQUITOUS SODA
>
> In Costa Rica the word *soda* has nothing to do with a carbonated beverage. (That's a *gaseosa* here.) Instead, a soda is a small, often family-run restaurant frequented by locals that you'll find in every town and city. Don't expect anything as fancy as a menu. A board usually lists specials of the day. The lunchtime *casado* (literally, "married")—a "marriage" of chicken, pork, or beef with rice, beans, cabbage salad, and natural fruit drink—sets you back about $2. No one will bring you a bill; just pay the cashier when you're done.

NIGHTLIFE

"Wild nightlife" takes on its own peculiar meaning here. You can still get up close with nature after the sun has gone down. Several of the reserves have guided evening walks—advance reservations and separate admission are required—and the Ranario, Serpentario, and Bat Jungle keep evening hours. Noted area biologist Richard LaVal presents a slide show called "*Sounds and Scenes of the Cloud Forest*" at the Monteverde Lodge nightly at 6:15 ($5). Advance reservations are required.

The area has a splendid concert venue, the **Anfiteatro Monteverde** (*Monteverde Amphitheater*) ✉*100 m east of CASEM, Monteverde* ☎*2645–6272*). The semi-open-air facility adjoins the Bromelias shop and resembles a giant cocoon with 200 concrete terraced seats. Dress warmly: evenings get chilly here.

CAÑO NEGRO REFUGE AREA

Long a favorite among fishing enthusiasts and bird-watchers, this remote area is off the beaten track and may be difficult to get to if your time in Costa Rica is short. You can cross into Nicaragua, via Los Chiles, but there are almost no roads in this part of southern Nicaragua, making access to the rest of the country nearly impossible. The border crossing at Peñas Blancas, near the north Pacific coast, is far more user friendly (⇨ *Crossing into Nicaragua at Peñas Blancas, in Chapter 4*).

CLOSE UP

A Biological Superpower

Costa Rica's forests hold an array of flora and fauna so vast and diverse that scientists haven't even named thousands of the species found here. The country covers less than 0.03% of the Earth's surface, yet it contains nearly 5% of the planet's plant and animal species. Costa Rica has at least 9,000 plant species, including more than 1,200 types of orchids, some 2,000 kinds of butterflies, and 876 bird species.

Costa Rica's biological diversity is the result of its tropical location, its varied topography, and the many microclimates resulting from the combination of mountains, valleys, and lowlands. It can also be attributed to Costa Rica's geological youth. Five million years ago this patch of land didn't even exist—in its place was a huge canal separating North and South America, where the Pacific and Atlantic oceans flowed together. About three million years ago the movement of tectonic plates created the land bridge that is now Costa Rica and Panama, which became a pathway for flora and fauna that had never coexisted.

Costa Rica's enormous natural diversity is in many ways the result of the intercontinental exchange, but the country's flora and fauna actually add up to more than what has passed between the continents. Although it is a biological corridor, the isthmus also acts as a filter, a hospitable haven to many species that couldn't complete the journey from one hemisphere to the other. The rain forests of Costa Rica's Caribbean and southwestern lowlands, for example, are the most northerly home of such southern species as the crab-eating raccoon and the dreaded jungle pit viper known as the bushmaster. The tropical dry forests of the northern Pacific slope are the southern limit for such North American species as the white-throated magpie-jay and the Virginia opossum. And then there are the tourists—migrants, that is—such as the dozens of northern bird species that spend their winter holidays in Costa Rica, among them the Tennessee warbler, western tanager, and yellow-bellied sapsucker. Costa Rica's many physical barriers and microclimates have also fostered the development of indigenous plants and animals, such as the mangrove hummingbird and mountain salamander.

CAÑO NEGRO NATIONAL WILDLIFE REFUGE

FodorsChoice ★ *91 km/57 mi (1½ hrs) northwest of La Fortuna.*

A lowland rain-forest reserve in the far northern reaches of Costa Rica near the Nicaraguan border, Refugio Nacional de Vida Silvestre Caño Negro covers 98 square km (38 square mi). Caño Negro has suffered severe deforestation over the years, but most of the Río Frío is still lined with trees, and the park's vast lake is an excellent place to watch such waterfowl as jabiru, anhinga, and the roseate spoonbill, as well as a host of resident exotic animals. In the dry season you can ride horses, but the visit here chiefly entails a wildlife-spotting boat tour. Caño Negro can be reached from the Nuevo Arenal–La Fortuna area, or you can approach via Upala (a bus from here takes 45 minutes). Visiting with a tour company is the best way to see the park. ⊠*180 km/108 mi north of La Fortuna* ⊴*$7* ⊙*Daily 7–4.*

GETTING HERE & AROUND

The highway from La Fortuna to Los Chiles is one of the best-maintained in the northern lowlands. You can catch public buses in San José at Terminal Atlántico Norte twice a day, a trip of about five hours, with many stops. Public buses also operate between La Fortuna and Los Chiles. If they have room, many tour companies (Sunset Tours included) will allow you to ride along with them on their shuttles, for a cost of around $10. If you're not staying way up here, an organized tour of the reserve is the best way to get to and from it.

OUTDOOR ACTIVITIES

Several La Fortuna–area tour companies have trips to Caño Negro. **Sunset Tours** (☎*2479–9800, 866/417–7352 in North America* ⊕*www. sunsettourscr.com*) pioneered tours to the reserve, and runs top-notch, informative daylong or half-day tours, among the best in the country, to Caño Negro for $48. Bring your jungle juice: the mosquitoes are voracious. **Jacamar Naturalist Tours** (☎*2479–9767* ⊕*www.arenaltours. com*) is a well-established tour operator with three-hour boat trips ($50) on the Río Frío in the Caño Negro preserve.

WHERE TO STAY

$$ 🛏**Caño Negro Natural Lodge.** That such an upscale property exists in this remote place might amaze you, but this Italian-designed, family-operated resort on the east side of the reserve is never pretentious. Rooms have high ceilings, colorful drapes and bedspreads, and huge showers; some rooms have bunk beds. There are two- and three-day packages available for anglers and non-anglers alike. The lodge has a variety of meal options; most guests opt for taking all meals here, since there are few other restaurants in town. Horseback riding can be arranged and miniature golf, croquet, and badminton are a few of the on-site diversions. **Pros:** Secluded location, close to reserve. **Con:** Need car to get here. ⊠*Caño Negro village* ☎*2471–1426, 2265–3302 in San José* 🖷*2265–4310* ⊕*www.canonegrolodge.com* ⊲*22 rooms* ♿*In-room: no phone, safe, no TV. In-hotel: restaurant, bar, pool, laundry service* ▤*AE, MC, V* ⊙|*CP.*

$$ 🛏**Hotel de Campo Caño Negro.** All are welcome here, though the lodge is best known for its fishing tours, equipment and boat rental, and nearby lake filled with tarpon and bass. Seven white bungalows of high-quality wood each contain two bright, sparkling rooms with terra-cotta tile floors, and are arranged around the wooded property. The produce from the lodge's citrus orchard ends up on your breakfast plate. In addition to credit cards and cash, the lodge accepts American Express traveler's checks. **Pros:** Secluded location, close to reserve. **Con:** Need car to get here. ⊠*Caño Negro village* ☎*2471–1012* 🖷*2471–1490* ⊕*www.hoteldecampo.com* ⊲*14 rooms* ♿*In-room: no a/c, no phone, no TV. In-hotel: restaurant, bar* ▤*AE, MC, V* ⊙|*BP.*

THE SARAPIQUÍ LOOP

The area immediately north of the San José metro area doesn't leap to mind when discussing ecotourism in Costa Rica, but it should. The Sarapiquí River gave its name to this region at the foot of the Cordillera Central mountain range. To the west is the rain forest of Braulio Carrillo National Park, and to the east are Tortuguero National Park and Barra del Colorado National Wildlife Refuge. These splendid national parks share the region with thousands of acres of farmland, including palm, banana, and pineapple plantations, as well as cattle ranching. Cheap land and rich soil brought a wave of Ticos to this area a half-century ago. Until the construction of Highway 126 in 1957, which connects the area to San José, this was one of the most isolated parts of Costa Rica, with little or no tourism. Government homesteading projects brought many residents, who cleared massive swaths of the rain forest for cattle grazing and agriculture. Now, ironically, old-growth lowland rain forest, montane cloud forest, and wetlands exist only within the borders of the national parks and several adjoining private reserves. A growing selection of nature lodges have set up shop here, and you can enjoy their offerings 60–90 minutes after you leave the capital. (Just try getting to the Osa Peninsula on the Southern Pacific coast in that same time.)

> ## VOLCANO VIEWING ON AN EMPTY STOMACH
>
> No question: the earlier you get to Poás, the better the views you'll be afforded. If that means skipping breakfast, a number of roadside stands on the way up the volcano sell strawberry jam, *cajeta* (a pale fudge), and rather bland corn crackers called *biscochos* to tide you over until you can have a hearty *típico* breakfast in the park visitor center's cafeteria.

VOLCÁN POÁS

37 km/23 mi (45 mins) north of Alajuela, 57 km/35 mi (1 hr) north of San José.

Towering to the north of Alajuela, the verdant mass of the Poás Volcán is covered with a quilt of farms and topped by a dark green shawl of cloud forest. Arenal may be Costa Rica's most famous volcano, but you walk right up to the crater here at Poás. (Authorities are closely monitoring the volcano's activity following several eruptions in March 2006, the first significant activity since 1994. Access is nearly always open at this writing, but closes on those rare occasions of activity deemed "irregular.") A paved road leads all the way from Alajuela to its 8,800-foot summit, winding past coffee fields, patches of forest, pastures, fern farms, and increasingly spectacular views of the Central Valley. Most of the volcano's southern slope is covered with coffee, but the higher altitudes, which are too cold for that crop, hold screened-in fern and flower farms, neat rows of strawberries, and the light green pastures of dairy farms. Only the volcano's upper slopes and summit are still covered with cloud forest, which stretches northward toward Cerro Congo and east toward Volcán Barva. The road divides at Poasito, not far from the summit, where the route to the left leads to the national park, and the one to the right heads toward the intersection of Vara Blanca. At Vara Blanca, you can turn left for the La Paz Waterfall Gardens and Northern Zone, or continue straight to wind your way down the slopes of Volcán Barva to Heredia.

GETTING HERE & AROUND

■TIP➔Avoid taking a public bus to the park, as it can take up to five hours. Taxis from San José are around $80 (and around $40 from Alajuela). From the Pan-American Highway north of Alajuela, follow the signs for Poás. The road is in relatively good condition. A slew of tours from San José take in the volcano and combine the morning excursion with an afternoon at the La Paz Waterfall Gardens, or tours of Café Britt near Heredia or the Doka Estate near Alajuela. (F Chapter 2).

EXPLORING

Fodor's Choice
★
The 57-square-km (22-square-mi) **Poás Volcano National Park** *(Parque Nacional Volcán Poás)* protects epiphyte-laden cloud and elfin (small-tree) forest near the summit as well as a blue-green crater lake and the volcano's massive active crater. The main crater, nearly 1½ km (1 mi) across and 1,000 feet deep, is one of the largest active craters in the world. The sight of this vast, multicolor pit with smoking fumaroles and a gurgling, gray-turquoise sulfurous lake is captivating. All sense of scale is absent here, as the crater is devoid of vegetation. No one is allowed to venture into the crater or walk along its edge.

The peak is frequently shrouded in mist, and many who come here see little beyond the lip of the crater. Be patient and wait awhile, especially if some wind is blowing—the clouds can disappear quickly. ■TIP➔The earlier in the day you go, the better your chance of a clear view. Aim to get there before 10 AM. Also, take periodic breaks from peering over the edge. Step back at least every 10 minutes, so that the sulfur fumes don't overcome you. If you're lucky, you'll see the famous geyser in action, spewing a column of gray mud high into the air. Poás last had a series of major eruptions in 2006; at any sign of danger the park is closed to visitors. It can be very cold and wet up top, so dress accordingly. If you come ill equipped, you can duck under a *sombrilla de pobre* (poor man's umbrella) plant, the leaves of which grow to diameters of 4 to 5 feet.

The park has a paved road that leads from the visitor center to the edge of the active crater, from which two trails head into the forest. The second trail, on the right just before the crater, winds through a thick mesh of shrubs and dwarf trees to the eerie but beautiful Botos Lake (**Laguna Botos**), which occupies an extinct crater. It takes 30 minutes to walk here and back. Note that Volcán Poás is a popular spot and gets quite crowded, especially on Sunday. It's not the place to go to commune with nature in solitude, but it is definitely worth seeing. The large visitor center has a scale model of the park, a display on vulcanology, a modest gift shop, and a cafeteria that serves hot coffee, perfect for those chilly afternoons. ✉*From Alajuela, drive north through town* *and follow signs* ☎*2482–2424, 192 (national parks hotline) in Costa Rica* ✉*$10* ⊙*Daily 8:30–3:30.*

★ Five magnificent waterfalls are the main attractions at **La Paz Waterfall Gardens,** on the eastern edge of Volcán Poás National Park, but they are complemented by the beauty of the surrounding cloud forest, an abundance of hummingbirds and other avian species, and the country's biggest butterfly garden. A concrete trail leads down from the visitor center to the multilevel, screened butterfly observatory and continues to gardens where hummingbird feeders attract swarms of these multicolor creatures. The trail then enters the cloud forest, where it leads to a series of metal stairways that let you descend into a steep gorge to viewing platforms near each of the waterfalls. A free shuttle will transport you from the trail exit back to the main building if you prefer to avoid the hike uphill. Several alternative paths lead from the main trail through the cloud forest and along the river's quieter upper stretch, providing options for hours of exploration—it takes about two hours to hike the entire complex. (Enter by 3:00 to give yourself adequate time.) The visitor center has a gift shop and open-air cafeteria with a great view. The gardens are 20 km (12 mi) northeast of Alajuela, and are a stop on many daylong tours from San José that take in the Poás volcano or area coffee tours. ✛*6 km (4 mi) north of Vara Blanca* ☎*2482–2720, 2225–0643 in San José* 🖷*2225–1082* ⊕*www.waterfallgardens.com* ✉*$32, $41 with lunch, $65 with round-trip transportation from San José* ⊙*Daily 8–5.*

OUTDOOR ACTIVITIES

HORSEBACK RIDING Guided horseback tours with **Poás Volcano Lodge** (✛*6 km (4 mi) east of Chubascos restaurant, on road to Vara Blanca* ☎*2482–2194*) are available in the cloud forest of Finca Legua, a private reserve 5 km (3 mi) north of the lodge. Daily tours ($65), which include lunch, run from 9 AM to 2 PM. Make reservations.

WHERE TO STAY & EAT

$ ✕**Chubascos.** Amid tall pines and colorful flowers on the upper slopes
Fodor'sChoice of Poás Volcano, this popular restaurant has a small menu of tradi-
★ tional Tico dishes and delicious daily specials. Choose from the full selection of casados and platters of *gallos* (homemade tortillas with meat, cheese, or potato fillings). The *refrescos* (fresh fruit drinks) are top-drawer, especially the ones made from locally grown *fresas* (straw-berries) and *moras* (blackberries) blended with milk. ✛*1 km (½ mi) north of Laguna de Fraijanes* ☎*2482–2280* ▤*AE, D, DC, MC, V* ⊙*Closed Tues.*

$ ✕**Jaulares.** Named after the *jaul,* a tree common in the nearby cloud forest, this spacious restaurant specializes in grilled meat, though there are also several fish dishes and *chicharrones* (deep-fried meaty pork rinds). All the cooking is done with wood, which adds to the rustic ambience of terra-cotta floors, bare wooden beams, and sylvan sur-roundings. The house specialty, *lomito Jaulares* (Jaulares tenderloin), is a strip of grilled meat served with *gallo pinto* (rice and beans) and a mild *salsa criollo* (creole sauce). Though primarily a lunch spot, Jaula-res stays open until midnight on weekends for concerts—Latin music

Certificate of Sustainable Tourism

One trip to Costa Rica and you'll swear everything here is eco-lodges, ecotourism, eco-this, eco-that. But "sustainability," the buzzword in Costa Rican tourism these days, also has to do with conserving cultural, as well as natural, resources. The Certification for Sustainable Tourism (CST) program, administered jointly by the Costa Rican Tourism Institute, National Chamber of Tourism, Ministry of the Environment, and University of Costa Rica, recognizes businesses that adhere to those ideals. Those that submit to a rigorous assessment are evaluated on their employment of local people, respect for local culture, contribution to the economic and social well-being of the community, and preservation of natural resources. Businesses that rely heavily on foreign investment and whose earnings are mostly repatriated outside Costa Rica don't make the cut (but probably don't submit to an evaluation in the first place).

Instead of stars, 74 hotels have earned one to five leaves for their efforts. At this writing, Finca Rosa Blanca, north of Heredia in the Central

Valley; Lapa Ríos, at Cabo Matapalo on the South Pacific; Sí Como No, at Manuel Antonio on the Central Pacific; and Hotel Villablanca, near San Ramón in the Northern Plains, are the only four lodgings to hold five leaves. The resorts and hotels that are recognized are not all small "mom-and-pop" places: the Four Seasons on the Papagayo Peninsula and Arenal's Tabacón have been recognized as well. Nor are they only places in the middle of the rain forest: San José's large but unobtrusive Clarion Hotel Amón Plaza is among several city lodgings proudly displaying awards.

Although other countries have their own rating systems for eco-friendly lodgings, many of these suffer from corrupt policies that allow ratings to be bought. The CST is one of the best and most thorough awards programs in the world. In fact, the World Tourism Organization has adopted it as its model, and countries from Mexico to Malawi now employ similar standards. You'll find a list of Costa Rica's CST holders at the program's Spanish-English-French Web site, ⊕ www.turismo-sostenible. co.cr.

---

on Friday night and rock on Saturday night. Four basic cabinas in back are an inexpensive overnight option, though you'll need to reserve them early for concert nights. ✛ 2 km (1 mi) north of Laguna de Fraijanes ☎ 2482–2155 ☰ AE, D, DC, MC, V.

$$$–$$$$ ▦ **Peace Lodge.** These rooms overlooking the misty forest of La Paz
★   Waterfall Gardens seem like something out of the *Lord of the Rings*, with their curved, clay-stucco walls, hardwood floors (note that all but the top floors can be noisy due to creaky stairs), stone fireplaces (gas), and four-poster beds made of varnished logs, complete with mosquito-net canopy. They are proper abodes for elfin kings, especially the spacious, grottolike bathrooms with two showers, a whirlpool tub, tropical gardens, and private waterfall. Most hotels settle for a room with a bath. Peace Lodge gives you a bath with a room. And as if that weren't enough, you can soak in your second whirlpool tub on a porch with a cloud-forest view. Being able to explore the waterfall gardens before they open is another perk; room rates include admission. The

cuisine here is a couple of notches below the accommodations. The entire place is an old favorite of posters to the fodors.com discussion boards. **Pros:** Many activities included in rates, whimsical furnishings. **Cons:** Popular with tour groups, sometimes difficult to find space. ⊹6 *km (4 mi) north of Vara Blanca* ☎482–2720, 225–0643 in San José, 954/727–3997 in North America 🖷2482–2722, 2225–1082 in San José ⊕www.waterfallgardens.com ⟲17 rooms, 1 villa ⌂In-room: no a/c, no phone, refrigerator. In-hotel: restaurant, no elevator ⊟AE, DC, MC, V ⎮O⎮BP.

$–$$ ⊞**Poás Volcano Lodge.** The rustic architecture of this former dairy farm-house, with rough stone walls and pitched beam roof, fits perfectly into the rolling pastures and forests that surround it. The interior mixes Persian rugs with textiles from Latin America, and Guaitil Indian pottery with North American pieces. The oversize sunken fireplace may be the lodge's most alluring feature. All rooms are different, so if possible, look at a few before you decide: one has an exquisite stone bathtub. The less expensive rooms, though not as opulent, have a more dependable supply of hot water. A small dairy farm and garden supply the kitchen with ingredients for the hearty breakfasts. **Pros:** Cozy rooms, close to volcano. **Con:** Rustic rooms. ⊹6 *km (4 mi) east of Chubascos restaurant, on road to Vara Blanca* ⎕Apdo. 5723–1000, San José ☎2482–2194 🖷2482–2513 ⊕www.poasvolcanolodge.com ⟲11 rooms, 9 with bath ⌂In-room: no a/c, no phone, no TV. In-hotel: restaurant, laundry service, public Internet, airport shuttle ⊟AE, DC, MC, V ⎮O⎮BP.

SHOPPING

The **Neotrópica Foundation** sells nature-theme T-shirts, cards, and posters in the national park's visitor center and devotes a portion of the profits to conservation projects.

BRAULIO CARRILLO NATIONAL PARK

30 km/19 mi (45 mins) north of San José.

In a country where deforestation is still rife, hiking through Parque Nacional Braulio Carrillo is a rare opportunity to witness dense, primary tropical cloud forest. The park owes its foundation to the public outcry provoked by the construction of the highway of the same name through this region in the late 1970s—the government bowed to pressure from environmentalists, and somewhat ironically, the park is the most accessible one from the capital thanks to the highway. Covering 443 square km (171 square mi), Braulio Carrillo's extremely diverse terrain ranges from 108 feet to about 9,500 feet above sea level and extends from the central volcanic range down the Caribbean slope to La Selva research station near Puerto Viejo de Sarapiquí. The park protects a series of ecosystems ranging from the cloud forests on the upper slopes to the tropical wet forest of the Magsasay sector; it is home to 6,000 tree species, 500 bird species, and 135 mammal species.

For all its immense size and proximity to the capital, visitor facilities in the park are limited. Your exposure will most likely take place when you pass through on the way to the Caribbean, or when you stay at any of the lodgings that fringe Braulio Carrillo. Penetrating the park's depths is a project only for the truly intrepid:

The **Zurquí ranger station** is to the right of the highway, ½ km (¼ mi) before the Zurquí Tunnel. Here a short trail loops through the cloud forest. Hikes are steep; wear hiking

boots to protect yourself from mud, slippage, and snakes. The main trail through primary forest, 1½ km (1 mi) long, culminates in a *mirador* (lookout point), but alas, the highway mars the view. Monkeys, tapirs, jaguars, kinkajous, sloths, raccoons, margays, and porcupines all live in this forest, and resident birds include the quetzal and the eagle. Orchids, bromeliads, heliconias, fungi, and mushrooms live closer to the floor. Another trail leads into the forest to the right, beginning about 17 km (11 mi) after the tunnel, where it follows the Quebrada González, a stream with a cascade and swimming hole. There are no campsites in this part of the park. The **Carrillo ranger station**, 22 km (14 mi) northeast along the highway from Zurquí, marks the beginning of trails that are less steep. Farther north on this highway, near the park entrance/exit toward Guápiles is the **Quebrada González** ranger station. To the east of Heredia, a road climbs **Barva Volcano** (⇨ *below*) from San Rafael. ☎2290–8202 *Sistemas de Areas de Conservación, 192 (national parks hotline)* ☒$10 ⊙ *Daily 7–4.*

The 9,500-foot summit of **Barva Volcano** is the highest point in Braulio Carrillo National Park. Dormant for 300 years now, Barva is massive: its lower slopes are almost completely planted with coffee fields and hold more than a dozen small towns, nearly all of which are named after saints. On the upper slopes are pastures lined with exotic pines and the occasional native oak or cedar, giving way to the botanical diversity of the cloud forest near the top. The air is usually cool near the summit, which combines with the pines and pastures to evoke the European or North American countryside.

Barva's misty, luxuriant summit is the only part of Braulio Carrillo where camping is allowed, and it's a good place to see the rare resplendent quetzal early in the morning. Because it's somewhat hard to reach, Barva receives a mere fraction of the crowds that flock to the summits of Poás and Irazú. A two- to four-hour hike in from the Barva ranger station takes you to the main crater, which is about 540 feet in diameter. Its almost vertical sides are covered in sombrillas de pobre, a plant that thrives in the highlands, and oak trees laden with epiphytes (nonparasitic plants that grow on other plants). The crater is filled with an otherworldly black lake. Farther down the track into the forest lies a smaller crater lake. ■TIP➔**Bring rain gear, boots, and a warm shirt. Stay on the trail when hiking anywhere in Braulio Carrillo; even experienced hikers who know the area have lost their way up here, and the rugged** terrain makes wandering through the woods very dangerous. In addition, muggings of hikers have been reported in the park. (This is the closest national park to San José and its attendant urban problems.) Go with a ranger if possible.

For access to the volcano, start from Sacramento, north of Heredia. North of Barva de Heredia the road grows narrow and steep. At Sacramento the paved road turns to dirt, growing worse as it nears the Barva ranger station. We recommend a 4WD vehicle, especially during the rainy season. From the ranger station you can take a 4WD vehicle over the extremely rocky road to the park entrance (dry season only), or hike up on foot. The walk through the cloud forest to the crater's two lakes takes two to four hours, but your efforts should be rewarded by great views (as long as you start before 8 AM, to avoid the mist). ✉*Access via the park's Barva ranger station* ☎*2283–5906, 192 (national parks hotline) in Costa Rica* 🖃*$10 (in addition to $6 Braulio Carrillo Park entrance)* ☉*Tues.–Sun. 7–4.*

San Rafael de Heredia, 2 km (1 mi) northeast of Heredia, is a quiet, mildly affluent coffee town with a large church notable for its stained-glass windows and bright interior. The road north from the church winds its way up Barva Volcano to the Hotel La Condesa, ending atop the Monte de la Cruz lookout point.

GETTING HERE & AROUND
From San José, travel northeast on Calle 3, which becomes the Guápiles Highway (Hwy. 32), toward Limón. This highway winds through the park, entering at the main ranger station, Zurquí, and exiting at the Quebrada González ranger station. The Barva station is on the west side of the park, north of Zurquí, and is the easiest to access. From Heredia, drive north to Sacramento on Highway 114. The station is 4 km (2½ mi) northeast of Sacramento on a trail that's accessible on foot or by 4WD (except during heavy rains).

Any bus going to Guapiles, Siquirres, and Puerto Viejo de Sarapiquí can drop you off at the Zurquí ranger station. Buses ($2) depart from San José Monday through Saturday from the Atlántico Norte bus station (for Guápiles) or the Gran Terminal del Caribe (for Siquirres or Puerto Viejo de Sarapiquí) several times daily. A cab from San José costs $40–$50. A number of tour companies offer one-day tours from San José.

OUTDOOR ACTIVITIES
HIKING The upper slopes of **Barva Volcano** have excellent hiking conditions: cool air, vistas, and plentiful birds. The crater lakes topping the volcano can be reached only on foot, and if you haven't got a 4WD vehicle, you'll also have to trek from Sacramento up to the entrance of Braulio Carrillo National Park. The trails are frequently muddy; ask about their condition at the ranger station. The **Sendero Botello** trail, on the east side of the park (entrance near the Quebrada González ranger station off the Guápiles Highway), is a better choice for casual hikers.

WHERE TO STAY

$$–$$$ 📺 **Hotel & Villas La Condesa Monte de la Cruz.** The stone fireplace surrounded by armchairs and a small bar in the La Condesa lobby is one of the many facets of the hotel that suggest a lodge you'd expect to find in a more northern latitude. In the central courtyard, topped by a giant skylight, is one of the hotel's two restaurants. A tropical garden is similarly enclosed in the pool area. Guest rooms are carpeted and tastefully furnished, and each has a picture window. Suites have bedroom lofts, sitting areas, and the hotel's best views. **Pros:** Rustic luxury, easily reached from San José. **Cons:** Isolated, not much within walking distance. ✉ *Next to Castillo Country Club* ⊕ *10 km (6 mi)*

north of San Rafael de Heredia ☎ *2267–6000* 🖷 *2267–6200* ⊕ *www. hotellacondesa.com* 🛏 *70 rooms, 36 suites* ♿ *In-room: no a/c, safe, kitchen (some), refrigerator, Wi-Fi. In-hotel: 2 restaurants, bars, pool, laundry service, public Internet* 🖃 *AE, D, DC, MC, V* 🍽 *BP.*

$ 📺 **Las Ardillas.** Surrounded by old pines on a country road, these unpretentious log cabins are inviting retreats for those looking to lock themselves up in front of a fireplace and tune out the world. The small on-site spa is a good reason to venture from the comfortable, romantic rooms. The restaurant specializes in meats roasted over a wood fire and has a nice selection of Spanish wines. All rooms have modest wood furniture and queen-size beds. **Pro:** Secluded location. **Con:** Rustic rooms. ✉ *Main road, Guacalillo de San José de la Montaña* ✉ *Apdo. 44–309, Barva* ☎ *2260–2172* 🖷 *2266–0211* 🛏 *19 cabins* ♿ *In-room: no a/c, no phone, kitchen, no TV (some). In-hotel: restaurant, bar, spa* 🖃 *MC, V* 🍽 *BP.*

PUERTO VIEJO DE SARAPIQUÍ

6½ km (4 mi) north of La Selva.

In the 19th century, Puerto Viejo de Sarapiquí was a thriving river port and the only link with the coastal lands straight east, now Barra del Colorado National Wildlife Refuge and Tortuguero National Park. Fortunes nose-dived with the construction of the coastal canal from the town of Moín, and today Puerto Viejo has a slightly run-down air. The activities of the Nicaraguan Contras made this a danger zone in the 1980s, but now that the political situation has improved, boats once again ply the old route up the Río Sarapiquí to the Río San Juan on the Nicaraguan frontier, from where you can travel downstream to Barra del Colorado or Tortuguero. A few tour companies have Sarapiquí

River tours with up to Class III rapids in the section between Chilamate and La Virgen, with plenty of wildlife to see. If you prefer to leave the driving to them, many of the lodges operate boat tours on the tamer sections of the river.

GETTING HERE & AROUND

The Carretera Braulio Carrillo (Braulio Carrillo Highway) runs from Calle 3 in San José and passes the Zurquí and Quebrada González sectors of Braulio Carrillo National Park. It branches at Santa Clara, north of the park, with the paved

> ### CAUTION
>
> Don't confuse Puerto Viejo de Sarapiquí with Puerto Viejo de Talamanca on the south Caribbean coast (⇨ *Puerto Viejo de Talamanca, in Chapter 7*). Locals refer to both as simply "Puerto Viejo." Buses for both towns depart from San José's Gran Terminal del Caribe with nothing more than a PUERTO VIEJO sign in the station to designate either.

Highway 4 continuing north to Puerto Viejo de Sarapiquí. Alternatively, an older winding road connects San José with Puerto Viejo de Sarapiquí, passing through Heredia and Vara Blanca. The former route is easier, with less traffic; the latter route is more scenic but heavily trafficked. (If you are at all prone to motion sickness, take the newer road.) The roads are mostly paved, with the usual rained-out dirt and rock sections; road quality depends on the time of year, the length of time since the last visit by a road crew, and/or the amount of rain dumped by the latest tropical storm. Heavy rains sometimes cause landslides that block the highway near the Zurquí Tunnel inside the park, in which case you have to go via Vara Blanca. Check conditions before you set out. Get an early start; fog begins to settle in on both routes by midafternoon. ■TIP➡There are gas stations on the Braulio Carrillo Highway at the turnoff to Puerto Viejo de Sarapiquí, as well as just outside of town. Fill the tank when you get the chance.

Buses travel several times daily via both routes and leave from San José's Gran Terminal del Caribe.

PUERTO VIEJO DE SARAPIQUÍ ESSENTIALS

Bank/ATM **Banco Nacional** (⊠*Across from post office* ☏*2766–6012*). **Banco Popular** (⊠*West corner of soccer field* ☏*2766–6814*).

Medical Clinic **Red Cross** (⊠*West end of town 2766–6901*).

Internet **Internet Sarapiquí** (⊠*Next to Joyería Mary* ☏*2766–6223*).

Post Office **Correos** (⊠*50 m north of soccer field*).

EXPLORING

Bats are not blind, contrary to popular belief, and most have no interest in sucking your blood. These are just a couple of things you learn on the **Bat Tour** at the nonprofit **Tirimbina Rainforest Center.** Also in the "did you know?" category, touching frogs will not give you warts. You'll learn that on Tirimbina's evening Frog Tour. The center encompasses 750 acres of primary forest and 8 km (5 mi) of trails, some of them traversing hanging bridges at canopy level. Reservations are required for all tours. ⊠*La Virgen de Sarapiquí* ✛*17 km (11 mi) southwest of Puerto Viejo* ☎*2761–1579* ⊕*www.tirimbina.org* ≊*$15, $20 guided tour, $17 bat tour, $20 frog tour, $22 bird-watching tour* ☉*Daily 7–5, bat tour: daily 7:30 PM, frog tour: daily 7:30 PM, guided tours: daily 8 AM and 2 PM.*

Costa Rica's indigenous peoples don't get the visibility of those in Guatemala or Mexico, probably because they number only 40,000 out of ★ a population of 4 million. The **Dr. María Eugenia Bozzoli Museum of Indigenous Cultures** (Museo de Culturas Indígenas Doctora María Eugenia Bozzoli), part of the Centro Neotrópico Sarapiquís, provides a well-rounded all-under-one-roof introduction to the subject. Nearly 400 artifacts of the Boruca, Bribri, Cabécar, Guaymí, and Maleku peoples are displayed, including masks, musical instruments, and shamanic healing sticks. Start by watching a 17-minute video introduction, *Man and Nature in Pre-Columbian Costa Rica.* A botanical garden next door cultivates medicinal plants still used by many traditional groups. In 1999 researchers discovered an archaeological site on the grounds that contains pre-Columbian tombs and petroglyphs dating from the 15th century. The site is still under study. ⊠*La Virgen de Sarapiquí* ✛*17 km (11 mi) southwest of Puerto Viejo* ☎*2761–1418* ⊕*www.sarapiquis.org* ≊*$12 (includes guide)* ☉*Daily 9–5.*

The newest of Costa Rica's serpentaria is the aptly named **Snake Garden,** with some 50 species of reptiles on display, including all the poisonous snakes (and most of the nonpoisonous ones) found here in Costa Rica, as well as pythons, anacondas and rattlesnakes from elsewhere in North and South America. You can handle a few specimens (the nonvenomous varieties, at least) upon request and under supervision. ⊠*La Virgen de Sarapiquí, 400 m south of Centro Neotrópico Sarapiquís* ☎*2761–1059* ≊*$6, $5 children under 6* ☉*Daily 9–5.*

A working dairy farm and horse ranch, the **Hacienda Pozo Azul** runs guided tours of the ecologically sound 360-cattle dairy operation. It also has many adventure tours *(*⇨*Outdoor Activities, below).* ⊠*La Virgen de Sarapiquí* ✛*17 km (11 mi) southwest of Puerto Viejo* ☎*2761–1360, 877/810–6903 in North America* ⊕*www.hacienda pozoazul.com* ≊*$10* ☉*By reservation.*

Heliconias abound at the aptly named **Heliconia Island** in the Sarapiquí River. Some 70 species of the flowering plant, a relative of the banana, are among the collections that populate five acres of botanical gardens here. Expect to see ample bird and butterfly life, too. ⊠*La Chaves* ✛*8 km (5 mi) south of Puerto Viejo de Sarapiquí* ☎*8397–3948* 🖷*2766–6247* ⊕*www.heliconiaisland.com* ≊*$7.50* ☉*Daily 9–5.*

OUTDOOR ACTIVITIES

Hacienda Pozo Azul (⊠*La Virgen de Sarapiquí* ✛*17 km (11 mi) southwest of Puerto Viejo* ☎*2761–1360, 877/810–6903 in North America* ⊕*www.haciendapozoazul.com*) is a dairy farm and ranch with biking, horseback riding, rafting, canopy tours, float tours, and rappelling excursions that allow you to combine several activities in a day. **Hotel Gavilán Río Sarapiquí** (☎*2766–6743* ⊕*www.gavilanlodge.com*) runs wildlife- and bird-watching tours from its site near Puerto Viejo de Sarapiquí up to the San Juan River. Passports are required for the trip, since the San Juan lies entirely within Nicaragua.

CANOPY TOUR The canopy tour ($45) at **Hacienda Pozo Azul** (⇨ *above)* has twelve zip lines, ranging in height from 60–90 feet.

HORSEBACK RIDING Dairy farm **Hacienda Pozo Azul** (⇨ *above)* is also a horse ranch and has riding excursions for all experience levels through the region around La Virgen. A two-hour tour is $35; a half-day is $45. Check out the multiday tours, too, if you're an experienced rider.

MOUNTAIN BIKING **Aventuras de Sarapiquí** (☎2766–6768 ⊕*www.sarapiqui.com)* has made-to-order half-day and multiday biking trips for casual and serious riders. **Costa Rica Biking Adventure** (☎2235–4982 *in San José* ⊕*www.bikingincostarica.com)* runs one-day mountain-biking tours of the area. **Hacienda Pozo Azul** (⇨ *above)* has half-day, full-day, and two-day rough-and-tumble back-roads bike tours ($45–$75).

RAFTING The Virgen del Socorro area is one of the most popular "put-in points" for white-water rafters, and offers both Class II and III rapids. Trips leaving from the Chilamate put-in are more tranquil, with mostly Class I rapids. The put-in point depends on the weather and season.

Several operators lead tours on the Sarapiquí River. Old standby **Costa Rica Expeditions** (☎2222–0333 📠2257–1665 ⊕*www.costaricaexpeditions.com)* offers full-day trips on the Sarapiquí from San José. La Fortuna–based **Desafío** (☎2479–9464 ⊕*www.desafiocostarica.com)* brings you in from the west to the Sarapiquí River, but the distance is no longer than making the trip from San José. **Ríos Tropicales** (☎2233–6455 ⊕*www.riostropicales.com)* takes in the Sarapiquí on day excursions from San José.

RAPPELLING **Hacienda Pozo Azul** (⇨ *above)* guides you on a 90-foot river canyon descent ($28).

WHERE TO STAY

$$–$$$ ★ **Selva Verde Lodge.** Built on stilts over the Río Sarapiquí, this expansive complex stands on the edge of a 2-square-km (1-square-mi) private reserve of tropical rain forest and caters primarily to natural-history tours. The buildings have wide verandas strung with hammocks, and the rooms come with polished wood paneling and mosquito blinds. Activities include guided walks, boat trips, canoeing, rafting, and mountain biking. Room prices include a bird-watching tour. Reserve a few weeks ahead, especially in high season; the place is very popular with tour groups. **Pro:** Ecology-minded staff. **Cons:** Popular with tour groups, sometimes difficult to find space. ✛*7 km (4 mi) west of Puerto Viejo de Sarapiquí* ⌂*Apdo. 55, Chilamate* ☎2766–6800, 800/451–7111 *in North America* 📠2766–6011 ⊕*www.selvaverde.com* ⏏*40 rooms, 5 bungalows* ⌂*In-room: no a/c (some), no phone, no TV. In-hotel: restaurant, bar, pool, no elevator, laundry service* ▭*AE, MC, V* ⏁⏁*EP, FAP.*

$$ ☺ **Centro Neotrópico Sarapiquís.** Overlooking the Río Sarapiquí, the CNS is an environmental educational center, museum, garden, and hotel all

rolled into one. Three indigenous-inspired circular *palenque* (indigenous huts) buildings with palm-thatch roofs house the ample-size rooms. All come with a tile floor, pre-Columbian-style decor, wrought-iron fixtures, and a private terrace. There's an extra cost to visit the center's numerous attractions. **Pros:** Good value, many activities, whimsical furnishings. **Con:** No a/c. ⊠*La Virgen de Sarapiquí* ⊠*17 km (11 mi) southwest of Puerto Viejo* ☎*2761–1004* 📠*2761–1415* ⊕*www. sarapiquis.org* 🛏*47 rooms* ⚿*In-room: no a/c, no phone (some), no TV. In-hotel: restaurant, bar, laundry service, public Internet* ☱*AE, D, DC, MC, V* ⍾*EP.*

¢–$ 🏨**Hotel Gavilán Río Sarapiquí.** Beautiful gardens run down to the river, and colorful tanagers and three types of toucan feast in the citrus trees. The two-story lodge has comfortable rooms with white walls, terra-cotta floors, and decorative crafts. The food, Costa Rican *comida típica* (typical fare), has earned its good reputation. Prime activities are horseback jungle treks and boat trips up the Río Sarapiquí. **Pros:** Lovely gardens, activities. **Con:** Rustic rooms. ⊠*700 m north of Comando Atlántico (naval command)* ✉*Apdo. 445–2010, San José* ☎*2766–6743, 2234–9507 in San José* 📠*2253–6556* ⊕*www.gavilanlodge.com* 🛏*17 rooms* ⚿*In-room: no a/c, no phone, no TV. In-hotel: restaurant* ☱*AE, D, DC, MC, V* ⍾*BP.*

¢ 🏨**Posada Andrea Cristina.** The Martinez family owns and operates this friendly and comfortable B&B. High-ceiling rooms have private bathrooms and hot water. Two A-frame bungalows share a (cold-water-only) bathroom. All bungalows and rooms have private gardens with hammocks. **Pros:** Good value, secluded location, attentive owners. **Con:** Rustic rooms. ✛*½ km (¼ mi) west of town, La Guaria* ☎📠*2766–6265* ⊕*www.andreacristina.com* 🛏*7 rooms, 2 bungalows with shared bath* ⚿*In-room: no a/c* ☱*No credit cards* ⍾*BP.*

LA SELVA BIOLOGICAL STATION

⏱ *6 km (3½ mi) south of Puerto Viejo de Sarapiquí, 79 km/49 mi (2–4 hrs) northeast of San José.*

At the confluence of the Puerto Viejo and Sarapiquí rivers, La Selva packs about 420 bird species, 460 tree species, and 500 butterfly species into just 15 square km (6 square mi). Spottings might include the spider monkey, poison dart frog, agouti, collared peccary, and dozens of other rare creatures. ■TIP➜**If you want to see wildlife without having to rough it, skip Rara Avis and come here.** Extensive, well-marked trails and swing bridges, many of which are wheelchair accessible, connect habitats as varied as tropical wet forest, swamps, creeks, rivers, secondary regenerating forest, and pasture. The site is a project of the Organization for Tropical Studies, a research consortium of 63 U.S., Australian, and Latin American universities, and is one of three biological stations OTS operates in Costa Rica. To see the place, take an informative three-hour morning or afternoon nature walk with one of La Selva's bilingual guides, who are some of the country's best. Walks start every day at 8 AM and 1:30 PM. You can add a noontime lunch to your walk for $12; schedule it in advance. For a completely different view of the forest, set off on a guided dawn two-hour walk at 5:45 AM, or the night tour at 7 PM. If you get a group of at least five together you can enroll in the Saturday-morning Bird-watching 101 course or one of the nature photo workshops, which can be arranged anytime—either is $40 per person. Or get a group of at least six together and tag along with one of the resident research scientists for a half-day. Young children won't feel left out either, with a very basic nature-identification course geared to them. Even with all the offerings, La Selva can custom-design excursions to suit your own special interests, too. Advance reservations are required for the dawn and night walks as well as for any of the courses. *6 km (3½ mi) south of Puerto Viejo de Sarapiquí* ☜*OTS, Apdo. 676–2050, San Pedro* ☎*2766–6565, 2524–0607 in San José, 919/684–5774 in North America* 🖷*2766–6535, 2524–0604 in San José* ⊕*www.ots.ac.cr* ✉*Nature walk $34, morning and afternoon walks $40, dawn or night walk $40* ☉ *Walks: daily at 8 AM and 1:30 PM.*

GETTING HERE & AROUND
To get here, drive south from Puerto Viejo, and look for signs on the west side of the road. For those without wheels, La Selva is a $4 taxi ride from Puerto Viejo de Sarapiquí.

WHERE TO STAY
$$$ 🏨 **La Selva.** Other lodges provide more comfort for the money, but none can match La Selva's tropical nature experience. The dorm-style rooms have large bunk beds, tile floors, and lots of screened windows. Newer family-style cabins can sleep up to four people and offer a greater level of comfort and privacy. The restaurant, something like a school cafeteria, serves decent food but has a very limited schedule (reserve ahead). It's a good idea to pay the full-board fee, which includes a guided nature walk and three meals a day with your room rate, since there's nowhere else to eat. Priority is given to researchers, so advance reservations are essential. **Pros:** Many activities, ecology-minded staff. **Cons:** Rustic rooms, no a/c. ⊕ *6 km (3½ mi) south of Puerto Viejo de Sarapiquí* ☜*OTS, Apdo. 676–2050, San Pedro* ☎*2766–6565, 2524–0607 in San José* 🖷*2524–0604* ⊕*www.ots.ac.cr* ☞*60 bunk beds share 12 baths, 18 cabins* ⚒*In-room: no a/c, no phone, no TV. In-hotel: restaurant, laundry facilities* ▭*AE, MC, V* ☺|*FAP.*

NORTHERN PLAINS ESSENTIALS

TRANSPORTATION

BY AIR

ARRIVING &   NatureAir and SANSA have daily flights from their respective airports
DEPARTING   in San José to La Fortuna (FTN). Most travelers to this region fly into San José's Juan Santamaría Airport or Liberia's Daniel Oduber Airport. Monteverde and Arenal are equidistant from both. *For more information, see By Air in Costa Rica Essentials.*

BY BUS

ARRIVING & DEPARTING *For more information about bus travel between the Northern Plains and San José, see By Bus in Costa Rica Essentials.*

GETTING AROUND Buses in this region are typically large, clean, and fairly comfortable, but often crowded Friday through Sunday. Don't expect air-conditioning. Service tends toward the agonizingly slow: even supposedly express buses marked *directo* (direct) often make numerous stops.

BY CAR

ARRIVING & DEPARTING Road access to the northwest is by way of the paved two-lane Pan-American Highway (Carretera Interamericana, or CA1), which starts from the west end of Paseo Colón in San José and runs northwest to Peñas Blancas at the Nicaraguan border. Turn north at Naranjo or San Ramón for La Fortuna; at Lagarto for Monteverde; and at Cañas for Tilarán. Calle 3 heading north from downtown San José becomes the Braulio Carrillo Highway and provides the best access to Puerto Viejo de Sarapiquí and environs.

GETTING AROUND This region manages to mix some of the country's smoothest highways with some of its most horrendous roads. (The road to Monteverde is legendary in the latter regard, but the final destination makes it worth the trip.) Four-wheel-drive vehicles are best on the frequently potholed roads. If you don't want to pay for 4WD, at least rent a car with high clearance. (Many rental agencies insist you take a 4WD vehicle if you mention Monteverde as part of your itinerary.) You'll encounter frequent one-lane bridges; if the triangular CEDA EL PASO faces you, yield to oncoming traffic.

It is possible to rent a car in La Fortuna or Monteverde, but for a far better selection, most visitors pick up their rental vehicles in San José or Liberia.

Major Rental Agencies Alamo (✉ *100 m west of church, La Fortuna* ☎ *2479–9090* ⊕ *www.alamocostarica.com*). **Hertz** (✉ *Cerro Plano, Monteverde* ☎ *2645–6555* ⊕ *www.hertz.com*).

Local Rental Agencies Mapache Rentacar (✉ *800 m west of church, La Fortuna* ☎ *2479–0010* ⊕ *www.mapache.com*). **Poás Rentacar** (✉ *25 m south of church, La Fortuna* ☎ *2479–8027* ⊕ *www.poasrentacar.com*).

BY SHUTTLE VAN

ARRIVING & DEPARTING If you prefer a speedier, more private form of travel, consider taking a shuttle. Gray Line has daily service between San José, La Fortuna and Arenal ($27), and Monteverde ($38). Comfortable air-conditioned vans leave various San José hotels early in the morning and return mid-afternoon. Purchase tickets at least a day in advance. Service is also provided from Arenal and Monteverde to several Pacific-coast beaches. Interbus also connects San José with La Fortuna, Ciudad Quesada, San Ramón, and Monteverde (all $29) daily, with connections from here to a few of the North Pacific beaches. Apart from their schedules, there's little difference between Gray Line and Interbus.

Shuttle Van Services Gray Line Tourist Bus (☎ *2220–2126* ⊕ *www.graylinecostarica.com*). **Interbus** (☎ *2283–5573* ⊕ *www.interbusonline.com*).

CONTACTS & RESOURCES

Banks and emergency contacts follow each town listed in the chapter.

BANKS & EXCHANGE SERVICES

Most larger hotels, tour companies, and retailers accept credit and debit cards. Visa and MasterCard predominate; a few retailers accept American Express, with some businesses also taking Diners Club and Discover. Changing U.S. dollars or traveler's checks is possible at the state Banco Nacional branches scattered throughout the region, but lines are long. A few branches of private banks—BAC San José, HSBC, and Scotiabank—have set up shop in this region; opt for them and their quicker service if you see one. Most hotels and larger businesses are prepared to accept U.S. dollars (although may give you change in colones); smaller businesses usually will not.

You'll find a small but growing number of *cajeros automáticos* (ATMs) out here; Banco Nacional offices in La Fortuna and Santa Elena, as well as HSBC in Ciudad Quesada and CooTilarán in Tilarán, are affiliated with the ATH (A Toda Hora) network, and accept Cirrus- and Plus-linked cards. BAC San José branches in Ciudad Quesada and La Fortuna have ATMs affiliated with the Red Total network—look for the red sign with the lion's head—and accept Cirrus- and Plus-linked cards, with some machines taking American Express and Diner's Club, too.

INTERNET

Internet cafés are easy to find in most areas of the Northern Plains, with hourly rates averaging around $1.50–$4. Some still have dial-up service, but broadband connections are becoming more common up here. At upscale hotels or resorts, rates can run as high as $6–$7 per hour.

North Pacific

Conchal Beach

WORD OF MOUTH

"Having visited the northwest (province of Guanacaste) during both rainy and dry seasons, we really prefer the rainy season when everything is greener. But there are some colors that show up in some of the trees during the dry season that you don't see otherwise. Those gorgeous yellow flowering trees. . .In the national park of that area, Rincon de la Vieja, the green season definitely enhances the beauty, but supposedly you can see more wildlife in the trees when there aren't so many leaves!"

—shillmac

WELCOME TO NORTH PACIFIC

TOP REASONS TO GO

★ **Beaches:** White sand; black sand; beaches for swimming, partying, surfing, and sunbathing—you can't beat Guanacaste's beaches for sheer variety.

★ **Endangered nature:** Guanacaste's national parks protect some of Central America's last patches of tropical dry forest, an ecosystem where you might spot magpie jays, or howler monkeys in the branches of a gumbo-limbo tree.

★ **Surfing:** The waves are usually excellent at more than a dozen North Pacific beaches, including Playa Avellanas, Playa Grande, Playa Negra, and remote Playa Naranjo, in Santa Rosa National Park, guarded by Witch's Rock.

★ **Big wind:** From December to May, the trade winds whip across northern Guanacaste with a velocity and consistency that makes the Bahía Salinas a world-class sailboarding and kitesurfing destination.

★ **Scuba diving:** Forget the pretty tropical fish. Sharks, rays, sea turtles, and moray eels are the large-scale attractions for divers on the Guanacaste coast.

1 Far Northern Guanacaste. Dry, hot Far Northern Guanacaste is traditionally ranching country, but it does include the impressive wildernesses of Santa Rosa and Rincón de la Vieja national parks, the latter of which holds one of Costa Rica's five active volcanoes. Farther to the north is Bahía Salinas, second only to Lake Arenal for wind- and kitesurfing.

2 The Nicoya Coast. The number and variety of beaches along the Nicoya Coast make it a top tourist destination. Each beach has its specialty, be it surfing, fishing, diving, or just plain relaxing. Hotels and restaurants are in generous supply.

3 The Tempisque River Basin. National parks Palo Verde and Barra Honda are the main attractions in the Tempisque River Basin. The former is a prime bird-watching park; the latter has caves and tropical forest ripe for exploration.

Ostional Wildlife Refuge

CRI

Guanacaste

La Cruz

4

Bahía Salinas

Bahía Junquillal

Santa Rosa National Park

1

Hacienda Santa Rosa

Puerto Culebra

Papagayo Peninsula

Playa Hermosa

21

Filadel

Playa Flamingo

Belén

Playa Brasilíto

155

Playa Grande

Huacas

Tamarindo

Playa Langosta

Villa Real

Playa Avellanas

Santa Cruz

Playa Junquillal

Lagarto

160

Nosa

Playa Ostional

Garza

Pacific Coast

Nicoya Coast

Pacific Ocean

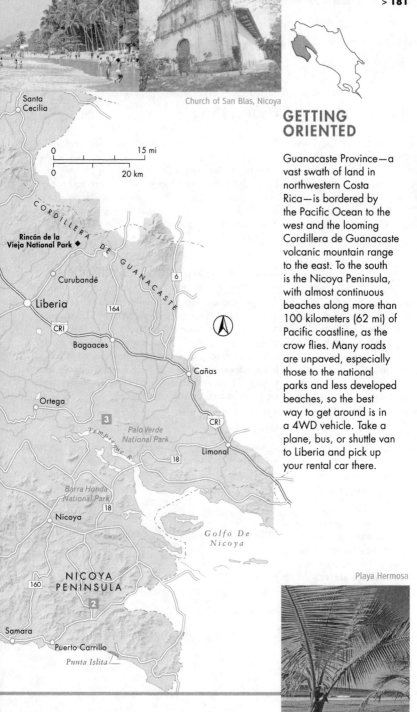

Church of San Blas, Nicoya

GETTING ORIENTED

Guanacaste Province—a vast swath of land in northwestern Costa Rica—is bordered by the Pacific Ocean to the west and the looming Cordillera de Guanacaste volcanic mountain range to the east. To the south is the Nicoya Peninsula, with almost continuous beaches along more than 100 kilometers (62 mi) of Pacific coastline, as the crow flies. Many roads are unpaved, especially those to the national parks and less developed beaches, so the best way to get around is in a 4WD vehicle. Take a plane, bus, or shuttle van to Liberia and pick up your rental car there.

4

Santa Cecilia

0   15 mi

0   20 km

C O R D I L L E R A

Rincón de la Vieja National Park ◆

D E   G U A N A C A S T E

Curubandé

Liberia

164

CR1

Bagaaces

6

Cañas

Ortega

3

Palo Verde National Park

Tempisque R.

CR1

Limonal

18

Barra Honda National Park

18

Nicoya

Golfo De Nicoya

NICOYA PENINSULA

160

2

Samara

Puerto Carrillo

Punta Islita

Playa Hermosa

NORTH PACIFIC PLANNER

When to Go

Guanacaste is the driest region of the country, with only 65 inches of average annual rainfall, and the hottest, with average temperatures around 30°C–35°C (86°F–95°F). The best time to visit is the shoulder season (mid-November–January), when the landscape is green, the evening air is cool, and hotels and restaurants energetically prepare for the tourist influx. Rainy-season travel (May–September) means lower prices, fewer crowds, and a lush green landscape—though most afternoons bring downpours. From February to March skies are clear, but the heat is intense and the landscape is brown and parched. Fishing and scuba diving are their best during this period. The beaches and trails can get packed during the dry months, especially mid-December to February, when school is out in Costa Rica.

■TIP→ Always apply bug repellent if you're going to be on the beach around sunset, when no-see-ums feast on unprotected ankles.

Getting There

The Pan-American Highway heads northwest from San José to Liberia, then due north to the Nicaraguan border. It's poorly maintained, with many potholes and hills. Trucks and buses create heavy traffic. The airport outside Liberia provides easy access to the region. Fly directly from the United States or Canada, or hop on a domestic flight from San José and save yourself four to five hours of difficult driving.

Ground Transportation from Liberia

At Daniel Oduber Airport in Liberia, official red taxis and hotel vans wait to meet each flight. When you make your hotel reservation for the first night, ask if your hotel can provide a cab or shuttle. If not, ask how much you should expect to pay for ground transportation from the airport, because fares vary widely. In Guanacaste it's usually safe to take *pirata* (pirate, or unofficial) taxis, but always negotiate the price before getting into the cab.

What to Do

ACTIVITY	WHERE TO DO IT
Fishing	Playa Flamingo, Tamarindo, Puerto Carrillo, Playas del Coco
Diving	Playa Hermosa, Playa Flamingo, Playa Potrero, Playas del Coco, Ocotal
Surfing	Tamarindo, Playa Langosta, Playa Grande, Playa Avellanas, Playa Negra, Santa Rosa National Park, Playa Guiones
Volcanoes	Rincón de la Vieja National Park
Turtle-watching	Playa Grande, Playa Ostional
Wildlife-watching	Palo Verde National Park, Rincón de la Vieja National Park, Santa Rosa National Park, Barra Honda National Park

How Much Time?

We recommend visiting for about 10 days to get a taste of the North Pacific. Ideally, schedule at least a week to get into the rhythm of beach life. Logistically, you also need time for slow travel over bumpy roads. A beach with lots of restaurants and nightlife can keep you entertained for a week or more, whereas a more solitary beach might merit only a couple of days. Outdoorsy types should consider spending a few days around Rincón de la Vieja National Park, hiking, bird-watching, horseback riding, and doing canopy tours.

Great Combinations

You can easily stop at Monteverde (⇨Chapter 3) en route to the coast from San José. From here, shuttle-van connections to the beach are excellent. Most North Pacific beaches are just a few hours' drive from the Arenal Volcano area (⇨Chapter 3), so the region can be combined with the Northern Plains. Macaw Air flies directly from Tamarindo or Liberia to Puerto Jiménez, where you can spend a few days in a jungle lodge off the grid in the Osa Peninsula, a contrast to developed Nicoya beaches.

Recommended Tour Operators

Swiss Travel Service (☎2282–4898 ⊕www.swisstravelcr. com) specializes in Guanacaste. Despite the name, it's operated by Costa Ricans with lots of local experience. Custom-design a guided private or small-group tour.

The excellent **Horizontes** (☎2222–2022 ⊕www.horizontes.com) has independent, private tours with your own guide/driver and small-group tours.

Choosing a Place to Stay

Super-expensive resorts like the Four Seasons are well balanced with budget hotels that charge less than $50 per night. As in all of Costa Rica, the places we most recommend are the small owner-operated hotels and bed-and-breakfasts that blend in with unspoiled nature and offer one-on-one attention from the staff and owners.

4

WHAT IT COSTS IN DOLLARS				
¢	$	$$	$$$	$$$$
Restaurants				
under $5	$5–$10	$10–$15	$15–$25	over $25
Hotels				
under $50	$50–$75	$75–$150	$150–$250	over $250

Restaurant prices are per person for a main course at dinner. Hotel prices are for two people in a standard double room in high season, excluding taxes (16.4%).

FAR NORTHERN GUANACASTE

Updated
by David
Dudenhoefer

The mountains, plains, and coastline north of Liberia up to the border of Nicaragua make up Far Northern Guanacaste. Liberia, the capital of Guanacaste province, is the closest town to Costa Rica's second-largest airport. You'll most likely pass through it on your way to the beaches southwest of the city or to the nearby national parks of Guanacaste, Santa Rosa, or Rincón de la Vieja. This last park is home to Volcán Rincón de la Vieja, an active volcano that last erupted in 1991.

Northwest of Rincón de la Vieja, on the coast, Santa Rosa National Park is a former cattle ranch where Costa Ricans defeated the invading mercenary army of American William Walker in 1856. Together with adjacent Guanacaste National Park, Santa Rosa protects the country's largest remnant of tropical dry forest, as well as an important nesting beach for olive ridley sea turtles, which lay their eggs in the sand between July and November. Closer still to the Nicaraguan border is the town of La Cruz, overlooking the lovely Golfo de Santa Elena, and the remote beaches and windswept hotels of Bahía Salinas.

RINCÓN DE LA VIEJA NATIONAL PARK

★ *25 km (15 mi) northeast of Liberia.*

Parque Nacional Rincón de la Vieja is Costa Rica's mini-Yellowstone, with volcanic hot springs and boiling, bubbling mud ponds. The park protects more than 177 square km (54 square mi) of the volcano's upper slopes, which are covered with forest. Often enveloped in clouds, the volcano dominates the scenery to the east of the Pan-American Highway. It has two peaks: Santa María (1,916 m [6,284 ft]) and the barren Rincón de la Vieja (1,806 m [5,924 ft]). The latter has an active crater and fumaroles on its lower slope that constantly let off steam, making an eruption unlikely anytime soon. The wildlife here is diverse: more than 250 species of birds, including long-tailed manakins and blue-crowned motmots; plus mammals such as white-tailed deer, coyotes, howler and capuchin monkeys, and armadillos. The Las Pailas park entrance is the most common place to enter the park because it has the most accessible trails and there are several hotels along the road leading up to it. ■TIP→If you want to explore the slopes of the volcano, go with a guide—the abundant hot springs and geysers have given unsuspecting visitors some very nasty burns. In addition, the upper slopes often receive fierce and potentially dangerous winds—before ascending, check at either ranger station for conditions. The park does not have guides; we recommend the guides at Hacienda Guachipelín and Rincón de la Vieja Volcano Mountain Lodge (⇨*below*). You must sign in and pay at the ranger station. Many of the attractions people visit in Rincón de la Vieja are accessible without actually entering the park, since the ranches that border it also hold significant forest and geothermal sites. ☎2661–8139 ✉$10 ☉*Tues.–Sun. 7–5, last entry at 3* PM.

GETTING HERE & AROUND

There are two park entrances on the volcano's southern slope: the less traveled one at Hacienda Santa María on the road leading northeast from Liberia (1 hour); and at Las Pailas, past Curubandé off the Pan-American Highway. To get to the Las Pailas entrance from Liberia, take the first entrance road 5 km (3 mi) northwest of Liberia off the Pan-American Highway. The turnoff is easy to miss—follow signs for Hacienda Guachipelín or the town of Curubandé. It's a rough 23-km (14-mi) dirt road, and you have to pay a small toll. The Santa María entrance is 25 km (15 mi) northeast of Liberia along the Colonia Blanca route, which follows the course of the Río Liberia. The turnoff from the Pan-American Highway to the hotels on the western slope of the volcano is 12 km (7 mi) northwest of Liberia, turning right at the road signed for Cañas Dulces. A 4WD vehicle is recommended, though not essential, for all these slow and bone-rattling rides.

OUTDOOR ACTIVITIES

Borinquen Mountain Resort & Spa (✛ *13 km [8 mi] northwest of Liberia on the Pan-American Hwy., then 29 km [18 mi] north on the dirt road toward Cañas Dulces* ☎2690–1900) offers a day package ($90) that begins with a horseback ride and a 90-minute canopy tour, followed by lunch and free time in the hotel's hot springs and natural steam bath. **Buena Vista Lodge & Adventure Center**(✉ *Western slope of volcano ✛10 km [6 mi] north of Cañas Dulces* ☎2690–1414 📠2661–8156 ⊕*www.buenavistalodgecr.com*), located west of the park, lies on a large ranch contiguous with the park where visitors enjoy horseback riding, waterfall hikes, a canopy tour, hanging bridges, a 1,600-foot (long, not steep) waterslide through the forest, and hot springs. Tours are $20 to $35 per person; a combo ticket is $80, including lunch. **Hacienda Guachipelín Adventure Center** (✉ *Road to Rincón de la Vieja National Park* ☎2666–8075 or 2442–2818 ⊕*www.guachipelin.com*) has horseback riding, river tubing, hot springs and mud baths, and guided waterfall and volcano hikes. The popular canyon tour includes rock climbing, rappelling, zip lines, suspension bridges, and a Tarzan swing. A one-day, all-you-can-do adventure pass is $80, including lunch. Tours are designed for ages 8 to 80. Playa Hermosa–based Maynor Lara Bustos of **Tours Your Way** (☎2820–1829 ⊕*www.tours-your-way.com*) guides tours to Rincón de la Vieja or Palo Verde for $80, including transportation, entrance fees, lunch, and snacks.

CANOPY TOURS
The zip-line canopy tour ($35) with **Buena Vista Lodge & Adventure Center**(⇨*above*) has cables that are up to 90 feet off the ground and up to 450 feet long ($35). **Rincón de la Vieja Canopy** (✉*Rincón de la Vieja Volcano Mountain Lodge* ☎2200–0238) runs four-hour horseback and canopy tours ($45), which include a 16-platform zip line, a ride to the Los Azufrales sulfur springs, or a forest hike to a waterfall with a box lunch.

HIKING
Nearly all the lodges and outfitters in the area have guided hikes through the park to the fumaroles, hot springs, waterfalls, summit, or the edge of the active crater.

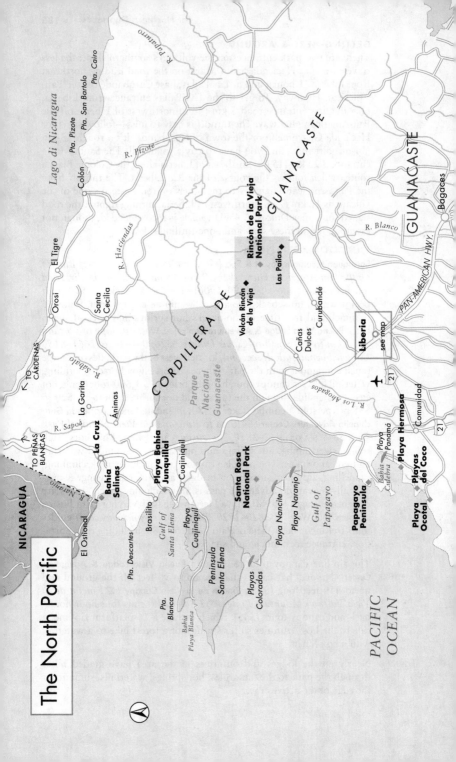

The North Pacific

More Texan than Tropical

Guanacaste, Costa Rica's "Wild West," looks different from the rest of Costa Rica. It was originally covered in dry tropical forests, but beginning in early colonial times, and then picking up speed in the 1950s (when cattle ranching became big business), the dry forest was cleared to create vast cattle ranges. Harder-to-access forests covering the volcanic slopes survived as well. The resulting flat, sunbaked landscape makes the inland parts of the province look a little like the American Southwest. Cowboy culture still takes center stage during seasonal fiestas and a few rodeos. But these days more and more *sabaneros* (cowboys) are trading in their horses for pickup trucks.

If you're doing a self-guided hike, stop for trail maps and hiking information at the park stations at both entrance gates. The 8-km (5-mi) **trail to the summit** heads up into the forest from the Las Pailas park entrance, then emerges onto a windy, exposed shale slope that's slippery and hard going, and has poor visibility owing to clouds and mist. It's a trip for serious hikers, best done in dry season with preparation for cold weather at the top. A less strenuous option is the fascinating 3-km (2-mi) **loop through the park,** which takes about two hours to complete, starting at the Las Pailas entrance. Along the well-marked trail you'll see fumaroles exuding steam, a *volcáncito* (baby volcano), and Las Pailas, the boiling mud fields named after pots used for boiling down sugarcane. If you tread softly in the nearby forest, you may spot animals such as howler, capuchin, and spider monkeys, as well as raccoonlike coatis looking for handouts. ■TIP➔**Remember the cardinal rule of wildlife encounters: don't feed the animals.** Another popular hike is a four-hour, 10-km (6-mi) **La Cangreja Waterfall loop,** passing through beautiful primary forests and windswept savannahs. The *catarata* (waterfall) has a cool swimming hole below; the surrounding rocks have pockets of hot springs.

HORSEBACK
RIDING
Borinquen Mountain Resort & Spa *(⇨above)* offers horseback tours ($80) on a 494-acre ranch that holds patches of forest and ridges with views of nearby Rincón de la Vieja that can be combined with a hike to waterfalls, or a canopy tour. The tour includes lunch and use of hot springs, and ranges in price from $80 to $100.

Buena Vista Mountain Lodge & Adventure Center *(⇨above)* has horseback trips to hot springs ($25) and to Borinquen Waterfall ($35). If not everyone in your party is a horse lover, tractor transport ($35) is available to the hot springs as well. **Rincón de la Vieja Volcano Mountain Lodge** (☎2200–0238) has guides for hiking or horseback riding near the park. **Hacienda Guachipélin** (✉ *Road to Rincón de la Vieja National Park* ☎2442–2818 ⊕ *www.guachipelin.com*) is a working ranch with 120 horses and miles of trails to three waterfalls, tropical dry forest, and hot springs. Fees range from $20 for an hour to $60 for a 10-hour tour.

WHERE TO STAY

$$$–$$$$ 🏨**Borinquen Mountain Resort & Spa.** The spacious villas on this 12,000-acre ranch overlook lawns shaded by tropical trees on the volcano's windy west slope. They are the nicest accommodations in the area, with sloping wooden ceilings, large porches, and plenty of amenities, but they are by far the most expensive as well. Elegant deluxe bungalows have king-size canopy beds, whereas the junior suites have amazing views. Though 90 minutes from the park entrance, the ranch holds most of the same natural attractions, including three waterfalls and patches of forest that hold monkeys, parrots, deer, and other wildlife. The spa has volcanic mud baths, hot springs, and a wooden sauna heated by steam from a fumarole, all included in room rates. Activities include hiking, horseback riding, ATV trips, a canopy tour, and a trip to the park in a Land Rover followed by a hike. The rooms are separated from the restaurant and spa by steep climbs, but the staff can transport you in a golf cart. **Pros:** Attractive, peaceful, well-equipped bungalows, lovely grounds and spa, lots of outdoor activities. **Cons:** Far from park entrance, overpriced, restaurant a notch below accommodations. ✛*13 km (8 mi) northwest of Liberia on Pan-American Hwy., then 29 km (18 mi) north on the dirt road toward Cañas Dulces* ☎*2690–1900* 📠*2690–1903* ⊕*www.borinquenresort.com* 🛏*22 villas, 17 bungalows* ⚬*In-room: refrigerator. In-hotel: restaurant, bar, pool, spa, no elevator, laundry service, public Internet* ▭*AE, DC, MC, V* ⦿*BP.*

$ 🏨**Hacienda Guachipelín.** Day-trippers come here, perhaps one of the best
★ values in the Rincón area, for hair-raising adventure tours (⇨*Outdoor Activities, above*), but this 3,706-acre working ranch is also famous for its horses—all 120 of them—and its nature trails leading to several waterfalls, hot springs, and mud baths. Rugged ranch hands swaggering around give the place a real cowboy flavor. Rooms are large and pleasantly furnished, with windows front and back to let in cool mountain air. The newer rooms, numbers 32 and up, are more colorful and larger, though a bit of a walk from the restaurant. Avoid Rooms 24–31, right beside the corral, unless you enjoy the aroma of horses; try to get one between 32 and 39, which have volcano views from the front terrace. Hearty buffet meals are served in the open-air restaurant, which has valley views. Dairy and beef products come fresh from the hacienda's own herd; vegetarians may have trouble finding meat-free dishes here. Large groups often stay here, but you can always find a quiet trail on the vast, partially forested property. The hotel's spa offers an array of treatments, from mud wraps to massages. **Pros:** Near park entrance, lots of activities, good value. **Con:** Caters to lots of large groups and day visitors. ✛*17 km (10 mi) northeast of the Pan-American Hwy., on road to Las Pailas park entrance* ☎*2666–8075 or 2442--1828* 📠*2442–1910* ⊕*www.guachipelin.com* 🛏*50 rooms* ⚬*In-room: no a/c, no phone, safe, no TV. In-hotel: restaurant, bar, pool, spa, no elevator, laundry service, public Internet* ▭*AE, DC, MC, V* ⦿*BP.*

$ 🏨**Rincón de la Vieja Mountain Lodge.** This is the closest you can stay to the Las Pailas park entrance, which makes it a good spot for hikers and nature lovers who aren't terribly demanding. Hiking and horse trails lead to a hot sulfuric pool, and farther through the forest, to a blue lake and waterfall, and the volcano's crater deep in the park. The sunny log cabins (room numbers 39 and up), with colorful tiled bathrooms and porches with hammocks, are the best choices. Avoid the rows of connected older rooms (1 to 28), which are dark and gloomy. The dining room is claustrophobic, with mediocre food served buffet-style, but the alfresco bar is lively in the evening, usually filled with small groups of international ecotourist types. The grounds are shaded by giant malinche trees, and there is a tiny dipping pool. **Pros:** Close to park, lots of tour options, reasonably priced. **Cons:** Rustic rooms, mediocre food. ✛*21 km (12 mi) northeast of Pan-American Hwy.; 5 km (3 mi) north of Hacienda Guachipelín; 2 km (1 mi) south of the Las Pailas park entrance* ☎*2200–0238* 🖷*2666–2441* ⊕*www.rincon delaviejalodge.net* ⇘*49 rooms* ⌂*In-room: no a/c, no phone, no TV. In-hotel: restaurant, bar, no elevator, public Internet* ⊟*AE, DC, MC, V* ⍠*BP.*

SANTA ROSA NATIONAL PARK

35 km (22 mi) northwest of Liberia.

Renowned for its wildlife, which is easy to spot in the dry season, thanks to sparser foliage, Santa Rosa protects the largest swath of tropical dry forest in Central America. Camping expeditions serving bird-watchers, naturalists, and backpackers often venture deep in the interior, but it's possible to experience a good bit of its impressive flora and fauna on a full-day or half-day visit. Treetop inhabitants include spider, capuchin, and howler monkeys, as well as hundreds of bird species. If you station yourself next to water holes during the dry season, you may also spot deer, coyotes, coatis, or armadillos. Typical dry-forest vegetation includes kapok, guanacaste, mahogany, calabash, bull-horn acacia, and gumbo-limbo trees.

Santa Rosa's wealth of flora and fauna is due in part to its remoteness, since much of it is still inaccessible to the common tourist. To get anywhere in the park, you must have a vehicle—preferably 4WD. The park headquarters, historic ranch house of La Casona, and camping area are 8 km (5 mi) from the Pan-American Highway via a paved road. Within this dense, shady forest, temperatures drop by as much as 5°C (9°F).

In rainy season the park's rough road to the beach cannot be accessed by even 4WD vehicles, but several short trails head into the forest from its first, flat stretch, and day hikers can easily explore the first stretch of the steep part on foot. Park off the road just before it descends into the forest. From the park headquarters it's 13 km (8 mi) to **Playa Naranjo,** where famed Witch's Rock surf break is located (surfers get there by boat). **Playa Nancite**—the world's only totally protected olive ridley turtle *arribada,* or mass nesting beach (accessible primarily to biologists and students; permit required), is an additional 5 km (3 mi) by footpath north of Playa Naranjo. Only the first 12 km (7 mi) of the road are accessible by vehicles. ⊠*Km 269, Pan-American Hwy.* ✛*35 km (22 mi) north of Liberia* ☎*2666–5051* 💲*$10* ⊙*Daily 8–4.*

GETTING HERE & AROUND

The turnoff for Santa Rosa National Park from the Pan-American Highway is well marked, about 30 minutes out from Liberia. From Liberia you can hop on a bus heading north to La Cruz and get off at the park entrance, but you'll have to hike hours in the hot sun, or hitchhike, to La Casona from here.

OUTDOOR ACTIVITIES

HIKING The short (about half a mile) **La Casona nature-trail loop** from the park headquarters is worth taking to get a brief sampling of the woods. Look for the INDIO DESNUDO, or "Naked Indian," path, named after the local word for gumbo-limbo trees. ■TIP➔**Carry plenty of water and insect repellent.**

> ### WALKER'S LAST STAND
>
> Santa Rosa Park was the site of the 1856 triumph over American invader William Walker in the famous Battle of Santa Rosa—one of the few historic military sites in this army-less country. The rambling colonial-style ranch house called **La Casona** was the last stand of a ragged force of ill-equipped Costa Ricans who routed the superior mercenary army of the notorious Walker. Disgruntled poachers burned La Casona to the ground in 2001, but it has since been rebuilt.

Several other short trails lead off the road **to the beaches** before it becomes impassable to vehicles. The hike to Playa Naranjo (13 km [8 mi] west of La Casona) and Playa Nancite (5 km [3 mi] north of Naranjo) requires good physical condition and lots of water. You can get a map of the trails at the park entrance.

SURFING **Witch's Rock,** one of the oldest rock formations in the country, towers
★ offshore over a near-perfect beach break off Playa Naranjo in Santa Rosa Park. If you are interested in surfing Witch's Rock, take a boat tour from Playas del Coco, Playa Hermosa, or Playa Tamarindo, to the south.

WHERE TO STAY

There are basic, dormitory-style lodgings and a camping area near the park's administrative center and at a biological station at Playa Naranjo. You can also camp within Santa Rosa Park at the beaches of Nancite and Murcielego—but those campsites are very basic and quite remote. Call the park headquarters (☎2666–5051) for information. Most people visit the park on day trips from Liberia, or nearby Cuajiniquil.

PLAYA BAHÍA JUNQUILLAL

26 km (16 mi) northwest of Santa Rosa National Park entrance.

This 2½-km (1½-mi), tree-fringed, Blue Flag beach is as close as you can get to white-sand beach in this part of Guanacaste. The warm, calm water makes it one of the best swimming beaches on the Gulf of Santa Elena. Not to be confused with the Playa Junquillal on the western coast of the Nicoya Peninsula farther south, this beach is part of the Guanacaste National Wildlife Refuge to the north of Santa Rosa. Stay for the day or camp out in the well-kept, shaded camping area with cold-water showers, grills, and picnic tables. You can snorkel if you've got your own gear. *18 km (11 mi) west of Pan-American Hwy. Cuajiniquil turnoff* ☎2679–9692 ☎$6 ⊙7 AM–7 PM.

GETTING HERE & AROUND
From the Pan-American Highway, take the road signed for Cuajiniquil, 43 km (26 mi) northwest of Liberia and 8 km (5 mi) north of Santa Rosa Park. Follow the paved road 14 km (8 mi) to the beach turnoff, along a dirt road for another 4 km (2½ mi). From the Bahía Salinas area, take the scenic dirt road (4WD recommended); then follow the road near Puerto Soley (signed for Cuajiniquil) 7 km (4 mi) to the beach entrance. It's about 30 minutes from the Pan-American turnoff and one hour from Bahía Salinas.

WHERE TO STAY
$ ☒ **Santa Elena Lodge.** This simple family-run lodge on the outskirts of Cuajiniquil provides the closest accommodations to both Playa Bahía Junquillal and Santa Rosa National Park, making it a good option for nature lovers and anyone who wants to stray from the vacationing crowds. The owner, Manuel Alán, is a former fisherman who switched to tourism a few years ago, converting his family home into a B&B. The rooms have varnished hardwood walls and ceilings, plenty of windows, and small bathrooms—Rooms 5 and 6 are the nicest, since they overlook the garden. Breakfast is served in back, whereas lunch and dinner are available at the adjacent seafood restaurant. Manuel rents bikes, kayaks, and snorkeling equipment, and offers an array of tours that include horseback riding, a hike through the Murcielago sector of Santa Rosa National Park, a boat tour of a mangrove estuary, and whale-watching from August to February. **Pros:** Friendly, near beach and park, lots of outdoor options. **Cons:** Little English spoken, basic accommodations, close to road. ☒*Cuajiniquil* ✛*10 km (6 mi) west of Pan-American Hwy., 8 km (5 mi) east of Junquillal* ☎2679–1038 ✍*santaelenalodge@gmail.com* ↩*10 rooms* ⌂*In-room: no phone, safe, no TV. In-hotel: restaurant, water sports, bicycles, no elevator, laundry service, public Internet* ▤*AE, DC, MC, V* ⦿ ☒☏.

LA CRUZ

65 km (40 mi) northwest of Liberia.

North of Santa Rosa National Park on the west side of the highway is the turnoff to La Cruz, a scruffy, bustling little town. For travelers, it's noteworthy only for the stunning views of Bahía Salinas from its bluff and its proximity to the nearby windswept beaches on the south shore of Bahía Salinas, in the hamlet of Jobo, and in the Golfo de Santa Elena. The Nicaraguan border lies just north of La Cruz at Peñas Blancas. ■TIP➔**All travelers are stopped at two checkpoints south of La Cruz for passport and cursory vehicle inspection. Police vigilance is heightened in the region.**

Guanacaste National Park

The 325-square-km (125-square-mi) Parque Nacional Guanacaste, bordering the east side of the Pan-American Highway 30 km (18 mi) north of Liberia, was created in 1989 to preserve rain forests around Cacao Volcano (5,437 feet) and Orosi Volcano (4,847 feet), which are seasonally inhabited by migrant wildlife from Santa Rosa. The park isn't quite ready for tourism yet. There are no facilities (not even a toilet) and no well-marked trails. In rainy season, roads are impassable; a 4WD vehicle is required year-round. The park is a mosaic of interdependent protected areas, parks, and refuges; the goal is to eventually create a single Guanacaste megapark to accommodate the migratory patterns of animals, from jaguars to tapirs. Much of the park's territory is cattle pasture, which, it is hoped, will regenerate into forest. Today the park has more than 300 different birds and more than 5,000 species of butterflies.

To really explore the park, you must stay in the heart of it, at one of three biological stations. They are mostly reserved for students and researchers, but you can request accommodations from the **park headquarters** (☎ *2666–5051*).

GETTING HERE & AROUND

La Cruz is a straight shot one hour north of Liberia on the Pan-American Highway. Buses leave Liberia for La Cruz or you can flag down a bus that says LA CRUZ on its windshield anywhere along the highway north of Liberia.

LA CRUZ ESSENTIALS

Bank **Banco Nacional** (⊠ *Pan-American Hwy. across from Ursa gas station* ☎ *2679–9389*). **Banco Popular** (⊠ *1 block east of Central Park* ☎ *2679–9352*).

Hospital **Hospital Area de Salud La Cruz** (⊠ *Main highway at entrance to town* ☎ *2679–9311*).

Pharmacy **Farmacia La Cruz** (⊠ *1 block north of Central Park* ☎ *2679–8048* ☉ *Weekdays 8–8, weekends 9–4*).

Internet **Internet Café** (⊠ *Beside Banco Popular*).

Post Office **Correo** (⊠ *Behind police station on west side of Central Park*).

CROSSING INTO NICARAGUA AT PEÑAS BLANCAS

Costa Rica and Nicaragua share a busy border crossing at Peñas Blancas, 12 km (7 mi) north of La Cruz along a paved highway. ■TIP→ **Rental vehicles may not leave Costa Rica.** Tica Bus and Transnica bus companies (⇨ *Bus Travel in Travel Smart Costa Rica*) travel direct between San José and Managua via this route. You can also take a Tralapa bus to the border from other points in Costa Rica. You'll make your crossing, then catch a Nicaraguan bus or taxi to Rivas, 30 km (18 mi) farther, which is the regional hub for buses departing to other parts of Nicaragua. The fee to cross the border is $7 (paid on the Nicaraguan side), plus a $2 surcharge if you cross from noon to 2 PM or on weekends. Nicaraguan shuttle taxis transport people between the border posts. Returning to Costa Rica is basically the same process in reverse; you are charged a $1 municipal tax and $2 exit tax to leave Nicaragua by land. The crossing is open daily 6 AM–8 PM; get there with time to spare or you *will* be stranded. Banks on both sides of the border change their own currency and U.S. dollars. Colones are not accepted or exchanged in Nicaragua; likewise for córdobas in Costa Rica. Overland border crossing procedures can be confusing if you don't speak Spanish.

BAHÍA SALINAS

15 km (9 mi) west of La Cruz.

The large windswept bay at the very top of Costa Rica's Pacific coast is the second-windiest area in the country, after Lake Arenal, making it ideal for windsurfing and kitesurfing. Strong breezes blow from November to May, when only experienced surfers are out on the water and the water grows steadily cooler. The south (bay) side has the strongest winds, and choppy, cold water from January to May.

In July and August the wind is more appropriate for beginners, whereas any time of year you can enjoy the area's diving and beaches. On the sheltered Golfo Santa Elena, to the west, are two beaches that rank among the most beautiful in all of Costa Rica: Playas Rajada and Jobo, a far cry from the overdeveloped beaches of Guanacaste's gold coast farther to the south.

GETTING HERE & AROUND

From a high point in La Cruz, the road to Salinas descends both in altitude and condition. It's only 15 km (9 mi) southwest to Hotel Ecoplaya, but the road can be jilted and broken, so may take up to 45 minutes or an hour. Signs direct you to Puerto Soley and Jobo, an end-of-the-road hamlet, about 2 km (1 mi) past the turnoff for Ecoplaya. Playa Copal is about 13 km (8 mi) along the same road from La Cruz.

EXPLORING

Playa Copal (✥ *About 2 km [1 mi] east of the branch road that leads to Ecoplaya*) is a narrow, dark-beige beach that wouldn't be worth visiting except for the fact that it is one of the main venues for kitesurfing. There are villas and rooms for rent. A couple of kilometers to the east, Playa Papaturro also has kitesurfing and simple accommodations.

Gorgeous, horseshoe-shape **Playa Rajada** (✥ *5 km [3 mi] west of Ecoplaya Beach Resort or 3 km [2 mi] north of the town of Jobo*) is a wide sweep of almost-white, fine-grain sand. Shallow, warm waters make it perfect for swimming, and an interesting rock formation at the north end invites snorkelers. It's also a favorite beach for watching sunsets.

★ **Playa Jobo** (✥ *3 km [2 mi] walk or drive, west from Ecoplaya Beach Resort*) is a gem with fine sand, calm water, and rocky claws at each end of its horseshoe. It's fringed with acacia trees that have sharp thorns, so keep your distance. There's a shady parking area about 500 feet off the beach where you have to leave your car.

OUTDOOR ACTIVITIES

Inshore fishing is quite good in the bay during windy months, when snapper, roosterfish, wahoo, and other fighters abound. Scuba divers also encounter plenty of big fish from December to May, though visibility can be poor then. From May to December the snorkeling is good around the rocky points and Isla Bolaños. **Ecoplaya Beach Resort** (⊠*La Coyotera Beach* ⊕*15 km (10 mi) west of La Cruz on a rough dirt road* ☎*2676–1042* ⊕*www.ecoplaya.com*) organizes local adventure tours that include kayaking to Isla Bolaños (a tiny bird-preserve island), inshore fishing, horseback riding, hiking, and scuba diving, as well as farther-afield adventure tours to Santa Rosa National Park, Hacienda Guachipelín, and the historic city of Granada, in nearby Nicaragua.

> ### THIEVES ON THE BEACHES
>
> The North Pacific's idyllic landscapes and friendly people belie an ever-present threat of theft. Though a tiny minority, Costa Rica's thieves manage to ruin a lot of vacations by absconding with backpacks, cameras, wallets, and passports; the last of which necessitates a trip to San José. Keep your valuables in your hotel safe and don't ever leave anything in an unattended car, even while checking into your hotel. Hotel parking lots are popular spots for local kleptomaniacs, as is the beach.

KITESURFING & WINDSURFING The **Kite Surfing Centre and School** (☎*8826–5221* ⊕*www.bluedreamhotel. com*) on Playa Papaturro (9 km [5½ mi] west of La Cruz, turn left at sign for Papaturro) is run by Nicola, a multilingual instructor with lots of experience; eight hours of kitesurfing lessons cost $240, including equipment. The school has 10 inexpensive rooms on a ridge with ocean views and a restaurant, called Blue Dream Hotel. **Cometa Copal Kite Surfing Centre and School,** (☎*2676–1192*) on Playa Copal (10 km [6 mi] west of La Cruz), is run by an American who provides kitesurfing lessons and rents equipment

WHERE TO STAY

$$ ⊡ **Ecoplaya Beach Resort.** Set between La Coyotera Beach and a mangrove estuary, this small resort has a sprawling collection of villas and two-story cement buildings (with several types of spacious rooms) that dot ample grounds. Be warned—it's in a high-wind zone. Even with glass buffers and windbreak trees and shrubs, the large swimming pool usually has waves. The 1-km-long (½-mi-long) beach has coarse brown sand flecked with broken shells, and the water is extremely shallow and murky during the windy months. Jobo, Copal, and Rajada beaches are just a short drive away. The hotel organizes activities and tours that include fishing, diving, horseback riding, and full-day tours to the province's national parks, or historic towns in nearby Nicaragua. Since the resort is also a timeshare, it's often packed with Costa Rican families, and is full during the holidays. The restaurant, set beneath a massive thatch roof, serves good food, though the service is inconsistent. **Pros:** Friendly, quiet, lots of activities. **Cons:** Timeworn, service inconsistent, pool gets packed during holidays. ⊠ *La Coyotera Beach* ⌖*15 km (10 mi) west of La Cruz on a rough dirt road* ☎*2676–1010, 2228–7146 in San José* 🖷*2289–4536 in San José* ⊕*www.ecoplaya.com* ⇔*16 villas, 20 rooms* ⌂*In-room: safe, kitchen (some). In-hotel: restaurant, bar, pool, beachfront, diving, water sports, no elevator, laundry service, public Internet* 🞖*AE, MC, V* ⫍◯⫌*FAP.*

¢   ⌖**Restaurante Copal & Pura Vida Residence.** An affordable base for exploring the area, this Italian-built and -managed hilltop residence overlooks Playa Copal, the premier beach for windsurfing and kitesurfing. Studio rooms are in a white cement building on a ridge overlooking a small pool. Fully equipped villas are perfect for groups. High ceilings, lots of cool stone and tile, and huge windows to catch the winds off the bay help you keep your cool despite the lack of air-conditioning in the rooms and some of the villas. The small restaurant above those rooms serves the best food in the area ($), such as fresh pastas, baked whole fish, risottos, stuffed calamari, and a selection of pizzas. It's a great lunch option, since the view from its rustic wooden tables is impressive. **Pros:** Good value, near surfing beach. **Cons:** Isolated, weatherworn. ⊠*Playa Copal* ⌖*13 km (8 mi) west of La Cruz* ☎*8389–6794* 🖷🖷*2676–1055* ⊕*www.progettopuravida.com* ⇔*7 rooms, 5 villas* ⌂*In-room: no a/c (some), no phone, kitchen (some), no TV. In-hotel: restaurant, pool* 🞖*No credit cards* ⫍◯⫌*EP.*

LIBERIA

234 km/145 mi (4 hrs) northwest of San José.

Once a dusty cattle-market town, Liberia is now galloping toward modernization. Though you can spot the occasional *sabanero* (cowboy) on horseback, the capital of Guanacaste province is well on its way to becoming one big shopping mall, complete with fast-food restaurants and a multiplex theater. The whitewashed adobe houses for which Liberia was nicknamed the "White City" are the only traces of its colonial past. Today Liberia is essentially a good place to have a meal and make a bank stop, though it can serve as a base for day trips to Santa Rosa and Rincón de la Vieja national parks. The drive from San José takes between four and five hours, so it makes sense to fly directly into Liberia if you're going to the North Pacific. It's easy to rent a car near the airport.

NAVIGATING   The *avenidas* (avenues) officially run east–west, while the *calles* (streets)
LIBERIA   run north–south. Liberia is not too big to walk easily, but there are always taxis lined up around the central park.

GETTING HERE & AROUND
From San José, follow the Pan-American Highway west past the Puntarenas exit, then north past Cañas to Liberia. The road is paved but is poorly maintained in places. It's a heavily traveled truck and bus route, and there are miles and miles where it is impossible to pass, but many drivers try, making this a dangerous road. Hourly direct buses leave San José for Liberia each day, and there are half a dozen daily

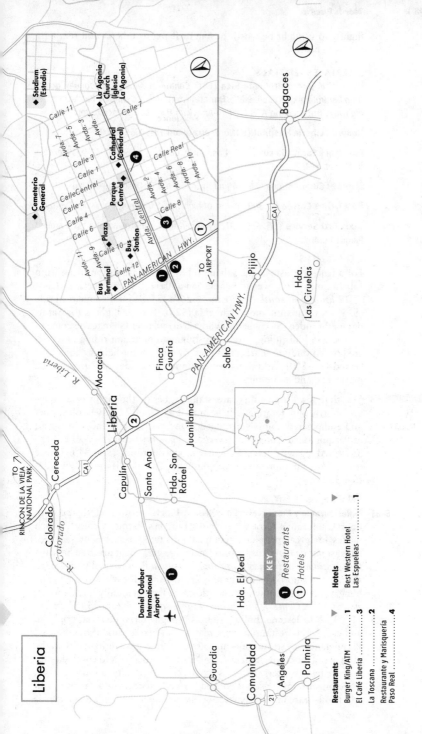

Liberia

4

KEY

▶ Restaurants
① Hotels

Restaurants

Burger King/ATM **1**
El Café Liberia **3**
La Toscana **2**
Restaurante y Marisquería
Paso Real **4**

Hotels

Best Western Hotel
Las Espuelas **1**

flights, so it might be worth busing or flying to Liberia and renting a car from here.

LIBERIA ESSENTIALS

Bank/ATM **Banco de Costa Rica** (⊠ *C. Central at Avda. 1; diagonally across from Central Park* ☎ *2666–9002*). **Bancredito** (⊠ *Avda. Central, 2 blocks north of highway*). **Burger King ATH** (⊠ *Pan-American Hwy., at entrance to town*).

Hospital **Liberia Hospital** (⊠ *North end of town* ☎ *2666–4250*).

Pharmacy **Farmacia Lux** (⊠ *C. 4 and Avda. Central* ☎ *2666–0061* ⊙ *Weekdays 8–10, Sat. 8–4*).

Internet **Ciber Enl@ce** (⊠ *C. 4 and Avda. Central* ⊙ *Daily 8 AM–10 PM*).

Post Office **Correo** (⊠ *300 m west of highway, 200 m north of Avda. Central*).

Taxis **Taxi Service** (☎ *2666–7070*); you can find a line of waiting taxis around Parque Central.

EXPLORING

For a true-grit taste of the sabanero life that is fast disappearing from Liberia, mosey on over to **Rancho Santa Alicia** (⊠ *Pan-American Hwy.* ✛ *12 km [7 mi] south of Liberia* ☎ *2671–2513*) for a scenic trail ride ($25) or a romantic moonlight ride ($25). The highlight is the Saturday-night **rodeo** ($4), when cowboys from all over Guanacaste come to compete in bull riding, bronco busting, and precision riding in a covered rodeo stadium. Barbecued beef, ribs, and some lighter choices are served ($6–$10). Additional entertainment includes *ranchero* music, mariachis, and a late-night disco.

EN ROUTE Yes, that is a life-size dinosaur standing beside the highway 20 minutes north of Puntarenas. It is one of 26 lifelike models of extinct and endangered animals arranged along a 1½ km (1-mi) forest trail at Parque MegaFauna Monteverde ⊠ *Pan-American Hwy.* ☎ *$$645–5029*). Along with the spectacular models outdoors, the $4 entrance fee includes an impressive insect museum. The park is open daily 8 AM to 4:30 PM.

WHERE TO STAY & EAT

$–$$ ✕ **Restaurante y Marisquería Paso Real.** A Liberia institution, this second-floor restaurant's terrace overlooks Liberia's Parque Central, which makes for great people-watching. Fresh, tangy ceviches or seafood-laden *sopas de mariscos* (seafood soup) are great light lunches. Save the *filet gratinado al brandy con camarones* (fish fillet topped with grilled shrimp and smothered in a brandy cream sauce) for when you're really hungry. Service is efficient and pleasant. It's open daily 11 AM to 10 PM. ⊠ *Avda. Central, south side of main square* ☎ *2666–3455* ▤ *AE,*

$ *MC, V.* ✕ **La Toscana.** Billing itself as "spaghetteria, pizzeria, grigliata, and cafe," this restaurant uses real Italian ingredients. Properly aged Parmigiano cheese and prosciutto from Parma give authenticity to the 40 types of wood-oven pizzas. Tender tuna carpaccio and ensalada caprese are tasty starters. Risottos are the chef's specialty; a nutty, brown, three-mushroom version is cooked perfectly *al dente* and flavored with truffle oil—rare in these parts. ⊠ *Centro Comercial Santa Rosa, across*

FODOR'S FIRST PERSON

Dorothy MacKinnon
Writer

We were rolling along the nearly deserted highway near Liberia when an aluminum ladder came loose from an open-bed truck and cartwheeled across the highway, heading straight for our windshield. My colleague swerved, catching the concrete abutment, flipping our rented KIA Sportage. We landed right side up, inches from a large tree.

Seconds later the highway was alive with people rushing to our aid. Two men, including the flying-ladder truck's driver, pried open our crumpled doors and pulled us out.

Amazingly we had only minor cuts, but the car was totaled and my driver was passing out from shock. An ambulance arrived in under five minutes. A passerby reported the accident to the traffic police and called my rental company. An elderly woman ran home to fetch salve for my injuries. A neighbor offered a glass of cold water and stayed with me for two hours.

Everyone, officials or not, was efficient. But more importantly, they were warm, treating two *extranjeras* (foreigners) like family. Within five hours of a potentially fatal accident our new KIA was loaded up and we were on our way with a better appreciation for Tico culture.

from Burger King, on road to airport ☎2665–0653 🖃*AE, DC, MC, V.*

¢ ✕**El Café Liberia.** The smell of roasting coffee is the best advertisement for this sophisticated café in the center of Liberia. New owners have kept some of the former French-Canadian owner's excellent dishes, including refreshing soups—the mint pea is a winner—savory quiches, and hot sandwiches. Save room for homemade desserts like ice cream in exotic fruit flavors. The casual bar is a cool place to relax, sip a glass of wine, and browse through the paperbacks in the book exchange. 🖃*C. 8, 75 m south of Banco Nacional* ☎2665–1660 🖃*No credit cards* C *Closed Sun.*

$$ 🏨**Best Western Las Espuelas.** From the gigantic guanacaste tree that shades its parking lot to the local paintings and indigenous stone statues that decorate its lobby, this motel just south of town has more character than one might expect. Rooms are a little institutional, but the grounds are verdant and the rectangular pool is quite large. Two suites, by the pool, have private whirlpool tubs. Rooms facing the highway can be a little noisy; numbers 17 and up are quieter. The restaurant, which resembles a coffee shop, serves complimentary buffet breakfasts, but you're best off heading into town for dinner. The hotel's casino is popular with locals. **Pros:** Reasonable rates, big pool. **Cons:** Highway noise, mediocre rooms, insects sometimes a problem. 🖃*Pan-American Hwy.* ✛*2 km (1 mi) south of Liberia* ☎2666–0144 🖷2666–2441 ⊕*www.bestwestern.co.cr* ⬎*44 rooms, 2 suites* ⚒ *In-room: safe. In-hotel: restaurant, bar, pool, no elevator, laundry service, public Wi-Fi* 🖃*AE, D, MC, V* ❏*BP.*

ICOYA COAST

Strung along the coast of the Nicoya Peninsula are sparkling sand beaches lined with laid-back fishing communities, and hotels and resorts in every price category. As recently as the 1970s, fishing and cattle ranching were the area's mainstays. Development is barreling ahead full speed, though, bringing with it sophisticated restaurants, hotels, and shops, along with congestion, construction chaos, water pollution, and higher prices. Roads are only starting to catch up, so you'll find the interesting anomaly of a trendy restaurant or upscale hotel plunked at the end of a tortuous dirt road. The key to enjoying Nicoya is to slow down. You'll soon be as mellow as the locals.

PAPAGAYO PENINSULA

The Papagayo Peninsula, a crooked finger of land cradling the west side of Bahía Culebra (Snake Bay), is the site of a government-sponsored development scheme modeled after Cancún. Five large hotels are already situated around the Papagayo Bay, and upward of 15 others are slated to be built here. Although the hotels are modeled on their Caribbean counterparts, the beaches are distinctly Costa Rican, with brown sand and aquamarine water that grows cool from January to April. Isolation is the name of the game, which means that getting out of man-made "paradise" to explore anything off-property often entails a pricey tour.

High season here coincides with dry season. There's guaranteed sun January to April, but there's also intense heat, and the landscape becomes brown and brittle. In the rainy season (August to December), the landscape is greener and lusher. Sparkling water and spectacular sunsets are beautiful year-round.

GETTING HERE & AROUND

All hotels here have airport pickup. To get to the Four Seasons from the Liberia airport (the hotel refuses to put up directional signs in order to "protect its privacy"), drive 10 km (6 mi) south of Guardia, over the Río Tempisque Bridge, then take the turn on the right signed for Papagayo Allegro Resort. Follow this road about 20 km (12 mi) to its end at the entrance to the resort.

OUTDOOR ACTIVITIES

CANOPY TOUR   Taking advantage of one of the few remaining patches of dry tropical forest on the Papagayo Peninsula, **Witch's Rock Canopy Tour** (☎8371–3685 ✎witchsrockcanopytour@hotmail.com) gives you your money's worth: 23 platforms, with a thrilling 450-meter cable zip between two of them; four hanging bridges; a waterfall in rainy season; and hiking trails. The 1½-hour tour is $65 per person.

WHERE TO STAY

$$$$ ⬚**Four Seasons Resort Costa Rica.** By far the most luxurious hotel in Costa Rica, the Four Seasons is extremely secluded (it's nearly 30 minutes from the main road). Service, provided by a cream-of-the-crop,

Continued on page 205

CHOOSING A BEACH

Tamarindo Beach, Guanacaste, Costa Rica

Each beach along Nicoya's coast, most lined with coconut palm or buttonwood trees, has its distinct merits. Sand varies from pulverized black volcanic rock (Playa Negra) to crushed white shells (Playa Conchal) to picture-perfect, soft white sand (Playa Carrillo), with every shade of brown in between. Atmospherically, beaches vary from tranquil, secluded, Robinson Crusoe–like strands (Playa Rajada) to civilized beaches with restaurants so close to the ocean the surf spray salts your food (Playa Brasilito) to family-friendly spots with calm, swimmable waters and shade (Playas Hermosa and Sámara) to beaches with buff and beautiful, tattooed surfers (Playas Tamarindo and Negra) to those made for contemplative walks or dramatic sunsets (Playas Langosta and Pelada).

Playa Hermosa

BEACHES KEY

🔲	Diving
🔲	Snorkeling
🔲	Fishing
🔲	Surfing
🔲	Kayaking
🔺	Sailing
🔲	Swimming
🚩	Blue Flag Ecological Award

The main attraction on the **Papagayo Peninsula** beaches is the resorts that inhabit them.

Playa Hermosa is one of the few Costa Rican beaches with calm, crystal-clear waters.

Surfing, diving, and fishing are the name of the game at **Playas del Coco** and its scruffy beach town.

Playa Ocotal is a quiet beach with great views and good snorkeling.

Playa Pan de Azúcar is practically deserted, and lined with tropical dry forest.

Shells sprinkle the sand at chilled-out **Playa Conchal**, near a small fishing village.

Busy white-sand **Playa Flamingo** is ideal for swimming and sunning.

Lively **Tamarindo** is a hyped-up surfing and water-sports beach with wild nightlife.

Aeropuerto Internacional Daniel Oduber

Gulf of Papagayo
Puerto Culebra
Bahía Culebra
Guardia
Comunidad
Palmira
Playa Panamá
Panama
Playa Hermosa
Sardinal
Playas del Coco
El Coco
Playa Ocotal
Nuevo Colon
Playa Pan de Azúcar
Potrero
Tempate
Coya
Playa Potrero
Isla Sta. Catalina
Playa Flamingo
Brasilito
Portegolpe
Playa Conchal
Llano
Brasilito
Huacas
Playa Real
Matapalo
Salinas
Playa Grande
Villarreal
Las Baulas Marine National Park
Tamarindo
Tamarindo
Playa Langosta

0 — 8 miles
0 — 12 km

Playa Langosta

Nosara

Playa Carrillo

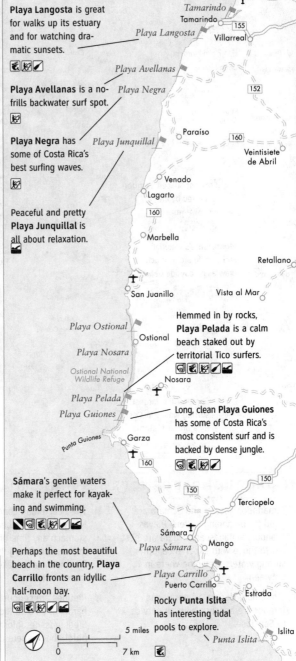

Playa Langosta is great for walks up its estuary and for watching dramatic sunsets.

Playa Avellanas is a no-frills backwater surf spot.

Playa Negra has some of Costa Rica's best surfing waves.

Peaceful and pretty **Playa Junquillal** is all about relaxation.

Hemmed in by rocks, **Playa Pelada** is a calm beach staked out by territorial Tico surfers.

Long, clean **Playa Guiones** has some of Costa Rica's most consistent surf and is backed by dense jungle.

Sámara's gentle waters make it perfect for kayaking and swimming.

Perhaps the most beautiful beach in the country, **Playa Carrillo** fronts an idyllic half-moon bay.

Rocky **Punta Islita** has interesting tidal pools to explore.

Tamarindo
Tamarindo
Playa Langosta — 155
Villarreal

Playa Avellanas
Playa Negra — 152

Paraíso — 160
Veintisiete de Abril
Playa Junquillal

Venado
Lagarto
160
Marbella

Retallano

San Juanillo
Vista al Mar

Playa Ostional
Ostional
Playa Nosara
Ostional National Wildlife Refuge
Nosara

Playa Pelada
Playa Guiones

Punta Guiones Garza
160
150

150
Terciopelo

Sámara
Playa Sámara Mango

Playa Carrillo
Puerto Carrillo
Estrada

Punta Islita Islita

0   5 miles
0   7 km

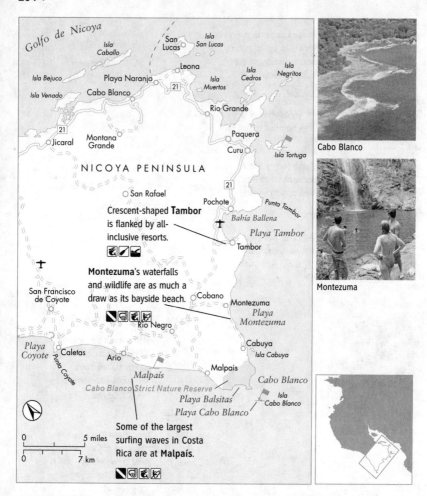

Golfo de Nicoya

NICOYA PENINSULA

Crescent-shaped **Tambor** is flanked by all-inclusive resorts.

Montezuma's waterfalls and wildlife are as much a draw as its bayside beach.

Some of the largest surfing waves in Costa Rica are at **Malpaís**.

Cabo Blanco Strict Nature Reserve

0   5 miles
0   7 km

Cabo Blanco

Montezuma

MAKING THE MOST OF YOUR BEACH VACATION

■ Tamarindo, Nosara, and Sámara are good for beginning surfers. Playas Grande, Avellanas, and Negra are best left to those with experience; other surfing waters are somewhere in between.

■ Tamarindo, Nosara, Sámara, and Tambor are beaches with air service to San José.

■ The beach road connecting most Nicoya Peninsula beaches is hard to stomach any time of year, and virtually impassable during the August through December rains. Take easier inland routes instead.

■ Riptides are seriously dangerous and hardly any Costa Rican beaches have lifeguards; get information from your hotel about where to swim.

Semana Santa

Don't underestimate how completely Costa Rica shuts down for Holy Week, the week preceding Easter. Cities become ghost towns—San José turns beguilingly peaceful—save for religious processions. Many businesses close the entire week; little opens on Thursday or Friday. Tourists, local and international, flock to the beaches. Make reservations weeks in advance if you plan to be here during that week, and expect greatly inflated room rates. Know that Holy Thursday and Good Friday are, by law, dry days. Bars and liquor stores must close, and no one, including restaurants or your hotel dining room, is permitted to sell alcohol.

bilingual staff, is faultless. The decor is tasteful and arty. Huge rooms have king-size beds, marble baths, and screened-in living-room terraces. The breezy 18-hole Arnold Palmer signature golf course has breathtaking views—and prices ($185 per round). The state-of-the-art spa is impressive but a little sterile. Dishes created at the dinner-only Di Mare restaurant are worth their wildly expensive price tags, but the rest of the hotel's food has been disappointing. **Pros:** Impeccable service, lovely beach. **Cons:** Isolated, expensive. ✛ *25 km (15 mi) west of Guardia; follow signs to Papagayo Allegro Resort, and continue to end of road* ☎2696–0000 ☐2696–0010 ⊕*www.fourseasons.com* ⤴*123 rooms, 36 suites, 21 villas* △*In-room: safe, refrigerator, Wi-Fi. In-hotel: 4 restaurants, room service, bars, golf course, pools, gym, spa, beachfront, water sports, children's programs (ages 4–12), laundry facilities, concierge, public Internet, airport shuttle, no-smoking rooms* ⊟*AE, DC, MC, V* ⏧*EP.*

PLAYA HERMOSA

27 km (17 mi) southwest of Liberia airport.

Beautiful Playa Hermosa is one of the last laid-back beach towns on this part of the coast. It's the kind of place where the beach is still the town's main thoroughfare, filled with joggers, people walking their dogs, and families out for a stroll. Not to be confused with the mainland surfers' beach of the same name south of Jacó, this Playa Hermosa is experiencing heavy development pressures, with new crops of sunny villas and high-rise condos filling up with American and Canadian expatriates. Luckily, though, the full length of the beach has long been occupied by small hotels, restaurants, and homes, so the newer hotel behemoths and other developments are forced to set up shop off the beach or on other beaches in the area.

Hermosa's mile-long crescent of dark gray volcanic sand attracts heat, so the best time to be out on the beach is early morning or late afternoon, in time for the spectacular sunsets. The beach fronts a line of trees, so there's a welcome respite from the heat of the sun. The crystal-clear water—it's a Blue Flag beach—is usually calm, with no strong currents and with comfortable temperatures of 74°F–80°F (23°C–27°C). Sea views are as picturesque as they get, with bobbing fishing boats, jagged profiles of coastline, rocky outcroppings, and at night the twinkling lights of the Four Seasons Resort across the bay. At the beach's north end, low tide creates wide, rock-lined tidal pools.

GETTING HERE & AROUND

From the Comunidad turnoff of Highway 21, heading from Liberia, Playa Hermosa is about 15 km (9 mi) northwest. The paved road forks after the small town of Sardinal, the right fork heading into Hermosa and the left leading to Playas del Coco. Local directions usually refer to the first and second entrance roads to the beach, the first entrance being the southern one. There is no through beachfront road, so you have to approach the beach from either of these two roads. Transportes La Pampa buses leave from Liberia for Playa Hermosa daily at 5:30, 7:30, and 11:30 AM and 1, 3:30, 5:30, and 7:30 PM. A taxi to Playas del Coco costs about $12.

PLAYA HERMOSA ESSENTIALS

Playa Hermosa has few resources. Get what you need in Liberia or Playas del Coco, to the south.

Internet **Villa Acacia** (✉ *Second entrance to Playa Hermosa; south on beach road* ☎ *2672–1000*).

OUTDOOR ACTIVITIES

Aqua Sport (✉ *Beach road; heading south, take second entrance to Playa Hermosa and follow signs* ☎ *2672–0050* ⊕ *www.costa-rica-beach-hotel.com*) organizes fishing, surfing, and snorkeling trips and rents every kind of boat and board. **Charlie's Adventure** (✉ *Hotel Condovac, north end of beach* ☎ *2672–1041* ⊕ *www.papagayotours.typepad.com*) organizes ATV tours ($75), horseback riding ($45), and sunset sails ($50), as well as boat tours of Hermosa Bay ($75, including drinks). **Velas de Papagayo** (✉ *Hotel Playa Hermosa Bosque del Mar* ☎ *2223–2598* ⊕ *www.velasdepapagayo.com*) runs morning and sunset cruises of Papagayo Bay that include snorkeling, drinks, and snacks ($100). **Hotel El Velero** (✉ *100 m north of Aqua Sport* ☎ *2672–0036* ⊕ *www.costaricahotel.net*) will take you out for a five-hour sunset cruise on a 38-foot sailing yacht ($50 per person). Daytime tours include snorkeling, cave exploring, and sunbathing ($70).

DIVING &
SNORKELING
Average temperatures of 75°F to 80°F (23°C–27°C), 20 to 60 feet of visibility, and frequent sightings of sea turtles, sharks, manta rays, moray eels, and very big fish make Hermosa a great place to dive. There is little coral in the area, but rock reefs attract large schools of fish, and countless critters lurk in their caves and crannies.

Charlie's Adventure (⇨ *above*) organizes snorkeling and diving trips. **Diving Safaris** (✉ *Second entrance road to Playa Hermosa, almost at beach on left side* ☎ *2672–1259* ⊕ *www.costaricadiving.net*) has a range of scuba activities, from beginner training to open-water PADI certifica-

Making a Difference

Your national-park or -reserve entrance fee helps support the preservation of Costa Rica's wildlife and places. You can also make your visit beneficial to the people living nearby by hiring local guides, horses, or boats; eating in local restaurants; and buying things (excluding wild-animal products) in local shops. You can go a few steps further by making donations to local conservation groups or to such international organizations as Conservation International, the Rainforest Alliance, and the Worldwide Fund for Nature, all of which support important conservation efforts in Costa Rica. It's also helpful to explore private preserves off the beaten path, and stay at lodges that contribute to environmental efforts and to nearby communities. By planning your visit with an eye toward grassroots conservation efforts, you join the global effort to save Costa Rica's tropical ecosystems and help ensure that the treasures you traveled so far to see remain intact for future generations.

tion courses. Multi-tank dives are organized at more than 20 sites. Guides and trainers are very good, and their safety standards have the DAN (Divers Alert Network) seal of approval. This dive shop has also earned the coveted five-star, gold-palm status from PADI. Prices range from $75 for two-tank morning dives to $425 and up for the PADI open-water certification course.

FISHING The fishing at Playa Hermosa is mostly close to the shores, and yields edible fish like *dorado* (mahimahi), amberjack, and yellowfin tuna. Local restaurants are happy to cook your catch for you. You can rent a boat with **Aqua Sport** (⇨*above*). **Charlie's Adventure** (⇨*above*) runs fishing trips.

WHERE TO EAT
A few of Playa Hermosa's best restaurants are at hotels (⇨ *Where to Stay, below*).

$ ✕ **Ginger.** This tapas restaurant, in a modernistic glass-and-steel tree
★ house cantilevered on the side of a hill, is a big hit. The chef has created an Asian-fusion menu with a few Mediterranean dishes. It includes such intriguing appetizer-size offerings as chicken satay with a macadamia-nut rub, mahimahi with a ginger mango sauce, and a taco basket filled with seared pepper-crusted tuna and pickled ginger slaw. Portions are small, but layers of condiments and garnishes make them surprisingly satisfying. The fun thing to do is order several dishes and share. ⊠*Main highway, south of Hotel Condovac* 📞*2672–0041* ⚑*Reservations essential* ▤*MC, V* ⊗*Closed Mon.*

WHERE TO STAY
$$$ 🏨 **Casa Conde del Mar.** Spread over verdant grounds just behind rela-
★   tively pristine Playa Panama—a mile north of Playa Hermosa—this is
☾   the place to head for privacy and relaxation. Rooms are in one-story buildings with a traditional Costa Rican decor: Spanish tile roof; redtile floors; high, sloping ceilings; and covered front terraces offering

a glimpse of the sea through the forest that lines the nearby beach. Standard rooms are spacious and equipped with amenities you might expect from any big luxury hotel, whereas the suites are bigger, and more elegant, with a Jacuzzi in the bathroom and pull-out couch in the living room. There's a large pool with a waterfall and swim-up bar, and an elegant, airy restaurant ($$) that serves pizza, pastas, and other Italian fare as well as local seafood and beef. The people at the tour desk offer an array of tours, and placid, tree-lined Playa Panama is mere steps away. ⊠*Playa Panama* ✛*2 km (1 mi) north of Playa Hermosa* ☎*2226–0808, 2672–1001* ⊕*www.grupocasaconde.com* ⤴*20 rooms, 6 junior suites* ⌂*In-room: safe, Wi-Fi. In-hotel: restaurant, room service, bars, pool, beachfront, no elevator, laundry service, public Internet.* ▤*AE, DC, MC, V* ⎡⊙⎤*EP.*

$$ ▦ **La Finisterra.** From its perch 250 meters up the ridge that defines the southern end of Playa Hermosa, this hotel enjoys a commanding view of the beach and bay. The restaurant ($$), which overlooks the pool and sea, is popular with local expats, who come for the Peruvian-style ceviche (fish cooked with lime juice), Thai curries, octopus sautéed in a tomato sauce, macadamia-encrusted sea bass, and Mediterranean chicken. The rooms, above the restaurant, are simple but comfortable, with two doubles or one king-size bed, picture windows, and nature paintings by local artists. Rooms on the north side of the building have the best view, though the vista from the common balcony and pool area below are even more impressive. **Pros:** Good food, great view. **Con:** Steep road up from beach. ⊠*First entrance to Playa Hermosa, left before Hotel Playa Hermosa, 250 m up hill* ☎*2672--0227* ⊕*www.lafinisterra.com* ⤴*10 rooms* ⌂*In-room: no phone, no TV, Wi-Fi. In-hotel: restaurant, pool, no elevator, public Wi-Fi* ▤*AE, MC, V* ⎡⊙⎤*EP.*

$$ ▦ **Hotel El Velero.** This laid-back hotel is right on the beach, and though ♻ nothing fancy, it's an excellent option if you're watching your expenses. The open-air bar and restaurant, hemmed by exuberant greenery and a small pool, is often hopping with local expats and visitors exchanging fishing, boating, and real-estate stories. The Canadian general manager is an ebullient host, full of local lore and advice. Spacious, attractive rooms have tropical decor with terra-cotta tiles, bamboo furniture, and large windows. Those on the second floor are nicer, with high, sloping wooden ceilings. Only two have ocean views, but you're likely to spend plenty of your time in one of the many chairs and hammocks overlooking the beach, some of which are a shell's toss from the surf at high tide. The hotel runs daily snorkeling and sunset cruises on its own handsome 38-foot sailboat. In the restaurant, jumbo shrimp and always-fresh mahimahi are fixtures. Come on Wednesday or Saturday for beach barbecues. Saturday night there's live music. Drinks are two-for-one every day during Happy Hour, 4 to 6 PM. **Pros:** On the beach, competitive rates, friendly, informal. **Cons:** Tiny pool, most rooms have lousy views, can be noisy. ⊠*Second entrance to Playa Hermosa, on beach road* ☎*2672–0036* 🖷*2672–0016* ⊕*www.costaricahotel.net* ⤴*22 rooms* ⌂*In-room: safe. In-hotel: restaurant, bar, pool, water sports, no elevator, laundry service* ▤*AE, MC, V* ⎡⊙⎤*EP.*

$$ ▦ **Hotel Playa Hermosa Bosque del Mar.** Century-old trees shade this low-
★   lying hotel on the southern end of Playa Hermosa. The most popular
☪   activity here is lounging in hammocks strung around the garden, but
floating in the blue-tile pool surrounded by lush landscaping is a close
second. Flashes of sunlit ocean, just a few barefoot steps away, periodi-
cally penetrate the cool greenery, and now and then an iguana, bird, or
monkey rustles the foliage above. Rooms complement the surrounding
nature, with trees growing through porches, stained-wood furniture,
earth tones, and ceramic bathrooms. Beachfront rooms are the nic-
est, since you can open the screened windows at night and catch the
breeze and the sound of the ocean. The restaurant serves truly fresh
fish and beef tenderloin raised on the owner's own ranch. ⊠*End of
first entrance to Playa Hermosa* ☎*2672–0046* ⎙*2672–0019* ⊕*www.
hotelplayahermosa.com* ⇥*32 rooms* ⌂*In-room: safe, refrigerator. In-
hotel: restaurant, bar, beachfront, water sports, no elevator, public Wi-
Fi* ⊟*AE, DC, MC, V* ⦙○⦙*EP.*

$$ ▦ **Villa del Sueño.** Although the handsome garden restaurant ($$$) is
the main attraction at this elegant hotel, the spacious rooms are quite
nice, too, though it's about a block from the beach. Rooms have up-to-
date bathrooms, comfortable mattresses, and tropical color schemes.
The smaller "standard" rooms around the pool are a good deal, and
they open onto small terraces with chairs. Larger "superiors" above the
restaurant sleep more people, but aren't as nice. If you need more room,
spring for a one- or two-bedroom suite in the development across the
street, which have kitchenettes, large balconies, or terraces, and are
steps away from a larger pool. The restaurant has formal food and
polished service, but a casual atmosphere. Filet mignon with a brandy-
and-peppercorn sauce, perfectly cooked mahimahi in shrimp sauce, and
garlicky butterfly shrimp are among the options. **Pros:** Excellent res-
taurant, good value. **Con:** Not on the beach. ⊠*First entrance to Playa
Hermosa, 350 m west of main highway* ☎*2672–0026* ⎙*2672–0021*
⊕*www.villadelsueno.com* ⇥*14 rooms, 16 junior suites, 12 suites*
⌂*In-room: safe, kitchen (some), refrigerator (some), no TV (some).
In-hotel: restaurant, room service, bar, pools, no elevator, laundry
service, concierge, public Internet, public Wi-Fi, no-smoking rooms*
⊟*AE, MC, V* ⦙○⦙*EP.*

NIGHTLIFE

Hotel El Velero (⊠*Second entrance to Playa Hermosa, then 100 m north
of Aqua Sport on beach road*) hosts beach barbecues with live music
on Wednesday and Saturday nights in high season. The crowd is 30-
ish and up. In high season there's live music on Tuesday, Friday, and
Sunday nights at **Villa del Sueño** (⊠*First entrance to Playa Hermosa,
350 m west of main highway*).

SHOPPING

You can shop for a beach picnic at **Aqua Sport** (⊠*Second entrance to
Playa Hermosa; follow signs heading south on beach road*) mini-mar-
ket and liquor store and buy souvenirs in the gift shop. The gift shop
at **Villa del Sueño** (⊠*First entrance to Playa Hermosa, 350 m west of
main highway*) has original oil paintings, exotic crafts from around the

world, locally made mother-of-pearl jewelry, and unique ivory bracelets made of local Brahma cow bones. **Kaltak Art and Craft Market** (⊠*South of airport on road to Santa Cruz*) has five rooms of high-quality crafts and gifts, including organic-cotton blouses and dresses and traditional leather-and-wood rocking chairs, which they will ship for you.

PLAYAS DEL COCO

25 km (16 mi) southwest of Liberia airport.

Messy, noisy, colorful, and interesting, Playas del Coco is first and foremost a fishing port, with a port captain's office, a fish market, and an ice factory for keeping the catch of the day fresh—not for cooling margaritas, although many are drunk here. The town (called "El Coco" by locals) is not particularly scenic. The dark-sand beach is mostly a workplace, and it hasn't yet met the Blue Flag standards of cleanliness. The main street becomes a sea of mud when it rains and a dust bowl when it doesn't. So why do visitors flock here? Although fresh seafood, myriad souvenir shops, and plenty of bars draw some tourism, the primary reasons to come to Playas del Coco are the diving, fishing, and surfing at remote breaks such as Olies Point and Witch's Rock. Because El Coco is mere minutes from Playa Hermosa, however, you can just as easily enjoy those sports while staying at that more pleasant beach. If you like to party, and want some local color, Coco's slightly down-at-the-heels ambience can be appealing.

GETTING HERE & AROUND

It's an easy drive from the Liberia airport to Playas del Coco. This is the first major town south of Liberia, about a 30-minute drive. The paved highway turns into a grand, divided boulevard as you enter town and then dissolves into the dusty main street that leads directly to the beach. If you don't have a car, the best way to get here from Playa Hermosa is in a taxi, for about $12 each way.

PLAYAS DEL COCO ESSENTIALS

Bank/ATM Banco Nacional (⊠*Main street, at entrance to town* ☎*2670–0801*).

Hospital Public Health Clinic (⊠*Next to Hotel Coco Verde* ☎*2670–0987*).

Pharmacy Farmacia Cocos (⊠*100 m east of Banco Nacional* ☎*2670–1186* ☾*Mon.–Sat. 8:30–8, Sun. 10–6* ☞*Resident doctor*).

Post Office Correo (⊠*Beachfront, beside police station*).

OUTDOOR ACTIVITIES

BOATING   You can sail off into the sunset for $55, including drinks and appetizers, on **Drums of Bora** (☎*2845–9448*), a 50-foot teak yacht. The company also offers snorkeling and diving trips

DIVING & SNORKELING   Half a dozen dive shops crowd into this small town. The standard price for a two-tank dive is $70; Catalina Island dives are $95. This coast doesn't have the coral reefs or the clear visibility of the Caribbean coast, but it does have a lot of plankton (hence the lower visibility) that feeds legions of fish, some of them really, really big. Manta rays and sharks (white-tipped, nurse, and bull varieties) are among the stars of the undersea show. It takes about 20 to 45 minutes to reach most dive sites.

Most of the dive shops have instruction, including **Summer Salt Dive Center** (✉ *Main street* ☎ *2670–0308* ⊕ *www.summer-salt.com*). **Deep Blue Diving Adventures** (✉ *Main street, in Hotel Coco Verde parking lot* ☎ *2670–1004* ⊕ *www.deepblue-diving.com*) is a reliable option. **Rich Coast Diving** (✉ *Main street, across from A&A office* ☎ *2670–0176* ⊕ *www.richcoastdiving.com*) has enthusiastic guides and instructors and limits tours to 5 divers per instructor and 15 divers per boat.

FISHING Fishing charter boats go out 15 to 40 mi seeking yellowfin tuna, mahimahi, grouper, and red snapper close-in, and sailfish, marlin, and roosterfish offshore (beyond 64 km [40 mi]). Boats, moored here and in nearby Ocotal, can pick you up from a beach near your hotel. **Tranqui-laMar** (✉ *Behind Louisiana Bar & Grill, off main street* ☎ *2670–0833* ⊕ *www.tranquilamar.com*) has three 28-foot Cummins diesel-power boats moored in nearby Ocotal. They can pick you up at any local beach. Just bring sunscreen and your hat, says the owner. Trips are $400 for a half day and $600 for a full day. **Blue Marlin Service** (✉ *Main street* ☎ *2670–0707 or 8348–6510*) goes out in either a 25-foot boat for close-in fishing ($285 half day) or in a luxury 52-footer for a full day offshore ($1,700).

GOLF The brand-new **Papagayo Golf & Country Club** (⊹ *2 km [1 mi] south of Sardinal on road to San Blas* ☎ *2697–0168* ⊕ *www.papagayo-golf. com*) is an 18-hole, par-72 course. It's also affordable; you can play the whole course for $70, including golf cart and a cooler with ice, or play nine holes for $40. There's a restaurant and bar and a tournament every Sunday morning.

SURFING Legendary **Witch's Rock and Ollie's Point** surfing spots are a one-hour boat
★ ride away from Playas del Coco off the coast of Santa Rosa National Park. You can surf as long as you pay the $6 park entrance fee.

You can sign up for a surfing trip with any beach-town tour operator, but local authorities only allow excursions to Witch's Rock and Ollie's Point to originate from the main dock at Playas del Coco, in boats owned by local boat owners, in order to curb overcrowding and undue environmental stress. **Roca Bruja Surf Operation** (✉ *Main street, about 3 blocks from beach* ☎ *2670–0952* ⊕ *www.costaricasurftrips.com*) is the operator that officially represents the local association of boat operators. The trips cost $75 to $100 per person, depending on the destination and number of people, plus the park entrance fee of $10.

WHERE TO STAY & EAT

$$–$$$ ✕ **Louisiana Bar & Grill.** This second-story restaurant is cool and breezy, but the Cajun cuisine is hot, with the most authentic jambalaya in town and a spicy gumbo loaded with shrimp, crab, and sausage. The fish is fresh, and it's served any way you like it, with a choice of 10 intriguing sauces, including macadamia pesto or orange-chipotle sauce.

⊠*Main street, across from Hotel Coco Verde Casino* ☎*2670–0400* ▤*AE, MC, V.*

\$\$–\$\$\$ ✕**Restaurante Papagayo Seafood.** The food here is straightforward, reliably fresh, and flavorful. Start with fish ceviche, or fish soup generously packed with shrimp, squid, fish, and crab. Then sink your teeth into the catch of the day (including lobster most notably), prepared any one of a dozen ways, or Papagayo seafood au gratin, which is a mix of sautéed seafood in a tarragon cream sauce. Meat lovers can order from the menu of the contiguous Papagayo Steakhouse, which has local and USDA beef, as well as a kids menu. Seating is available downstairs, between the stuffed fish and potted plants, or on the cooler, quieter second floor. ⊠*Main street, across from Hotel Coco Verde* ☎*2670–0298* ▤*AE, DC, MC, V.*

\$\$ ✕**El Sol y La Luna.** Playas del Coco's most pleasant surprise comes in the
★   form of this romantic alfresco restaurant serving haute-Italian cuisine. Host Alessandro Tolo brought his design ideas and superb jazz CD collection from Rome, but the food is what draws the crowd. Fans return for homemade pasta and homegrown basil and other distinctively Italian tastes, including a wide selection of Italian wines, sparkling San Pellegrino mineral water, and aromatic Sambuca liqueur. The house specialties include homemade cannelloni, salmon ravioli with a vodka cream sauce, and a fresh fish filet a la pizzaiola (in a tomato sauce). For dessert, try the homemade tiramisu, or Arenal, a moist, chocolate cake floating in a lake of chocolate sauce. If you're staying nearby, there's also pizza to go. ⊠*La Puerta del Sol hotel, last right from main road to Playas del Coco* ☎*2670–0195* ▤*MC, V* ☽*Closed Tues.*

\$\$ ▥**La Puerta del Sol.** Facing a formal garden with sculpted shrubs and a
☺   lovely pool just two blocks from the beach, this tranquil enclosure of stylish suites has modern, airy Mediterranean-style guest rooms shot through with hot, tropical colors. Each room has high ceilings, plenty of windows, and gleaming white, tiled bathrooms. King-size beds roost atop adobe platforms, whereas single beds nearby double as sofas by day. Pasha, the resident Newfoundland dog, can usually be found lolling around the reception area, and there are various pet cats prowling in the garden. The restaurant, El Sol y La Luna (⇨*above*), is excellent. ⊠*180 m to right (north) off main road to town* ☎*2670–0195* 🖷*2670–0650* ✎*lapuertadelsolcostarica@hotmail.com* ⬐*9 rooms* ☽*In-room: safe, refrigerator. In-hotel: restaurant, pool, gym, no elevator, laundry service, public Wi-Fi* ▤*MC, V* ⎟⊙⎟*BP.*

NIGHTLIFE

Most local expats prefer **Coconutz** (⊠*Main road, across from Hotel Coco Verde*), which is usually packed around happy hour (4–6), when they often have live music. They also have pool tables, lots of big TVs for games, and bar food. At the **Lizard Lounge** (⊠*Main road, west of Hotel Coco Verde*) there's dancing every night on a big thatch-roof dance floor. The reggae, techno, and rap beats appeal to a very young crowd. **Zouk Santana** (⊠*Main road, west of Hotel Coco Verde*) is a split-level lounge with a funky ambience that combines bars, couches, and small dance floors for moving to the eclectic mix of music.

SHOPPING

If you can't find it at **Galería & Souvenirs Susy** (✉*Main street, next to Coco Verde Hotel*), chances are they don't make it in Costa Rica. Along with a huge selection of interesting notebooks and albums made of botanical materials, the place also sells locally made shell belts.

PLAYA OCOTAL

3 km (2 mi) north of Playas del Coco.

One of the most dramatic beaches in the country, this serene crescent is ringed by rocky cliffs. The sparkling, clean turquoise water contrasts with the black sand. It's only ½-km (-mi long), but the vistas are endless, with offshore islands and the jagged profile of the Santa Elena Peninsula 34 km (21 mi) away. Right at the entrance to the Gulf of Papagayo, it's a good place for sportfishing enthusiasts to hole up between excursions. There's good diving at Las Corridas, just 1 km (½ mi) away, and excellent snorkeling in nearby coves and islands, as well as right off the beach around the rocks at the east end of the beach.

GETTING HERE & AROUND

The drive 10 minutes from Playas del Coco is on a paved road to the gated entrance of Playa Ocotal. The road winds through a heavily populated Tico residential area, so be on the lookout, especially at night, for bicyclists without lights, children, dogs, cows, and horses on the road. There are no buses from Playas del Coco to Ocotal, but it's about $7 by taxi.

OUTDOOR ACTIVITIES

DIVING & SNORKELING
The rocky outcrop at the north end of the beach near Los Almendros is good for close-in snorkeling. The dive shop at the **Ocotal Beach Resort** (✉*3 km [2 mi] south of Playas del Coco* ☎*2670–0321* ⊕*www. ocotaldiving.com*) is the only PADI Instruction Development Center in Costa Rica, offering the highest-level diving courses. The shop has excellent equipment, safety standards, and instruction. A regular dive costs $72; equipment rental is another $25. The shop also rents snorkeling equipment for $10 per day.

FISHING
Ocotal Beach Resort (⇨*above*) has a sportfishing operation with three 32-foot Morgan hulls powered by twin 260HP Cummins engines ($499 half day; $800 full day for up to four fishers). Marlins are catch-and-release, but you can keep—and eat—the mahimahi, yellowfin tuna, grouper, and amber jack you catch.

HIKING
Take an exhilarating and engrossing morning walk ($15) in the hills of Ocotal with retired vet and very active naturalist **Dr. Will Abrams** (☎*2670–0553*). The energetic, knowledgeable Kentucky native entertains and educates with stories about the secret lives of trees, plants, and animals spotted along the way.

WHERE TO STAY & EAT

$$$ ✕ **Picante.** It's hot and it's tropical and, as the name warns (*picante* means "spicy"), everything here makes your taste buds tingle. The menu spices up (literally) local fish and tropical fruits in dishes like fresh-tuna *salade niçoise* and grilled mahimahi with a picante mango sauce. (There's also a milder kids' menu.) The large terrace restaurant is poolside, facing the gorgeous beach backed by a cookie-cutter condominium development at Bahía Pez Vela. The cheap dinette furniture is out of sync with the innovative food, but you'll forgive the furniture faux pas when you taste the tart margarita pie or mango cobbler. Their Sunday brunch (10–2) is quite popular. ⊠ *At the beach, Bahía Pez Vela* ✛ *1½ km (1 mi) south of Ocotal* ☎ *2670–0901* ▤ *MC, V.*

$$$ ⬚ **Ocotal Beach Resort.** This resort has the best sea views hereabouts and is one of the best dive and sportfishing resorts in the country. All rooms have ocean views, but those with the nicest views are on the hilltop, even though they may be a bit cramped with furniture. Down the hill to the beach, comfortable triangular bungalows each have two separate suites that share a semiprivate pool. Swimming pools dot the property; be prepared, though, for a steep hike to the biggest one down at the beach, or call for a golf cart to take you there. The best feature of the restaurant, which specializes in Mediterranean and Asian flavors, is the 270° view from the terrace. ✛ *3 km (2 mi) south of Playas del Coco, down newly paved road* ☎ *2670–0321* 🖷 *2670–1112* ⊕ *www.ocotal resort.com* ⬚ *42 rooms, 4 suites, 12 bungalow suites* ⬙ *In-room: safe. In-hotel: 2 restaurants, room service, bars, tennis court, pools, spa, diving, no elevator, laundry service, public Internet, public Wi-Fi* ▤ *AE, MC, V* ❏ *BP.*

$$ ⬚ **Hotel Villa Casa Blanca.** For romance, you can't beat this Victorian-★   style, all-suites B&B in a hillside building buried in a bower of tropical plantings. Four-poster beds, plush furniture, and Victorian detailing set the mood. The honeymoon suites have deep soaking tubs built for two. The pool is small but pretty. There's no room service, but the obliging staff can arrange for local restaurants to deliver dinners *á deux*, to be enjoyed by candlelight at the pool or on the terrace. Waffles, pancakes, muffins, and savory dishes provide fuel in the morning. Breakfast entertainment is provided by various pet parrots who are vociferous as well as notorious moochers. Judging by the guest comments, people love them. ⊠ *Just inside gated entrance to El Ocotal Beach Resort* ⬚ *Apdo. 176–5019, Playas del Coco* ☎ *670–0448* ⊕ *www.hotelvilla casablanca.com* ⬚ *12 suites* ⬙ *In-room: no phone, safe, no TV. In-hotel: pool, no elevator, laundry service, public Internet, public Wi-Fi, no-smoking rooms* ▤ *AE, MC, V* ❏ *BP.*

NIGHTLIFE

Enjoy a quiet margarita with an ocean view at **Father Rooster Sports Bar & Grill** (⊠ *Next door to El Ocotal Beach Resort* ✛ *3 km [2 mi] south of Playas del Coco*) on the beach. The action heats up later in the evening with big-screen TV, music, pool, beach volleyball, and Tex-Mex bar food. During peak holiday weeks, crowds of partiers descend on the bar to dance by torchlight.

PLAYA PAN DE AZÚCAR

8 km (5 mi) north of Flamingo Beach.

Playa Pan de Azúcar (Sugar Bread Beach) has a quality that can be hard to come by in this area: privacy. With only one built-up property, the entire stretch of brown-sugar sand feels practically deserted. The north end of the beach has some good snorkeling when the sea is calm—usually around low tide—and the swimming out from the middle of the beach is relatively safe. But if the swell is big, children and weak swimmers shouldn't go in past their waist. Playa Penca, a short walk south along the beach, can be a good swimming beach as well. A large part of the attraction here is the forest that hems the beach, where you may see howler monkeys, black iguanas, magpie jays, trogons, and dozens of other bird species.

GETTING HERE & AROUND

Getting to this beach is an adventure in itself. It's still a very bumpy road 20 minutes from Flamingo Beach. If you have a 4WD vehicle and an excellent sense of direction, you can attempt to drive (dry season only) the 16-km (11-mi) Monkey Trail, which cuts through the mountains from Coco to Flamingo. But even some Ticos get lost on this route, so keep asking for directions along the way. There are no buses to Playa Pan de Azúcar; a taxi from Playa Flamingo costs about $15.

OUTDOOR ACTIVITIES

Most of the operators who work out of Flamingo (⇨ *below*) can pick up guests at the Hotel Sugar Beach for skin diving, sportfishing, sailing, horseback riding, and other excursions. The Hotel Sugar Beach (⇨ *below*) offers outrigger tours to a secluded beach 40 minutes to the north, which has a large reef and calm water for snorkeling.

WHERE TO STAY

$$–$$$ **Hotel Sugar Beach.** The theme of this secluded hotel with a shimmering pool and thin, curving beach is harmony with nature. Its owners have gone to great lengths to protect the surrounding environment, as the abundant wildlife on its 25-acres of protected forest attests. Spacious one- and two-bedroom suites, with high ceilings and private terraces with idyllic sea views, are great for couples and families (kids under 12 are free). If you like serenity and want to spend a little less on lodging, opt for a standard room in one of the duplexes scattered through the forest. Each room is decorated in earth tones, with elegant wicker furniture, a wooden door with a hand-carved local bird or animal, and a veranda with a garden or ocean view (the best ocean views are from Rooms 21 and 22). The open-air rotunda restaurant serves good seafood dishes ($$$) and there's a kids' menu. The hotel's recycling, energy and water conservation, and community service programs are exemplary. **Pros:** Friendly, natural setting, practically private beach. **Con:** Waves and rocks can make ocean dangerous for kids. ⊕ *8 km (5 mi) north of Playa Flamingo* ☎2654–4242 ⊟2654–4239 ⊕*www.sugar-beach.com* ⇝*22 rooms, 6 suites, 2 houses* ⚭*In-room: safe, kitchen (some), refrigerator. In-hotel: restaurant, room service,*

Fodor's Choice
★

bar, pool, water sports, no elevator, laundry service, airport shuttle (from Liberia), public Internet, public Wi-Fi ⊟*AE, D, MC, V* ⦿l*BP.*

PLAYA POTRERO

4 km (2½ mi) north of Flamingo.

The small town of Potrero is a classic Tico community, with a church, school, and supermarket arranged around a soccer field. But Potrero Beach stretches for 4 km (2½ mi) all the way south from the village to the skyline of Flamingo. Development is picking up speed, with large houses and condominium developments springing up on any hill with a view. There's a large Italian contingent here, adding some style and flavor to area hotels. The brown-sand beach is safe for swimming, but Potrero is neither the prettiest, nor cleanest, of this region's beaches. The best area for swimming is midway between Flamingo and Potrero town, near the hotel Bahía del Sol. The best beach view and best breeze are from a bar stool at Bar Las Brisas. About 10 km (6 mi) offshore lie the Catalina Islands, a barrier-island mecca for divers and snorkelers, which dive boats based in Flamingo reach in 10 minutes.

GETTING HERE & AROUND

Just before crossing the bridge at the entrance to Flamingo, take the right fork signed for Potrero. The road, which is alternately muddy or dusty, is rough and follows the shoreline. Local buses run from Flamingo to Potrero, but it's so close that you're better off taking a taxi.

OUTDOOR ACTIVITIES

DIVING Marked as Santa Catarina on some maps, the **Catalina Islands,** as they are known locally, are a major destination for dive operations based all along the coast. These barrier islands are remarkable for their diversity, and appeal to different levels of divers. On one side, the islands have 20- to 30-foot drops, great for beginners. The other side has deeper drops of 60 to 80 feet, better suited to more experienced divers. The top dive sites around the Catalina Islands are **The Point** and **The Wall.** From January to May, when the water is colder, you are almost guaranteed manta-ray sightings at these spots. Cow-nosed and devil rays are also spotted here in large schools, as well as white-tipped sharks, several types of eels, and an array of reef fish. Dive operators from Playa Hermosa south to Tamarindo offer trips to these islands. Reserve through your hotel.

Costa Rica Diving (✛ *1 km (½ mi) south of Flamingo on the main highway* ☎*2654–4148* ⊕*www.costarica-diving.com*) has been specializing in Catalina Islands dives for 16 years, with two-tank, two-location trips limited to five divers costing $75. The German owners also offer courses and are noted for their precision and high safety standards.

WHERE TO EAT

$ ✕**El Castillo Gourmet Eatery.** You won't find a better peanut-butter cookie in the country. This bakery/restaurant is also famous for its gooey cinnamon buns and pizza, which you can pick up to eat on the beach, or back at your hotel. A mix of Latin and American food—from breakfast eggs Benedict through sandwiches and salads, Tex-Mex standards, shrimp skewers, and fish-and-chips—is served at casual terrace tables shaded by an ancient fig tree. The only drawback is the location on a busy corner, since the traffic tends to kick up a lot of dust. There's live music on Thursday night, and karaoke on Friday night. ⊠*Across from Club Bahía Potrero* ☎2654–4271 ⊟*MC, V.*

$ ✕**Ristorante Marco Polo.** They came, they saw, they built a whole Tuscan-style village and imported a chef from Italy to cater to a demanding Italian clientele. Marco Polo, the main restaurant at the Villagio Flor de Pacífico mega-development of red-roof villas east of Potrero, serves properly *al dente* pasta with homemade sauces and a dozen different wood-oven pizzas. They also serve more substantial dishes such as grilled tuna, chicken cordon bleu, and tenderloin with a béarnaise sauce. There's even a pool in back that you can use while you wait for lunch. ✛*1 km (½ mi) east of Potrero* ☎254–5504 ⊟*AE, MC, V.*

¢–$ ✕**Bar Las Brisas.** The perfect beach bar, Las Brisas is a shack with a view of the entire sweep of Playa Potrero. The kitchen serves up fairly basic bar fare and some fresh seafood such as rice with shrimp, and a grilled mahimahi sandwich. The fish tacos are outstanding—breaded strips of fish smothered in lettuce, tomato, and refried beans and encased in both a crisp taco and a soft tortilla shell. Wednesday is ladies night, when the joint really jumps. The place is decorated with old surfboards, rusty U.S. license plates, and wall murals. ⊠*100 m west of soccer field, across from supermarket* ☎2654–4047 ⊟*V.*

WHERE TO STAY

$$–$$$ ⊞**Bahía del Sol.** It has the premier location on the beach, with rooms
★ surrounding lush gardens shaded by tropical trees. But this luxury hotel doesn't rest on its well-situated laurels. The service matches the unbeatable surroundings. At the restaurant ($$$), next to the gorgeous palm-fringed pool, smartly uniformed waiters serve jumbo shrimp, lobster, fresh fish, and various meat dishes prepared in an eclectic mix of ways, from blackened tuna to Moroccan lamb. Seating is under a massive thatch roof, or at several tables on the lawn overlooking the beach. Rooms are spacious and elegant, with Costa Rica wicker and wood furniture, patterned ceramic-tile floors, and paintings by Costa Rican artists. They open onto a portico with chairs, hammocks, and views of the garden; deluxe rooms also have a back patio with a Jacuzzi hemmed by greenery. Spacious one- and two-bedroom suites also have kitchens and living rooms. **Pros:** On the beach, lovely grounds, excellent restaurant, friendly. **Con:** Noise from nearby bars. ⊠*South end of Potrero Beach, across from El Castillo* ☎2654–4671 ⊞2654–5182 ⊕*www.potrero bay.com* ⇆*28 rooms, 15 suites* ⊟*In room: safe, refrigerator, Wi-Fi. In-hotel: restaurant, room service, bar, pool, beachfront, bicycles, no elevator, laundry service, concierge, public Internet, public Wi-Fi* ⊟*AE, MC, V* ⊧O⊧*BP.*

$ ⊞**Bahía Esmeralda Hotel & Restaurant.** Although it's not on the beach, this Italian-run hotel has style at an affordable price. It's a great place for families or groups. Ochre-color villas are spread out around pretty pool gardens and lawn. Large glass doors bring in lots of light, and the fans hung from high wooden ceilings keep things cool. The well-equipped

A Cavalcade of Stars

Costa Rica has rolled out the red carpet in recent years for a growing number of celebrities. Singers Sting, Ricky Martin, Enrique Iglesias, and Marc Anthony appended a bit of R&R onto concert performances here. (Much speculation ensued about the likelihood of Anthony's equally famous wife, Jennifer Lopez, singing with him. She didn't, but she received as much media attention as he did.) Angelina Jolie, Brad Pitt, and Paul Newman have visited to publicize humanitarian work. Actors Drew Carrey, Doris Roberts, Mel Gibson, and Matthew McConaughey have vacationed here (with McConaughey drawing much interest from paparazzi photographers). Keep your eyes peeled. You never know who you might spot.

apartments sleep four, six, or eight people, and have handsome fabrics and bathrooms tiled in cool green. An alfresco restaurant serves breakfast and light Italian dishes. The friendly owner-manager is always on the premises. It's a five-minute walk through the village to the beach. ⊠*1 block east of Potrero village* ☎*2654-4480* 🖷*2654-4479* ⊕*www. hotelbahiaesmeralda.com* ⇨*4 rooms, 14 apartments* ⚘*In-room: no phone, kitchen (some). In-hotel: restaurant, pool, laundry service, public Wi-Fi* ⊟*AE, MC, V* ⎰◎⎱*EP apartments, BP rooms.*

PLAYA FLAMINGO

80 km (50 mi) southwest of Liberia.

Flamingo was the first of the northern Nicoya beaches to experience the wonders of overdevelopment, a fact immortalized in the concrete towers that straggle up the hill above Flamingo Bay. The place is still abuzz with real-estate activity, and any ledge of land with a view is a building site. The beach, hidden away to the southwest of the town, is one of the loveliest strands in Costa Rica, with light-beige sand sloping into a relatively calm sea and buttonwood trees separating it from the road. This beach is great for swimming, with a fine-sand bottom and no strong currents, though there are a few submerged rocks in front of the Flamingo Beach Resort, so you should swim a bit farther south. There's sometimes a bit of surf, so if the waves are big, keep your eye on little paddlers. There is little shade along the beach's kilometer-long stretch, and no services, though there are restaurants in the beach resort and the adjacent town. To find the beach, go straight as you enter town, instead of going up the hill, and turn left after the Flamingo Beach Resort.

Flamingo is perhaps most famous for its large sportfishing fleet, temporarily moored out in the bay while the government grants a new concession to update and operate the marina here. Lured by boatloads of single-for-the-week fishermen, working girls abound here, adding a faint salacious whiff to the nightspots.

GETTING HERE & AROUND

To get to Playa Flamingo from Liberia, drive 45 km (28 mi) south to Belén and then 35 km (22 mi) west on a good, paved road. The trip takes about three hours. If you're coming from the Playas del Coco and Ocotal area, you can take a 16-km (10-mi) shortcut, called the Monkey Trail, starting near Sardinal and emerging at Potrero. It's then 4 km (2½ mi) south to Flamingo. Only attempt this in dry season and in a 4WD. You can also take a bus from Liberia *(⇨ Bus Travel in Travel Smart Costa Rica).*

PLAYA FLAMINGO ESSENTIALS

Bank/ATM **Banco de Costa Rica** (⊠ *Right from main street, halfway up hill, in Condominio Marina Real* ☎ *2654–4984*).

Hospital **Pacific Emergencies** (⊠ *Crossroads at Huacas* ☎ *2653–8785* ⊘ *Daily 8–8*).

Pharmacy **Santa Fe Medical Center & Pharmacy** (⊠ *Halfway up hill* ☎ *2654–9000* ⊘ *Daily 8–8*).

Internet **Shark Point at Costa Rica Diving** (⊹ *1 km [½ mi] south of town* ☎ *2654–4148* ⊘ *Daily 10–6*).

OUTDOOR ACTIVITIES

Flamingo offers the quickest access to the **Catalina Islands,** visible from its beach, where big schools of fish, manta rays, and other sea creatures gather. Coastal reefs to the north are visited on day trips that combine snorkeling with time on undeveloped beaches. **Aquacenter Diving** (⊠ *Below Flamingo Marina Resort* ☎ *8352–4031 or 2654–4141* ⊕ *www.aquacenterdiving.com*) runs two-tank dives at the Catalina Islands ($70) and snorkeling trips ($45), as well as offering a range of PADI certification courses.

BOATING **Lazy Lizard Catamaran Sailing Adventures** (☎ *2654–4192* ⊕ *www.lazylizardsailing.com*) offers a morning or afternoon snorkeling and sunbathing tour on a 38-foot catamaran. The four-hour tours starts at 9:30 AM and 2 PM and cost $75, with snorkeling equipment, kayaks, drinks, and food included. If you're up for a more energetic sea expedition, paddle with **Guanacaste Outriggers** (☎ *8383–3013* ⊕ *www.guanacasteoutriggers.com*) to remote beaches for snorkeling, swimming, and beachcombing ($57, including fruit buffet). Canoes seat seven, plus two guides.

Sail off for an afternoon of snorkeling, snacking, and sunset drinks on **Samonique III** (☎ *2654–5280, 8388–7870* ⊕ *www.costarica-sailing.com*), a *trés jolie* 52-foot French ketch ($75). The ship sails daily at 2 and returns at 6:30 PM.

FISHING Although the marina is still closed down while officials consider bids to rebuild it, there are plenty of sportfishing boats bobbing in Flamingo Bay. In December the wind picks up and many of the smaller, 31-foot-and-under boats head to calmer water farther south. But the wind brings cold water and abundant bait fish, which attract marlin (blue, black, and striped), Pacific sailfish, yellowfin tuna, wahoo, mahimahi, grouper, and red snapper. January to April is consequently prime catch-and-release season for billfish. One of the established fishing operations that sticks around all year is **Billfish Safaris** (⊠ *Lower level, Mariner Inn, at entrance to town* ☎ *2654–5244* ⊕ *www.bill fishsafaris.com*). Its 42-foot boat

THE GUANACASTE TREE

Massive and wide-spreading, with tiny leaflets and dark brown, ear-like seed pods, the guanacaste is common through this region, and is Costa Rica's national tree.

with twin 350-horsepower diesel engines can go anywhere in any kind of sea. Trips on a smaller 35-foot boat are also available. Half-day trips are $825--$900 for up to seven anglers; full-day trips run $1,150--$1,250. You can also go out night fishing for snapper and grouper ($100 per person).

WHERE TO EAT

$$$ ✕ **Mar y Sol.** Come early to catch the sunset from the second-floor tapas
★ lounge here, then linger over a fine French-accented dinner at this elegant, torchlighted terrace restaurant perched on a hillside. The chefs/owners Alain and Jean LucTaulere represent the fifth and sixth generations of a family of French restaurateurs, so of course there's bouillabaisse on the menu, along with escargots and Chateaubriand for two, sliced tableside. More interesting, though, are their fusions of French traditions with tropical flavors in dishes such as grilled mahimahi with a mango salsa and buerre blanc sauce, or seared tuna with an Asian reduction, wakame, and wasabi mashed potatoes. The succulent rack of lamb is served with a rosemary Bordelaise sauce, and the crispy duck, with a Cognac guava sauce. A Sunday brunch menu, served from 10:30 AM to 2:30 PM, has omelets, quiches, and scallops au gratin. There's an extensive wine cellar to match the sophisticated menu, and they serve two-dozen wines by the glass. Service is smoothly professional. ⊠ *150 m uphill (west) from the Banco de Costa Rica* ☎ *2654–4151* ⊟ *AE, MC, V* ☉ *Closed Sun.* and *Oct.*

$ ✕ **Marie's Restaurant.** A Flamingo institution, serving beachgoers and locals for more than two decades, this popular restaurant serves an array of sandwiches and salads, as well as reliably fresh seafood in large portions at reasonable prices. Settle in at one of the wooden tables beneath the ceiling fans and massive thatched roof for a traditional Costa Rican ceviche, avocado stuffed with shrimp, or heart of palm and pejivalle (palm fruit). The main fare includes whole-fried red snapper, shrimp and fish shish kebabs, and a delicious *plato de mariscos* (shrimp, lobster, and fish served with garlic butter, potatoes, and salad). Save room for Marie's signature banana-chocolate bread pudding. At breakfast, try unusual papaya pancakes, French toast made with cream cheese and jam, or Marie's special omelet with cheese, onion, sweet pepper, bacon, and ham. ⊠ *Main road, near north end of beach* ☎ *2654–4136* ⊟ *AE, MC, V.*

WHERE TO STAY

$$–$$$ ☷**Flamingo Marina Resort.** Though a short walk from Flamingo beach, this collection of hillside villas has lots to do. There are four pools, tennis courts, a beach, a dive shop, and a tour desk. The fashionably decorated rooms, color-washed in a mango hue, have terra-cotta lamps, hand-carved wooden furniture, and shell-shape sinks. The luxurious condos have modern kitchens and spacious sitting areas with leather couches. Nearly all rooms and condos have large verandas with views of the sea and Playa Potrero. **Pros:** Spacious rooms, sea views, ample grounds. **Con:** Not on main beach. ⊠*Hill above Flamingo Bay* ☝*Apdo. 321–1002, San José* ☎*2654–4141* ☐*2654–4035, 2231–1858 in San José* ⊕*www.flamingomarina.com* ⊅*22 rooms, 8 suites, 57 condos* ♿*In-room: safe, kitchen (some), Wi-Fi. In-hotel: restaurant, room service, bar, pools, beachfront, diving, laundry service, public Internet* ☰*AE, DC, MC, V* ⦿*EP.*

$$ ☷**Flamingo Beach Resort.** This three-story concrete hotel has a great
☼ location overlooking beautiful Flamingo Beach, and though few of its rooms have ocean views, they are all mere steps away from the sand and surf. A family-friendly inn, it has the comfortable, if slightly anonymous, look of an international hotel. You can't beat its beach-accessible location, though, or the huge, centerpiece swimming pool with Olympic-length lap lanes along one side. The kids' pool has a sunburn-preventive thatch roof, and is close enough to the swim-up bar that you could save a toddler without spilling your piña colada. There's a dive shop on-site, water-sports equipment, several pool tables, and children's activities. Rooms are standard size, with high ceilings and private balconies or terraces. Get a pool view, preferably on the second or third floor; those with higher numbers have ocean views. The restaurants are not exciting, so don't take the all-inclusive option. There are good restaurants within walking distance or a quick shuttle trip away. **Pros:** Beachfront, big pool, good value. **Cons:** Inconsistent service, mediocre food. ⊠*Hotel entrance on left just past Marie's Restaurant* ☎*2654–4444, 2283–8063 in San José* ☐*2654–4060, 2253–1593 in San José* ⊕*www.resortflamingobeach.com* ⊅*88 rooms, 32 suites* ♿*In-room: safe, kitchen (some), refrigerator, Wi-Fi. In-hotel: restaurant, room service, bars, tennis court, pools, gym, beachfront, diving, children's programs (ages 2–12), laundry service, public Wi-Fi* ☰*AE, MC, V* ⦿*EP, AI.*

$ ☷**Hotel Guanacaste Lodge.** On the outskirts of Flamingo, a short drive from the beach, this Tico-run lodge offers basic accommodations for a fraction of what the town's big hotels charge. Ten simple, duplex bungalows have high beamed ceilings, wood furniture, walk-in closets, and spacious bathrooms. Each room has a picture window looking out onto a garden that holds the pool, a thatched shelter, and a cascading fountain. ⊠*200 m south of the Potrero-Flamingo crossroads* ☎*2654–4494* ☐*2654–4495* ⊅*10 rooms* ♿*In-room: no phone. In-hotel: pool, no elevator* ☰*V* ⦿*BP.*

NIGHTLIFE

The **Mariner Inn Bar** (⊠*Bottom of hill, entering Flamingo*) is often boisterous and thick with testosterone, as fishermen trade fish tales. If you're interested in fishing of a different sort, or just like to watch, restaurant/disco/casino **Amberes** (⊠*Halfway up hill in Flamingo*) is the late-night meeting place.

PLAYA CONCHAL

8 km (5 mi) south of Flamingo.

Lovely, secluded Playa Conchal is named for the bits of broken shells that cover its base of fine white sand (the Spanish word for shell is concha). It's an idyllic strand of sugar sand sloping steeply into aquamarine water and lined with an array of trees. The point that defines Conchal's northern end is hemmed by a lava-rock reef that is a popular snorkeling area—locals rent equipment on the beach—whereas the beach's southern extreme is often deserted. Although the sprawling Paradisus Playa Conchal resort covers the hinterland behind the beach, you don't need to stay at that all-inclusive resort to enjoy Conchal, since it's a short walk, or drive, south to Brasilito.

GETTING HERE & AROUND

The drive south from Flamingo is 10 minutes on a paved highway. Both town and beach are just 1 km (½ mi) north of the entrance to Paradisus Playa Conchal. To reach Playa Conchal, turn left at the end of the town square and follow the dirt road across a stretch of beach and over a steep hill; the beach stretch is impassable at high tide. Buses run from Flamingo to Conchal three times daily, at 7:30 and 11:30 AM and 2:30 PM. A taxi from Flamingo is about $6.

PLAYA CONCHAL ESSENTIALS

The closest bank and ATM are in Flamingo.

Hospital **Pacific Emergencies** (⊠*Crossroads at Huacas* ☎*2653–8787 or 8378–8265* ⊙*Daily 8–8*).

Pharmacy **Farmacia El Cruce** (⊠*Crossroads at Huacas* ☎*2653–8787* ⊙*Daily 8–10*).

Internet **Internet Café** (⊠*Near Supermarket López, 200 m south of school* ⊙*Daily 9 AM to 8 PM*).

EXPLORING

A small, scruffy fishing village just 1 km (½ mi) north of Conchal, **Brasilito** has ramshackle houses huddled around its main square, which doubles as the soccer field. It's cluttered, noisy, and totally Tico, a lively contrast to the controlled sophistication of the Playa Conchal resort and residential development. Fishing boats moor just off a wide beach, about 3 km (2 mi) long, with golden sand flecked with pebbles and a few rocks. The surf is a little stronger here than at Flamingo Beach but the shallow, sandy bottom keeps it swimmable. The sea is cleaner off nearby Playa Conchal, which is also a more attractive beach. A few casual *marisquerias* (seafood eateries) and a couple of notable restaurants line Brasilito's beach.

OUTDOOR ACTIVITIES

GOLF One of the best golf courses in the country, the Paradisus Playa Conchal megaresort's **Garra de Léon Golf Course** (✉*Paradisus Playa Conchal, entrance, less than 1 km [½ mi] south of Brasilito* ☎*2654–4123*) is a par-72 course designed by Robert Trent Jones Jr. Hotel guests, and nonguests who reserve at least a day in advance, can try out their swing on 18 holes for $150 ($175 for nonguests), cart included.

WHERE TO STAY & EAT

$$ ✕**El Camarón Dorado.** Much of the appeal of this open-air bar-restaurant whose name translates as "The Golden Shrimp" is its shaded location on Brasilito's beautiful beach. Some tables are practically on the beach, with the surf lapping just yards away, making it the perfect spot for sunset drinks. The white-plastic tables and chairs are not up to the standards of the food, which is mostly locally caught fish and seafood served in bountiful portions. The house specialties include mahimahi prepared various ways, arroz a la marinera (rice with seafood), grilled lobster, and either jumbo, or the smaller pinky shrimp al ajillo (sautéed with garlic). If you have a reservation, a van can pick you up from Flamingo or Tamarindo hotels. ✉*200 m north of Brasilito Plaza* ☎*2654–4028* ▤*AE, DC, MC, V.*

$–$$ ✕**Il Forno Restaurant.** For a break from seafood, try lunch or dinner at this romantic Italian garden restaurant. There are 17 versions of thin-crust pizzas, plus fine homemade pastas and risotto. Vegetarians have lots of choices (if you can get past the thought that veal is on the menu), including an eggplant lasagne and interesting salads. They also serve some tasty seafood and meat dishes. At dinner, fairy lights and candles glimmer all through the garden, and some private tables are set apart under thatched roofs. Spanish and Italian wines are available by the glass or bottle. ✉*Main road, 200 m east of the bridge in Brasilito* ☎*2654–4125* ▤*No credit cards* ⊘*Closed Mon. and Oct.*

$$$$ ▦**Paradisus Playa Conchal Beach & Golf Resort.** So vast that guests ride around in trucks covered with striped awnings and the staff gets around on bicycles, this all-inclusive resort, the top of the line of the Spanish Melía hotel chain, is luxurious, if lacking a bit in personality. The grounds encompass almost 4 square km (1½ square mi) that include a distant, picture-perfect beach. But in the labyrinthine guest village, the ocean disappears and the only views are of gardens and other buildings exactly like yours. The split-level Spanish Colonial–style villas have huge marble bathrooms and elegant sitting rooms. More than 100 "Royal Service" rooms are closer to the beach and have a private concierge. There's a kids' club and the largest—and perhaps warmest—pool in Central America. Grownups can amuse themselves sailing, snorkeling, kayaking, gambling at the casino, playing the gorgeous 18-hole golf course, or rejuvenating at the spa. If you're into the beach, try to get booked into a building between 1–5, or 33–40. More expansive Royal Service rooms are far from the beach. **Pros:** Lovely rooms, beach access, abundant activities. **Cons:** Expensive, massive,

most rooms far from beach. ⊠*Entrance less than 1 km (½ mi) south of Brasilito* ☎*2654–4123* 🖳*2654–4181* ⊕*www.paradisusplayaconchal. travel* 🛏*292 villas, 122 Royal Service villas* ⎘*In-room: safe, refrigerator, Wi-Fi. In-hotel: 7 restaurants, room service, bars, golf course, tennis courts, pools, gym, spa, beachfront, water sports, bicycles, children's programs (ages 3–12), laundry service, concierge, public Internet, public Wi-Fi* ⊟*AE, DC, MC, V* ⎮⚬⎮*AI.*

¢ 🏨**Hotel Brasilito.** Backpackers and travelers who don't need amenities will love this vintage, two-story, wooden hotel's seafront location, if not its no-frills rooms. Those rooms are a bit devoid of decor, though they do have hot water and either air-conditioning or a fan. Be prepared for some noise: kids playing, dogs barking, and motors revving. Ask for one of the two larger rooms above the restaurant; they share a veranda with unobstructed sea views. You can't beat the price for seaside rooms. Outback Jack's ($$), the Australian restaurant that occupies the open-air lobby, is a colorful, lively spot that specializes in grilled meat and seafood. **Pros:** Inexpensive, across the street from beach, good restaurant. **Cons:** Very basic rooms, can be noisy. ⊠*Between soccer field and beach, Brasilito* ☎*2654–4237* 🖳*2654–4247* ⊕*www.brasilito.com* 🛏*15 rooms* ⎘*In-room: no a/c (some), no phone, no TV. In-hotel: restaurant, beachfront, no elevator, laundry service, public Wi-Fi* ⊟*MC, V* ⎮⚬⎮*EP.*

NIGHTLIFE

Live music, both acoustic guitar and rowdier dance bands, keeps **The Happy Snapper** (⊠*On main street across from beach in Brasilito*) hopping from Wednesday to Saturday nights. Owner Mike Osborne often mans the bar and spikes the drinks with his own brand of wry humor.

EN ROUTE Gas stations are few and far between in these hinterlands. If you're heading down to Tamarindo from the Flamingo/Conchal area, fill up first. Your best bet is the 24-hour Oasis Exxon, 3 km (2 mi) east of Huacas.

TAMARINDO

82 km (51 mi) southwest of Liberia.

Once a funky beach town full of spacey surfers and local fishermen, Tamarindo has become a pricey, hyped-up hive of commercial development and real-estate speculation, with the still-unpaved roads kicking up dust and mud alternately, depending on the season. On the plus side, there's a dizzying variety of shops, bars, and hotels, and probably the best selection of restaurants of any beach town. Strip malls and high-rise condominiums have obscured views of the still-magnificent beach, and some low-life elements are making security an issue. But once you're on the beach, almost all the negatives disappear (just keep your eyes on belongings). Wide and flat, the sand is packed hard enough for easy walking and jogging. How good it is for swimming and surfing, however, is questionable, since the town has twice lost its Blue Flag clean-beach status (due to overdevelopment and the total absence of water treatment). The water quality is especially poor during the rainy months, when you'll want to do your swimming and surfing at nearby Playa Langosta, or Playa Grande. ■TIP➔**Strong currents at the north end of the beach get a lot of swimmers into trouble, especially when they try to cross the estuary without a surfboard.**

Surfing is the main attraction here, and there's a young crowd that parties hard after a day riding the waves. Tamarindo serves as a popular base for surfing at the nearby Playas Grande, Langosta, Avellanas, and Negra. There are plenty of outdoor options in addition to surfing, though, among them diving, sportfishing, wildlife-watching, and canopy tours. You can play 18 rounds at the nearby Hacienda Pinilla golf course, or simply stroll the beach and sunbathe.

GETTING HERE & AROUND
Both Nature Air and SANSA fly to Tamarindo from San José. Macaw Air flies between Liberia and Tamarindo and to other Nicoya Peninsula towns. By car from Liberia, travel south on the highway to the turn-off for Belén, then head west and turn left at the Huacas crossroads to Tamarindo. Stretches of the paved road from Belén are in deplorable states of disrepair. There are no direct bus connections between Playa Grande or Playa Avellanas and Tamarindo. A taxi is the way to go from nearby towns if you don't have wheels. The **Tamarindo Shuttle** (☎2653–1326) ferries passengers between the various beaches in a comfortable van.

TAMARINDO ESSENTIALS
Bank/ATM **Banco Nacional** (✉*Across from Tamarindo El Diria Hotel* ☎2653–0366).

Hospital **Pacific Emergencies Clínic** (✉*Next to Farmacia Tamarindo* ☎2653–1226). **Emergencias 2000** (✚*4 km [2½ mi] east of Tamarindo at Villa Real crossroad* ☎8380–4125 *or* 2653–0611).

Pharmacy **Farmacia Tamarindo** (✉*Main road into town* ☎2653–1239).

Internet **Internet Café** (✉*Road to Hotel Pasatiempo, next to ABC Realty* ☎2653–1011).

Taxis **Olman Taxi** (☎2653–1143 *or* 8356–6364 *[cell]*); the SANSA shuttle van from the airport into town (☎2653–0244) charges $4 per person.

OUTDOOR ACTIVITIES
BOATING Rocky Isla El Capitán, just offshore, is a close-in kayaking destination, full of sand-dollar shells. Exploring the tidal estuaries north and south of town is best done in a kayak at high tide, when you can travel farther up the temporary rivers. Arrange kayaking trips through your hotel. **Iguana Surf** (✉*Road to Playa Langosta* ☎☎2653–0148 ⊕*www.iguana surf.net*) has an office with information on guided kayaking tours of the San Francisco Estuary and a full roster of local tours, including snorkeling. Sail off into the sunset aboard a 50-foot traditional schooner with cruise company **Mandingo** (☎2653–2323). Soft drinks, beer and wine, and bocas (snacks) are included on the three-hour cruise.

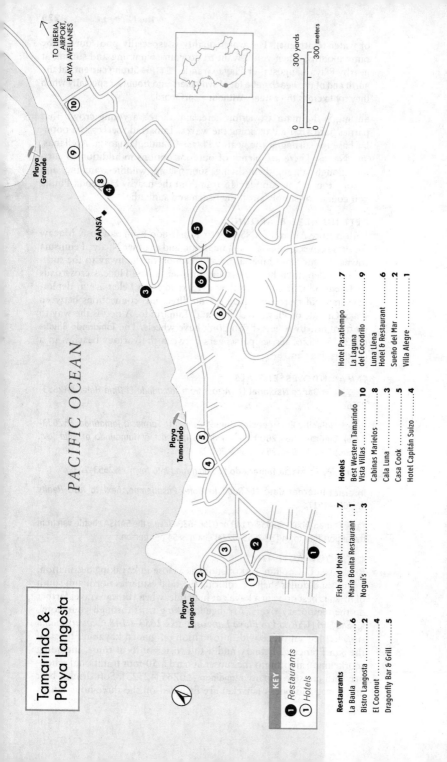

Tamarindo & Playa Langosta

KEY

1 Restaurants

① Hotels

Restaurants

La Baula **6**
Bistro Langosta **2**
El Coconut **4**
Dragonfly Bar & Grill ... **5**

Fish and Meat **7**
María Bonita Restaurant ... **1**
Nogui's **3**

Hotels

Best Western Tamarindo
Vista Villas **10**
Cabinas Marielos **8**
Cala Luna **3**
Casa Cook **5**
Hotel Capitán Suizo **4**

Hotel Pasatiempo **7**
La Laguna
del Cocodrilo **9**
Luna Llena
Hotel & Restaurant **6**
Sueño del Mar **2**
Villa Alegre **1**

PACIFIC OCEAN

TO LIBERIA,
AIRPORT,
PLAYA AVELLANES

Playa Grande

SANSA

Playa Tamarindo

Playa Langosta

300 yards

300 meters

The boat leaves at 3 PM from in front of El Pescador restaurant on the beach ($65 per person).

FISHING A number of fishing charters in Tamarindo cater to saltwater anglers. The most experienced among them is **Tamarindo Sportfishing** (☎2653–0090 ⊕*www.tamarindosportfishing.com*), run by Randy Wilson, who has led the way in developing catch-and-release techniques that are easy on the fish. Wilson has roamed these waters since the 1970s, and he knows where the big ones lurk. His 38-foot *Talking Fish* is equipped with a marlin chair and a cabin with a shower, and costs $1,300 for a full day, $750 for a half. A fishing trip for up to four anglers on one of two 28-foot boats costs $780 to $880 for a full day; $480 to $550 for a half.

GOLFING Mike Young, who has designed some of the best golf courses in the southern United States, designed the par-72 championship course at **Hacienda Pinilla** (⊹*10 km [6 mi] south of Tamarindo via Villa Real* ☎2680–7062 ⊕*www.haciendapinilla.com*). It has ocean views and breezes, and plenty of birds populate the surrounding trees. Guests pay $165 for 18 holes in high season.

SURFING **Iguana Surf 2** (⊠*At beach near Frutas Tropicales* ☎☎2653–0613) rents surfboards and Boogie boards and offers lessons (for ages 3 to 88). **Maresias Surf Shop** (⊠*Next to Banco Nacional* ☎2653–0224) has equipment, lessons, and lots of local knowledge. Check out **Robert August Surf Shop** (⊠*Tamarindo Vista Villas* ☎2653–0114) for boards to buy or rent, surfing gear, swimsuits, and sunblock. The shop operates a kids' surfing school as well as offering adult lessons. **High Tide Surf Shop** (⊠*Road to Langosta, about 200 m west of Hotel Pasatiempo* ☎2653–0108) has high-end surfing equipment and clothing and a large selection of beachwear in a second-story shop.

WILDLIFE TOURS **ACOTAM** (☎2653–1687), a local conservation association, conducts turtle-viewing tours with local guides for $28. The group picks you up at your hotel and briefs you at their headquarters on the estuary that separates Tamarindo and Playa Grande. An open boat then takes you across the estuary, where you wait at the park station until a turtle has been spotted. The turtle nesting season runs from mid October to February. They also offer mangrove tours year-round. They don't speak much English.

WHERE TO EAT

$$$$ ✕**El Coconut.** The red, black, and dark-wood interior of this high-gloss, dinner-only restaurant with giant stone sculptures and a coconut tree growing through the roof feels like a lacquered Japanese *bento* box. Seafood is the main event, with the catch of the day—usually mahimahi—served half a dozen ways, but they also serve a good tenderloin, with a choice of sauces, and the classic surf and turf. The innovative jumbo shrimp or lobster in a pineapple, raisin, and ginger sauce are delicious, and the list of sauces for the fish include the traditional Norwiegan sandelfjords smor (a cream sauce with lime)—the owner is from Norway. Service is smooth and more formal than at most beach restaurants, and they have a good wine list, but the food and drink

are much more expensive here than at the competition. ⊠*Main street, 150 m south of Tamarindo Vista Villas* ☎*2653–0086* ▤*AE, MC, V* ⊘*Closed Mon. No lunch.*

$$ ✕**Dragonfly Bar & Grill.** A low-key, natural ambience with tree-trunk
★ columns, sculptural hanging lamps, and a cool soundtrack make this immensely popular, friendly restaurant a great place to spend an evening. The chef offers a limited but enticing menu of innovative dishes that combine the flavors of Asia and Latin America, with a few Mediterranean accents. Settle in and tingle your taste buds with spicy shrimp rolls, or a roasted beet, gorgonzola, and walnut salad. Then sink your incisors into a pork chop over roasted garlic potato puree, or a Thai-style crispy fish cake with curried sweet corn. There are various vegetarian options, and the daily fish specials are always a good bet. ⊠*100 m east of Hotel Pasatiempo* ☎*2653–1506* ⊕*www.dragonflybarand grill.com* ⌕*Reservations recommended* ▤*AE, DC, MC, V* ⊘*Closed Sun. and Sept. No lunch.*

$$ ✕**Fish & Meat.** An Argentine chef cooks Thai, Indian, Middle Eastern, and makes the best sushi in town—that's about as multicultural as Tamarindo gets. Against an arty red, white, and black setting, Chef Federico rustles up pad thai, a spicy chicken curry, or a fusion explosion of tenderloin in a red curry sauce. Coconut milk figures prominently on the menu. Stick to sushi with the seaweed on the inside because in this humidity the *nori* quickly gets chewy. A wide choice of wines includes dry or sweet sake. ⊠*Across from Hotel Pasatiempo* ☎*2653–0535* ▤*MC, V* ⊘*Closed Mon.*

$$ ✕**Nogui's.** Pleasing a loyal legion of local fans since 1974, Nogui's offers a hearty Costa Rican menu and an ocean view. It is one of Tamarindo's best options for lunch, with a good selection of sandwiches and huge salads. It's also a good spot for dinner, when they offer a full seafood menu and various meat dishes. The recipes and presentation are nothing fancy, but the seafood is fresh and the price is right. Instead of the ubiquitous rice and beans on the side, Nogui's has a puree of *tiquisque,* a potato-like tuber. The homemade pies are legendary, notably the coconut cream. They also serve a signature margarita made with tamarind fruit. On weekends the restaurant on Nogui's second floor, called the Sunset Lounge, offers a small selection of innovative tapas, with a strong oriental influence, and a hipper ambience. ⊠*South side of Tamarindo Circle, on beach* ☎*2653–0029* ▤*AE, MC, V* ⊘*Closed Wed. and 2 wks in Oct.*

$ ✕**La Baula.** Popular with the locals, this alfresco pizzeria on a quiet side
☾ street has plenty of cars parked outside most nights. Families are especially fond of La Baula—the Costa Rican name for the "leatherback turtle"—because of its reasonable prices and adjacent playground. Everyone enjoys the consistently delicious thin-crust pizzas, though if you don't like pizza, stay away. It's about the only thing on the menu, which consists of two dozen pies and a mixed salad. They also offer a tasty little tiramisu. ⊠*100 m north of Hotel Pasatiempo* ☎*2653–1450* ▤*AE, MC, V* ⊘*No lunch.*

WHERE TO STAY

$$–$$$$
Fodor's Choice
★

Hotel Capitán Suizo. For folks who like nature, intimacy, and a beautiful beach setting, this is the best choice in town. Nestled in the forest on the relatively quiet southern end of Tamarindo's beach, elegant balconied rooms and airy bungalows surround a lovely pool shaded by large trees and greenery. Second-floor rooms have high, angled ceilings and lots of screens, which keeps them relatively cool despite their lack of air-conditioning. Lower rooms are smaller and darker, but have air-conditioning, and terraces with views of the forested grounds, which are home to iguanas, raccoons, howler monkeys, and an array of birds. All rooms are decorated with fascinating vintage sepia photos depicting early-20th-century Costa Rican life. The two-level bungalows have king-size four-poster beds, futon couches, and sensuous bathrooms with sunken whirlpool tubs, and outdoor garden showers—only two have an ocean view. The four-bedroom apartment has a kitchen and whirlpool tub. A beautifully decorated terrace restaurant overlooking the pool and beach serves contemporary cuisine and hosts lively beach barbecues on Friday night. Service is friendly and polished. **Pros:** Beachfront, secluded, friendly, lovely gardens and pool. **Con:** Sand fleas and mosquitoes can be a problem. ⊠ *Right side of road toward Playa Langosta* ⌂ *Apdo. 22–5159, Villa Real, Guanacaste* ☎ *2653–0075 or 2653–0353* 🖷 *2653–0292* ⊕ *www.hotelcapitansuizo.com* 🛏 *22 rooms, 8 bungalows, 1 apartment* ⚒ *In-room: no a/c (some), safe, refrigerator, no TV. In-hotel: restaurant, room service, bar, pool, beachfront, water sports, bicycles, no elevator, laundry service, public Internet, public Wi-Fi* ⊟ *AE, MC, V* ⧖ *BP.*

$$$
★

Casa Cook. With just a few rooms on the quiet, southern end of the beach, this friendly, family-run place is one of Tamarindo's most secluded lodging options. Two cabinas on the beach have sleeping areas separated by five-foot-high walls from living rooms with futon couches and kitchenettes. Narrow front terraces have ocean views through a high iron fence—security first—with hammocks hung between the trees on the other side of the gate. Behind those bungalows is a small tile pool hemmed by gardens, and the casita, which occupies the ground floor of the building that holds the owners' apartment. Though less private than the cabinas, the casita is slightly larger, with two futon couches, a kitchen, and glass doors that open onto the pool area. There are several restaurants and a supermarket within walking distance. **Pros:** Small, secluded, beachfront, friendly. **Con:** Usually full. ⊠ *Road to Playa Langosta, 100 m before Hotel Capitán Suizo,* ☎ *2653–0125* ⊕ *www.casacook.net* 🛏 *2 cabinas, 1 casita, 1 apartment* ⚒ *In-room: no phone, safe, kitchen. In-hotel: pool, beachfront, water sports, no elevator, laundry service, public Wi-Fi, no kids under 12, no-smoking rooms* ⊟ *AE, MC, V* ⧖ ⊠ 🖷.

$$

Best Western Tamarindo Vista Villas. If you're into surfing, this is where you want to be. Even though it's across the street from the beach, it's quite close to Tamarindo's beach break, and a quick paddle to the river-mouth break and Playa Grande. Around the pool and bar the talk is all about waves. There's a surf school and a surf shop, and surfing legends Robert August and Wing Nuts, of *Endless Summer* movie fame, are frequent guests. The large villas with kitchens have a bedroom with a double bed and two futon couches; they are slowly being redecorated. Avoid Rooms 101–107, which face the pool's supporting wall. Poolside rooms can be noisy when the pool is filled with frolicking kids. The hotel has a helpful tour desk. **Pros:** Near beach break, villas view ocean. **Con:** Not on the beach. ⊠ *Main road entering Tamarindo, on left* ☎ *2653–0114, 800/536–3241 in U.S.* 🖷 *2653–0115* ⊕ *www.tamarindo vistavillas.com* 🛏 *17 rooms, 16 villas* ⟐ *In-room: safe, kitchen (some). In-hotel: restaurant, room service, bar, pool, water sports, no elevator, laundry service, public Wi-Fi* ⊟ *AE, MC, V* ⊙ *CP.*

$$ 🏨 **Hotel Pasatiempo.** Come for Sunday football, open mike on Tuesday night, or great eggs Benedict any morning. One way or another, you are bound to pass some time at this friendly, laid-back place. This is one of the last relatively tranquil hotels in the sea of Tamarindo construction. Duplex bungalow rooms are scattered around lushly landscaped grounds and the pool, next to which towers the restaurant's thatch roof. Each unit, named after a Guanacaste beach, has a small patio with a hammock or swinging chair and a hand-painted beach mural; newer deluxe rooms are nicer and more secluded. Suites are good for young families, since they have one bedroom and small daybeds in the living room. The Oasis Restaurant ($$) serves a mix of above-average bar food and pizza, along with more sophisticated fare, such as maca-damia-encrusted mahimahi with a mango sauce, or chicken in a Stro-ganoff sauce. **Pros:** Lush grounds, relatively quiet. **Cons:** Several blocks from beach, noisy Sunday and until late on Tuesday night. ⊠ *Off dirt road to Playa Langosta, 180 m from beach behind Tamarindo Circle* ☎ *$$653–0096* 🖷 *$$653–0275* ⊕ *www.hotelpasatiempo.com* 🛏 *15 bungalows, 2 suites* ⟐ *In-room: no phone, safe, no TV (some). In-hotel: restaurant, bar, pool, laundry service, public Internet, public Wi-Fi* ⊟ *AE, MC, V* ⊙ *BP.*

$$ 🏨 **Luna Llena Hotel & Residence.** This place looks a little like a Fellini film set of a fantasy tropical village. Bright-yellow conical thatch-roof huts on different levels circle a small pool and tropical gardens. Interiors are colorful and whimsical, with unusual fabrics, furniture, and walls painted by co-owner Simona Daniela, who, along with husband Pino Trimarchi, adds Italian panache to the place. They also serve good Italian food in the tiny restaurant on the grounds. Four bright double rooms on the second floor have queen-size beds, high ceilings, spacious bathrooms, and colorful, creative decors. Bungalows with their own kitchens are great for families. The ground floor holds a kitchenette, bathroom, and a queen bed, whereas a steep, curving stair leads to a wooden loft with two single beds. The hotel is a 10-minute walk from the beach, in a relatively quiet area. **Pros:** Secluded, lush grounds. **Cons:** Several blocks away from beach, small pool. ⊠ *From road to Playa Langosta, first left (uphill); one block past Iguana Surf* ☎ *2653–0082* 🖷 *2653–0120* ⊕ *www.hotellunallena.com* 🛏 *5 rooms, 7 bungalows* ⟐ *In-room: safe, kitchen (some). In-hotel: restaurant, room service, pool, no elevator, laundry service, public Internet, public Wi-Fi* ⊟ *AE, MC, V* ⊙ *CP.*

$-$$** La Laguna del Cocodrilo. This hotel's name, which translates as "The Crocodile's Lagoon," refers to a pond between the hotel and the beach that is frequented by one of those giant lizards. A short trail leads from past that pond to the north end of Playa Tamarindo and the estuary. Standard rooms here should be avoided, since they are too close to Tamarindo's main road and are dark, but the ocean views and junior suites are a good deal, especially since they're practically on the beach. The only problem is their proximity to the restaurant and bar, which stays open till 11 PM, so this isn't the place for early-to-bed types. No matter where you stay, though, you should dine at the hotel's restaurant ($$$), where tables are scattered amid tropical greenery and coconut palms decorated with light spirals. The young American chef produces some tasty seafood inventions such as red snapper stuffed with a cognac mousse, potato-wrapped sea bass, and a decent bouillabaisse. The French bakery in front serves good breakfasts, light lunches, and sweets. **Pros: Almost beachfront, good restaurant. **Cons:** Standard rooms dark, can be noisy. ⊠*Main street, on right entering town* ☎*2653–0255* ⊕*www.lalagunadelcocodrilo.com* ⇥*8 rooms* △*In-room: no phone, safe, refrigerator. In-hotel: restaurant, bar, no elevator.* ⊟*MC, V* ⦿⊠⊞.

¢ Cabinas Marielos. Rooms at this well-situated, local-owned hotel are among the best of the budget category in Tamarindo. Two wings, decorated with floral motifs in the style of the artisans of Sarchí, are well back from the busy main road, on grounds with colorful gardens, coconut palms, and other trees. The beach and surf break are a short walk away. Rooms are quite basic, with cold-water showers and either a fan or air-conditioning. Guests sometimes share meals in the well-equipped common kitchen. The atmosphere is surprisingly serene, and the friendly staff can arrange turtle-watching, horseback riding, and other tours. **Pros:** Cheap, near beach, relatively quiet. **Con:** Very basic rooms. ⊠*Across main dirt road from beach,on left after Best Western* ☎*2653–0141* ✐*cabinasmarielos@hotmail.com* ⇥*24 rooms* △*In-room: no a/c (some), no phone, safe, refrigerator (some), no TV. In hotel: no elevator, no-smoking rooms* ⊟*AE, MC, V* ⦿*EP.*

NIGHTLIFE

Tamarindo is one of the few places outside of San José where the nightlife really jumps. In fact, it has the dubious distinction of being featured on Entertainment Television's explicit *Wild On* series, which spotlights the rowdiest party scenes around the world.

While party-hearty hot spots come and go with the tides, Tamarindo does have some perennial, low-key options. For a pleasantly sedate Friday evening, try barbecue on the beach at the **Hotel Capitán Suizo** (⊠*Right side of road toward Playa Langosta; veer left before circle*), starting at 6:30 with a cocktail, then on to a lavish barbecue buffet and live folk music and dancing ($29, reserve in advance). During the week, **Hotel Pasatiempo** (⊠*Off dirt road to Playa Langosta*) has wildly popular Tuesday open-mike sessions. Friday nights at **The Monkey Bar** (⊠*Tamarindo Vista Villas, main road entering Tamarindo*) is ladies' night. The live music attracts a crowd of locals who really know how to move. **Restobar La Caracola** (⊠ *Tamarindo Circle, beside Nogui's* ☎ 2653–0583) often has live music and dancing on weekends. There are tango, salsa, and merengue dance lessons for novices.

SHOPPING

Most stores in the strip malls lining the main road sell the same souvenirs. It's hard to leave town without at least one sarong in your suitcase. At **Calypso** (⊠ *Main Street at Tamarindo El Diria Hotel* ☎ 2653–1436), Parisian Anne Loriot has raised the bar on beach fashion with fabulous Indonesian- and Mexican-style cover-ups and elegant, cool dresses, all available in real women's sizes.

★ You'll also find original clothing and jewelry at **Azul Profundo** (⊠ *Main street, Plaza Tamarindo* ☎ 2653–0395), designed by a talented young Argentine woman. All her jewelry is made with real and semiprecious stones. For a good selection of swimsuits and a wide range of kiddie beachwear, check out **Tienda Bambora** (⊠ *On beach, south side of Tamarindo Circle* ☎ 2653–0029).

PLAYA LANGOSTA

2 km (1 mi) south of Tamarindo.

Playa Langosta is actually two beaches divided by the San Francisco Estuary, the mouth of which is a knee-high wade at low tide, and a deep river with dangerous currents around high tide. To the north is residential Langosta, where every foot of beachfront has been built up, but the contractors' hammers are now ringing out in every building space inland as well. It is sort of a bedroom community of Tamarindo, just five minutes away by car. To the south of the estuary is pristine Langosta, a protected annex of Las Baulas National Marine Park, where leatherback turtles nest at night and beachcombers roam by day. Luckily, most of the development on the northern half is tucked behind the buttonwood trees, so you can enjoy an unsullied dramatic beachscape, with surf crashing against rocky outcroppings. The beach here is rather narrow, since the coast is lined with rocks, and the light-gray sand is rather coarse. There's a wider, less rocky stretch in front of the Barceló Resort, where you can walk across the San Francisco Estuary at low tide to stroll and swim on the beach's southern half. If you walk a ways up that shallow tidal river at low tide you may see snowy egrets, baby blue herons, tail-bobbing spotted sandpipers, and if your eyes are sharp, tiny white-lored gnatcachers, endemic to these parts.

GETTING HERE & AROUND

The dirt road from Tamarindo is alternately dusty or muddy, but reliably rough. Or you can walk along the beach, at low tide, all the way from Tamarindo Beach. Most car-free visitors get picked up from Tamarindo by their hotels. Or you can take a taxi.

OUTDOOR ACTIVITIES

Tour operators in Tamarindo, just a few miles north, offer activities in the Playa Langosta area.

WHERE TO EAT

$$–$$$ ✕**Bistro Langosta.** Perfect for a light lunch or dinner, this friendly alfresco tapas bar is within walking distance from all of Playa Langosta's hotels. Though most people head here for the extensive tapas menu, which ranges from fried calamari to tuna carpaccio to lamb chops, they also offer a good selection of salads and panini at lunch, and half a dozen full dinners. Patio furniture dots the room around the large, cane-and-hardwood bar, or in the adjacent dining room, where white tablecloths add a touch of formality to this extremely casual place. There's free Wi-Fi for anyone who wants to hang out and work, and live music on Thursday night, when the place hops. ⊠*Main road, across from Hotel Cala Luna* ☎*2653–2025* ▤*AE, MC, V* ☻*Closed Sun. and Oct.*

$$ ✕**Maria Bonita Restaurant.** This popular Latin-Caribbean restaurant is
★ owned by a couple with years of hotel and restaurant experience in Cuba and throughout the Caribbean. Cheerful Adela serves (and makes delicious desserts) while Tom slaves away in the kitchen, turning out mouthwatering, perfectly spiced dishes such as smoked pork chops smothered in a tart tamarind sauce, coconut chicken casserole, and daily seafood specials. The wine list focuses on South American and Spanish vintages. There are just six tables in the pretty patio garden and four tables inside the intimate dining room—and they fill up fast. ⊠*Beside the Playa Langosta supermarket* ☎*2653–0933* ♨*Reservations essential* ▤*MC, V* ☻*Closed Sun. and Oct. No lunch.*

WHERE TO STAY

$$$–$$$$ ▦**Sueño del Mar.** The name of this place means "Dream of the Sea,"
Fodor'sChoice and the front gate opens into a dreamy world of intimate gardens,
★ patios, frescoes, hand-painted tiles, and a jungle of Latin American *objets d'art*. This nearly flawless B&B occupies an adobe-style house with spacious double rooms, two larger "casitas" with kitchens and loft bedrooms and a second-floor suite. The downstairs rooms are a little dark, but are full of interesting, often amusing folk art, and have Balinese showers that open to the sky. All rooms but the suite have queen-size beds, while the casitas have couches that convert into two single beds. If privacy is paramount, opt for the breezy honeymoon suite, a sensuous sultan's lair with rich, red fabrics, rugs, and hanging glass lamps and an ocean view. A lavish breakfast is served on the patio next to a tiny garden pool. Or you can take your morning coffee on the beach, with chairs and hammocks amid the trees and driftwood—it's also the perfect spot for sunsets. At low tide a large snorkeling pool forms in the rocks that surround the beach; but the swimming area is a 10-minute walk to the south. The hotel often plans and hosts beach weddings ⊠*130 m south of Capitán Suizo, veer right for 45 m, then right again for about 90 m to entrance gate, across from back of Cala Luna Hotel* ⚘*Sueño del Mar, detras de Cala Luna Hotel, Playa LangostaGuanacaste* ☎*2653–0284* 🖷*2653–0558* ⊕*www.sueno-del-mar. com* ⇆*3 rooms, 1 suite, 2 casitas* ♨*In-room: no phone, kitchen (some), no TV, Wi-Fi. In-hotel: restaurant, pool, beachfront, water sports, no elevator, laundry service, public Internet, no-smoking rooms* ▤*MC, V* ⦿*BP.*

4

$$$　🏠**Cala Luna.** This gorgeous collection of bungalows sequestered in a private jungle can be alternately as lifeless as a tomb and raucously noisy, with parties around the extravagantly landscaped pool. Standard rooms in ocher-color bungalows—reached via a labyrinth of high hibiscus hedges—have king-sized beds, high wooden ceilings, softly lighted alcoves, and oversize bathrooms with sunken, tiled tubs. The secluded villas, with hidden driveways and private pools, have two or three bedrooms and kitchens. The beach is a short walk away, across a road and through the forest, but it's narrow and lined by rocks here. The glorious pool is overlooked by the pretty, Provençal-style Cala Moresca restaurant ($$$), where the cuisine is Mediterranean with Asian touches. On the other end of the pool is an excellent sushi bar, making this a good place to dine if you stay at one of the B&Bs nearby. ⊠*100 m south of Hotel Capitán Suizo, veer right.* ☎2653–0214 📠2653–0213 ⊕*www. calaluna.com* ✍*20 rooms, 28 villas (3 3-bedroom, 18 2-bedroom)* △*In-room: safe. In-hotel: restaurant, bar, pool, no elevator, laundry service, public Internet, public Wi-Fi,* ☰*AE, MC, V* ⏹CP.

$$$　🏠**Villa Alegre.** A visit here is like coming to stay with friends who just
★　happen to have a really terrific house on the beach. Owned by congenial and helpful Californians Barry and Suzye Lawson, this homey but sophisticated Spanish-style B&B overlooks a small forest reserve and a somewhat rocky section of Langosta Beach, which is only visible from the terrace and pool. Rooms, villas, and casitas are furnished with souvenirs from the Lawsons' international travels, including Japan, Russia, and Guatemala. The Mexican honeymoon suite has a Frida Kahlo–esque canopy bed and a huge outdoor bathroom/patio. Spacious villas have kitchens, living rooms with several futons, and terraces overlooking the forest. Lavish breakfasts are served family style at 8:30 on a terrace overlooking the small pool—they're a chance to meet other guests, and ask the Lawsons for travel advice, or other help, which they happily provide. The hotel often plans and hosts weddings; ceremonies take place at a huge boulder on the beach dubbed Marriage Rock. ⊠*Playa Langosta, 300 m south of Hotel Capitán Suizo* ☎2653–0270 📠2653–0287 ⊕*www.villaalegrecostarica.com* ✍*4 rooms, 2 villas, 1 casita* △*In-room: no phone, no TV, Wi-Fi. In-hotel: pool, beachfront, no elevator, laundry service, public Internet, no-smoking rooms* ☰*AE, MC, V* ⏹BP.

PLAYA GRANDE

21 km (13 mi) north of Tamarindo.

A largely paved 34 km (21 mi) from Tamarindo by road, but only five minutes by boat across a tidal estuary, lies beautiful Playa Grande. The beach has thus far escaped the overdevelopment of nearby Tamarindo, and is consequently lined with thick vegetation instead of hotels and strip malls. It is one of the world's most important nesting beaches for the massive leatherback turtle, and is consequently protected within a national park, though admission is free unless you go on a turtle tour during the nesting season (Oct. 20–Feb. 15). The beach's protected status is in part due to a surfer who arrived here more than 30 years ago and was so upset by the widespread turtle-egg poaching that he adopted a conservationist's agenda. Louis Wilson, owner of Las Tortugas Hotel, spearheaded a campaign to protect the nesting *baulas* (leatherback turtles) that eventually resulted in the creation of Las Baulas Marine National Park. The long Blue Flag beach is also a paradise for surfers and sunbathers by day, and the forest that lines it holds howler monkeys and an array of birds, whereas the mangrove estuary on the north end of the beach has crocodiles. The only problem with Playa Grande is the abundance of mosquitoes during the rainy months, especially near the estuary, so bring plenty of repellent. .

Playa Grande isn't immune to development, though; developers have sold hundreds of lots, and there are at least 100 finished houses. The good thing is that the homes are well back from the beach, thanks to a legislated buffer zone and a decree that no lights can be visible from the beach, to avoid annoying the turtles. A few hotels and restaurants make this a pleasant, tranquil alternative to Tamarindo. And if you want to go shopping, Tamarindo is only a boat ride away.

4

GETTING HERE & AROUND
The road from Tamarindo, about 21 km (13 mi) away, is paved for the duration of the 30-minute drive. Palm Beach Estates, where most hotels are, is about 3 km (2 mi) south of the main Playa Grande entrance on a dirt road. Alternatively, you can take a small boat across the Tamarindo Estuary for about $2 per person and walk 30 minutes along the beach to the surf break; boats travel between the guide kiosk at the north end of Tamarindo and either Villa Baulas, or Hotel Bula Bula in Playa Grande.

EXPLORING
Both **Las Baulas Marine National Park** *(Parque Nacional Marino Las Baulas)*, which protects the long Playa Grande, and the **Tamarindo Wildlife Refuge,** a mangrove estuary with some excellent bird-watching, have been under some developmental pressure of late. Playa Grande hosts the world's largest visitation of nesting giant leatherback turtles. From October 15 to February 15, during the peak nesting season, the beach is strictly off limits from 6 PM to 5 AM. You can only visit as part of a guided tour, waiting your turn at the park entrance, beside Hotel Las Tortugas, until spotters find a nesting turtle. At their signal, you'll walk down the beach as silently as you can, where in the darkness you'll witness the remarkable sight of a 500-pound creature digging a hole in the sand large enough to deposit up to 100 golf ball–size eggs. About 60 days later, the sight of hundreds of hatchlings scrambling toward open water in the early morning is equally impressive. Turtle-watching takes place around high tide, which can be shortly after sunset, or in the early morning. From December to mid-February, try to reserve your tour a week ahead of time, or stop by the ranger station early the morning of the day you want to do the tour, since they only allow 40 people on the beach per night, half of which can register that day. Plan on spending one to four hours at the ranger station waiting for a turtle to come up, during which time you can watch a video on the turtles in English (the guides speak mostly Spanish). ⊠ *Playa Grande, 100 m east of main*

beach entrance ☎2653–0470 ✉$20, *includes guided tour* ◷Oct. 20–Feb. 15 by reservation made between 8 AM and 5 PM.

OUTDOOR ACTIVITIES

■TIP➔Unless you are a strong swimmer attached to a surfboard, don't go in any deeper than your waist here. There is calmer water for snorkeling about a 20-minute walk north of Las Tortugas, at Playa Carbón.

All the hotels can arrange boat tours of the estuary, where you may see crocodiles, monkeys, herons, kingfishers, and an array of other bird-life; go either early in the morning or late in the afternoon, and bring insect repellent.**Hotel Las Tortugas** (✉*Las Baulas Marine National Park* ☎2653–0423 ⊕*www.lastortugashotel.com*) has a full menu of nature tours, including guided nature walks, and canoeing on the estuary; they also rent snorkeling equipment and explain how to get to Playa Carbón, the nearest skin-diving spot ($25–$55).

SURFING Playa Grande is renowned for having one of the most consistent surf breaks in the country. Only experienced surfers should attempt riding this beach break, which often features big barrels and off-shore winds. The waves are best at high tide, especially around a full moon. **Hotel Las Tortugas** (⇨*above*) rents boards for $20 a day. **Hotel Bula Bula** (✉*Palm Beach Estates* ✚*2 km [1 mi] east of Playa Grande* ☎2653–0975 ⊕*www.hotelbulabula.com*) rents both long and short boards for $25 a day.

WHERE TO EAT

$$$ ✕**Hotel Cantarana.** Chef Manfred Margraf brings to the table 30 years of cooking experience in Switzerland, Germany, and the Caribbean. The menu changes depending on availability of local ingredients—think lots of seafood—and on the chef's inspired whims, but is always classically continental, with elegant presentation. ✉*Palm Beach Estates* ✚*2 km (1 mi) east of park headquarters* ☎2653–0486 ⊟2653–0491 ⊟MC, V

$$$ ✕ **Rip Jack Inn.** Located a block from the beach, this place usually has
★ an ocean breeze to complement the ceiling fans, which are best enjoyed from the hammock in the corner. They have rooms for rent downstairs, but most people who head here come to eat, or party at the long bar, which occupies about a third of the restaurant. The food is quite good, and the menu ranges from sesame-crusted tuna with rice and tempura vegetables to slow-cooked pork ribs slathered in barbecue sauce. The lunch menu has a good selection of salads and sandwiches. Save room for a mud pie, or cheesecake with strawberries. ✉*100 m south of park headquarters* ☎2653–0480 ⊟AE, DC, MC, V ◷*Closed Wed.*

$ ✕**Big Mama's.** You can get a taste of the Caribbean coast's distinctive cuisine at this colorful little restaurant run by a woman who grew up in Costa Rica's port city of Limón. This place serves authentic dishes such as patacones (plaintain chips with black bean puree), and "rice and beans," which consists of coconut rice, red beans, and chicken in a slightly spicy sauce. They also serve American-style breakfasts. Despite the name's connotations, the owner, Grettel Solorzano, is young and

petite. ✉*Road from Tamarindo, 200 m east of Kike's* ☎*2652–92*◟
▤*V* ☾*Closed Mon.*

$$ 📷**Hotel Bula Bula.** At the eastern edge of the estuary near Palm Beach Estates, Bula Bula ("happy, happy" in Hawaiian) has its own dock and boat for ferrying guests and restaurant patrons the short distance to and from Tamarindo. The hotel forms a 45-degree angle to the curvy pool bordered by a garden. (Be careful of the cactus!) Rooms have king-size beds, high ceilings, and open onto a portico with wicker rocking chairs, with walls painted in brilliant colors and hung with Central American art. They don't offer a lot of privacy, but the friendly American owners provide complimentary sarongs, fluffy pool towels, coffeemakers, DVD players, and other amenities. They can arrange a two-hour boat tour of the estuary, or rentals of nearby houses. The menu at the alfresco Great Waltini Restaurant & Bar ($$–$$$) reads like that of a U.S.-style eatery: peel-and-eat shrimp, lobster tails, filet mignon, and New York strip steak. They have good fresh seafood specials. **Pros:** Friendly, good food, lots of amenities. **Cons:** Rooms small for price, 10-minute walk from beach, far from surf break. ✉*Palm Beach Estates* ⬦*3 km (2 mi) east of Playa Grande* ☎*2653–0975, 877/658–2880 in U.S.* ⊕*www. hotelbulabula.com* 🛏*10 rooms* ⚲*In-room: no phone, refrigerator. In-hotel: restaurant, bar, pool, laundry service* ▤*AE, MC, V* ⑩*BP.*

¢–$$ 📷**Hotel El Manglar.** If you like cooking for yourself, consider the apartments at this French-run hotel. Painted in tropical colors, they also have a Provençal touch, with French doors and lace curtains. Sitting rooms, kitchens, and terraces give you lots of room to relax, and there is even a grill on the terrace. The cheaper upstairs guest rooms are much more basic, with minimalist decor and loft bedrooms with fans instead of air-conditioners. The hotel has a pretty garden and a pool inlaid with bright mosaic tile. It's a short walk from the beach. **Pros:** Quiet, near beach. **Cons:** Foam mattresses, no restaurant, far from surf break. ✉*Palm Beach Estates* ⬦*2 km (1 mi) south of Playa Grande, just south of Hotel La Cantarana* ☎*2653–0952* ⊕*www.hotel-manglar. com* 🛏*5 rooms, 4 apartments* ⚲*In-room: no a/c (some), no phone, safes, kitchen (some), no TV (some). In-hotel: pool* ▤*MC, V* ⑩*EP.*

¢–$$ 📷**Hotel Las Tortugas.** With a prime location on the beach, steps away
★ from Playa Grande's famous surf break, this place is perfect for surfers, nature lovers, and sun worshippers. The name, which means "The Turtles," is no accident; this hotel was designed with turtles in mind. Owner/conservationist Louis Wilson made sure, for instance, that room and restaurant lights don't shine on the beach, since light disorients the turtles. Rooms are spacious, with good beds, stone floors, and colorful tile bathrooms. Most have either a terrace or a balcony. Las Tortugas accommodates all budgets, with rooms ranging from spacious suites to dorm-style rooms in an annex that Louis built for student groups and volunteers. They also offer an array of apartments up the hill, some with kitchenettes, that rent by the night, week, or month. All of this adds up to the best value in Playa Grande, and one of the best deals on the Pacific coast. The main surf break is just to the south of the hotel, and turtle tours start at the nearby ranger station. Rip currents are a

4

danger on the beach here, which is why many guests prefer the pool shaped like a leatherback turtle (the turtle's head is the kiddie pool). Lush gardens slung with hammocks round out the grounds' appeal. The restaurant ($$$) serves a good selection of fresh seafood and grilled meat dishes. **Pros:** On the beach, friendly owners, good value. **Cons:** Busy spot. ⊠ *Entrance to Las Baulas Marine National Park* ✛ *33 km (20 mi) north of Tamarindo* ☎ *2653–0423* ⊕ *www.lastortugashotel. com* ➪ *10 rooms, 3 dorms, 17 apartments* ♿ *In-room: no phone, safe (some), kitchen (some), refrigerator (some), no TV. In-hotel: restaurant, bar, pool, beachfront, water sports, no elevator, laundry service, public Internet, public Wi-Fi* ⊟ *MC, V* ⦿| *EP.*

PLAYA AVELLANAS

17 km (11 mi) south of Tamarindo.

Traditionally a far cry from Tamarindo's boom of real-estate development, this relatively undeveloped beach's main claim to fame is surfing. As you bump along the rough beach road, most of the cars you pass have surfboards on top. Nevertheless, Avellanas (pronounced ah-vey-ya-nas) is a lovely spot for anyone who likes the sea and sand, though you shouldn't go in deeper than your waist when the waves are big, due to rip currents. Tamarindo escapees have been slowly encroaching on Avellanas for years, building private houses and a smattering of small hotels, but the inauguration of a massive Marriott here in 2008 marked the beginning of major development. The beach itself is a beautiful, 1-km (½-mi) stretch of pale-gold sand with rocky outcroppings at its southern end, a small river mouth, and a mangrove swamp behind its northern half. It is also home to a very big pig named Lola, who likes to cool off in the surf. Unfortunately, security is an issue here, as at most Costa Rican beaches; posted signs warn visitors not to leave anything of value in parked cars or unattended on the beach.

GETTING HERE & AROUND

You have to drive 30 minutes inland from Tamarindo to Villa Real, where you turn right for the 13-km (8-mi) trip down a bumpy road to reach Playa Avellanas. There are rivers to cross in rainy season, when you may want to drive via Paraíso and Playa Negra. If you're without a car, take the **Tamarindo Shuttle** (☎ *2653–1326*) van, $20 one way for one to four people.

OUTDOOR ACTIVITIES

SURFING Locals claim there are eight breaks here when the swell is big, which means Avellanas doesn't suffer the kind of overcrowding the breaks at Playas Negra and Langosta often do. Tamarindo-based surf schools can arrange day trips here. You can rent boards and find kindred surfing spirits at **Cabinas Las Olas** (⊠ *Main road, on right* ☎ *2652–9315*), $2 an hour or $25 a day.

WHERE TO STAY & EAT

$–$$ ✗**Lola's.** In deference to Lola, the owners' free-roaming pet pig, the
★ menu at this hip beach café is heavily vegetarian. It has exactly the kind
of ambience one comes to Costa Rica for, with tables scattered along
the beach amid palms and Indian almond trees, hammocks swinging in
the wind, palm fronds rustling, and surfers riding the glistening waves
in front. Seating, or more precisely, lolling, is all on the sand at low
hardwood tables and reclining chairs, or on colorful cushions on rat-
tan mats. Along with the fresh-fruit smoothies and ultra-thin vegetarian pizzas, the menu includes organic chicken and "responsible fish"
(fish caught in nets that don't also trap turtles). Seared ahi tuna with
sun-dried tomato and olive tapenade served on ciabatta bread is a winner, as are the ceviche, fish-and-chips, and assorted salads. You can
arrange in advance for private beach dinners by candlelight (the pig
isn't invited). ⊠*At main entrance to Playa Avellanas* ☎*2652–9097*
▤*No credit cards* ⊘*Closed Mon. Lunch only.*

$ ⊞**Cabinas Las Olas.** Frequented mainly by surfers, this place is a good
option for anyone seeking beach access and relative solitude. The
hotel's spacious glass-and-stone bungalows are scattered across a leafy
property behind Playa Avellanas, which guests reach via an elevated
boardwalk through a protected mangrove estuary. Each cabina has
a queen and a single bed, high wooden ceiling, and a covered terrace
with a hammock. There's no air-conditioning, but high ceilings, a shady
location, and good cross ventilation keep the rooms cool at night.
Monkeys, iguanas, and other critters lurk in and around the extensive,
forested grounds. The restaurant, under the shade of a giant guanacaste
tree, serves a good selection of Costa Rican and continental cuisine
at reasonable prices ($$) for breakfast, lunch, and dinner. **Pros:** Near
beach, in forest, secluded. **Con:** Mosquitoes a problem in rainy season.
⊹*1 km (½ mi) before Avellanas, on right* ☎*2652–9315* ▤*2652–*
9331 ⊕*www.cabinaslasolas.co.cr* ⊠*10 rooms* ⚒*In-room: no a/c, no*
phone, safe, no TV. In-hotel: restaurant, water sports, laundry service,
public Wi-Fi ▤*AE, MC, V* ⊘*Closed 15 days in Oct.* ⊙❘*EP.*

PLAYA NEGRA

3 km (2 mi) south of Playa Avellanas.

Surfer culture is apparent here in the wave of beach-shack surfer camps
along the beach road. But there's also a big residential development
here called Rancho Playa Negra, with more upscale development on
the drawing boards. Contrary to the name, the beach is not black, but
rather beige with dark streaks. It's not a great swimming beach, since
it tends to have big waves and is lined with rocks, though there is one
short stretch of clear sand to the south of the hotel, and at low tide a
large tidal pool forms in front of the hotel. The spindly buttonwood
trees that edge the beach provide sparse shade.

GETTING HERE & AROUND

From Playa Avellanas, continue south 10 minutes on the rough beach
road to Playa Negra. If it's rainy season and the road is too rough,

you can approach along a slightly more civilized route from Santa Cruz. Drive 27 km (16½ mi) west, via Veintisiete de Abril, to Paraíso, then follow signs for Playa Negra for 4 km (2½ mi). Taxis are the easiest way to get around if you don't have a car.

> ### A SURF CLASSIC
>
> Americans—surfer Americans, at least—got their first look at Playa Negra in 1994's *The Endless Summer II*, a film by legendary surf documentarian Bruce Brown.

OUTDOOR ACTIVITIES

SURFING Surfing cognoscenti dig the waves here, which are almost all rights, with beautifully shaped barrels. It's a spectacular, but treacherous, rock-reef break for experienced surfers only. There's also a small beach break to the south of the rocks where neophytes can cut their teeth. Both breaks can be ridden from mid- to high tide. The point break is right in front of the **Hotel Playa Negra** (✛ *4 km (2½ mi) northwest of Paraíso on dirt road, then follow signs carefully at forks in road* ☎2652–9134 ⊕*www.playanegra.com*), which can arrange surfing classes ($35 per hour), and rents boards ($20 per day).

WHERE TO STAY

$$ ⌘**Hotel Playa Negra.** Brilliantly colored thatch-roof cabinas are sprin-
★   kled across sunny lawns strewn with tropical plantings at this gorgeous ocean-front place. Each hut has curvaceous tile bathrooms plus built-in sofas that can double as extra beds. There's no air-conditioning, but conical thatch roofs keep the cabinas cool. Ocean tidal pools, swimming holes, and rock reefs provide plenty of opportunities for lazy afternoon exploration. This is paradise for surfers, with a good swell running right in front of the hotel. The round restaurant serves typical food with a few continental dishes under a giant thatch roof, but the ocean view is more of an attraction than the food. There's also an air-conditioned Internet café in the beach boutique, which arranges kayaking and horseback tours. **Pros:** In front of reef break, friendly. **Con:** Not a great swimming beach. ✛*4 km (2½ mi) northwest of Paraíso on dirt road (watch signs for Playa Negra), then follow signs carefully at forks in road* ☎2652—9134 ⎙2652—9035 ⊕*www.playanegra.com* ⇋*10 cabinas* ⌂*In-room: no a/c, no phone, safe, no TV. In-hotel: restaurant, bar, pool, beachfront, water sports, no elevator, laundry service* ▭*AE, DC, MC, V* ⊘*Restaurant closed Sept. 15–Nov. 1* ⎮⊙⎮*EP.*

PLAYA JUNQUILLAL

⟳ *4 km (2½ mi) south of Paraíso, 34 km (22 mi) south of Santa Cruz.*

Seekers of tranquillity need look no farther than Junquillal (pronounced hoon-key-*yall*). A short drive to the south of Playa Negra, this wide swath of light brown sand stretches about 3 km (2 mi), with coconut palms lining much of it and hardly a building in sight. Two species of sea turtle nest here, and a group of young people collect and protect their eggs, releasing the baby turtles after sunset. Although it qualifies as a Blue Flag beach, the surf here is a little strong, so watch children carefully. There's a kids' playground right at the beach, and a funky little restaurant with cement tables amid the palms. If you're child-free, it's a perfect beach for taking long, romantic strolls. Surfers head here to ride the beach break near Junquillal's northern end, since it rarely gets crowded. A surprisingly cosmopolitan *mélange of expats has* settled in this area, as the selection of goods in the small supermarket in town confirms, but Junquillal is still barely on the tourist map. Its handful of hotels consequently offers some of the best deals on the North Pacifc coast.

GETTING HERE & AROUND

In rainy season, the 4-km-long (2½-mi-long) beach road from Playa Negra to Playa Junquillal is sometimes not passable. The alternative is driving down from Santa Cruz one hour on a road that's paved part of the way. The Castillos bus company runs a bus to Junquillal from the central market in Santa Cruz four times a day (at 5 and 10:30 AM, and 2:30 and 5:30 PM); the trip takes about an hour. A taxi from Santa Cruz costs about $25; from Tamarindo, $35.

PLAYA JUNQUILLAL ESSENTIALS

The closest town for most services is Santa Cruz, 33 km (21 mi) east.

Hospital Clínica (⊠ *Veintisiete de Abril* ✛ *16 km [10 mi] northeast of Playa Junquillal*).

Internet Supermercado Junquillal (⊠ *Near beach entrance*).

OUTDOOR ACTIVITIES

HORSEBACK RIDING At German-run **Paradise Riding** (☎ *2658–8162* ⊕ *www.paradiseriding. com*) the 14 horses are in tip-top shape, as is the impressive tack room, with top-quality saddles lined up in a neat row. There are two-hour trail rides (about $50), or you can set off for a whole day of riding. The maximum number of riders they can handle is 10. You'll saddle up at the friendly owner's house, across from the entrance to Guacamaya Lodge.

WHERE TO EAT

$$$ ✕ **La Puesta del Sol.** Italian food aficionado Alessandro Zangari and his
★ wife Silvana have created what he modestly calls "a little restaurant in my home." But regulars drive all the way from Tamarindo to sit at one of his five tables and enjoy the dinner-only, haute-Italian menu. It's one of the priciest restaurants on the coast, but Alessandro spares no expense or effort to secure the best ingredients, buying only locally caught seafood and importing his own truffles from Italy. The pasta is made from scratch, and the sauces are prepared to order. The fettucine *boscaiolo* contains a woodsy trio of cremini, porcini, and Portobello mushrooms and the ravioli al tartufo (with truffle) is simply sublime. Another favorite is fresh fish livornesca (in a caper, olive, and tomato

sauce). The softly lighted patio restaurant, tinted in tangerine and deep blue, overlooks a lush garden within earshot of the surf. ⊠ *Just north of main entrance to Playa Junquillal* ☎2658–8442 ⚠*Reservations essential* ▤*No credit cards* ⊘*Closed end of Easter week to mid-Nov. No lunch.*

$ ✕**Restaurante Playa Junquillal.** This funky, open-air restaurant with cement tables amid the coconut palms is a classic Costa Rican beach bar. It regularly fills up in the evening, when local expats gather to watch the sunset. The lunch options include a small selection of appetizers, a fish sandwich, and the typical Costa Rican casado (fish fillet, or barbecued steak with rice and beans). At dinner, you can also get a fish fillet, or shrimp sautéed with garlic, barbecued chicken, or beef, and a few vegetarian options. It's basically just a good spot for a drink and snack on the beach. ⊠ *Main entrance to Playa Junquillal* ☎2658–8432 ▤*MC, V.*

WHERE TO STAY

$$ ▦**Hotel Villa Serena.** Serenely spread across verdant grounds a short walk from the beach, this hotel is certainly aptly named. The rooms are slightly old, but bright and spacious, with high wooden ceilings, big bathrooms, and soothing pastels and local art on the walls. They open onto narrow terraces with wooden chairs, most of which overlook the gardens; only Rooms 1 and 2 have ocean views. A large, rectangular pool is surrounded by coconut palms, and across the street is a small shelter at the edge of the beach, perfect for watching the sunset. The second-floor bar and restaurant ($$$) also have a nice ocean view. The menu ranges from fish-and-chips to filet mignon, with daily seafood specials. Coffee is delivered to rooms in the morning, and free snorkeling gear and kayaks are available to guests. **Pros:** Closest rooms to beach, quiet. **Con:** Only TV is at the bar. ⊠*Main Junquillal road, south of main beach access* ☎2658–8430 ⊕*www.land-ho.com/villa/* ⌑*12 rooms* ⚠*In-room: no phone, no TV. In-hotel: restaurant, bars, pool, gym, spa, water sports, no elevator, laundry service, public Wi-Fi* ▤*AE, DC, MC, V* ⅋*EP.*

$–$$ ▦**Guacamaya Lodge.** Spread across a breezy hill with expansive views of
Fodor'sChoice the surrounding forest and the sea above the treetops, the Guacamaya
★   is a real find. Spacious cabinas surround a generous-sized pool, lawn,
☾   and tropical plants. The large restaurant ($–$$) shaded by a conical thatch roof serves excellent continental cuisine, including such Swiss specialties as *Rösti* (hashbrowns with bacon and cheese) and Zürcher Geschnetzeltes (beef medallions and mushrooms in a creamy sauce), various pastas, fresh seafood dishes, and a good salad selection. Meals come with deliciously dense homemade bread. The spacious duplex bungalows with plenty of windows and small terraces are a real deal. Screened windows let in the cooling evening breezes, so you probably won't need the quiet air-conditioners in each room. Well-equipped studios in a two-story building have kitchenettes, big bathrooms, and covered porches; those on the second floor are more spacious, and have better views. The modern house, with a full kitchen and a large covered veranda, is perfect for rental by families. There's also a kids' pool, a playground, and a resident little girl happy to have playmates. The

place fills up fast, so book early. **Pros:** Good value, clean, friendly. **Con:** 1,000 feet from the beach. ⊠ *275 m east of Playa Junquillal* ⌂ *Apdo. 6, Santa Cruz* ☎ *2658–8431* 🖷 *2658–8164* ⊕ *www.guacamayalodge. com* ⇆ *6 cabinas, 4 studios, 1 house* & *In-room: no phone, kitchen (some), no TV. In-hotel: restaurant, bar, tennis court, pool, no elevator, laundry service, public Internet, public Wi-Fi* ⊟ *AE, MC, V* ⊘ *Closed Sept. and Oct.* ⊚ *EP.*

¢ 🏨 **Hotel TaTanka.** This attractive Italian-run hotel has tasty food and very comfortable rates. Ten big rooms are lined up under a tile-roof veranda facing a kidney-shape pool. They have Mayan-style wall paintings, arty bamboo closets, and large tiled bathrooms. Wood-oven pizzas and homemade pastas—the *spaghetti a la carbonara* is *delicioso*—are served in a huge alfresco restaurant with elegant furniture. The beach is a three-minute walk away. **Pros:** Inexpensive, near beach. **Cons:** Rooms a bit dark, musty. ⊠ *Main Junquillal road, just south of Guacamaya Lodge* ☎ *2658–8426* 🖷 *2658–8312* ⊕ *www.hoteltatanka.com* ⇆ *10 rooms* & *In-room: no phone, no TV. In-hotel: restaurant, pool, no elevator, laundry service, public Internet* ⊟ *MC, V* ⊘ *Closed Sept. and Oct.; restaurant closed Mon.* ⊚ *BP.*

NOSARA

28 km (17 mi) southwest of Nicoya.

One of the last beach communities for people who want to get away from it all, Nosara's attractions are the wild stretches of side-by-side beaches called Pelada and Guiones, with surfing waves and miles of sand on which to stroll, and the tropical dry forest that covers much of the hinterland. The town itself is inland and not very interesting, but the surrounding flora and fauna keep nature lovers entertained. Regulations here limit development to low-rise buildings 600 feet from the beach, where they are thankfully screened by trees. Americans and Europeans, with a large Swiss contingent, are building at a fairly rapid pace, but there appears to be an aesthetic sense here that is totally lacking in Tamarindo and Sámara.

For years, most travelers headed here for the surf, but the Nosara Yoga Institute, which offers instructor training, and daily classes for all levels, is increasingly a draw for health-conscious visitors. Birdwatchers and other nature enthusiasts can explore the tropical dry forest on hiking trails, on horseback, or by boating up the tree-lined Nosara River. The access roads to Nosara are abysmal, and the labyrinth of woodsy roads around the beaches and hard-to-read signs make it easy to get lost, which is why most hotels here provide local maps for their guests.

GETTING HERE & AROUND

From Nicoya, drive south, almost to Sámara, but take the very first road signed for Nosara, 1 km (½ mi) south of the big gas station before Sámara. This high road is rough for about 8 km (5 mi), but there are bridges over all the river crossings. When you join up with the beach road near Garza, you still have a very bumpy 10 km (6 mi) to go. The

THE ECOLOGICAL BLUE FLAG

The world gives high marks to Costa Rica for its environmental awareness, but a visit here shows that the accolades don't always match the reality. Deforestation occurs at an alarming rate, and the country has major trash-disposal issues. Recognizing that three-quarters of visitors to Costa Rica make a beach excursion, the national water utility, Aqueductos y Alcantarillados, in conjunction with the Instituto Costarricense de Turismo, began evaluating and ranking water and environmental quality in coastal communities in 1996. Those that achieved a 90% score were awarded a Bandera Azul Ecológica (Ecological Blue Flag) to fly as a symbol of excellence.

The program, modeled on one begun in Spain in 1986 and now used in the European Union, awards flags as prizes for communities, rather than to individual hotels. Participating areas are required to form a Blue Flag committee, a move that brings together diverse sectors of an area's population, many of which otherwise fiercely compete for tourist dollars. In true developing-country fashion, Costa Rica's wealth concentrates in the capital and the Central Valley. But the Blue Flag program has prompted less affluent lowland and coastal communities to put resources into improving environmental quality of life for themselves and for their guests.

Only 10 beaches earned a Blue Flag that first year, a fact that Costa Rica sheepishly decided not to publicize, not wanting to call attention to the high number of communities that *didn't* make the cut. When 19 succeeded the following year, the results went public. Officials inspect heavily visited beaches once a month. More isolated communities get bimonthly assessments. They evaluate water quality—both ocean and drinking water—trash cleanup, waste management, security, signage, and environmental education. In 2002 the competition was opened to inland communities.

Blue flags fly proudly in the following communities covered in this book:

Central Valley: Carrizal (Alajuela).

Northern Plains: La Fortuna, Las Horquetas de Sarapiquí, San Rafael de Heredia, Vara Blanca.

North Pacific: Bahía Junquillal, Nosara (Playa Guiones, Playa Pelada), Ostional, Playa Avellanas, Playa Carrillo, Playa Conchal, Playa Grande, Playa Hermosa, Playa Junquillal, Playa Langosta, Playa Ocotal, Playa Pan de Azúcar, Playa Panamá, Punta Islita.

Central Pacific: Barú, Isla Tortuga, Malpaís, Manuel Antonio (Playa Manuel Antonio, Playa Espadilla Sur, Puerto Escondido, Playa Gemelas), Puntarenas, Punta Leona (Playa Blanca, Playa Limoncito, Playa Mantas).

South Pacific: Ballena National Marine Park (Playa La Colonia, Playa Piñuela, Playa Ballena, Punta Uvita), Dominical, San Gerardo de Rivas, San Marcos de Tarrazú.

Caribbean Coast: Cahuita (Puerto Vargas, Playa Blanca, Playa Negra), EARTH, Puerto Viejo de Talamanca (Playa Negra, Playa Chiquita, Playa Cocles, Punta Uva), Gandoca-Manzanillo National Wildlife Refuge.

roads into Nosara are in really bad shape, so a 4WD vehicle is definitely recommended. Budget about one hour for the trip. You can also fly directly to Nosara on daily scheduled SANSA and Nature Air flights, or take an air-conditioned shuttle van from San José. Several major rent-a-car companies have offices in Nosara.

NOSARA ESSENTIALS

Bank/ATM **Banco Popular** (⊠ *In strip mall next to Café de Paris on road to Playa Guiones* ☎ *2682–0267*).

> ### CAUTION
>
> To approach Nosara along the coast from Junquillal to the north, you have to ford many rivers, including the Río Ostional, which is sometimes impassable during the wet season. This beach road requires 4WD. If you have a compact car, or it has been raining a lot, you are better off driving via Nicoya on the paved road.

Hospital **Centro Médica Nosara** (⊠ *In front strip mall next to Café de Paris, on road to Playa Guiones* ☎ *2682–1212*).

Pharmacy **Farmacia Nosara** (⊠ *In front strip mall next to Café de Paris, on road to Playa Guiones* ☎ *2682–1212* ☯ *Mon.–Sat. 8–4*).

Internet **Café de Paris** (⊠ *At entrance to Playa Guiones* ☎ *2682–0087*).

Post Office **Correo** (⊠ *Next to soccer field*).

Taxis Independent drivers provide taxi service. **Abel's Taxi** (☎ *8812–8470*) is reliable.

EXPLORING

With some of the most consistent surf on the Pacific coast, **Playa Guiones** attracts a lot of surfboard-toting visitors. But the breezy beach, with vegetation rising up from the high-tide mark for its length, is also a haven for shell seekers, sun lovers, and anyone who wants to connect with nature. The only building in sight is the bizarre Hotel Nosara, which was originally the only choice for lodging in town, but which is now a rambling private residence complete with observation tower. Otherwise, this glorious beach has 7 km (4 mi) of hard-packed sand, great for jogging and riding bikes. Since there's a nine-foot tide, the beach is expansive at low tide, but rather narrow at high tide, when waves usually create strong currents that can make the sea deadly for non-surfers. Most hotels post tide charts. Guiones is at the south end of the Nosara agglomeration, with three public accesses. The easiest one to find is about 1,000 feet past the Hotel Harmony, heading straight at the intersection.

North along the shore, Playa Guiones segues seamlessly into crescent-shape **Playa Pelada,** where the water is a little calmer. There are tide pools to explore and a blowhole that sends water shooting up when the surf is big. Lots of trees provide shade. This is the locals' favorite vantage point for watching sunsets. Olga's Bar, a ramshackle Tico beach bar, is a great place for a cool beer; or sip a sunset cocktail at the funky La Luna Bar & Grill, next door.

Ostional National Wildlife Refuge
(Refugio Nacional de Fauna Silvestre Ostional) protects one of
Costa Rica's major nesting beaches
for olive ridley turtles. Locals have
formed an association to run the
reserve on a cooperative basis, and
during the first 36 hours of the
arribadas (mass nesting) they are
allowed to harvest the eggs, on the
premise that eggs laid during this
time would likely be destroyed by
subsequent waves of mother turtles. Though turtles nest here year-
round, the largest arribadas, with
thousands of turtles nesting over
the courses of several nights, occur

> **HELP ON THE ROAD**
>
> The more remote the area, the
> more likely that someone will stop
> to help you change a tire or tow
> you out of a river. Usually, good
> Samaritans won't accept any pay-
> ment and are more trustworthy
> than those who offer to "help" in
> the States. Near Ostional, there's a
> farmer named Valentin who regu-
> larly pulls cars out of the flooded
> river with his tractor. So he is
> known as Valentin *con chapulin*
> (with a tractor).

from July to December, though smaller arribadas take place between
January and May. They usually take place around high tide, the week
of a new moon. People in Nosara usually know when an arribada has
begun. Guided tours of the nesting and hatching areas cost $7 per per-
son, plus the $7 entrance fee. Stop at the kiosk at the entrance to the
beach to arrange a tour. ✚*7 km (4½ mi) north of Nosara* ☎*2682–
0428, 2682--0400* ✉*$7* ☾*June--Dec., by tour only.*

★ **Nosara Biological Reserve** (Reserva Biológica Nosara) is a treasure. The
90-acre private reserve includes trails through a huge mangrove wetland and old-growth forest along the Nosara River. A concrete walkway passes over an eerily beautiful mangrove swamp, with fantastical
stilt roots and snap-crackling sound effects from respiring mollusks.
More than 250 bird species have been spotted here, and there's an
observation platform for watching birds. There are always crabs, lizards, snakes, and other creatures rustling in the grass and howler monkeys and iguanas in the trees. Pick up a self-guided trail map from
the Lagarta Lodge when you pay your admission fee, or better yet,
hire the resident nature guide; call ahead if you want to hire a guide.
The best times to do the hike, which takes about two hours, are early
in the morning or late in the afternoon, which means you can follow
your trek with breakfast, or sunset cocktails at the Lagarta Lodge.
✉*Trailhead 168 steps down from Lagarta Lodge, top of hill at the
north end of Nosara* ☎*2682–0035* ✉*$6, $3 for kids under 12, $12
with guide.*

MASSAGE &
YOGA
The Nosara Yoga Institute (✉*Southeast end of town, on main road to
Sámara* ☎*2682–0071, 866/439–4704 in U.S.* ⊕*www.nosarayoga.
com*) focuses on teacher certification, but also offers several daily yoga
classes to the public ($10), weeklong workshops, and retreats. Relaxing
massages in a jungle setting ($55 per hour) are available by appoint-
ment at **Tica Massage** (✉*Across from the Hotel Harmony [formerly
the Hotel Villa Taype]* ☎*2682–0096*), plus spa services such as facials
and salt glows.

OUTDOOR ACTIVITIES

Iguana Expeditions (✉*Gilded Iguana, Playa Guiones* ☎2682–4089 ⊕*www.iguanaexpeditions.com*) organizes kayaking on the Nosara River, a hike to a waterfall, horseback riding, fishing, and nature tours. The **Harbor Reef Surf Resort** (✉*Follow signs from Café de Paris turnoff, Playa Guiones* ☎2682–0059 ⊕*www.harborreef.com*) has an excellent tour desk that can arrange fishing, surfing, nature tours, and a day trip to the Tempisque River that combines a boat and canopy tour.

BIRD-
WATCHING
☯

On river trips with **Nosara Boat Tours** (✉*Boat moored at bottom of hill leading to Lagarta Lodge, follow signs to the boca [mouth] of Nosara River* ☎2822–1806 or 2682–0610), you glide up the Nosara and Montaña rivers in a flat-bottom catamaran with an almost noise-less electric motor. Wading herons, egrets, roseate spoonbills, ospreys, and kingfishers are common sights. The German-born naturalist guide also knows where river otters play and crocodiles hunker down in mud caves along the riverbank. Trips are $30 per person ($15 for kids under 14).

HORSEBACK
RIDING
☯

German equestrienne Beate Klossek and husband Hans-Werner take small groups of up to six people on 3½-hour horseback nature tours through the jungle and along the beach ($60 to $90 per person, accord-ing to group size) with **Boca Nosara Tours** (✉*150 m below Lagarta Lodge, at mouth of Nosara River* ☎2682–0280). Horses are well man-nered and well treated. There are smaller saddles for kids over eight.

SURFING

If you ever wanted to learn to surf, Nosara is the place. Guiones is the perfect beginners' beach, with no rocks to worry about. Local surf instructors say that the waves here are so consistent that there's no week throughout the year when you won't be able to surf. In March and April, the Costa Rican National Surf Circuit comes here for surf trials. Espe-cially recommended for beginners, **Safari Surf School** (✉*Road to Playa Guiones; ask for directions at Casa Tucán* ☎2682–0573 ⊕*www.safari surfschool.com*) is run by two surfing brothers from Hawaii, one of whom lives here year-round. A one-hour private lesson costs $40, equip-ment included. The school is closed in October. **Corky Carroll's Surf School** (✉*Near Casa Romántica, on the Playa Guiones road* ☎2682–0385 ⊕*www.surfschool.net*) has its own hotel for surfing students. **Coconut Harry's Surf Shop** (✉*Main road, across from Café de Paris* ☎2682–0574) has boards ($20 per day), gear, and lessons ($35 per hour). **Nosara Surf Shop** (✉*Café de Paris, road to Playa Guiones* ☎2682–0186) rents boards by the day ($15 to $20) and has lots of gear, too.

WHERE TO EAT

$$ ✕**Café de Paris.** The French-Swiss owners have turned this corner res-taurant into a chic, alfresco eatery. Fresh-baked pastries and desserts are a major draw. Sweet and savory croissants are excellent, as is the divine chocolate tart. In addition to the tried-and-true wood-oven piz-zas, nachos, and hearty sandwiches, they have such continental treats as fish and vegetables baked in papillote, jumbo shrimp flambé, and lamb stew with mushrooms. ✉*Main road at Playa Guiones entrance* ☎2682–0087 ▭*AE, MC, V.*

$$ ✕**Giardino Tropicale.** Famous for
★ its crispy-crust, wood-oven pizzas
loaded with toppings as well as the
bowls of homemade chili-pepper
sauce that grace every table, this
thatch-roof multilevel restaurant
casts a wide net to include daily
fresh seafood and fish specials.
Sit on one of the upper decks by
day, and you'll dine amid the tree-
tops. Service is always fast and
very friendly. ⊠ *Giardino Tropical
Hotel, main street, past entrance to
Playa Guiones* ☎2682–0258 ⊟*AE, MC, V.*

> **CAUTION**
>
> Many restaurants do not include
> the legally required 13% tax and
> 10% service in their menu prices,
> but tack them onto the bill at
> the end. It might be indicated
> somewhere on the menu that tax
> and tip are not included, but that's
> not always the case. If you're not
> sure, ask.

$$ ✕**Marlin Bill's.** Sink your teeth into classic rib-eye steak, pork chops,
and lobster in American-size portions at this open-air restaurant with
a distant ocean view. Lighter choices include eggplant Parmesan and
delicious "dorado fingers"—battered fish fillet strips served with tartar
sauce. The decor is decidedly fishy, with a mounted marlin, fish murals,
and a photo wall of happy fishers and their prize catches. Fishing and
real estate talk over beer and chicken wings keeps the U-shape bar
abuzz. ⊠ *Hilltop above main road, near Coconut Harry's Surf Shop*
☎2682–0458 ⊟*MC, V* ⊗ *Closed Sun.*

WHERE TO STAY

$$$ ▦**Harmony Hotel.** Surf's up... upscale, that is. This formerly frayed surf-
★ er's haunt has been reborn as an ultra-cool hipster's retreat. The Ameri-
can owners are surfers, but of an age where comfort and quiet are more
appealing than partying. The rooms surround a huge garden that holds
a gorgeous, chlorine-free pool and sundeck—an oasis of tranquillity.
Every room, villa, and bungalow has soft sage-and-cream-color walls,
a king-size bed dressed in white linen, and natural and polished wood
trim and furniture. Enclosed back decks with hammocks expand what
are otherwise standard-size rooms. The slightly larger duplex bunga-
lows in back offer a little more privacy for an extra $60. The retro
'60s lounge bar with basket chairs and adjacent restaurant add to the
sophisticated ambience, but chic is not cheap—this place is markedly
more expensive than its neighbors. For the health-conscious traveler
there's a "healing center" complete with spa, yoga classes, and juice
bar. The best surf breaks are just 600 feet away, down a shaded path.
Pros: Near beach, chic, nice details. **Con:** Pricey. ⊠ *From Café de Paris,
take road almost all the way to Playa Guiones, on right,* ☎2682–4114
🖷2682–4113 ⊕ *www.harmonynosara.com* ➭ *10 rooms, 15 bunga-
lows* ⚹ *In-room: safe, refrigerator, no TV, Wi-Fi. In-hotel: restaurant,
bar, pool, spa, beachfront, laundry service, no-smoking rooms* ⊟*AE,
DC, MC, V* ⦿*BP.*

$$ ▦**Harbor Reef Surf Resort.** Lose yourself in the junglelike garden grounds
centered around two small pools, one presided over by a concrete croc-
odile, the other by a tiny waterfall. Your wake-up call is the bellowing
of a resident howler monkey, and you can bird-watch at breakfast.
Rooms and suites cater to surfers of every age, with plenty of space for

boards and gear inside, but the decor is rudimentary. "Surf city" rooms have two queen beds in slightly separate alcoves, whereas larger suites are great for families, with two bedrooms, two baths, a loft with twin beds, and a kitchen. The surf break at Playa Guiones is a 1,000-foot walk away. The open-air restaurant ($–$$) serves an American menu, with fresh fish, steak, chicken, pastas, and some Tex Mex dishes. A large souvenir shop and also a beachwear shop are on the grounds. Owner Randy Bombard has a wealth of information about the area. **Pros:** Attractive grounds, near beach, good restaurant. **Con:** Bland rooms. ⊠ *Follow signs from Café de Paris turnoff, Playa Guiones* ☎ *2682–0059 or 2682–1000* 🖷 *2682–0060* ⊕ *www.harborreef.com* 🛏 *13 rooms, 9 suites, 18 houses* 🛇 *In-room: no phone, kitchen (some), refrigerator. In-hotel: restaurant, bar, pools, no elevator, laundry service, public Internet, public Wi-Fi* ⊟ *AE, DC, MC, V* ⊺⊙⊦*EP.*

$$ 🖼 **Luna Azul.** Sequestered in the hills above Playa Ostional, several miles
★ north of Nosara, Luna Azul is a tranquil, tasteful spot full of clever design and healthful attributes—supplied by the zoologist and homeopathist Swiss owners. Abundant birds and wildlife, thanks to the surrounding private nature reserve, make this an excellent spot for nature lovers; it is also the most convenient lodge for seeing turtles nesting. Rooms are spacious, and the bathrooms are elegant, with hot-water showers open to nature. Three separate rooms have very private decks, cooled by overhead fans; four others have their own gardens. Acupuncture and homeopathic treatments and massages are available. The chic seafood restaurant overlooking the small tile pool and treetops draws customers from Nosara, with perfectly prepared seafood, fresh fish, tenderloin, and organic chicken. The only drawback to this picture-perfect place is that it's hard to get to when the Lagarto River swells in rainy season, but you can always reach it via Veintisiete de Abril, near Tamarindo. **Pros:** Isolated in a picturesque environment, good restaurant. **Con:** Off the beaten path. ✛ *1 km (½ mi) north of Ostional, 5 km (3 mi) north of Nosara* ☎ *2821–0075* ⊕ *www.hotellunaazul.com* 🛏 *3 bungalows, 4 rooms* 🛇 *In-room: no phone, safe, refrigerator, no TV. In-hotel: restaurant, bar, pool, no elevator, laundry service* ⊟ *AE, DC, MC, V* ⊙ *Closed Oct.* ⊺⊙⊦*BP.*

$–$$ 🖼 **Casa Romántica Hotel.** The name ("Romantic House") says it all: the
★ Spanish Colonial–style house has a balustraded veranda upstairs and a graceful arcade below. The young Swiss owners renovated the original rooms and built new rooms in separate wings. All are bright, with big bathrooms and shared terraces with views of the glorious gardens. There's a kidney-shape pool next to a thatch shelter with hammocks, and a short path through the surrounding forest leads to the beach. The small patio restaurant where the complementary buffet breakfast is served becomes a truly romantic, candlelighted restaurant ($–$$) at night, when the menu includes such continental favorites as chicken cordon bleu, beef Stroganoff, a creamy shrimp curry, and daily fish and seafood specials. **Pros:** Near beach, good restaurant, good value. **Con:** Rooms not spectacular. ⊠ *100 m west of Giardino Tropical, on left, Playa Guiones* ☎ *2682–0272* ⊕ *www.casa-romantica.net* 🛏 *12 rooms* 🛇 *In-room: no a/c (some), no phone, safe, refrigerator, no TV.*

In-hotel: restaurant, pool, beachfront, no elevator, laundry service, public Wi-Fi ⊟*MC, V* ⊙*|BP.*

$–$$ 🔲 **Giardino Tropicale Hotel.** In the lush gardens downhill from the popular restaurant *(⇨above)*, shaded by large trees, are comfortable cabinas and a sparkling 40-foot swimming pool—the only good lap pool in town. The handsome suites have everything you need to make breakfast: electric kettles, coffeemakers, refrigerators, and sinks. Two spacious apartments also have full kitchens. The four smaller cabinas have solar-heated hot water, ceiling fans, coffeemakers, and refrigerators; use of air-conditioning costs extra. Inexpensive, hearty breakfasts are served by the pool, and the restaurant is one of the best in town. **Pros:** Good value, environmentally friendly, helpful owners. **Cons:** Road noise, short walk to beach. ⊠*Main street, past entrance to Playa Guiones* ☎*2682–4000* 🖶*2682–0353* ⊕*www.giardinotropicale.com* ⇱*4 cabinas, 4 suites, 2 apartments* ♿*In-room: no phone, kitchen (some), no TV (some). In-hotel: restaurant, pool, no elevator, public Wi-Fi* ⊟*AE, DC, MC, V* ⊙*|EP.*

$ 🔲 **The Gilded Iguana.** This lively hotel/bar/restaurant has been a Nosara fixture for more than 15 years. Televised sports, live music, and lots of friendly regulars make the open-air bar a popular place. The on-site tour desk can arrange almost any outing you can imagine. Six large, air-conditioned rooms are lined up behind a small, kidney-shape pool with a refreshing waterfall. For traditionalists, the original rooms have more character, in a shaded wooden building with louvered, screened windows letting in fresh breezes in lieu of air-conditioning. ⊠*Playa Guiones, Nosara* ☎*2682–0259* ⊕*www.gildediguana.com* ⇱*12 rooms, 1 suite* ♿*In-room: no a/c (some), no phone, refrigerator, no TV. In-hotel: restaurant, bar, pool, no elevator, laundry service* ⊟*MC, V* ⊙*|EP.*

$ 🔲 **Lagarta Lodge.** A birders' and nature-lovers' Valhalla, this magnifi-
★ cent property on a promontory has amazing views of the forest, river, and coast north of Nosara. The private Nosara Biological Reserve is directly below the lodge. A 10-minute walk down a steep path takes you through a monkey-filled forest to beautiful Playa Guiones and surfing waves. The bright, spacious rooms are simple but comfortable, with balconies and terraces perfect for admiring the sweeping vista. Swiss managers Regina and Amadeo Amacker oversee the eagle's-nest lobby-restaurant ($–$$, reservations essential), which features a Swiss-inspired menu that is strong on fresh fish and seafood, such as skewered prawns with bacon, and poached fish with a lemon sauce. There is also a cocktails-and-canapés Sunset Bar that you must visit even if you stay elsewhere. The breakfast buffet is delicious, with fresh breads and homemade jams. ⊠*Top of hill at north end of Nosara* ☎*2682–0035* 🖶*2682–0135* ⊕*www.lagarta.com* ⇱*6 rooms* ♿*In-room: no a/c, no phone, no TV. In-hotel: restaurant, bar, pool, no elevator, public Internet* ⊟*MC, V* ⊙*|EP.*

NIGHTLIFE
There's always plenty of surfing talk at **Kaya Sol**, (⊠*Playa Guiones* ☎*2682–0080*) a friendly, laid-back bar near the beach with a pool table, tree-trunk tables, and a light, inexpensive menu. **The Gilded Iguana** (⊠*Playa Guiones* ☎*2682–0259*) has live acoustic music on Tuesday

night that draws a big crowd. Sip a margarita or one of the other cocktails and watch the sun set at tony **La Luna Bar & Grill** (✉ *Playa Pelada* ☎ *2682–0122*).

Sunset is the main event in the evening, and people gather to watch it at **Olga's Bar** (✉ *Playa Pelada* ☎ *No phone*), a ramshackle beach shack.

Saturday night, the popular **Tropicana** (✉ *Downtown Nosara, beside the soccer field* ☎ *No phone*) is where the action is.

SHOPPING

Arte Guay (✉ *Commercial center, just past Café de Paris on road to Playa Guiones* ☎ *2682–0757*) has local crafts and beachwear. Along with surfing wear and gear, **Coconut Harry's Surf Shop** (✉ *Main road, across from Café de Paris*) has an interesting selection of jewelry and bottled hot sauces made by Harry himself. (The Iguana Atomic Hot Sauce will rip your tongue out!) At the **Chenoa Boutique** (✉ *Commercial center, just past Café de Paris on road to Playa Guiones*) has an interesting selection of jewelry, handbags, and beachwear.

SÁMARA

36 km (23 mi) southwest of Nicoya, 26 km (16 mi) south of Nosara.

The drive to Sámara from Nicoya may be one of the most scenic in Costa Rica, passing rolling hills and green vistas before descending to a wide, south-facing bay hemmed by palm-shaded sand. Long a favorite summer-home spot with well-off Costa Ricans, Sámara's combination of safe swimming water and relative proximity to San José make it a popular destination for working-class Ticos as well. The town of Sámara has an abundance of budget accommodations, which makes it a good destination for travelers with limited budgets. It can be a lively place on weekends, with bars on the beaches and handicraft venders on the main drag, but it isn't the cleanest of beaches (no Blue Flag), and those seeking solitude should head to the beach's western or eastern ends. Though it lacks the rip currents that make many Costa Rican beaches dangerous, Sámara has pollution problems, and is thus is not the best beach for swimming from September to December, when daily rains flush plenty of things you wouldn't want to swim with into the sea.

Sámara's wide sweep of light-gray sand is framed by two forest-covered hills jutting out on either side. It's the perfect hangout beach, with plenty of natural shade, bars, and restaurants to take refuge in from the sun. There is, however, a sandy roadway running through the coconut palms and Indian almond trees that line the beach, so be sure to look both ways when you move between the surf and margaritaville. The waves break out on a reef that lines the entrance of the cove, several hundred yards offshore, which keeps the water calm enough for safe swimming, but leaves enough surf to have fun in. The reef holds plenty of marine attractions for diving and snorkeling excursions. Isla Chora, at the south end of the bay, provides a sheltered area that is especially popular for kayakers and snorkelers—it even has a tiny beach at lower tides.

GETTING HERE & AROUND

The road from Nicoya is paved all the way for the scenic one-hour drive to Sámara. ■TIP→Potholes are spreading, so keep your eyes on the road instead of the beautiful views. A rough beach road from Nosara is passable in dry season (it's more direct, but takes just as long); do not attempt this road when it rains. To get from Nosara to Sámara via the paved road, drive south, 5 km (3 mi) past Garza. At the "T" in the road, ignore the road toward Sámara (the beach road) and take the road to the left, toward Nicoya. This will take you uphill to merge with the main Nicoya–Sámara highway. No matter which way you go, the drive to Sámara is long and bumpy. Sámara-bound buses leave Nicoya from a stop 300 meters east of the central park. They depart hourly from 5 AM to 3 PM and then at 4:30, 6:30, 8, and 9:45 PM.

SÁMARA ESSENTIALS

Bank/ATM **Banco Nacional** (⊠ 50 m west of church, 100 m west of main road ☎ 2656–0089).

Hospital **Medical Care Beach Services** (☎ 8304–2121 ⊙ 24-hour emergency hotline).

Pharmacy **Farmacia Sámara** (⊠ North end of soccer field ☎ 2656–0123).

Internet **Se@net** (⊠ Across from soccer field ☎ 2656–0302 ⊙ Daily 8 AM–9 PM).

Post Office **Correo** (⊠ Beside church, across from soccer field).

OUTDOOR ACTIVITIES

Sámara is known more for gentle water sports such as snorkeling and kayaking than for surfing, although there are a couple of surf schools in town. There are also two high-flying adventures here: zip-line tours and ultralight flights and flying lessons. ATV tours, tearing along dirt roads, are popular with travelers who are particularly fond of dust, or mud, according to the season. For information on area activities, visit the town's official Web site at ⊕ www.Samarabeach.com.

Tío Tigre Tours (⊠ 50 m east of school and 100 m north ☎ 2656–0098) has a full line of guided outdoor activities, including kayaking ($25), snorkeling ($30), horseback riding ($30), and dolphin- and whale-watching tours ($35). **Sámara Travel Center** (⊠ Main street, across from Century 21 ☎ 2656–0922) offers an array of local tours, bus and plane tickets to other parts of the country, and rents bikes and motorcycles.

CANOPY TOURS **Wing Nuts Canopy Tour** (⊠ In the hills above Sámara ☎ 2656–0153) has a three-hour, 12-platform zip-line tour through a patch of tropical forest just south of town, with ocean views from some of the platforms ($55).

DIVING & SNORKELING The reef offshore is the best place to snorkel. Kayakers also paddle out to Isla Chora to snorkel on the leeward side of the island. The lone dive shop here, French-run **Pura Vida Dive** (⊠ Sámara, 600 m west of church ☎ 8843–2075 or 8398–8655), takes a maximum of five divers ($85 each) about 8 km (5 mi) out to explore rock formations off Playa Buena Vista and Playa Carrillo. Turtles, white-tipped sharks, and lots of big fish are the star sightings. The company also rents scuba equipment and arranges snorkeling trips.

KAYAKING Plastic sit-on-top kayaks can be rented at Villas Playa Sámara *(⇨below)*, which is quite close to Isla Chora and the reef. **C&C Surf Shop** (⊠*On beach across from Casa del Mar* ☎2656–0628) runs kayak snorkeling tours to Isla Chora and the nearby reef ($30). **Tío Tigre***(⇨above)* offers various kayaking tours.

SURFING The surf is relatively gentle at Sámara, so it's a good place for beginners. The challenging waves for more experienced surfers are farther south, at Playa Camaronal, which has both left and right breaks. **C&C Surf Shop** *(⇨above)* has a beachfront surf school ($40 per lesson), and rents boards ($4 per hour).

ULTRALIGHT **Flying Crocodile Lodge** (⊠*Playa Buena Vista ✢6 km [4 mi] northwest*
FLIGHTS *of Sámara* ☎2656–8048 ⊕*www.flying-crocodile.com*) gives ultralight flights and flying lessons ($60 for 20-minute tour).

WHERE TO EAT

$$$ ✕**El Lagarto.** With varnished wooden tables scattered across the sand
★ amid ficus and Indian almond trees, close enough to the sea to hear the surf above the mix of Latin music on the stereo, El Lagarto has Sámara's best ambience by far. But its big draw is the food—fresh local seafood and quality meat grilled to perfection on a massive, open-air barbecue. The name means "The Crocodile," but you won't find croc steaks on the menu. You can, however, sink your teeth into juicy tenderloin, lamb chops, mahimahi, prawns, tuna, veal ribs, mussels, chicken breast stuffed with mushrooms and cheese, Portobello mushrooms, or a whole-grilled lobster. You won't find any barbecue sauce on the meat here; everything is simply brushed with extra-virgin olive oil seasoned with a bit of garlic, salt, and pepper to complement the flavor of the wood. Dinners include grilled vegetables and potatoes; a salad is à la carte. They have a kids' menu, an ample wine list, and an extensive cocktail selection, not to mention the banana split. ⊠*200 m west and 200 m south of Banco Nacional* ☎2656–0750 ▭AE, DC, MC, V ⊗*No lunch. Closed Sept. and Oct.*

$–$$ ✕**Restaurante Las Brasas.** Seafood and meat grilled over hot *brasas* (coals), and served with a selection of sauces, are the specialties at this Spanish restaurant in the heart of town. They serve such Spanish standards as paella, gazpacho, and a variety of *tortillas* (hearty omelets), as well as pastas and various Mediterranean dishes. Avocado stuffed with shrimp salad makes an excellent shared starter or a light lunch. An upstairs balcony is a perfect place for sipping Spanish wines. Downstairs, enormous green elephant-ear leaves frame the rustic wooden-railed restaurant, decorated with ox horns and yokes. ⊠*Main road to beach, beside soccer field* ☎2656–0546 ▭AE, DC, MC, V ⊗ *Closed Fri.*

$ ✕**El Manglar.** Hidden on a rutted side street, this informal Italian eat-
★ ery beneath a large thatch roof doesn't look like much, but there are usually plenty of cars parked in front, since it's a favorite of local expatriates. The owner, Letizia Vendittelli, is invariably in the kitchen,

preparing fresh pasta, fish, and meat dishes to order, or sliding another one of her super-thin, crispy pizzas out of the oven. She makes the best pizza in town, with two dozen varieties to choose from. The ricotta-and-spinach ravioli with porcini mushrooms and zucchini have made many a mouth water, as have the homemade gnocchi—but ask for the mahimahi ravioli, which isn't on the menu but is often available, and have Letizia smother them in her creamy shrimp sauce. She makes nearly everything fresh, which means you have to wait a little longer here than at the competition, but she is happy to modify recipes to suite your taste. ⊠ *200 m west and 150 m south of Banco Nacional* ☎ *2656–0096* ⊟ *MC, V* ⊙ *No lunch. Closed 2 wks in May and 2 wks in Sept.*

$ ✕ **Pizza & Pasta a Go-Go.** An ample selection of quality Italian food, including 25 fabulous pizzas, 26 pastas, generous salads, and a lengthy Italian wine list are just a few reasons to drop in at this sidewalk trattoria. Unlike the checkered tablecloths you'd find elsewhere, here you have glass tabletops showcasing shells, or plain wooden tables by the pool. Save room for a tiramisu that transcends the tropics and delivers your taste buds to Italy. ⊠ *Hotel Giada lobby, main strip, 150 m north of beach* ☎ *2656–0132* ⊟ *AE, MC, V.*

WHERE TO STAY

$$$ 🏨 **Villas Playa Sámara.** Families come back to this property year after
☿   year for good reason: there's lots to do, the villas are spacious and practical, and the setting is fabulous. It is spread along the picture-perfect southern end of the beach, where the ocean is cleaner than it is near town, and shallow and safe enough for swimming. The spacious, Spanish-style one-, two-, and three-bedroom villas of white stucco are sprinkled across the property's gardens and wide lawns. They have kitchens and dining areas with day beds that are perfect for kids (under 12 are free), and shaded terraces with either a hammock or chairs, but they are quite timeworn and lack such basics as a phone and a TV. Most have ocean views through the palms, but the duplex villas 2 A/B and 11A/B are especially close to the beach, and thus cost an extra $20; 17 A/B is a close second. The restaurant food is not terrific; it's best to cook for yourself, or dine in town. **Pros:** Great location, spacious villas, ample grounds. **Cons:** Villas timeworn, cleaning inconsistent. ⊠ *Off main road* ⬦ *2 km (1¼ mi) south of town* ☎ *2656–0372, 2256–8228 in San José* ⊕ *www.villasplayaSamara.com* ➴ *57 villas* ⚙ *In-room: no phone, kitchen, no TV (some). In-hotel: restaurant, bar, pool, beachfront, water sports, bicycles, no elevator, laundry service, concierge, public Internet, public Wi-Fi* ⊟ *AE, MC, V* ⏐○⏐ *EP.*

$$ 🏨 **Villas Kalimba.** You may never want to leave this tranquil oasis hid-
★   den behind scrolled white-and-orange walls. The architecture is Mexican but the style is all Italian. Ochre-washed villas with hammocks and dining tables on their front porches circle an exuberant garden and pool with a cool waterfall. Rooms have state-of-the-art kitchens, and you can dine alfresco at a long wooden table on your own tiled terrazza. All the comforts of a luxury home—king-size bed, cable TV, a personal portable phone—are here, just across the street from the beach. Barbecues and pasta dinners for guests are offered several times

a week beneath a Spanish-tile roof by the pool. **Pros:** Spacious villas, lovely gardens, quiet. **Con:** Not on beach. ✉*200 m east of the Sámara Police Station, along beach road* ☎*2656–0929* 🖷*2656–0930* ⊕*www. villaskalimba.com* ⇱*6 villas* ♨*In-room: kitchen. In-hotel: pool, no elevator, laundry service* ▭*MC, V* ℺*EP.*

$–$$ ⊡ **Las Brisas del Pacífico.** One of the few beachfront hotels in Sámara, Las Brisas has been here for nearly two decades, and much of the place shows its age. The standard rooms, in two rows of white, Spanish-style bungalows hugging the bottom of a steep hill, can be hot and stuffy. "Sky rooms," in the two-story building at the top of the hill, are more expensive, but much nicer, with ocean-view balconies and a nearby pool, as well as a separate parking lot, so that you don't have to climb up and down the steep hill. Newer "on-top" rooms above the office are closer to the beach, and have balconies, but most view the restaurant's roof. You'll want to eat everything but breakfast in town. The receptionist can arrange diving trips and other outings. **Pros:** Great location, two nice pools. **Cons:** Rooms and grounds somewhat neglected, service inconsistent. ✉*Just south of town* ☎*2656–0250* 🖷*2656–0076* ⊕*www.brisas.net* ⇱*55 rooms* ♨*In-room: no a/c (some), no phone, safe. In-hotel: restaurant, bar, pools, beachfront, no elevator, laundry service, public Wi-Fi* ▭*AE, D, MC, V* ℺*BP.*

$ ⊡ **Hotel Giada.** Giada means "jade," in Italian, and this small hotel in the heart of town has been decorated with the artistic Italian owners' precious, polished creations. Watermelon, terra-cotta, and yellow washes give the walls an antique Mediterranean look, while the terraces of the back rooms overlook a curvaceous blue pool surrounded by tropical greenery. The rooms have whimsical bamboo furniture and sea creatures on the hand-pained bathroom tiles. Pizza & Pasta a Go-Go (⇨*above), the hotel's restaurant,* is an excellent Italian restaurant. The hotel's drawback is noise from the restaurant and the street, which is why roadside rooms should be avoided; ask for a room overlooking the pool. ✉*Main strip, 250 m from beach* ☎*2656–0132* 🖷*2656–0131* ⊕*www.hotelgiada.net* ⇱*24 rooms* ♨*In-room: safe, refrigerator (some). In-hotel: restaurant, pool, no elevator* ▭*AE, DC, MC, V* ℺*BP.*

¢–$ ⊡ **Casa del Mar.** Less than a block from the beach, this pleasant, well-tended hotel is one of Sámara's best values. The bright, tidy rooms have dark-wood furniture, white walls, and ceramic floors. Eleven of the rooms have private bath, and some have queen-size beds. Six of the rooms lack air-conditioning and share baths, but they share a common balcony with an ocean view, and sea breezes help to cool them. The hotel has a giant cold-water whirlpool in a small garden and a big cage holding a parrot named Lolita. ✉*Main strip, 45 m east of school* ☎*2656–0264* 🖷*2656–0129* ⊕*www.casadelmarSamara.com* ⇱*17 rooms, 11 with bath* ♨*In-room: no a/c (some), no phone, refrigerator (some), no TV (some). In-hotel: no elevator, no-smoking rooms* ▭*AE, MC, V* ℺*BP.*

NIGHTLIFE

The liveliest, noisiest beach bar is **Las Olas** (⊠ *On beach, 200 m west and 200 m south of Banco Nacional* ☎2656–1100). Three pool tables, bright lights, and a pulsing Latin soundtrack attract a mix of locals and young backpackers. **Tutifruti** (⊠ *50 m west of police station*), on the beach, is the local dance club. It only opens Friday and Saturday, when it gets packed with young Costa Ricans. **Shake Joe's** (⊠ *On beach, center of town*) is the place for music, drinks, and an international menu.

★ **La Vela Latina** (⊠ *Across from Villas Kalimba, on beach*) is the cool place for grown-up soft music and cocktails on the beach.

SHOPPING

Souvenir stands set up along the main street and at the entrance to the beach. Most shops here have pretty much the same beachwear and souvenirs for sale. **Tienda Licia** (⊠ *Main street*) has a wall hung with pretty glass fish and butterfly ornaments made by a San José artist. Arts-and-crafts gallery **Dragonfly Galería** (⊠ *Across the street from Licia*) sells local paintings and carvings, and shell, feather, and bead jewelry. It also paints temporary henna tattoos.

PLAYA CARRILLO

Fodor'sChoice

★

7 km (4 mi) southeast of Sámara.

With its long, reef-protected beach backed by an elegant line of swaying palms and sheltering cliffs, Playa Carrillo (interchangeably called Puerto Carrillo) is a candidate for the most picturesque beach in Costa Rica. Unmarred by a single building, it's ideal for swimming, snorkeling, walking, and lounging—just remember not to sit under a loaded coconut palm. There are some concrete tables and benches, but they get snapped up quickly. This is a popular beach with locals, and it gets quite busy on weekends. The main landmark here is the Hotel Guanamar, high above the beach. Unfortunately the former private fishing club and previously grand hotel has been bought and sold so often that its charm has faded. But its bar still has the best view.

GETTING HERE & AROUND

You can fly into Playa Carrillo on SANSA or Nature Air and land at the airstrip, or head south 15 minutes on the smooth, paved road from Sámara. If you're not staying at a hotel in Carrillo you'll have to park your car either in a sunbaked concrete lot halfway along the beach or on the grassy median at the south end of the beach. You can also leave the driving to Interbus (⇨ *North Pacific in Essentials, at end of chapter*) and get here in an air-conditioned van.

PLAYA CARRILLO ESSENTIALS

Sámara is the closest town for banks and other services.

EXPLORING

Most nature lovers are no fans of zoos, but **La Selva Zoo & Bromeliad Garden,** a small zoo with mostly rescued small animals, is a great chance to see them up close in chest-high corrals under the shade of trees. The zoo's focus is on hard-to-see nocturnal animals, so the best time to visit is at sunset when the roly-poly armadillos and big-eyed kinkajous are starting to stir. There are also skunks, spotted pacas, raccoons, and scarier species like bats, boas, poison dart frogs, caimans, and crocodiles. A bromeliad and orchid collection is artistically arranged around the zoo. If you come early in the day, your ticket is also good for a return evening visit. ⊠ *Road behind Hotel Esperanza* ☎ *8305–1610* 💳 *$8* 🕙 *Daily 10–9.*

OUTDOOR ACTIVITIES

FISHING   From January to April, the boats moored off the beach take anglers on fishing expeditions. Experienced local skipper Rob Gordon lives right in Puerto Carrillo and runs fishing trips on the five-passenger *Kitty Kat* (☎ *2656–0170 or 8359–9039* ⊕ *www.sportfishcarrillo.com*), a 28-foot aluminum boat with twin diesels ($900 full day, $500--$600 half day). He offers catch-and-release marlin and sail fishing as well as good-eating dorado, yellowfin tuna, and wahoo. There are also dolphins and occasional whales to watch if the fishing is slow.

PUNTA ISLITA

8 km (5 mi) south of Playa Carrillo in dry season, 50 km (31 mi) south of Carrillo by alternate route in rainy season.

Punta Islita is named for a tiny tuft of land that becomes an island at high tide, but the name is synonymous in Costa Rica with Hotel Punta Islita, one of the country's most luxurious and gorgeous resorts. The curved beach is rather rocky but good for walking, especially at low tide when tidal pools form in the volcanic rock. Another interesting stroll is through the small village, which has become a work in progress, thanks to a community art project led by renowned Costa Rican artists who use town buildings as their canvas. Everything—from outdoor activities to food—revolves around, and is available through, the resort.

GETTING HERE & AROUND

During the dry season, it's a quick trip south of Playa Carrillo in a 4WD vehicle, but in the rainy season, it's often impossible to cross the Río Ora, so you have to make a much longer detour along rough dirt roads with spectacular mountain views. Most guests consequently fly into the hotel's private airstrip.

WHERE TO STAY

$$$$ **Hotel Punta Islita.** Overlooking the ocean from a forested ridge, this
Fodor'sChoice   secluded hotel is luxury incarnate. Hidden around the hillside are vil-
★   las, casitas, suites, and spacious rooms, each with a private porch and a hammock. Beds have rough-hewn wooden bedposts, and bathrooms are tiled, with deep tubs. Casitas have their own private plunge pools

or outdoor whirlpools and private gardens, one of the main attractions for the many honeymooners. A massive thatched dome covers the restaurant and opens onto an infinity-edge pool with a swim-up bar. If you overdo it with the activities here—including golfing, mountain biking, and zip-line tours—stop by the spa for massage treatments using local herbs. **Pros:** Gorgeous views, lots of activities. **Cons:** Isolated, mediocre beach. ✛ *8 km (5 mi) south of Playa Carrillo* ⬜ *Apdo. 242–1225, Plaza Mayor, San José* ☎ *2661–4044, 2231–6122 in San José* 🖨 *2661–4043, 2231–0715 in San José* ⊕ *www.hotelpuntaislita.com* ↘ *14 rooms, 8 suites, 8 casitas, 17 villas* 🛇 *In-room: DVD (some), VCR (some). In-hotel: 2 restaurants, bars, golf course, tennis courts, pools, gym, spa, beachfront, no elevator, laundry service, public Wi-Fi, no-smoking rooms* ⊟ *AE, DC, MC, V* ⏀ *BP.*

THE TEMPISQUE RIVER BASIN

The parks in and around the Río Tempisque are prime places to hike, explore caves, and spot birds and other wildlife. The town of Nicoya is the commercial and political hub of the northern Nicoya Peninsula. By road, Nicoya provides the best access to Sámara, Nosara, and points south and north and is linked by a smooth, well-paved road to the artisan community of Guaitil and the northern Nicoya beach towns.

The Friendship Bridge, built with donated funds from Taiwan and more commonly referred to as the Río Tempisque Bridge, crosses the Río Tempisque just north of where passengers used to weather long waits for a ferry. To get to the bridge, head north from San José on the Pan-American Highway, turn left about 48 km (30 mi) north of the Puntarenas turnoff, and drive 27 km (17 mi) west.

PALO VERDE NATIONAL PARK

52 km (32 mi) south of Liberia.

One of the best wildlife- and bird-watching parks in Costa Rica, Palo Verde is bordered on the west by the Río Tempisque. Extending over 198 square km (76 square mi), the park protects a significant amount of deciduous dry forest. The terrain is fairly flat—the maximum elevation in the park is 268 meters (879 ft)—and the forest is less dense than a rain forest, which makes it easier to spot the fauna. The park holds seasonal wetlands that provide a temporary home for thousands of migratory birds toward the end of the rainy season, whereas crocodiles ply the Tempisque's waters year-round. From September through March you can see dozens of species of migratory and resident aquatic birds, including herons, wood storks, jabirus, and elegant, flamingo-like roseate spoonbills. ■TIP→A raised platform near the ranger station, about 8 km (5 mi) past the park entrance, gives you a vantage point over a marsh filled with ducks and jacanas. But be prepared to climb a narrow metal ladder. Lodging in rustic dormitory facilities ($10) and meals ($5 breakfast; $7 for lunch or dinner) can be arranged through the park headquarters. ✢20 km (12 mi) southwest of Bagaces ☎2200–0125 ✉$10 ⊙Daily 6–6; entrance gates open 8–noon and 1–4.

GETTING HERE & AROUND

To get to Palo Verde from Liberia, drive south along the Pan-American Highway to Bagaces, then turn right at the small, easy-to-miss sign for Palo Verde, along a rough dirt road for 28 km (17 mi). Count on an hour to drive the distance from the main highway to the park entrance; it's a very bumpy road. You'll have to pay the $10 park entrance fee to get to the Organization for Tropical Studies station. The OTS station is about 7 km (5 mi) beyond the park entrance; the park headquarters is just another kilometer farther. The gatekeeper takes lunch from noon to 1 PM, so don't arrive then. The drive should take a total of about three hours.

EXPLORING

Just 3 km (2 mi) north of the Palo Verde road at Bagaces, take the dirt road signed for **Llanos de Cortés** to get to this hidden waterfall less than 2 km (1 mi) off the highway. About half a kilometer along the dirt road you'll see on your right a large rock with CATARATAS scrawled on it. Follow this bumpy road about 1.3 km (.8 mi) to its end and then clamber down a steep path to the pool at the bottom of a spectacular, wide, 50-foot waterfall. This is a great place for a picnic. ■TIP➡Don't leave anything of value in your car.

Sad but sobering, one of the few places left in the country where you are guaranteed to see large wild cats, including a jaguar, is **Las Pumas Rescue Shelter** (✢4½ km [3 mi] north of Cañas on main highway ☎2669–6044 ⊕www.laspumas.org). The small enclosures also hold jaguarundis, pumas, margays, ocelots, and oncillas. Some small animals and birds are rehabilitated and released into the wild. The larger cats are probably here for life, as it's dangerous for them to be released. The refuge relies on contributions. It's open daily 8 to 4.

OUTDOOR ACTIVITIES

The **Organization for Tropical Studies** (☎2524–0607 ⊕www.ots.ac.cr), a nonprofit, scientific consortium, offers overnight packages with a guided walk, meals, and lodging in rustic, bunk-bedded double rooms with private bath ($62 per person). Their biological research station overlooks the Palo Verde wetlands, and they also offer a boat tour plus longer hikes as affordable add-ons to the package.

BIRD-
WATCHING
The best bird-watching in Palo Verde is on the wetlands in front of the Organization for Tropical Studies' (OTS) biological station. The OTS has expert guides who can help you see and identify the varied birds in the area, but if you have good binoculars and a bird book, you can identify plenty of species on your own. A boat excursion to Isla Pájaros south of the Río Tempisque is interesting for birders. Toward the end of rainy season this 6-acre island near Puerto Moreno is an exciting place to see hundreds of nesting wood storks, cormorants, and anhingas. You can get close enough to see chicks being fed in nests. ■TIP➡The best time to go is very early in the morning, to avoid heat and to guarantee the most bird sightings. **Aventuras Arenal** (☎2479–9133 ⊕www.arenal

adventures.com) guides have good eyes and usually know the English names for birds. The company specializes in ecological tours and runs $30 bird-watching boat tours to Isla Pájaros. Tours depart from docks along the Río Tempisque, including the dock at Palo Verde. **CATA Tours** (☎2674–0180, 2296–2133 *in San José*) runs $59 wildlife- and bird-watching boating adventures down the Río Bebedero into Palo Verde. Arrange hotel pickup from Nicoya beaches and Papagayo Peninsula when you book.

Safaris Corobicí(☎2669–6192 ⊕*www.nicoya.com*) is a small company that specializes in the class I–II floats down the Río Corobicí ($35–$60) that start from (and end at) the Restaurante Rincón Corobicí, on the Pan-American Highway 5 km (3 mi) north of Cañas.

WILDLIFE WATCHING ☼ On a calm adventure trip with **Safaris Corobicí** (✉*Main highway to Liberia at Km 193, just south of Corobicí* ☎2669–6192 🖷2669–6091 ⊕*www.nicoya.com*), guides do the rowing on large inflatable rafts while you look at the flora and fauna. Two- or three-hour float trips ($35 to $60) cover wildlife-rich territory not far from Palo Verde. Trips require two or more passengers, and they start from the Restaurante Rincón Corobicí, on the Pan-American Highway 5 km (3 mi) north of Cañas. **Ríos Tropicales** (☎2233–6455 ⊕*www.riostropicales.com*) lets you paddle down the easy Class I–II rafting route on the Río Corobicí. Those two- to three-hour trips ($50) are great for bird- and monkey watching and are safe enough for kids ages seven and older.

WHERE TO STAY NEAR PALO VERDE

$ 🏨 **La Ensenada Lodge.** This is the most comfortable base for bird-watching and nature appreciation near the Río Tempisque. Part of a national wildlife refuge, the property is also a 1,000-acre cattle ranch and salt producer. The salt flats and nearby shallow waters attract wading birds (and crocodiles that snack on them). The Isla Pájaros Biological Reserve, the country's largest breeding ground for black-crowned night herons, is a short boat ride away. The wood cabins are comfortable, with verandas and big screened windows that let the light and breeze in, but because most of them are duplexes they don't afford a lot of privacy, so see if you can get a free-standing one. The rancho restaurant serves buffet-style Italian and Costa Rican meals, including beef raised on the ranch. ✛*13 km (8 mi) southwest of Pan-American Hwy. along a dirt road, 40 km (25 mi) north of the Puntarenas turn-off* ☎2289–6655 🖷2289–5281 ⊕*www.laensenada.net* ➫*26 cabin rooms* ✂*In-room: no a/c, no phone, no TV. In-hotel: restaurant, bar, pool, laundry service* ▭*No credit cards* ⦿*EP.*

EN ROUTE The approach to the town of Santa Cruz from the east is like a giant pit stop, with one car-parts shop after another. One of the few reasons to visit is to eat at **Coope-Tortillas** (✉*Drive through business district, 200 m past church turn right and look for peaked-roof metal structure, Santa Cruz* ☎2680–0688), where you can watch hand-rolled corn tortillas being cooked the old-fashioned way over an open fire. Friendly women in blue uniforms, members of a local women's cooperative, heap your plate with your choice of traditional *Guanacasteco* foods and bring it to one of the picnic tables in a high-ceiling, corrugated-metal building. Try the delicious *arroz de maiz,* a corn stew. The restaurant is open 4 AM to 5 PM. Tortillas sometimes run out before 4 PM.

BARRA HONDA NATIONAL PARK

100 km (62 mi) south of Liberia, 13 km (8 mi) west of Río Tempisque Bridge.

Once thought to be a volcano, 1,184-foot **Barra Honda Peak** actually contains an intricate network of caves, a result of erosion after the ridge emerged from the sea. Some caves on the almost 23-square-km (14-square-mi) park remain unexplored, and they're home to abundant animal life, including bats, birds, blindfish, salamanders, and snails.

GETTING HERE & AROUND
From the Río Tempisque Bridge, drive west along a paved highway. Then follow a dirt road (signed off the highway) for 10 km (6 mi) to the park entrance. There are buses that come here from the town of Nicoya, but they don't leave until 12:30 and 4 PM, a little late to start a hike. You can also take a taxi from Nicoya to the park entrance or go with one of many tour companies in beach towns on the Nicoya Peninsula.

EXPLORING
Every day from 7 AM to 1 PM local guides take groups rappelling 58 feet down into **Terciopelo Cave,** which shelters unusual formations shaped (they say) like fried eggs, popcorn, and shark's teeth. You must wear a harness with a rope attached for safety. The tour costs $26, including equipment rental, guide, and entrance fee. Kids under 12 are not allowed into this cave, but they can visit the kid-size La Cuevita cavern ($6), which also has interesting stalagmites. Both cave visits include interpretive nature hikes.

If you suffer a fear of heights, or claustrophobia, the cave tour is not for you, but Barra Honda still has pleny to offer, thanks to its extensive forests and abundant wildlife. You can climb the 3-km (2-mi) Los Laureles trail (the same trail that leads to the Terciopelo cave) to Barra Honda's summit, where you'll have sweeping views over the surrounding countryside and islet-filled Gulf of Nicoya. Wildlife you may spot on Barra Honda's trails includes howler monkeys, white-faced monkeys, skunks, coatis, deer, parakeets, hawks, dozens of other bird species, and iguanas. Local guides charge $6 for hiking tours. An off-site **park office** (✉ *Across from colonial church, Nicoya* ☎2686–6760) provides information and maps of the park. It's open weekdays 7–4. It's a good idea to hire a local guide from the **Asociación de Guias Ecologistas** (☎2659–1551). The park has camping facilities, and the guide association runs a

THE FIRST GUANACASTECOS

The Chorotega tribe first settled the Guanacaste area and grew corn and fished. Chief Nicoya was the Chorotegan leader who greeted the conquistadors in 1523 and bequeathed his name to the town and peninsula.

rustic, inexpensive lodge ($6 per person) near the park entrance. Make reservations for weekend lodging in the park. *13 km (8 mi) west of Río Tempisque Bridge,* ☎*2659–1551* ✉*$10* ⊙*Daily 7:30–4.*

NICOYA

27 km (15 mi) west of the Río Tempisque Bridge.

Once a quaint provincial town, Guanacaste's colonial capital is now bustling due to tourism and real-estate booms along the nearby coast. With all the commercial bustle, Nicoya is rapidly losing what small-town charm it once had. But there are still a few historical remnants around the central park. A noticeable Chinese population, descendants of 19th-century railroad workers, has given Nicoya numerous Chinese restaurants. The town has Internet cafés and ATMs that take international cards.

GETTING HERE & AROUND

The town of Nicoya is 40 minutes west of the Río Tempisque Bridge on a paved road. If you're running out of gas, oil, or tire pressure, the Servicentro Nicoyano on the north side of Nicoya, on the main road, is open 24 hours.

NICOYA ESSENTIALS

Bank/ATM Banco de Costa Rica (✉*West side of central park* ☎*2685–5110*). **Coopmani ATH** (✉*Main street, beside Fuji Film store*).

Hospital Hospital de L'Anexion (✉*Main road into town from highway* ☎*2685–5066*).

Pharmacy Farmacia Clinica Medica Nicoyana (✉*Main street, near Restaurante Nicoya* ☎*2685–5238* ⊙*Weekdays 8–7:30, Sat. 8–6*).

Internet CiberClub (✉*Across from Hotel Yenny, 1 block south of central park* ☎*2686–6063* ⊙*Mon.–Sat. 8:30 AM–9 PM*).

Post Office Correo (✉*Southwest corner of park*).

Taxis Taxi Service (☎*2686–2466*).

EXPLORING

Nicoya's only colonial landmark is the whitewashed, mission-style **Church of San Blas.** Originally built in 1644, the current church was reconstructed after the original was leveled by an 1831 earthquake. The spare interior is made grand by seven pairs of soaring carved-wood columns. Inside are folk-art wood carvings of the Stations of the Cross arrayed around the stark white walls, a small collection of 18th-century bronze mission bells, and some antique wooden saints. Arched doorways frame verdant views of park greenery and distant mountains. ✉*North side of central park* ☎*No phone* ✉*By donation* ⊙*Erratic hours.*

Understanding Costa Rica's Climate

Although you may associate the tropics with rain, precipitation in Costa Rica varies considerably, depending on where you are and when you're here. This is a result of the mountainous terrain and regional weather patterns. A phenomenon called rain shadow—when one side of a mountain range receives much more than the other—plays an important ecological role in Costa Rica. Four mountain ranges combine to create an intercontinental divide that separates the country into Atlantic and Pacific slopes; because of the trade winds, the Atlantic slope receives much more rain than the Pacific. The trade winds steadily pump moisture-laden clouds southwest over the isthmus, where they encounter warm air or mountains, which make them rise. As the clouds rise, they cool, lose their ability to hold moisture, and eventually dump most of their liquid luggage on the Caribbean side.

During the rainy season—mid-May to December—the role of the trade winds is diminished, as regular storms roll off the Pacific Ocean and soak the western side of the isthmus. Though it rains all over Costa Rica during these months, it often rains more on the Pacific side of the mountains than on the Atlantic. Come December, the trade winds take over again, and while the Caribbean prepares for its wettest time of the year, hardly a drop falls on the western side until May.

Climate variation within the country results in a mosaic of forests. The combination of humidity and temperature helps determine what grows where; but whereas some species have very restricted ranges, others seem to thrive just about anywhere. Plants such as strangler figs and bromeliads grow all over Costa Rica, and animals such as the collared peccary and coati—a long-nose cousin of the raccoon—can pretty much live wherever human beings let them. Other species have extremely limited ranges, such as the mangrove hummingbird, restricted to the mangrove forests of the Pacific coast, and the volcano junco, a gray sparrow that lives only around the highest peaks of the Cordillera de Talamanca.

OUTDOOR ACTIVITIES

Hiking in Barra Honda is the main outdoor adventure here. If that's too strenuous for you, **Tempisque Eco Adventures** (✛ *4 km [2½ mi] southwest of Río Tempisque Bridge* ☎*2687–1212* ✐*ecoaventuras@racsa.co.cr*) can show you flora and fauna similar to Barra Honda's on a seven-cable canopy tour ($35). For a fun day, you can combine the canopy tour with a Palo Verde boat tour. Lunch is in a charming open-air restaurant accompanied by traditional marimba music ($70).

WHERE TO STAY & EAT

$ ✕**Restaurante Nicoya.** There are many Chinese restaurants from which to choose in Nicoya. This one is the most elegant, with hanging lanterns, a colorful collection of international flags, and an enormous menu with 85 Asian dishes, such as stir-fried beef with vegetables. The fresh sea bass sautéed with fresh pineapple, chayote, and red peppers is excellent. ✉*Main road, 70 m south of Coopmani Bldg.* ☎*2685–5113* ▭*AE, DC, MC, V* ☾*Closed daily 3–5.*

¢ ✕ **Soda Colonial.** One of the town's last vestiges of local color is this vintage all-day restaurant with white-adobe walls. Facing the shady central park, it's a great place to watch small-town life go by. Sit at a wooden bench in the wainscotted interior and sip a tamarindo refresco or order hearty portions of typical Tico food, heavy on the beans and rice. ⊠*Southeast corner of central park* ⊟*No credit cards.*

$ ▥ **Hotel de Lujo Río Tempisque.** There aren't many reasons to stay over-night in Nicoya, but if you get stuck here, this "luxury" lodge is the best option. The rooms here, with high wooden ceilings and big pic-ture windows, are comfortable by any standards. Huge white-tile bath-rooms have mirrored closets and showers big enough for two. The best thing about the place, though, is its tranquil location north of town, and its ample gardens and small pool. ⊠*Highway north to Santa Cruz, just outside Nicoya* ☎*2686–6650* ↘*30 rooms* ⌂*In-room: no phone, refrigerator. In-hotel: restaurant, pool* ⊟*AE, MC, V* �aⓄ*EP.*

¢ ▥ **Hotel Mundiplaza.** This hotel is the town's most modern. On the sec-ond floor above a medical clinic, it doesn't have much personality. But if you need a bed for the night, it has fresh rooms with all the modern conveniences. There's also a small restaurant and Internet café in the same building. ⊠*Main road into Nicoya, near hospital* ☎*2685–3535* ↘*25 rooms* ⌂ *In-room: no phone. In-hotel: no elevator, laundry ser-vice* ⊟*AE, DC, MC, V* Ⓞ*EP.*

NORTH PACIFIC ESSENTIALS

TRANSPORTATION

BY AIR

ARRIVING & DEPARTING
International Aeropuerto Internacional Daniel Oduber (LIR) in Libe-ria is a good gateway to the coast. Tamarindo, Playa Nosara, Playa Sámara, Playa Carrillo, and Punta Islita also have airstrips. Flying in from San José to these airports is the best way to get here if you are already in the country. If your primary destination lies in Guanacaste or Nicoya, make sure you or your travel agent investigates the pos-sibility of flying directly into Liberia instead of San José, which saves some serious hours on the road. *For more information, see By Air in Costa Rica Essentials.*

GETTING AROUND
SANSA and Nature Air have scheduled flights between San José and destinations on the Nicoya Peninsula. Macaw Air flies small planes between Liberia and Tamarindo, as well as between destinations on the Nicoya Peninsula and to mainland destinations like Quepos and Puerto Jiménez.

BY BUS

ARRIVING & DEPARTING
For information about bus travel to and from the North Pacific, see By Bus Travel in Costa Rica Essentials.

GETTING AROUND
Bus service connects the larger cities to each other and to the more popular beaches, but forget about catching a bus from beach to beach; you'll generally have to backtrack to the inland hubs of Nicoya and

Liberia unless you take a minibus, which may take just as long as a bus, although they're usually more comfortable. Your hotel front desk should be able to confirm which station specific buses and lines depart from. Buses don't serve Rincón de la Vieja National Park.

BY CAR

ARRIVING & DEPARTING
The northwest is accessed via the paved two-lane Pan-American Highway (CA1), which begins at the top of Paseo Colón in San José. Take the bridge across the Río Tempisque to get to the Pacific beaches south of Liberia. Paved roads run down the spine of the Nicoya Peninsula all the way to Playa Naranjo, with many unpaved and potholed stretches. Once you get off the main highway, dust, mud, potholes, and other factors come into play, depending on which beach you visit. The roads to Playa Flamingo, Playa Conchal, Playa Brasilito, Tamarindo, Playa Grande, Playa Sámara, Playas del Coco, Hermosa, and Ocotal are paved all the way; every other destination requires some dirt-road maneuvering.

GETTING AROUND
If you want to drive around the Nicoya Peninsula, be prepared to spend some serious time in the car. The road to Nicoya's southern tip is partly paved and partly just gravel, and it winds up and down and around various bays. Some roads leading from Liberia to the coast are intermittently paved. As you work your way toward the coast, pay close attention to the assorted hotel signs at intersections—they may be the only indicators of which roads to take to your lodging.

Stick with the main car-rental offices in San José and their branches in Liberia—they have more cars available and you're more likely to reach an English-speaking agent on the phone; some have local satellite offices. Alamo has pickup and car delivery in Liberia. Budget has branches in San José and also 6 km (4 mi) west of Liberia's airport. Economy, Alamo, and Elegante rent cars in Tamarindo; Economy has a good supply of automatic 4WD vehicles.

■TIP→Four-wheel-drive vehicles are recommended, but not essential, at least not in the dry season, for most roads. If you don't rent a 4WD vehicle, at least rent a car with high clearance—you'll be glad you did.

Major Rental Agencies **Alamo** (✛ 2 km [1 mi] northeast of Liberia airport, Liberia ☏ 2668–1111, 800/462–5266 in U.S. ✉ Hotel Diría, main road, Tamarindo ☏ 2653–0727 ✉ Café de Paris, main road, Nosara ☏ 2682–0052 ✉ C. Principal, Sámara ☏ 2656–0958). **Budget** (✛ 1 km [½ mi] southwest of Liberia airport, Liberia ☏ 2668–1118 ✉ Hotel Zullymar, main road, Tamarindo ☏ 2653–0756 ✉ 100 m east of Hotel Giada, Sámara ☏ 2436–2000). **Economy** (✛ 3½ km [2 mi] southwest of Liberia airport, Liberia ☏ 2666–2816 or 2666–7560 ✉ Main road entering Tamarindo, next to Restaurant Coconut, Tamarindo ☏ 2653–0752 ✉ Flamingo Shopping Center, Playa Flamingo ☏ 2654–4543 ✉ Café de Paris shopping center, Nosara ☏ 2682–0944).

Local Rental Agencies **Payless Car Rental** (✛ 5 km [3 mi] southwest of Liberia airport, Liberia ☏ 2667–0511). **Hola Rentacar** (✛ 2 km [1 mi] southwest of Liberia airport, Liberia ☏ 2667–4040 ✉ Hacienda Pinilla, Tamarindo ☏ 2653–2000).

BY SHUTTLE VAN

ARRIVING &
DEPARTING

You can ride in a comfortable, air-conditioned minibus with Gray Line Tourist Bus, connecting San José, Liberia, Playa Flamingo, Playa Conchal, Playa Potrero, Playa Brasilito, Playa Hermosa, Playas del Coco, Ocotal, Tamarindo, and Playa Langosta. Fares range from $33 to $43, depending on destination. The Gray Line Tourist Bus from San José to Liberia and Tamarindo begins picking up passengers from hotels daily around 8 AM. The return bus leaves the Tamarindo and Flamingo areas around 8:30 AM and 3:30 PM, then passes through Liberia about an hour later. Interbus has door-to-door minivan shuttle service from San José to all the major beach destinations (Papagayo, Panamá, Hermosa, Flamingo, Tamarindo, Cocos, Ocotal, Nosara, and Sámara in Nicoya), for $35 to $43 per person. Reserve at least one day in advance.

Shuttle Van Services **Gray Line Tourist Bus** (☎ 2232–3681 or 2220–2126 ⊕ www.graylinecostarica.com). **Interbus** (☎ 2283–5573 ⊕ www.interbusonline. com).

CONTACTS & RESOURCES

Banks, Internet cafés, post offices, and emergency contacts follow each town listing in the chapter.

BANKS & EXCHANGING SERVICES

ATMs that accept international bank cards are few and far between in Guanacaste. ATH (A Todas Horas) machines are the most reliable, although even they may be out of cash during peak holiday times. You can get a cash advance on a Visa card at a bank, but be prepared for a long wait and be sure you have your passport (not a copy) with you. Your best bets for ready cash are the Burger King ATH near Liberia and the Coopmani ATH in Nicoya. Branches of Banco Nacional and Banco de Costa Rica can be found in Filadelfia, Liberia, Nicoya, and Santa Cruz. Banco Nacional also has a branch in Playas del Coco. Banco de Costa Rica is in Playa Flamingo and at the Liberia airport.

INTERNET

Most mid-range to expensive hotels on the coast offer public Wi-Fi or Internet access to guests, and some restaurants are also wired. Apart from beach communities, public Internet access is not widespread in this part of the country. Expect to pay about $2 per hour of access time at Internet cafés, where connections are pretty slow.

MAIL & SHIPPING

Finding a post office in beach towns is almost impossible, since most beach areas are not incorporated towns. Liberia, La Cruz, Nicoya, Nosara, Playas del Coco, Sámara, and Santa Cruz all have post offices.

Central Pacific

Scarlet Macaw

WORD OF MOUTH

"We love the Osa, but it's a pretty undeveloped area. If you're look-ing for something uncomplicated, Manuel Antonio would fit the bill. It's really easy to get around there, offers the beautiful beach and good wildlife inside the national park, and also has lots of restaurant choices. Very few people go to the Osa for only 3 days. We haven't made it to Guanacaste yet."

–volcanogirl

WELCOME TO CENTRAL PACIFIC

Surfing at Playa Jacó

TOP REASONS TO GO

★ **Nature and wildlife:** Explore seaside flora and fauna at Manuel Antonio National Park, Curú National Wildlife Refuge, and Cabo Blanco Absolute Nature Reserve.

★ **Fishing:** Deep-sea fishing at Quepos, Tambor, Jacó, or Herradura is a chance to hook a sailfish, marlin, wahoo, or yellowfin tuna.

★ **Sunsets:** Whether you view it from the beach in Malpaís or while sipping hilltop cocktails in Manuel Antonio, this region has some of the country's best venues for watching the sunset.

★ **Surfing:** This is Costa Rica's surf central. Jacó, Malpaís, and Playa Hermosa swarm with surfers, from beginners to pros.

★ **Adventure sports:** Snorkel among colorful fish, get muddy on ATV mountain rides, and zip through treetops near Jacó, Manuel Antonio, or Montezuma.

Carara National Park

Golfo De Nicoya

Puntarenas

Leona

21

San Rafael

Curu

1

160

Pachote

Tambor

Carmen

160

Montezuma

Malpais

Kayaking, Quepos

Waterfalls, Montezuma

1 The Southern Nicoya Tip. On the Southern Nicoya Tip, across the gulf from the "mainland," towns are more tranquil and more spread out. Beaches and surfing dominate.

2 Inland. Humid evergreen forests, coffee fields, and cattle pastures blanket the Inland portions of the Central Pacific. Carara National Park is home to a very impressive collection of plants and animals.

3 The Coast. From Tárcoles, the highway along the Coast connects lively tourist hubs Jacó, Quepos, and Manuel Antonio, and on down to the South Pacific. This is the place to surf, do a multitude of active tours, laze on the beach, and explore Manuel Antonio National Park.

GETTING ORIENTED

Most of the Central Pacific is mountainous, and beach towns are backed by forested peaks. Humid evergreen forests, oil-palm plantations, and cattle pastures blanket the land. The coastal highway connects all towns from Tárcoles to the southern Pacific. The hub town of Jacó makes a good base for visiting surrounding beaches and wildlife areas. Farther south are Quepos and its neighbor, Manuel Antonio, followed by smaller towns barely touched by tourism. Across the Gulf of Nicoya, the more tranquil southern tip of the Nicoya Peninsula is also surrounded by impressive mountains, but with dry tropical forests that change radically from the rainy to the dry season.

5

Carara Biological Reserve

Tárcoles

34

2

Jacó

Pavona

Esterillos Este

Parrita

Esterillos Oeste

Playa Bejuco

3

Quepos

Manuel Antonio

Pacific Ocean

34

Manuel Antonio National Park

Rey

| 0 | | | | 15 mi |
| 0 | | | 20 km | |

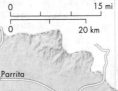

Manuel Antonio National Park

CENTRAL PACIFIC PLANNER

When to Go

Masses arrive during the dry season (late December–May), driving hotel prices up; in Manuel Antonio high-season prices kick in even earlier. Holy Week and the last week of December are the hardest times to find a room. Consider July and August, when the weather tends to sunny days and occasional light rain. Avoid the tip of Nicoya in September and October—heavy rains make road crossing difficult, and many businesses close.

Crowd Control

Most tourist towns in Costa Rica spring into action after Christmas, but Manuel Antonio's high season activates at the start of December, with long park entrance lines, and plenty of bodies on the beaches. To avoid the crunch, go between June and November. To beat the crowds at the park, get there early—around 7 AM.

Getting There

If you're not pressed for time, rent a car or travel by bus, shuttle, or private driver instead of flying from San José to experience beautiful landscapes and typical rural towns. Distances from San José are not overwhelming, and the ferry ride across the Gulf of Nicoya has great views of the mountainous coast and its islands. Buses are timely and economical, but if you prefer an air-conditioned ride, shuttles leave from San José and can drop you off at your hotel's doorstep. Most travelers heading to the southern tip of the Nicoya Peninsula arrive by car via the ferry from Puntarenas to Paquera. You can also fly into Tambor's airstrip and taxi to your beach from here.

What to Do

ACTIVITY	WHERE TO DO IT
Fishing	Quepos, Manuel Antonio, Playa Herradura, Tambor, Jacó
Snorkeling	Isla Tortuga, Manuel Antonio, Montezuma
Surfing	Jacó, Playa Hermosa, Malpaís
Wildlife-viewing	Manuel Antonio National Park, Tárcoles River, Cabo Blanco Absolute Nature Reserve, Curú National Wildlife Refuge, Carara National Park
Yoga	Montezuma, Malpaís, Jacó, Manuel Antonio
Zip-line tours	Malpaís, Montezuma, Jacó, Playa Herradura, Playa Hermosa, Manuel Antonio, Quepos

Choosing a Place to Stay

The Central Pacific has a good mix of high-quality hotels, nature lodges, and *cabinas* (low-cost Tico-run hotels, often laid out like motels), including some of the country's priciest lodgings. As a rule, prices drop 20% to 30% during the rainy season. Reserve as far in advance as possible during the busy dry season. Near Manuel Antonio National Park, Manuel Antonio is the more activity-rich, attractive, and expensive place to stay (though we've culled the best budget options).

Recommended Tour Operators

Costa Rica's Temptations (CRT ☎2777–0607 ⊕www. costarica4u.com) has a variety of Central Pacific tours, plus car rentals, private drivers, shuttle vans, and a 4WD off-the-beaten-path "adventure" transfer between San José and Manuel Antonio.

Cruise West (☎800/397–3348 ⊕www.cruisewest.com) runs four 11- to 15-day cruises that visit coastal reserves in Panama and Costa Rica.

King Tours (☎2637–7343 or 2643–2441 ⊕www. kingtours.com) arranges trips to the top Central Pacific attractions, including Manuel Antonio National Park and Carara National Park.

Ríos Tropicales (☎2233–6455 or 888/722–8273 ⊕www.riostropicales.com), a high-quality adventure tour company, runs a four-day, three-night sea-kayaking trip ($600) based at Curú National Wildlife Refuge and meanders among the islands of the Gulf of Nicoya. White-water rafting trips on rivers near Manuel Antonio cost $70–$98.

WHAT IT COSTS IN DOLLARS				
¢	$	$$	$$$	$$$$
Restaurants				
under $5	$5–$10	$10–$15	$15–$25	over $25
Hotels				
under $50	$50–$75	$75–$150	$150–$250	over $250

Restaurant prices are per person for a main course at dinner. Hotel prices are for two people in a standard double room in high season, excluding service and tax (16.4%).

Spring Break All Year

Nightlifers of all ages, Ticos as well as tourists, flock to Jacó to party till sunrise, making it the country's liveliest beach town. Jacó draws everyone from partying college kids to groups of men seeking to savor the local beer and ladies of the night.

How Much Time?

A week gives you enough time to visit several beaches on the central coast or get a good grasp of the tip of Nicoya.

Great Combinations

South of Quepos along the coastal highway lie tranquil beaches, where time seems to stand still, a real contrast with the busy Manuel Antonio area. Dominical makes a great surf spot after Jacó, whereas Punta Uvita has a vast beach and more wildlife than people. From the southern tip of Nicoya, head up the west coast to hop along the endless stretch of beaches. Or ferry back to the mainland to explore Monteverde's cloud forest.

5

THE SOUTHERN NICOYA TIP

Updated
by David
Dudenhoefer

Reached by a one-hour ferry ride from Puntarenas, the southern tip of the Nicoya Peninsula is one of Costa Rica's less-developed regions, where some of the country's most gorgeous beaches, rain forests, waterfalls, and tidal pools lie at the end of some of its worst roads. Within the region are quiet, well-preserved parks where you can explore pristine forests or travel by boat or sea kayak to idyllic islands for bird-watching or snorkeling. Other outdoor options include horseback riding, gliding through the treetops on a canopy tour, or surfing on some of the country's most consistent waves. In the laid-back beach towns of Montezuma, Santa Teresa, and Malpaís, an international cast of surfers, nature lovers, and expatriate massage therapists live out their dreams in paradise.

PUNTARENAS

110 km (68 mi) west of San José.

A docking point for international cruise ships and the launching pad for ferries heading to the southeast coast of the Nicoya Peninsula, Puntarenas could easily be relegated to what you see from your car as you roll through town. Unless you're waiting to catch the ferry, there's really no reason to stay in Puntarenas. Parts of its urban beach look almost like a dumpster. How this stretch of shoreline got a Blue Flag for cleanliness is a mystery. Nonetheless, it's a city with a past as an affluent port town and principal vacation spot for San José's wealthy, who arrived by train in the last century. Once the port was moved and roads opened to other beaches, Puntarenas's economy crashed. Recent attempts by politicians and hotel owners to create tourism-boosting diversions have been unsuccessful thus far. But if you have some down-time here, head for the Paseo de los Turistas, a beachfront promenade lined with concrete benches. From this narrow spit of sand—*punta de arenas* literally means "point of sand"—which protrudes into the Gulf of Nicoya, you get impressive sunsets and vistas of the Nicoya Peninsula. On days when cruise ships arrive, local artisans sell their wares at a market near the dock.

GETTING HERE & AROUND

The drive from San José to Puntarenas takes about two hours. From downtown San José, take the General Cañas Highway (CA1) west toward the airport, then continue west on CA1 for another 90 minutes to the turnoff for Puntarenas. From here it's another 15 minutes to the ferry dock. Buses run every hour between San José and Puntarenas. If you travel to Puntarenas by bus, take a taxi to the ferry dock.

Ferries shuttle passengers between Puntarenas and Paquera on the Nicoya Peninsula, where they are met by buses bound for Cóbano, Montezuma, and Santa Teresa. The passenger and car ferries run by **Naviera Tambor** (☎2661–2084) depart both Puntarenas and Paquera at 5, 7:30, and 10 AM, and 12:30, 3, 5:30, and 10 PM. The trip takes about 60 minutes.

Asociación de Desarrollo Integral Paquera (☎2641–0118) runs a small passenger-only ferry that departs from behind Puntarenas Mercado daily at 11:30 AM and 4 PM, with return trips at 7:30 AM and 2 PM. The trip takes 90 minutes.

PUNTARENAS ESSENTIALS

Bank/ATM**Banco de Costa Rica** (*BCR* ✉*100 m north of municipal market*). **Banco Nacional** (✉*200 m west of municipal market* ☎*2661–0233*). **Mutual Alajuela ATH** (✉*Across from Ferretería Tung Sing, near municipal market*).

Hospital**Hospital Monseñor Sanabria** (⊕*8 km (5 mi) east of Puntarenas* ☎*2663–0033*).

Pharmacy**Farmacia Andrea** (✉*75 m east of Victoria Park* ☎*2661–2866*).

Internet**Millennium Cyber Café** (✉*Paseo de Los Turistas, east of Hotel Tioga* ☎*2661–4759*).

Post Office**Correos** (✉*Avda. 3, near Parque Victoria*).

Tourist Information**La Camara de Turismo** (✉*Plaza de las Artesanías, in front of Muelle de Cruceros* ☎*2661–2980* ⊙ *Weekdays 8–12:30 and 1:30–5:30; weekends when cruise ships are in port*). **La Oficina de Información Turistica** (✉*Near car ferry terminal* ☎*2661–9011* ⊙ *Daily 8–5*).

WHERE TO STAY & EAT

$–$$ ✕**Restaurante La Yunta.** In a 1928 wooden building that originally served as a vacation home for San José's upper class, this old-fashioned steak house is presided over by mounted ox heads (*yunta* means a yoked pair of oxen). Seating is on a large veranda with a view of the ocean and of passersby strolling down the Paseo de los Turistas. The specialty is *churrasco* (tenderloin), but the diverse menu includes seafood dishes like lobster and sea bass cooked 10 different ways. The liquor list is impressively long. ✉ *West end of Paseo de los Turistas, east of Hotel Tioga* ☎*2661–3216* ═*AE, DC, MC, V*.

$$ ⊡**Hotel Las Brisas.** Close to the ferry docks, this white, three-story motel-style building wraps around its pool, where the views of the sun setting over the Nicoya Peninsula are terrific. Superior rooms have balconies with views of the ocean, and a few of them also have Jacuzzis. Standard rooms on the third floor cost a little bit more, but they are worth it for the ocean view. Pictures of Greece taken by the owner hang in the hallways and a few rooms. The restaurant menu ($$–$$$) reflects the owners' nationalities with Greek-influenced seafood and meat and some Mexican dishes. **Pros:** Ocean views, decent restaurant. **Con:** Expensive considering location. ✉ *West end of Paseo de los Turistas* ☎*2661–4040* ⊟*2661–2120* ⊕*www.lasbrisashotelcr.com* ⇆*19 rooms* ��*In-room: safe (some), Wi-Fi (some). In-hotel: restaurant, room service, bar, pool, gym, no elevator, laundry service, public Wi-Fi* ═*AE, DC, MC, V* ⦿*BP*.

$–$$ ⊡**Hotel Tioga.** Across the street from a tree-filled park and the cleanest part of the city's beach, Hotel Tioga opened in 1959 and is run by the original owner's son. Face-lifts over the years have modernized it a bit, but it's still rather timeworn. Glimpses of the past hang in hallways of the first to third floors with black-and-white photographs of Puntar-

A Darker Side of Tourism

Despite Costa Rica's relative affluence in Central America—in large part due to its thriving tourism industry—the fact remains that 10% of the country's population still lives in poverty. And while burgeoning tourism has benefited portions of the population, it has manifested itself in less fortunate ways in more impoverished sectors of society by giving rise to a sex-for-sale trade that some experts say rivals that in Thailand.

The case is bleak for impoverished Costa Ricans, but is worst for women and young girls. Forty percent of girls do not attend school, and 41% of births in Costa Rica are to unwed mothers. Prostitution is legal for those over 18 in Costa Rica, but pimping is not, and prostitution of minors certainly is not. There are no statistics on the number of minors involved in prostitution, but it's clear from the many Web sites promoting travel to Costa Rica as a sex-tourism paradise

with plenty of young girls available, that the problem is ongoing. In 1996 the National Institute for Children (PANI) targeted Limón, San José, and Puntarenas as the places where poor children are most susceptible to entering into prostitution.

In 2004 the U.S. Human Trafficking Report listed Costa Rica as one of the world's worst offenders in the trafficking of women and children into prostitution. To their credit, the administrations of Presidents Abel Pacheco and Oscar Arias have taken steps to combat the problem of the underage sex trade, a refreshing change from their predecessor, Miguel Angel Rodríguez, who famously denied in an interview on the ABC News program *20/20* in 2001 that such a problem existed. Steps taken thus far have included crackdowns on brothels, closer surveillance, harsher penalties for offenders, and a Web site that lists photos of missing children.

enas in the early 1900s. Your best bets are the 11 "executive" guest rooms upstairs, with balconies overlooking the gulf, pleasantly decorated with colorful, tropical prints and heavy varnished dark-wood furniture. Rooms around the courtyard, which holds a small pool, can be noisy. The second-floor restaurant is open to cool breezes off the gulf. **Pros:** Good value, across street from beach. **Cons:** Timeworn, a bit cramped, busy on weekends. ⊠*Paseo de los Turistas, 8 blocks west of dock* ☎2661–0271 🖷2661–0127 ⊕*www.hoteltioga.com* ⤶*52 rooms* ☼*In-room: safe (some). In-hotel: restaurant, bar, pool, no elevator, laundry service, public Wi-Fi* ☰*AE, DC, MC, V* ⦿*BP.*

EN ROUTE

If you take the ferry from Puntarenas to the southern tip of the Nicoya Peninsula, you'll arrive at a ferry dock 5 km (3 mi) north of the small community of **Paquera.** The only reason to stop here is to pick up supplies or fill up your tank on the way to the beach.

CURÚ NATIONAL WILDLIFE REFUGE

☾ *7 km (4½ mi) south of Paquera, 1½ to 2 hrs southwest of Puntarenas by ferry.*

Established by former farmer and logger-turned-conservationist Federico Schutt in 1933, Refugio Nacional de Vida Silvestre Curú was named after the indigenous word for the pochote trees that flourish here. Trails lead through the forest and mangrove swamps where you see hordes of phantom crabs on the beach, howler and white-faced capuchin monkeys in the trees, and plenty of hummingbirds, kingfishers, woodpeckers, trogons, and manakins (including the coveted long-tailed manakin). The refuge is working to reintroduce spider monkeys and scarlet macaws into the wild. Some very basic accommodations, originally designed for students and researchers, are available by the beach ($8 per person); call ahead to arrange for lodging, guides, horseback riding, and early-morning bird-watching walks. ⊠ *7 km (4½ mi) south of Paquera on road to Cóbano, left side of road* ☎ *2641–0100* ⊕ *www.curuwildliferefuge.com* ⊠ *$8* ⊗ *Daily 7–3.*

GETTING HERE & AROUND
From the town of Paquera it's a short drive to Curú National Wildlife Refuge. You can also take a bus bound for Cóbano, asking the driver to drop you off at the refugio.

OUTDOOR ACTIVITIES
Luis Schutt Tours (⊠ *Main road, across from Esso station, Paquera* ☎ *2641–0004* ⊕ *www.curutourism.com*) gives horseback tours of the refuge ($13) and also has a ride to sparkling-white Quesera Beach ($40). The company also offers inexpensive kayaking trips ($20) and tours to Tortuga Island ($17).

EN ROUTE Paquera is the closest city to Tambor, but if you're headed to Montezuma or Malpaís, you'll pass through **Cóbano,** 12 km (7½ mi) southwest of Tambor. The town has a supermarket, gas station, and a Banco Nacional with the area's only ATM.

PLAYA TAMBOR AREA

27 km (17 mi) south of Paquera.

Known for massive, all-inclusive hotels and housing developments, Playa Tambor runs along the large half-moon Bahía Ballena, whose waters are more placid than those of other beaches on Nicoya's southern tip. Playa Tambor is one of the country's least attractive beaches, although there are two small but lovely ones to the south. The tiny fishing village hasn't developed as much as Montezuma or Malpaís, which makes it a better destination for those who want to get away from the crowds. It can serve as a convenient base for fishing excursions, horseback-riding trips, and day trips to Curú National Wildlife Refuge and Isla Tortuga.

GETTING HERE & AROUND
You can fly directly to Tambor from San José on SANSA and Nature Air. Taxis meet every flight and can take you to a nearby hotel ($10 to $15), to Montezuma ($30), or to Malpaís ($40).

The Central Pacific

Isla Chira

Refugio Silvestre de Peñas Blancas

San Ramón

Esparza

San Mateo

Orotina

CA1

PAN-AMERICAN HWY

Puntarenas

Caldera

27

Playa Naranjo

R. Cuarros

R. Tárcoles

Carara Biological Reserve

Paquera

Curú National Wildlife Refuge

San Rafael

Tárcoles

Playa la Pita

Agujas

Isla Tortuga

Punta Leona

Nicoya Peninsula

Herradura

Playa Tambor Area

Playa Herradura

Cobano

Jacó
see map

34

Santa Teresa

Carmen

Montezuma

Playa Santa Teresa

Cabuya

Playa Hermosa

Malpaís

Cabo Blanco Absolute Nature Preserve

Cabo Blanco

Isla Cabo Blanco

PACIFIC OCEAN

KEY

 Ferry lines

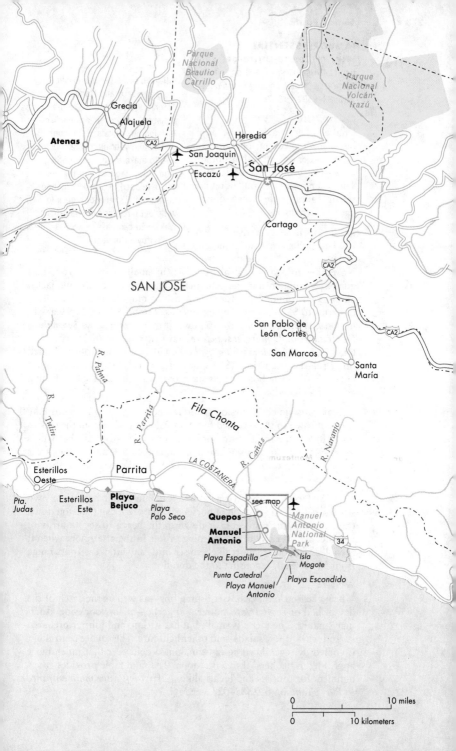

TAMBOR ESSENTIALS

Internet Compu-Office del Pacífico (⊠ *In small strip mall on left after Costa Coral Hotel, coming from Paquera* ☎ *2683–0582* ⊗ *9–7*).

OUTDOOR ACTIVITIES

Unlike other beach towns, Tambor doesn't have tour operators on every corner or rental shops of any kind—not even for a basic bike. The receptionist at your hotel can set up tours of the area's diverse natural attractions.

FISHING In the open sea off the Gulf of Nicoya, sailfish, marlin, tuna, and wahoo are in abundance from November to March. Local fishermen in small boats are your best guides to finding fish in the gulf, including snapper, sea bass and jacks, almost year-round. Prices for inshore fishing range from $250 for half-day trips to $500 for full-day excursions. Tambor's best deep-sea fishing boat is the 29-foot *Phoenix,* owned by **End of the Line Sportfishing** (⊠ *Road from Paquera, just before Playa Tambor's entrance* ☎ *2683–0453* ⊘ *endofthelinefishing@yahoo.com*). Captain Robert Ranck offers full-day excursions ($950) or half-day trips that last around five hours ($500). The boat carries six people. Lunch, drinks, and fishing gear are included.

HIKING An easy and quick excursion from Tambor is the 1-km (½-mi) hike south of town to the secluded beach of Palo de Jesús. From the town's dock, follow the road south until it becomes a shady trail that winds its way over rocks and sand around Punta Piedra Amarilla. The trees along the way resound with squawks of parakeets and the throaty utterings of male howler monkeys.

HORSEBACK RIDING Both the Hotel Tambor Tropical and the Tango Mar have their own stables and offer a selection of horseback tours that can take you down trails through the rainforest or down to the beach to see an array of wildlife. Set off early in the morning or late in the afternoon, when it is cooler and you are more likely to see birds and animals. Tours range from $30 to $60, according to the duration.

WHERE TO EAT

$ ✕**Bahía Ballena Yacht Club.** Get fishing tips—as well as the catch of the day grilled or served with butter and garlic—at this dockside fisherman's haunt. The menu is small, but has shrimp and lobster prepared several ways, a few salads, and other light fare. The square central bar is cooled by several ceiling fans, making a cold beer that much more appealing in the heat of the afternoon. The pool table provides entertainment for tourists and locals alike. ⊠ *First left after main entrance to Playa Tambor* ☎ *2683–0213* ▭ *MC, V*.

$ ✕**Trattoria Mediterránea.** This colorful restaurant in an old wooden
★ house is often packed with local epicureans who come to savor the
homemade pastas, thin-crust pizzas, and fresh seafood. The young Italian owners, Maurizio and Sandra, welcome guests with complimentary
bruschetta made with fresh-baked bread, and everything is made to
order, so the food can take awhile to arrive. They offer a selection of
about a dozen pizzas and such authentic dishes such as linguine con
gamberi (with shrimp), scaloppini con esparagi (chicken medallions
with asparagus) and pescado de la trattoria (baked fish with olive oil,
lemon, garlic, and spices). ⊠ *On left after main entrance to Playa Tambor* ☎ *2683–0400* ⚑ *Reservations essential* ☰ *MC, V C Closed Mon.
and Sept. and Oct. No lunch*

WHERE TO STAY

$$$ 🏨 **Tambor Tropical.** Though a stone's throw from the beach, this small
hotel isn't a great place for beach lovers, because it isn't a great beach,
but is a convenient base for anyone interested in sportfishing, horse-
back riding, or who simply seeks an intimate setting in which to loll
by the pool. The attractive, spacious suites have floors, ceilings, walls,
and even toilet seats made of varnished tropical hardwoods. The large
windows running across the front give them a great view of the sea and
surrounding gardens—second-floor rooms have the best. Platform beds
provide sunrise views. The sea breeze and ceiling fans cool the rooms
better than air-conditioning, and the lack of televisions inspires rest and
relaxation. Meals are served by a lovely, blue-tile pool, or in the thatch
dining room during the rainy months; on Monday they have a popu-
lar barbecue. **Pros:** Lovely rooms, tranquil. **Con:** Not on nice beach.
⊠ *Main street of Tambor, turn left at beach* ☎ *2683–0011* 📠 *2683–
0013* ⊕ *www.tambortropical.com* 🛏 *12 suites* ⚘ *In-room: no a/c, no
phone, kitchen, no TV, Wi-Fi. In-hotel: restaurant, room service, bar,
pool, beachfront, no elevator, laundry service, airport shuttle, no kids
under 16* ☰ *AE, MC, V* ⚑|*CP.*

$$$ 🏨 **Tango Mar Resort.** This idyllic resort south of Tambor was featured on
☾ the TV series *Temptation Island.* The 150-acre grounds include a small
Fodor'sChoice nine-hole golf course, exuberant gardens, tropical forests, and stunning
★ Playa Quitzales, a beach lined with coconut palms and lush foliage.
There is a large rock reef just offshore, and an impressive waterfall on
the beach a short hike away. Colorful villas with two to five bedrooms
and ample porches overlook the beach. Smaller suites are housed in
raised octagonal wooden bungalows with whirlpool tubs and ocean
views. The standard rooms are in a three-story cement building that is
a stone's throw from the surf. Two restaurants serve Costa Rican and
continental cuisine. On-site activities include snorkeling, horseback riding, hiking through a private nature reserve, and golf (greens fee $20).
They also offer a dozen tours to nearby attractions, as well as sportfishing excursions. **Pros:** Gorgeous setting, friendly, quiet, lots of activity
options. **Con:** Not the place for partiers. ⚓ *3 km (2 mi) south of Tambor* ⚐ *Apdo. 1–1260, Escazú* ☎ *2683–0001* 📠 *2683–0003* ⊕ *www.
tangomar.com* 🛏 *18 rooms, 17 suites, 4 villas* ⚘ *In-room: safe, kitchen
(some), refrigerator. In-hotel: 2 restaurants, bars, golf course, tennis
courts, pools, spa, beachfront, water sports, bicycles, no elevator, laun-*

5

dry service, concierge, airport shuttle, public Internet, public Wi-Fi ▭*AE, DC, MC, V* ¶❘*BP.*

$ 🏨**Costa Coral.** On the road from Paquera, a few meters from Tambor's entrance, stands this festive blue-and-orange hotel with spacious and tastefully decorated, Mexican-theme rooms. Those with terraces face the pool and hot-tub area and all have well-kept kitchenettes. The top floor holds a restaurant and bar, with karaoke on Thursday night. The beach lies about 300 meters away. This place makes for a good overnight stop on your way to or from Paquera. ✉*Road to Cóbano, 200 m from Tambor's cemetery, left-hand side* ☎*2683–0105 or 2683–0280* 🖨*2683–0016* ⬥*10 rooms* 🔑*In-room: kitchen. In-hotel: restaurant, bar, pool, laundry service* ▭*MC, V* ¶❘*BP.*

ISLA TORTUGA

🕐 *90 mins by boat from Puntarenas.*

Soft white sand and casually leaning palms fringe this island of tropical dry forest off the southern coast of the Nicoya Peninsula. Sounds heavenly? It would be if there weren't quite so many people. Tours from Jacó, Herradura, San José, Puntarenas, and Montezuma take boatfuls of visitors to drink from coconuts and snorkel around a large rock. You'll see a good number of colorful fish, though in the company of many tourists. But it does make for an easy day trip out to sea. On the boat ride from Playa Tambor or Montezuma you might spot passing dolphins. A 40-minute hiking trail wanders past monkey ladders, strangler figs, bromeliads, orchids, and the fruit-bearing *guanabana* (soursop) and *marañón* (cashew) trees up to a lookout point with amazing vistas. Though state-owned, the island is leased and inhabited by a Costa Rican family. Day trips here cost $17 to $99, according to the duration and departure point.

GETTING HERE & AROUND

Every tour operator in Playa Tambor and Montezuma (⇨*below*) offers trips to Isla Tortuga, one of the area's biggest attractions, or you can kayak from the nearby Curú National Wildlife Refuge. Admission to the island is $7 (included in tour prices).

OUTDOOR ACTIVITIES

KAYAKING   **Luis Schutt Tours** (✉*Main road, across from Esso station, Paquera* ☎*2641–0004* ⊕*www.curutourism.com*) arranges year-round kayak excursions to Isla Tortuga for $17. Snorkeling equipment is available for an additional fee. **Calypso Cruises Island Tours** (☎*2256–2727* ⊕*www.calypsocruises.com*) takes you to Isla Tortuga from San José, Jacó, Manuel Antonio, or anywhere in between with bus and boat transportation included ($99, kids under 12 $50).

MONTEZUMA

7 km (4½ mi) southeast of Cóbano, 45 km (28 mi) south of Paquera, 18 km (11 mi) south of Tambor.

Beautifully positioned on a sandy bay, Montezuma is hemmed in by a precipitous wooded shoreline that has prevented the overdevelopment that so many other beach towns are affected by. Its small, funky town center is a pastel cluster of New Age health-food cafés, trendy beach-wear shops, jaunty tour kiosks, noisy open-air bars, and older *sodas* (casual eateries). Most hotels are clustered in or around the town's center, but the best ones are on the coast to the north and south, where the loudest revelers are the howler monkeys in the nearby forest. The beaches north of town, especially Playa Grande, are lovely.

Montezuma has been on the international vagabond circuit for years, attracting backpackers and alternative-lifestyle types. At night, the center of town often fills up with tattooed travelers and artisans who drink in the street and entertain each other and passersby. When college students are on break, the place can be a zoo.

North and south of the town center, however, are always quiet, and the attractions here include swaths of tropical dry forest, waterfalls, and beautiful virgin beaches that stretch across one national park and two nature preserves. One especially good walk (about 2½ hours) or horseback ride leads to a small waterfall called El Chorro that pours into the sea, where there is a small tidal pool at lower tides.

GETTING HERE & AROUND
Most people get here via the ferry from Puntarenas to Paquera, which is an hour's drive from Montezuma. The quickest way to get here, however, is to fly to nearby Tambor *(⇨ By Air in Travel Smart Costa Rica)*. One of the taxis waiting at the airstrip will take you to Montezuma for $35, about an hour-and-a-half drive. There are also one-hour water taxis ($35) that travel every morning between Herradura, near Jacó, and Montezuma, departing from Montezuma at 6:30 AM and 9:30 AM, and Herradura at 7:45 AM and 10:45 AM.

MONTEZUMA ESSENTIALS
ATM **Banco Nacional** (⊠ *Main road, Cóbano* ☏ *2642–0210*).

Internet **Surf the Banana Internet Café** (⊠ *Main road, next to El Sano Banano* ☏ *2642–0944*).

Post Office **Librería Topsy** (⊠ *Next door to school*).

OUTDOOR ACTIVITIES
In Montezuma it seems that every other storefront is occupied by a tour operator. The town's oldest and most experienced tour company, **Cocozuma Traveller** (⊠ *Main road, next to El Sano Banano, Montezuma* ☏ *2642–0911* ⊕ *www.cocozumacr.com*), offers horseback riding to a beachfront waterfall ($40), a full-day snorkeling trip to Isla Tortuga with lunch ($50), various sportfishing options ($170–$750), scuba diving ($120–$200), and a canopy tour ($40).

HIKING ★ Hiking is one of the best ways to explore Montezuma's natural treasures, including beaches, jungles, and waterfalls. There are plenty of options around town or in nearby parks and reserves. Just over a bridge, 10 minutes south of town, a slippery path patrolled by howler monkeys leads upstream to two waterfalls and a fun swimming hole. If you value your life, don't jump or dive from the waterfalls. Guides from any tour operator in town can escort you, but save your money. This one you can do on your own. To reach the beachfront waterfall called **El Chorro,** head left from the main beach access and hike about two hours to the north of town along the sand and through the woods behind the rocky points. The trip takes you across seven adjacent beaches, on one of which there is a small store where you can buy soft drinks. Bring water and good sunblock. El Chorro can also be reached on a horseback tour.

WHERE TO EAT

$$$ ✕**Playa de los Artistas.** This open-air restaurant with driftwood tables
Fodor'sChoice   scattered along the beach specializes in modern Mediterranean-style
★   seafood, meat dishes, and pizza. Flickering lanterns combine with crashing surf to create a romantic and relaxed dinner experience. Portions are plentiful and dramatically presented on huge platters. The eclectic menu changes daily, and on weekends they fire up a barbecue. An outdoor, coffee-wood oven gives a tropical aroma to pizza, fish, and pork. Meals are accompanied with freshly baked, savory focaccia. ⊠*275 m south of town, near Los Mangos Hotel, Cóbano* 🕾*Apdo. 72, Cóbano* ☎*2642–0920* ▭*No credit cards* ⊗*Closed Sun., mid-May–mid-June, and mid-Sept.–mid-Nov.*

$$–$$$ ✕**Ylang-Ylang Restaurant.** One of Montezuma's best restaurants, Ylang-
★   Ylang is nestled between the beach and the jungle. The lunch menu—a selection of sushi, salads, and sandwiches—makes it well worth the 10-minute walk down the beach. The inventive dinner menu ranges from a Thai-style teriyaki tuna steak and stir-fries to penne in a seafood sauce. There are also various vegan and raw live dishes. Whatever you choose, you'll want to save room for one of the scrumptious desserts, such as the tiramisu espresso crepe. At night, they provide free transportation from the Sano Banano, in town. ⊠*On beach, ½ km (¼ mi) north of town* ☎*2642–0636* ▭*AE, DC, MC, V.*

$$ ✕**El Sano Banano Restaurant.** Freshly caught seafood, organic chicken, sushi, Thai dishes, and a half-dozen pasta dishes are included on the menu at Montezuma's first natural-food restaurant. Named after the dried bananas sold by the owners, the eatery serves mostly vegetarian fare, including some excellent salads. On the terrace, which is a popular people-watching spot, you can enjoy a delicious Mocha Chiller, made with frozen yogurt, or a wide variety of coffee drinks. A battalion of ceiling fans keeps the air moving in the spacious, adobe-style dining room. A free movie is shown nightly at 7:30 PM in the dining room, which is a popular diversion, but don't expect a romantic dinner during this time. Rooms to rent on the second floor are a comfortable option if the other hotels are full. ⊠*Main road* ☎*2642–0944* ▭*AE, MC, V.*

$–$$ ✕**Cocolores.** Follow the line of multicolor lanterns to this open-air eatery. The simple wooden tables are on a patio bordered with gardens or, during the drier months, on the beach. The Italian and Argentine owners serve an eclectic menu ranging from shrimp curry to seafood pasta to tenderloin with porcini mushrooms. They also have a good selection of pizzas. ✉ *Behind Hotel Pargo Feliz* ☎ *2642–0348* ▤ *AE, DC, MC, V* ☺ *Closed Mon. and Oct. No lunch June–Dec.*

WHERE TO STAY

$$–$$$ 🏨 **Ylang-Ylang Beach Resort.** Secluded and quiet, this tropical resort with
Fodor's Choice a holistic slant is a 10-minute beach walk from town. Nestled between
★ the sea and a lush forest, the geodesic-dome bungalows are snug but
charming, with outdoor showers and terraces. Some have sea views and
cozy loft sleeping areas. Facing the beach, a three-story building has
two-story suites with balconies and simple but colorful standard rooms
below. Rustic "jungalows"—large tents with beds and decks—offer a
back-to-nature experience, but they share bathrooms. The grounds are
covered with trees that hold iguanas, howler monkeys, tricolor squir-
rels, and an array of birds. Adding to the romance is a jungle-fringed
pool with a waterfall. Yoga classes and spa services are offered, and a
restaurant with tables under the stars serves some of the tastiest fusion
dishes in Montezuma. **Pros:** Gorgeous, natural setting, great restaurant, friendly. **Con:** Jungalows offer limited privacy ✉ *700 m north of
school in Montezuma* ⌖ *El Sano Banano, Montezuma,* ☎ *2642–0636*
🖷 *2642–0068* ⊕ *www.elbanano.com* 🛏 *3 rooms, 3 suites, 8 bungalows, 6 tents* ⚒ *In-room: no a/c, no phone, safe, refrigerator (some),
no TV. In-hotel: restaurant, bar, pool, beachfront, water sports, no
elevator, laundry service, public Internet, public Wi-Fi* ▤ *AE, MC, V*
⦿ *MAP.*

$$ 🏨 **Hotel El Jardín.** Spread across a hill several blocks from the beach, this
hotel has rooms with ocean, pool, and garden views. True to its name,
the rooms are scattered around a lush garden populated with bright red
ginger flowers and faux stone indigenous sculptures. Teak paneling and
furniture, stained-glass pictorial panels, and terraces with hammocks
give this hotel style as well as comfort. If you don't mind the climb,
ask for an upper room and you'll get a better view. There's no formal
breakfast, but fresh fruit and coffee are laid out in the reception area
each morning. **Pros:** Central location, good value. **Con:** Noise from
bars in town. ✉ *West end of main road* ☎ *2642–0548* 🖷 *2642–0074*
⊕ *www.hoteleljardin.com* 🛏 *14 rooms, 1 house* ⚒ *In-room: no phone,
refrigerator, no TV. In-hotel: pools, no elevator* ▤ *AE, DC, MC, V*
⦿ *EP.*

$$ 🏨 **Nature Lodge Finca los Caballos.** A dirt road leads to this cozy eques-
trian paradise high on a hill, just a short ride from Montezuma center.
Horses graze on the 14-acre estate when they aren't taking guests to
nearby waterfalls, mountains, or beaches. The open-air restaurant and
pool terrace have bird's-eye views of the ocean and the surrounding valley. The small, simple rooms have pastel walls decorated with stencils
of lizards and frogs; all have hammocks in front. Only four have forest
views, so ask for one of these when you reserve. Massages and other
spa services are available to guests. ⊕ *3 km (2 mi) north of Montezuma
on main road* ☎ *2642–0124* ⊕ *www.naturelodge.net* 🛏 *12 rooms*
⚒ *In-room: no a/c, no phone, safe, refrigerator, no TV. In-hotel: restaurant, bar, pool, no elevator, laundry service, airport shuttle, no-smoking
rooms* ▤ *AE, MC, V* ☺ *Closed Oct.* ⦿ *BP*

5

¢-$$ 🛏 **Hotel Amor de Mar.** About ½ *km* (¼ mi) south of town, this ruggedly handsome hotel sits across from the entrance to Montezuma's famous waterfall. A grassy lawn stretches to the rocky seashore, where you can cool off in a natural tidal pool at low tide, or lounge about in one of the palm-shaded hammocks. The place has a peaceful and intimate atmosphere in which to savor the homemade breakfasts served each morning. Wood-panel rooms are rustic but comfortable; second-floor rooms have more windows. Two rooms share a bathroom and are considerably cheaper. The two-story oceanfront houses next door have four bedrooms, making them great for larger groups. ✉ *300 m south of town, just past bridge* 📠 *2642–0262* ⊕ *www.amordemar.com* 🛏 *11 rooms, 9 with bath; 2 houses* ♿ *In-room: no a/c (some), no phone, no TV. In-hotel: restaurant, no elevator* ☰ *MC, V* ❗❶*EP.*

¢-$$ 🛏 **Los Mangos Hotel.** Within sight and sound of the sea, these affordable
★   octagonal wood bungalows are spread across a shady mango grove. Hammocks and rocking chairs furnish the wraparound decks on each. Less attractive, though cheaper, are the rooms in a two-story, orange-and-blue building by the road. Here you'll find verandas and rocking chairs facing the sea. Four of the second-floor rooms share baths, for half the price. The secluded, scenic pool with a waterfall overlooks the ocean. Yoga classes are given in an open-air pavilion. ✉ *Near entrance to waterfall trail, ½ km (¼ mi) south of town* 📠 *2642–0076* 📠 *2642–0259* ⊕ *www.hotellosmangos.com* 🛏 *10 rooms, 6 with bath; 9 bungalows* ♿ *In-room: no a/c, no phone, refrigerator (some), no TV. In-hotel: pool, no elevator* ☰ *AE, MC, DC, V* ❗❶*EP.*

NIGHTLIFE

Though options are extremely limited, Montezuma's nightlife scene is growing. Locals and foreigners mix at pool tables or late-night clubs, a refreshing change from larger beach towns where the clientele tends to be more segregated. Street-side artisans selling their creations often animate the area with drumming and dancing that draws passersby to stop and shake their hips, too.

Chico's Bar (✉ *Next to Hotel Moctezuma*) blasts music from its dark, uninviting entrance, but farther back is a brighter, spacious deck with pool tables and dancing. Directly behind is an open-air beach bar with a more laid-back atmosphere. The bar at **Restaurante Moctezuma** (✉ *Under Hotel Moctezuma* 📠 *2643–0657*) serves the cheapest beers in town. At night, tables in the sand are lit by candles and moonlight.

SHOPPING

Beachwear, banana paper, wooden crafts, and indigenous pottery are some of what you find in colorful shops in the town's center. During the dry season, traveling artisans from around the world unfold their street-side tables just before the sun begins to set; candles light up the handmade leather-and-seed jewelry, dream catchers, and knit tops. For some intellectual stimulation at the beach, head to **Librería Topsy** (✉ *Next door to school* 📠 *2642–0576*), where you can buy, exchange, or rent a book—one whole room is devoted to a lending library. Some foreign newspapers are available.

CABO BLANCO ABSOLUTE NATURE PRESERVE

10 km (6 mi) southwest of Montezuma, about 11 km (7 mi) south of Malpaís.

Conquistadores named this area Cabo Blanco on account of its white earth and cliffs, but it was a more benevolent pair of foreigners—Nicolas Wessberg and his wife Karen, arriving here from Sweden in 1950—who made it a preserve (Reserva Natural Absoluta Cabo Blanco, in Spanish). Appalled by the first clear-cut in the Cabo Blanco area in 1960, the pioneering couple launched an international appeal to save the forest. In time their efforts led not only to the creation of the 12-square-km (4½-square-mi) reserve but also to the founding of Costa Rica's national park service, the National Conservation Areas System (SINAC). Wessberg was murdered on the Osa Peninsula in 1975 while researching the area's potential as a national park. A reserve just outside Montezuma was named in his honor. A reserve has also been created to honor his wife, who dedicated her life to conservation after her husband's death.

Informative natural-history captions dot the trails in the moist evergreen forest of Cabo Blanco. Look for the sapodilla trees, which produce a white latex used to make gum; you can often see V-shape scars where the trees have been cut to allow the latex to run into containers placed at the base. Wessberg catalogued a full array of animals here: porcupine, hog-nosed skunk, spotted skunk, gray fox, anteater, cougar, and jaguar. Resident birds include brown pelicans, white-throated magpies, toucans, cattle egrets, green herons, parrots, and blue-crowned motmots. A fairly strenuous 4-km (2½-mi) hike, which takes about two hours in each direction, follows a trail from the reserve entrance to **Playa Cabo Blanco.** The beach is magnificent, with hundreds of pelicans flying in formation and paddling in the calm waters offshore—you can wade right in and join them. Off the tip of the cape is the 7,511-square-foot **Isla Cabo Blanco,** with pelicans, frigate birds, brown boobies, and an abandoned lighthouse. As a strict reserve, Cabo Blanco has restrooms and a visitor center but no other tourist facilities. Rangers and volunteers act as guides. ⊠ *10 km (6 mi) southwest of Montezuma via Cabuya* ☎ *2642-0093* 🖾 *$8* ⊙ *Wed.–Sun. 8–4.*

GETTING HERE & AROUND

Roads to the reserve are usually passable only in the dry season, unless you have a 4WD. From Montezuma or Malpaís, take the road to Cabuya. Taxis can take you to or from Montezuma, but buses toward the park also leave from Montezuma daily at 8 and 9:50 AM and 2 PM, returning at 9 AM, and 1 and 4 PM.

MALPAÍS & SANTA TERESA

12 km (7½ mi) southwest of Cóbano, 52 km (33 mi) south of Paquera.

This remote fishing village was once frequented only by die-hard surfers in search of some of the country's largest waves and by naturalists en route to the nearby Cabo Blanco Absolute Nature Preserve. The town and its miles of beach are accessible only down a steep and bumpy dirt road. But now hotels, restaurants, and shopping centers are springing up at an alarming rate, especially toward the Santa Teresa side. Still, the abundant forest, lovely beaches, and consistent surf make this a great place to spend some time.

Coming from Montezuma, the road hits an intersection, known locally as El Cruce, marked by hotel signs and a strip mall on the right. To the left is the rutted route to tranquil Malpaís, and to the right is the road to Santa Teresa, with plenty of hotels, restaurants, and shops. Playa Carmen, straight ahead, is the area's best place for surfing, though swimmers will want to be careful of rip currents there. Malpaís and Santa Teresa are so close that locals disagree on where one begins and the other ends. You could travel up the road parallel to the ocean that connects them and not realize you've moved from one town to the other.

GETTING HERE & AROUND
From Paquera it's a 90-minute drive to Malpaís via Cóbano. After Cóbano, the road quickly deteriorates. It can become quite muddy in the rainy season, so you'll want a 4WD vehicle. There are no direct buses between Paquera and Malpaís; to get here you have to change buses in Cóbano. Taxis waiting at Tambor's airstrip will take up to four people to Malpaís for $40. The trip between Jacó and Malpaís takes about two hours, thanks to the daily boat service from Montezuma. **Tropical Tours** (⊠ *North of El Cruce, Santa Teresa* ☎ *2640–1900*) can set you up with a shuttle to San José ($35), or a taxi and boat from Malpaís and to Jacó ($55).

MALPAÍS & SANTA TERESA ESSENTIALS
ATM **Banco Nacional** (⊠ *Centro Comercial Playa Carmen* ☎ *2640-0598*).

Internet **Tropical Tours** (⊠ *50 m. north of El Cruce, Santa Teresa* ☎ *2640-1900*) has two Internet cafés in Santa Teresa.

Pharmacy **Farmacia Amiga** (⊠ *Centro Comercial Playa Carmen* ☎ *2640-0463*).

OUTDOOR ACTIVITIES
CANOPY TOUR **Canopy del Pacífico** (⊠ *In front of fisherman's village, Malpaís* ☎ *2640-0360 or 8817–1679*) is the only canopy tour in the area ($35 for two-hour, nine-platform tour). You can walk, glide, or rappel through 64 acres of forest. **Tropical Tours** (⊠ *North of El Cruce, Santa Teresa* ☎ *2640–1900*) can set you up with a canopy tour, horseback-riding jaunt, or day trip to Isla Tortuga.

SURFING From November to May, the Malpaís area has some of Costa Rica's most consistent surf, as well as clear skies and winds that create idyllic conditions. **Playa Carmen** is the area's most consistent surf spot for all levels, and has dozens of beach breaks scattered along its shores. The sea grows rough and dirty during the May to December rainy season, with frequent swells that make it impossible to get out. **Playa**

Santa Teresa is a better option when the waves at Playa Carmen are too gnarly. In Malpaís, at **Mar Azul,** more advanced surfers can try the break over a rock platform. **Corduroy Horizon** (⊠*20 m east of Playa Carmen, Malpaís* ☎*2640–0173*), Malpaís's original surf shop, rents surfboards ($10 per day); arranges lessons ($30 per hour); and sells wax, boards, and beachwear.

WHERE TO EAT

$$$ ✕**Nectar.** Resort Florblanca's alfresco restaurant by the pool has some
★   tables that provide calming sea views through the tropical foliage. Fresh seafood is the specialty here, with inventive daily specials that focus on the day's catch. Asian and Mediterranean influences shine through in dishes ranging from spicy prawn fettuccine, to succulent pork ribs, to seared tuna with sweet Thai rice and braised bok choy. There's always a pizza of the day and a small sushi menu. ⊠*Resort Florblanca* ✛*2 km (1 mi) north of soccer field, Santa Teresa* ☎*2640–0232* ☖*Reservations essential* ▤*AE, DC, MC, V.*

$$$ ✕**Soma.** This small, tranquil restaurant within the Milarepa hotel serves
★   up delicious and creative Asian-inspired plates based on fresh local ingredients. The menu changes each night, but usually has fresh tuna, mahimahi, or other seafood, plus a chicken or beef dish. Any of the dishes can be prepared without meat, so vegetarians can choose from a wide selection. Tables are arranged under an open-air poolside deck a short walk from the beach. ⊠*Milarepa hotel* ✛*2 km (1 mi) north of soccer field, Santa Teresa* ☎*2640–0663* ☖*Reservations essential* ▤*MC, V* ⊗*Closed Oct.*

$ ✕**Piedra Mar.** With all the new restaurants popping up along the beach road, the favorite standby is still this old shack down on the beach. Tables and plastic chairs are set up under a corrugated tin roof, and the only decor is the rocky seascape, 10 feet away. Your shrimp or lobster (just $15) comes flavored with garlic and—on windy days—the sea spray crashing against the rocks. Sunset is popular with locals, so come early. Or come for breakfast at 7 and watch the early-morning sun lighting up the ocean. ⊠*275 m south of Blue Jay Lodge, Malpaís* ☎*2640–0069* ▤*No credit cards* ⊗*Closed Sun.*

$ ✕**Pizzeria Playa Carmen.** This restaurant's location, under the trees on the area's most popular beach, makes it the perfect choice for lunch. It's extremely casual, so you don't even have to put on a shirt. Oven-baked pizza is the house specialty, and these thin-crust pies are big enough for two people, especially if you start with one of the oversize salads. The kitchen also serves shrimp scampi, various pastas, and other dishes. ⊠*Playa Carmen, east of El Cruce, Malpaís* ☎*2640–0110* ▤*No credit cards* ⊗*Closed Tues. and Sept.–Nov. No dinner.*

WHERE TO STAY

$$$$ ▦**Florblanca.** Named for the white flowers of the frangipani trees grow-
Fodor'sChoice ing between the restaurant and the beach, this collection of luxurious
★   villas is scattered through the forest mere steps from the surf. It's a tasteful, friendly resort dedicated to relaxation and rejuvenation. The wonderfully decorated and spacious villas have an Asian feel, especially in the outdoor Balinese-inspired bathrooms with rain showers

and sunken tubs. Airy living rooms open onto porches with large hammocks. Most villas have one air-conditioned bedroom with a king-size bed; two-bedroom villas have a second room with twin beds. Only three villas have sea views through the trees, so request one of these when you book. Free yoga classes are given in a studio that faces the ocean, and the massage therapist at the beachfront spa will happily work out your kinks. The only TV is in a comfortable lounge. Two pools flow into each other near the beach and Nectar ($$$), the hotel's restaurant (⇨*above*). **Pros:** Gorgeous villas and grounds, friendly, great yoga classes. **Cons:** Very expensive, on rocky stretch of beach, insects sometimes a problem.   ✛*2 km (1 mi) north of soccer field, Santa Teresa* ⌂*Apdo. 131–5361, Cóbano* ☎*2640–0232* ☎*2640–0226* ⊕*www.florblanca.com* ⊲*10 villas* ⌂*In-room: safe, refrigerator, no TV, Wi-Fi. In-hotel: restaurant, room service, bar, pools, gym, spa, beachfront, water sports, bicycles, no elevator, laundry service, public Internet, public Wi-Fi, no kids under 14* ▤*AE, DC, MC, V* ⊧⊙*EP.*

$$$ 🏯 **Milarepa.** Named after a Tibetan Buddhist saint who gained enlight-
★ enment in just one lifetime, Milarepa is a perfect place for peaceful renewal, whether romantic or spiritual. The four bamboo bungalows are spaced apart to ensure privacy and are furnished in ascetic but exquisite taste, with carved Indonesian wooden beds draped with mosquito netting, and bamboo armoires. Bathrooms are open to the sky, with alcoves for Buddhist deities. Each bungalow has a veranda looking out onto the beach, shaded by a grove of palms and lined with volcanic rocks. Beachfront bungalows cost a bit more than those with ocean views set farther back. A large pool lies next to Soma (⇨*above*), the hotel's excellent restaurant ($$$). **Pros:** Secluded, small, beachfront, great restaurant. **Cons:** Loosely managed, insects can be a problem, on rocky section of beach.   ✛*2 km (1 mi) north of school, beside Resort Florblanca, Santa Teresa* ☎*2640–0023* ☎*2640–0168* ⊕*www. milarepahotel.com* ⊲*4 cottages* ⌂*In-room: no a/c, no phone, safe, no TV. In-hotel: restaurant, bar, pool, beachfront, water sports, no elevator, laundry service, public Wi-Fi, no-smoking rooms* ▤*MC, V* ⊧⊙*BP.*

$$ 🏯 **Luz de Vida.** This laid-back, beachfront lodge owned by a group of
☾ Israeli surfers is a good value. Simple bungalows, spread around forested grounds, have sloping wooden ceilings, lofts, a couch, or extra beds downstairs (kids under 10 are free). Smaller standard rooms in two-story cement buildings close to the road are not nearly as good a deal. The pool has a waterfall and is surrounded by trees, gardens, and thatch parasols. The open-air restaurant, nearby, has an ocean view and serves everything from falafel to filet mignon. Good waves break right in front of the hotel, so when the staff offers to arrange surfboard rentals and lessons, be sure to take them up on it. **Pros:** Beachfront, nice grounds, friendly. **Cons:** Service inconsistent, standard rooms too close to road. ✉*From El Cruce, 800 m south toward Malpaís* ☎*2640–0568 or 2640–0320* ☎*2640–0319* ⊕*www.luzdevida-resort.com* ⊲*6 bungalows, 8 rooms* ⌂*In-room: safe, refrigerator, no TV. In-hotel: restaurant, bar, pool, beachfront, water sports, no elevator, laundry service, public Wi-Fi* ▤ *MC, V* ⊧⊙*EP.*

$ ⬚ **Blue Jay Eco-Lodge.** Perched along a forested mountainside, these wooden bungalows feel like tree houses; you'll hear howler monkeys and an array of birdsong from your bed. Steep trails lead to the rustic aeries built on stilts, with screens for walls on three sides, comfortable beds, and balconies hung with hammocks. Once you drag your luggage up the hill you will be rewarded with great views from the upper rooms. Blankets buffer you against the sometimes cool, breezy nights. Blue Jay's three lower cabins are larger, but lack the arboreal charm of the rest. Breakfast is in the open-air restaurant, next to an attractive, blue-tile pool. Head to the nearby beach, or climb the mountain trail behind the cabins, to look for birds. **Pros:** Natural setting, good value. **Con:** Not well maintained. ⊠*From El Cruce, 800 m south toward Malpaís* ☎*2640–0089 or 2640–0340* 🖷*2640–0141* ⊕*www.bluejay lodgecostarica.com* ⇴*10 cabins* ⚘*In-room: no a/c, no phone, safe, no TV. In-hotel: pool, no elevator, laundry service, no-smoking rooms* ▤*AE, D, MC, V* ⟠*BP.*

¢ ⬚ **Ritmo Tropical.** Tranquil, comfortable, and nicely priced, this small
⟳ hotel a short walk from the beach is the best deal in Malpaís. Red-tile-
★ roof bungalows here are simple yet tasteful, with high wooden ceilings, large bathrooms, lots of windows, and front terraces. Some cabins, arranged in a semicircle around the large pool and gardens, have views of the sea and the jungle. A couple of rooms in back are even cheaper than the others. The reasonably priced Italian restaurant ($) in front of the property serves two dozen types of pizza, fresh fish with a selection of sauces, and tasty pasta dishes such as farfalle with fish and shrimp curry sauce. ⊠*100 m south of El Cruce on road toward Malpaís* ☎*2640–0174* ✎*ritmotropical_mp@yahoo.com* ⇴*7 bungalows, 2 rooms* ⚘*In-room: no a/c, no phone, safe, no TV. In-hotel: restaurant, bar, pool, no elevator, laundry service* ▤*MC, V* ⟠*EP.*

INLAND

Beaches may be this region's biggest draw, but the countryside holds some splendid scenery, from the steep coffee farms around Atenas to the tropical forests of the lowlands. In the wilderness of Carara National Park and surroundings, you might encounter white-faced capuchin monkeys in the trees or crocodiles lounging on a riverbank. The region is extremely biologically diverse, making it an excellent destination for bird-watchers and other wildlife enthusiasts.

ATENAS

42 km (26 mi) west of San José.

Known for its excellent climate, Atenas is a pleasant, friendly town surrounded by a hilly countryside of coffee and cane fields, cattle ranches, and patches of forest. The small city is off the tourist circuit, which means that here, unlike other highly popular destinations, you'll walk alongside more locals than foreigners and get a more authentic idea of the country. Gazing at the tree-covered peaks and exploring the coffee farms are the main activities in this traditional town. Atenas's center has a concrete church, some well-kept wooden and adobe houses, and a park dominated by royal palms.

GETTING HERE

Atenas lies about one hour west on the route between San José and beaches such as Herradura, Jacó, and Manuel Antonio. Take the Pan-American Highway past the airport and turn right at the overpass with the signs for beach resorts and Zoo

> **BASE CAMP**
>
> Visitors to Costa Rica prefer using Atenas as their first- and last-night base camp instead of San José, since Atenas is smaller, friendlier, and more tranquil. The international airport is geographically closer to Atenas, but the hilly roads make the ride slightly longer than on San José's express highway.

Ave. Turn left from the exit and stay on the main road. Buses to Atenas leave frequently from the Coca-Cola terminal in San José and arrive near the center of town.

ATENAS ESSENTIALS

Bank/ATM Banco de Costa Rica (⊠ *200 m west of Catholic church* ☎ *2446–6034*). **Banco Nacional** (⊠ *Northern corner of central park* ☎ *2446–5157*).

Hospital Clínica Pública (⊠ *150 m south of the fire station* ☎ *2446–5522*).

Pharmacy Farmacia Don Juan (⊠ *West corner of Catholic church* ☎ *2446–5055*).

Internet C@fé K-puchinos (⊠ *Northwest corner of Parque Central* ☎ *2289–0082*).

Post Office Correos (⊠ *50 m southeast of northeast corner of market*).

WHERE TO STAY & EAT

$ ✕ **Mirador del Cafetal.** An obligatory stop even if it's just for a cup of coffee, this open-air restaurant next to the road between Atenas and Jacó is a great spot to enjoy the view of steep hillsides covered with coffee trees. The best view is from the long countertops with stools that line the edge of the building, but the wooden tables and chairs might be more comfortable. The food is a mix of Costa Rican and Mexican cuisine, including burritos, chicken with rice, and *sopa azteca* (a tomato-base soup). The restaurant's own brand of coffee is sold by the pound. ⊠ *Road to Jacó ✛ 6 km (3 mi) west of Atenas* ☎ *2446–7361* ⊟ *AE, MC, V.*

$$ ▨ **El Cafetal Inn.** This charming B&B feels and looks more like a home than a hotel, since they go out of their way to help with your travel plans. On a hilltop coffee farm, the two-story concrete lodge has comfortable accommodations with fabulous vistas. Most rooms have balconies, and those on the corners of the second floor have curved windows offering panoramic views. They also have a bungalow near the pool, and two small houses for rent nearby. Breakfast, which includes home-grown and -roasted coffee, is served on the back garden patio. The fact that it lies just 25 minutes from the airport makes this a tran-

quil place to begin or end a Costa Rica trip. ✛ *8 km (5 mi) north of Atenas; heading west from San José on highway to Puntarenas, turn left (south) just before bridge 5 km (3 mi) west of Grecia, Santa Eulalia de Atenas* ☎ *2446–5785* 🖷 *2446–44850* ⊕ *www.cafetal.com* ⍰ *14 rooms, 1 bungalow, 2 houses* ⚒ *In-room: no a/c, no phone, no TV. In-hotel: restaurant, bar, pool, no elevator, laundry service, no-smoking rooms* ⊟ *AE, MC, V* ◎ *BP.*

CARARA NATIONAL PARK

43 km (25 mi) southwest of Atenas, 85 km (51 mi) southwest of San José.

On the east side of the road between Puntarenas and Playa Jacó, Parque Nacional Carara protects one of the last remnants of an ecological transition zone between Costa Rica's drier northwest and the more humid southwest. It consequently holds a tremendous collection of plants and animals. Much of the 47-square-km (18-square-mi) park is covered with primary forest on steep slopes, where the massive trees are laden with vines and epiphytes. The sparse undergrowth makes wildlife easier to see here than in many other parks, but nothing is guaranteed. If you're lucky, you may glimpse armadillos, basilisk lizards, coatis, and any of several monkey species, as well as birds such as blue-crowned motmots, chestnut-mandibled toucans, and trogons.

The first trail on the left shortly after the bridge that spans the Río Tárcoles (a good place to spot crocodiles) leads to a horseshoe-shape *laguna meandrica* (oxbow lake). The small lagoon covered with water hyacinths is home to turtles, crocodiles, and waterfowl such as the northern jacana, roseate spoonbill, and boat-billed heron. It is a two- to four-hour hike from the trailhead to the lagoon and back, depending on how much bird-watching you do. ■**TIP**➡**Cars parked at the trailhead have been broken into. If you don't see a ranger on duty at the** *sendero laguna meandrica* **trailhead, avoid leaving anything of value in your vehicle. You may be able to leave your belongings at the main ranger station (several miles south of the trailhead), where you can also buy drinks and souvenirs and use the restroom. Otherwise, visit the park as a day trip from a nearby hotel.**

Two trails lead into the forest from the parking lot. The shortest one can be done in 15 minutes, while the longer one that connects with the Quebrada Bonita loop takes one to three hours to hike. The latter can be quite muddy during the rainy months, when you may want rubber boots. Carara's proximity to San José and Jacó means that tour buses arrive regularly in high season, scaring some animals deeper into the forest. Come very early or late in the day to avoid crowds. Bird-watchers can call the day before to arrange admission before the park opens. Camping is not permitted.

Local travel agencies and tour operators arrange transport to and guides through the park *(*⇨ *Park Tours, below).* The park itself has guides, but you must arrange in advance. ⊠*East of Costanera just to the south of bridge over Tárcoles River* ☎*8383–9953* 🎫*$10* 🕐*Daily 7–4.*

GETTING HERE

From Atenas, pass through Orotina and follow the signs to Jacó and Quepos. The reserve is on the left after you cross Río Tárcoles. From San José, hop on a bus to Jacó, Quepos, or Manuel Antonio and ask to be dropped off near the entrance of the park, about a two-hour drive.

PARK TOURS

Johnny Marin at **Jaguar Riders** (☎*2634–0180, 8393–6626*), in Jacó, has been guiding people through the forests of Carara for years. **Costa Rica Expeditions** (☎*2222–0333* ⊕*www.costaricaexpeditions.com*), the country's original ecotour operator, offers day trips to Carara from San José, and includes the park in several of its multiday trips. **Horizontes** (☎*2222–2022* ⊕*www.horizontes.com*) , the country's premier nature-tour operator, can arrange visits to Carara as a day trip from San José or as part of a longer tour.

THE COAST

Along a short stretch of Costa Rica's Pacific coast from Tárcoles to Manuel Antonio are patches of undeveloped jungle, the popular Manuel Antonio National Park, and some of the country's most accessible beaches. The proximity of these strands to San José leads Costa Ricans and foreigners alike to pop down for quick beach vacations. Surfers have good reason to head for the consistent waves of Playas Jacó and Hermosa, and anglers and golfers should consider Playa Herradura for its golf courses and ocean access. You might find Herradura and Jacó to be overrated and overdeveloped. Manuel Antonio could be accused of the latter, but nobody can deny its spectacular natural beauty.

TÁRCOLES

90 km (54 mi) southwest of San José.

Crocodile boat tours on the Río Tárcoles are this small town's claim to fame. In fact, you don't actually have to drive to Tárcoles to do the tour, since operators can pick you up in Herradura or Jacó. The muddy river has gained a reputation as the country's dirtiest, thanks to San José's inadequate sewage system, but it amazingly remains an impressive refuge for wildlife. A huge diversity of birds results from a combination of transitional forest and the river, which houses crocodiles, herons, storks, spoonbills, and other waterbirds. This is also one of the only areas in the country where you can see scarlet macaws, which you may spot on a boat tour or while hiking in a private reserve nearby.

GETTING HERE

By car, head through Atenas to Orotina and follow the signs to Herradura, Jacó, and Quepos. After crossing the bridge over the Tárcoles River, look for the entrance to the town of Tárcoles on the right. On the

CLOSE UP

Diving the Deep at Coco Island

Rated one of the top diving destinations in the world, Isla del Coco is uninhabited and remote, and its waters are teeming with marine life. It's no place for beginners, but serious divers enjoy 100-foot visibility and the underwater equivalent of a big-game park: scalloped hammerheads, white-tipped reef sharks, Galápagos sharks, bottlenose dolphins, billfish, and manta rays mix with huge schools of brilliantly colored fish.

Encompassing about 22½ square km, or 14 square mi, Isla del Coco is the largest uninhabited island on earth. Its isolation has led to the evolution of dozens of endemic plant and animal species. The rocky topography is draped in rain forest and cloud forest and includes more than 200 waterfalls. Because of Isla del Coco's distance from shore (484 km [300 mi]) and its craggy topography, few visitors to Costa Rica—and even fewer Costa Ricans—have set foot on the island.

Costa Rica annexed Coco in 1869, and it became a national park in 1978. Today only extremely high-priced specialty-cruise ships, park rangers and volunteers, and scientists visit the place Jacques Cousteau called "the most beautiful island in the world." The dry season (November–May) brings calmer seas and is the best time to see silky sharks. During the rainy season large schools of hammerheads can be seen, but the ocean is rougher.

Two companies offer regular 10-day dive cruises to Isla del Coco that include three days of travel time on the open ocean and cost roughly $3,400–$4,200, according to the boat and dates. The *Okeanos Aggressor* (☎ 2289–2261, 800/348–2628 in U.S. ⊕ www.aggressor.com) offers 8- and 10-day dive safaris to Coco Island in December and January. *Undersea Hunter* (☎ 2228–6613, 800/203–2120 in U.S. ⊕ www.underseahunter. com) runs 10-day dive trips to the island year-round.

left is the dirt road that leads to the Hotel Villa Lapas and the waterfall reserve. Any bus traveling to Jacó can drop you off at the entrance to Tárcoles. Let the driver know in advance.

OUTDOOR ACTIVITIES

BOAT TOURS On the two-hour riverboat tours through the mangrove forest and Tarcoles River you might see massive crocodiles, Jesus lizards, iguanas, and some of roughly 50 colorful bird species, including the roseate spoonbill and boat-billed heron. Tours reach the river's mouth, providing nice sea views, especially at sunset. ■TIP→ **Around noon is the best time to spot crocs sunbathing; bird enthusiasts prefer afternoon rides to catch scarlet macaws. During the rainy season (May–November), the river may grow too rough for boats in the afternoon.**

Two brothers run **Crocodile Man Tour** (✉ *Main road into Tárcoles* ☎ *2637–0426, 2637–0771, or 8822–9042* ⊕ *www.crocodilemantour. com*). The small scars on their hands are the result of the tour's most original (and optional) attraction: feeding fish to the crocs. The boats are small enough to slide up alongside the mangroves for a closer look. Transportation is provided from nearby beaches, but not from San José.

CANOPY TOUR **Hotel Villa Lapas** (✉*Off Costanera, after bridge over Tárcoles River* ☎*2637–0232* ⊕*www.villalapas.com*) manages a suspension-bridge nature walk and a zip-line tour. **Sky Way** consists of five suspension bridges spread out over a 2½-km (1½-mi) old-growth-forest nature trail. You can do the trail with a guide ($30). A shuttle picks you up at the Hotel Villa Lapas. **Villa Lapas Canopy** has zip lines through primary forest. The tour is $40 per person.

WHERE TO STAY & EAT

$$ ✕**Steve n' Lisa's.** A convenient location, an ocean view, and good food make this roadside restaurant overlooking Playa La Pita, just south of the entrance to Tárcoles, a popular pit stop for those traveling between San José and the Central Pacific beaches. Sit on the covered porch or at one of the concrete tables on the adjacent patio, and enjoy the view of the Gulf of Nicoya through the palm fronds. The menu includes breakfast options and a wide selection of lunch and dinner entrées that ranges from tacos and hot dogs to a pricy surf and turf. ✉*On the Costanera* ✛*1 km (½ mi) south of Tárcoles turnoff, on right* ☎*2637–0594* ▤*AE, DC, MC, V.*

$$ ▦**Hotel Villa Lapas.** Within a tranquil rain-forest preserve, far from
☾ other hotels (and the beach), Villa Lapas is a great escape for nature lovers, but also has on-site entertainment to keep you busy, such as a large-screen television, a pool table, and foosball. You can cross a suspension bridge to reach a small replica of a Costa Rican colonial village with a restaurant, cantina, church, and gift shops. Follow the river flowing through the protected forest for a pleasant hike. There is a canopy tour on the property *(see Canopy Tour, above)*. The austere rooms are nothing special, but have terra-cotta floors, hardwood ceilings, and large baths. An all-inclusive meal plan is available, but you're better off eating your lunch and dinner elsewhere. **Pros:** Surrounded by forest, lots of activities, birds, kid-friendly. **Cons:** Rooms sometimes musty, air conditioners old, mediocre buffets. ✉*Off Costanera* ✛*3 km (2 mi) after bridge over Tárcoles River, turn left on dirt road, up 600 m* ☎*2637–0232* 🖷*2637–0227* ⊕*www.villalapas.com* ⇆*55 rooms* ☾*In-room: safe, no TV (some). In-hotel: 2 restaurants, bars, pool, no elevator, laundry service, public Wi-Fi* ▤*AE, DC, MC, V* ▮◯❙*BP.*

EN ROUTE Even if you choose to bypass Tárcoles and its crocodile tours, you can still get a peek of the huge reptiles as they lounge on the riverbanks: on the Costanera, pull over just after crossing the Río Tárcoles bridge and walk back onto it. Bring binoculars if you have them. ▮TIP➔**Be sure to lock your car—vehicles have been broken into here.**

BETWEEN TÁRCOLES AND PLAYA HERRADURA

Past Tárcoles, the first sizable beach town of the Central Pacific coast is Playa Herradura. In between, you'll pass two exclusive hotels, hidden from view at the end of long winding roads.

About a kilometer (½ mi) south after the entrance to Tárcoles, the Costanera passes a small beach called **Playa La Pita,** which provides your first glimpse of the Pacific if you're coming down from San José or the Central Valley. The beach is rocky, and its proximity to the Tárcoles River makes the water murky and unfit for swimming, but it's a nice spot to stop and admire the ocean. From here the road heads inland again, and you'll come across the entrance to Punta Leona, a vast hotel and residential complex. The road then winds its way up a steep hill, atop which is the entrance to the luxury hotel Villa Caletas. On the other side of that ridge is the bay and beach of Herradura.

WHERE TO STAY & EAT

$$$–$$$$ ✕ **El Mirador Restaurant.** White tablecloths, glass walls, and yellow-and-blue-checked curtains contribute to the sophisticated but not overly stuffy atmosphere of this restaurant at Villa Caletas. Expensive prix-fixe meals include your choice of appetizer, main dish, and dessert. Appetizers range from the traditional escargots to a shrimp and lobster bisque. The entrées include beef tenderloin with a red wine and espresso sauce, jumbo shrimp sautéed with coconut and vanilla, and a combination of a veal chop and roast duck. A covered terrace below the restaurant is popular for sunset viewing over a cocktail, and the tapas menu is much less expensive than the main restaurant. ⊠ *Villa Caletas hotel, off coastal highway ✛3 km (1½ mi) south of Punta Leona* ☎*2637–0505* ▤*AE, DC, MC, V.*

$$$–$$$$ 🏨 **Villa Caletas.** Perched 1,200 feet above the sea on a promontory south ★ of Punta Leona, this collection of elegant rooms sequestered in the jungle has jaw-dropping views of the surrounding foliage and sea below. Spectacular sunset views should be enjoyed from the bar, even if you stay elsewhere. Freestanding suites and villas are gorgeous, but rooms in the main building are far inferior; if a villa isn't within your budget, do try to get a deluxe room. Victorian, French colonial, and Hellenistic motifs are combined throughout, with Ionic columns, varied artwork, cookie-cutter trims, and cane chairs. The regular pool is rather small and chilly, but the new Zephyr Palace complex has amazing views and an impressive infinity pool. The closest beach, Playa Caletas, is attractive, but small and rocky. Though a great place for romance or relaxation, this hotel has little to offer kids or active travelers. **Pros:** Gorgeous views, forest, and sunsets, good food. **Cons:** Abundant insects, little to do, lots of stairs, inconsistent service. ⊠ *Off coastal highway ✛3 km (1½ mi) south of Punta Leona, on right* 🏠*Apdo. 12358–1000, San José* ☎*2637–0505 or 2630–3000* 🖷*2637–0404* ⊕*www.villacaletas. com* 🛏*10 rooms, 14 villas, 7 junior suites, 13 suites* ⚐*In-room: safe. In-hotel: 2 restaurants, bars, pool, gym, spa, no elevator, laundry service, concierge, no-smoking rooms* ▤*AE, DC, MC, V* ⊠⦿*EP.*

$$–$$$ 🏨 **Hotel Punta Leona.** This 740-acre private reserve and resort community ☾ is an odd and overwhelming mix of nature, residential development, and vacation spot. Punta Leona's attractions include three beaches, a tropical forest, a butterfly farm, and guided bird-watching hikes. Punta Leona (Lion's Point) made headlines as the setting of the Ridley Scott film *1492: Conquest of Paradise* and more recently for blocking public access to its beaches, which is illegal in Costa Rica. The little

"city" contains everything from restaurants and pools to a grocery store and church, plus plenty of amusements, including a zip-line tour, tennis court, and mini–golf course. Frequent shuttles travel between the rooms, restaurants, and beaches. Hotel guests, home owners, and time-share members contribute to crowded beaches on weekends, especially in the dry season, when this place can be a bit of a zoo. ✥ *15 km (9 mi) south of Tárcoles on west side of road to Jacó* ☎ *2231–3131 or 2630–1000* 🖶 *2282–0791* ⊕ *www.hotelpunta-leona.com* 🛏 *108 rooms, 13 suites, 27 apartments* ⚙ *In-room: safe, refrigerator. In-hotel: 3 restaurants, room service, bars, tennis court, pools, beachfront, water sports, no elevator, laundry service, public Wi-Fi* ☰ *AE, DC, MC, V* ⫶◉⫶ *BP.*

> ### THE HAUNTED CART
>
> If you're out late one night and hear a slow scraping of wheels against the road, it just might be the *carreta sin bueyes* (cart without oxen) of ghostly legend. Its owner reputedly stole building materials from a church, and was condemned to perpetually traversing the country's highways and byways in the cart he used to transport his stolen goods. (The oxen were blameless for their role and escaped the curse.)

PLAYA HERRADURA

20 km (12 mi) south of Tárcoles.

If sportfishing and golf are your priorities, this is a good option. If you're looking for nature, seclusion, a beautiful beach, or a bargain, keep driving. Rocky Playa Herradura, a poor representative of Costa Rica's breathtaking beaches, gets its name from the Spanish word for "horseshoe," referring to the shape of the deep bay in which it lies. Its tranquil waters make it considerably safer for swimming than most central and southern Pacific beaches, and that, coupled with its proximity to San José, has turned it into a popular weekend getaway for Josefinos, who compete for shade beneath the sparse palms and Indian almond trees that line the beach. On the north end of the beach is the Los Sueños development, which includes a large marina, shopping center, hundreds of condos, a golf course, and a massive Marriott hotel.

GETTING HERE

By car, head 20 minutes straight down the Central Pacific highway. The town's entrance is on the right-hand side, where a long paved road leads to the beach. Follow the signs to the Marriott.

OUTDOOR ACTIVITIES

Few activities are available directly in Playa Herradura, but that doesn't mean you have to settle for less. Most of the area's diverse outfitters can pick you up at your hotel for activities near Jacó and Playa Hermosa. Your hotel's reception desk is often a good source of information.

King Tours (✉ *Main road into Playa Herradura, in front of Los Sueños* ☎ *2643-2441 or 800/213-7091* ⊕ *www.kingtours.com*) arranges trips to renowned attractions like Manuel Antonio National Park and Carara National Park, as well as crocodile boat tours, deep-sea and coastal fishing trips, horseback rides, and canopy tours. The company can also book tours to destinations elsewhere in the country, such as Poás and Arenal volcanoes, Monteverde Cloud Forest, and Isla Tortuga. **Costa Rica Dreams** (⊠ *Los Sueños Marina* ☎*2637–8942, 732/901–8625 Ext. 46 in the U.S.*) is one of the area's oldest and most reputable sportfishing outfitters.

WHERE TO STAY

$$$$ ▦ **Marriott Los Sueños Ocean and Golf Resort.** This mammoth multimillion-dollar resort in a palatial colonial-style building has a gorgeous view of Herradura Bay. It combines modern amenities with traditional Central American decorative motifs, such as barrel-tile roofing and hand-painted tiles. Rooms here, though attractive and some of the country's most expensive, are nothing special compared with those at smaller hotels in the same price range. They have marble baths, wooden furniture, and tiny balconies. Be sure to get a room with an ocean view, or you'll be contemplating condos. An enormous pool with islands and swim-up bars, a Ted Robinson golf course, a modern marina, and various diversions are designed to keep you on-site and entertained. ⊠*800 m west of road to Jacó from San José, follow signs at entrance of road to Playa Herradura* ☎*2630–9000, 800/228–9290 in U.S.* 🖷*2630– 9090* ⊕*www.marriott.com* ⇖*191 rooms, 10 suites* ♿*In-room: safe, refrigerator, Ethernet. In-hotel: 5 restaurants, room service, bars, golf course, tennis courts, pool, gym, spa, beachfront, children's programs (ages 5–15), laundry service, concierge, public Internet, public Wi-Fi, airport shuttle, no-smoking rooms* ☰*AE, DC, MC, V* ⏀*EP.*

JACÓ

2 km (1 mi) south of Playa Herradura, 114 km (70 mi) southwest of San José.

Its proximity to San José has made Jacó the most developed beach town in Costa Rica. Nature lovers and solitude-seekers should skip this place, which is known mostly for its nightlife, surf scene, and prostitution. More than 50 hotels and cabinas back its long, gray-sand beach, and the mix of restaurants, shops, and bars lining Avenida Pastor Diaz (the town's main drag), give it a cluttered appearance devoid of any greenery. Any real Costa Rican–ness evaporated years ago; U.S. chain hotels and restaurants have invaded, and you can pretty much find anything you need, from law offices and dental clinics to DVD-rental shops and appliance stores. It does have a bit of everything in terms of tours and outdoor activities, and makes a convenient hub for exploring neighboring beaches and attractions.

GETTING HERE & AROUND

The drive from San José takes about three hours; take the Pan-American Highway past the airport to the exit for Atenas, then follow the signs to Orotina, Jacó, and Quepos. The exit, on the right after Herradura, is well marked. Buses leave from San José's Coca-Cola station five times daily. **Pacific Travel** (☎2643–2520) brings passengers across the Gulf of Nicoya to Montezuma.

JACÓ ESSENTIALS

Bank/ATM BAC San José (✉ *Il Galeone mall*). **Banco Nacional** (✉ *Avda. Pastor Diaz* ☎2643–3621).

Hospital Ambulance (☎2643–1690) **Clínica Pública** (✉ *In front of Plaza de Deportes* ☎2643–1767)

Pharmacy Farmacia Jacó (✉ *Diagonally across from Mas X Menos supermarket* ☎2643–3205).

Internet Centro de Computación (✉ *Avda. Pastor Diaz, center of town* ☎2643–2713).

Post Office Correos (✉ *Avda. Pastor Diaz*).

Taxis Taxi services (☎2643–2020, 2643–2121, or 2643–3030).

Tourist Information Pacific Travel & Tours (✉ *Centro Comercial La Casona [La Casona shopping center]* ☎2643–2520 or 2643–2449 ⊕ *www.pacifictravelcr. com*).

EXPLORING

Long, palm-lined **Playa Jacó**, west of town, is a pleasant enough spot in the morning, but can burn the soles of your feet on a sunny afternoon. Though the gray sand and beachside construction make it less attractive than most other Costa Rican beaches, it's a good place to soak up the sun or enjoy a sunset. Playa Jacó is popular with surfers for the consistency of its waves, but when the surf is up swimmers should beware of dangerous rip currents. During the rainy months the ocean here is not very clean.

OUTDOOR ACTIVITIES

You don't have to physically step into any tour office, since everyone from a reception desk attendant to a boutique salesperson can book you a local adventure. Almost every tour can pick you up at your hotel's doorstep. ■TIP➔**Keep in mind that part of your price tag includes the salesperson's commission, so if you hear higher or lower prices from two different people, it's likely a reflection of a shift in the commission. You can try negotiating a better deal directly from the outfitter.**

Jaguar Riders (☎2643–0180 *or* 8393–6626) specializes in ATV tours of the mountains east of town and trips to Carara National Park, but can arrange all kinds of personalized excursions. **Fantasy Tours** (✉ *Best Western Jacó Beach Resort* ☎2643–2231 ⊕ *www.graylinecostarica. com*) deals primarily with large groups, arranging day trips from Jacó to Arenal and Poás volcanoes, Manuel Antonio National Park, Sarchí, Tortuga Island, and raft trips on the Savegre River. **Pacific Travel and Tours** (✉ *Centro comercial La Casona [La Casona shopping center]* ☎2643–2520 *or* 2643–2449) sells an array of tours in and around Jacó.

ATV TOURS Since ATV tours are fairly new here, the vehicles are in good condition. But they're not exactly the most eco-friendly way to see the area's rain

Jacó

Restaurants ▼
El Hicaco **7**
Las Sandalias ... **8**
Rioasis **3**
Tsunami Sushi ..**2**
Wishbone **1**

Hotels ▼
Aparthotel
Flamboyant **7**
Aparthotel
Girasol **10**
Club del Mar .. **12**
Docelunas **11**
Hotel Canciones
del Mar **1**
Hotel Tangerí ...**4**
Las Orquideas ...**9**
Mar de Luz **3**
Tropical Garden
Hotel **8**

Nightlife ▼
Jungle **2**
Nacho Daddy's . **13**
Restaurante
El Colonial **6**
Tabacón **5**

Shopping ▼
Cocobolo **6**
El Cofre **4**
Guacamole **5**

PACIFIC
OCEAN

KEY

1 *Restaurants & Shopping*

① *Hotels & Nightlife*

forest and wildlife. Some operators will ask you to put up a credit card voucher of roughly $500. **ATV Tours** (☎2778–8172 or 8812–1789) runs two- or three-hour tours ($65–$85) through rain forests, rivers, and waterfalls that lie about 15 minutes south of Jacó. **Ricaventura** (✉*In the center of Playa Jacó, behind Subway* ☎2818–6973 or 2643–3395) is considered by locals to be the best ATV tour with the longest routes. Ricaventura offers three options: a two-hour sunset tour ($65), a four-hour Carara Park and nearby river tour ($90), and a six-hour Pacayal Waterfall trip ($150).

CANOPY
TOURS

In the hills across the highway from Jacó Beach, **Chiclets Canopy Tour** (☎2643–3271) takes you sliding through one of the area's more pristine forests along cables strung between 14 treetop platforms between 60 and 130 feet above the ground. The price is $60 per person. **Waterfalls Canopy Tour** (☎2643–3322 ⊕*www.waterfallscanopy.com*), in a private reserve 4 km (2½ mi) from Jacó, is a zip-line tour with a view of rain forest and waterfalls. You can combine the tour, which costs $60 per person, with nature walks and a visit to a butterfly and frog garden, or do it at night.

A modified ski lift offers easy access to the rain-forest canopy, with six-seat gondolas that float through the treetops at the **Rain Forest Aerial Tram** (☎2257–5961 ⊕*www.rainforestram.com*). This tram lies within a 222-acre private reserve 3 km (2 mi) west of Jacó. The company offers guided tours that explain a bit of the local ecology ($46), as well as early morning bird-watching tours ($79). There is also a small serpentarium and medicinal plant garden.

HANG GLIDING

A truly unique experience, hang gliding gives you the chance to see not just Jacó, but a huge expanse of Pacific coastline. With **Hang Glide Costa Rica** (☎8353–5514) you can take a tandem hang-gliding flight or fly in a three-seat, open cockpit ultralight plane. You are picked up in Jacó and taken to the airstrip 6 km (4 mi) south of Playa Hermosa. Prices start at around $70 per person.

HORSEBACK
RIDING

Discovery Horseback Tours (☎8830–7550) is owned by a British couple who run two-and-a-half-hour trail rides on healthy horses. You'll spend some time in the rain forest and also stop at a small waterfall where you can take a dip ($60). **Horse Tours at Hacienda Agujas** (☎243–2218 or 8838–7940) are serene enough for all ages and skill levels. Late-afternoon tours are on a cattle ranch about 25 minutes north of Jacó, where the trail winds through a rain forest and down a beach. The ride ends with a colorful sunset bang ($50).

KAYAKING AND
CANOEING

Kayak Jacó Costa Rica Outriggers (☎2643–1233 ⊕*www.kayakjaco.com*) takes you to calmer waters than those at Jacó Beach. Instead, you'll visit Playa Agujas for sea-kayaking tours and Hawaiian-style outrigger canoe trips ($60). The half-day tours include snorkeling (conditions permitting) at secluded beaches.

SURFING

Jacó has several beach breaks, all of which are best around high tide. Surfboard-toting tourists abound in Jacó, but you don't need to be an expert to enjoy the waves—the swell is often small enough for beginners, especially around low tide. Abundant surf shops rent boards and give lessons. Prices range from $25 to $45 an hour and usually include a board and transportation. If you plan to spend more than a week surfing, it might be cheaper to buy a used board and sell it before you leave (⇨*Shopping, below*). If you don't have much experience, don't go out when the waves are really big—Jacó sometimes gets very powerful swells, which result in dangerous rip currents. During the rainy season, waves are more consistent than in the dry months, when Jacó sometimes lacks surf.

> **CAUTION**
>
> Riptides (or rip currents), common in Jacó and Manuel Antonio's Playa Espadilla, are dangerous and have led to many deaths in the area. If you get caught in one, don't panic and don't try to swim against it. Let the current take you out just past the breakers, where its power dissipates, then swim parallel to shore. Once the current is behind you, swim back to the beach. The best policy is not to go in deeper than your waist when the waves loom large.

5

SWIMMING The big waves and dangerous rip currents that make surfing so popular here can make swimming dangerous. Lifeguards are on duty only at specific spots, and only sporadically. If the ocean is rough, stay on the beach—dozens of swimmers have drowned here over the years.

When the ocean is calm, especially around low tide, you can swim just about anywhere along Jacó Beach. The sea is always calmer near the beach's northern and southern ends, but the ocean bottom is littered with rocks there, as it is in front of the small rivers that flow into the sea near the middle of this beach.

WHERE TO EAT

$$$ ✕**El Hicaco.** One of Jacó's best restaurants—and by far its most expen-★ sive—El Hicaco is known for serving copious servings of seafood. The house specialty is lobster, but the kitchen also offers fresh mahimahi, sea bass, tuna, shrimp, and other fruits of the sea with seasonings ranging from a teriyaki glaze to a papaya-ginger sauce. Seating is in a simple but elegant open-air dining room or in plastic chairs on a gravel patio near the beach. Wednesday night brings a sumptuous buffet known as the "lobster feast," with lobster and other seafood cooked to order, an open bar, and a calypso band ($60). ⊠*End of Calle Hicaco* ☎2643–3226 ⊟*AE, DC, MC, V.*

$$-$$$ ✕**Las Sandalias.** Located in the Club del Mar, at the southern end of the ★ beach, this colorful restaurant overlooking a pool and gardens serves consistently good food. Its short, eclectic menu ranges from grilled sea bass to chateaubriand, and includes such treats as seafood crepes and mahimahi sautéed with white wine, tomatoes, peppers, and hearts of palm. The nightly specials are also a good bet. Lunch consists of salads, sandwiches, and a few heartier dishes like fish-and-chips. It's a pleasant walk down the beach from the center of town by day, but you'll want to take a taxi here for dinner. ⊠*Costanera, south of gas station* ☎2643–3194 ⊟*AE, DC, MC, V.*

$$–$$$ ✕**Tsunami Sushi.** This small sushi bar on the second floor of the Il Galeone shopping center takes advantage of the area's steady supply of fresh fish and seafood to create more than 20 kinds of maki rolls, nigiri, and sashimi. They also offer a few cooked items, such as shrimp and vegetable tempuras, chicken teriyaki, and an unusual blackened filet mignon, but it's the sushi that keeps this place full. Simple but chic decor makes the air-conditioned dining room a pleasant place to spend some time; there are also a few outdoor tables. ⊠*Avda. Pastor Diaz, 2nd fl of Il Galeone shopping center* ☎*2643–3678* ▤*MC, V* ⊘*No lunch.*

$–$$ ✕**Rioasis.** This large, colorful place in the heart of town is the best ♺ pizzeria in Jacó. The eclectic menu includes Tex-Mex dishes, seafood, and salads, but the pizza is your best bet, with 34 varieties baked in an outdoor wood-burning oven. You can eat in the front garden, which is nicely candle-lit by night, or under a high roof dotted with ceiling fans. There's a long bar in back, and a pool and foosball tables for after-dinner entertainment. ⊠*Avda. Pastor Diaz, north of Banco Nacional* ☎*2643–3354* ▤*MC, V* ⊘*Closed Sept.*

$–$$ ✕**Wishbone.** This popular eatery in the heart of Jacó's commercial district serves great seafood, mainly fresh tuna and mahimahi. You can have your tuna as sashimi, grilled, blackened, or as "spicy tuna," which is seared with a wasabi soy sauce, chopped into pieces, and served over sticky rice. Other good options are filet mignon, garlic shrimp, or sautéed vegetables. They also offer a selection of pizzas and Tex-Mex dishes, but the best bet is the seafood listed on a separate, paper menu. The portions are generous, the staff is friendly, and the owner, Caliche, is usually there chatting with guests. ⊠*Avda. Pastor Diaz, across from Il Galeone shopping center* ☎*2643–3406* ▤*AE, DC, MC, V* ⊘*Closed Wed.*

WHERE TO STAY

$$–$$$ ▦**Club del Mar.** Secluded at the beach's southern end, far from Jacó's Fodor'sChoice crowds, Club del Mar is the area's priciest, and nicest, lodging option. ★ In the main building, above the restaurant, bar, and reception, standard green-and-cream-hue rooms have private teak balconies with screen doors that keep the sea breeze circulating. Comfortable condos, clustered in two-story buildings amid massive trees and verdant lawns, are considerably nicer. One- and two-bedroom apartments have abundant windows, modern kitchens, and pleasant furnishings; two-bedroom condos are a bargain for two couples. The nicest condos are those nearest the sea (Nos. 13–16). Las Sandalias restaurant ($$–$$$) serves some of the area's finest food (⇨*above*). **Pros:** Beachfront, tranquil, friendly, lush grounds, tasteful decor. **Con:** Some highway noise reaches back condos. ⊠*Costanera, 275 m south of gas station* ✑*Apdo. 107–4023, Jacó* ☎*2643–3194, 866/978–5669 in U.S.* ☐*2643–3550* ⊕*www.clubdelmarcostarica.com* ➟*8 rooms, 22 condos, 2 suites* ⌂*In-room: safe, kitchen (some). In-hotel: restaurant, room service, bar, pool, beachfront, water sports, no elevator, laundry facilities, concierge, public Wi-Fi* ▤*AE, DC, MC, V* ⦿*EP.*

$$–$$$ ▦**Docelunas.** Most of Jacó's hotels and visitors huddle around the beach, but "Twelve Moons" sits a couple of miles from the sea and sand. With a mountainous green backdrop, this hotel spreads out across 5 acres of lawns shaded by tropical trees and luxuriant gardens. Spacious teak furniture–filled rooms have large bathrooms with showers, bathtubs, and double sinks. Yoga classes are given daily in a hilltop, hardwood-floor room with windows for walls. The full-service spa uses the hotel's own homemade beauty products, and the open-air restaurant ($$–$$$) serves up creative seafood, meat, vegetarian, and vegan dishes. ✉ *On coastal highway from San José, pass the first entrances to Jacó; take dirt road on left with signs for Docelunas* ☎ *2643–2211* 📠 *2643–3633* 🌐 *www.docelunas.com* *20 rooms* *In-room: safe, refrigerator, Wi-Fi. In-hotel: restaurant, room service, bar, pool, spa, no elevator, laundry service, no-smoking rooms* 💳 *AE, DC, MC, V* 🍽 *BP.*

$$–$$ **Hotel Tangerí.** One of Jacó's older hotels, the Tangerí has an excellent beachfront location and ample grounds shaded by coconut palms. The accommodations range from spacious rooms by the sea to villas big enough for a large family. The bright but bland standard rooms in a two-story cement building by the beach are a good deal for couples. Beachfront rooms have balconies or terraces with lovely ocean views through the palms. Ocean-view rooms are over the lawn, and some have a rather distant glimpse of the sea. The villas, complete with kitchens and one to three bedrooms, are set back from the beach; avoid Nos. 5, 6, and 8, which are too close to the road. This is a popular spot with Costa Rican families, thanks to its convenient beach access, several pools, a playground, Ping Pong, and pool table, which means it can be quite busy during the holidays. There's a snack bar by the pool and a steak house ($$$) near the entrance. **Pros:** Beachfront, spacious rooms, centrally located. **Cons:** Rooms a bit timeworn, musty. ✉ *Avda. Pastor Diaz, north of river* ☎ *2643–3001 or 2258–4012* 🌐 *www.hoteltangeri.com* *14 rooms, 11 villas* *In-room: kitchen (some), refrigerator. In-hotel: restaurant, bar, pools, gym, beachfront, no elevator, laundry service, public Wi-Fi* 💳 *AE, MC, V* 🍽 ✉ ☎.

5

$$ **Apartotel Girasol.** A great option for families, or small groups of friends looking for comfort and quiet, Girasol is a quiet beachfront hotel with a neighborly feel. The cozy apartments face the small pool and grill area and include a bedroom with a queen and single bed, a living and dining room with another bed, a complete kitchen, and a terrace with chairs. A winding pathway crosses the well-maintained front lawn with an impressive ficus tree in the middle, and leads to a small gate that opens directly onto the beach, where you should take at least one evening to enjoy a spectacular sunset. **Pros:** Beachfront, quiet grounds, big apartments. **Cons:** Far from town center, often full. ✉ *100 m west of Motoshop, end of C. Republica Dominicana* ☎📠 *2643–1591* 🌐 *www.girasol.com* *16 apartments* *In-room: safe, kitchen, Wi-Fi. In-hotel: pool, beachfront, no elevator, laundry service* 💳 *MC, V* 🍽 *EP.*

$$ **Hotel Canciones del Mar.** The poetically named "Songs of the Sea" is a tranquil, intimate, and charming hotel with rooms that are among the closest to the ocean of any hotel in the area. Tastefully and individually decorated, the one- and two-bedroom suites are in a two-story cream-color building, with well-equipped kitchens. Five ocean-view rooms cost a bit more, but the rest have porches overlooking the lush

Fodor's Choice ★

gardens and blue-tile pool. Breakfast and drinks can be enjoyed under a thatch roof next to the beach or in the shade of palms on the beach itself, whereas the roof-top tapas bar is a great spot to watch the sunset. A communal tree house–like space behind the pool makes a pleasant reading or relaxing spot. **Pros:** Close to ocean, rooms have kitchens. **Con:** Perhaps a bit too close to Jacó for comfort. ⊠*End of C. Bri Bri* ◻*Apdo. 86–4023, Jacó* ☎*2643–3273* 🖷*2643–3296* ⊕*www. cancionesdelmar.com* ⮂*12 suites* ⬧*In-room: safe, kitchen, refrigerator, Wi-Fi. In-hotel: restaurant, bar, pool, beachfront, no elevator, laundry service* ▤*AE, MC, V* ⧫|*BP.*

$$ ▦**Mar de Luz.** It may be a few blocks from the beach, and it doesn't �l look like much from the street, but Mar de Luz is a surprisingly pleasant place full of flowering plants and shady, bird-attracting trees. The Dutch owner is dedicated to cleanliness and providing lots of amenities, such as poolside grills, a kids' game room, plentiful common areas—like the large open-air reading lounge—and inexpensive tours. Rooms vary in decor: the bright, pastel-hue rooms have two queen-size beds and kitchenettes; top-floor rooms have a small living room with checkered sofas and a double bed; the cozy split-level rooms with kitchenettes and stone walls are reminiscent of European B&Bs. **Pros:** Attentive owner, plenty to do. **Con:** Rooms a bit dark. ⊠*Just east of Avda. Pastor Diaz, behind Jungle bar* ☎*2643–3000 or 877/623–3198* 🖷*2643–3259* ⮂*27 rooms, 2 suites* ⬧*In-room: safe, kitchen (some), refrigerator, Wi-Fi (some). In-hotel: pool, no elevator, laundry service, public Internet, no-smoking rooms* ▤*AE, DC, MC, V* ⧫|*BP.*

$–$$ ▦**Aparthotel Flamboyant.** Though nothing special, this small beachfront ★ hotel is a good deal, especially if you take advantage of the cooking �l facilities. Half the rooms have small kitchenettes; the others have air-conditioning instead. Larger apartments can fit five to six people. Terraces with chairs overlook a garden and pool area, where there's a grill for your use. Second-floor rooms have balconies with sea views. It's all just a few steps from the surf, and a block east of Jacó's busy main strip. **Pros:** Beachfront, good value, quiet, centrally located. **Con:** Very simple rooms. ⊠*100 m west of Centro Comercial Il Galeone* ☎*2643–3146* 🖷*2643–1068* ⮂*20 rooms, 3 apartments* ⬧*In-room: no a/c (some), safe, kitchen (some), Wi-Fi (some). In-hotel: pool, beachfront, no elevator, laundry service, public Wi-Fi* ▤*AE, DC, MC, V* ⧫|*EP.*

$ ▦**Tropical Garden Hotel.** As its name suggests, this hotel's special charm comes from the impressive lush gardens that fill almost every inch of its property, making it one of the most verdant places in Jacó. Meters from the beach and from the main strip, rooms lack style but have very basic kitchenettes and front porches for iguana- and bird-spotting. It's one of Jacó's original hotels (formerly known as Villas Miramar), and the rooms show their age, but it's competitively priced. **Pro:** Pleasant grounds. **Con:** Timeworn. ⊠*50 m west of Il Galeone mall, toward the beach* ☎*2643–3003* 🖷*2643–3617* ⊕*www.tropicalgardenhotel. com* ⮂*11 rooms, 1 suite* ⬧*In-room: no a/c (some), no phone, safe, kitchen. In-hotel: pool, no elevator* ▤*AE, MC, V* ⧫|*EP.*

¢–$ ▦**Las Orquídeas.** Just far enough from the beach and main tourist beat to be a bargain, but close enough to be convenient, this pleasant little hotel provides cleanliness and comfort at reasonable rates. Colorful, narrow rooms have tile floors, two beds, and the basic amenities; air-conditioning costs $10 extra. Small front terraces overlook the gardens and small pool, where the predominantly surfer guests tend to congregate. **Pro:** Good location. **Con:** No frills. ☒*Just east of Frutastica supermarket* ☎*2643–4056* ⤴*10 rooms* ♿*In-room: no phone, safe, refrigerator, Ethernet. In-hotel: pool, laundry service, no elevator* ⊟*AE, MC, V* ⧈*EP.*

NIGHTLIFE & THE ARTS

While other beach towns may have a bar or two, Jacó has an avenue full of them, with enough variety for many different tastes. After-dinner spots range from restaurants perfect for a quiet drink to loud bars with pool tables to dance clubs or casinos.

BARS For a laid-back cocktail, people-watching, and a tropical feel, head to **Restaurante El Colonial** (☒*Avda. Pastor Diaz, across from Il Galeone mall* ☎*2643–3326*) on the main drag, which has a large circular bar in the center and lots of wicker chairs and tables in the front. Sometimes it has live music. A mix of bar and disco, **Nacho Daddy's** (☒*Avda. Pastor Diaz, 1st fl of Il Galeone mall* ☎*2643–2270*) is Jacó's after-hours nightspot, open from 10 PM to 4 AM. The restaurant, **Tabacón** (☒*Avda. Pastor Diaz, north of Il Galeone mall* ☎*2643–3097*), is a nice place for a cocktail, after-dinner drinks, or a late-night meal. It has a big bar in back, pool tables, and live music on weekends. **Jungle** (☒*Avda. Pastor Diaz, across from Hotel Tangerí, above Subway* ☎*2643–3911*), a large, second-floor bar, has wide-screen TVs, several pool tables, dart boards, a large bar, and a dance floor in back.

CASINOS **Jazz Casino and Sportsbook** (☒*Hotel Amapola, 130 m east of the Municipalidad government building, southern end of town* ☎*2643–2316*), Jacó's first casino, has rummy, slot machines, and craps. There's also a roomy bar area.

SHOPPING

Souvenir shops with mostly the same mass-produced merchandise are crowded one after the other along the main street in the center of town. Most of the goods, like wooden crafts and seed jewelry, are run-of-the mill souvenir fare, but a few shops have more unusual items. The two neighboring shops at **Cocobolo** (☒*Avda. Pastor Diaz, next to Banana Café* ☎*2643–3486*) are jam-packed with merchandise hanging from the ceiling, walls, and shelves. It's much of what you find in other stores, but with more international and tasteful items and a richer variety. **El Cofre** (☒*Avda. Pastor Diaz, across from Banco Nacional* ☎*2643–1912*) claims to sell only handmade goods and specializes in mostly wooden furniture, including heavy Guatemalan pieces and Indonesian teak; it also sells masks, drums, Moroccan lamps, and even carved doors. Curious religious statues of saints and angels from Central America are big sellers. **Guacamole** (☒ *Centro Comercial Costa Brava, just south of Il Galeone mall* ☎*2643–1120*) sells beautiful and comfortable batik clothing produced locally, along with Brazilian bathing suits, Costa Rican leather sandals and purses, and different styles of jewelry.

SURFBOARDS **Carton** (✉ *Calle Madrigal* ☎2643–3762) sells new and used boards
& GEAR and has a selection in surf wear, sunglasses, and accessories. **El Pana Bikinis and Surf** (✉ *Avda. Pastor Diaz, next to Cocobolo* ☎2612–2803) has less variety than the other shops in town, but more affordable prices. It rents and sells new and used surfboards and Boogie boards, and fixes small dings. **Jass** (✉ *Centro Comercial Ureña* ☎2643–3549) has a good variety of surf gear at decent prices. It sells new and used boards. ■ TIP➡ **Most shops that sell boards also buy used boards.**

PLAYA HERMOSA

5 km (3 mi) south of Jacó, 113 km (70 mi) southwest of San José.

On the other side of the rocky ridge that forms the southern edge of Jacó Beach is Playa Hermosa, a swath of gray sand and driftwood stretching southeast as far as the eye can see. Despite its name—Spanish for "Lovely Beach" —Playa Hermosa is hardly spectacular. The southern half of the wide beach lacks palm trees or other shade-providing greenery; its sand is scorchingly hot in the afternoon; and frequent rip currents make it unsafe to swim when there are waves. But board-riders find beauty in its consistent surf breaks. The beach's northern end is popular because it often has waves when other spots are flat, and the ocean is cleaner than at Jacó. There is also plenty of forest covering the hills, and scarlet macaws sometimes gather in the Indian almond trees near the end of beach. For non-surfers, outdoor options include horseback and canopy tours in the nearby, forested hills or ultralight and hang-gliding flights over the coast. But all of these can be done from other beaches. As for the town itself, there's really not much, which is part of the attraction for travelers who want to escape Jaco's crowds and cement towers. Most of the restaurants, bars, and hotels have cropped up one after the other on a thin stretch separating the highway and the beach. From June to December, olive ridley turtles nest on the beach at night, especially when there's not much moonlight.

GETTING HERE

If you have a car, take the coastal highway 5 km (3 mi) past Jacó. You'll see the cluster of businesses on the right. If you don't, take a taxi from Jacó or a local bus toward Quepos.

PLAYA HERMOSA ESSENTIALS

Internet **Goola Café and Internet** (✉ *Costanera, north of soccer field* ☎2643–3696).

OUTDOOR ACTIVITIES

You can arrange activities throughout the Central Pacific from Playa Hermosa. Most tour operators and outfitters include transportation in their prices. *For more options than we list here, see Outdoor Activities in Jacó, above, or consult your hotel's reception.* Raul Fernandez of **Playa Hermosa Turtle Tours** (✉   ☎8817–0385) takes small groups to look

Catch the Wave

Costa Rica gets high marks among surfers for its warm, clean ocean water, beautiful tropical scenery, consistent waves, and not-too-crowded conditions. (The place hasn't yet turned into California or Hawaii.)

Tamarindo anchors a popular surfing region on the North Pacific coast. Its protected bay offers smaller waves that translate into great conditions for beginners. The exception is December and January, when the bay is exposed to southern swells that create bigger waves. North of town to Playa Grande and south to Playas Avellanas and Negra the swells are always dangerous: these are experts-only destinations year-round.

Farther down the coast, **Sámara** is little mentioned in surfing circles, but is a good beginner's beach for its small waves.

Some of the country's finest dry-season surfing is at **Malpaís** and nearby **Santa Teresa,** near the tip of the Nicoya Peninsula. They are gradually becoming more popular, despite their remoteness.

The Central Pacific town of **Jacó** gets mixed reviews. As the closest surfing destination to San José, it draws the crowds. Surfers say its waves close out early (good for beginners) but tend toward quick shore breaks (conditions best negotiated by experts).

Playa Hermosa, just to the south, is enormously popular, but there are plenty of breaks, so crowding is rarely a problem. Because of its angle, Hermosa often has waves when other beaches are flat.

The South Pacific's **Dominical** is a nice alternative to Jacó. It's considerably farther from San José and has a bigger, more consistent break. A cool surf-town atmosphere makes it worth the trip.

Staring at each other from across the entrance to the Golfo Dulce are the point breaks and resulting big waves at **Matapalo** and **Pavones.** The former is an experts-only right that breaks over a rocky platform. The latter is famed in surfing circles for being one of the world's longest lefts, and the waves are consistently big.

While the Pacific has consistent year-round conditions, the Caribbean coast has a narrower window (January through April) of top-notch surfing. The difficult access, tendency for waves to close out, and shark-infested waters make the northern half of the Caribbean coast a no-go. Heading south, the reef break at **Playa Bonita,** just north of **Limón,** is popular with locals, but not as convenient to surf as the Puerto Viejo area. The coast to the south of Limón has several beach breaks, but don't leave any valuables in your car when you surf them. Cahuita's **Playa Negra** has a fairly consistent beach break that has the advantage of nearby hotels.

Puerto Viejo de Talamanca, south of Cahuita, is the Caribbean coast's surf mecca. The consistent beach break at **Playa Cocles,** a short walk south of town, is good for most levels, though rip currents can be a real danger. The famed—and revered—**Salsa Brava,** an experts-only reef break, is just off the point on the southern end of the town of Puerto Viejo, but it only breaks when the waves are five feet or higher.

5

for nesting sea turtles on Playa Hermosa between July and December ($35), as part of a project to collect the eggs and raise them in a hatchery. Tour times vary according to the tide; he can provide transportation from hotels in Jacó.

CANOPY TOUR **Chiclets Canopy Tour** (⊠ *West of Costanera* ✛ *½ km (¼ mi) north of Hermosa* ☎2643–3271 ⊕*www.jacowave.com*) runs four guided tours daily that take you through the rain-forest canopy ($60). Cables strung between platforms perched high in a dozen trees have views of tropical foliage, wildlife, and the nearby coast.

HORSEBACK **Discovery Horseback** (☎8838–7550 ⊕*www.discoveryhorsetours.com*)
RIDING runs various tours through the nearby mountains to a waterfall and along the beach. Their most popular tour is a 2½-hour ride through the rain forest ($6). You can also arrange riding lessons.

SURFING Most people who bed down at Playa Hermosa are here for the same reason—the waves that break just a shell's toss away. There are a half-dozen breaks scattered along the beach's northern end, and the surf is always best around high tide. Because it is a beach break, though, the waves here often close out, especially when the surf is big. If you don't have much experience, don't go out when the waves are really big—Hermosa sometimes gets very powerful swells, which result in dangerous rip currents. If you're a beginner, don't go out at all. Surf instructors in Hermosa take their students to Jacó, an easier place to learn the sport.

Reggae-theme **Restaurante Jammin'** (⊠*Next to Cabinas Las Arenas* ☎ 2643–1853) offers surf lessons ($45) and buys, rents, and sells boards as they're available. Andrea Díaz, a professional surfer with **Waves Costa Rica** (⊠*Next to the Backyard* ☎ 2643–7025 *or* 8829– 4610 ⊕*www.wavescr.com*), takes surf students to calmer Playa Jacó for two-hour lessons ($45; $100 for daylong package). She also offers surf-camp packages, which include room and board and yoga.

WHERE TO STAY & EAT

$–$$ ╳**The Backyard.** Playa Hermosa's original nightlife spot, the North American–style Backyard has two seating areas, each with its own bar. Television sets on the wraparound bar in the front room show sports matches and surf videos. A wooden deck in back overlooking the beach is great for lunch and sunset, mostly because of the pleasant sea breezes and view. The usual bar food—Tex-Mex standards and burgers—is complemented by fresh seafood, including ceviche, grilled tuna, lobster, and jumbo shrimp. It's popular especially on Friday and Saturday, when there's live music. ⊠*Costanera, southern end of town (next to the Backyard hotel, below)* ☎2643–7011 ▤*AE, DC, MC, V.*

$–$$ ╳**Jungle Surf Cafe.** This simple, open-air eatery decorated with a colorful rain-forest mural serves some of Hermosa's best food. Seating is on a patio and wooden deck hemmed by tropical trees, with views of the road and soccer field. Breakfasts are hearty—try the banana pancakes—and the eclectic lunch selection ranges from shish kebabs to fish sandwiches. The dinner menu changes nightly, but usually includes big portions of fresh tuna or mahimahi. ⊠*Costanera, north of soccer field* ☎*2643–1495* ▭*No credit cards* 🍴*BYOB* ⊘*Closed Wed.*

$$$ 🛏**The Backyard.** Surfers—not the budget backpacking kind—are the main clientele at this small, cream-color hotel on the beach. Rooms have high ceilings, clay-tile floors, and sliding-glass doors that open onto semiprivate balconies and terraces, most of which have good views of Playa Hermosa. Second-floor rooms have better views, as do the two spacious corner suites with separate bedrooms and large balconies—they're a good deal for small groups. There's a nice little pool surrounded by tropical foliage in back. **Pros:** Steps from the surf, nice views from second floor, friendly. **Cons:** Expensive, bar next door noisy on weekends. ⊠*Costanera, southern end of town* ☎*2643–7011* ⊕*www.backyardhotel.com* ➽*6 rooms, 2 suites* ⌂*In-room: safe, refrigerator, Wi-Fi. In-hotel: restaurant, bar, pool, no elevator, laundry service* ▭*AE, DC, MC, V* 🍴*CP.*

¢–$$ 🛏**Cabinas Vista Hermosa.** Playa Hermosa's original hotel, Cabinas Vista ⟳ Hermosa sits at the edge of a pleasant grove of coconut palms and almond trees. It can be a bit hard to find. The hotel was renovated in 2007, and the new rooms in a two-story cement building are simple but comfortable. Pay the extra $20 for an ocean-view room, with sliding doors that open onto a common terrace, since the ones in back overlook the road and parking lot. A separate building on the beach has rustic backpacker rooms that share a bathroom for half the price. The rooms and restaurant overlook two pools, a grill for guest use, and tables on the beach. Common areas have hammocks and diversions like foosball and Ping-Pong. ⊠*Costanera, 150 m south of soccer field* ☎*2643–7022* ⊕*www.vistahermosa.20m.com* ➽*12 rooms, 2 with shared bath* ⌂*In-room: no a/c (some). In-hotel: restaurant, pools, no elevator, laundry service* ▭*No credit cards* 🍴*BP.*

PLAYA BEJUCO

27 km (16 mi) south of Playa Hermosa, 32 km (19 mi) south of Jacó.

Surfers wanting to escape the crowds at Jacó and Playa Hermosa, or anyone simply seeking to stray from the beaten path, need only drive 20 minutes south to this relatively deserted palm-lined beach. One could stroll for an hour along the light-gray swath of sand and hardly encounter a soul. Several vacation homes and two small hotels sit behind the first part of the beach, and behind them is a large mangrove forest where you might see macaws or white-faced monkeys. The surf is as big and consistent as at Playa Hermosa, but with a fraction of the surfers. It's a Blue-Flag beach, but like Hermosa, it can develop dangerous rip currents, so swimmers should go in no deeper than their waist when the waves are big. Aside from surfing and beach-combing, there is little to do here, which makes it a good place for people wanting to do nothing at all. The mosquitoes can be quite fearsome during the rainy months.

GETTING HERE

If you have a car, take the coastal highway *27 km (16 mi) south* past Playa Hermosa to the turnoff for Playa Bejuco, which is 1 km (½ mi) west of the highway. If you don't, take a taxi from Jacó, or local bus toward Quepos.

OUTDOOR ACTIVITIES

SURFING There are various high-tide beach breaks scattered along Playa Bejuco. Waves tend to close out here when the swell is big, but then you can try the mouth of the estuary, half a mile (1 km) south of the hotels. Bejuco is a do-it-yourself beach, with neither surf schools nor board rental nearby, and because the waves break so close to shore, it's not a good spot for beginners.

WHERE TO STAY & EAT

$$ ☒ **Delfin Beach Front Resort.** Every room in this two-story hotel has an ocean view, and the surf breaks right in front of it. Tastefully decorated rooms are standard size, with one king or two queen beds, and a small bathroom. They all have either a large balcony or a terrace; those on the ground floor tend to have better views of the sea, past the skinny coconut palms. The bright, airy restaurant ($$) also overlooks the beach, but the menu is very limited, with tilapia instead of ocean fish, oddly enough. There's a small pool in back, near which hang a few hammocks. **Pro:** Beachfront. **Con:** Limited selection at restaurant. *⊠On beach, Playa Bejuco ☎2777–8054 or 2777–6045 ⊕www.delfinbeachfront.com ⇱12 rooms ☆In-room: no phone, safe. In-hotel: restaurant, bar, pool, beachfront, no elevator, laundry service ⊟AE, DC, MC, V ⎪○⎪CP.*

$$ ☒ **Playa Bejuco Hotel.** Playa Bejuco's less expensive accommodations are
☾ 50 meters away from the beach, so the views are of pool and gardens rather than surf and sand. The rooms are spacious and well equipped, and the hotel is nicely designed with ocher walls, lots of foliage, and a large, blue-tile pool. They cater to families by putting several beds in some rooms, such as the second-floor rooms with one king and a loft with two twin beds. The restaurant ($$–$$$) has an extensive menu that includes sea bass served with various sauces, pastas, pork loin, filet mignon, and jumbo shrimp. **Pros:** Big pool, decent restaurant. **Con:** Lacks ocean view. *⊠Road to Playa Bejuco, on left ☎2777—8181 ⊕www.hotelplayabejuco.com ⇱20 rooms ☆In-room: no phone, safe, refrigerator. In-hotel: restaurant, bar, pool, no elevator, laundry service, public Wi-Fi, no-smoking rooms ⊟AE, DC, MC, V ⎪○⎪BP.*

QUEPOS

23 km (14 mi) south of Parrita, 174 km (108 mi) southwest of San José.

This hot and dusty town serves as a gateway to Manuel Antonio. It also serves as the area's hub for banks, supermarkets, and other services. Because nearby Manuel Antonio is so much more attractive, there is no reason to stay here, but many people stop for dinner, for a night on the town, or to go sportfishing. Quepos's name stems from the indigenous tribe that inhabited the area until the Spanish conquest wiped them out. For centuries the town of Quepos barely existed, until the 1930s, when the United Fruit Company built a banana port and populated the area with workers from other parts of Central America. The town thrived for nearly two decades, until Panama disease decimated the banana plantations in the late 1940s. The fruit company then switched to less lucrative African oil palms, and the area declined. Only since the 1980s have tourism revenues lifted the town out of its slump, a renaissance owed to the beauty of the nearby beaches and nature reserves. Forests around Quepos were destroyed nearly a century ago, but the massive Talamanca Mountain Range, some 10 km (6 mi) to the east, holds one of the largest expanses of wilderness in Central America.

GETTING HERE

It's just over a three-hour drive from San José to Quepos; follow the directions for Jacó and continue south another 40 minutes. Buses from San José's Coca-Cola bus station drop you off in downtown Quepos. SANSA and Nature Air run 10 flights per day between San José and Quepos, as well as direct flights between Quepos and other tourist destinations.

QUEPOS ESSENTIALS

Bank/ATM **BAC San José** (⊠ *Avda. Central*). **Banco Nacional** (⊠ *50 m west and 100 m north of bus station* ☎ *2777–0113*).

Hospital **Ambulance** (☎ *2777–0118*). **Quepos hospital** (✢ *4 km [2½ mi] on road to Dominical* ☎ *2777–0020*).

Pharmacy **Farmacia Fischel** (⊠ *Near bus station, in front of municipal market* ☎ *2777–0816*).

Post Office **Correos** (⊠ *C. Central*).

Taxis **Taxi services** (☎ *2777–0425, 2777–1693, or 2777–1068*).

Travel Agency **Lynch Travel** (⊠ *Downtown, behind bus station* ☎ *2777–1170* ⊕ *www.lynchtravel.com*).

EXPLORING

Spread over Fila Chota, a lower ridge of the Talamanca Range 22 km (13 mi) northeast of Quepos, **Rainmaker** is a private nature reserve which protects more than 1,500 acres of lush and precipitous forest. The lower part of the reserve can be visited on guided tours from Manuel Antonio, or as a stop on your way to or from Quepos. Tours begin at 8:30 and 12:30. There are two tours available: a walk up the valley of the Río Seco, which includes a dip in a pool at the foot of a waterfall; or a hike into the hills above the waterfall and over a series of suspension bridges strung between giant tropical trees. The park also offers an early-morning bird-watching tour and a night hike. The best value is a half-day package ($70) that includes transport from Manuel Antonio or Quepos, a guided tour, a river swim, and breakfast and lunch. The reserve is home to many of Costa Rica's endangered species, and you may spot birds here that you won't find in Manuel Antonio. It isn't as good a place to see animals as the national park, but Rainmaker's forest is different from the park's—lusher and more precipitous—and the view from its bridges is impressive. It's best to visit Rainmaker in the morning, since—true to its name—it often pours in the afternoon. ⊹22 km (13 mi) northeast of Quepos ☎2777–3565, 504/349–9849 in U.S. ⊕www.rainmakercostarica.org ⊠$60–$90 for guided tours ⊙Mon.–Sat. 8–4.

OUTDOOR ACTIVITIES

There's a tour operator, or travel agency on every block in Quepos that can sell you any of about a dozen tours, but some outfitters give discounts if you book directly through them. The dry season is the best time to explore the area's rain forests. If you're here during the rains, do tours first thing in the morning.

There are many zip-line tours in the area that take you flying through the treetops, but **Canopy Safari** (⊠Downtown, next to the Poder Judicial ☎2777–0100 ⊕www.canopysafari.com) has earned a reputation for long and fast-paced rides. The company's privately owned forest is about a 45-minute car ride from Quepos, and the tour ($65) includes gliding down nine zip lines and a swim in a river pool.

FISHING Quepos is one of the best points of departure for deep-sea fishing in southwestern Costa Rica. The best months for hooking a marlin are from October to February and in May and June, whereas sailfish are abundant from November to May, and are caught year-round. From May to October you're more likely to catch yellowfin tuna, rooster fish, mahimahi, and snapper. **Bluefin Tours** (⊠Downtown, across from the soccer field ☎2777–2222 or 2777–1676 ⊕www.bluefinsportfishing. com) has catch-and-release sportfishing, conventional, and fly-fishing on a fleet of 25-, 28-, and 31-foot boats. Half-day charters run $500–$750, whereas a full day costs $700–$950. **Costa Mar Dream Catcher** (⊠Entrance to Quepos, next to Café Milagro ☎2777–0593 ⊕www. costamarsportfishing.com) has the largest fleet of boats in Quepos, with 11 boats ranging from 25 to 36 feet, and consequently has a wide range of rates. Half- and full-day charters run $500–$1,100. Half-, three-quarter-, and full-day catch-and-release fly and conventional trips ($600–$900 for a full day) with **Luna Tours Sport Fishing** (⊠Downtown, next to Casino Kamuk ☎2777–0725 or 888/567–5488 in the U.S. ⊕www.lunatours.net) are available on 27-, 32-, or 33-foot boats.

KAYAKING & **Iguana Tours** (⊠Downtown Quepos, across from soccer field ☎2777– RAFTING 2052 ⊕www.iguanatours.com) specializes in exploring the area's natural beauty through white-water rafting on the Naranjo and Savegre rivers and kayak adventures at sea or in a mangrove estuary. They also offer bird-watching, horseback riding, and canopy tours.

MOUNTAIN The area's green mountains are great for biking, but in the dry sea-
BIKING son it's hot—very, very hot. The rainy season is slightly cooler, but be prepared to get muddy. **Estrella Tour** (⊠Downtown, across the street from Restaurante El Pueblo ☎2777–1286 or 8843–6612 ⊕www. puertoquepos.com/ecotourism/mountain-biking.html) has an array of bike tours for intermediate and expert riders ranging from a couple of

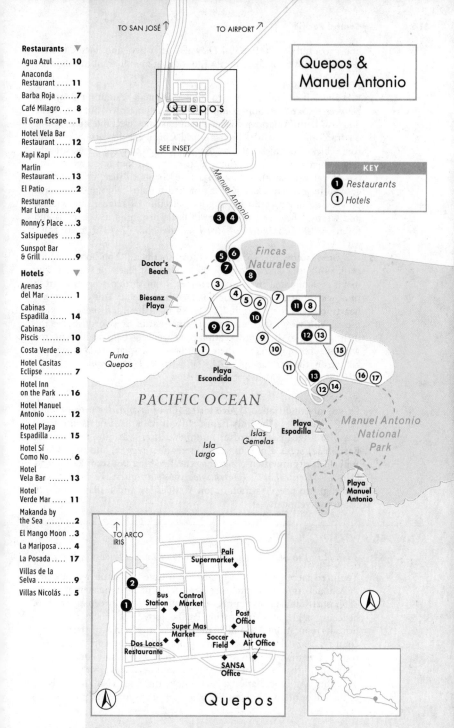

Quepos & Manuel Antonio

KEY
- **①** *Restaurants*
- **①** *Hotels*

TO SAN JOSÉ ↑
TO AIRPORT ↗

Quepos

SEE INSET

Manuel Antonio

Fincas Naturales

Doctor's Beach

Biesanz Playa

Punta Quepos

Playa Escondida

PACIFIC OCEAN

Isla Largo

Islas Gemelas

Playa Espadilla

Manuel Antonio National Park

Playa Manuel Antonio

Quepos (inset)

↑ TO ARCO IRIS

Palí Supermarket

Bus Station

Control Market

Post Office

Super Mas Market

Soccer Field

Nature Air Office

Dos Locos Resturante

SANSA Office

Quepos

hours to a full day ($40–$50). They also offer two- and three-day trips ($140–$310) that include meals and lodging in mountain cabins.

WHERE TO EAT

$$–$$$ ✕ **El Patio.** It would be easy to miss this small restaurant squeezed
★   between a couple of shops south of the bridge into town, but don't. The nouveau Latin American cuisine includes some delectable innovations on traditional Central American and Caribbean flavors. Start with some chicken tamales, ceviche, or a mango and chayote (green squash) salad, then sink your teeth into a slice of pork loin in a creole mojo (spicy tomato sauce), shrimp in a rum coconut sauce, or mahimahi cooked in a banana leaf with a smoked tomato mojo and a squash puree. The lunch menu has a good selection of salads, sandwiches, and wraps. The nicest tables are in back, around a lush garden and fountain. ✉*250 m north of Hotel Kamuk* ☎*2777–4982* ▭*AE, DC, MC, V* ✆*Closed Sun.*

$$ ✕ **El Gran Escape.** A favorite with sportfishermen ("You hook 'em, we cook 'em"), the Great Escape is the town's best place for seafood. The menu is dominated by seafood entrées, from shrimp scampi to fresh tuna with mushrooms to bouillabaisse and paella. You can also get hearty burgers, or a handful of Mexican dishes, and there's a kids' menu. You won't find any billfish, like marlin or swordfish, on the menu, owing to their conservation policy, but the back wall is covered with pictures of them (and their proud reelers). Weathered fishing caps hang from the bar's ceiling. ✉*150 m north of Hotel Kamuk* ☎*2777–0395* ▭*AE, DC, MC, V* ✆*Closed Tues.*

NIGHTLIFE

Large, air-conditioned **El Arco Iris** (✉*Over last bridge into Quepos* ☎*2777–0449*) is the only dance club in the area. Locals and tourists of all ages pack in after midnight, after warming up in other bars. A DJ spins a mix of salsa, merengue, reggae, and pop. Older American expats often congregate at Tex-Mex **Dos Locos Restaurante** (✉*Avda. Central at C. Central, near bus station* ☎*2777–1526*) day and night to people-watch or, on Wednesday and Friday nights, to listen to live music.

MANUEL ANTONIO

3 km (2 mi) south of Quepos, 179 km (111 mi) southwest of San José.

You need merely reach the top of the forested ridge on which many of Manuel Antonio's hotels are perched to understand why it is one of Costa Rica's most popular destinations. That sweeping view of beaches, jungle, and shimmering Pacific dotted with rocky islets confirms its reputation. And unlike the tropical forests in other parts of the country, Manuel Antonio's humid tropical forest remains green year-round. The town itself is spread out across a hilly and curving 5-km (3-mi) road that originates in Quepos and dead-ends at the entrance to Manuel Antonio National Park. Along this main road, near the top of the hill or on its southern slope, are the area's most luxurious hotels

Continued on page 320

MANUEL ANTONIO NATIONAL PARK

 GOOD THINGS COME IN SMALL PACKAGES. Case in point, Costa Rica's smallest park packs in an impressive collection of natural attractions: lots of wildlife, rain forest, white-sand beaches, and rocky coves with abundant marine life. Trails are short, well maintained, and easy to walk. The forest is dominated by massive ficus and gumbo-limbo trees, and is home to two- and three-toed sloths, green and black iguanas, agoutis, three species of monkeys, and more than 350 species of birds.

FAST FACTS

Size: 7 square km (3 square mi)

Established: 1972

Dry season: December–April

Wettest months: September–October

What to do: Nature hikes, bird-watching, wildlife-watching, kayaking, snorkeling, swimming

Geography: 5 km (3 mi) of coastline; 700 hectares (1,730 acres) of primary, secondary, and mangrove forest; 12 islands

Number of species catalogued: 184 birds, 109 mammals, 60 fish, 4 turtles

- One of two places in Costa Rica to see squirrel monkeys.
- One of the best places in Costa Rica to see white-faced Capuchin monkeys and three-toed sloths.
- Despite being Costa Rica's smallest national park, this is its second most-visited, after Poás Volcano.

Make no mistake about it: Manuel Antonio is no undiscovered wilderness. It's one of Costa Rica's most-visited attractions, so if you're looking for an undisturbed natural oasis, this is not it. But what Manuel Antonio *does* have is great diversity of wildlife, all easily spotted from the well-marked trails. And because animals are so used to humans, this is one of the best places to see them up close.

ATTRACTIONS

From the ranger station a trail leads through the rain forest behind **Playa Espadilla Sur**, the park's longest beach. It's also the least crowded because the water can be rough. The coral reefs and submerged volcanic rocks of white-sand **Playa Manuel Antonio** make for good snorkeling. The 1/2-mile-long beach, tucked into a deep cove, is safe for swimming. At low tide you can see the remains of a Quepos Indian turtle trap on the right—the Quepos stuck poles in the semicircular rock formation, which trapped turtles as the tide receded. Olive ridley and green turtles come ashore on this beach May through November. Espadilla and Manuel Antonio beaches lie on opposite sides of a tombolo, or a sandy strip that connects the mainland to **Punta Catedral** (Cathedral Point), which used to be an island. The steep

path that leads up Punta Catedral's rocky hill draped with thick jungle, passes a lookout point from which you can gaze over the Pacific at the park's islands. ■TIP→Theft is a problem on the beaches; don't leave your belongings unattended while you swim and don't leave anything of value in your car.

Farther east, **Playa Escondido** (Hidden Beach) is rocky and secluded, but it's also more difficult to access. Before you head out to Escondido, find out when the tides come in so you're not stranded.

It's quiet and secluded. Kayaking trips might take you down to **Punta Serrucho** near the southern border of the park, whose jagged peaks explain its name. (*Serrucho* means "saw.")

Trails from the entrance to Punta Catedral and Playa Manuel Antonio are in good shape. Trails farther east to Escondido and Playita are progressively rougher going.

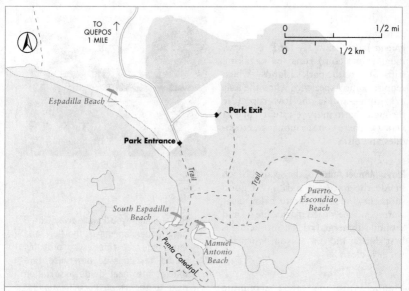

Squirrel Monkey

MONKEY BUSINESS

Monkeys are undoubtedly the superstars of Manuel Antonio wildlife. It's nearly impossible to tour the park without seeing at least one species. ■TIP➔Never feed or touch the monkeys: they have been known to bite overly friendly visitors and they can get sick, or even die from eating improper foods. Some monkeys are kleptomaniacs, so keep your backpack tightly zipped.

The **squirrel monkey** (*mono tití* in Spanish), the country's smallest monkey, is endangered, with only 1,200 to 1,500 remaining. Manuel Antonio is one of only two places in Costa Rica (the Osa Peninsula being the other) inhabited by squirrel monkeys.

Monkeys can't thrive only within the small park's border. To allow them to access areas outside the park, forested corridors have been built connecting the habitats. Suspended bridges allow monkeys to travel above roads around the park. Still, growing infrastructure around the park threatens the monkey population.

A SHAKY START

Before 1972 the land that now constitutes the park had a succession of foreign private owners intent on making a profit from tourism. These owners alienated the local community by cutting off their access to the park and, in the case of the final owner, razing tracts of forest and allegedly dumping pesticides to throw a wrench in the government's plan to create a protected area. The government seized the land shortly thereafter.

ACTIVITIES

KAYAKING

Iguana Tours (☎ 2777–1262 ⊕ www.-iguanatours.com) runs sea-kayaking trips ($65) to the park's islands—which require some experience when the seas are high—and a mellower paddle through the mangrove estuary of Isla Damas, where you see monkeys, crocodiles and birds.

SNORKELING

Playa Manuel Antonio, the second beach inside the national park, is a good snorkeling spot thanks to calm, clear waters and the varied marine life on and around submerged rocks. Snorkeling is best during the dry season, when the water is clear.

SWIMMING

Manuel Antonio's safest swimming area is sheltered **Playa Manuel Antonio,** whose white sand makes it attractive for lounging while keeping an eye on pint-sized swimmers.

TOP WILDLIFE

Top on our list of animals to see here are:

- howler monkeys
- white-faced capuchin monkeys
- squirrel monkeys
- two- and three-toed sloths
- agoutis
- coatis
- boat-billed heron
- black iguana

For information on these and other species, *see* the Wildlife & Plant Glossary *in* Understanding Costa Rica, at the back of the book.

Sloth

TIPS

- Hire a guide—you'll walk away with a basic understanding of the flora and fauna and see things you probably would have missed otherwise. Hire one at the local guide association next to the Mono Loco Restaurant (☎ 2777–5194) for $10 per hour per person.

- Beware of *manzanillo* trees (indicated by warning signs)—their leaves, bark, and applelike fruit secrete a gooey substance that irritates the skin.

- Get here as early as possible—between 7 and 8 AM is ideal. Rangers permit only 600 to 800 people inside at a time, and during peak season visitors line up to enter. Early morning is also the best time to see animals. Avoid weekends and major holidays, particularly around Christmas and the week before Easter, when the park is packed.

- Camping is not allowed in the park, and there are no lodges or food.

- Park beaches do not have lifeguards, but that doesn't mean that swimming is always safe.

A FRAGILE BEAUTY

Deforestation, development, cattle ranching, pollution, and tourism place environmental stress on the park. Tourism brings in enough revenue for the federal government to sustain the park, but the majority of the money goes to fund social programs. The major problems facing Manuel Antonio today are:

- Hotel and resort development that encroaches on natural wildlife corridors and traps animals within the park, diminishing their gene pool and threatening biodiversity

- Endangered squirrel-monkey population

- Solid-waste pollution

- Overwhelming growth that outruns development of infrastructure to handle it

- Lax regulations, corruption of park management, and poor relationship between the park and the municipality

PARK INFO

Hours of Operation: Tuesday–Sunday 7–4. Closed Monday.

Contacts: 2777–5185

Admission: $10

Getting There: From San José, 3 hours by car, 4 hours by bus, or a 30-minute flight to Quepos, then 25 minutes by car. Entrance at the end of the main road from Quepos. Parking is less than $2. ■**TIP→** The park entrance is across a shallow estuary that is so deep when the tide is high that you have to pay a boatman (less than $1) to ferry you across it.

HOW MUCH TIME? A few hours is sufficient to tour the short trails and see some wild animals, but we recommend an entire day that includes lounging on the beaches, and/or hiking the challenging trails toward Puerto Escondido.

and fine-dining restaurants, surrounded by rain forest with amazing views of the beaches and offshore islands. The only problem with staying in one of those hotels is that you'll need to drive or take public transportation to and from the main beach and national park, about 10 minutes away. More hotel and restaurant options are available at the bottom of the hill, within walking distance of the beach, but they lack the sweeping view.

Manuel Antonio is a very gay-friendly town. Many hotels and bars cater to gay travelers, and all of them offer a warm welcome to anyone walking in the door. The area doesn't especially cater to budget travelers, but there are a few cheap places near the end of the road, and various mid-range lodging options.

GETTING HERE

Manuel Antonio is a 15-minute drive over the hill from Quepos and 25 minutes from the Quepos airport. Between SANSA and NatureAir, there are 10 flights per day linking San José and Quepos, as well as direct flights between Quepos and other tourist destinations. Buses depart from San José's Coca-Cola bus station for Manuel Antonio three times a day, at 6 AM, 12 PM, and 6 PM, traveling the opposite direction at 6 AM, 12 PM, and 5 PM; they pick up and drop off passengers in front of hotels on the main Quepos–Manuel Antonio road. Gray Line offers door-to-door service to and from San José, Jacó, Monteverde, Arenal, and major North Pacific beaches. The trip from San José takes about three and a half hours by car or bus. A local public bus makes the 20-minute trip from Quepos to Manuel Antonio every half hour from 7 to 7, then hourly until 10 PM.

MANUEL ANTONIO ESSENTIALS

Bank/ATM Banco Proamerica (⊠ *Main road, next to Economy Rent A Car*).

Pharmacy Farmacia Manuel Antonio (⊠ *Main road, across from Marlin Restaurant* ☎ *2777–5370*). **Farmacia La Económica** (⊠ *Main road, across from soccer field* ☎ *2777–2130*).

Internet Cantina Internet (⊠ *Main road, across from Costa Verde* ☎ *2777–0548*). **Sí Como No Internet** (⊠ *Main road, inside Regalame Art Gallery* ☎ *2777–0777*).

Taxis Taxi services (☎ *2777–0425, 2777–0734, or 2777–1693*).

EXPLORING

As the road approaches the national park, it skirts the lovely, forest-lined beach of **Playa Espadilla,** which stretches for more than a mile north from the rocky crag that marks the park's border to the base of the ridge that holds most of the hotels. One of the most popular beaches in Costa Rica, Playa Espadilla fills up with sunbathers, surfers, volleyball players, strand strollers, and sand-castle architects on dry-season weekends and holidays, but for most of the year it is surprisingly quiet. Even on the busiest days it is long enough to provide an escape from the crowd, which tends to gather around the restaurants and lounge chairs near its southern end. Though it is often safe for swimming, beware of rough seas, which create deadly rip currents. Near the northern end of Playa Espadilla is a rocky ridge that separates the main beach from a short, secluded beach called **Playitas,** which has a decent surf break, and is the area's nude beach.

☙ **Fincas Naturales,** a former teak plantation, has been reforested to allow native trees to spring back among the not-so-native ones. A footpath winds through part of the 30-acre tropical forest, and naturalist guides do a good job of explaining the local ecology and identifying birds. The reserve is home to three kinds of monkeys, as well as iguanas, motmots, toucans, tanagers, and seed-chomping rodents called agoutis. Guided walks are given throughout the day: the first starts at 6:30 AM for bird-watching, then at 9 AM and 1 PM, plus a nighttime jungle trek that departs at 5:30 PM. The quickest and least expensive tour is an hourly walk through displays on butterflies, reptiles, and amphibians. Unfortunately, you can't explore the reserve at your own pace. ✉ *Entrance across street from Sí Como No Hotel* ☎ *2777–0850* ⊕ *www.butterflygardens.co.cr* ✂ *$20–$45, kids under 12 $10–$35, depending on the tour* ⊙ *Daily 7 AM–6 PM.*

> **IN THE THICK OF IT**
>
> There's more rain forest on private land than in Manuel Antonio National Park, which means it's not unusual to see many of the animals the park is famous for from the balcony of your hotel room or from your breakfast table. It also means that local landowners play an important role in conserving the area's flora and fauna.

OUTDOOR ACTIVITIES

Manuel Antonio's list of outdoor activities is almost endless. Tours generally range from $40 to $90 per person and can be booked through your hotel's reception desk or directly through the outfitter. During the rainy season, some outdoor options might lose their appeal, but clouds usually let loose in the afternoon, so take advantage of sunny mornings.

★ **Tití Canopy Tours** (☎ 2777–3130) has a relatively slow-paced zip-line tour ($55) through a forest reserve that is contiguous with the national park. Guides go above and beyond to make you feel comfortable and safe, and will help you spot animals.

TOUR OPERATORS A small company run by friendly young locals with a good grasp of the area's activities, **Espadilla Tours** (☎ 2777–5334 ✉ arellysmonge@yahoo.com) can arrange any kind of activity in the Manuel Antonio area, from surf lessons to sunset sails. The Internet café next to the Marlin Restaurant has information.

HIKING Highly visited Manuel Antonio National Park is the obvious place to go, but in private reserves like Fincas Naturales *(⇨above)* and Rainmaker *(⇨Quepos, above)* you can also gain a rich appreciation of the local forests' greenery and wildlife. ■TIP➔ **Bring binoculars!**

HORSEBACK RIDING **Brisas del Nara** (☎ 2779–1235 ⊕ www.horsebacktour.com) takes riders of all ages and levels through the protected Cerro Nara mountain zone,

32 km (20 mi) from Manuel Antonio, and ends with a swim in a natural pool at the foot of a 350-foot waterfall. Full-day tours ($65) include three hours on horseback, with breakfast and lunch included; the ride on the half-day tour ($50) lasts two hours, and there's no lunch. **Finca Valmy Tours** (☎2779–1118 ⊕*www.valmytours.com*) is known for its attentive service and healthy horses. Its six-hour horseback tours take you through the forested mountains above Villa Nueva, east of Manuel Antonio ($65). Lunch and swimming in a pool below a small waterfall on their property are included.

Beach riding is the specialty of **Rancho Savegre** (☎2779–4430 *or* 8834–8687 ✍*diegosolis@racsa.co.cr*). Run by two cowboy hat–wearing brothers, trips set out from a cattle ranch about 15 minutes south of Manuel Antonio and include a stop at a waterfall for swimming or trail walking. Of the two half-day tours, only the morning tour includes a meal.

KAYAKING **Iguana Tours** (☎2777–2052 ⊕*www.iguanatours.com*) runs sea-kayaking trips ($65) to the islands of Manuel Antonio National Park—which require some experience when the seas are high—and a mellower paddle through the mangrove estuary of Isla Damas, where you might see monkeys, crocodiles, and various birds.

SNORKELING AND DIVING The islands that dot the sea in front of Manuel Antonio are surrounded by volcanic rock reefs that are dotted with small coral formations and attract schools of snapper, jacks, barracudas, rays, sea turtles, moray eels, and other marine life. **Manuel Antonio Divers** (☎2777–3483 ⊕*www.manuelantoniodivers.com*) offers two-tank dives ($95) at half a dozen spots offshore where an array of fish and other marine life congregate around volcanic rocks. Full-day trips to Caño Island ($200), a 90-minute boat trip away, as well as snorkeling excursions ($60) to the Islas Gemelas, complement the complete selection of PADI certification courses they provide. **Oceans Unlimited** (☎2777–3171 ⊕*www.oceansunlimitedcr.com*) offers various offshore sites, an all-day diving excursion to Caño Island ($95–$200), PADI certification courses, and snorkeling. Several tour operators in town can put you on an organized snorkel excursion to the calm waters of Biesanz Beach.

SWIMMING When the surf is up, riptides are a dangerous problem on Playa Espadilla, Manuel Antonio's main beach, which runs parallel to the road to the park's entrance. For a less turbulent swim and smaller crowds, head to **Playa Biesanz** (✉*Near Hotel Parador*), which lies within a sheltered cove and also has good snorkeling. Manuel Antonio's safest swimming area is sheltered **Playa Manuel Antonio,** the second beach in the national park. Its white sand makes it attractive for lounging around, and it's also a good place for snorkeling. ■TIP➔**Never leave your valuables unattended while you're swimming.**

ULTRALIGHT FLYING **Sky Riders** (*2777–4101* ✍ *skyriders@amnet.co.cr*) has open-cockpit, slow-flying ultralights that glide between sea level and 1,000 feet. One tour is a one-passenger, 24-minute ride over Manuel Antonio and several surrounding beaches ($85). The other is a two-person 35-minute flight over Damas Island's canals and mangroves ($125).

The three white-water rivers in this area have limited seasons. The rains from August to October raise the rivers to their perfect peak. **Río Savegre,** which flows past patches of rain forest, has two navigable stretches: the lower section (Class II–III), which is a mellow trip perfect for neophytes, and the more rambunctious upper section (Class III–IV). It is usually navigable from June to March. **Río Naranjo** (Class III–IV) has a short but exciting run that requires some experience and can be done only from June to December. **Río Parrita** (Class II–III) is a relatively mellow white-water route, and in the dry season it can be navigated only in two-person, inflatable duckies.

Manuel Antonio's original rafting outfitter, **Amigos del Río** (☎2777–1084 ⊕www.adventuremanuelantonio.com), leads trips down the Savegre and Naranjo on full-day and half-day tours ($69–$98). Naranjo River tours can be combined with kayaking in the nearby estuary. **Ríos Tropicales** (☎2777–4092 ⊕www.h2ocr.com), the biggest rafting outfitter in the country, runs kayaking excursions and rafting trips on the Savegre and Naranjo ($70–$98).

WHERE TO EAT

$$$ ✕**Kapi Kapi.** This elegant restaurant at the edge of the forest offers
★   Manuel Antonio's best ambience for dinner, with low lighting, ocher walls, dark hardwoods, and potted palms. The name is a greeting in the indigenous Maleku language, but the menu is the cosmopolitan invention of a Californian chef. It includes such un-Costa Rican start-ers as a lemongrass, chicken, coconut soup and "seafood cigars"—a mix of fresh tuna, shrimp, and mahimahi deep fried in an egg-roll wrapper and served on a cabbage salad. The main courses include such Asian-inspired dishes as prawns with a tamarindo-coconut-rum glaze and macadamia-encrusted mahimahi with a plum chili sauce. Only in dessert does the chef reveal his nationality, with the chocolate s'more cake. ⊠*East side of main road, across from Pacífico Colonial condos* ☎2777–5049 ⚐*Reservations essential* ▤*MC, V* ⊗*No lunch.*

$$$ ✕**Restaurante Mar Luna.** Easy to overlook, this simple blue wooden res-taurant propped on the hillside is often packed. The decor is limited to illuminated plastic fish, ceramic mobiles, potted palms, and colorful tablecloths, but the restaurant has a pleasant view of treetops and the sea below. The fresh seafood, caught each morning by one of the cooks, is what draws the crowd. You might start with sashimi or seafood soup, and move on to one of the popular entrées: grilled tuna with peppers and onions, lobster in a brandy sauce, the humongous mariscada—a sautéed seafood platter for two—or one of the surf-and-turf options. They have live Latin music Thursday to Saturday, and a small bamboo bar in front. ⊠*East side of road, 100 m north of Manuel Antonio Elementary School* ☎2777–5107 ▤*AE, MC, V* ⊗*No lunch.*

$$–$$$ ✕**Agua Azul.** This simple second-floor restaurant with a small kitchen
★   in one corner offers a breathtaking view by day and a deliciously inven-tive selection of seafood at night. The lunch menu is strong on salads and sandwiches, but the dinner options include some of the best entrées in town. In addition to nightly fish and pasta specials, they offer such inventive delicacies as seared tuna over a tequila-and-lime cucumber

Getting Married in Costa Rica

Couples long ago discovered that Costa Rica's rain forests, volcanoes, beaches, and sunsets make the country a prime honeymoon destination. A growing number are deciding to start that honeymoon early and tie the knot here as well.

First the marriage legalities:

■ Any two people of the opposite sex at least 18 years old may marry in Costa Rica.

■ Your passport must have at least six months' remaining validity.

■ Your witnesses, who may not be your relatives, must meet the same requirements.

■ You need to demonstrate that any former marriage is no longer in effect by providing a copy of a divorce decree or death certificate of a prior spouse; a Costa Rican consulate in the country where those documents were issued must translate them into Spanish and notarize them.

Judges, attorneys, and Catholic priests have legal authority to certify a marriage in Costa Rica. While the law provides for complete freedom of religion, it grants the Catholic Church special "state church" status, meaning that if you have an official other than a Catholic priest preside over your service, a lawyer or judge will have to make it legal, either at the ceremony or at his or her office later. The priest (in a Catholic ceremony), a lawyer, or a judge will register the marriage with the Civil Registry and your own embassy. The license takes three months to issue and is sent to your home address. Virtually all Western countries recognize the legality of a Costa Rican marriage.

While the country offers no shortage of impressive backdrops for a ceremony, the Central Pacific coast sees the most tourist weddings, hands down. (May and June are the most popular months.) Manuel Antonio's Makanda by the Sea, La Mariposa, and Sí Como No and Punta Leona's Villa Caletas are among the many lodgings here with events staff well versed in planning ceremonies and tending to the legalities. You need only say, "I do." Private wedding planner **Tropical Occasions** (☎ 2249–0773 or 8810–7216 in U.S. ⊕ www.tropicaloccasions. com) has more than 450 weddings under its belt. It has also arranged same-sex commitment ceremonies, although Costa Rican law does not recognize these as legally binding.

---

salad, calamari sautéed with capers and olives, and coconut-crusted mahimahi. ⊠ *Main road, above the Villas del Parque office* ☎ 2777–5280 ⊟ V ☉ *Closed Wed. and Oct.*

$$–$$$ ╳ **Barba Roja.** Near the top of the hill, with a sweeping view of the sea and jungle, pirate-theme "Red Beard" is one of this town's original restaurants. Hardwoods furnish the open-air dining room and the sunset deck on the ridge below. The view, which is most impressive at sunset and equally good from any seat in the house, compensates for the sparse decor. The food and service here have had their ups and downs over the years, but the current Mexican-American managers seem to have a good team. Their extensive menu includes mahimahi with a light coconut curry in a banana leaf, red snapper à la Azteca (in a spicy tomato sauce), and a Moroccan seafood couscous. Meat lovers can sink their incisors into rack of lamb with green olives, beef tenderloin with a béarnaise sauce, or barbecued ribs. The bar fills up for a sunset happy hour, and the place becomes a dance club after dinner on Saturday. ⊠ *Main road to park, across from Hotel Divisamar, on right* ☎ 2777–0331 ⊟ *MC, V* ⊘ *No lunch.*

$–$$$ ✕ **Sunspot Bar and Grill.** The open-air, poolside restaurant of the exclu-
★   sive Makanda by the Sea hotel has tables beneath purple cloth tents overlooking the sea and surrounding jungle. Its kitchen, cleverly hidden beneath the bar, serves up such succulent treats as jumbo shrimp in a ginger sauce and grilled beef tenderloin with a choice of sauces. The menu also includes poultry, lamb, and pasta dishes, along with nightly specials. At lunch they offer great pizzas, salads, and sandwiches. You'll want to put on insect repellent at night. ⊠ *Makanda by the Sea hotel* ✚ *1 km (½ mi) west of La Mariposa* ☎ 2777–0442 ⚐ *Reservations essential* ⊟ *AE, DC, MC V.*

$$ ✕ **Anaconda Restaurant.** Named for the humongous snake whose skin is mounted on the wall behind the bar, this open-air restaurant is hidden in the rain forest. You won't see any anacondas (they are found in South America), but you may spot iguanas, squirrel monkeys, or various species of birds from one of the restaurant's oversize chairs. You are sure to enjoy the view of the coast. The eclectic menu ranges from Japanese-style tuna to Tuscan mahimahi. They also serve excellent pastas and salads. The restaurant is a short drive from the beach, making it an excellent option for a quiet lunch. ⊠ *Costa Verde Hotel* ☎ 2777–1973 ⊟ *AE, DC, MC, V.*

$$ ✕ **Hotel Vela Bar Restaurant.** This small, open-air restaurant retains an intimate atmosphere behind a hedge of tropical foliage and beneath a conical thatch roof. They serve a variety of dishes in generous proportions, including mahimahi with an array of sauces, shrimp with ginger, and pork chops in pineapple sauce. There are vegetarian options as well. Service can be slow when it gets busy. ⊠ *Up road from Marlin Restaurant* ☎ 2777–0413 ⊟ *AE, DC, MC, V.*

$–$$ ✕ **Ronny's Place.** A spectacular sunset view and friendly, attentive service are this simple, open-air restaurant's best qualities. The small menu includes such typical Tico dishes as *sopa negra* (black-bean soup), ceviche, shrimp and fish on a skewer, and filet mignon wrapped with bacon and topped with a mushroom sauce. Ronny's is somewhat secluded down a long dirt road that crosses a green valley on a narrow ridge in front of the sea. ✚ *1 km (½ mi) west of main road, down dirt road across from Amigos del Río* ☎ 2777–5120 ⊟ *AE, DC, MC, V.*

$–$$ ✕ **Marlin Restaurant.** The outdoor tables of this two-story concrete restaurant are pretty much always full, owing to its location on Manuel Antonio's busiest corner, across the street from the beach. It's a convenient place to grab breakfast after an early-morning hike through the park—be it banana pancakes or a *típico,* with eggs and *gallo pinto* (black beans and rice). The lunch and dinner menu ranges from the ubiquitous *arroz con pollo* (rice with chicken) to tenderloin with french fries, and jumbo shrimp in garlic and lemon butter, The fresh mahimahi and tuna are always a good bet. ⊠ *Main road, south of the hill, on*

5

corner across from bus stop and beach ☎2777–1134 ▤AE, DC, MC, V ☺Breakfast served.

$ ✕**Café Milagro.** The only place in town that serves its own fresh-roasted coffee, Café Milagro is a colorful, cozy choice for breakfast food any time of the day, or to satisfy a chocolate-chip-cookie craving. The North American menu includes bagels, breakfast burritos, baked goods like brownies and muffins, an inventive selection of sandwiches, and a fruit plate with granola. Tables on the front porch overlook the road, but there's also seating in the back garden. ⊠Main road to park, across from La Mariposa ☎2777–0794 ▤AE, DC, MC, V ☺No dinner.

$ ✕**Salsipuedes.** This colorful, friendly tapas bar nestled behind a rock formation at the edge of the forest has one of the best sunset views in town, making it a great cocktail and appetizer option. The tapas are fun to share, three to five per couple, according to how hungry you are. They range from sashimi and grilled tuna or mahimahi to fajitas. Such Costa Rican favorites as frijolitos blancos (white beans stewed with chicken) and chicharrones con yuca (fried pork and cassava root) are also available. They offer half a dozen full dinners, including larger cuts of fish, and some rice and pasta dishes, plus they're willing to turn any of the tapas dishes into a full meal. ⊠ Main road, across from Banco Proamerica ☎2777–5091 ▤MC, V ☺Closed Tues. No lunch.

WHERE TO STAY

$$$$ 🏨**Makanda by the Sea.** Hypnotic views of the jungle-framed Pacific
Fodor's Choice Ocean make this secluded rain-forest retreat perfect for honeymooners.
★ The bright, spacious, white-and-cream villas are among the country's most tasteful (and expensive). They have a comfortable seating area and king-size bed facing the sliding glass doors that lead to large balconies with ocean views and hammocks. The modern kitchens won't be necessary for breakfast, which is delivered to your room. Windows behind the bed maximize natural light, and the small Japanese-style garden out back adds to the subtle, well-designed touches. The smaller studios are darker, and have less impressive views, but they have access to the lovely, colorful pool and the Sunspot Bar and Grill (⇨above), one of the best restaurants in town. Adventurous hikers can make the 20-minute trek through the jungle to a tiny, private beach. **Pros:** Secluded, tranquil, surrounded by nature, ocean views. **Con:** Far from beach. ✛1 km (½ mi) west of La Mariposa ✉Apdo. 29, Quepos ☎2777–0442, 888/625–2632 in North America ☎2777–1032 ⊕www.makanda.com ☞6 villas, 5 studios ⚖In-room: safe, kitchen, Ethernet. In-hotel: restaurant, room service, pool, beachfront, no elevator, laundry service, concierge, public Internet, no kids under 16 ▤AE, DC, MC, V ⧄BP.

$$$–$$$$ 🏨**Arenas Del Mar.** Nestled between the rain forest and the sea at the
Fodor's Choice north end of Playa Espadilla, this charming and environmentally
★ friendly hotel is one of the few places in Manuel Antonio that combine ocean views with convenient beach access. Rooms in three-story buildings, on a bluff, or a hillside behind the beach, are tastefully decorated with cane and wicker furniture, and have wide porches overlooking the sea or forest. Details such as hand-carved doors with images of local wildlife, colorful tile showers, ceramic vases, and paintings of tropical

flora add to their charm. Suites have pull-out beds in the living room and extra-large terraces with Jacuzzis; a suite and superior room can be combined as an apartment that sleeps up to six. The main restaurant ($$–$$$) serves Caribbean cuisine with an ocean view; a beachfront bar serves light lunches; and there are two pools, one of which is a short walk from the surf; and a full spa. The hotel is surrounded by a 10-acre, private forest reserve where guests can see plenty of wildlife, and the management has taken pains to make the place sustainable through recycling, solar energy, sewage treatment, training of staff, and other means. **Pros:** Beachfront, lovely rooms, environmentally sustainable, wildlife. **Con:** On a popular nude beach. *+2 km (1 mi) southwest of La Mariposa, veer left.* 2777–2777 *www.arenasdelmar.com* *18 rooms, 20 suites In-room: safe, refrigerator, Wi-Fi. In-hotel: 2 restaurants, room service, bars, pools, spa, beachfront, water sports, no elevator, laundry service, concierge, public Wi-Fi, no-smoking rooms AE, DC, MC, V BP.*

$$$–$$$$
Fodor'sChoice
★

La Mariposa. The best view in town—a sweeping panorama of verdant hills, the aquamarine ocean, and offshore islands—is Mariposa's claim to fame. A confusing array of accommodations ranges from standard rooms overlooking the rain forest to bright suites with ocean-view balconies, to a penthouse. All are spacious, and are located in a series of buildings between the jungle and gardens ablaze with colorful flowers. The four-story main building holds the lobby and restaurant, above which are three floors of ocean-view rooms reached by external spiraling stairways, which aren't for people who have trouble with stairs, or who suffer from vertigo. They are big, though rather plain, and have semiprivate balconies with amazing views; book a bright corner room on an upper floor (Nos. 31, 35, 36, or 40). Older ocean-view rooms on the hillside have low ceilings, Spanish decor, and big balconies overlooking the coast and park. Newer standard ocean-views, down the hill, have lesser vistas, but TV sets. Larger premier rooms offer more privacy, great views, and have day beds for kids (under 10 free), though the modern, new units suffer design flaws. The sundeck and wraparound pool are lovely. Transportation is provided to and from the beach, 4 km (2½ mi) away, several times a day. **Pros:** Gorgeous views, decent restaurant, central location. **Cons:** Two miles from beach, ocean-view balconies separated by cane barriers. ✉ *West of main road, right after Barba Roja* *Apdo. 4, Quepos* 2777–0355, 800/572–6440 *in U.S.* 2777–0050 *www.hotelmariposa.com* *60 rooms In-room: safe, kitchen (some), no TV, Ethernet. In-hotel: restaurant, room service, bars, pools, no elevator, laundry service, concierge, public Wi-Fi AE, DC, MC, V BP.*

$$$–$$$$
★
☾

Hotel Sí Como No. This luxury resort goes to great lengths to be eco-friendly, and has earned a level-four Certificate of Sustainable Tourism (level five is the highest). It's also quite family-friendly, with a separate kids' pool, complete with waterslide, and an in-house cinema. Rooms of varying sizes (and prices) are in two-story buildings scattered through the rain forest, decorated in earth tones to complement the surrounding nature. Spring for a spacious deluxe room for a sea view, which you can enjoy from your private balcony. Smaller "superior"

5

rooms, in the ground floors, have less impressive views, whereas standard rooms view the forest. There is live music nightly at the Claro Que Sí restaurant (dinner only; $$$), which specializes in Caribbean-style seafood, and the Rico Tico ($$) grill, which serves lighter fare. A free shuttle makes scheduled trips to the beach, about two miles away. **Pros:** Friendly, nice views, environmentally sustainable, good restaurants. **Cons:** Two miles from beach, standards overpriced, several suites too close to road. ⊠ *Road to park, just after Villas Nicolás, right-hand side* 🕾 *2777–0777* 📠 *2777–1093* ⊕ *www.sicomono.com* 📮 *38 rooms, 19 suites* ⛄ *In-room: safe, kitchen (some), refrigerator, no TV. In-hotel: 2 restaurants, bars, pools, spa, no elevator, laundry service, concierge, public Wi-Fi* ⊟ *AE, MC, V* ⊙| *BP.*

$$$ 🏨 **El Mango Moon.** This B&B's intimate atmosphere and hospitable staff make you feel like you're staying with a friend rather than at a hotel. The comfy, open living-room area extends to a balcony lined with a wooden counter and stools with views to the mango-shape pool below and a tranquil cove framed by the rain forest. The cream-color rooms vary in size and amenities; more expensive rooms have semiprivate balconies. Rooms on the top floor can connect for families. Monkey-attracting mango trees surround the building, and a steep 20-minute trail leads to a secluded beach. **Pros:** Nice view, tranquil area, friendly. **Cons:** Far from main beaches, not much privacy, some rooms dark, relatively expensive. ⊠ *Between La Mariposa and Makanda* 🕾 *2777–5323* 📠 *2777–5128* ⊕ *www.mangomoon.net* 📮 *9 rooms, 2 suites* ⛄ *In-room: no phone. In-hotel: restaurant, bar, pool, no elevator, no kids under 12, no-smoking rooms* ⊟ *AE, MC, V* ⊙| *BP.*

$$–$$$ 🏨 **Costa Verde.** You're likely to see monkeys, iguanas, and all kinds of
★ birds on the forest trails surrounding this extensive hotel's buildings, which are scattered on both sides of the main road. Adult-only studios are spacious, with large balconies and screened walls that let the breeze through. Those in the other buildings are smaller, but are air-conditioned. Splurge for a "Studio-Plus," which all have ocean views. Three fully equipped bungalows are also available for groups of up to six. The cheaper "efficiencies" are a mixed lot—only those in building D, in the jungle overlooking the sea, are recommended; buildings B and C aren't. The hotel's Anaconda Restaurant (⇨ *above*) is excellent. The dinner-only La Cantina ($$), across the street, serves good grilled meats and seafood, and has live music. **Pros:** Great ocean views, wildlife, restaurants, studios and building D efficiencies a good value. **Cons:** Most efficiencies suffer road noise, no beach access, service inconsistent. ⊠ *Road to park, south side of hill, on left* 🕾 *2777–0584, 2777–0187, or 866/854–7958* 📠 *2777–0560* ⊕ *www.costaverde.com* 📮 *10 efficiencies, 29 studios, 3 bungalows* ⛄ *In-room: no a/c (some), no phone (some), kitchen. In-hotel: 2 restaurants, bars, pools, no elevator laundry service, public Internet* ⊟ *AE, MC, V* ⊙| *EP.*

$$–$$$ 🏨 **Hotel Playa Espadilla.** A short walk from the beach, this friendly hotel
☻ spreads across grounds bordered on two sides by the tall trees of Manuel Antonio National Park, and it has a trail through an area of the park that few people visit. The simple but spacious mint-green rooms with big windows are housed in two-story buildings surrounded by

green lawns; for a bit more money, some rooms have good-size kitchens with modern appliances. A small blue-tile pool and patio have a pleasant adjacent bar area with a billiard table. Directly behind are a large, open-air restaurant and a tennis court, but there are better places to dine in the area. **Pros:** Surrounded by forest, close to beach. **Con:** Service inconsistent. ✉ *150 m up side road from Marlin Restaurant, first left* ☎ *2777–0903* 🖷 *2777–5052* ⊕ *www.espadilla.com* ⬅ *16 rooms* ⚲ *In-room: safe, kitchen (some), Wi-Fi. In-hotel: restaurant, room service, bar, tennis court, pool, no elevator, laundry service, public Wi-Fi, no-smoking rooms* ▭ *AE, DC, MC, V* ¹⊙¹*BP.*

\$\$–\$\$\$

Fodor'sChoice

★

🏨 **Villas Nicolás.** On a hillside about 3 km (2 mi) from the beach, terraced Mediterranean-style villas have impressive views. Villas on the upper levels have ocean views, while those on the lower level overlook the jungle, where you may spot monkeys, iguanas and an array of birds. (Avoid units 1 and 2, which overlook the hotel next door.) Each room is decorated differently, but the predominant motif is tropical. Most have balconies, some of which are large enough to hold a table, chairs, and hammock. Narrow walkways wind through this tranquil property's lush grounds to the villas and blue-tile pool. During the high season a tiny restaurant by the pool offers breakfasts and light meals. ✉ *Road to park, across from Hotel Byblos* ✑ *Apdo. 236, Quepos* ☎ *2777–0481* 🖷 *2777–0451* ⊕ *www.villasnicolas.com* ⬅ *19 villas* ⚲ *In-room: no a/c (some), safe, kitchen (some), refrigerator, no TV. In-hotel: pool, no elevator, laundry service, no-smoking rooms* ▭ *AE, DC, MC, V* ¹⊙¹*EP.*

\$\$

☪

🏨 **Cabinas Espadilla.** Owned by the same family that runs the nearby Hotel Playa Espadilla, these quiet cabinas close to the beach are more affordable but have fewer amenities. Rooms open onto porches overlooking tropical gardens and a wide lawn, shaded by hammock-strung palm trees, and a large pool. The rooms with kitchenettes cost \$10 more, but are a bit cramped. Guests have access to the hotel's restaurant, tennis court, and forest trail. **Pros:** Good value, short walk from beach, nice grounds. **Cons:** Mediocre rooms, not very friendly. ✉ *On road beside Marlin Restaurant* ☎ *2777–2113* ⊕ *www.espadilla.com* ⬅ *16 cabinas* ⚲ *In-room: no phone, safe, kitchen (some), refrigerator, no TV. In-hotel: pool, no elevator, laundry service* ▭ *AE, MC, V* ¹⊙¹*EP.*

\$\$

☪

🏨 **Hotel Inn on the Park.** This family-friendly inn has a quiet location near the beach and national park. The papaya-color building has three floors with two rooms each. Half are master suites with separate bedrooms, kitchens, and pull-out couches, which can be a deal for small families (kids under 12 are free). Upper rooms share balconies with verdant views. A small pool area with a wooden deck has a grill and tables where complimentary Continental breakfast is served. The rain forest rises up just behind it. **Pro:** Good for families. **Con:** No frills. ✉ *200 m up side road from Marlin Restaurant* ☎ *2777–5115 or 2777–5232* 🖷 *2777–3468* ⊕ *www.innontheparkhotel.com* ⬅ *6 rooms* ⚲ *In-room: safe, kitchen (some). In-hotel: pool, no elevator, laundry service, public Internet, no-smoking rooms* ¹⊙¹*CP.*

$$ Hotel Verde Mar. This whimsical little hotel and its helpful staff are in the rain forest, with direct access to the beach and minutes away from the park. The rooms in a long two-story concrete building are on the small side, with one queen bed, but have colorfully artistic interiors, kitchenettes, and large windows with views of the ubiquitous tropical foliage. Suites are a bit bigger than standard rooms and have two queen beds and a walk-in closet. There's a small pool, from which a wooden catwalk leads through the woods to the beach. **Pros:** Good value, mere steps from beach, in forest, friendly. **Cons:** Rooms smallish, very basic. ⊕ ½ km (¼ mi) north of park 🕾 2777–1805 🖷 2777–1311 ⊕ www. verdemar.com ☞ 22 rooms ঌ In-room: no phone, safe, kitchen (some), no TV. In-hotel: pool, no elevator, public Internet, no-smoking rooms ☰ AE, DC, MC, V ⫶ EP.

$$**   La Posada. Nestled on the edge of the national park, this cluster of bungalows is also just a short walk from the beach. Each bungalow has its own name—Fisherman's Wharf, Birds of Paradise, Jungle—and is decorated accordingly. The palm-thatch terraces face the small pool and lush greenery of the rain forest, which is regularly animated by troops of squirrel monkeys and other animals. As the charming North American owner, Michael, says, it's as close as you'll get to sleeping in the park. The main building holds three spacious apartments and a fully equipped casita (small house) on the second floor with two bedrooms, two baths, and a futon. Complimentary breakfast and cheap pizza are served in a small restaurant ($) in front. **Pros: Good value, near beach and park, wildlife, friendly. **Con:** A bit isolated. ✉ 250 m up side road from Marlin Restaurant ⊕ Apdo. 155–6350, Quepos 🕾🕾 2777–1446 ⊕ www.laposadajungle.com ☞ 4 bungalows, 3 apartments, 1 casita ঌ In-room: no phone, safe, refrigerator. In-hotel: pool, no elevator, laundry service, no-smoking rooms ☰ MC, V ⫶ BP.

$$ Villas de la Selva. Hidden from the main road behind a mural of monkeys, this unique hillside hotel has comfortable accommodations and great views of the ocean. Straight down the long stairway, and perched on a cliff facing the ocean, are three airy rooms, each with its own color scheme, kitchenette, and ample terrace. There's also a casita that fits several people. Up the side of the hill, two much smaller rooms with balconies have nice views, but tiny bathrooms. A 300-meter trail leads to the beach. **Pros:** Nice views, beach access, good value. **Cons:** Unfriendly owner, not much privacy. ✉ Road to park, past Costa Verde and La Arboleda hotels 🕾 2777–1137 🖷 2777–1018 ⊕ www.villasdelaselva.com ☞ 7 rooms, 1 casita ঌ In-room: no a/c (some), no phone, safe (some), kitchen (some), refrigerator. In-hotel: pool, no elevator, laundry service ☰ MC, V ⫶ EP.

¢–$$ Hotel Manuel Antonio. One of Manuel Antonio's original hotels, this economical place is close to the national park entrance and across the street from the beach. The rooms, in two-story cement buildings, have tile floors, simple pastel drapes and bedspreads, and large balconies or terraces, many of which have ocean views. Unfortunately, the ocean view is often obstructed by souvenir vendors' stalls and cars lining the road. The rooms are comfortable but not fancy, equipped with air-conditioning and cable TV, and just steps away from the beach and park.

Backpackers can stay in one of the rustic wooden rooms above the restaurant, which lack air-conditioning and TV, but are a third of the price. **Pros:** Near beach, park, a real bargain. **Cons:** Busy area on weekends, service inconsistent. ☒*End of road to park* ☎*2777–1237 or 2777–1351* ☒*2777–5172* ✑ *hotelmanuelantonio@racsa.co.cr* ➳*28 rooms* ⟲*In-room: safe. In-hotel: restaurant, room service, bar, no elevator, laundry service, no-smoking rooms* ▤*AE, MC, V* ⊙*EP.*

¢–$ ▦ **Hotel Vela Bar.** Abutting the jungle not far from Playa Espadilla, this
★ low-key, eclectic hotel has small but attractive rooms and very competitive rates. Though a bit cramped, each room has its own rustic charm, with white stucco walls, simple wooden furniture, and terracotta tile or wood floors. Room 7 is particularly nice, thanks to large windows and a bathtub. Shared front terraces with rocking chairs and hammocks overlook lush gardens. Two bungalows with private patios, air-conditioning, and TV sleep four. The restaurant, under a conical thatch roof in front, serves an eclectic mix of seafood and meat dishes with an array of sauces. ☒*Up road from Marlin Restaurant, on left* ☎*2777–0413* ☒*2777–1071www.velabar.com* ➳*8 rooms, 2 bungalows, 1 apt* ⟲*In-room: no a/c (some), no phone, safe, kitchen (some), refrigerator (some), no TV (some). In-hotel: restaurant, bar, no elevator, public Internet* ▤*AE, DC, MC, V* ⊙*EP.*

¢ ▦ **Cabinas Piscis.** A short walk through the woods from the beach, this tranquil hotel shaded by tall trees is one of the area's best options for budget travelers. Most rooms are in a concrete building with a wide porch; they are simple but spacious, with small bathrooms and lots of windows. The tiny, lower-price rooms that share a separate, cold-water bathhouse are marketed to backpackers. Also available are a separate cabin with a refrigerator, and an open-room, fully equipped *casita* for four. A small restaurant serves breakfast and light lunches. Bathrooms do not have hot water. **Pros:** Forested property on the beach, inexpensive. **Cons:** Spartan rooms, soft beds. ☒*Road to park, just past Hotel Karahe* ☎*2777–5320* ☒*2777–0046* ➳*15 rooms, 10 with bath; 1 casita; 1 cabin* ⟲*In-room: no a/c, no phone, no TV. In-hotel: no elevator* ▤*MC, V* ⊙*EP.*

NIGHTLIFE

BARS The **Billfish Bar** (☒*Main road, across from Barba Roja* ☎*2777–0411*), with large-screen TVs and pool tables, fills up on game nights.

★ **Salsipuedes** (☒*Main road, north of Barba Roja* ☎*2777–5019*), a colorful tapas bar hidden behind tropical foliage, is a great sunset venue. It's one of the few places you can enjoy a quiet drink.

DANCE CLUB **Barba Roja** (☒*Main road, across from Hotel Divisamar* ☎*2777–0331*) has a popular sunset happy hour. The bar becomes a dance club late on Saturday night. **Tutu** (☒*Above Gato Negro, Casitas Eclipse* ☎*No phone*) is Manuel Antonio's late-night gay bar. It's an elegant place, with light reflected off a deep blue pool. **The Lounge** (☒*Main road, above La Hacienda Restaurant* ☎*2777–5143*), is a popular late-night spot, with reggae playing Monday and Wednesday and a mix of Latin rhythms other nights.

SHOPPING

There's no shortage of shopping in this town. The beach near the entrance to the park is lined with a sea of vendors who sell T-shirts, hats, and colorful beach wraps. More authentic handicrafts, like seed jewelry, are sold at night by artisans positioned along the sidewalk in central Manuel Antonio.

La Buena Nota (⊠ *Main road, past Hotel Karahe* ☎2777–1002) has an extensive selection of beachwear, souvenirs, sunscreen, hats, postcards, and English-language books and magazines. **Regalame** (⊠ *Next to Sí Como No Hotel* ☎2777–0777) is primarily an art gallery, with paintings, drawings, pottery, and jewelry by dozens of artists, but it also sells wood handicrafts and other souvenirs.

HIGH-WIRE ACTS

Though the construction of hotels and other buildings has altered the natural landscape, the surrounding forest has largely been left intact. The greatest danger most animals face is the traffic that flows between Quepos and Manuel Antonio, which is why local conservationists have strung ropes over the road between large trees, so that monkeys can cross the street without risking their simian necks. The Association for the Conservation of the Mono Tití (⊕www.ascomoti.org) is working with local landowners to preserve forest corridors for the monkeys between remaining islands of wilderness.

CENTRAL PACIFIC ESSENTIALS

TRANSPORTATION

BY AIR

ARRIVING & DEPARTING

The 30-minute flight between San José and Quepos can save you the three-hour drive or bus trip, which involves a serpentine mountain road. Flights from San José to Tambor take 20 minutes—a fraction of the time it takes to drive to Puntarenas and ferry over, and from here it's a reasonable taxi trip to Montezuma and Malpaís. *For more information about flights between the Central Pacific and San José, see By Air in Costa Rica Essentials.*

BY BUS

ARRIVING & DEPARTING

Buses are very inexpensive and easy to use. From San José to Puntarenas you'll pay about $4, and from San José to Quepos or Manuel Antonio you'll pay about $7. *For more information about bus travel between the Central Pacific and San José, see By Bus in Costa Rica Essentials.*

GETTING AROUND

Local buses are run-down, and the ride might wrack your nerves, especially as they slowly rattle up the hills (sometimes reversing to gain more momentum). Don't sweat it, you'll make it. Not every town has direct buses, so you may have to hop on a connecting bus to get to some destinations. Ask any local or your hotel's reception where the often unmarked bus stop is located; they'll also know what the fare and departure times are.

BY CAR

ARRIVING & DEPARTING From San José the best way to get to the southern tip of Nicoya is to take the Pan-American Highway (CA1) west to Puntarenas (2 hours), and board a car ferry bound for Paquera (1 hour). Take the road to Cóbano, which passes Tambor. Turn left in Cóbano to reach Montezuma (40 minutes), or drive straight to reach Malpaís and Santa Teresa (1 hour).

The quickest way to the Central Pacific coast from San José is to take the Pan-American Highway (CA1) west to the exit for Atenas, where you turn left (south). Once you leave the highway, the road is one lane in each direction for the rest of the route. Between Atenas and Orotina it is steep and full of curves. If you don't have experience in mountain driving, you're better off taking a bus, shuttle van, or flight to the coast. The coastal highway, or Costanera, heads south from Orotina to Tárcoles, Jacó, Hermosa, Bejuco, and Quepos. It is well marked and paved. An asphalt road winds its way over the hill between Quepos and Manuel Antonio National Park. It takes about two and a half hours to drive to Jacó and three to Quepos.

GETTING AROUND It's best to stick with the main rental offices in San José, because they have more cars available and you're more likely to reach an English-speaking agent on the phone; some have local satellite offices. Payless is the best of the local rental companies and has offices in Jacó and Quepos.

Major Rental Agencies **Alamo** (⊠ *Downtown, 50 m south of Korean school, Quepos* ☎ *2777–3344, 800/462–5266 in U.S.* ⊕ *www.alamo.com*). **Budget** (⊠ *Avda. Pastor Diaz, Jacó* ☎ *2643–2665* ⊠ *Centro Comercial Playa Carmen, Malpaís* ☎ *2640–0500* ⊕ *www.budget.com*). **Economy** (⊠ *Avda. Pastor Diaz, Jacó* ☎ *2643–1098* ⊠ *Next to Banca Proamerica, Manuel Antonio* ☎ *2777–5353* ⊕ *www.economycarrental.com*). **National** (⊠ *Avda. Pastor Diaz, Jacó* ☎ *2643–1752* ⊕ *www.nationalcar.com*).

Local Rental Resources **Payless** (⊠ *Avda. Pastor Diaz, Jacó* ☎ *2643–3224* ⊠ *Main road between Quepos and Manuel Antonio, Quepos* ☎ *2777–0115* ⊕ *www.paylesscarrental.com*).

BY SHUTTLE VAN

ARRIVING & DEPARTING A more comfortable, air-conditioned alternative to regular bus service to Montezuma, Tambor, Puntarenas, Punta Leona, Playa Herradura, Jacó, Manuel Antonio, and some destinations in between is the hotel-to-hotel shuttle service offered by Gray Line, which serves Jacó and Manuel Antonio. Prices from San José are $25 to Jacó and $33 to Manuel Antonio, and there are departures every morning and afternoon. You can request that vans to Jacó drop you off at Carara National Park. Vans to Manuel Antonio can drop you off at Playa Hermosa's hotels. There is also once-daily service connecting Jacó and Manuel Antonio to the major North Pacific beaches, Monteverde, and Arenal; rates range from $33 to $43.

Shuttle Van Services **Gray Line** (☎ *2220–2126 or 2643–3231* ⊕ *www.gray linecostarica.com*).

CONTACTS & RESOURCES

Banks, Internet cafés, post offices, and emergency contacts follow each town listing in the chapter.

BANKS & EXCHANGING SERVICES

There are ATMs in Puntarenas, Cóbano, Malpaís, Atenas, Herradura, Jacó, Quepos, and Manuel Antonio that accept either Visa, Master-Card, or both. Ask the receptionist at your hotel where the nearest one is located. In the unlikely event that you come upon an ATM that's out of order, you should be able to find another one nearby. Banks in Jacó, Puntarenas, Herradura, Cóbano, Atenas, Manuel Antonio, and Quepos exchange U.S. dollars, though it's quicker to get Costa Rican currency directly from an ATM. Most hotels, restaurants, tour operators, taxi drivers, gift shops, and supermarkets will accept or change U.S. dollars, though at slightly less than the bank rate. Canadian, Australian, and New Zealand dollars, English pounds, and euros must be exchanged in banks.

INTERNET

There are plenty of Internet cafés in Jacó, Montezuma, Puntarenas, and the Quepos/Manuel Antonio area, and at least one each in Atenas, Tambor, Malpaís, and Playa Hermosa. They charge the equivalent of $1–$3 per hour.

South Pacific

Matapalo Beach

WORD OF MOUTH

"I would recommend the Osa Peninsula for lush rain forests, hiking, beaches (some have strong rip tides, so be sure to ask before swimming . . .), boating activities, and just communing with nature. The Osa is a more remote, pristine destination [than the Arenal area]; definitely more off-the-beaten-path and very special."

—cmerrell

WELCOME TO SOUTH PACIFIC

TOP REASONS TO GO

★ **Enormous Corcovado National Park:** The last refuge of such endangered species as jaguars and tapirs.

★ **Mountain hikes:** Hikes that range from easy daytime treks from luxurious lodges to Costa Rica's toughest: 12,500-foot Cerro Chirripó.

★ **Kayaking:** Head to the Golfo Dulce or along the Sierpe or Colorado rivers' jungly channels.

★ **Bird-watching:** Yields such beauties as scarlet macaws and the resplendent quetzal.

★ **Wild places to stay:** Relax in the top eco-lodges, platform tents on the beach, and mountain retreats.

1 Central Highlands. The main road climbs more than 7,000 feet over mountains and above the clouds of the Central Highlands before descending into the huge Valle de El General agricultural region. Highlights are fabulous mountain lodges and Chirripó National Park.

2 The Coast. The Coast consists of miles of beaches and small beach communities, including unassuming surfer town Dominical.

3 The Osa Peninsula. The wild Osa Peninsula consists almost entirely of Corcovado National Park, 445 square miles of primary and secondary rain forest straight out of a Tarzan film.

4 Golfo Dulce. The eastern Golfo Dulce draws anglers to Golfito, slow-paced beach bums to Zancudo, and serious surfers to Pavones.

Iguana-crossing road sign, Dominical

Howler monkeys, Corcovado National Park

GETTING ORIENTED

The most remote part of Costa Rica, the South Pacific encompasses the southern half of Puntarenas Province and La Amistad National Park. The region descends from mountainous forests just an hour south of San José to the humid Golfo Dulce and the richly forested Osa Peninsula, 8 to 10 hours from the capital by car.

6

Cabagra

La Amistad National Park

Paso Real

237

San Vito

Chacarita

16

245

C2   Río Claro   Ciudad Neily

Piedras Blancas National Park

Golfito

14

Golfo Dulce

Puerto Jiménez

Zancudo

OSA PENINSULA

Conte

Carate

El Higo
Pavones
Punto Banco   Banco

Cabo Matapolo

Pacific Ocean

0 — 15 mi
0 — 20 km

SOUTH PACIFIC PLANNER

When to Go

The May to December rainy season is the worst in the Osa Peninsula, where rains usually last through January, and roads flood and lodges might close in the rainiest months (Oct.–Nov.). Elsewhere, mornings tend to be brilliant and sunny, with rain starting in mid-afternoon. Climate swings wildly in the south, from frigid mountain air to steamy coastal humidity. In the mountains it's normally around 24°C (75°F) during the day and 10°C (50°F) at night, though nighttime temperatures on the upper slopes of Cerro de la Muerte can be close to freezing. Temperatures in coastal areas are usually 24°C–32°C (76°F–90°F), but it's the humidity that does you in.

Driving Tips

The Cerro de la Muerte is often covered with fog in the afternoon. If you're driving, plan to cross the mountains in the morning.

Don't try to cover too much ground. You can't easily hop from one destination in the south to the other. It is impossible to underestimate how long it takes to drive the roads or make transportation connections in this part of the country.

What's Your Beach Style?

Family	Playa Platanares
Relaxation	Playa Zancudo
Water Sports	Ballena Marine Park, Playa Dominical, Playa Pavones
Safe Swim	Playa Platanares, Playa Uvita

What to Do

ACTIVITY	WHERE TO DO IT
Bird-watching	San Gerardo de Dota, Hacienda Barú, San Vito, Corcovado Park
Fishing	Dominical, Ballena Marine Park, Golfito, Playa Zancudo, Puerto Jiménez, Cabo Matapalo
Diving	Ballena Marine Park, Caño Island
Hiking	San Gerardo de Dota, Chirripó Park, Corcovado Park
Snorkeling	Ballena Marine Park, Caño Island
Surfing	Dominical, Playa Pavones, Cabo Matapalo
Whale-watching	Ballena Marine Park, Puerto Jiménez, Drake Bay
Wildlife-viewing	La Amistad Park, Corcovado Park

Choosing a Place to Stay

Expect reasonable comfort in unbelievably wild settings. Small hotels and lodges are run by hands-on owners, many of them foreigners who fell in love with the place on a visit and stayed. Generally speaking, the farther south and more remote the lodge, the more expensive it is. Bad roads (causing supply problems) and lack of electricity and communications make hotel-keeping costly, especially in the Osa Peninsula and Golfo Dulce. But most of these places include meals, transport, and guides in the price.

How Much Time?

You need at least a week to truly experience any part of the Osa Peninsula. Even if you fly, transfers to lodges are slow, so plan two days for travel. Choose one home base and take day trips. In three weeks you can experience the entire Southern Zone: mountains, beaches, and the Osa Peninsula. If you have only a few days you could make a quick mountain sortie from San José to tour the Route of the Saints and go hiking on Cerro de la Muerte.

Recommended Tour Operators

Horizontes Nature Tours (☎2222–2022 ⊕www.horizontes.com) is an expert ecotourist company that can arrange custom tours with excellent naturalist guides and ornithologists.

Costa Rica Expeditions (☎2257–0766 ⊕www.costaricaexpeditions.com) is the original ecotourist outfit in Costa Rica, specializing in countrywide nature tours with local naturalist guides and trips with overnights at their flagship Corcovado Lodge Tent Camp.

WHAT IT COSTS IN DOLLARS				
¢	$	$$	$$$	$$$$
Restaurants				
under $5	$5–$10	$10–$15	$15–$25	over $25
Hotels				
under $50	$50–$75	$75–$150	$150–$250	over $250

Restaurant prices are per person for a main course at dinner. Hotel prices are for two people in a standard double room in high season, excluding service and tax (16.4%).

Living off the Grid

Many hotels in the South Pacific generate their own electricity, so don't count on air-conditioning, using a hair dryer, or paying with a credit card (unless it's arranged in advance). Pharmacies are few, and often low on supplies. Pack with Mother Nature in mind. Bring:

■ Flashlight with extra batteries

■ Insect repellent (lots of it)

■ Sunscreen (ditto)

■ All toiletries or medicine that you might conceivably need

■ Sturdy, breathable hiking shoes and lots of socks (your feet will get wet)

■ Waterproof walking sandals

■ Binoculars

■ Sun hat

■ Water bottle

Getting There

For points between San José and San Vito, driving is a viable option, as long as you have lots of time. Direct buses to San Isidro, Golfito, and Puerto Jiménez are cheap and reliable and most are quite comfortable. But the best and fastest way to get to the far south is to fly directly to Golfito, Puerto Jiménez, Drake, Palmar Sur, or Carate. Many lodges arrange flights, taxi, and boat transfers all the way from San José.

THE CENTRAL HIGHLANDS

By Dorothy
MacKinnon

Less than an hour south of San José the Pan-American Highway climbs up into the scenic Central Highlands of Cerro de la Muerte, famous for spectacular mountain vistas, high-altitude coffee farms, cloud-forest eco-lodges, and challenging mountain hikes.

ZONA DE LOS SANTOS

Santa María de Dota is 65 km (40 mi) south of San José. The Route of the Saints is 24 km (15 mi) long.

Empalme, at Km 51 of the Pan-American Highway, marks the turnoff for Santa María de Dota, the first of the blessed coffee-growing towns named after saints that dot this mountainous area known as the Zona de Los Santos (Zone of the Saints).

★ The scenic road that winds through the high-altitude valley from Empalme to San Pablo de León is appropriately called **La Ruta de Los Santos** *(Route of the Saints)*. It's well paved to facilitate shipping the coffee produced in the region, which is central to Costa Rica's economy. On the 30-minute (24-km [15-mi]) drive from Empalme to San Pablo de León Cortés, you see misty valleys ringed by precipitous mountain slopes terraced with lush, green coffee plants. The route also captures the essence of a traditional Tico way of life built around coffee growing. Stately churches anchor bustling towns full of prosperous, neat houses with pretty gardens and 1970s Toyota Landcruisers in a rainbow of colors parked in front.

NAVIGATING
THE ROUTE OF
THE SAINTS

From San José, drive an hour and a half southeast on the paved Pan-American Highway, heading toward Cartago, then follow the signs south for San Isidro de El General. The two-lane road climbs steeply and there are almost no safe places to pass heavy trucks and slow vehicles. Make an early start, because the road is often enveloped in mist and rain in the afternoon. At Km 51 turn right at Empalme to reach Santa María de Dota, 14 km (8½ mi) along a wide, curving, paved road.

WHERE TO STAY & EAT

¢ ✕**Café de Los Santos.** This pretty café serves more than 30 different local coffees, using high-altitude *arabica* Tarrazú, the "celestial drink" for which this area is famous. The café also has homemade sweet and savory pastries. It's open weekdays 9–6:30, weekends 2–5:30. There's also a conveniently located outpost on the highway at Empalme called La Ruta del Café, open Tuesday to Sunday, 9–6. ✉ *100 m east of church ✚ 6 km (4 mi) west of Santa María de Dota, San Marcos de Tarrazú* ☎ *2546–7881* ▭ *No credit cards* ✉ *Pan-American Hwy. at entrance to Ruta de Los Santos, Empalme* ☎ *2571–1118* ▭ *No credit cards* ☉ *Closed Mon.*

$-$$ ▦**El Toucanet Lodge.** For serenity and mountain greenery, you can't beat this family-run lodge with plenty of pastoral scenery on view from the glassed-in dining room. Each of the six large rooms in three wooden cabins above the main lodge has its own private veranda and tile bathroom with skylight. Two new junior suites have fireplaces, whirlpool baths, and king-size beds. There's also a rustic three-bedroom cabin with a kitchen and fireplace. Owners Gary and Edna Roberts are known for hearty breakfasts, baked trout dinners, and creative vegetarian dishes. Gary leads a free

quetzal hunt every day at 7 AM. He also arranges horseback rides, mountain hikes, and tours of neighboring coffee *fincas* (farms). With at least six hours' notice, he can fire up the natural-stone hot tub for an end-of-day soak under the stars. **Pros:** Fresh mountain air, tranquillity, low-key, affordable. **Cons:** Simple furnishings, limited menu. ✛ *7 km (4½ mi) east of Santa María de Dota along steep, winding paved road, Copey; or from Km 58 of the Pan-American Hwy., turn right at sign for Copey and follow dirt road 8 km (5 mi)* ☎ *2541–3131* ☎☎ *2541–3045* ⊕ *www.eltoucanet.com* ✒ *6 rooms, 2 suites, 1 cabin* ♿ *In-room: no a/c, no phone, no TV. In-hotel: restaurant* ▤ *AE, MC, V* ☾ *Closed Sept.* ⭘*BP.*

SHOPPING

The best—and cheapest—place to buy local coffee is where the farmers themselves bring their raw coffee beans to be roasted and packed into jute bags, the **Coopedota Santa María** (⊠ *Main road, just after the bridge as you enter Santa María de Dota* ☎ *2541–2828*). You can buy export-quality coffee here for about $8 per kilo (2.2 pounds). Choose between *en grano* (whole bean) or *molido* (ground), and between light or dark roast. It's open Monday to Saturday 8 to 6, Sunday 8 to 1. You can also reserve a tour ($12) of the coffee co-op by calling ahead.

SAN GERARDO DE DOTA

89 km (55 mi) southeast of San José, 52 km (32 mi) south of Santa María de Dota.

Cloud forests, invigorating, cool mountain air, well-kept hiking trails, and excellent bird-watching make San Gerardo de Dota one of Costa Rica's premier nature destinations. The tiny hamlet is in the narrow Savegre River valley, 9 km (5½ mi) down a twisting, partially asphalted track that descends abruptly to the west from the Pan-American Highway. The peaceful surroundings look more like the Rocky Mountains than Central America, but hike down the waterfall trail and the vegetation quickly turns tropical again. Beyond hiking and bird-watching, activities include horseback riding and trout fly-fishing.

GETTING HERE

The drive from San José takes about three hours, and from Santa María de Dota about one hour. At Km 80 on the Pan-American Highway, turn down the dirt road signed SAN GERARDO DE DOTA. It's a harrowing, twisting road for most of the 9 km (5½ mi), with signs warning drivers to gear down and go slow. Some newly paved sections help to

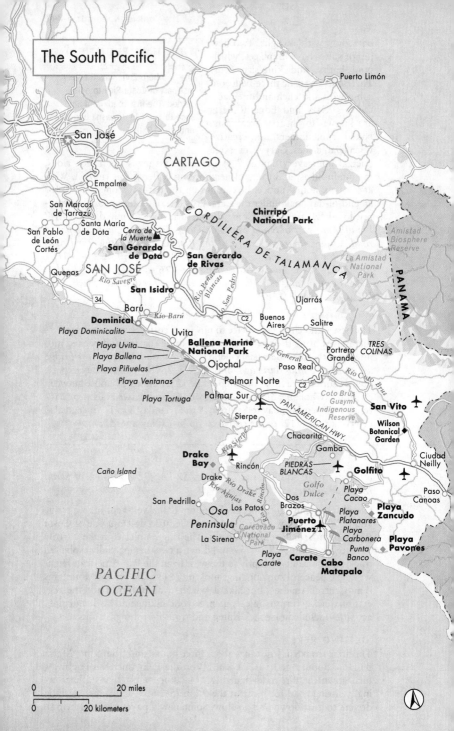

The South Pacific

Puerto Limón

San José

CARTAGO

Empalme

San Marcos
de Tarrazú

Santa María
de Dota

San Pablo
de León
Cortés

San Pablo
de León
Cortés

Cerro de
la Muerte

**San Gerardo
de Dota**

**San Gerardo
de Rivas**

Chirripó
National Park

CORDILLERA DE TALAMANCA

Amistad
Biosphere
Reserve

La Amistad
National
Park

PANAMA

SAN JOSÉ

Quepos

Río Savegre

San Isidro

Río Peñas
Blancas

San Pedro

Ujarrás

Barú

34

Río Barú

Dominical

Playa Dominicalito

Uvita

C2

Buenos
Aires

Salitre

Playa Uvita

Playa Ballena

**Ballena Marine
National Park**

Ojochal

Playa Piñuelas

Playa Ventanas

Playa Tortuga

Palmar Norte

Palmar Sur

Río General

Paso Real

Portrero
Grande

TRES
COLINAS

C2

Río Coto Brus

San Vito

PAN-AMERICAN HWY.

Coto Brus
Guaymí
Indigenous
Reserve

**Wilson
Botanical
Garden**

Sierpe

Río Sierpe

Chacarita

Gamba

**Drake
Bay**

Rincón

PIEDRAS
BLANCAS

Ciudad
Neilly

Caño Island

Drake

Río Drake

Río Agujas

Río Rincón

Golfo
Dulce

Golfito

Paso
Canoas

San Pedrillo

Los Patos

Dos
Brazos

Playa
Cacao

Playa
Platanares

**Playa
Zancudo**

**Osa
Peninsula**

Corcovado
National
Park

La Sirena

**Puerto
Jiménez**

Playa
Carbonera

Punta
Banco

**Playa
Pavones**

Playa
Carate

Carate

**Cabo
Matapalo**

PACIFIC
OCEAN

0   20 miles

0   20 kilometers

ease the worst curves. Tourist vans often stop along the road when the guides spot birds; grab your binoculars and join them!

OUTDOOR ACTIVITIES

BIRD-WATCHING ★ This area is a must for bird-watchers, who flock here with small package tours (⇨ *Tours in Travel Smart Costa Rica*). Individual birders can choose from a roster of expert local guides; check with your hotel for recommendations. **Savegre Hotel de Montaña** (☎2740–1028 ⊕*www.savegre.co.cr*) has the best bird guides in the area ($70 for a half day) and organizes hiking tours in the surrounding mountains.

Although you can see many birds from your cabin porch, most bird-watching requires hiking, some of it along steep paths made extra challenging by the high altitude (from 7,000 to 10,000 feet above sea level). Come fit and armed with binoculars and layers of warm clothing. The early mornings are brisk up here, but you'll warm up quickly with the sun and the exertion of walking.

HIKING Some of the best hiking in the country is in this valley. Expert birder Marino Chacón of Savegre Hotel (⇨*below*) leads a daylong natural-history hike (about $150 for up to 9 people, including transportation and a packed lunch) that starts with a drive up to the *páramo* (high-altitude, shrubby ecosystem) of **Cerro de la Muerte.** The trail begins at the cluster of communication towers, near Km 89, and descends through the forest into the valley. Miles of prime bird-watching/hiking trails wind through the forest reserve belonging to the Chacóns. ■TIP→**Night temperatures on the slopes of Cerro de la Muerte can approach freezing— it's called the Mountain of Death for the very simple reason that long-ago travelers attempting to cross it on foot often froze to death during the night. Pack accordingly.**

★ The most challenging trail in the area is the one that begins at the Hotel Savegre and follows the **Río Savegre** down to a spectacular waterfall. To get to the trailhead, follow the main road past Savegre Hotel to a fork, where you veer left, cross a bridge, and head over the hill to a pasture that narrows to a footpath. Although it is only 2 km (1¼ mi) each way, the hike is steep and slippery, especially near the bottom, and takes about three hours.

WHERE TO STAY

$$ ⊞**Dantica Lodge and Gallery.** High style at a high altitude, this avant-garde lodge clinging to the side of a mountain has unbeatable valley views. Spacious white-stucco casitas with two bedrooms and baths are perfect for families. New casitas in a forest clearing provide the ulti-

---

THE RESPLENDENT QUETZAL

The damp, epiphyte-laden oak-tree forest around San Gerardo de Dota is renowned for resplendent quetzals, considered by many to be the most beautiful bird in the Western world. Male quetzals in full breeding plumage are more spectacular than females, with metallic green feathers, crimson stomachs, helmetlike crests, and extravagantly long tail feathers. Ask guides or hotel staff about common quetzal hangouts; early morning during the March-to-May nesting season is the best time to spot them.

6

mate in seclusion and close-to-nature experiences. There's also a cozy honeymoon hideaway with a whirlpool tub big enough for two. All the casitas have living rooms with huge picture windows, private terraces, kitchenettes, and electric heaters, along with fluffy, warm duvets. Some have the added luxury of whirlpool tubs and fireplaces. Mixing modern European style with Latin American antiques, the young Dutch/Colombian owners have an unerring eye for style, reflected in their stunning, glassed-in gallery of *artesanía* (arts and crafts). Enjoy a hearty breakfast or light lunch served on exquisite china in a glass house with a heart-stopping view. **Pros:** Stylish, comfortable casitas; gorgeous natural setting. **Cons:** No dinner served, so bring your own food or go off-property; steep access to forest casitas along narrow trails. ⊠ *Road to San Gerardo de Dota* ⊹ *4 km (2 mi) west of Pan-American Hwy.* ☎ *2740–1067* 📠 *2740–1071* ⊕ *www.dantica.com* 🛏 *7 casitas, 1 suite, 1 house* ⚘ *In-room: kitchen, refrigerator. In-hotel: restaurant, no-smoking rooms* ⊟ *AE, MC, V* �‖ *BP.*

$$ ▦ **Trogón Lodge.** Overlooking the same cloud forest and boulder-strewn river as Savegre Hotel de Montaña, Trogón Lodge is more a relaxing hideaway than a hiking-heavy destination. The green wooden cabins encircle a fantasy garden bursting with color and a riot of roses, calla lilies, and geraniums. Each cabin has two separate rooms with big windows, queen-size beds, white-tile baths with hot showers, and gas heaters and extra blankets for chilly mountain nights. The only drawback is shared verandas. A honeymoon cabin perched in solitary splendor has a king-size bed and a whirlpool tub with a panoramic view. Meals are served in a restaurant with tree-trunk tables, adjoined by a bar and a new dining terrace with a river view. Quetzal-watching, horseback riding, waterfall hikes, and an 11-platform canopy tour are some of the diversions, or you can relax with a massage at the new spa. **Pros:** Pretty, lush garden; pleasant, convivial public area. **Cons:** Steep, short trails that end at road; little privacy except in honeymoon suite. ⊹ *Turn right at sign to San Gerardo de Dota on Pan-American Hwy., about 80 km (50 mi) southeast of San José, and follow signs; lodge is 7½ km (4½ mi) down a dirt road* ⚲ *Apdo. 10980–1000, San José* ☎ *2740–1051, 2293–8181 in San José* 📠 *2239–7657 in San José* ⊕ *www.grupomawamba.com* 🛏 *22 rooms, 1 suite* ⚘ *In-room: no a/c, no phone, no TV. In-hotel: restaurant, bar, bicycles* ⊟ *AE, MC, V* ❖ *EP.*

$–$$ ▦ **Savegre Hotel de Montaña.** Famous for its miles of bird-watching trails
Fodor's Choice and expert guides, this once-rustic lodge has been upgraded to luxury,
★ including new cabins with handsome wood furniture, fireplaces, and deep bathtubs—unthinkable luxuries back in the 1950s when Don Efraín Chacón first bushwhacked his way through these mountains. Still run by Efraín's children and grandchildren, the main lodge has a big fireplace, a cozy bar, and a veranda buzzing with hummingbirds. Breakfast and lunch can be served on a sunny terrace also abuzz with hummingbirds. Homegrown trout is the restaurant's specialty. You can avoid the twisting drive here by taking a bus to Km 80 on the Pan-American Highway and arranging to get a lift to the hotel ($10). **Pros:** Great trails, amazing bird life, excellent guides. **Cons:** Buffet-style meals when hotel has lots of groups, older cabins are very simple

and lack privacy, very cold here at night. ✛*Turn right at sign to San Gerardo de Dota on Pan-American Hwy., about 80 km (50 mi) southeast of San José, and travel 9 km (5½ mi) down very steep gravel road* ✆*Apdo. 482, Cartago* ☎*2740–1028* 🖷*2740–1027* ⊕*www.savegre. co.cr* ⮑*25 cabinas, 20 cabin-suites* ⌂*In-room: no a/c, no TV. In-hotel: restaurant, bar, public Internet* ▤*AE, MC, V* ⫯⦿*BP.*

$ 🏨**Albergue de Montaña Paraíso del Quetzal.** Nestled in a cloud forest just minutes off the main highway, this rustic lodge is, indeed, a paradise for resplendent quetzals and for the visitors who want to see this most beautiful and sought-after bird in Costa Rica. Even if you don't catch sight of a quetzal, the vistas of cloud-enshrouded mountains and valleys will keep you busy, as will the hiking and birding trails through ancient oak forests dripping with moss and epiphytes. Each cozy cabin, set in splendid isolation, has a double bed plus a bunk bed, and lots of blankets. Night-time temperatures drop into the 40s at this altitude (about 7,800 feet above sea level) and you'll be happy for the tiny, tiled bathrooms with steaming-hot showers. The main lodge has a wood-burning stove and a deck abuzz with brilliant hummingbirds. Meals are simple comida tipica, cooked on a wood stove. All the family pitches in, cooking, serving, and guiding. This is the first hotel in this world-renowned birding area to receive the country's coveted Blue Flag for eco-friendliness. Per-person rates include dinner and breakfast, and guided hiking and birding tours. Pros: Scenic views, pristine cloud forest, amazing bird-watching and hikes. Cons: Very simple lodging and food, steep paths to some cabins, very cold nights. ✉*Km 70, Pan-American Hwy., Cerro de la Muerte* ☎*2200–0241 or 8865–0263* ⊕*www.paraisodelquetzal.com* ⮑*8 cabins* ⌂*In-room: no a/c, no phone, no TV. In-hotel: restaurant* ▤*MC, V* ⫯⦿✉🖷*.*

$ 🏨 **Las Cataratas.** One of the best deals—and meals—in the valley is at this rustic restaurant and cabins run by a Tico family, who all join in (kids, too) to help serve meals. Three simple, wooden cabins, one with a wood-burning fireplace, have red-velvet decor reminiscent of a bordello, but they are cheap and comfortable. There are some short, steep forest trails to explore. At the restaurant ($) you can dine on fresh trout—pulled directly out of the adjoining pond when you place your order—with salad, vegetables, dessert, and juice for under $10. If you haven't got the time or the courage to face the steep road all the way down to San Gerardo, this is a good compromise, only 3 km (2 mi) in from the highway. It's a good idea to call ahead on a weekday, and Bernardo, the owner, will be ready for you. **Pros:** Cheap, excellent fresh trout, authentic Tico culture. **Cons:** Rustic, simple. ✛*3 km (2 mi) down steep road to San Gerardo de Dota* ☎*8393–9278 or 2740–1064* ⊕*www.cataratas.guiapz.com* ⮑*3 cabins* ⌂*In-room: no a/c, no phone, no TV. In-hotel: restaurant* ▤*MC, V* ⫯⦿✉🖷*.*

VALLE DE EL GENERAL REGION

The Valle de El General (The General's Valley) is bounded to the north and west by the central highlands of the massive Cordillera de Talamanca and to the south by La Amistad International Park, above San

Vito. The valley is named for the Río de El General, one of the many rivers that rise in the Talamancas and run down through the valley, making it ideal for farming. This area includes vast expanses of highland wilderness on the upper slopes of the Cordillera de Talamanca and the high-altitude *páramo* (shrubby ecosystem) of Chirripó National Park, as well as prosperous agricultural communities amid vast, sunbaked fields of pineapple and sugarcane.

SAN ISIDRO

54 km (34 mi) south of San Gerardo de Dota.

Although San Isidro has no major attractions, the bustling market town is a good place to have lunch, get cash at one of the many ATMs (most accept only Visa/Plus cards), or fill your tank—the main highway into town is lined with service stations, some operating 24 hours.

GETTING HERE & AROUND
The Pan-American Highway takes you straight into San Isidro. It's 129 km (80 mi) south of San José and about one and a half hours' drive south of the San Gerardo de Dota highway exit. Truck traffic can be heavy. Buses to Dominical leave San Isidro from the Quepos bus terminal, 100 meters south and 200 meters east of the cathedral, near the main highway. Buses to San Gerardo de Rivas, the starting point of the trail into Chirripó National Park, depart from San Isidro at 5 AM from the central park and at 2 PM from a stop at the central market.

SAN ISIDRO ESSENTIALS
Bank/ATM **Banco de Costa Rica** (⊠*1 block south of southwest corner of park* ☎*2229–2231*). **ATH Coopealianza** (⊠*South side of central park, beside Hotel Chirripó* ☞*ATM only*).

Hospital **Hospital Escalante Pradilla** (⊠*North end of town* ☎*2661–3122*).

Pharmacy **Farmacia Santa Marta** (⊠*Across from cultural center* ☎*2771–4506*).

Internet **Internet El Balcón** (⊠*150 m east of Central Market, near Banco de Costa Rica* ☎*2771–6300*).

Post Office **Correo** (⊠*200 m south of City Hall, south side of park*).

Visitor Information **Ciprotur** (⊠*Behind the MUSOC bus station, where San José buses arrive* ☎*2771–6096*). **Selva Mar** (⊠*45 m south of central park* ☎*2771–4582* ⊕*www.exploringcostarica.com*).

EXPLORING
The **National Parks Service** (⊠*Across from Cámara de Cañeros* ☎*2771–3155*) has an office in town where you can get information on Chirripó National Park.

☾ In a lush valley 7 km (4½ mi) northeast of San Isidro, the community-managed **Las Quebradas Biological Center** is a *centro biológico* (nature reserve) that protects 1,853 acres of dense forest in which elegant tree ferns grow in the shadows of massive trees, and colorful tanagers and euphonias flit about the foliage. A 3-km (2-mi) trail winds through the forest and along the Río Quebradas, which supplies water to San Isidro and surrounding communities. ✛*At bottom of mountain as you approach San Isidro, take sharp left off Pan-American Hwy. at sign for Las Quebradas, go 7 km (4½ mi) northeast; center is 2 km (1 mi) north of town, along unpaved road. No phone* ⊠*$5* ⏲ *Tues.–Sun. 8–3.*

Los Cusingos Neotropical Bird Sanctuary was the home of the late Dr. Alexander Skutch, Central America's preeminent ornithologist/naturalist and a co-author of *A Guide to the Birds of Costa Rica,* the birders' bible. His 190-acre estate,

HITTING THE TRAILS

The hiking in the south is simply spectacular, so don't leave home without your boots. The most challenging hike in the country is Chirripó Mountain, a 6- to 10-hour haul up to the national-park hostel, a base camp for exploring surrounding peaks. Dramatic but less challenging hikes include the well-maintained, wide trails in the cool high-altitude forests of the Savegre Valley; the narrow Coastal Path south of Drake; and forest trails to waterfalls and swimming holes in the Golfo Dulce, Osa Peninsula, and around Dominical.

an island of forest amid a sea of new farms and housing developments, is now run by the nonprofit Tropical Science Center, which has improved the trails and restored the simple house where Dr. Skutch lived—without electricity—from 1941 until his death in 2004, just a week shy of his 100th birthday. Bird species you might see include fiery-billed araçaris—colorful, small members of the toucan family—and mixed tanager flocks. ✛*12 km (7½ mi) southeast of San Isidro, Quizarrá* ☎*2200–5472* ⊕*www.cct.or.cr* ⊠*$10* ⏲ *Daily 7–3, by reservation only.*

OUTDOOR ACTIVITIES

Selva Mar (⊠ *Half a block south of the cathedral* ☎*2771–4582*) is the most experienced Southern Zone tour operator.

BIRD-WATCHING **Sunny Travel/Tropical Feathers** (☎*2771–9686 or 2772–3275* ⊕*www.costaricabirdingtours.com*), run by expert birder Noel Urena, has multiday bird-watching packages and arranges customized tours in the San Isidro and Dominical area.

HIKING The major tourist draw is climbing Mount Chirripó (the highest peak is 3,820 m or about 12,530 feet high) in Chirripó National Park. **Costa Rica Trekking Adventures** (☎*2771–4582* ⊕*www.chirripo.com*), run by Selva Mar, can arrange everything you need to climb the mountain, including transportation, guide, porters to carry your gear, meals, snacks, and beverages. But you still have to make the tough climb yourself, about eight hours uphill to the park lodge, and five hours to come down. The two-night, three-day packages are $379 per person, with at least two people.

CLOSE UP

A Mosaic of Forests

Though the rain forest is the most famous region in Costa Rica, there are other types of forests here equally rich in life and well worth exploring. The **tropical dry forests** of the northwestern lowlands are similar to rain forests during the rainy season, but once the weather turns dry, most trees lose their leaves, and some burst simultaneously into full flower, notably the yellow-blossom buttercup tree and the pink tabebuia. Cacti, coyotes, and diamondback rattlesnakes can be found, in addition to typical rain-forest flora and fauna.

The **cloud forests** on the upper reaches of many Costa Rican mountains and volcanoes are so deeply lush that it can be hard to find the bark on a tree for all the growth on its trunk and branches. Vines, orchids, ferns, aroids, and bromeliads are everywhere. More light reaching the ground means plenty of undergrowth,

too. Cloud forests are home to a multitude of animals, ranging from delicate glass frogs, whose undersides are so transparent that you can see many of their internal organs, to the legendary resplendent quetzal. The foliage and mist can make it hard to see wildlife.

Along both coasts are extensive **mangrove forests**, extremely productive ecosystems that play an important role as estuaries. Mangroves attract animals that feed on marine life, especially fish-eating birds such as cormorants, herons, pelicans, and ospreys. The forests that line Costa Rica's northeastern coast are dominated by the water-resistant *jolillo* palm or *palma real*. Mangroves are home to many of the same animals found in the rain forest—monkeys, parrots, iguanas—as well as river dwellers such as turtles and crocodiles.

WHERE TO STAY & EAT

$ ✕ **Taquería Mexico Lindo.** Locals, expats, and tourists crowd into this casual cantina, famous for its authentic Mexican food cooked and served by an extended Mexican family. It's cheap and cheerful, with hearty servings of burritos (including veggie options), enchiladas, chiles rellenos, tuna-stuffed avocadoes, and daily specials served on terra-cotta dishes under a flutter of festive paper cutouts on the ceiling. Unusually for a Mexican place, the desserts are standouts and all homemade. ⊠*Shopping arcade beside Hotel Chirripó, outside of Central Park in downtown San Isidro* ☎2771–8222 ☰*AE, MC, V* ☾*Closed Sun.*

¢–$ ✕ **El Trapiche de Nayo.** This rustic open-air restaurant with a panoramic valley view serves the kind of food Ticos eat at *turnos* (village fundraising festivals), including hard-to-find *sopa de mondongo* (tripe soup). Easier to stomach are the *gallos* (do-it-yourself filled tortillas), which you can stuff with hearts of palm, other root vegetables, and wood-fire-cooked chicken. On Saturdays, raw sugarcane is pressed in an antique mill and boiled in huge iron cauldrons to make smooth *sobado*, a molasses-flavor fudge. Service is leisurely, to say the least, and the restrooms—with seatless toilets—leave much to be desired. ⊠*Pan-American Hwy.* ✛*6 km (4 mi) north of San Isidro* ☎2771–7267 ☰*AE, MC, V.*

‹ 🛏 **Hotel Los Crestones.** Flowers in window boxes give this pleasant, two-story, motel-style building near the local stadium a homey feel. Affordable rooms are large and comfortable, and some have bathtubs. There's a small pool where you can cool off. **Pros:** Affordable, pleasant rooms, secure parking for car. **Cons:** Can be noisy since it is near soccer stadium and busy shopping area, a few rooms have ceiling fans but no a/c. ✉ *Southwest side of stadium, on road to Dominical* ☎ *2770–1200* 🖷 *2770–5047* ⊕ *www.hotelloscrestones.com* ➟ *27 rooms* ♿ *In-room: no a/c (some), Wi-Fi. In-hotel: restaurant, pool* ⊟ *AE, MC, V* ⊠ *EP.*

‹ 🛏 **Hotel Zima.** Close to the main bus station and especially popular with backpackers heading up to Chirripó, this hotel's pleasant rooms are in a nicely landscaped row, reminiscent of a 1950s motel, complete with swimming pool. Some have queen-size beds and air-conditioning; others have double or single beds and ceiling fans. Have breakfast at the small terrace restaurant or cross the highway and forage among the inexpensive eateries. **Pro:** Handy to bus station and restaurants in town. **Cons:** Not a scenic location, just off main highway; smallish rooms. ✉ *Half a block east of main highway into San Isidro, across from MUSOC bus terminal* ☎ *2770–1114* 🖷 *2770–9394* ➟ *14 bungalows, 13 rooms* ♿ *In-room: no a/c (some), no phone. In-hotel: restaurant, pool, laundry service, public Internet* ⊟ *AE, MC, V* ⊠ *EP.*

SAN GERARDO DE RIVAS

20 km (12½ mi) northeast of San Isidro.

Chirripó National Park is the main reason to venture to San Gerardo de Rivas, but if you aren't up for this physically challenging adventure it's still a great place to spend a day or two. Spread over steep terrain at the end of the narrow valley of the boulder-strewn Río Chirripó, San Gerardo de Rivas has a cool climate, good bird-watching, spectacular views reminiscent of Nepal, and an outdoor menu that includes waterfall hikes.

GETTING HERE

More than half the one-hour drive from San Isidro is on a very rocky, very hilly, dirt road; 4WD is strongly recommended. There is a bus from San Isidro and it is a slow, dusty ride up the mountain.

EXPLORING

☉ The **Hot Springs** (Aguas Termales), on a farm above the road to Herradura, are a favorite tourist stop. To get here, you must cross a river on a rickety bridge, then manage a steep climb on foot or by 4WD vehicle to a combination of natural rock and concrete pools in a forested area. It's nothing fancy and it can be crowded with locals on weekends, so aim for a weekday soak. ✉ *Above road to Herradura* ⊹ *About 1½ km (1 mi) past the ranger station, north of town* ☎ *2742–5210* 🖭 *$3* ⊙ *Daily 7–5:30.*

☉ **Cloudbridge Private Nature Reserve,** a private nature reserve staffed by volunteers, has an easy trail to a waterfall, plus almost 20 km (12 mi) of river and ridge trails bordering Chirripó National Park. It's a pleasant alternative for hikers who aren't up to the challenge of Chirripó. ✛*2 km (1 mi) northeast of San Gerardo de Rivas* ⊕*www.cloudbridge.org* 🖃*By donation* ☉*Daily, sunrise to sunset.*

OUTDOOR ACTIVITIES

Selva Mar *(⇨San Isidro, above)* also runs tours around San Gerardo de Rivas.

WHERE TO STAY

$–$$ 🏨**Río Chirripó Retreat.** A popular place for yoga retreats, this lodge has clear mountain air, a rushing river, and a huge conical-roof adobe temple hung with a monastery bell and Tibetan prayer flags. You'll feel as though you have arrived in the Himalayas. The bougainvillea-bedecked B&B is a great place for bird-watching, clambering along the river rocks strewn with Druidic-looking stone seats and altars, or acclimatizing before climbing Chirripó. Or you can relax in the hot tub or the swimming pool overlooking the tumultuous river. Two-story wood cabins are cantilevered over a steep ravine, with twig-railing porches. The comfortable rooms have large bathrooms and walls stenciled with mysterious symbols. A new yoga platform with a view also doubles as a palatial guest room. **Pros:** Dramatic scenic location, extravagant breakfasts with copious fresh fruits. **Cons:** No lunch or dinner, smallish rooms with two single beds each, shared balconies. ⊠*Down a steep drive, just past cemetery* 🕾*2742–5109* ⊕*www.riochirripo.com* 📞*8 rooms, 2 cabins* ♨*In-room: no a/c, no phone, no TV. In-hotel: restaurant, pool, Wi-Fi* 🖃*No credit cards* 🍴*BP.*

¢ 🏨**Albergue de Montaña El Pelícano.** On a precipitous ridge south of town, this wooden lodge is named for a chunk of wood that resembles a pelican—one of dozens of idiosyncratic wooden sculptures carved out of tree roots by owner Rafael Elizondo. Above the restaurant, which has a gorgeous view of the valley below San Gerardo, are economical small rooms with shared bath. A more comfortable option are the two private wooden cabins with kitchenettes near the pool. The owners can help arrange everything for a climb up Chirripó. The climb to the hotel itself is quite steep and 4WD is advisable. **Pros:** Proximity to Chirripó and a free ride to the trailhead, very cheap. **Cons:** Shared bath, very tiny rooms, but most visitors are only here to sleep before setting off early to climb Chirripó. ⊠*260 m south of national park office* 🕾*2742–5050* ⊕*www.hotelpelicano.net* 📞*10 rooms with shared bath, 2 cabins* ♨*In-room: no a/c, no phone, no TV. In-hotel: restaurant, tennis court, pool, Internet* 🖃*MC, V* 🍴*EP.*

CHIRRIPÓ NATIONAL PARK

The park entrance is a 5-km (3-mi) hike uphill from San Gerardo de Rivas.

The ascent to Mount Chirripó, the highest mountain in Costa Rica, is the most popular and challenging hike in the country. Unfortunately, it is also the most exclusive. A recent environmental-impact study led officials to limit the number of hikers in the park each day to 35. Twenty-five reservations are booked months ahead and usually snapped up by tour companies, leaving only 10 spaces for hikers who show up at the park. Without reservations, you can check in at the San Gerardo ranger station, which grants entrance on a first-come, first-served basis. To access the challenging trail, you must first hike about 2 km (1 mi) uphill from San Gerardo de Rivas to the park's official boundary. From here it's a tough climb to the base camp—6 to 10 hours from the official park entrance, depending on your physical condition—so most hikers head out of San Gerardo at the first light of day. There is a modern but unheated (and chilly) **hostel** near the top ($10 a night). This will be your base for a night or two if you want to continue your hike up to the peaks. The hostel has small rooms with four bunks each, cold-water bathrooms, and a cooking area. You need to bring your own sleeping bag, pillow, and provisions, but you can hire porters to lug it all up and down for you. A new generator and some solar panels provide some electricity, but the hostel is still bare-bones rustic. ■ TIP➜**Pack plenty of warm clothes.** Trails from the hostel lead to the top of Chirripó—the highest point in Costa Rica—and the nearby peak of Terbi, as well as to glacier lakes and the *páramo*—a highland ecosystem common to the Andes, with shrubs and herbaceous plants.

GETTING HERE

You are required to report to the **San Gerardo de Rivas National Parks Service** (⊠ *Main street* ☎ *2742–5085, 2742–5083 reservations* ✎ *parquechirripo@racsa.co.cr*) before you start, either the day before, or the morning of your climb. The office is open 6:30–4, admission is $10, and they have trail maps. Don't try to sneak in: a park ranger will stop you at a checkpoint on the trail and ask to see your reservation voucher. You can reserve and pay for lodgings over the phone or email.

OUTDOOR ACTIVITIES

Hikes and other activities in the park are arranged by **Selva Mar** (⇨ *San Isidro, above*).

SAN VITO

110 km (68 mi) southeast of San Isidro, 61 km (38 mi) northeast of Golfito.

Except for the tropical greenery, the rolling hills around the bustling hilltop town of San Vito could be mistaken for a Tuscan landscape. The town actually owes its 1952 founding to 200 Italian families who converted forest into coffee, fruit, and cattle farms. The Italian flavor lingers in outdoor cafés serving ice cream and pastries and an abundance of shoe stores. A statue dedicated to the *pioneros* stands proudly in the middle of town. San Vito is also the center of the Coto Brus coffee region. Many of the coffee pickers are from the Guaymí tribe, who live in a large reserve nearby and just over the border in Panama. They're easy to recognize by the women's colorful cotton dresses.

GETTING HERE & AROUND

If you are driving south from San Isidro, your best route is along the wide, smooth Pan-American Highway via Buenos Aires to Paso Real, about 70 km (43 mi). Then take the scenic high road to San Vito, 40 km (25 mi) farther along. This road has recently been paved and it's the most direct and prettiest route. Another route, which many buses take, is via Ciudad Neily, about 35 km (22 mi) northeast of Golfito, and then 24 km (15 mi) of winding steep road up to San Vito, at almost 1,000 meters (3,280 feet) above sea level. At this writing, the road is potholed and in mal estato (bad shape). There are direct buses from San José four times a day; and buses from San Isidro seven times a day. You can also fly to Coto 47 and take a taxi to San Vito.

SAN VITO ESSENTIALS

Most of the banks in town have cash machines that accept foreign cards.

Bank/ATM **Banco Nacional** (⊠ *Across from central park* ☎ *2773–3601*). **ATH Coopealianza** (⊠ *Center of town, north of hospital* ☞ *ATM only*).

Hospital **Hospital San Vito** (⊠ *South end of town on road to Wilson Botanical Garden* ☎ *2773–3103*).

Pharmacy **Farmacia Coto Brus** (⊠ *Center of town across from La Flor pastry shop* ☎ *2773–3076*).

Internet **Cybershop** (⊠ *1 block west of main street at north end of town* ☎ *2773–3521*).

Post Office **Correo** (⊠ *Far north end of town, beside police station*).

Taxis **Taxi service** (⊠ *Taxi stand beside park at center of town* ☎ *2773–3939*).

EXPLORING

Fodor'sChoice ★ The compelling tourist draw here is the world-renowned **Wilson Botanical Garden,** a must-see for gardeners and bird-watchers and enchanting even for those who are neither. Paths through the extensive grounds are lined with exotic plants and shaded by avenues of palm trees and 50-foot-high bamboo stalks. In 1961 U.S. landscapers Robert and Catherine Wilson bought 30 acres of coffee plantation and started planting tropical species, including palms, orchids, bromeliads, and heliconias. Today the property extends over 635 acres, and the gardens hold around 2,000 native and more than 3,000 exotic species. The palm collection—more than 700 species—is the second-largest in the world. Fantastically shaped and colored bromeliads, which usually live in the tops of trees, have been brought down to the ground in impressive mass plantings, providing one of many photo opportunities. The property was transferred to the Organization for Tropical Studies in 1973, and in 1983 it became part of Amistad Biosphere Reserve. Under the name **Las Cruces Biological Station,** Wilson functions as a research and educational center, so there is a constant supply of expert botanists and biologists to take visitors on natural-history tours in the garden and the adjoining forest trails. If you spend a night at the garden lodge, you have the garden all to yourself in the late afternoon and early morning, when wildlife is most active. ✛ *6 km (4 mi) south of San Vito on road to Ciudad Neily* ✉ *Apdo. 73–8257, San Vito* ☎ *2773–4004* 🖷 *2773–4109* ⊕ *www.esintro.co.cr* 💲 *$8* ⊙ *Daily 8–4.*

OUTDOOR ACTIVITIES

BIRD-
WATCHING

In addition to its plants, **Wilson Botanical Garden** (⇨ *Exploring, above*) is renowned for its birds. There are about 250 species of birds in the garden alone, including half of the country's hummingbird species, and 410 species total in the immediate area. Competing with the birds for your attention are more than 800 butterflies. Naturalist guides lead visitors on birding and natural-history tours through the garden ($18 per person). The Río Java trail, open only to overnight guests of Wilson, is a great place to see birds.

WILDLIFE-
WATCHING

If you are an overnight guest at **Wilson Botanical Garden** (⇨ *Exploring, above*), you can walk the Río Java trail, through a forest thick with wildlife, particularly monkeys.

WHERE TO STAY & EAT

$ ✕ **Pizzería Liliana.** Follow the locals' lead and treat yourself to authen-
★ tic pizza at the classiest restaurant in town or dig into the macaroni *sanviteña*-style: with white sauce, ham, and mushrooms. The classics are here as well, and they're all homemade—lasagne, cannelloni, and ravioli. The authentically Italian vinaigrette salad dressing is a welcome change from more acidic Tico dressings. In true Italian fashion, the friendly, family-run restaurant can be noisy, but it's a happy buzz. For a more romantic dinner, ask for a table on the pretty garden terrace. ✉ *150 m west of central square* ☎ 2773–3080 ▭ MC, V.

$$$ ▦ **Hacienda La Amistad.** Here's a rare opportunity to explore La Amis-
tad Park, which borders this 25,000-acre family estate, most of which is primary forest studded with rivers and waterfalls. The alpine-style lodge offers comfortable quarters, great home-cooked food, and the best cappuccino and espresso in the country, made from the estate's own organic coffee beans. New junior suites are a little more luxurious. Daylong guided hikes or horseback rides traverse the property's 57 km (35 mi) of trails. The really adventurous can take the Feel Green hiking tour, walking to four camps over the course of five days. The staff, including a cook, carries all your gear and food in the truck and meets you at each camp. The cabins are as rustic as it gets; the shared baths have only (very) cold water. But the wildlife and walks are beyond exhilarating, and the food cooked in a wood-fire stove is simple but delicious. Bring along a really good sleeping bag for the cold mountain nights. ✛ *32 km (20 mi) east of San Vito along a rough, rocky road* ☎ 2200–5037, 2289–7667 in San José ⊕ *www.laamistad.com* ⌂ 12 *rooms in lodge, 6 cabins at each camp* ⌂ *In-room: no a/c, no phone, no TV. In-hotel: restaurant, bar* ▭ AE, MC, V ▮◯▮ FAP.

$–$$ ▦ **Wilson Botanical Garden.** A highlight of any Costa Rican visit, this
Fodor'sChoice magical botanical garden has comfortable rooms in two modern build-
★ ings built of glass, steel, and wood that blend into a forested hillside. The smaller rooms have two single beds and larger ones have three singles. Private balconies cantilevered over a ravine make bird-watching a snap even from your room. Each room is named after the exotic plant growing at the doorway. Room rates include three excellent home-style meals, a guided tour of the grounds, and 24-hour access to the garden. Staying overnight is the only way to see the garden at dusk and dawn

6

or to walk the Sendero Río Java, a trail that follows a stream through a forest teeming with birds and monkeys. The staff here is cheerful and professional, and the youthful enthusiasm of visiting research students is contagious. **Pros:** Unparalleled setting with 24-hour access to garden and nature trails, excellent birding and wildlife-viewing. **Cons:** Rooms are becoming a little shabby; meals are served family-style, precisely on time, so be on time or go hungry! ✈6 km (4 mi) south of San Vito on road to Ciudad Neily ☝OTS, Apdo. 676–2050, San Pedro ☎2524–0628 San José office, 2773–4004 lodge ☎2524–0629 ⊕www.esintro. co.cr ⌨12 rooms ⌂In-room: no a/c, no TV. In-hotel: restaurant, public Internet ☐AE, MC, V ⦿FAP.

¢ 🏨**Hotel El Ceibo.** The best deal in town, El Ceibo is tucked in a quiet cul-de-sac behind the main street, an Italian-style oasis with graceful arcades and decorative balustrades overlooking potted palms. Rooms are compact but tidy, bright, and comfortable. Rooms 1–10 and 21–32 have small balconies opening onto a wooded ravine alive with birds. The restaurant, illuminated by a skylight, serves home-style Italian and Tico food at reasonable prices. **Pros:** Central location, good price, relative quiet. **Cons:** Some rooms are quite small, furnishings are nothing special. ✉140 m east of San Vito's central park, behind Municipalidad ☎2773–3025 ☎2773–5025 ⌨40 rooms ⌂In-room: no a/c, no phone. In-hotel: restaurant, bar ☐MC, V ⦿EP.

SHOPPING

In an old farmhouse on the east side of the road between San Vito and the botanical garden, **Finca Cántaros** (✉Road to Ciudad Neily ✈3 km [2 mi] south of San Vito ☎2773–3760) sells crafts by indigenous artisans from near and far, including Guaitil ceramic figures and *molas* (colorful appliqué work) made by Kuna women from the San Blas Islands in Panama. You can also find a great selection of colorful, high-glaze ceramics from San José artists. Profits help support the adjacent children's library.

EN ROUTE The 33-km (21-mi) road from **San Vito to Ciudad Neily** is twisting and spectacular, with views over the Coto Colorado plain to the Golfo Dulce and Osa Peninsula beyond. Watch out for killer potholes, though. The road from **San Vito to Paso Real** is equally scenic, traveling along a high ridge with sweeping valley views on either side. As you descend, the wide valley of the El General River opens up before you, planted with miles of spiky pineapples and tall sugarcane. The road has recently been repaved and once again even drivers can enjoy the scenery without falling into potholes.

THE COAST

On the other side of a mountain ridge, just a scenic hour-long drive west of San Isidro, you reach the southern Pacific coast with its miles of beaches for sunning, surfing, kayaking, and snorkeling. Ballena National Marine Park alone encompasses almost 10 km (6 mi) of protected beaches. Scattered along the coast are small communities with

La Amistad National Park

By far the largest park in Costa Rica, at more than 1,980 square km (765 square mi), La Amistad is a mere portion of the vast La Amistad Biosphere Reserve that stretches into western Panama. Altitudes range from 1,000 meters (3,280 feet) to 3,500 meters (11,480 feet). There are miles of rugged, densely forested trails and plenty of wildlife (two-thirds of the country's vertebrate species live here), but because access is extremely difficult, it's not worth visiting the park unless you plan to spend several days, making this a trip only for experienced hikers. Tour operators don't do trips yet, but you can if you plan ahead.

Unless you're comfortable being lost in the wilderness, hire a park guide. The three-day guided trips have overnights at a ranger station with potable water and rest rooms. The alternative is rustic camp sites (bring your own tent) for $5 per person. Reserve space about a week in advance. To get to the park (4WD essential), drive 31 km (20 mi) west from San Vito along the road to Paso Real. Turn right at the park sign at Guacimo, near two small roadside restaurants. Then drive about 20 km (13 mi) uphill on a rough road. There is no public transport. ☎2730–0846 💲$10 per day ⊙ Daily 8–4.

6

increasing numbers of international residents and interesting restaurants and lodging options.

DOMINICAL

34 km (21 mi) southwest of San Isidro, 40 km (25 mi) south of Quepos.

Sleepy fishing village turned scruffy surfer town, Dominical is changing again, as luxury villas pop up all over the hillsides above the beaches, bringing new wealth that is boosting the local economy. For now, it's still a major surfing destination, with a lively restaurant and nightlife scene. Bars and restaurants come and go with the waves of itinerant foreigners, so don't hesitate to try something new. Dominical's real magic lies beyond the town, in the surrounding terrestrial and marine wonders: the rain forest grows right up to the beach in some places, and the ocean offers world-class surfing.

GETTING HERE & AROUND

The road west over the mountains and down to Dominical is scenic at its best and fog-shrouded and potholed at its worst. It has recently been repaved, but there are lots of curves, and potholes pop up unexpectedly, so take your time and enjoy the scenery along the hour-long drive from San Isidro. From Quepos, the road south is the only section of the Costanera still not

MAKING OUT

Kissing in public, among heterosexual couples at least, is rarely frowned upon, with parks a favorite venue. But a growing number of locally patronized restaurants have posted signs: ESCENAS AMOROSAS PROHIBIDA, literally "Amorous scenes prohibited."

paved, and it's a bumpy, dusty ride past palm-oil plantations. Buses from San Isidro and Quepos leave four times a day. If you want to avoid driving altogether, Easy Ride *(⇨ By Shuttle Van in Travel Smart Costa Rica)* has air-conditioned minibuses with room for six to eight passengers that make two trips to and from San José daily ($35).

DOMINICAL ESSENTIALS

Bank/ATM Banco de Costa Rica (⊠ *Plaza Pacífica* 🕾 *2787–0381).*

Hospital Clínica González Arellano (⊠ *Next to pharmacy* 🕾 *2787–0129).*

Pharmacy Farmacia Dominical (⊠ *Pueblo del Río Center at entrance to town* 🕾 *2787–0197).*

Internet Dominical Internet Cafe (⊠ *Above San Clemente Bar, main street* 🕾 *2787–0191).* Super Diuwak (⊠ *Next to Hotel Diuwak on road to beach* 🕾 *2787–0143).*

Post Office San Clemente Bar (⊠ *Main stree, at bus stop).*

Visitor Information Southern Expeditions (⊠ *On Main Street across from San Clemente Bar* 🕾 *2787–0100).*

Taxis (⊠ *Taxi stand on main street, at bus stop in front of San Clemente Bar).*

EXPLORING

★ The **Hacienda Barú** nature reserve is a leader in both ecotourism and
☼ conservation, with a turtle protection project and nature education program in the local school. The bird-watching is spectacular, with excellent guides. You can stay at the cabins or just come for the day to walk the forest and mangrove trails, zip through the canopy on cables, climb a tree, or stake out birds on an observation platform. *⊹3 km (2 mi) north of bridge into Dominical* 🕾*2787–0003* ⊕*www.hacienda baru.com* ☜*$6, tours $20–$60* ☯*Daily 7 AM–dusk.*

☼ Five years in the making, **Parque Reptilandia** is an impressive reptile house with more than 150 specimens of snakes, lizards, frogs, turtles, and other creatures in terrariums and large enclosures. You can even catch a glimpse of Central America's only Komodo dragon, or the newly arrived Gila monsters. Kids love the maternity ward showcasing newborn snakes. More mature snakes live under a retractable roof that lets in sun and rain. They become much more active when it rains, so this is a great rainy-day-at-the-beach alternative activity. Night tours ($12) can also be arranged to watch nocturnal animals at work. If you're not squeamish, feeding day is Friday. *⊹11 km (7 mi) east of Dominical on road to San Isidro* 🕾*2787–8007* ⊕*www.crreptiles.com* ☜*$10* ☯*Daily 9–4:30.*

☼ The **Nauyaca Waterfalls** (Cataratas de Nauyaca), a massive double cascade tumbling down 45 meters (150 feet) and 20 meters (65 feet), are one of the most impressive sights in Costa Rica. The waterfalls—also known as Barú River Falls—are on private property, so the only way to reach them is to take a hiking or horseback tour *(⇨Outdoor Activities, below).*

Playa Dominical is long and flat, rarely crowded, and good for beach-combing among all the flotsam and jetsam that the surf washes up onto the brown sand. Swimmers should beware of fatally dangerous rip currents. In high season, flags mark off a relatively safe area for swimming, under the watchful gaze of a professional lifeguard.

Playa Dominicalito, just 1 km (½ mi) south of Playa Dominical, is usually calmer and more suited to Boogie boarding.

> **PACK YOUR BOARD**
>
> The surfing is great in Dominical, thanks to the runoff from the Barú River mouth, which constantly changes the ocean bottom and creates well-shaped waves big enough to keep intermediate and advanced surfers challenged.
> The best surfing is near the river mouth, and the best time is two hours before or after high tide, to avoid the notorious riptides.

A considerably smaller waterfall than Cataratas de Nauyaca, **Pozo Azul** is in the jungle about 5 km (3 mi) south of town. Off the main highway, head up the road toward Bella Vista lodge and take the first road to the right, past the new school and through a stream; follow the road straight uphill for about 300 meters to where the road widens. You can park here and climb down the steep trail to the river on the right, where there is a lovely swimming hole and waterfall, often populated by local kids when school is out. Be sure not to leave anything of value in your parked car.

OUTDOOR ACTIVITIES

Southern Expeditions (⊠ *On main street, across from San Clemente Bar & Grill* ☎ *2787–0100* ⊕ *southernexpeditionscr.com*), a major tour operator in the area, can arrange kayaking, white-water rafting, scuba diving, fishing, and nature tours in and around Ballena Marine National Park, Caños Island, and all the way down to Corcovado National Park.

Much of the lush forest that covers the steep hillsides above the beaches is protected within private nature reserves. By leading hikes and horseback tours, several of these reserves, such as Hacienda Barú and La Merced (⇨ *Ballena Marine National Park below*), are trying to finance preservation of the rain forest.

FISHING
Angling options range from expensive sportfishing charters to a trip in a small boat to catch red snapper and snook for supper. The five most common fish species here, in the order in which you are likely to catch them, are sailfish, dorado, yellowfin tuna, wahoo, and marlin. **Mark Hendry** (☎ *2787–8224*) runs trips 28 nautical miles out to the Furuno Bank, which he claims is the most reliable area for finding the big ones, including sailfish and marlin. Trips ($600) are in a 21-foot Mako boat and include food, drinks, and gear. **Costa Brava** (☎ *2787–8437* ⊕ *www.cunadelangel.com*), can take you out on Capt. Rudy "Record" Dodero's 31-foot boat with flying bridge, tuna tower, and 260hp engine. Dodero has won six Costa Rican championships. A full day costs $700, half day $550, for a maximum of six guests, three of whom are fishing.

HORSEBACK RIDING **Don Lulo** (☎2787–8137 or 2787–8013) operates tours to Nauyaca Falls that depart Monday to Saturday at 8 AM from the road to San Isidro, 10 km (6 mi) northeast of Dominical. The tour is $45 and includes breakfast and lunch at Don Lulo's family homestead near the falls. You can swim in the cool pool beneath the falls, so bring a bathing suit. There is a river to cross, but otherwise the ride is easy; horses proceed at a walk. Be sure to reserve a day in advance.

☾ Friendly, well-trained horses at **Bella Vista Lodge** (✛5 km (3 mi) southeast of Dominical ☎2787–8069) also take riders to the Nauyaca, following a shorter route, with lunch and a ride in an aerial tram included for $45. For the same price you can go for a gallop on the beach in the morning or afternoon, depending on tides. These tours include lunch. The three- to four-hour tours start at the lodge, then head down the steep Escaleras road 2 km (1 mi) passing Pozo Azul. Riders staying in hotels on the beach can also pick up the ride right on the beach.

SURFING **Green Iguana Surf Camp** (☎2787–0157 ⊕www.greeniguanasurfcamp. com) gives 2–3 hour individual lessons ($50) and has weeklong packages that include lodging, board rental, lessons, and transport to whichever nearby beach has the best waves each day (from $495). These longer packages include transportation to and from San José.

WHERE TO EAT

$–$$$ ✕**Coconut Spice.** If you like rice with spice, you've come to the right place. This sophisticated restaurant has authentic Southeast Asian flavor in both food and furnishings. Try the hot-and-sour tom yan goong soup, tart with lemongrass and lime and heated up with chilies. The jumbo shrimp vary in price and can get quite expensive, but they're worth it: buttery, sweet, and cooked in spicy coconut sauce. There are also satays, curries, and other Indian standards. The restaurant recently moved to a larger location by the river, so bring along repellent. ✉*Pueblo del Río at entrance to Dominical* ☎2787–0073 ▭MC, V ☾Daily from 1 PM

$$ ✕**ConFusione.** The location—on a dead-end road at the southern end of the beach—may confound you on your first visit, but there's nothing confusing about the sophisticated Italian food. Along with the usual dishes, the menu has some interesting local twists: pork instead of veal in the saltimbocca, fettucine with consommé and chicken livers, and lots of Gorgonzola. Appetizers are big enough to share, and pizzas are popular among the more budget-conscious surfers. The terrace dining room, though, is all grown up, glowing with gold light and warm earth tones. The wine list concentrates on Italian wines at modest prices. ✉*Domilocos Hotel, south end of Dominical Beach* ☎2787–0244 ▭AE, MC, V ☾No lunch.

$ ✕**San Clemente Mexican-American Bar & Grill.** Signs you're in the local surfer hangout: dozens of broken surfboards affixed to the ceiling, photos of the sport's early years adorning the walls, and a big sound system and dance floor. Fresh seafood, sandwiches, and Tex Mex standards like burritos and nachos make up the menu. The bargain "starving surfer's breakfast"—two eggs with gallo pinto or pancakes, plus coffee—is always popular. Owner Mike McGinnis is famous for making a blistering hot sauce and for being a super source of information about the area. ⊠*Middle of main road* ☎*2787–0055* ☰*AE, MC, V.*

$ ✕**Tortilla Flats.** Another popular surfer hangout, this casual place has the advantage of being right across from the beach. Fresh-baked baguette sandwiches are stuffed with interesting combinations; the grilled chicken, avocado, tomato, and mozzarella California sandwich is the most popular. Light eaters can buy half a sandwich. Fresh-fish specials and typical Mexican fare round out the casual menu. The margaritas are excellent, and ladies drink free anise-and-*guaro* (sugarcane liquor) shots on Thursday night. ⊠*On beach, Dominical* ☎*2787–0033* ☰*AE, MC, V.*

SOUTH OF ✕**La Parcela.** Picture a dream location: a high headland jutting out into
DOMINICAL the sea with vistas up and down the coast. Throw in a breeze-swept
$–$$$ terrace, polished service, and some fine seaside cuisine. This restaurant has had its ups and downs, often relying on its unmatched location, but the current management has got it right: a wide-ranging menu of pastas, salads, and seafood. Generous servings of perfectly cooked fish are topped with some interesting sauces, including a standout roasted red pepper sauce with almonds. Desserts here are rich—mud pie and a delectable chocolate cake—and substantial enough to share. If you're just passing through Dominical, this is a good place for a cold beer or a *naturale,* a tall glass of freshly whipped fruit juice. Sunsets here are spectacular. ✛*4 km (2½ mi) south of Dominical* ☎*2787–0016* ☰*AE, DC, MC, V.*

WHERE TO STAY

Lodgings in the lowlands of Dominical and the area a little to the north tend to be hot and muggy and not as comfortable as the more luxurious, private, and breezy places up in the hills above Dominicalito, to the south.

$ ▦**Hacienda Barú National Wildlife Refuge and Ecolodge.** Base yourself in
☾ these spacious but simple cabinas to explore the surrounding forests, mangroves, and Blue Flag beach. The six cabins have sitting rooms with wood furniture, screened-in porches, and pretty flower borders. Each sleeps three or four people. Linger for an hour or two atop a lofty bird observation platform in the hotel's rain-forest canopy, zip along the canopy tour, climb a 114-foot-high tree with ropes, or stay overnight at a shelter in the heart of the forest. Excellent local guides interpret the miles of trails, or you can follow the self-guided trail with the help of a handbook. There's a great gift shop here with lots of local crafts and nature books. **Pros:** Prime wildlife viewing, excellent guides, trails and outdoor activities, spacious cabins with kitchens. **Cons:** Cabins are not fancy and can get quite hot, with only fans to cool them; bathrooms are small and pretty basic. ✛*3 km (2 mi) north of bridge into Dominical* ⌂*Apdo. 215–8000, Pérez Zeledón* ☎*2787–0003* ▤*2787–0057* ⊕*www.haciendabaru.com* ➴*6 cabinas* ⌂*In-room: no a/c, no phone, kitchen, no TV. In-hotel: restaurant, beachfront* ☰*AE, MC, V* ⦿*CP.*

$ ▦**Villas Río Mar.** Upriver from the beach on exquisitely landscaped
★ grounds, this hotel is awash in clouds of terrestrial orchids and aflame

with bright bougainvillea and hibiscus. Rooms are in adobe-style cabinas with thatched roofs and cane ceilings, and have clean white-tile bathrooms. The newer junior suites have king-size beds, cable TV, and air-conditioning—a must, since the cabinas bake in the sun. Four suites also have whirlpool tubs. Every room has a private porch screened with mosquito netting and furnished with bamboo chairs and hammocks. Plants and elegant table settings fill the thatch-roof restaurant where the breakfast buffet ($6) is a good deal. A luxurious, large pool has a swim-up bar and handsome teak pool furniture. **Pros:** Huge pool, lovely grounds, good restaurant. **Cons:** About half the rooms have no a/c, and it can get hot here; there are small beaches along the river, but it's a 15-minute walk along an alternately dusty/muddy road to town and the ocean beach. ⊕ *1 km (½ mi) west of Dominical; turn right off highway into town and then right again under bridge and follow bumpy river road* ☎*2787–0052* ☎*2787–0054* ⊕*www.villasriomar. com* ⇆*40 rooms, 12 junior suites* ⌂*In-room: no a/c (some), refrigerator, no TV (some). In-hotel: restaurant, bar, tennis court, pool, spa, bicycles, public Wi-Fi* ⊟*AE, MC, V* ⦙◎⦙*EP.*

SOUTH OF
DOMINICAL
$$$

▦ **Casí el Cielo.** The name, which means "almost heaven," is accurate at this luxury B&B with a twist: a full staff at your service all day long. The views from the lofty terraces alone are worth the price tag, stretching south to the Osa Peninsula and north to Manuel Antonio. The four rooms, all with queen beds topped with pillow-soft mattresses, have themes of shells, birds, jungle, or fish. Exquisite details echo each motif down to the towel racks in the bathrooms. A coffee tray appears at 6 AM on your private terrace with a garden and ocean view. The friendly staff prepares creative breakfasts and elegant dinners on a breezy terrace. Enticing you to leave your room is a pretty but petite pool. **Pros:** Charming decorative touches and spectacular views; warm, friendly owner and staff. **Cons:** Once you're up here, it's a steep trek down to town or the beach, so your own transportation is a good idea; minimum stay is three days. ⊠*South of Km. 151 on the Costanera; turn left on San Martin road, head uphill to crossroads, then turn right and follow signs* ☎*8813–5614* ⊕*www.casielcielo.com* ⇆*4 rooms* ⌂*In-room: no phone, safe, no TV. In-hotel: pool, public Internet* ⊟*MC, V* ⦙◎⦙*MAP.*

$$$

▦ **Cuna del Angel Hotel and Spa.** Hosts of decorative angels abound at this made-in-heaven fantasyland for grown-ups. The over-the-top decor may not suit everyone, but this is a perfect spot for those who like to indulge themselves. The luxurious rooms are chock-full of delightful touches, including luxurious linens and towels, stained-glass windows, and spectacular lamps. The spa is small and intimate, with a sensual Turkish bath, a selection of soothing massages, and a full-service hair salon. Once you feel rejuvenated, a lush garden, a terrace restaurant, and a pretty pool with an ocean view draw you outdoors. Dinner in the terrace restaurant is pleasant, with a sophisticated menu and, if your timing is right, there's entertainment by top national musicians at the hotel's once-a-month dinner concerts. **Pros:** Endlessly amusing decor to keep you talking, admiring, and laughing; friendly service in hotel and spa, which is small and intimate. **Cons:** Room balconies and terraces are quite close together, so not a lot of privacy; rooms all face the pool, and if there are kids playing, you can't escape their squeals. ⊠*Puertocito* ✢*9 km (5 mi) south of Dominical* ☎*2787–8012* 🖷*2787–8015 Ext. 304* ⊕*www.cunadelangel.com* ☞*16 rooms* ⅃*In-room: Wi-Fi. In-hotel: restaurant, bar, pool, spa, no-smoking rooms* ⅥⓄ*CP.*

\$–\$\$ 🖼**Coconut Grove Oceanfront Cottages.** Right on the beach, this well-maintained cluster of cabins and beach houses is ideal for couples or families who want to fend for themselves. The two bamboo-furnished beach houses sleep two to six and have full kitchens; the smaller cabins have kitchenettes and room for three. At night you can turn off the a/c, open the screened windows, and fall asleep to the sound of the sea. The largest cottage, #5, is also closest to the beach. There's a pretty pool and yoga classes twice a week. The American owners have dogs, including two very large but lazy Great Danes. **Pros:** Best location in town: right on beach, close to cool ocean breezes; communal BBQ; friendly owner/hosts. **Cons:** Furnishings are simple, not fancy; guests must love dogs. ⊠*Turn off main highway at Km 147* ✢*3 km (2 mi) south of Dominical* 🖷☎*2787–0130* ⊕*www.coconutgrovecr. com* ☞*3 cabins, 2 beach houses* ⅃*In-room: kitchen (some). In-hotel: pool, beachfront* ▭*No credit cards* ⅥⓄ*EP.*

\$–\$\$ 🖼**Necochea Inn.** The forest setting feels primeval, but the decor at this
★ handsome mountain retreat is a sophisticated mix of plush, contemporary furniture. Downstairs living and dining rooms face a wall of sliding glass doors looking onto a stone-deck pool in the jungle and a slice of ocean for a view. Two streams run through the forested property, supplying a natural, burbling sound track. A curved stone stairway leads up to two luxurious, large rooms that share a spacious bath. Two upstairs suites have private porches, decadent bathrooms with deep tubs, antique armoires, and gleaming hardwood floors. A new creek-side suite has its own TV and a whirlpool on a private terrace. Hosts Yvonne and Carlos are full of energy and make every guest feel at home. **Pros:** Luxurious accommodation with a personal touch, including Yvonne's mural-size wildlife paintings; excellent breakfasts; and, if you ask, a rollicking night of karaoke with your hosts. **Cons:** Up a steep road that can be muddy, need your own car to get down hill to restaurants and beaches. ⊠*Just south of Km 147, turn 2 km (1 mi) up, past the Pozo Azul, Dominicalito* ☎*2787–8072 or 8395–2984* ⊕*www.thenecocheainn.com* ☞*3 rooms with shared bath, 3 suites, 1 room with private bath* ⅃*In-room: no a/c, no phone, no TV. In-hotel: restaurant, pool* ▭*MC, V* ⅥⓄ*BP.*

¢–\$ 🖼**Pacific Edge.** Unbeatable views and affordable prices set these styl-
★ ishly rustic cabins apart. The forest grows right up to the edge of the property, high on a mountain ridge south of town. Private, spacious wood cabinas—one sleeps six; others sleep four—have newly tiled bathrooms, hammocks strung on wide porches, and comfortable orthopedic mattresses covered with colorful Guatemalan bedspreads. Host Susie Atkinson serves great breakfasts in the lodge's bamboo-roof, pagoda-style dining room. Dinner—Thai-style shrimp, perhaps—is cooked on request. Two lookout towers at each end of the tiny pool catch the spectacular sunsets and passing whale pods. The road up to this lofty perch

requires a 4WD vehicle, but a hotel shuttle can pick you up in town with advance notice. Be prepared for a barky welcome; Susie and her husband, George, love big (but gentle) dogs. The reception desk closes at 6 PM. **Pros:** Fabulous views, bargain prices, serene setting, can make your own breakfast and simple snacks. **Cons:** Very steep road that requires 4WD to get back and forth to town restaurants and beaches, must love dogs. ⊠ *Turn inland 4 km (2½ mi) south of Dominical at Km 148, up a rough road 1.2 km (1 mi)* 🖭🖭*2787–8010* ⊕*www.pacific edge.info* ⌐*4 cabinas* ⌂*In-room: no a/c, no phone, refrigerator, no TV. In-hotel: restaurant, bar, pool* ☰*AE, MC, V* ⦶|*EP.*

NIGHTLIFE

During the high season, Dominical hops at night, and when the surfers have fled to find bigger waves there are enough locals around to keep some fun events afloat. At Friday night's **Movies in the Jungle** (⊠*High up on Marina Dr. at Cinema Escaleras in a private house with no sign; call for directions* ☎*2787–8065*), after a potluck dinner at 5, the movies start at 6, except during the depths of the rainy season. Movie buff Harley "Toby" Toberman presents self-proclaimed weird shorts from his huge collection plus a full-length feature on a huge screen, with state-of-the-art equipment. Admission is $4, which goes into a projector-bulb fund. Saturday night the dance action is at the **Roca Verde** (⊹*1 km [½ mi] south of Dominical* ☎*2787–0036*), with a mixed crowd that doesn't usually get warmed up until 11 PM. Friday night there's live music at **San Clemente Bar** (⊠*On main road* ☎*2787–0055*). At **Maracatu World Music Bar** ⊠*Main street, across from San Clemente* ☎*2787–0091*) the crowd is young and edgy, with an open mike on Tuesday, salsa music on Wednesday ladies' night, reggae and pasta on Thursday, and DJ dancing on Friday. An older crowd gathers at **Río Lindo Resort** (⊠*At entrance to town* ☎*2787–0028*) for dance music and live bands in the Rum Bar on Thursday from 8 *to* 12 PM. On Sunday from 4 *to* 9 PM, an alfresco fiesta by the pool includes BBQ, horseshoes, and calypso and bluesy music. Bring your swimsuit.

SHOPPING

★ **Banana Bay Gallery & Gifts** (⊠*Plaza Pacífica shopping center, highway just above Dominical* ☎*2787–0106* ⊙ *Closed Sun.*) is not only airconditioned, but also stocked with an always-intriguing and -amusing mix of arts and crafts and unusual items, along with indigenous crafts such as tropical masks and lots of insect-theme toys for kids of all ages.

BALLENA MARINE NATIONAL PARK

20 km (12 mi) southeast of Dominical.

There's great snorkeling and whale-watching at Parque Nacional Marino Ballena (Whale Marine National Park), which protects several beaches stretching for about 10 km (6 mi), a mangrove estuary, a recovering coral reef, and a vast swath of ocean with rocky isles and islets. Along with the tropical fish you'll see while snorkeling, you may be lucky enough to see humpback whales with their young, from December to April and again in late July through late October. Dolphins are also common sights. Above the water there are frigate birds and brown boobies, a tropical seabird, nesting on the park's rocky islands. ⊠ *Park begins at Playa Uvita, about 16 km/10 mi south of Dominical* ☎*2743–8236* ✉*$6 ($1 if you enter at Playa Uvita)* ⊘*Daily 6–6.*

GETTING HERE & AROUND

The park area encompasses the communities of Uvita, Bahía Ballena, and Ojochal, all easily accessed off the Costanera. The park officially begins 20 km (12 mi) south of Dominical along a wide, newly paved highway. As soon as you get off the highway, however, the roads are bumpy and dusty. Alternatively, take a taxi or bus from Dominical. Buses leave Dominical at 10:30 AM and 5:30 PM daily, and there are longer-haul buses that pass along the Costanera and can drop you off in Uvita.

★ The park has four sectors, each with a small ranger station. At the northern end, palm-fringed **Playa Uvita** stretches out along a *tombolo*, or long swath of sand, connecting a former island to the coast. At low tide the brown sandbar resembles a whale's tail, hence the name of the bay: Bahía Ballena, or Whale Bay. Pods of migrating whales are spotted here, too. Although there are no park services here, there are plenty of restrooms in the nearby restaurants lining the main street of the town of Bahía Ballena.

Playa Colonia, 2 km (1¼ mi) south of Playa Uvita, has a safe swimming beach with a view of rocky islands. It's the only beach in the park where cars can park on the beach.

Playa Ballena, 4 km (2½ mi) to the south of Playa Colonia, is a lovely strand backed by lush vegetation. The price to enter the park here is $6.

Tiny **Playa Piñuela**, 3 km (2 mi) south of Playa Ballena, is the prettiest of the park beaches, in a deep cove that serves as the local port. You can camp here, for the price of park admission, and also at Playas Ballena and Colonia (but not at Playa Uvita).

Playa Ventanas, just 1½ km (1 mi) south of Ballena Marine Park, is a beautiful beach that's popular for sea-kayaking, with some interesting tidal caves. The mountains that rise up behind these beaches hold rain forests, waterfalls, and wildlife. There is guarded, private parking here for 350 colones (about 75¢) an hour.

At **La Merced National Wildlife Refuge,** owned by Selva Mar, you can ride the range on horseback, explore the forest on a nature hike, or go bird-watching with an excellent guide. Tours, which are the only way to visit, include transportation from your hotel and a guide; the full-day tour includes lunch. ⊠*Km 159 on the Costanera, north of Uvita* ☎*8861–5147* ⊕*www.rancholamerced.com* ✉*$35 half-day tour, $65 full-day tour* ⊘*By reservation only.* You'll find more excellent bird-watching and hiking a little farther up the hill in the **Oro Verde Private Nature Reserve**, which offers daily two-hour birding tours at 6 AM and 2 PM ($30), as well as guided hikes through their primary forest reserve

($15–$35) and a three-hour morning or afternoon horseback tour to a waterfall ($35). ✢ *3 km (2 mi) uphill from Rancho La Merced, north of Uvita* ☎*2743–8072* ⊕*www.costarica-birding-oroverde.com* ⊗*By reservation only.*

OUTDOOR ACTIVITIES

Outfitters in Dominical *(⇨above)* run tours to the park and surrounding beaches. **La Merced National Wildlife Refuge** *(⇨above)* has birding, forest hikes, and horseback riding. For local bookings and information, contact the Uvita Information Center (☎8843–7142 ⊕www. uvita.info).

DIVING & SNORKELING
Mystic Dive Center (☎*2786–5217* ⊕*www.mysticdivecenter.com*) specializes in dive and snorkel trips to Caño Island, about 50 km (31 mi), or an hour and 15 minutes, from Playa Ventanas ($90 full-day snorkeling; $145 full-day diving including equipment, lunch, park fees, and guide).**Crocodive** has complete PADI-certified diving and snorkeling courses, including introductory dive courses in a pool ($60) or at Caño Island ($159). A four-hour dive or snorkeling trip around Ballena Marine Park is $50 per snorkeler or $86 per diver (with two tanks). They also have night dives and trips to Caño Island ($80–$128). ⊠*At entrance to Ojochal, Playa Tortuga* ☎*2786–5417* ⊕*www.crocodive.com.*

The best spot for snorkeling in the park is at the north end of Playa Ballena, near the whale's tail. **Dolphin Tours of Bahía Ballena** (☎*2743–8013* ⊕*www.dolphintourcostarica.com*), with an office very close to the beach, takes you on 2½-hour snorkeling tours ($50). It also offers kayaking trips for the same price.Mystic Dive Center and Crocodive also offer snorkeling tours.

FISHING
Dolphin Tours of Bahía Ballena *(⇨ Diving & Snorkeling, above)* offers half-day fishing trips for snook and red snapper that cost $400 for up to four anglers; $550 for a full day inshore and $650 offshore.

ULTRALIGHT FLIGHTS
For a bird's-eye view of Bahía Ballena and the park, take off in an ultralight flying machine with aeronautical engineer Georg Kiechle
☾ and **Ultralight Tour** (⊠*Road into Bahía Ballena* ☎*2743–8037* ⊕*www. ultralighttour.com*). Tours cost $75 to $150 for trips lasting 20 to 60 minutes.

WHERE TO EAT

$$ ✕**Exotica Restaurant.** Nestled in the tiny French-Canadian enclave of Ojochal, this thatch-roof restaurant with only nine tables has been serving tropical fare with a French accent for 10 years now. For starters, there's a tangy refreshing avocado, pineapple, lime, and cilantro appetizer or an intriguing Tahitian fish carpaccio with bananas. Or try a hearty serving of fish or shrimp in a spicy banana-curry sauce. French favorites include cognac liver pâté, and duck breast with an orange or pineapple sauce. Presentation is artistic, with flourishes of flowers and sprigs of exotic greenery. Desserts are all homemade and luscious. Chocoholics won't want to miss the chocolate chiffon cake with chocolate sauce and an accompanying shot glass of cocoa liqueur.

⊠ *Main road into Ojochal* ✢*15 km (9 mi) south of Uvita* ☎*2786–5050* ▭*MC, V* ⊗*Closed Sun.*

$-$$ ✕**Pizzeria El Jardín Tortuga.** Ordering a pizza doesn't get any simpler
★ than this: vegetarian or meat. The German pizza baker can make only
six individual pizzas at a time in his wood-fired clay oven, but it's
worth the wait for thin-crust pies heaped with toppings. In high season
there's also grilled fish on the menu, along with year-round lasagne,
roast pork, and curried chicken. While you wait for your meal, you
can enjoy the restaurant's bar, popular with locals. ⊠*Ojochal, past
supermarket, left on bridge and first right* ☎*2786–5059* ▭*No credit
cards* ⊗*Closed Tues.*

$ ✕**Tilapias El Pavón.** To enjoy an authentically Tico day in the country,
follow a winding river road up to this family-run tilapia fish farm.
You can work up an appetite on a short hike to a spectacular waterfall
with a swimming hole (bring your suit and binoculars for bird-watching), then catch your own tilapia. The cooks at the open-air wooden
restaurant overlooking the tidily kept fish ponds will fry up your fish
in 10 minutes, and present it whole or filleted, with rice, salad, yucca,
and patacones (fried, mashed plantains), a feast for only $7. They also
serve wine and beer. Open 9 AM to 6 PM, till 8 PM on weekends. ⊠*Just
before bridge in Punta Mala (2 km [1 mi] south of Ojochal), follow a
dirt road 4 km (2½ mi) uphill to hamlet of Vergel* ☎*8356–6051* ▭*No
credit cards* ⊗*Closed Mon.*

WHERE TO STAY

$-$$$ ▥**Cristal Ballena Hotel Resort.** High on a hillside with spectacular ocean
★ views, this Austrian-owned hotel is the most luxurious base for explor-
ing the area. The jewel in this blue-and-white Mediterranean-style hotel
is a sparkling, 400-square-meter swimming pool that commands both
mountain and sea views. If the setting doesn't relax you enough, a new
spa offers holistic therapy and massages. Spacious, elegant rooms and
suites set in carefully landscaped grounds have canopy beds, large tile
bathrooms with sinks for two, and sliding-glass doors leading out to
private terraces. If you tire of the view (not likely), there are large tele-
visions on swivel bases. A pair of rustic cabins are set close together in
a lush garden, but they get quite hot and don't have an ocean view (or
TV). Breakfasts are hearty at the poolside Pura Vida restaurant, which
also serves lunch. Dinner, featuring excellent fish (sushi on Thursday),
along with some tasty Austrian specialties, is served in the upstairs, ele-
gant, air-conditioned El Cristal restaurant, overlooking the pool. Ser-
vice is on the slow side, but with an ocean vista and refreshing breezes,
who cares? **Pros:** Wonderful swimming pool for serious swimmers and
loungers; great ocean, mountain, and sky views; luxurious rooms.
Cons: Restaurant service can be slow; steep walk/drive to beach; bar-
gain-price rustic garden cabins do not have a/c or TV. ✢*7 km (4 mi)
south of Uvita on the Costanera* ☎*2786–5354* 🖷*2786–5355* ⊕*www.
cristal-ballena.com* ⇔*18 suites, 2 cabins* ⚙*In-room: refrigerator. In-
hotel: restaurant, bar, pool, spa, public Wi-Fi* ▭*AE, MC, V* ⦿*EP.*

$-$$ ▥**Villas Gaia.** Conveniently just off the highway, these spacious, tasteful villas owned by a sophisticated Dutch couple, are spread around
the jungle on a ridge behind Playa Tortuga, overlooking forest ravines.

6

Most of the recently remodeled villas now have air-conditioning, plus handsome wood furniture and breezy terraces with ceiling fans. A luxurious house has air-conditioning and satellite TV. The restaurant, with chandeliers made of mangrove roots hanging from above, has an eclectic menu ranging from Mexican to Thai. There's also a new breakfast terrace under tall palms, and a lovely rancho/bar by the pool where you can enjoy ocean views and breezes. The pool also has comfortable, contoured teak lounges for sunbathing. A forest trail leads from the villas down to the beach, where you can swim safely. The hotel happily arranges horseback, mangrove, and sea-kayaking tours. **Pros:** Easy access, right off the highway; serene setting; proximity to beaches and Ballena Park. **Cons:** You must climb some stairs to get to the villas, pool is small and beach is a bit of a walk down a steep path. ✛ *15 km (9 mi) south of Uvita on coastal highway, Playa Tortuga* ☎ *2786-5044* 🖷 *2786-5009* ⊕ *www.villasgaia.com* 📞 *14 cabinas, 1 house* ⚒ *In-room: no a/c (some), no phone, no TV. In-hotel: restaurant, bar, pool, laundry service* ⊟ *AE, MC, V* ⧖ *EP.*

¢–$ 🏠**Diquis del Sur Resort.** An ideal—and affordable—tropical retreat for the winter-weary, this formerly run-down hotel in the hills above Ojochal has been given new life by a creative French-Canadian couple. Renée and Pierre Beaupré are just as delighted as their guests to be in this "earthly paradise," and their enthusiasm shows in the welcome you'll receive. The views look to mountains and the ocean and a garden full of mature fruit trees and flowering shrubs. Five bungalows are spread around the pretty grounds. Some have kitchens and air-conditioning; some have only a fan, but shady trees keep them cool. The full breakfast has a French accent—crepes, French toast, omelets—and is served in a thatch-roof dining room overlooking an inviting pool with a waterfall. There is a two-day minimum stay. **Pros:** Bargain rates, great breakfasts, lots of privacy in well-spaced bungalows. **Cons:** Some bungalows have no a/c, spare but adequate furnishings, rough road up from main highway. ✛ *1 km (½ mi) up dirt road signed* CALLE PAPA-GAYO, *off Ojochal main road* ☎ *2786-5013* ⊕ *www.diquiscostarica. com* 📞 *5 bungalows* ⚒ *In-room: no a/c (some), no phone, kitchen (some), no TV. In-hotel: restaurant, bar, pool, public Internet* ⊟ *No credit cards* ⧖ *BP.*

SHOPPING

Next door to Mystic Dive Center is **Green Leaf Arts & Artesania** (✉ *Centro Comercial Ventanas, near Km 174* ✛ *1 km (½ mi) north of Ojochal* ☎ *2786-5221*), with a great selection of quality local art, indigenous crafts and Asian home accessories plus a wide selection of field guides, jewelry, and home accessories. Next door, at the Licorera Feliz (same owner) you can pick up imported snacks, cheeses, and treats for a beach picnic, as well as wine from the best selection available in the area. Both stores are open daily from 9 to 6.

THE GOLFO DULCE

One of only three tropical fjords in the world, the Golfo Dulce has 600-foot-deep waters in the center of a usually placid gulf that attract humpback whales. At Chacarita, 33 km (20 mi) south of Palmar Sur, the southern coast assumes a multiple personality. Heading west, you reach the Osa Peninsula and, eventually, the Pacific Ocean and the wildest region of Costa Rica. Continuing due south is the Golfo Dulce, which means Sweet Gulf and suggests tranquil waters. This gulf creates two shorelines: an eastern shore that is accessible only by boat above Golfito, and a western shore, which is the eastern side of the Osa Peninsula. South of Golfito the coast fronts the Pacific Ocean once again (rather than the tranquil gulf), with wilder beaches that beckon surfers and nature lovers.

GOLFITO

339 km (212 mi) southeast of San José.

Overlooking a small gulf (hence its name) and hemmed in by a steep bank of forest, Golfito has a great location. Sportfishing has taken off in this area, and many lodges run world-class fishing trips. The gulf water is warm, salty, and crystal-clear in the early mornings. When the sun sets behind the rolling silhouette of the Osa Peninsula, you can sometimes spot phosphorescent fish jumping. Golfito was a thriving banana port for several decades—United Fruit arrived in 1938—with elegant housing and lush landscaping for its plantation managers. After United Fruit pulled out in 1985, Golfito slipped into a state of poverty and neglect. The town itself consists of a pleasant older section and a long, ugly strip of newer buildings. Visiting U.S. Navy ships dock here, and small cruise ships moor in the harbor. The Costa Rica Coast Guard Academy is also here.

NAVIGATING GOLFITO

Taxis and boats take you wherever you need to go in and around Golfito. You can hire taxi boats at the city dock in Golfito (about $60 round-trip to go to area lodges or across to Puerto Jiménez). The only way to reach the remote Golfo Dulce lodges above Golfito is by boat. Early morning is the best time, when the water in the gulf is at its calmest. Most lodges include the boat transport in their rates.

GETTING HERE

From San José the trip is a long and often grueling eight-hour drive along paved roads crossing over often-foggy mountains. Your best bet, especially if you are visiting one of the lodges on the gulf, is to fly to Golfito, which only takes about one hour. Direct buses from San José leave twice daily.

GOLFITO ESSENTIALS

Bank/ATM **ATH Coopealianza** (⊠ *Across from hospital, north end of town*). **Banco Nacional** (⊠ *South of hospital* ☎ *2775–1101*).

Hospital **Regional Hospital** (⊠ *American Zone, near Deposito* ☎ *2775–1001*).

Going Fishing?

Costa Rica teems with a constant supply of *pescado* (fish), some of which might seem unique to North Americans. Below are some local catches and where you'll find them.

Gaspar (alligator gar), found in Barra del Colorado River and Lake Arenal, looks like a holdover from prehistoric times and has a long narrow snout full of sharp teeth; they make great sport on light tackle. Gar meat is firm and sweet (some say shrimplike), but the eggs are toxic to humans.

Guapote (rainbow bass) make their home in Lake Arenal. It's a hard-hitting catch: 5- to 6-pounders are common. Taxonomically, guapote are not related to bass, but are caught similarly, by casting or flipping plugs or spinner bait. Streams near the Cerro de la Muerte, off the Pan-American Highway leading south from San José, are stocked with guapote. The fish tend to be small, but the scenery makes a day here worthwhile.

Marlin and sailfish migrate northward through the year, beginning about November when they are plentiful in the Golfito region. From December into April they spread north to Quepos, which has some of the country's best deep-sea fishing, and are present in large numbers along the Nicoya Peninsula at Carrillo and Sámara from February to April, and near Tamarindo and Flamingo from May to September. Pacific sailfish average over 45 kilos (100 pounds), and are usually fought on a 15-pound line or less. Costa Rican laws require that all sails, except record catches, be released.

Tarpon and snook fishing is big on the Caribbean coast, centered at the mouth of the Barra del Colorado River. The acrobatic tarpon, which averages about 85 pounds here, is able to swim freely between salt water and freshwater and is considered by many to be the most exciting catch on earth. Tarpon sometimes strike like a rocket, hurtling 5 meters (16 feet) into the air, flipping, and twisting left and right. Anglers say the success rate of experts is to land about one out of every 10 tarpon hooked. In the Colorado, schools of up to 100 tarpon following and feeding on schools of *titi* (small, sardinelike fish) travel for more than 160 km (100 mi) to Lake Nicaragua. Snook also make this long swim. The long-standing International Game Fishing Association all-tackle record was taken in this area.

Pharmacy Farmacia Golfito (⊠ *Main street, across from city park* ☎ *2775-2442*).

Internet Golfito on Line (⊠ *Main street, between city dock and gas station, next to Servicentro Pacifico Sur* ☎ *2775-2424*).

Post Office Correo (⊠ *Across from soccer field; climb flight of stairs off the main road, just south of central park*).

Taxis Taxi service (☎ *2775-2020*).

Visitor Information Land Sea Services (⊠ *Next to Banana Bay Marina on left as you enter town* ☎ *2775-1614*); they also sell SANSA tickets. **Visitor Information Center** (⊠ *At municipal dock* ☎ *2775-1820* ⊗ *Mon.-Sat. 8-noon*).

EXPLORING

The northwestern end of town is the so-called **American Zone,** full of wooden houses on stilts, where the expatriate managers of United Fruit lived amid flowering trees imported from all over the world. Some of these vintage houses, built of durable Honduran hardwoods, are now being spruced up.

Golfito doesn't have a beach of its own, but **Playa Cacao** is a mere five-minute boat ride across the bay from town. Hire a boat at the city dock or from a mooring opposite the larger cruise-ship dock, north of Golfito's center. Playa Cacao has two casual restaurants and one collection of basic cabinas, but it makes a cooler, quieter option when the heat and noise in Golfito get unbearable.

Piedras Blancas National Park has some great birding. The park is verdant forest, home to many species of endemic plants and animals. It's also an important wildlife corridor because it connects to Corcovado National Park. Follow the main road northwest through the old American Zone, past the airstrip and a housing project: the place where a dirt road heads into the rain forest is ground zero for bird-watchers. ✉*Adjacent to Golfito National Wildlife Refuge* ☎*No phone* 💲*Free* 🕐*Daily dawn–dusk.*

A Garden of Eden with mass plantings of ornamental palms, bromeliads, heliconias, cycads, orchids, flowering gingers, and spice trees, ★ **Casa Orquideas** has been tended with care for more than 25 years by American owners Ron and Trudy MacAllister. The 2½-hour tour, available Sunday and Thursday at 8:30 AM, includes touching, tasting, and smelling, plus spotting toucans and hummingbirds. Trudy is also a font of information on local lore and medicinal plants. Guided tours, given for a minimum of three people, are $8 per person. Self-guided visits cost $5. The garden is accessible only by boat; a water taxi from Golfito to the garden (about $60 round-trip for up to four people) is a tour in itself. ✉*North of Golfito on the Golfo Dulce* ☎*8829–1247* 💲*$5–$8* 🕐*Tours: Sat.–Thurs. at 8:30 AM.* 🕐 *Closed Fri.*

OUTDOOR ACTIVITIES

FISHING The open ocean holds plenty of sailfish, marlin, and roosterfish during the dry months, as well as mahimahi, tuna, and wahoo during the rainy season; there's excellent bottom fishing any time of year. Captains are in constant radio contact with one another and tend to share fish finds.

Banana Bay Marina (☎*2775–0838 or 2775-1111* ⊕*www.bananabay marina.com*) has a fleet of five boats skippered by world-record-holding captains. A day's fishing for up to four averages $850. **C-Tales** (✉*Las Gaviotas Hotel* ☎*2775–0062* ⊕*www.c-tales.com*) operates fishing boats with English-speaking captains and mates. With 11 boats, **Golfito Sailfish Rancho** (☎*8380–4262, 800/450–9908 in U.S.* ⊕*www. golfitosailfish.com*) has the area's largest fishing charter operation. **Land Sea** (✉ *Waterfront next to Banana Bay Marina* ☎*2775–1614* ⊕*www. marinaservices-yachtdelivery.com*) can hook you up with independent captains in the area.

6

WHERE TO EAT

GOLFITO
$–$$$

✕ **Banana Bay.** For consistently good American-style food, you can't beat this breezy marina restaurant with a view of expensive yachts and fishing boats. Locals complain that the prices are high, but portions are hefty, and include generous salads, excellent chicken fajitas wrapped in homemade tortillas, and a delicious grilled dorado fish sandwich with a mountain of fries—a deal at $7. Jumbo shrimp, for which the town's commercial fleet is famous, are expensive at $15, but worth it. While you're waiting for your order, check your e-mail at their high-speed Internet café, or take advantage of the Wi-Fi. It's open for breakfast, too. ⊠ *Golfito main street, south of town dock* ☎ *2775–0838* ⊟ *MC, V.*

$

✕ **Restaurante Mar y Luna.** Strings of buoys, nets, and fishing rods give a nautical air to this casual, affordable terrace restaurant jutting out into Golfito Harbor. Twinkling fairy lights frame a pleasant harbor view. The seafood-heavy lineup includes shrimp and grilled whole fish. Chicken fillets smothered in a mushroom sauce and vegetarian dishes round out the menu. The quality varies, depending on who's in the kitchen, but during a recent visit the kitchen was in top form. ⊠ *South end of Golfito main street, just north of Hotel Las Gaviotas* ☎ *2775–0192* ⊟ *AE, MC, V* ⊘ *Closed Mon.*

WHERE TO STAY

The atmosphere of the in-town hotels differs dramatically from that of the lodges in the delightfully remote east coast of the Golfo Dulce. The latter is a world of jungle and blue water, birds and fish, and desert-island beaches, with lodges accessible only by boat, from either Golfito or Puerto Jiménez.

$
☼

🏨 **Hotel Samoa del Sur.** Nautical kitsch at its best, this dockside hotel has a ship-shape restaurant ($–$$$), complete with a billowy sail and a mermaid figurehead. This is definitely fisherman territory, with a pool table, loud music, and big TVs. Unexpectedly, the breakfast omelets may be the best in Costa Rica. The seaside theme carries through to spacious rooms, from shell-pattern bedspreads to shell-shape hand soap. Rooms have two double beds, remote-control air-conditioning, and tile bathrooms with hot water (a rarity in these parts). The mattresses are a little soft, and you are at the mercy of adjoining neighbors and the thumping music from the bar, but things usually quiet down by 11 PM. The eccentric French owner designed a swimming pool in the shape of butterfly wings, plus a kids' pool and play area. Guests who want to get out on the water can paddle complimentary kayaks. After midnight you are warned not to leave your room to avoid a nasty encounter with the guard dogs. **Pros:** Affordable and fun, lively restaurant. **Cons:** Can be lots of rambunctious kids in pool, noisy bar in evenings, guard dogs may scare off some guests. ⊠ *Main street, 1 block north of town dock* ☎ *2775–0233* 🖷 *2775–0573* ⊕ *www.samoadelsur.com* 🛏 *14 rooms* ☁ *In-room: no phone. In-hotel: restaurant, bar, pool, bicycles, laundry service* ⊟ *AE, MC, V* ⦿ *EP.*

GOLFO DULCE
$$$
Fodor's Choice
★

🏨 **Playa Nicuesa Rainforest Lodge.** Hands-down, this is the best lodge on the gulf, with an emphasis on adventure on both land and sea. Out the front door of the lodge are beach, bay, and mangroves, with kayaks, snorkeling, fishing, sailing, and swimming; out the back door is a forested mountain with hiking trails, a waterfall, and plenty of wildlife and a resident naturalist to interpret the trails. For more contemplative types, there is a resident yoga instructor in high season. The two-story main lodge is a palatial tree house, crafted from 15 kinds of wood. Luxurious, hexagonal wooden cabins with open-air showers are scattered around a lush garden that ensures privacy. A stucco guesthouse with four large, comfortable rooms is shaded by mango trees. Solar power ensures a steady supply of electricity and there's always lots of hot water. Imaginative meals are served in the second-story dining room–cum–lounge with an unbeatable tropical-garden view. The owners are active ex–New Yorkers devoted to running an eco-friendly operation and delivering top-level service. **Pros:** Everything you need to have an active vacation; excellent food and service; idyllic setting; friendly, intelligent owners who interact with guests. **Cons:** No a/c; cabins are fairly open to nature, so there will be some insects outside the mosquito netting at night. ⊠ *Golfo Dulce, north of Golfito; accessible only by boat from Golfito or Puerto Jiménez* ⊕ *Apdo. 56, Golfito* ☎ *8824–6571, 2256–0085 in San José, 866/504–8116 in U.S.* ⊕ *www.nicuesalodge.com* ⋑ *6 cabins, 4 rooms* ⅍ *In-room: no a/c, no phone, no TV. In-hotel: restaurant, bar, beachfront, water sports, no kids under 6* ⊟ *MC, V* ⊘ *Closed Oct.–Nov. 15* ⍓*AI.*

$$ ⚏**Esquinas Rainforest Lodge.** This well-managed eco-lodge is a model conservation project run by Austrians who have tried to instill a sense of Teutonic order. (More than 80% of the guests here are from Germany and Austria.) But the tidy gravel paths winding past wooden cabins in manicured gardens are constantly being encroached upon by wild forest, with the garden looking wilder every year. A spring-fed pool is delightful, and. fragrant white ginger and ylang-ylang encircle a pond that is home to contented, well-fed caimans. Another nearby pond has a new lookout for bird-watchers. Local guides lead visitors along thrilling trails that head to the waterfalls and primary forest of Piedras Blancas National Park. Rooms have tile floors, good reading lamps, and airy bathrooms with plenty of hot water. The dining room, romantically candlelit at night, serves excellent food. If you have 4WD, you can get here by following the dirt road from Golfito through the heart of Piedras Blancas National Park. In the dry season when it's passable, this back route can cut miles off a trip from the north, and it passes through some gorgeous wilderness. **Pros:** Excellent trails and wildlife-viewing opportunities in unique natural setting, hearty meals. **Cons:** No a/c and it can get hot here, some trails are challenging and you need to be steady on your feet, lodge is geared to nature lovers who aren't looking for luxury. ⊠ *Near La Gamba* ⊹ *5 km (3 mi) west of Villa Briceño turnoff* ☎ *2741–8001, 2775-0140 in Golfito* ⊕ *www. esquinaslodge.com* ⋑ *14 rooms in 7 bungalows* ⅍ *In-room: no a/c, no phone, no TV. In-hotel: restaurant, bar, pool* ⊟ *AE, MC, V* ⍓*FAP.*

¢–$ ⚏**Hotel Las Gaviotas.** Just south of town on the water's edge, this hotel has wonderful views over the inner gulf. Rooms have terra-cotta floors, teak furniture, and a veranda with chairs overlooking the well-tended tropical gardens and the shimmering gulf beyond. A pleasant open-air restaurant with fresh-tasting food looks onto the large pool, whose terrace is barely divided from the sea. The restaurant has an extensive wine and cocktail list, and the weekend barbecue buffets ($15) are the best deal in town. The hotel offers sportfishing trips from its own dock and has a good gift shop. **Pros:** Great location and large pool, safe parking. **Cons:** Fairly utilitarian furniture and spare decor, bathrooms are a little dreary. ⊕*3 km (2 mi) south of Golfito town center* ⌂*Apdo. 12–8201, Golfito* ☎*2775–0062* 🖷*2775–0544* ⊕*www.resortlasgaviotas.com* 🛏*18 rooms, 3 cabinas* ↺*In-room: safe. In-hotel: restaurant, bar, pool* ▤*AE, MC, V* ⫿◎*EP.*

> ### TO FLUSH OR NOT TO FLUSH?
>
> Costa Rican toilets *do* flush, but in most of Costa Rica, septic systems weren't designed to accommodate toilet tissue (the pipes are too narrow). If you don't want to be the *gringo* who clogs up the works, watch for signs asking you not to put anything in the toilet. A wastebasket (*basurero*) is almost always provided to hold used tissue. Even upscale resorts and other places with modern septic systems have the basket, since the habit has been ingrained in locals.

SHOPPING

Ticos are drawn to Golfito's duty-free bargains on such imported items as TV sets, stereos, tires, wine, and liquor. To shop at the **Depósito Libre** you have to spend the night in Golfito, because you have to register in the afternoon with your passport to shop the next morning. Shopping is sheer madness in December. It's closed on Mondays. **Tierra Mar** (⊠*Waterfront next to Banana Bay Marina*) has an excellent selection of painted wood masks. It also has one-of-a-kind local crafts, such as woven straw hats, cotton purses, and painted gourds.

★ In a class all its own, the **Mercado Artesania** (⊠*Hotel Samoa Sur, main street, 1 block north of town dock*) is filled with every imaginable— and unimaginable—souvenir. Large paintings by local artists, huge painted fans from Thailand, hammocks, beach clothes, and life-size snake carvings are just a few of the offerings here. Even if you don't buy a thing, it's fun to look. Ask the hotel manager to unlock the door and visit the Shell Museum, the hotel owner's personal, lifelong collection of shells.

NIGHTLIFE

The bar at **Banana Bay Marina** (⊠*Main street, south of town dock*) is usually full of English-speaking fishermen in the evening. Every night, **Bar Los Comales** (⊠*Near the large dry dock at north end of town*) has dancing and karaoke until 2 AM. It's in a rougher section of town, so go with a group and leave in a taxi.

The bar at **Samoa del Sur** (⊠*1 block north of town dock*) has a mix of Ticos and foreigners, mostly of the male persuasion, who gather for the loud music until 11 PM.

PLAYA ZANCUDO

51 km (32 mi) south of Golfito.

For laid-back beaching involving hammocks strung between palms and nothing more demanding than watching the sun set, you can't beat breezy Playa Zancudo, with its miles of wide, flat beach and views of the Osa Peninsula. It isn't picture-perfect: the 10 km (6 mi) of dark brown sand is often strewn with flotsam and jetsam. But there's a constant breeze and a thick cushion of palm and almond trees between the beach and the dirt road running parallel. The standout feature is the magnificent view across the gulf to the tip of the Osa Peninsula. The beach runs almost due north–south, so you have center-stage seats for sunsets, too. Away from the beach breezes, be prepared for biting *zancudos* (no-see-ums).

There's a flurry of new construction here, with Canadians and Americans building substantial beachfront homes. Most hotels and restaurants are within sight of the beach. Life here is laid-back and very casual, centering on walking the beach, fishing, kayaking, swimming, and hanging out at the local bars and restaurants. Zancudo has a good surf break at the south end of the beach, but it's nothing compared with Playa Pavones a little to the south. Swimming is good two hours before or after high tide, especially at the calmer north end of the beach, and if you get tired of playing in the surf and sand, you can arrange a boat trip to the nearby mangrove estuary to see birds and crocodiles. Zancudo is also home to one of the area's best sportfishing operations, headquartered at the Zancudo Lodge.

GETTING HERE & AROUND

The road from Golfito is paved for the first 11 km (7 mi), but after the turnoff at El Rodeo the trip entails almost two hours of bone shaking and a short ride on—but sometimes long wait for—a cable river ferry (600 colones, about $1.10). You are much better off without a car here. You can hire a boat at the municipal dock in Golfito for the 25-minute ride ($30 for two) or take a $5 *collectivo* boat that leaves Zancudo Monday to Saturday at 6:30 AM; the return boat leaves Golfito's Hotel Samoa del Sur at noon. **Cabinas Los Cocos** (⊠ *Beach road* ☎*2776–0012*) has water-taxi service to Golfito ($15 per person; minimum 2 people) and service to Puerto Jiménez ($15 per person; minimum 4 people).

Getting around Playa Zancudo doesn't take much, since there's really only one long, dusty road parallel to the beach. You can rent a bike at Cabinas Sol y Mar or Tres Amigos Supermercado, both on the main road in Zancudo, for about $10 per day.

PLAYA ZANCUDO ESSENTIALS

Internet**Oceano Internet Café** (⊠ *In Oceano Cabinas, 50 m south of Supermercado Bellavista* ☎*2776-0921).*

OUTDOOR ACTIVITIES

FISHING   If you've got your own gear, you can do some good shore fishing from the beach or the mouth of the mangrove estuary, or hire a local boat to take you out into the gulf. The main edible catches are yellowfin tuna, snapper, and snook; catch-and-release fish include marlin, roosterfish, and swordfish.

The Zancudo Lodge (⊠*North end of town on main road* ☎*2776–0008* ⊕*www.thezancudolodge.com*) runs the biggest charter operation in the area, with 15 boats ranging in length from 25 feet to 36 feet. Packages include gear, food, and drinks, and you can arrange to be picked up in Golfito, Puerto Jiménez, or San José. Captain John Olson at **Sportfishing Unlimited** (☎*2776–0036* ⊕*www.sportfishing.co.cr*) offers 28-foot center-console boats with both fly and conventional tackle. The rate is $650 per day for two fishers, which includes lunch, drinks, and gear. Born and raised in Golfito, **Captain Ronny** (☎*2776–0048* ✎*golfitocr@ yahoo.com*) has worked at all the area fishing lodges. The daily rate is an all-inclusive $700 for a maximum of four fishers.

KAYAKING   The kayaking is great at the beach and along the nearby Río Colorado, lined with mangroves. **Cabinas Los Cocos** (⊠*Beach road* ☎*2776–0012*) has a popular tour ($45) that takes you for a 1½-hour motorboat ride up the river, then a two-hour kayak tour along a jungly mangrove channel. The company also rents user-friendly sit-on-top kayaks with back rests for $5 per hour.

WHERE TO EAT

$–$$ ✕**Macondo.** There's absolutely nothing fancy about this tiny restaurant, but it serves the best homemade pasta in the Southern Zone. Chef Daniel Borello comes from the Piemonte region in northern Italy, and his pasta is light, almost tissue-paper thin, and perfectly sauced. There's no written menu, just a recitation of pasta shapes available with your choice of sauce. There's also meat or spinach-and-cheese ravioli and, sometimes, lasagna, as well as jumbo shrimp and beef tenderloin. But stick to the pasta—it's a sure bet. The only disappointment is that none of the wine choices is worthy of the food. End your meal with an authentic espresso or cappuccino. ⊠*Across from Ferreteria, on beach road, center of town* ☎*2776–0157* ⊟*No credit cards* ☉*Closed Sept.–Nov.*

$–$$ ✕**Oceano Bar & Restaurant.** This popular new beachfront restaurant has a wide-ranging menu that gets raves from the locals. You can choose from seafood, steaks, salads, and Greek specialties. The young Canadian owners make what is probably the country's only *poutine* (a Quebecois comfort food with French fries, gravy, and chunks of cheese). There's also an alfresco tapas bar and a lounge where you can sip martinis. ⊠*Beach road, 50 m south of Supermercado Bellavista* ☎*2776– 0921* ⊟*MC, V* ☉*Closed Oct.*

$–$$ ✕**Restaurant Sol y Mar.** On a breezy porch with a palm-fringed beach
★   view, this restaurant has the most cosmopolitan food in Zancudo, with an eclectic menu of spicy *quesadillas* and super-stuffed burritos, savory chicken *cordon bleu,* and fresh fish with elegant French sauces. There's a touch of Thai here, too; one of the most popular dishes is mahimahi

in a coconut-curry sauce. Desserts are decadent and delicious, including a standout carrot cake. As at a lot of restaurants catering to tourists, prices do not include tax and service, so be sure to factor in an extra 23% to the bill. ⊠ *Hotel Sol y Mar, main road* ☎2776–0014 ▭*No credit cards.*

WHERE TO STAY

$–$$ ⊞ **Oasis on the Beach.** The three wooden cabins at this laid-back beach hotel are reminiscent of old Nantucket cottages. Each has bright ceramic bathrooms and porches where you can catch the constant breeze and admire the view of coconut palms, blue sky, and white surf. Mini-fridges are stocked with water. The newest additions are the two air-conditioned rooms in a two-story villa. The contemporary restaurant/bar ($–$$$) is the coolest place in Zancudo, meaning it has air-conditioning at night. It's also the best choice for breakfast, with ocean breezes and the most creative breakfast menu in town. ⊠ *Main beach road, as you enter town* ☎2776–0087 ☏2776–0052 ⊕*www. oasisonthebeach.com* ⤳*3 cabins, 2 rooms* ⌂*In-room: no a/c (some), no phone, refrigerator, no TV. In-hotel: restaurant, bar, beachfront* ▭*MC, V* ⊠*EP.*

$$–$$$ ⊞ **The Zancudo Lodge.** Most people who stay here are anglers on all-inclusive sportfishing packages, taking advantage of the lodge's 15 fishing boats. But new owners are making the comfortable beachfront hotel a good choice even if you've never caught anything but a cold. Kayaks and surfboards are available for guests to enjoy the gulf without dropping a fishing line. The verdant grounds surround an inviting pool and an open-air restaurant that serves both buffet and table-service meals. The rate includes all meals and drinks, including alcohol. Women are more than welcome here, but remember this place is usually full of rowdy fishermen—which can be a good or bad thing, depending on your tastes. The sea foam–green two-story hotel, enlivened with colorful murals, has huge rooms with hardwood floors, firm queen beds, and ocean views. The four suites are in cozy private cabinas. **Pros:** Fishers' delight with excellent boats and captains; most luxurious hotel in Zancudo, with a/c, a rarity in these parts. **Cons:** If you don't like a testosterone-charged fisherman atmosphere, this is not the place for you; evenings can get a little rowdy. ⊠ *Main road, north end of town, 200 m past police post, Playa Zancudo* ⌂*Apdo. 41, Golfito* ☎2776–0008 ☏2776–0011 ⊕*www.thezancudolodge.com* ⤳*14 rooms, 4 cabinas* ⌂*In-room: refrigerator. In-hotel: restaurant, bar, pool, beachfront* ▭*AE, MC, V* ⊠*FAP.*

$ ⊞ **Cabinas Los Cocos.** This cluster of castaway-island, self-catering cabins is designed for people who want to kick back and enjoy the beach. Artist Susan England and her husband, Andrew Robertson, are Zancudo fixtures and can organize any activity, including river safaris, kayaking tours, and visits to nature preserves. Two idyllic tropical cabins have thatch roofs and hammocks. The others are renovated 40-year-old banana-company houses moved here from Palmar Norte. These charming pastel wooden cottages give you the rare chance to share a little bit of Costa Rican history. Book early, because so many guests return the same time every year. **Pros:** Like having your own beach house on

6

a practically deserted, idyllic beach, with everything you need to live well; friendly, funny hosts who help you get the most out of your stay. Cons: No a/c, but there are ceiling fans and ocean breezes. ⊠*Beach road, about 200 m north of Sol y Mar* ☎☎*2776–0012* ⊕*www.los cocos.com* ⏎*4 cabins* ♿*In-room: no a/c, no phone, kitchen, no TV. In-hotel: beachfront, laundry service* ▭*No credit cards* ¶◎*EP.*

¢   ▦**Cabinas Sol y Mar.** As its name implies, Cabinas Sol y Mar has sun and sea, plus a beach fringed by coconut palms. Wooden cabinas painted leaf green have porches and high ceilings looking onto the gulf with spectacular views of the Osa Peninsula. Each breezy, roomy cabina has a sunny bathroom with a pebble-panel shower and sleeps four. The alfresco restaurant (⇨*above*) consistently serves the best food in town. The popular U-shape bar is an easy place to meet new friends, including Laurie and Rick, the friendly Canadian-American owners. A well stocked gift shop sells colorful sarongs and clothing from Thailand. ⊠*Main road, south of Cabinas Los Cocos, Playa Zancudo* ☎*2776–0014* ⊕*www.zancudo.com* ⏎*5 cabinas, 1 house* ♿*In-room: no a/c, no phone, no TV. In-hotel: restaurant, bar, beachfront* ▭*No credit cards* ¶◎*EP.*

PLAYA PAVONES

53 km (33 mi) south of Golfito.

One of the most scenic beaches to drive past is remote Playa Pavones, on the southern edge of the mouth of Golfo Dulce. Through a fringe of palms you catch glimpses of brilliant blue water, white surf crashing against black rocks, and the soft silhouette of the Osa Peninsula across the gulf. The area attracts serious surfer purists, but also has pristine black-sand beaches and virgin rain forest. The coast is very rocky, so it's important to ask locals which beach to try. One of the best places to swim is in the Río Claro, under the bridge or at the river mouth (dry season only). The town of Pavones itself is an unprepossessing collection of *pensiones* and sodas clustered around a soccer field.

GETTING HERE

There's no avoiding the bumpy road from Golfito to Conte, where the road forks north to Zancudo and south to Pavones. But the dirt road to Pavones is usually well graded. A public bus leaves from Golfito very early in the morning, and the drive takes about two and a half hours. A taxi from the airstrip in Golfito costs more than $60.

OUTDOOR ACTIVITIES

SURFING   Pavones is famous for one of the longest waves in the world, thanks to the mouth of the Río Claro, which creates ideal sand banks and well-shaped waves. The ocean bottom is cobblestone where the surfing waves break. The most consistent waves are from April to September, and that's when the surfing crowd heads down here from the Central Pacific coast beaches. But even at the crest of its surfing season Pavones is tranquillity central compared to the surfing hot spots farther north.

Most surfers here are serious about their sport and bring their own boards, but you can rent soft surfboards—$20 long, $15 short—and Boogie boards at **Sea Kings Surf Shop** (⊠*In town, by soccer field* ☎*8393–6982 or 8829–2409* ⊕*www.surfpavones.com*). **Cabinas La Ponderosa** (⇨ *Where to Stay & Eat, below*) rents surfboards ($15) and Boogie boards ($5), as well as bicycles ($10). **Río Claro Sports & Adventures** (☎*2776–2015*) offers surf lessons ($50), including board rental; they also rent snorkeling gear for $15 a half day, and bicycles for $5 per hour.

WHERE TO EAT

$ ✕**Cafe de la Suerte.** Fortunately for food lovers, the "Good Luck Café" serves truly astonishing vegetarian food that even a carnivore could love, along with intriguing exotic juice combinations and thick fruit smoothies. The homemade yogurt is a revelation: light, almost fluffy, and full of flavor. The Israeli owners serve it over a cornucopia of exotic fruits, sprinkled with their own granola, and mix it into refreshing fruit-flavor *lassis* (a yogurt-base drink from India). Healthy sandwiches are heavy on excellent hummus, and hot daily specials might include curried hearts of palm. Don't leave without buying a fudgy brownie or a brown-sugar oatmeal square for the road. ⊠*Next to soccer field* ☎*2776–2388* ▭*No credit cards.*

WHERE TO STAY

$$ ▦**Riviera.** If you like being self-sufficient, each of these spacious, one-bedroom villas next to the Río Claro has a large modern kitchen, and single, double, or king-size bed. Huge tiled patios look out onto a garden, and there's a trail to the river, where you can enjoy a cool swim. You're a two-minute walk from the beach, close enough to hear the surf. **Pros:** Good for families or cash-strapped surfer buddies to share, safe parking. **Cons:** You're on your own for meals. ⊠*300 m southwest of Supermercado Siete Mares* ☎*2776–2396* ⚲*5 villas* ⚘*In-room: no phone, kitchen, no TV. In-hotel: beachfront* ▭*No credit cards* ⏀*EP.*

$$ ▦**Tiskita Jungle Lodge.** This last outpost lodge is one of the premier attractions in the Southern Zone for nature lovers. Peter Aspinall, a passionate farmer and conservationist, and his wife, Lisbeth, homesteaded here in 1977 and today the property includes a vast fruit orchard, with more than 100 varieties of trees that attract monkeys, coatis, birds, and other wildlife. Surrounding the orchard are 800 acres of primary and secondary forest, a habitat for the more than 275 species of birds and a 90-strong troop of squirrel monkeys. Peter leads tours of the orchard, and expert naturalist guide Luis Vargas leads bird-watching

Fodor'sChoice
★

6

and nature tours. Comfortable screened wooden cabins on stilts have rustic furniture and tiled bathrooms, some of them open-air. Trails invite you to explore the jungle and a cascading waterfall with freshwater pools. Very simple buffet meals are served in an open-air dining room. Throughout the day you can help yourself to freshly squeezed tropical juices in the fridge, and the cookie jar is always full. Cabins are spread out, with lots of steps to climb. No. 6 has the most privacy, and a beautiful ocean view. The beach, with swimmable waters, is a steep 15-minute downhill walk. Most guests arrive by air taxi at the hotel's private airstrip. **Pros:** Unrivalled wildlife viewing and birding; splendid natural isolation; excellent guides and opportunity to get to know the friendly, knowledgeable owners. **Cons:** Some steep walks to cabins in forest; no a/c, and expect some insect visitors in rustic cabins; not a lot of privacy in joined double and triple cabins, which share verandas; food is simple and there's not a whole lot of it. ✢ *6 km (4 mi) south of Playa Pavones* 🖉 *Apdo. 13411–1000, San José* ☎ *2296–8125* 📠 *2296–8133* ⊕ *www.tiskita.com* 🛏 *17 rooms arranged in 4 single cabins, 3 doubles, and 1 triple* ⚷ *In-room: no a/c, no phone, no TV. In-hotel: restaurant, bar, pool, beachfront, bicycles* ▭ *No credit cards* ⊘ *Closed Sept. 15–Oct. 31* ⏐⊙⏐ *AI.*

$ 🖥 **Cabinas La Ponderosa.** The world-famous Playa Pavones surfing break is just a 10-minute walk from this surfer-owned hotel. It's a cut above the usual surfer place, and a bargain, with an optional meal plan for just $20 extra per person. Screened porches overlook a lush garden and a new swimming pool, and nature trails wind through 14 acres. The house has two bedrooms that sleep up to six and a screened balcony but no kitchen. The common area has a Ping-Pong table, and there are volleyball and basketball courts. Everything is within walking distance, including a swimmable beach and restaurants, so you don't need a car. **Pros:** A surfer's haven, with gear for rent and lots of local knowledge, courtesy of surfing owners and other guests; affordable and close to beach and town. **Cons:** Tends to attract a younger crowd, no land phone yet. ✉ *On beach* ☎ *8824–4145 for voice mail, 954/771–9166 in U.S.* ⊕ *www.cabinaslaponderosa.com* 🛏 *5 rooms, 1 house* ⚷ *In-room: no a/c (some), no phone, refrigerator (some). In-hotel: restaurant, beachfront, bicycles* ▭ *No credit cards* ⏐⊙⏐ *EP.*

$ 🖥 **Casa Siempre Domingo.** High on a breezy hill, this spacious B&B has ♻ the town's best view of the Golfo Dulce. Two of the four enormous rooms have 20-foot ceilings and double beds set high to catch the view out the large windows. The other two have pretty garden views. Even the big outdoor stone shower has narrow slits to capture the view. A new swimming pool gives guests yet another opportunity to enjoy the view poolside. (If you tire of the view, each room has a DVD player.) The owners have a young son and welcome visiting playmates. Substantial breakfasts, prepared by owner Heidi, a food professional in her former life, are served at a large communal table in a screened-in great room, and there's a communal fridge for storing food and drinks. The steep driveway up to this lofty perch can be a little daunting. You'll need 4WD or else you can build up a set of steely muscles climbing up on foot. **Pros:** The view, the view, the view; spacious, well-appointed

FODOR'S FIRST PERSON

Dorothy MacKinnon
Writer

In search of local nightlife, I set out with entomologist Tracie Stice one moonless night on the Osa Peninsula. Equipped with headlamps and night-vision optics, we carefully moved along the jungle trail. After studying, then steering clear of a venomous fer-de-lance snake, we came across a whip scorpion and a dozen huge, industrious spiders. At a rickety suspension bridge, Stice felt a vibration. She signaled for silence while she scanned the bridge with her infra-red flashlight for an animal large enough to make the bridge move. In a flash we recognized the creature. Eyes wide with terror, we silently beat a hasty retreat, narrowly escaping an encounter with the most dreaded animal in the forest: the skunk.

rooms; great breakfasts; kids welcome. **Con:** A very steep drive uphill and a thigh-cramping walk up and down to the beach. ✣*2 km (1 mi) south of town; follow signs after Río Claro Bridge* ☎*8820–4709* 🌐*www.casa-domingo.com* ⇨*4 rooms* ♨*In-room: no phone, no TV. In-hotel: pool* ▭*No credit cards* ¶⊙*BP.*

NIGHTLIFE

The town's main watering hole is **Cantina Esquina del Mar** (✉*Beachfront, center of town*). It's nothing fancy, but it's lively.

THE OSA PENINSULA

If you came to Costa Rica seeking wilderness and adventure, this is it. You'll find the country's most breathtaking scenery and most abundant wildlife on the Osa Peninsula, a third of which is protected by Corcovado National Park. You can hike into the park on any of three routes or fly in on a charter plane. Corcovado also works for day trips from nearby luxury nature lodges, most of which lie within private preserves that are home for much of the same wildlife you might see in the park. And complementing the peninsula's lush forests and pristine beaches is the surrounding sea, with great fishing and surfing.

There are two sides to the Osa: the gentler Golfo Dulce side, much of it accessible by car, albeit along rocky roads; and the much wilder and dramatic Pacific side, which is only accessible by boat, by charter plane, or by hiking a sublimely beautiful coastal trail.

PUERTO JIMÉNEZ

130 km (86 mi) west of Golfito, 364 km (226 mi) from San José.

You might not guess it from the rickety bicycles and ancient pickup trucks parked on the main street, but Puerto Jiménez is the largest town on the Osa Peninsula. This one-iguana town has a certain frontier charm, though. New restaurants, hotels, and "green" newcomers are lending an interesting, funky edge. It's also the last civilized outpost on the peninsula. Heading south, you fall off the grid. That means no public electricity or telephones. So make your phone calls, send your e-mails, get cash, and stock up on supplies here. Be prepared for the humidity and mosquitoes—Puerto Jiménez has plenty of both. If you need a refreshing dip, head south of the airport to Playa Platanares, where there is a long stretch of beach with swimmable, warm water.

The main reason to come to Puerto Jiménez is to spend a night before or after visiting Corcovado National Park, since the town has the best access to the park's two main trailheads and an airport with flights from San José. It's also the base for the *collectivo* (public transport via pickup truck) to Carate.

GETTING HERE & AROUND

Most visitors fly to Puerto Jiménez from San José, since the drive is grueling and long. The drive from Golfito is not recommended either— although the road from Chacarita to Rincón has recently been paved, the road from Rincón to Jiménez is dust-filled dirt all the way. A better option from Golfito is the motorboat launch. A rickety old passenger launch ($1.50 each way) leaves Golfito at 11:30 AM every day and takes 1½ hours. Faster motorboat launches (4$) make the trip in 45 minutes, leaving Golfito seven times a day starting at 5:10 AM. The fast launches heading to Golfito leave Puerto Jiménez at 6 AM, noon, and 4 PM. You can also hire private taxi boats at the city dock. Prices are $50 to $65 between Golfito and Puerto Jiménez. Water taxis can also take you to beachfront lodges.

A *collectivo,* an open-air communal truck ($8), leaves Puerto Jiménez twice daily for Cabo Matapalo and Carate. It's the cheapest way to travel, but the trip is along a very bumpy road—not recommended in rainy season (May–December). The collectivo leaves from a stop 200 meters west of the Super 96, at 6 AM and 1:30 PM.

Once you get to the main street in town, you can get around on foot or by bicycle. You can rent a bike for $10 a day ($15 for mountain bikes) at **Tom's Bike Rentals** (⊠ *100 m east of Cabinas Marcellina* ☎ *2735-5414*). If you don't have a car and are staying outside of town, you are at the mercy of taxis to get anywhere. Water taxis, hired at the city dock, can take you to waterfront lodges, nearby beaches, or Golfito. There are also daily passenger launches speeding across the Gulf to Golfito, starting at 6 AM.

PUERTO JIMÉNEZ ESSENTIALS

Bank/ATM Banco Nacional (⊠ *500 m south of Super 96, directly across from church* ☎ *2735-5020).*

Hospital Public Clinic and First Aid Station (⊠ *25 m west of post office* ☎ *2735-5063).*

Pharmacy Farmacia Hidalgo (⊠ *Main street, across from Carolina Restaurant* ☎ *2735-5564* ☉ *Mon.–Sat. 8–8).*

Internet **CaféNet El Sol** (✉ *Main street, next to Juanita's* ☎ *2735–5702*).

Café Internet Osa Corcovado (✉ *1 block east of Tom's Bikes* ☎ *2735–5230* ☽ *Closed Sun.*) has a more reliable high-speed connection, plus laptop data ports and, best of all, really strong air-conditioning.

The **National Parks Service Headquarters** (✉ *Next to airport* ☎ *2735–5036*) has information about hiking trails in Corcovado National Park. The office is open weekdays 8 to 4.

Post Office **Correo** (✉ *West side of soccer field*).

Visitor Information **Osa Tropical** (✉ *Across from Banco Nacional on main street* ☎ *2735–5062* ⊕ *www.osatropical.com*).

OUTDOOR ACTIVITIES

Escondido Trex (✉ *Restaurante Carolina, 200 m south of soccer field* ☎ *2735–5210* ⊕ *www.escondidotrex.com*) arranges kayaking, charter-fishing, and small-boat outings for watching wildlife, and land-based outings, including a half-day hike around Matapalo ($45). Isabel Esquivel at **Osa Tropical** (✉ *Main road, across from Banco Nacional* ☎ *2735–5062* ⊕ *www.osatropical.com*) runs the best general tour operation on the peninsula. Whatever travel question you ask the locals, they will usually say: "Ask Isabel." Along with arranging flights, ground transport, hotel bookings, tours, and car rentals, Osa Tropical is the radio communications center for many of the off-the-grid Osa lodges and tour operators.

BIRD-WATCHING The birding around the Osa Peninsula is world renowned, with more than 400 species. Endemic species include Baird's trogon, yellow-billed cotinga, whistling wren, black-cheeked ant tanager, and the glorious turquoise cotinga. There have even been sightings of the very rare harpy eagle in the last couple of years. One of the best spots on the peninsula to find a yellow-billed cotinga or a white-crested coquette is the bridge over the river at **Rincón** (⊹ *40 km [25 mi] north of Puerto Jiménez*), if you get there before 7 AM.

★ The best English-speaking birding guides are Liz Jones and Abraham Gallo, who run **Bosque del Río Tigre Lodge** (✉ *Dos Brazos del Tigre* ⊹ *12 km [7½ mi] northwest of Puerto Jiménez* ⊕ *www.osaadventures.com*). They lead birding trips all around the peninsula, including visits to Corcovado National Park.

FISHING Along with Golfito across the water, Puerto Jiménez is a major fishing destination, with plenty of billfish and tuna, snapper and snook, almost all year, with the exception of June and July, when things slow down. The best offshore fishing is between December and April.

Parrot Bay Village (☎ *2735–5180* ⊕ *www.parrotbayvillage.com*) is one of the biggest operations around. Its state-of-the-art boats have quiet four-stroke engines and custom rods and lures. A full-day offshore fishing trip for up to four costs $875. **Taboga Aquatic Tours** (☎ *2735–5265, 8379–0705*), a more modest local fishing outfit, offers half-day inshore fishing for up to four for $400; a whole day offshore costs $500.

HIKING

If you have 4WD, it's just a 30-minute ride west to the village of Dos Brazos and the **Tigre Sector** of Corcovado Park. Few hikers come to this pristine part of the park because it's difficult to access, which means you'll likely have it to yourself. You can take a taxi to Dos Brazos and hike from here, or use rustic but comfortable Bosque del Río Tigre Lodge as a base.

★ **Osa Aventura** (☎*2735–5758* ⊕*www.osaaventura.com*) specializes in multiday Corcovado hiking adventures led by Mike Boston, an ebullient tropical biologist who sounds like Sean Connery and looks like Crocodile Dundee. Mike also employs three young bilingual biologists to lead hikes and conduct scientific research projects, in which visitors can sometimes participate.

HORSEBACK RIDING

The most popular horse trails in the area are at remote **Río Nuevo Lodge** (⊠*Office next to La Carolina Restaurant, main street* ☎*2735–5411* ⊕*www.rionuevolodge.com*), about 12 bumpy km (7½ mi) west of town. Rides along the river and up onto scenic forested ridges last from three to seven hours and include transportation there and back and a home-cooked hot meal for $50 per person.

KAYAKING

Puerto Jiménez is a good base for sea-kayaking trips on the calm Golfo Dulce and for exploring the nearby mangrove rivers and estuaries. Alberto Robleto, an enterprising local, has amassed an impressive fleet of kayaks with excellent safety equipment at **Aventuras Tropicales Golfo Dulce** (⊠*South of airport on road to Playa Platanares* ☎*2735–5195* ⊕*www.aventurastropicales.com*). Tours include snorkeling, dolphin-watching, and bird-watching. The most popular is the three-hour mangrove tour ($30). A three- to five-day kayaking tour ($90 per day) teaches survival skills in the tropical forest. Outrigger canoe trips ($40 half day) are also offered. **Escondido Trex** (⇨*above*) has kayak fishing trips ($35), mangrove tours ($40), and popular sunset dolphin tours ($40).

Finca Köbö Chocolate Tour (⊹*18 km (11 mi) west of Puerto Jiménez, near La Palma* ☎*8398–7604* ⊕*www.fincakobo.com* ✆*$28, free for kids under 6* ☉*Tours: 9 am and 2 pm*) Go right to the source and see how cacao grows and becomes chocolate at this organic cacao plantation. The two-hour tour includes a naturalist-guided walk around the roughly 50-acre property, which includes gardens, orchards, and both primary and secondary forest. The highlight of the tour is the tasting—dipping an array of tropical fruits grown on-site into a pot of melted, homemade chocolate fondue.

WHERE TO EAT

$-$$

✕ **Il Giardino.** Northern Italian cooking, in the form of tasty homemade pastas and excellent salads, is alive and well in Puerto Jiménez at this popular garden restaurant. Sadly, wood-oven pizzas are not the restaurant's forte, and service can be painfully slow. The owner is also a master carpenter, so the curvy blond-wood bar and hand-carved detailing in the casual restaurant are handsome indeed. Choose a table in the back garden if you're in the mood for a leisurely, romantic dinner. Oddly enough, sushi makes a guest appearance on the menu. It's open

erty. Abraham, a lifelong local, can show you hidden mountain trails into Corcovado National Park, less than a mile away. Miners still pan for gold in the nearby river, which has a great swimming hole. **Pros:** A birder's paradise, great hiking trails, fabulous food. **Cons:** Shared bathroom (except in one separate cabin) and outdoor showers, limited electricity, must love the outdoors. ✉*Dos Brazos del Tigre* ✛*12 km (7 mi) west of Puerto Jiménez* ☎ *888/875–9543 in U.S.* ⊕*www. osaadventures.com* ⛴*4 rooms with shared bath, 1 cabin with private bath* ⚒*In-room: no a/c, no phone, no TV. In-hotel: restaurant, airport shuttle* ▤*No credit cards* ⊘*Closed Sept. and Oct.* ⍟*FAP.*

$$ 🏨 **Parrot Bay Village.** A storybook collection of octagonal cottages in a tropical garden opening out onto a beach, this hotel also has caimans lurking in the nearby mangrove lagoon. The main event here is fishing, both onshore and offshore, and the hotel has fishing packages that also include some nature activities off the water. The cozy cabinas have comfortable king-size beds, wicker furniture, tile floors, hot-water showers, and intricately carved mahogany doors. They are also comfortably air-conditioned. The attractive alfresco restaurant ($) has a view of fishing boats in the gulf and the distant hills of Piedras Blancas. The short dinner menu changes daily (the fish is excellent), and full breakfasts are served. **Pros:** Price includes airport pickup, welcome drink, and use of kayaks; great fishing operation; close to beach. **Cons:** Close to beach and ferry dock but a bit of a walk to town. ✉*500 m southeast of airport, on Puerto Jiménez beachfront* ☎*2735–5180, 866/551–2003 in U.S.* 🖷*2735–5568* ⊕*www.parrotbayvillage.com* ⛴*8 cabinas, 1 house* ⚒*In-room: no phone, no TV. In-hotel: restaurant, bar, beachfront, water sports, laundry service, airport shuttle, no-smoking rooms* ▤*AE, D, MC, V* ⍟*BP.*

¢–$ 🏨 **Cabinas Jiménez.** Overlooking the harbor, these creatively renovated rooms and bungalows have the best water views in town. You can enjoy the sound of the surf from your own terrace or the new hammock hut, or jump right into the gulf when it laps up against the hotel garden at high tide. Colorful wall murals, fresh tiled bathrooms, and air-conditioning make this affordable place a cut above the others in town. The owner is a keen fishermen and offers fishing trips on his own boat. **Pros:** Watery views; a/c; bungalows have pleasant, private terrace with hammock. **Cons:** Rooms are on the small side, no food service. ✉*200 m west of town dock* ☎*2735–5090* 🖷*2735–5152* ⊕*www.cabinasjimenez.com* ⛴*7 rooms, 3 bungalows* ⚒*In-room: no phone, safe, refrigerator, no TV. In-hotel: beachfront, water sports* ▤*AE, D, MC, V* ⍟*EP.*

¢–$ 🏨 **Danta Corcovado Lodge.** This artistically rustic lodge within walking
⟳ distance of the western edge of Corcovado National Park is reminiscent of an Adirondacks camp, with creatively designed twig chairs and headboards, twisted-branch windows, and furniture made of leftover tree stumps. Kids of all ages will like the cabin-in-the-woods atmosphere. An ideal place to start a hike into Corcovado, the 100% locally run lodge offers accommodations to suit all budgets, from bunk-bed rooms with shared bath to spacious forest cabins, to a wheelchair-accessible master suite with a spacious, semi-alfresco bathroom, paved with smooth river stones. Traditional Costa Rican meals are served in

6

an alfresco restaurant, joined to the lodge by a covered breezeway. The Los Patos entrance to the park is 8 km (5 mi) away; if you'd rather not walk, the lodge offers a horseback tour to the park entrance, with lunch by a waterfall. You can enjoy much of the same national park wildlife by walking the trails of this 35-hectare (86-acre), reforested property. ⊠*Guadalupe* ✛*3 km (2 mi) northwest of La Palma* ☎*2735–1111* ⊕*www.dantacorcovado.net* ⌂*3 rooms, 1 suite, 4 cabins sleeping 3–8 people* ☌*Restaurant, no a/c, some shared bath* ▤*AE,MC,V* ⦶*EP.*

¢ ⊡**Cabinas Marcelina.** Two elderly Italian sisters run the best bargain hotel in town. Fresh, spotlessly clean rooms look out onto the pleasant garden and have homey, old-fashioned touches like lace shower curtains. All have private bathrooms and hot water, and half are air-conditioned. If you're traveling solo or need a break from your traveling companion, two single rooms with fans are $18 each. The lavish continental breakfast, served in the garden, is an additional $4. **Pros:** Affordable, some rooms have a/c, pleasant garden oasis in middle of town. **Cons:** Rooms are quite small, fan-only rooms are very cheap but can be hot and sticky. ⊠*Main street, north side of Catholic church* ☎☎*2735–5007* ✎*cabmarce@hotmail.com* ⌂*8 rooms* ☌*In-room: no a/c (some), no phone, no TV* ▤*No credit cards* ⦶*EP.*

NIGHTLIFE

The sidewalks are usually rolled up by 9 PM in Puerto Jiménez, but there are a few evening options. **Bar La Taberna** (⊠*1 block east of El Tigre Mini Mercado, downtown* ☎*2735–9533* ☉*5 PM to 2 AM*). Every night of the week, this surprisingly sophisticated hangout is where the action is. Locals and visitors mingle around the curvy, polished wood bar, knocking back exotic cocktails or local beers; snacking on bocas at the tree-trunk tables; or playing darts or foosball on the adjoining terrace. The music is eclectic and always tuanis (cool). At **Juanita's** (⊠*Next to CaféNet El Sol in middle of town*) there's occasional karaoke and live music, along with its signature margaritas. With live salsa music, **Pearl of the Osa** (⊠*Next door to Iguana Lodge on Playa Platanares*) attracts a big crowd Friday night. The crowd is a mix of ages, and the music is loud and a lot of fun.

SHOPPING

Jewelry maker **Karen Herrera** (⊠*Beside airport*) has collected the finest arts and crafts in the area and displayed them in an impressive shop.

★ **Jagua Arts & Crafts** (⊠*Beside airport*) has some rare items, including colorful cotton dresses and woven Panama hats made by the Guaymí people. Other interesting items are exquisitely detailed bird carvings made by a family in Rincón, stained-glass mosaic boxes, mirrors, and trivets made by a San José artist, local paintings, and serious art ceramics. There's also a selection of natural-history field guides and books.

CABO MATAPALO

21 km (14 mi) south of Puerto Jiménez.

The southern tip of the Osa Peninsula, where virgin rain forest meets the sea at a rocky point, retains the kind of natural beauty that people

CLOSE UP

Wildlife-Watching Tips

If you're accustomed to nature programs on TV, with visions of wildebeest and zebra swarming across African savannah, your first visit to a tropical forest can be a bewildering experience. If these forests are so diverse, where are all the animals? Web sites, brochures, and books are plastered with lovely descriptions and close-up images of wildlife that give travelers high hopes. Reality is much different but no less fascinating. Below are some tips to make your experience more enjoyable.

■ Don't expect to see rarely sighted animals. It might happen; it might not. Cats (especially jaguars), harpy eagles, and tapirs are a few rare sightings.

■ Monkeys can be the easiest animals to spot, but while they are as reliable as the tides in some locations, in others they are rare indeed.

■ Remember that nearly all animals spend most of their time avoiding detection.

■ Be quiet! Nothing is more unsettling to a wary animal than 20 *Homo sapiens* conversing as they hike. It's best to treat the forest like a house of worship—quiet reverence is in order.

■ Listen closely. Many visitors are surprised when a flock of parrots overhead is pointed out to them, despite the incredible volume of noise they produce. That low-pitched growl you hear is a howler monkey call, which is obvious if nearby, but easily missed over the din of conversation. Try stopping for a moment and closing your eyes.

■ Slowly observe different levels of the forest. An enormous caterpillar or an exquisitely camouflaged moth may be only a few inches from your face, and the silhouettes in the tree 100 meters away may be howler monkeys. Scan trunks and branches where a sleeping sloth or anteater might curl up. A quick glance farther down the trail may reveal an agouti or peccary crossing your path.

■ In any open area such as a clearing or river, use your binoculars and scan in the distance; scarlet macaws and toucans may be cruising above the treetops.

■ Cultivate some level of interest in the less charismatic denizens of the forest—the plants, insects, and spiders. On a good day in the forest you may see a resplendent quetzal or spider monkey, but should they fail to appear, focus on an intricate spiderweb, a column of marching army ants, mammal footprints in the mud, or colorful seeds and flowers fallen from high in the canopy.

travel halfway across the world to experience. From its ridges you can look out on the blue Golfo Dulce and the Pacific Ocean, sometimes spotting whales in the distance. The forest is tall and dense, with the highest and most diverse tree species in the country, usually draped with thick lianas. The name Matapalo refers to the strangler fig, which germinates in the branches of other trees and extends its roots downward, eventually smothering the supporting tree by blocking the sunlight. Flocks of brilliant scarlet macaws and troops of monkeys are the other draws here.

GETTING HERE & AROUND

If you drive one hour south from Puerto Jiménez, be prepared for a bumpy ride and a lot of river crossings. In rainy season cars are sometimes washed out along rivers to the ocean. Most hotels arrange transportation in 4WD taxis or their own trucks. The cheapest—and the roughest—way to travel is by *collectivo,* an open-air communal truck ($8) that leaves Puerto Jiménez twice a day (at 6 AM and 1:30 PM). Buses do not serve Cabo Matapalo.

OUTDOOR ACTIVITIES

Ⓒ Outfitters in Puerto Jiménez run tours in this area. Each of the lodges listed has resident guides who can take guests on nature hikes. For extreme forest sports, **Everyday Adventures** (☎8353–8619 ⊕*www. psychotours.com*) takes you on not-so-everyday adventures: rappelling down waterfalls ($85), climbing up a 140-foot strangler fig tree ($65), ocean kayaking (with an optional 30-foot dive, $55), and rainforest hiking ($35). Or you can go all out with a combination one-day tour for $120.

FISHING **Cabo Matapalo Sportfishing** (☎8382–7796 ⊕*www.cabo-matapalo.com*) has excellent, experienced fishing captains and top-of-the-line, well-equipped boats ($1,200 full day; $950 half day).

SURFING On the eastern side of Cabo Matapalo, waves break over a platform Ⓒ that creates a perfect right, drawing surfers from far and wide, especially beginners. Local surf expert **Richard Gardela** (☎2735–5857 *or 8866–4657*) will take you to where the best waves are on any given day, at Matapalo, or in Pavones directly across the gulf, for $200–$400, including transportation, lunch, and drinks for one to three surfers.

WHERE TO STAY

$$$$ 🏠 **Bosque del Cabo.** Atop a cliff at the tip of Cabo Matapalo, this lodge
Fodor'sChoice   has unparalleled views of the Golfo Dulce merging with the endless blue
★   of the Pacific. The property, with hundreds of acres of animal-rich primary forest, also has the most beautiful landscaping on the peninsula. Deluxe thatch-roof cabins have king-size beds, with private, outdoor garden showers with hot water. Private decks are perfect for sunning by day and stargazing at night. A suspension bridge through the forest links the main lodge with three more rustic cabins set in a tropical garden that is great for bird-watching. Excellent meals are served in a rancho restaurant overlooking a garden alive with hummingbirds by day and serenaded by a chorus of frogs at night. Solar- and hydro-powered generators provide enough light to read by, and with the ocean breezes, you won't miss air-conditioning. Resident guides are on hand to lead you along forest trails—on foot or along a canopy zip line—and down to the beach with its natural warm tidal whirlpools and river waterfalls. The owners work hard to make their lodge as environmentally responsible as possible. **Pros:** luxurious, artistic bungalows; fabulous trails and guides; congenial atmosphere among guests at cocktail hour and dinner. **Cons:** steep trail to beach and back, very small pool, limited electricity supply. *⊕22 km (14 mi) south of Puerto Jiménez on road to Carate* 🏠*Box 02-5635, Miami, FL 33102* ☎☎*2735–5206* ⊕*www.bosquedelcabo.com* 📑*10 ocean-view cabins; 2 garden cabins;*

3 houses, one with pool ⑂*In-room: no a/c, no phone, kitchen (some), no TV. In-hotel: restaurant, bar, pool, beachfront* ▤*MC, V* ⑈*FAP.*

$$$$
Fodor'sChoice
★

Lapa Ríos. The most spectacular eco-resort in Costa Rica, Lapa Ríos has won numerous awards for its mix of conservation and comfort at the edge of civilization. After catching your breath when you see the view from the high, breezy jungle ridge rife with wildlife, your next sharp intake may be when you see the bill. But in this case the price is not inflated. Spacious, airy cabins built of gleaming hardwoods have four-poster queen beds, stylish bathrooms, and showers with one screened wall open to nature. Private teak-decked garden terraces allow you to view passing monkeys and toucans from a lounge chair. There's an infinity pool, a spa, and a yoga deck. Inspired meals, served under a soaring thatch roof, include lots of seafood, exotic local fruits and vegetables, and mouthwatering desserts. You can eat whenever—and as much as—you want. Resident naturalist guides lead tours through pristine wilderness and to nearby beaches on foot or on horseback. Along with the high cost of transporting and providing all these luxuries in a remote location, it's the exceptional service that justifies the high price tag, which includes transfers from Puerto Jiménez in new 4WD vehicles. Don't miss their free sustainability tour highlighting the resort's ingenious eco-friendly infrastructure, including pigs' contribution to energy fuels. **Pros:** Excellent, professional service; Tico-flavor atmosphere with local employees; delicious typical and international dishes. **Cons:** Steep price, but this is a once-in-a-lifetime experience; some steps to climb to farther cabins; steep trail to beach, but there is a shuttle service. ■TIP→**If you don't like to climb stairs, request a cabin close to the main lodge.** ⊹*20 km (12 mi) south of Puerto Jiménez* ✑*Apdo. 100–8203, Puerto Jiménez* ☎*2735–5130* 🖷*2735–5179* ⊕*www.laparios.com* ✑*16 cabinas* ⑂*In-room: no a/c, no phone, no TV. In-hotel: restaurant, bar, pool, spa, beachfront, laundry service* ▤*AE, MC, V* ⑈*AI.*

$$$$
★

El Remanso. You'll find tranquillity and elegant simplicity at this almost spiritual retreat in a forest brimming with birds and wildlife, 400 feet above a beach studded with tide pools. Luxurious two-person cabinas have screened windows, large verandas, and showers behind curving Gaudí-like walls. There's also a large family cabin and a very private deluxe two-story cabin, perfect for honeymoons. Four spacious rooms and two suites in a new two-story building have king-size beds and bathtubs overlooking a swimming pool. Excellent meals using local produce are served on a newly expanded deck restaurant. The property reflects the owners' conservationist ideals; the American-Spanish couple met as Greenpeace volunteers. Waterfall rappelling, zip-line access to a canopy platform, and biologist-guided nature walks are the highlights, apart from soaking in the serenity. This is the most relaxed lodge in the area. ✉*Just south of the entrance to Bosque del Cabo on road to Carate* ☎🖷*2735–5569* ⊕*www.elremanso.com* ✑*4 rooms, 2 suites, 5 cabinas* ⑂*In-room: no a/c, no phone, no TV. In-hotel: restaurant, bar, public Internet, beachfront* ▤*MC, V* ⑈*FAP.*

6

60 km (37 mi) west of Puerto Jiménez.

Carate is literally the end of the road. The black volcanic-sand beach stretches for over 3 km (2 mi), with surf that's perfect for Boogie boarding and body surfing but not for serious board surfing or safe swimming. The main entertainment at the beach is watching the noisy but magnificent scarlet macaws feasting on almonds in the beach almond trees that edge the shore. Carate has no phone service; a couple of lodges have satellite phones and iffy Wi-Fi and cell-phone connections.

GETTING HERE & AROUND

The road from Matapalo to Carate covers 40 suspension-testing km (25 mi); at this writing, the road is graded and relatively smooth, but that can all change with one drenching wet season. You're better off taking the *collectivo* from Puerto Jiménez (⇨ *To & From Puerto Jiménez, above).* Or give yourself a break and fly via charter plane to Carate's small airstrip, arranged through your lodge. From here it's just 3 km (2 mi), roughly a 40-minute walk along the beach to the La Leona ranger station entrance to Corcovado National Park. In rainy season (May–December) it is sometimes impossible to cross the raging Río Carate that separates the landing strip from the beach path to the park, and you may end up stranded on either side. Parking at the store in Carate is $5 per day.

OUTDOOR ACTIVITIES

Activities here revolve around Corcovado National Park and its environs. Hiking, horseback riding, canopy tours, and other adventures must be organized through your hotel.

WHERE TO STAY

$$$ 🏨 **Lookout Inn.** The only hotel on Carate's beach, this barefoot inn—shoes come off at the bottom step—is set on a precipitous hillside (steep stairs are plentiful here, including a 500-step "Stairway to Heaven" up to a lofty lookout). Luxurious rooms in the lodge have huge ceramic bathrooms. Two screened-in wooden cabins are perfect for those craving privacy and one new cabin is great for families, with a queen bed and two singles in a loft. Cheaper tentlike "tiki" cabinas sit on 10-foot platforms. Dozens of scarlet macaws frequent the garden, and monkeys come to feast on bananas. The new Monkey House guest cabin is under the monkeys' favorite treetop freeway. The place is full of quirky artistic touches, including a swinging bed in a new Spa Cabin. But the quirkiest element is owner Terry Conroy, an energetic host who makes sure everyone joins in on activities. His serene Tica wife, Katya, balances her husband and makes a mean margarita. Inventive meals with lots of fresh fish and Asian flavors are served on two breezy terraces with spectacular views of the coastline. There's also a spring-fed plunge pool with a hammock rancho, a yoga deck, a new spa, a bird-watching trail through primary forest, and a corral with horses for beach and trail rides. **Pros:** Proximity to beach and access on foot to Corcovado Park, good food, party atmosphere, guaranteed scarlet macaw sightings (or your money back!). **Cons:** Very steep drive/stair climb up to lodge, very limited communication with outside world, cabins have more privacy than main lodge rooms. ✉ *300 m east of Carate landing strip* ☎ *2735–5431, 815/955–1520 in U.S.* ⊕ *www.lookout-inn.com* ⇔ *3 rooms, 3 cabins, 2 cabins with shared bath* ⚙ *In-room: no a/c, no phone, no TV. In-hotel: restaurant, bars, pool, spa, beachfront, laundry service, some pets allowed* ⊟ *MC, V* ⍥ *AI.*

\$–\$\$ 🏕 **Corcovado Lodge Tent Camp.** Ecotourist pioneer Costa Rica Expe-
★ ditions owns this rustic, beachfront lodge set on 400 acres of forest
⚙ adjoining Corcovado National Park. At this camp you can fall asleep to the sound of surf pounding the beach in a tent on a wooden plat-form. Sitting side by side, the blue-top white tents have two single beds, no electricity, and share bathrooms in two separate thatch-roof bath-houses, each with eight showers and toilets. Excellent naturalist guides make this a prime destination for nature lovers. Family-style meals are served in an open-air thatch restaurant with communal tables over-looking the ocean. Bring a flashlight (there's no electricity after 9 PM), insect repellent, and sandals for river hikes. The package with all meals included is a great deal, especially since there's nowhere nearby to buy food. Packages usually include a charter flight to Carate. The 2-km (1-mi) walk from Carate is along a hot beach, so bring a sun hat. A horse and cart can pick up your luggage from the store with advance notice. **Pros:** Unique setting within short walk of park and right on beach, excellent guides. **Cons:** Shared bathrooms; bring a flashlight for night walks to the bathhouses; more tents crowded into same space is detract-ing from former castaway-island restfulness. ✉ *On beach* ⊹ *2 km (1 mi) north of Carate; 30–45 min on foot* ⌂ *Apdo. 6941–1000, San José* ☎ *2222–0333, 2257–0766 in San José* 🖷 *2257–1665, 800/886–2609 in U.S.* ⊕ *www.costaricaexpeditions.com* ⇔ *16 tents with shared bath* ⚙ *In-room: no a/c, no phone, no TV. In-hotel: restaurant, bar, beach-front, laundry service* ⊟ *AE, MC, V* ⍥ ✉ 🖷.

\$–\$\$ 🏕 **Luna Lodge.** Luna Lodge's ultimate charm lies in its remoteness and
★ tranquillity. On a mountaintop overlooking the ocean and the rain forest, it's a true retreat, with a huge hardwood pavilion for practic-ing yoga or contemplating magnificent sunsets. Just below the yoga platform there's an elegant massage hut with ethereal views. Round bungalows in the garden, spaced apart for privacy, have thatch roofs, garden showers, and decks for bird-watching or relaxing in wood-and-leather rocking chairs. Three deluxe rooms near the main lodge have private baths and share a spacious deck. You can also rough it in a well-ventilated, comfortable tent. Guided hikes to nearby water-falls and swimming holes are precipitous and thrilling, while lounging around the beautiful new, pebble-deck pool is pure nirvana. Health-ful meals have an imaginative vegetarian flair, tempered with servings of fish and chicken spiced with herbs from a hilltop organic garden. Host Lana Wedmore is a model of amiable helpfulness. **Pros:** Scenic setting for peace, yoga, and therapeutic massage; comfortable lodging and healthful food; excellent birding. **Cons:** Extremely steep road up to lodge, beach is quite a hike back down (and up!), no a/c and lim-ited electricity, open cabins mean there may be some encounters of the small wildlife kind. ⊹ *2 km (1 mi) up a steep, partially paved road*

6

from Carate ✉Box 025216–5216, Miami, FL 33102 ☎8380–5036 *or 8358–5848, 888/409–8448 in U.S.* ⊕www.lunalodge.com ⇆8 *bungalows, 3 rooms, 5 tents* ⚦In-room: no a/c, no phone, no TV. In-hotel: restaurant, bar, pool, spa ▤MC, V ⺣FAP.

DRAKE BAY

18 km (11 mi) north of Corcovado, 40 km (25 mi) southwest of Palmar Sur, 310 km (193 mi) south of San José.

This is castaway country, a real tropical adventure, with plenty of hiking and some rough but thrilling boat rides. The rugged coast that stretches south from the mouth of the Río Sierpe to Corcovado probably doesn't look much different from what it did in Sir Francis Drake's day (1540–96), when, as legend has it, the British explorer anchored here. Small, picture-perfect beaches with surf crashing against dark, volcanic rocks are backed by steaming, thick jungle. Nature lodges scattered along the coast are hemmed in by the rain forest, which is home to troops of monkeys, sloths, scarlet macaws, and hundreds of other bird species.

GETTING HERE & AROUND

The fastest way to get to Drake Bay is to fly directly to the airstrip. You can also fly to Palmar Sur and take a taxi to Sierpe and then a boat to Drake Bay. From the airport, it's a 25-minute taxi ride to Sierpe; small, open boats leave at low tide, usually 11–11:30 AM for the one-hour trip to Drake. Captains will often stop along the way to view wildlife in the river mangroves. Many lodges arrange boat transportation from Drake Bay or Sierpe. From Rincón you can drive to Drake on a 20-km (12-mi) graded dirt road. Buses leave Puerto Jiménez for La Palma every two hours from 6 AM to 8 PM, connecting in La Palma with buses to Drake Bay at 10:30 AM and 4 PM. Buses leave Drake at 4 AM and 1 PM for La Palma, to connect with buses to either Puerto Jiménez or San José. The drive from San José to Drake is scenic, but an exhausting seven hours long.

Exceptionally fit backpackers can hike to the northern entrance of Corcovado along an 18-km (11-mi) coastal path that follows the shoreline, cutting through shady forest when the coast gets too rocky. But it is impossible to walk during rainy season (September–December), when rivers flood and tides are too high.

DRAKE BAY ESSENTIALS

Drake just got electricity in 2004, so there are still very few services.

Internet **Internet Cafe** (✉*Corcovado Expeditions, Drake village* ☎*8818–9962* ⊙*Daily 10–8*).

Visitor Information **Corcovado Expeditions** (✉*Drake* ☎*8818–9962* ⊕*www. corcovadoexpeditions.net*).

The cheapest accommodations in the area can be found in the town of **Drake,** which is spread out along the bay. A trio of upscale nature

Continued on page 398

CORCOVADO NATIONAL PARK

FOR THOSE WHO CRAVE UNTAMED WILDERNESS, Corcovado is the experience of a lifetime. Covering one-third of the Osa Peninsula, the park is blanketed primarily by virgin rain forest and holds Central America's largest remaining tract of lowland Pacific rain forest. The remoteness of Corcovado and the difficult access to its interior results in its being one of the most pristine parks in the country—barely disturbed by human presence—where massive *espavel* and *nazareno* trees tower over the trails, thick lianas hang from the branches, and toucans, spider monkeys, scarlet macaws, and poison dart frogs abound.

FAST FACTS

Size: 445 square km (172 square mi)

Established: 1975

Dry season: January-April

Wettest months: October–November

What to do: Nature hikes, bird-watching, wildlife-watching, river walks, sea kayaking, camping, deep-sea fishing

Geography: 37 km (23 mi) of beach; 44,500 hectares (109,961 acres) of tropical wet forest

Number of species catalogued: 10,000 insects, 700 trees, 367 birds, 140 mammals, 123 butterflies, 117 amphibians and reptiles

- 17 of Costa Rica's 38 endangered animal species live here
- Corcovado has the largest population of scarlet macaws in Costa Rica
- Nearly 200 inches of rain falls here every year
- The hike between any two ranger stations takes at least a day
- The harpy eagle, thought to have been extinct, has been sighted a couple of times here since 2003

Your chances of spotting endangered species, such as boa constrictors, squirrel monkeys, and five wild cats, are better here than anywhere else in the country. The rarest and most sought-after are the jaguar and Baird's tapir. In and around the park are some of Costa Rica's most luxurious jungle lodges and retreats, all of which are contributing to the effort to save Corcovado's wildlife.

For day trips into the park, the most convenient place to base yourself is either in Drake Bay or at the Corcovado Lodge Tent Camp near Carate. There are three staffed entrances: **La Leona** (to the south), **San Pedrillo** (to the north), and **Los Patos** (to the east). The park has no roads, however, and the roads that approach it are dirt tracks that require 4WD most of the year.

ROUGHING IT

If you have a backpack, strong legs, and a reservation for a tent site or a ranger-station bunk, you can spend days deep in the wilds. Bunks at the Sirena ranger station (which is in a deplorable state of disrepair at the moment) are very limited; there's room for only 20 people. Bring your own sheets, a pillow, and a good mosquito net. Basic meals can be arranged at Sirena if you reserve in advance with the National Parks Service office in Puerto Jiménez.

You must make reservations for bunks and camping 30 days before you visit. All the information you need is at ⊕ www.procreorade.blogspot.com. You may be asked to deposit money into the National Park's account in the Banco Nacional to reserve space. Reconfirm your reservation a few days before you enter the park. Camping is allowed at the Sirena,

ENDANGERED ANIMALS

Corcovado has significant populations of species that are in danger of extinction, including:

- Baird's tapir
- American crocodile
- crested eagle
- harpy eagle
- howler monkey
- jaguar
- jaguarundi
- little spotted cat (*caucel*)
- margay
- ocelot
- poison-arrow frogs (various)
- puma
- scarlet macaw
- spider monkey
- squirrel monkey
- Sungrebe
- white-lipped peccary

BIRD CHECKLIST

Check the following off your "life list":

- Baird's trogon
- black-bellied wren
- black-hooded antshrike
- black-cheeked ant-tanager
- black-headed brush finch
- crested eagle
- fiery-billed aracari
- golden-naped woodpecker
- harpy eagle (very rare)
- mangrove hummingbird
- orange-collared manakin
- riverside wren
- scarlet macaw
- spotted-crowned euphonia
- turquoise cotinga
- whistling wren
- white-crested coquette
- yellow-billed cotinga

American crocodile

scarlet macaw

squirrel monkey

jaguar

purple gallinule

roseate spoonbill

hummingbird

brown pelican

laughing gull

howler monkey

three-toed sloth

Baird's tapir

SAVING THE CATS

The park has been under heavy pressure from poachers who have been killing the peccaries and pacas (small mammals) that the jaguars, ocelots, margays, and other cats feed on. Local and international groups are raising money to fund new park rangers to stop illegal hunting. In 2004 one non-profit conservation fund in the U.S. earmarked $8 million to protect and preserve the park. Much of the money has gone to hiring more park rangers.

ocelot

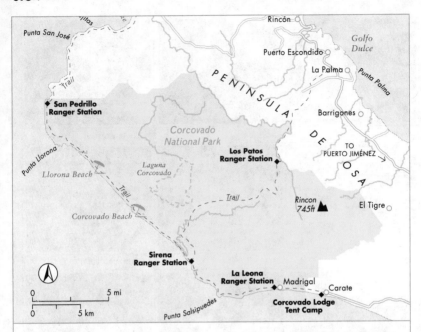

La Leona, Los Patos, and San Pedrillo stations, but only 30 people are allowed to camp at any given station (and only 15 at Sirena during the rainy season), so reservations with the National Parks Service are essential in high season.

⚠Swimming on the beach near Sirena is not advised due to rip currents and bull sharks. Also steer clear of the brackish Río Sirena, home to crocs, bull sharks, and snakes. The only advisable swimming area is the Río Claro.

HOW MUCH TIME?

Most first-time visitors to Corcovado come on a day-long boat tour or hike. But to get to the most pristine, primary growth areas, you need to walk, and that means a minimum of three days: one day to walk in; one day to walk out out; and one day inside.

HIRING A GUIDE

If your reason for coming to the Osa is Corcovado, choose a lodge that has resident naturalist guides. On the Drake Bay and gulf sides of the park, all the lodges arrange guided trips into Corcovado, most with their own guides, but some with freelance guides. Corcovado Lodge Tent Camp, on the southern edge of the park, has its own guides. Outdoors outfitters in Puerto Jiménez and Drake Bay also run guided trips in the park.

HIKING

There are three main hiking routes to Corcovado. One begins near Puerto Jiménez, at the **Los Patos** entrance. There are also two beach trails to the park: one begins in Drake Bay and follows the coast down to the **San Pedrillo** entrance to the park; the other is an easy 40-minute beach walk from Carate to the **La Leona** entrance. Hiking is always tough in the tropical heat, but the forest route (Los Patos) is cooler than the two beach hikes (La Leona and San Pedrillo), and the latter are accessible only at low tide.

The hike between any two stations takes all day or more, and the longest hike is

San Pedrillo to Sirena; it's 25 km (15 mi) along the beach, then 7 km (4 mi) on the forest trail. ■ TIP→This trail is open only in the dry season, from December to April, as the rivers get too high to cross in the rainy months and the river mouths are home to snakes, bull sharks, and crocodiles! But for hardy hikers who attempt it, the reward is walking through majestic forest as you approach Sirena.

The hike from **La Leona to Sirena** is about 16 km (10 mi) and requires crossing one big river mouth and a stretch of beach that can only be crossed at low tide. It takes planning ahead, and some guides do it at night, by the light of the moon and stars, to avoid the blistering heat along the beach.

The 17.4-km (10.8-mi) trail from **Los Patos to Sirena** is lovely and forested. But to get to the Los Patos station you first walk 8 km (5 mi) along the verdant Río Rincón valley. The **Sirena ranger station** has great trails around it that can easily fill a couple of days. Osa Aventura (⇨ Outdoor Activities *in* Puerto Jiménez, *above*) specializes in multiday wildlife tours.

ESSENTIALS

Hours of Operation: Ranger stations are officially open from 8 AM to 4 PM daily, but you can walk in almost any time as long as you pay in advance.

Contacts: 735–5036 (National Parks Service in Puerto Jiménez)

Admission: $8 per day.

Getting There: The easiest way to visit remote Corcovado is on a day trip via boat from a Drake Bay lodge or on foot from the Corcovado Lodge Tent Camp. The 20-minute boat trip from Drake Bay gets you to the San Pedrillo entrance in the dry season (January–April). The boat trip from Drake to Sirena takes 45 min. to 1 hour. The Corcovado Lodge Tent Camp

HIKING TIPS

- Stay on the trails, for your safety and for the well-being of animals and plants

- Animals here are less used to humans than those in more touristed parks; be quiet and keep your eyes and ears open

- Apply mosquito repellent only as needed. Repellent reduces your ability to sweat

- Take plenty of water with you, even on short hikes. Don't ever drink water from streams. Every ranger station has potable water.

- Bring a flashlight. Darkness falls quickly in the forest.

- Plan your hikes around high tides, which can block park entrances

- Bring a sun hat and sunblock, and wear comfortable shoes.

is a 10-minute walk from the La Leona entrance.

For getting to Corcovado from elsewhere, the most expensive option—but also the easiest way to get right to the heart of the park—is flying in on a small charter plane ($365 each way, up to 5 passengers) to the tiny La Sirena airstrip in the park. Contact **Alfa Romeo Aero Taxi** (✉ Puerto Jiménez airport ☎ 735–5178).

Less expensive is hiring a taxi in Puerto Jiménez ($60) to the Los Patos trailhead, or at least $45 to the first crossing of the Río Rincón (from which you hike a few miles upriver to the trailhead).

The cheapest, and least convenient, option is to take a morning bus for less than $1 from Puerto Jiménez to La Palma and then hike or take a taxi to the Los Patos entrance. Buses depart every two hours from 6 AM till 8 PM.

Snorkelers' Paradise

Most of uninhabited 2½-square-km (1-square-mi) **Caño Island Biological Reserve** is covered in evergreen forest that includes fig, locust, and rubber trees. Coastal Indians used it as a burial ground, and the numerous bits and pieces unearthed here have prompted archaeologists to speculate about pre-Columbian long-distance maritime trade. Occasionally, mysterious stones that have been carved into perfect spheres of varying sizes are discovered. The uninhabited island's main attraction now is the ocean around it, superb for scuba diving and snorkeling. The snorkeling is best around the rocky points flanking the island's main beach; if you're a certified diver you'll probably want to explore Bajo del Diablo and Paraíso, where you're guaranteed to encounter thousands of good-size fish.

The only way to get to the island, 19 km (12 mi) due west of the Osa Peninsula, is by boat arranged by your lodge or a tour company. Lodges and the Jinetes de Osa tour company in Drake Bay run day trips here, as do tour companies in Dominical and Uvita.

lodges—Drake Bay Wilderness Resort, Aguila de Osa Inn, and La Paloma Lodge—are also clumped near the Río Agujitas on the bay's southern end. They all offer comprehensive packages, including trips to Corcovado and Caño Island. Lodges farther south, such as Punta Marenco Lodge and Casa Corcovado, run excursions from even wilder settings. During the dry season you can reach the town of Drake via a graded dirt road from Rincón.

OUTDOOR ACTIVITIES

Jinetes de Osa (⊠ *Drake village, west side of bay* ☎2236–5637 ⊕*www. jinetesdeosa.com*) has diving ($95 plus $20 for gear) and snorkeling ($70) and dolphin-watching tours ($95), as well as a canopy tour ($55) with some interesting bridge, ladder, and rope transitions between platforms. **The Divine Dolphin Tour** allows you to spend a day with marine biologists following schools of dolphins—as many as 25 species are resident or pass through this area—and pods of humpback whales, who come here from both South and North America to nurture their young. The tour boat is equipped with hydrophones for listening to dolphin and whale songs. Tour includes an educational video and talk before setting out onto the bay, plus lunch onboard. *Drake Bay* ☎866/527–5558 in U.S. ⊕*www.divinedolphin.com* ☎$95 ☉*Open 4–5 days a week depending on conditions; call ahead.*

WHERE TO STAY

$$$$ **Aguila de Osa Inn.** A sportfisher's dream lodge, Aguila de Osa has spacious rooms with hardwood interiors, bamboo beds, and luxurious bathrooms. Stained-glass lamps with tropical themes and hand-carved doors add artistic flair. Be prepared for a steep climb up a concrete path to your room with a view of Drake Bay. Morning coffee arrives outside your room before 6 AM. Diving trips and excursions into Corcovado Park are also offered. Two-night packages include transfers from Drake Bay or Palmar Sur airports. **Pros:** Great for fishing enthusiasts; elegant

lodge and rooms; convivial, communal dining with wine included. **Cons:** Set back from ocean at river mouth, so no ocean views or breezes, and heat and humidity can be stifling; steep climb to some rooms. ⊠*South end of Drake at mouth of Río Agujitas* ⅅ*Interlink 898 Box 025635, Miami, FL 33102* ☎*2296–2190 in San José* 🖷*2232–7722* ⊕*www. aguiladeosa.com* ⮐*11 rooms, 2 suites* ⅃*In-room: no a/c, no phone, refrigerator (some), no TV. In-hotel: restaurant, bar, water sports, laundry service, public Internet, public Wi-Fi* ⊟*AE, MC, V* ⅉ*FAP.*

$$$$
★
La Paloma Lodge. Sweeping ocean views and lots of tropical-foliage privacy make these secluded cabinas the area's most romantic. Planted in a jungle garden on a ridge jutting into Drake Bay, the elegant wooden villas have bedroom lofts, spiffy bathrooms, and large porches with pretty green wicker furniture. All cabins have been renovated, but Numbers 1 and 3 have the best views. A small pool overlooks forest and ocean, or you can head down the hill to Playa Cocolito, the hotel's gem of a beach at the edge of the coastal path to Corcovado. The hotel runs a diving school and offers river kayaking. The flower-filled restaurant serves tropical fare, and there's always afternoon tea and banana bread when you can mingle with the other guests. Manager Nichole Dupont maintains a high standard of service. There's a three-night minimum stay; packages are the best bet, as they include transportation from San José, all meals, and some tours. **Pros:** Idyllic setting with ocean views and easy access to Coastal Footpath, great service, interesting guests from all over the world. **Cons:** Expensive, no a/c, open cabins mean you will have to contend with some insect visitors. ⊠*Drake Bay, 300 m past Drake Bay Wilderness Resort* ⅅ*Apdo. 97–4005, Heredia* ☎*2293–7502* 🖷*2239–0954* ⊕*www.lapalomalodge. com* ⮐*4 rooms, 7 cabinas* ⅃*In-room: no a/c, no phone, no TV. In-hotel: restaurant, pool, beachfront, diving, water sports* ⊟*AE, MC, V* ⊗*Closed Oct.* ⅉ*FAP.*

$$$–$$$$
★
Casa Corcovado Jungle Lodge. This hilltop jungle lodge has it all: a prime location on the edge of Corcovado National Park, resident naturalists, luxury accommodations, and first-class service and food. Spanish colonial–style cabinas are spread around a garden for maximum privacy. Guest rooms have elegant furniture, four-poster beds, and huge tile bathrooms plus open-air garden showers. There is laundry service for an extra charge, as well as clothes lines for drying your sure-to-be-damp clothes. The sunset margarita bar at the top of hill has excellent views. A tractor-towed cart transports guests and luggage. The new restaurant, studded with Art Deco stained glass, serves upscale dinners and packs picnic lunches. The minimum stay is two nights, but the best deal is a three-night package that includes transportation from San José, all meals, and a trip to Caño Island and Corcovado National Park. **Pros:** Unrivalled location adjoining national park and close to Caño Island, first-rate naturalist guides, excellent restaurant and facilities. **Cons:** An adventure to get here: be prepared for a hair-raising, wet landing; steep climb to lodge from beach, but there is a tractor-pulled cart. ⊠*Northern border of Corcovado* ⅅ*Apdo. 1482–1250, Escazú* ☎*2256–3181* 🖷*2256–7409* ⊕*www.casacorcovado.com* ⮐*14 rooms* ⅃*In-room:*

6

no a/c, no phone, no TV. In-hotel: restaurant, bars, pools, beachfront, water sports ▤*AE, MC, V* ☉*Closed Sept.–mid-Nov.* ⦷*AI.*

$$–$$$ ⌨**Jinetes de Osa.** The most comfortable and reasonably priced place to stay right in the village of Drake, this small bay-side hotel with a casual open-air restaurant has simple rooms, all with tile floors and hot-water showers. Rooms open out onto a pleasant terrace with a view of the town and the bay. The on-site diving operation is well run, so the lodge is often filled with groups of divers. **Pros:** Convenient location; affordable; adventuresome, active clientele. **Cons:** Standard rooms are smallish, so opt for the larger deluxe room if you can; no a/c. ✉*Drake village, west side of bay* ☎*8826–9757* 📠*2231–5801 in San José* ⊕*www.costaricadiving.com* ⇘*9 rooms* ⚴*In-room: no a/c, no phone, no TV. In-hotel: restaurant, beachfront* ▤*MC, V* ⦷*FAP.*

$$ ⌨**Punta Marenco Lodge.** This rustic lodge has the best location on the Pacific side of the Osa, and it's the best deal on the coast. South Seas island–style cabins with thatch roofs perch on the spine of a ridge overlooking the sea. Private porches are perfect for siestas, sunsets, and stargazing. There are also tents for the adventurous and standard rooms in the lodge for the more timid. Toucans and scarlet macaws visit every morning, and paths lead to the scenic coastal trail and deep into the Río Claro National Wildlife Refuge. A resident guide is on hand for nature walks, and the lodge can arrange oceangoing tours, including diving and dolphin-watching excursions. The rancho restaurant has a family feel, with communal tables and typical Tico food. There is electricity for only a few hours in the evening, and no hot water. Insects frequent the thatch roofs, but so do tiny lizards that eat them up. You can hike here from Drake or take a boat from Drake or Sierpe (included in packages). **Pros:** Castaway-island remoteness, trails are as good as those in Corcovado Park, very reasonable price. **Cons:** Very rustic, steep climb uphill to lodge after thrilling wet landing on beach, simple food, very limited electricity and contact with outside world. ✉*Beachfront, directly east of Caño Island and north of Casa Corcovado* ⬧*Apdo. 2133–1100, Tibas* 📠*2297-0771, 2241–4678 in San José* ⊕*www.puntamarenco.com* ⇘*15 cabinas, 8 tents* ⚴*In-room: no a/c, no phone, no TV. In-hotel: restaurant, beachfront* ▤*No credit cards* ⦷*FAP.*

$–$$ ⌨**Drake Bay Wilderness Resort.** On a grassy point between Río Agujitas and the ocean, this breezy resort has the best views of Drake Bay. It's also kid-friendly, with a pool, open ground for romping, and tidal pools to explore. Keep an eye out for precocious squirrel monkeys. The wooden cabins are camp-style, three rooms to a building. But with hot water, tile bathrooms, and carved animal bedposts supporting firm queen-size beds, this is very comfortable camping. There's no air-conditioning, but ocean breezes make for cool evenings. There are also five less expensive, tentlike cabanas on platforms with shared baths, right at the water's edge. Kayaks are at your disposal for exploring the river. Most guests come to see the rain forest, but you can also opt for mangrove, scuba-diving, sportfishing, and dolphin- and whale-watching tours. Resident marine biologist, guide, and dive master Shawn Larkin is renowned in Costa Rica for his knowledge of sea life and conservation efforts. Minimum stay is three nights. **Pros:** Great location, family-friendly and affordable, great sea-life tours with knowledgeable and personable marine biologist. **Cons:** Not a lot of privacy, no a/c, noisy generator provides the limited electricity. ⊠*On peninsula at mouth of Río Agujitas, on southern end of bay* ☊*Apdo. 1370010–1000, San José* ☎*8337–8004, 561/371–3437 in U.S.* ☎☎*2770–8012* ⊕*www. drakebay.com* ➫*20 rooms* ☖*In-room: no a/c, no phone, no TV. In-hotel: restaurant, bar, pool, laundry facilities, public Internet, public Wi-Fi* ▤*AE, MC, V* ♚*FAP.*

NIGHTLIFE

When you're on the Osa Peninsula, the wildest nightlife is outdoors. Join entomologist Tracie Stice, also known as the Bug Lady, on the **Night Tour**
★ (☎*8812–6673 or 8867–6143* ⊕*www.thenighttour.com*) of insects, bats,
☾ reptiles, and anything else moving around at night. Tracie is a wealth of bug lore, with riveting stories from around the world. Headlamps and infrared flashlights help you see in the dark. Tours are $35 per person.

THE SOUTH PACIFIC ESSENTIALS

6

TRANSPORTATION

BY AIR

SANSA and Nature Air have direct flights to Drake Bay, Palmar Sur, and Puerto Jiménez. SANSA has the monopoly on Golfito and Coto 47 (for San Vito). *For more information about air travel to the South Pacific from San José, see By Air in Costa Rica Essentials.*

Alfa Romeo Aero Taxi, at the Puerto Jiménez airport (really more of an airstrip), flies small charter planes to Carate, Tiskita, and Corcovado National Park's airstrip at La Sirena. The one-way price is $365 for up to five people.

Contacts **Alfa Romeo Aero Taxi** (☎2735–5178).

BY BUS

ARRIVING & Bus fares from San José range from about $3 to $8, depending on dis-
DEPARTING tance and number of stops. *For more information about bus travel, see By Bus in Costa Rica Essentials.*

GETTING The best way to get around the region's roads is by bus—let someone
AROUND else do the driving. Bus fares are cheap, and you'll meet the locals. But the going is generally slow, buses often leave very early in the morning, and schedules change frequently, so check the day before you want to travel.

BY SHUTTLE VAN

Based in Dominical, Easy Ride has two daily shuttle-van services in each direction between San José and the Dominical/Uvita/Ojochal area. The cost is $30 to $35 per person. For an extra $8 they will take you to the San José airport.

Shuttle-Van Services **Easy Ride** (☎2253–4444 ⊕www.easyridecr.com).

BY CAR

Owing to the dismal state of the roads and hazardous driving conditions—flooded rivers and potholes—we don't recommend driving to the South Pacific, especially in rainy season. If you decide to drive, make sure your vehicle has 4WD and a spare tire. Give yourself lots of time to get to where you are going.

Driving is fairly straightforward, if slow, around Cerro de la Muerte, San Isidro, Dominical, and Uvita. But as soon as you get off the main paved highways, the roads are rough and slow going, and most require 4WD. On the Osa Peninsula and around the Golfo Dulce, the last thing you want is a car. Boat taxis and land taxis will save you time, if not money, and preserve your energy for activities that are more fun than navigating rotten roads.

Solid Car Rental has an office in Puerto Jiménez with 4WD vehicles (including some with automatic transmission); it also has cars available in Golfito and Dominical. With Selva Mar you can pick up a car in San Isidro and drop it off anywhere down south. Alamo, in Dominical, allows drop-off at various points south. But you'll incur steep drop-off fees, which range from $50 to $125.

Rental Agencies **Alamo** (⊠ *Hotel Villas Río Mar* ☎ *2787–0052* ⊕ *www. alamocostarica.com*). **Solid Car Rental** (⊠ *150 m north of airport, Puerto Jiménez* ☎ *2735–5777* ⊕ *www.solidcarrental.com*); in Dominical, at the Hotel Diuwak (☎ *2787–1101*); in Golfito, at the Hotel Sierra (☎ *2775–3333*). **Selva Mar** (☎ *2771–4582* ⊕ *www.exploringcostarica.com*).

CONTACTS & RESOURCES

Banks, Internet cafés, post offices, and emergency contacts are listed at the end of each town entry.

BANKS & EXCHANGING SERVICES

In the major centers—San Isidro, Golfito, and San Vito—banks and ATMs are plentiful. But in Puerto Jiménez there is only one bank with one ATM, which may or may not be working. Many other places have no banking facilities at all. Don't count on being able to use a credit card, since phone lines—where they exist—are often out of order. Arrange to pay lodges in advance.

INTERNET

Internet cafés are popping up in all the major towns, but much of the south is still without phone service or even electricity. Internet service costs anywhere from $1 to $5 per hour, depending on the location and the type of connection.

MAIL & SHIPPING

Post offices are few and far between. You are better off saving up your postcards and mailing them from San José.

Caribbean

La Selva Biological Station

WORD OF MOUTH

"I could also spend several days [in Puerto Viejo], but that's probably because of the experience we had. We just met so many great
people and loved it there. The food was great and inexpensive.
Nice beaches, lots of places to wander and many hotels within
walking distance to town. Returning in March."

—hipvirgochick

WELCOME TO THE CARIBBEAN

TOP REASONS TO GO

★ **Turtles:** People from around the world flock to the northern Caribbean for the annual nesting of four species.

★ **Food and flavors:** Leave gallo pinto behind in favor of mouthwatering rondón (meat or fish stew), or caribeño (Caribbean) rice and beans, stewed in coconut milk.

★ **Dolphin-watching:** Bottlenose, tucuxi, and Atlantic-spotted dolphins ply the southern Caribbean coast.

★ **Music:** Mix reggae and calypso with your salsa. Rhythms waft in from the far-off Caribbean Islands; and home-grown musicians are making names for themselves, too.

★ **Sportfishing:** World-class tarpon and snook attract serious anglers to the shores off Barra del Colorado and Tortuguero national parks.

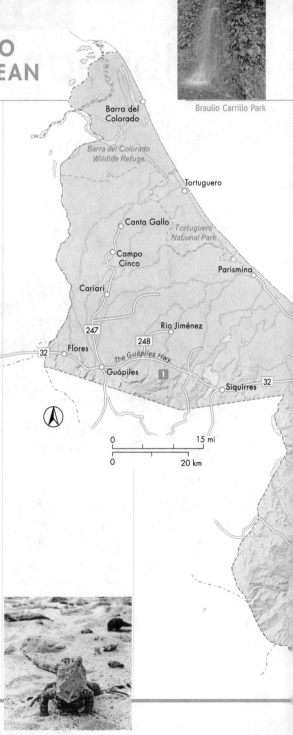

Braulio Carrillo Park

Barra del Colorado

Barra del Colorado Wildlife Refuge

Tortuguero

Canta Gallo

Tortuguero National Park

Campo Cinco

Parismina

Cariari

247

Rio Jiménez

248

32   Flores

The Guápiles Hwy.

Guápiles   1

Siquirres   32

0   15 mi

0   20 km

Limón, Central Caribbean

Pachira Lodge

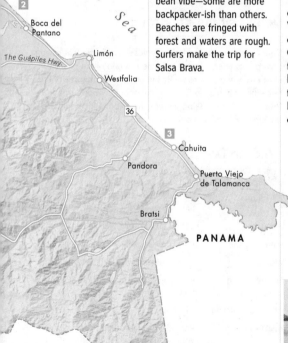

1 **The Northern Lowlands.** The Northern Lowlands have little to offer tourists in their own right, but are close to Braulio Carrillo Park and rafting-trip put-in points.

2 **The Northern Caribbean Coast.** encompasses the coastal jungles and canals of Tortuguero National Park and Barra del Colorado Wildlife Refuge. Boat and air travel are the only ways to reach this roadless region.

3 **Southern Caribbean Coast.** stretches south from port-of-call Limón to Panama. Towns along the coast have an Afro-Caribbean vibe—some are more backpacker-ish than others. Beaches are fringed with forest and waters are rough. Surfers make the trip for Salsa Brava.

GETTING ORIENTED

This flat, expansive region just a few meters above sea level stretches from the eastern slope of the Cordillera Central, east through banana-growing country, and down to pristine beaches. North to the Nicaragua border, it encompasses the coastal jungles and canals of Tortuguero National Park and Barra del Colorado Wildlife Refuge. In the central and southern Caribbean, nearly everything of tourist interest lies along the main artery to Limón (the Guápiles Highway) and the coastal highway south.

7

Punta Cocles, South Caribbean

CARIBBEAN PLANNER

Not That Caribbean

Costa Rica's Caribbean coast is sometimes called its Atlantic coast, so as not to confuse tourists looking for the white sand and clear-blue waters of the Caribbean Islands. This Caribbean is very different, with sands in shades of brown and black, waters that are rough and murky (ideal for surfing), dense jungle, heavy and frequent rain, and a less sophisticated, laid-back approach to tourism. It is beautiful and fascinating in its own way, but it's definitely not St. Barths.

The Complete Package

If you don't want to be bothered arranging the logistics of transportation to remote Tortuguero, consider booking a package tour. Many lodges listed in the chapter have similar packages, varying in length from one night to two weeks, that include transport from San José, overnights, meals, and guided tours.

Getting There

This historically isolated sector of Costa Rica is today one of the most accessible. The southern coast is a three- to four-hour drive from San José, over decent roads (by Costa Rican standards), and public transportation is frequent. The northern Caribbean coast is another story: the total absence of roads means you have to arrive by plane or boat. Most travelers go with a tour or book at one of the large hotels that include transport to and from San José.

DRIVING ALERT: When visiting the Caribbean coast by car, remember that fog often covers the Braulio Carrillo mountains after noon, making driving hazardous. Cross this area in the morning.

Don't Get the Runaround

Check road conditions before you set out for the Caribbean from points west. Most of the time it is one of the country's most easily reached regions, but occasional closures of the route through Braulio Carrillo National Park north of San José necessitate passing through Turrialba, which can add a couple of hours to your journey.

What to Do

ACTIVITY	WHERE TO DO IT
Fishing	Barra del Colorado, San Juan River, Tortuguero
Diving	Gandoca-Manzanillo Wildlife Refuge
Snorkeling	Gandoca-Manzanillo Wildlife Refuge
Surfing	Cahuita, Puerto Viejo de Talamanca, Limón
Turtle-watching	Gandoca-Manzanillo Wildlife Refuge, Tortuguero
White-water rafting	Siquirres
Wildlife-viewing	Barra del Colorado, Gandoca-Manzanillo Wildlife Refuge, Tortuguero

Choosing a Place to Stay

The glitzy resorts of the Pacific coast are nowhere to be found in the Caribbean, where the norm is small, independent lodgings, usually family owned and operated. Fewer tourists in this region means plenty of decent lodging at affordable prices. But tourism *is* growing, so it's risky to show up without reservations. Surprisingly few places here have air-conditioning; but sea breezes and ceiling fans usually provide sufficient ventilation. Smaller places don't take credit cards; those that do may give discounts if you pay with cash.

How Much Time?

Attractions near Guápiles and Siquirres lend themselves to long day trips from San José. Tour operators also have whirlwind daylong Tortuguero trips from San José. Avoid these—the area really deserves two or three days, which is the length of the classic Tortuguero package that includes transportation, lodging, food, and tours. Choose a single Caribbean destination and stay put if you have just a few days. (Cahuita and Puerto Viejo de Talamanca are ideal for that purpose.) If you have a week, you can tackle the north and south coasts.

Package Tours

Horizontes (☎2222–2022 ⊕www.horizontes.com) tours include naturalist guides and transport by 4WD vehicle.
Talamanca Adventures (☎2224–3570 ⊕www. talamanca-adventures.com) leads off-the-beaten-path tours familiarizing you with everything from Caribbean cooking to rain-forest conservation.

WHAT IT COSTS IN DOLLARS				
¢	$	$$	$$$	$$$$
Restaurants				
under $5	$5–$10	$10–$15	$15–$25	over $25
Hotels				
under $50	$50–$75	$75–$150	$150–$250	over $250

Restaurant prices are per person for a main course at dinner. Hotel prices are for two people in a standard double room in high season, excluding service and tax (16.4%).

Rain Check

Packing for wet weather is a necessity. Be sure to bring:

- a collapsible umbrella
- a poncho
- ziplock bags for cameras and other things you'll take on hikes and tours
- waterproof sandals
- quick-drying clothing

When to Go

The Caribbean lacks a true dry season, though February to April and September to October could be called *drier* seasons, with many sunny days and intermittent showers. The heaviest rains (and periodic road closures) come in December and January, prime tourist months elsewhere. During the rainiest months prices are lower and tourists fewer. Temperatures remain constant year-round, with daily highs of 29°C–31°C (84°F–88°F) and lows of 21°C–23°C (69°F –73°F). Yet, despite weather patterns that differ from the rest of Costa Rica, places here charge high-season rates from December to April, and again in July and August. Not to fear: prices skew a bit lower in the Caribbean than elsewhere in the country.

7

THE NORTHERN LOWLANDS

By Jeffrey Van
Fleet

That proverbial fork in the road presents you with a choice just beyond the immense Braulio Carrillo National Park north of San José. The highway branches at Santa Clara, having completed its descent onto the Caribbean plain. A left turn takes you north to Puerto Viejo de Sarapiquí and the forest-clad hills of the eastern slope of the Cordillera Central. (⇨ Chapter 3.) If you stay on the well-maintained main Guápiles Highway, you head southeast toward Limón and the Caribbean coast. The highway passes through sultry agricultural lowlands, home to large banana and cacao plantations, but bypasses the region's three main communities: burgeoning Guápiles and the smaller towns of Guácimo and Siquirres. You may not see any reason to stop when driving through the region—the Caribbean coast beckons, after all—but a couple of decent lodgings and lesser-known sights might be an incentive to take a break.

GUÁPILES

60 km (38 mi) northeast of San José.

Guápiles is fast becoming the hub of northeastern Costa Rica, and with all the facilities in town, residents of the region find little need to trek to San José anymore. The smaller town of Guácimo lies 12 km (7 mi) east on the Guápiles Highway.

GETTING HERE & AROUND

Guápiles lies just north of Braulio Carrillo National Park and straddles the highway to the Caribbean. It's an easy one-hour drive from San José just 60 km (38 mi) to the southwest, or Limón 84 km (50 mi) to the east. Empresarios Guapileños buses connect San José's Gran Terminal del Caribe with Guápiles every hour from early morning until late evening.

GUÁPILES ESSENTIALS

Bank/ATM **Banco Nacional** (⊠ *400 m east of Palí supermarket* ☎ *2713–2000*). **BAC San José** (⊠ *Across from Acueductos y Alcantarillados* ☎ *2710–7434*).

Hospital **Hospital de Guápiles** (⊠ *90 m south of fire station* ☎ *2710–6801*).

Pharmacy **Farmacia San Martín** (⊠ *Across from Palí* ☎ *2710–1115*). **Farmacia Santa Marta** (⊠ *Across from Banco Nacional* ☎ *2710–6253*).

Post Office **Correos** (⊠ *North of MUCAP*).

EXPLORING

Curious how those tropical houseplants you have at home started out? Ornamental plant farm **Costa Flores** conducts 1½-hour English-language tours—advance reservations are required—through its gardens and facilities. (Riotously colored heliconias are a specialty here.) The tour ends at the packing house, where you see how plants are prepared for export. You get to create your own floral bouquet to take with you as a souvenir. ⊹ *3½ km (2 mi) north of Guácimo on road to Río Jiménez* ☎ *2716–6430* 💲 *$18* ☉ *Daily 6–4.*

WHERE TO STAY

¢ ⬛ **Hotel Río Palmas.** Think of it as a hacienda motel. Close to EARTH (⇨*below*), near the town of Guácimo, the Río Palmas has an open-air restaurant with a red-tile roof that grabs your eye as you're speeding by on the highway. The restaurant is a popular stop for tour buses or individual travelers en route to and from the Caribbean. Behind an arched, whitewashed entry gate, one-story tile-roof cabinas wrap around a central courtyard with a fountain. Exotic plantings abound, and the staff can arrange hikes, farm and jungle tours, and horseback rides to private waterfalls. **Pros:** Good value, good restaurant. **Cons:** Far from sights, need car to stay here. ⊠*Pocora de Guácimo* ⊹*15 km (9 mi) east of Guápiles on Guápiles Hwy.* ☎2760–0330 🖷 2760–0296 ⬅*25 rooms* ⚴*In-room: no a/c (some), no phone, no TV (some). In-hotel: restaurant, pool, laundry service* ⊟*AE, D, DC, MC, V* ⏀⊠⬛.

EARTH

The nonprofit institution of higher education EARTH (Escuela de Agricultura de la Región Tropical Húmeda, or Agricultural School of the Humid Tropical Region) researches the production of less pesticide-dependent bananas and other forms of sustainable tropical agriculture, as well as medicinal plants. The university graduates some 100 students from Latin America and Africa each year. EARTH's elegant stationery, calendars, and other paper products are made from banana stems, tobacco leaves, and coffee leaves and grounds, and are sold at the on-site Oropéndola store and in many tourist shops around the country. The property encompasses a banana plantation and a forest reserve with nature trails. Half-day tours are $15; full-day, $25; and lunch is $12 for day visitors. Though priority is given to researchers and conference groups, you're welcome to stay in the school's 50-person lodging facility, with private bathrooms, hot water, and ceiling fans, for $60 a night, which includes the use of a swimming pool and exercise equipment. The site is a bird-watchers' favorite; some 250 species have been spotted here. Reservations are required. ⊠*Pocora de Guácimo* ⊹*15 km (9 mi) east of Guápiles on Guápiles Hwy.* ⏏*Apdo. 4442–1000, San José* ☎2713–0000 ⊕*www.earth.ac.cr.*

GETTING HERE & AROUND

The entrance to EARTH lies just east of the town of Guácimo. Stop and check with the guard at the gate off the highway. If you're taking the bus, drivers should drop you off at the stop in front of the gate.

SIQUIRRES

28 km (17 mi) east of Guápiles.

Its name is a corruption of the words *Si quieres* (if you want), fittingly impassive for this lackluster town. It anchors a fertile banana- and pineapple-growing region, and marks the transition point between the agricultural lowlands and the tropical, palm-laden coast. Siquirres has the unfortunate historical distinction of having once been the west-

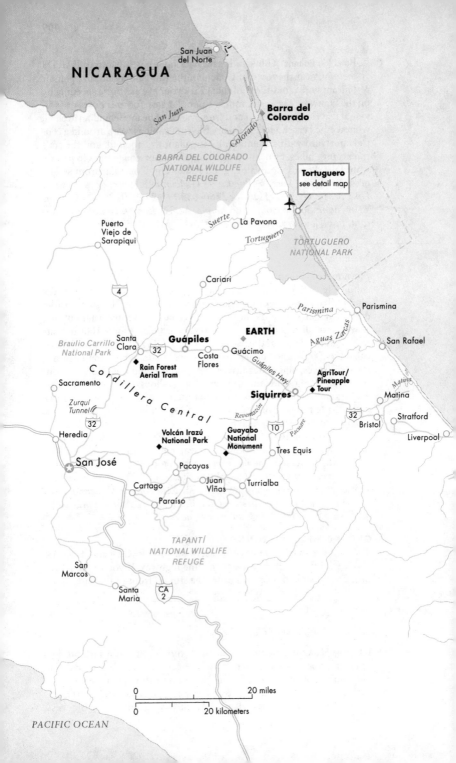

The Caribbean Coast

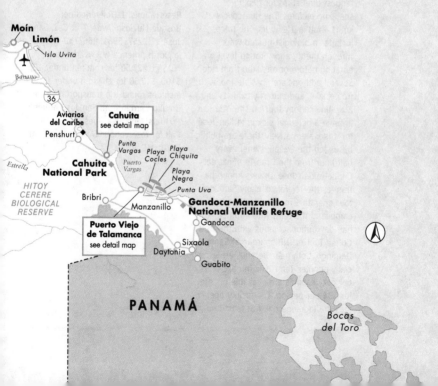

Caribbean Sea

Moín
Limón
Isla Uvita

Banano

36

Aviarios
del Caribe
Penshurt

Cahuita
see detail map

Punta
Vargas
*Puerto
Vargas*

**Cahuita
National Park**

Estrella

HITOY
CERERE
BIOLOGICAL
RESERVE

Bribri

Playa
Cocles

Playa
Chiquita

Playa
Negra

Punta Uva

**Gandoca-Manzanillo
National Wildlife Refuge**

Manzanillo

**Puerto Viejo
de Talamanca**
see detail map

Gandoca

Sixaola

Daytonia

Guabito

PANAMÁ

*Bocas
del Toro*

Rain Forest Aerial Tram

Just 15 km (9 mi) beyond the north-eastern boundary of Braulio Carrillo, a 4-square-km (2½-square-mi) preserve houses a privately owned and operated engineering marvel: a series of gondolas strung together in a modified ski-lift pulley system. (To lessen the impact on the jungle, the support pylons were lowered into place by helicopter.) The tram gives you a way of seeing the rain-forest canopy and its spectacular array of epiphyte plant life and birds from just above, a feat you could otherwise accomplish only by climbing the trees yourself. Though purists complain that it treats the rain forest like an amusement park, it's an entertaining way to learn the value and beauty of rain-forest ecology.

The 21 gondolas hold five people each, plus a bilingual biologist-guide equipped with a walkie-talkie to request brief stops for gaping or snapping pictures. The ride covers 2½ km (1½ mi) in 1½ hours. The price includes a biologist-guided walk through the area for ground-level orientation before or after the tram ride. Several add-ons are possible too, with frog, snake, and butterfly exhibits and a zip-line canopy tour on-site. You can arrange a personal pickup in San José for a fee; alternatively, there are public buses (on the Guápiles line) every half hour from the Gran Terminal del Caribe in San José. Drivers know the tram as the *teleférico*. Many San José tour operators make a daylong tour combining the tram with another half-day option; combos with the Britt Coffee Tour or INBioparque in Santo Domingo, both near Heredia, are especially popular. Ten rustic (no a/c or TV) but cozy cabinas are available on-site for $94 per person. The facility operates the lodging only if at least two

cabins are being rented at the same time. (Reservations are required.) Electricity shuts off after 9 PM. Cabin rates include meals, tram tours, and guided walks. A café is open to all for breakfast, lunch, and dinner. If you're traveling the Central Pacific coast, you'll find similar installations near the town of Jacó ($\Rightarrow$ *Chapter 5*) 3 km (2 mi) north of Supermercado Maxi Bodega, although without the accommodation, and a restaurant open for breakfast and lunch only. The admission price at the Pacific facility includes the tram ride, nature walk, snake exhibit, heliconia and medicinal plant gardens, and transport from Jacó-area hotels, as opposed to the à la carte pricing used at the Braulio Carrillo tram. The company also operates trams in the Caribbean-island nations of Dominica and St. Lucia, both outside the scope of this book.

Reservations: ⊠ Teleférico del Bosque Lluvioso, Avda. 7 at C. 7, San José ☎ 2257–5961, 866/759–8726 in North America w www.rfat.com ✉ $55, $27.50 for children under 12; $100, $72.50 for children under 12, includes round-trip transportation to Braulio Carrillo from San José hotels ☉ Tours: Mon. 9–4, Tues.–Sun. 6:30–4. Call for reservations 6 AM–9:30 PM c AE, D, DC, MC, V.

ernmost point to which Afro-Caribbeans could migrate. Costa Rica implemented the law in the late 1880s—when large numbers of Afro-Caribbeans immigrated (mainly from Jamaica) to construct the Atlantic Railroad—but abolished it in the 1949 constitution.

GETTING HERE

Siquirres lies just off the main highway and is easily accessible from the east, west, or south (if you're arriving from Turrialba). Autotransportes Caribeños buses connect San José's Gran Terminal del Caribe with Siquirres several times daily.

SIQUIRRES ESSENTIALS

Bank/ATM **Banco Nacional** (✉ *50 m south of Acón gas station* ☎ *2768–8128*).

Medical Clinic **Centro de Salud de Siquirres** (✉ *East side of soccer field* ☎ *2768–6138*).

Pharmacy **Farmacia Santa Lucía** (✉ *50 m west of fire station* ☎ *2768–9304*).

Post Office **Correos** (✉ *Next to Guardia Rural*).

EXPLORING

Pineapples don't get the same attention in world circles as Costa Rican coffee and bananas, but the **Agri Tours Pineapple Tour** (✉ *On highway ✛ 7 km (4 mi) east of Siquirres* ☎ *2282–1349 in San José* ⊕ *www.agritourscr. com*), affiliated with Del Monte Foods, can acquaint you with the life and times of the country's lesser-known crop, from cultivation to drying and packing at a farm just east of town. The two-hour tour is $17, samples included. Call to make a reservation.

OUTDOOR ACTIVITIES

RAFTING Siquirres's proximity to the put-in sites of several classic rafting excursions makes it an ideal place to begin a trip. Old standby **Ríos Tropicales** ★ (✉ *On the highway in Siquirres* ☎ *2233–6455, 866/722—8273 in North America* ⊕ *www.riostropicales.com*) has tours on a Class III–IV section of the Pacuare River between Siquirres and San Martín, as well as the equally difficult section between Tres Equis and Siquirres. Not quite so wild, but still with Class III rapids, is the nearby Florida section of the Reventazón. Day excursions normally begin in San José, but if you're out in this part of the country, you can kick off your excursion here at the company's operations center in Siquirres.

THE NORTHERN CARIBBEAN COAST

Some compare these dense layers of green set off by brilliantly colored flowers—a vision doubled by the jungle's reflection in mirror-smooth canals—to the Amazon. That might be stretching it, but there's still an Indiana Jones mystique to the journey up here, especially when you get off the main canals and into the narrower lagoons. The region remains one of those Costa Rican anomalies: roadless and remote, it's nevertheless one of the country's most-visited places. The tourism seasons here are defined not by the rains or lack thereof (it's wet most of the year) but by the months of prime turtle hatching in Tortuguero, or by what's biting in sportfishing paradise Barra del Colorado.

In 1970 a system of canals running parallel to the shoreline was constructed to provide safer access to the region than the dangerous journey up the seacoast. You can continue up the canals, natural and man-made, that begin in Moín, near Limón, and run all the way to Tortuguero and beyond to the less-visited Barra del Colorado Wildlife Refuge. Or you can embark at various points north of Guápiles and Siquirres, as do public transportation and most of the package tours. (The lodges' minivans bring you from San José to the put-in point, where you continue your journey by boat.)

TORTUGUERO

Fodor'sChoice North of the national park, the hamlet of Tortuguero is a pleasant
★   little place with 600 inhabitants, two churches, three bars, a handful of souvenir shops, and a growing selection of inexpensive lodgings. (And one more plus: there are no motor vehicles here, a refreshing change from the traffic woes that plague the rest of Costa Rica.) You can also take a stroll on the 32-km (20-mi) beach, but swimming is not recommended because of strong riptides and large numbers of bull sharks and barracuda.

The stretch of beach between the Colorado and Matina rivers was first mentioned as a nesting ground for sea turtles in a 1592 Dutch chronicle. Nearly a century earlier, Christopher Columbus compared traversing the north Caribbean coast and its swimming turtles to navigating through rocks. Because the area is so isolated—there's no road here to this day—the turtles nested undisturbed for centuries. By the mid-1900s, however, the harvesting of eggs and poaching of turtles had reached such a level that these creatures faced extinction. In 1963 an executive decree regulated the hunting of turtles and the gathering of eggs, and in 1970 the government established Tortuguero National Park; modern Tortuguero bases its economy on tourism.

GETTING HERE & AROUND

It's easier than you'd think to get to remote Tortuguero. Flying is the quickest (and most expensive) option. SANSA and Nature Air provide early-morning flights to and from San José. SANSA agent **Victor Barrantes** (☎ 2709–8055 or 8838–6330) meets both planes—they arrive and depart within 15 minutes of each other—and offers boat-taxi service to and from town for $3. Call and confirm with him the day before if you need a ride. If you're staying at one of the lodges, its boat will meet you at the airstrip.

The big lodges all have packages that include transportation to and from San José along with lodging, meals, and tours. Guide-staffed minivans pick you up at your San José hotel and drive you to the put-in site, usually somewhere north of Siquirres, where you board a covered boat for the final leg on the canals to Tortuguero. The trip up entails sightseeing and animal viewing. The trip back to San José stops only

Continued on page 419

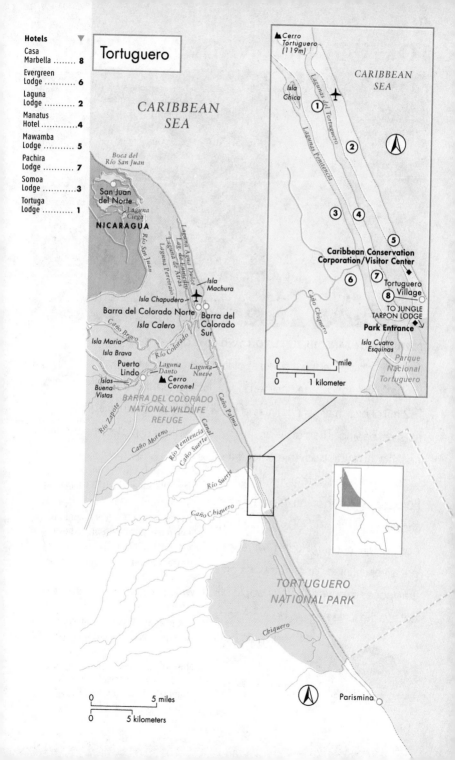

Hotels ▼

Tortuguero

**CARIBBEAN
SEA**

**CARIBBEAN
SEA**

▲Cerro
Tortuguero
(119m)

Isla
Chica

Lagunas del Tortuguero

Lagunas Penitencia

① ②

③ ④

⑤
**Caribbean Conservation
Corporation/Visitor Center**

⑥ ⑦ Tortuguero
⑧ Village

TO JUNGLE
TARPON LODGE

Park Entrance

Caño Chiquero

Isla Cuatro
Esquinas

*Parque
Nacional
Tortuguero*

0 _____ 1 mile
0 _____ 1 kilometer

Boca del
Río San Juan

San Juan
del Norte
*Laguna
Ciega*

NICARAGUA

Río San Juan

Lagunas Cuatro
Lag. de la Condesa
Laguna de Atras
Laguna Penitencia

Isla
Machura

Isla Chapudero

Barra del Colorado Norte

Isla Calero

Barra del
Colorado
Sur

Caño Bravo

Río Colorado

Isla Maria

Isla Brava

Puerto
Lindo

*Laguna
Danto*

*Laguna
Nueve*

Islas
Buena
Vistas

▲Cerro
Coronel

Caño Palma

Canal

*BARRA DEL COLORADO
NATIONAL WILDLIFE
REFUGE*

Río Zapote

Caño Penitencia

Caño Moreno

Caño Suerte

Río Suerte

Caño Chiquero

**TORTUGUERO
NATIONAL PARK**

Chiquero

0 _____ 5 miles
0 _____ 5 kilometers

Parismina

TORTUGUERO NATIONAL PARK

TORTUGUERO MEANS "TURTLE REGION," which is apt, since turtles are the main attraction. Four species of turtles—green, hawksbill, loggerhead, and giant leatherback—lumber up the 35 km (22 mi) of beach at various times of the year and deposit their eggs for safekeeping. The park was, in fact, established to protect the sea turtles' nesting habitat and to protect the turtles themselves. From the time that Europeans set foot on Costa Rican shores in the mid-1500s up until the early 20th century, turtles were aggressively hunted, and their eggs and carapaces exported. Some people still believe the turtle eggs to be a delicacy and some bars (illegally) serve them as snacks.

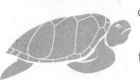

FAST FACTS

Size: 189 square km (73 square mi)

Established: 1975

"Dry" Season: February–April and September–October (But it's never *completely* dry here.)

Wettest months: January, June, July, and December

What to do: Turtle tours, canal tours, fishing

Geography: Lowland rain forests, swamp forests, beaches, canals, and lagoons

Number of species catalogued: 309 birds, 85 freshwater fish, 60 mammals, 7 river turtles, 4 sea turtles

Turtles have the limelight at Tortuguero, but also keep your eyes peeled for **non-turtle species** such as tapirs (in Jolillo groves), jaguars, anteaters, ocelots, howler monkeys, white-faced capuchin monkeys, three-toed sloths, collared and white-lipped peccaries, raccoons, otters, skunks, coatis, and blue morpho butterflies.

The palm-lined **beaches** of Parque Nacional Tortuguero stretch off as far as the eye can see. You can wander the beach independently, but riptides make swimming dangerous, and shark rumors persist.

Tours

It's entirely possible to get around Tortuguero on your own, but a package tour is the easiest way to go. Most Tortuguero tours are packaged through local lodges, with one- or two-night stays, and include transportation, meals, and guided tours. ■TIP→ Opt for at least two nights. The one-night tours give you a scant 18 hours to spend in Tortuguero, with the rest of your time spent coming and going.

Turtle watching is the name of the game most of the year here, and various guides in and around the village of Tortuguero can take you on excursions. For information on package tours, *see* The Caribbean Planner, at the start of this chapter.

River and rain forest tour

The Turtle-Nesting Ritual

Every two to four years, female turtles come ashore, nesting two to five times in a 12-day period. Each turtle digs a pit with her flippers and scoops out a chamber for depositing about 100 eggs. She fills and conceals the chamber before heading back out to sea. After a 60-day incubation period, the hatchlings emerge. In the ultimate in team effort, they scurry up the sides of the chamber, kicking sand down to the bottom, gradually raising the level of the base of the pit, allowing them to escape, and make a mad dash to the sea. Biologists believe that the nesting site's sand leaves an imprint on the hatchlings—though it's not known exactly how—that draws the females back as adults to the same stretch of beach, to continue the ritual that has taken place for thousands of years. Less than one percent of the hatchlings will make it to adulthood. Most fall victim to birds, dogs, sharks, and humans. That the turtle population survives at all is a remarkable feat of nature.

Tortuguero National Park

The Endangered Manatee

It is estimated that only about 100 manatees (*vacas marinas*, or "sea cows" in Spanish) remain in Tortuguero even though they were common here prior to 1950. It is thought that numbers have dwindled due to pesticides used on banana plantations, which seep into the water, killing the manatees' food supply and changing the aquatic environment. Also, because the manatees move extremely slowly, they are easy prey and often hit by motorboats.

SEA-TURTLE SPECIES	NESTING SEASON
▪ Giant Leatherback	February—July
▪ Green	July—October
▪ Hawksbill	March—October
▪ Loggerhead	Infrequently year-round

The green turtle is the most numerous species, so its nesting season is the most impressive to see.

Ironically, efforts to save Tortuguero's turtles have pushed manatees to the margins: Increased boat traffic bringing tourists to help guide turtle hatchlings to sea means more opportunities for manatees to be hit by boats, and scares them deeper into obscure canals. In another bit of irony, manatees provide a service to the very boats that threaten them by eating water hyacinths, which can clog up waterways if they grow unchecked.

Manatees, which are generally 3–3½ meters (10–12 feet) long and weigh 450–800 kilos (1,000–1,800 pounds), are vegetarians, and eat up to 75 kilos (150 pounds) of fresh- and saltwater plants every day. They are the only exclusively herbivorous marine mammals. Their slow digestion makes for lots of gas, so a good way to spot a manatee is to stop and look around for bubbles in the water! Count yourself lucky if you see one of these rare and cute (in a bulldog sort of way) creatures.

Park Info

Hours of Operation: Daily 6–6

Contacts: 2710–2929 or 2710–2939

Admission: $10

Getting There: The north entrance to the park lies at the southern edge of Tortuguero village. If you come here on a package tour with one of the lodges, your boat trip to and from will take you through the park. Hiking in the park is best accomplished on a guided tour that provides transportation.

for a lunch break. This is the classic "leave the driving to them" way to get to Tortuguero.

A boat from the port of Moín, near Limón, is the traditional budget method of getting to Tortuguero if you are already on the Caribbean coast. Arrive at the docks by 9 AM

and you should be able to find someone to take you there. The going price is $30 per person one way, $50 round-trip, and travel time is about three hours. **Alexis Soto and Sebastián Torres** (☎900/296–2626 *beeper*) partner to provide a reliable boat service between Moín and Tortuguero for about $50 round-trip. Arrange in advance. If you arrive in Moín in your own vehicle, JAPDEVA, Costa Rica's Atlantic port authority, operates a secure, guarded parking facility for your car while you are in Tortuguero.

It's entirely possible to make the trip independently from San José, a good option if you are staying in the village rather than at a lodge. A direct bus departs from San José's Gran Terminal del Caribe to Cariari, north of Guápiles, at 9 AM. At Cariari, disembark and walk five blocks to the local terminal, where you can board a noon bus for the small crossroads of La Pavona. From here, boats leave at 1:30 PM to take you to Tortuguero, arriving around 3 PM. The Cariari–La Pavona–Tortuguero bus-boat service is provided by **COOPETRACA** (☎2767–7137) or **Viajes Clic-Clic** (☎2709–8155, 8844–0463, or 8308–2006) for $10 one way. La Pavona has secure parking facilities. ■TIP➔**Avoid Rubén Bananero, a company that provides bus-boat transport from Cariari via an inconvenient route through the Geest banana plantation.** They begin to hustle you the minute you get off the bus in Cariari, insisting the La Pavona route does not exist. They also require that you buy a round-trip ticket, limiting your return options, and do everything they can to steer you toward hotels that pay them a commission. Others will also try to take you to their own dedicated "information dock" in the village, steering you toward their own guides. If you've made advance reservations for guides or hotels, stand your ground and say *"No, gracias."*

Water taxis provide transport from multiple points in the village to the lodges. Expect to pay about $2–$3 per trip.

TORTUGUERO ESSENTIALS

Internet La Casona (✉North side of soccer field ☎2709–8092).

Visitor Information Kiosk (✉Town center ☞Information on the town's history, the park, turtles, and other wildlife; unstaffed booth with free brochures). **Tortuguero Information Center** (✉Across from Catholic church ☎2709–8011 or 8833–0827 ✉tortugueroinfo@yahoo.com).

EXPLORING

The **Caribbean Conservation Corporation** *(CCC)* runs a visitor center and a museum with excellent animal photos, a video narrating local and natural history, and detailed discussions of the latest ecological goings-

A Province Apart

The capital's historic neglect of this region has given rise to an "us vs. them" outlook among the people here. It extends to the tourism industry as well, with complaints that the Instituto Costarricense de Turismo (Costa Rican Tourism Institute, or ICT) would rather promote the sunnier Pacific coast to international markets. Some here charge that subtle racism is at play. (Memories of early-20th-century government racial policies that segregated this region still remain.) The San José press doesn't help matters by splashing stories of crime in the Caribbean on front pages while giving little attention to comparable problems in Jacó, Tamarindo, or the capital. Any racial issues that *do* exist in Costa Rica—and that analysis goes way beyond the scope of this book—pale in comparison to those of many other countries. The true cause for the Caribbean's lighter tourism may be as non-sociological as the weather: the fact remains that it's rainier here than elsewhere in the country; it's just not the typical fun-in-the-sun mass-tourist destination. And it's exactly that road-less-traveled aspect of the Caribbean and its unique ethnic makeup that make the region worth visiting.

on and what you can do to help. There's a souvenir shop next door. For the committed ecotourist, the **John H. Phipps Biological Field Station,** affiliated with the CCC, has camping areas and dorm-style quarters with a communal kitchen. If you want to get involved in the life of the turtles, helping researchers to track turtle migration (current research, using satellite technology, has tracked turtles as far as the Florida Keys), or helping to catalog the population of neotropical migrant birds, arrange a stay in advance through the center. ⊠*From beach, walk north along path and watch for sign* 🏠*Apdo. 246–2050, San Pedro* ☎*2709–8091, 2297–5510 in San José, 352/373–6441 or 800/678–7853 in North America* ⊕*www.cccturtle.org* 🕮*$1* ⊘*Mon.–Sat. 10–noon and 2–5, Sun. 2–5:30.*

OUTDOOR ACTIVITIES

Tortuguero is one of those "everybody's a guide" places. Quality varies, but most guides are quite knowledgeable. If you stay at one of the lodges, guided tours are *usually* included in your package price (check when you book). If you hire a private guide, $5 per person per hour is the going rate, with most excursions lasting three hours.

TOUR GUIDES AND OPERATORS
Call or stop by the visitor center at the **Caribbean Conservation Corporation** (☎*2709–8091, 2297–5510 in San José* ⊕*www.cccturtle.org*) to get a recommendation for good local guides.

★ **Daryl Loth** (☎*8833–0827 or 2709–8011* ✉*safari@racsa.co.cr*) has a wealth of information about the area and conducts boat excursions on the canals and responsible turtle-watching tours in season with advance notice. **Victor Barrantes** (☎*2709–8055 or 8838–6330* ✉ *tortuguero_info@racsa.co.cr*) is the local SANSA agent who conducts hiking tours to Cerro Tortuguero and around the area when he's not meeting the early-morning flights.

FISHING You have your choice of mackerel, tarpon, snook, and snapper if you fish in the ocean; snook and calba if you fish in the canals. If you opt for the latter, the National Parks Service levies a $30 license fee (you are fishing in the confines of Tortuguero National Park), good for one month. Operators add the fee to your price.

Longtime area fishing expert **Eddie Brown** (☎2710–8016) is based out of Tortuga Lodge and has daylong fishing packages for $500. **Elvin Gutiérrez** (☎2709–8115 ⊕*www.tortuguerosportsfishing.com*), known as "Primo" to everyone in town, takes two passengers out for two hours or more, at $75 per hour, or for a full nine-hour day ($500). Prices include boat, motor, guide, and refreshments.

TURTLE-
WATCHING If you want to watch the *deshove* (egg laying), contact your hotel or the parks office to hire a certified local guide, required on turtle-watching excursions. Note that you won't be allowed to use a camera—flash or nonflash—on the beach, and only your guide is permitted to use a flashlight (and that must be covered with red plastic), because lights can deter the turtles from nesting. ■TIP→**A few unscrupulous locals will offer to take you on a turtle-watching tour outside the allowed February-through-November season, disturbing sensitive nesting sites in the process. If it's not the season, don't go on a turtle excursion. As the signs around town admonish:** DON'T BECOME ANOTHER PREDATOR.

WHERE TO EAT

The big lodges here offer one- or two-night excursion packages. (Given the choreography it takes to get up here, opt for a more leisurely two-night stay if you can.) Rates are expensive, but prices include everything from guides, tours, meals, and snacks to minivan and boat transport, and in some cases air transport to and from San José. If you stop and calculate what you get, the price may not be as bad as it first seems, and the tours are undeniably great fun. Usually *not* included in package prices? Alcoholic beverages, soda, bottled water, and the $10 entrance to Tortuguero National Park. Ask to be sure. Few of the lodges have phones, although all have radio contact with the outside world. All reservations must be made with their offices in San José. Be sure to travel light; you get a baggage allowance of 25 pounds.

$ ✕**Budda Café.** "Hip" was never a word that went hand in hand with Tortuguero, but this place has changed the rules. Pizza, crepes, pastas, and fresh fish are on the menu at this small, canal-side café in the center of town. Lattice wood over the windows, a thatched roof, and of course, a Buddha statue make up the furnishings. Jazzy cha-cha or a Dean Martin ballad might be playing in the background. ⊠*Next to police station, Tortuguero village* ☎2709–8084 ▬*No credit cards* ⊗*Closed Wed.*

$ ✕**Miss Junie.** Longtime Tortuguero doyenne Miss Junie has supposedly retired as the village's best-known cook, a tradition she learned at her mother's knee more than a half century ago, but still can be seen in the kitchen of the open-air restaurant adjoining her home. (Fidel Castro and Che Guevara were among the early diners here.) Selection is limited, and reservations are required, but you can usually count on a chicken, beef, or fish platter with rice and beans simmered in coconut milk. Your meal includes a beverage and dessert. ⊠ *150 m north of Paraíso Tropical, Tortuguero village* ☎ *2709–8102* ⌕ *Reservations essential* ▭ *No credit cards.*

¢ ✕ **The Vine Bakery.** Pastas, pizzas, and sandwiches are on the menu, but this small bakery and coffee shop is also a great place to stop for breads made with banana, carrot, and *natilla* (cream), for example. ⊠ *25 m north of Catholic church, Tortuguero village* ☎ *2709–8132* ▭ *No credit cards* ☉ *No dinner.*

WHERE TO STAY

$$$$ ▦ **Evergreen Lodge.** Owned by the Pachira Lodge people, the Evergreen
Fodor's Choice   offers an entirely different (and intimate) concept in Tortuguero lodg-
★   ing: while other lodges have cabins arranged around a clearing, at Evergreen they penetrate deep into the forest. A network of walking trails extends to Canal Chiquerito, the third waterway inland. Cabins are made from deep-red almond wood or gypsum wood. All have one double and one single, as well as venetian blinds for privacy. Honeymooners make up a substantial portion of the clientele here. Watch for the whimsical ANT CROSSING signs as you walk around the grounds. **Pro:** Seclusion from other lodges. **Con:** Rustic rooms. ⊹ *2 km (1½ mi) from Tortuguero village on Canal Penitencia* ⌂ *Apdo. 1818–1002, San José* ☎ *2257–2242, 800/644–7438 in North America* ⊕ *www. pachiralodge.com* ↬ *36 cabins* ⌕ *In-room: no a/c, no phone, no TV. In-hotel: restaurant, bar* ▭ *AE, D, DC, MC, V* ¶◎¶*AI.*

$$$$ ▦ **Laguna Lodge.** Laguna is the largest of the Tortuguero lodges, and it hums with activity. Jam-packed package tours begin in San José and embark boats at Caño Blanco, north of Siquirres. A mix of concrete and wood buildings spread out over 12 acres of grounds on a thin sliver of land between the ocean and the first canal inland. Rooms have wood paneling and floors, and tiled bathrooms. The property includes a butterfly garden and a small network of trails through secondary forest. Meals are served buffet style at the open-air restaurant that extends out over the canal. The snazzy combo reception–gift shop–meeting room building seems to have sprung straight from the mind of Gaudí. **Pro:** Many activities. **Con:** Large numbers of guests. ☎ *2709–8082, 2272–4943 in San José* ⊟ *2292–4927* ⊕ *www.lagunatortuguero.com* ↬ *80 rooms* ⌕ *In-room: no a/c, no phone, no TV. In-hotel: 2 restaurants, bars, pool, laundry service, public Internet* ▭ *AE, D, DC, MC, V* ¶◎¶*AI.*

$$$$ ▦ **Mawamba Lodge.** Nestled between the river and the ocean, Mawamba
★   is the perfect place to kick back and relax. It is also the only jungle lodge within walking distance (about 10 minutes) of town. Packages include transport from San José; when you arrive at the river town of Matina, you're whisked into a launch for a 2½-hour ride to a 15-acre site with comfortable (hot water!) rustic cabins with garden views. Meals are taken in the spacious dining room, and are included in the price, along

with transfers and guided tours of the jungle and canals; trips to turtle-heavy beaches cost $10 extra. Packages begin at $223 per person. **Pros:** Many activities, walking distance to village. **Con:** Rustic rooms. ⌖ *½ km (¼ mi) north of Tortuguero on ocean side of canal* ⌂*Apdo. 10980–1000, San José* ☎*2293–8181 in San José* ☎*2239–7657 in San José* ⊕*www.grupomawamba.com* ⟲*58 cabinas* ⌂*In-room: no a/c, no phone, no TV. In-hotel: restaurant, bar, pool, beachfront, laundry service, public Internet* ☰*AE, D, DC, MC, V* |◯|*AI.*

$$$$
Fodor'sChoice
★

⊡**Pachira Lodge.** This is the prettiest of Tortuguero's lodges, but not the costliest. Each almond-wood cabina in the lush, well-manicured gardens contains four guest rooms with high ceilings, king-size beds, and bamboo furniture. The stunning pool is shaped like a giant sea turtle: the head is a whirlpool tub, the left paw is a wading pool, and the right paw is equipped for swimmers with disabilities. There is no cross-river transportation into town. Package deals include transport from San José, a jungle tour, and all meals; rates begin at about $188 per person. Pachira is known for being the most competitive marketer of the lodges here, and the place is often full. **Pros:** Many activities, good value. **Con:** Large numbers of guests. ⊠*Across river from Mawamba Lodge* ⌂*Apdo. 1818–1002, San José* ☎*2223–1682 in San José, 800/644–7438 in North America* ☎*2223–1119 in San José* ⊕*www. pachiralodge.com* ⟲*88 rooms* ⌂*In-room: no a/c, no phone, no TV. In-hotel: restaurant, bar, pool, laundry service* ☰*AE, MC, V* |◯|*AI.*

$$$$

⊡**Samoa Lodge.** A location on the inland side of the second canal in from the ocean gives this place plenty of room to spread out, and indeed, a network of hiking trails on the lodge's grounds is one of the attractions here. Buildings are scattered around manicured gardens and contain rooms with vaulted ceilings, all with either one double and one single bed or three single beds. **Pro:** Seclusion from other lodges. **Con:** Rustic rooms. ⌖*2 km (1½ mi) from Tortuguero village on Canal Penitencia* ⌂*Apdo. 10736–1000, San José* ☎*2258–6244 in San José* ☎*2258–5687 in San José* ⊕*www.samoalodge.com* ⌂*In-room: no a/c, no phone, no TV. In-hotel: restaurant, bar, pool, no-smoking rooms* ☰*AE, D, DC, MC, V* |◯|*AI.*

$$$$
★

⊡**Tortuga Lodge.** Lush lawns, orchids, and tropical trees surround this thatched riverside lodge owned by Costa Rica Expeditions and renowned for its nature packages and top-notch, personalized service. Tortuga sets itself apart with its smaller size, and markets itself to a higher-budget clientele than do its major competitors here (Laguna, Mawamba, and Pachira). Tortuga's packages all include its own charter flights to Tortuguero rather than the land/boat combos from San José used by the other lodges. Guest rooms are comfortable, with much-appreciated mosquito blinds. The new penthouse suite, with two king-size beds and an extra smaller bed, has ample room for a family. The chefs do an excellent job preparing hearty food, which is served family style rather than in a buffet line as at other lodges. Tortuguero National Park is 20 minutes south by boat. **Pros:** Many activities, seclusion from other lodges. **Con:** Rustic rooms. ⊠*Across the river from airstrip* ⌖*2 km (1 mi) from Tortuguero* ☎*2710–8016, 2257–0766 in San José* ☎*2257–1655 in San José, 800/886–2609 in North America* ⊕*www.*

costaricaexpeditions.com ⇆26 rooms ⌂In-room: no a/c, no phone, no TV. In-hotel: restaurant, bar, pool, laundry service ☰AE, MC, V ⺽FAP.

$$$$ 🖼**Manatus Hotel.** Take one longtime budget lodging, give it a makeover worthy of a television reality show, reincarnate it as Tortuguero's luxurious hotel, and you've got yourself Manatus Hotel. Amenities such as air-conditioning, massage, and television are simply not found up here, but Manatus has them. Bright rooms with large windows each have two four-post queen-size beds with flowered quilted spreads, all under vaulted ceilings. Packages include round-trip van and boat transportation from San José, as well as all meals in the snazzy riverside restaurant. **Pros:** Intimate surroundings, numerous creature comforts. **Con:** Fills up quickly in high season, degree of luxury may feel out of place in Tortuguero. ⊹*Across river, about 1 km (½ mi) north of Tortuguero* ☎2709–8197, 2239–4854 in San José 📠2709–8198 ⇆12 rooms ⌂In-room: no phone, refrigerator. In-hotel: restaurant, room service, bar, pool, gym, laundry service ☰AE, D, DC, MC, V ⺽AI.

¢ 🖼**Casa Marbella.** This B&B, the best of the in-town lodgings, is a real
FodorśChoice find. Canadian owner and naturalist Daryl Loth is a respected authority
★ on all things Tortuguero, and one of the community's biggest boosters. If he's unable to take you out in his boat himself, he'll find someone who can. Immaculate rooms have tile floors and varnished-wood finishing with vaulted ceilings and skylights in the bathrooms. Ample breakfasts are served on the covered back patio facing the lodging's own private canal dock. The terrace is also a relaxing place for a coffee break on a rainy afternoon. There's a small kitchenette for your use. **Pros:** Knowledgeable owner, immaculate rooms. **Con:** Some street noise. ✉*Across from Catholic church, Tortuguero village* ☎8833–0827 or 2709–8011 ⊕*casamarbella.tripod.com* ⇆5 rooms ⌂In-room: no a/c, no phone, no TV ☰No credit cards ⺽BP.

SHOPPING

★ Octagonal **Jungle Shop** (✉*25 m north of Catholic church, Tortuguero village* ☎2709–8072) has the best selection of souvenirs in town. Tiles, feather paintings, and original-design T-shirts are the standouts, and they are things you won't find at every other store in Costa Rica. The town's largest souvenir emporium, **Paraíso Tropical** (✉ *West side of Tortuguero school, Tortuguero village* ☎2709–8095), has a huge selection of wood carvings and sandals in addition to the standard T-shirt and postcard fare. You can't miss it; it's right at the pier where the lodges' boats dock for their afternoon tours of the village. **Souvenirs Pura Vida** (✉*Across from police station, Tortuguero village* ☎2709–8037) is small but has a nice variety of colorful T-shirts and wood carvings.

BARRA DEL COLORADO

Up the coast from Tortuguero is the ramshackle hamlet of Barra del Colorado, a popular sportfishing hub characterized by plain stilted wooden houses, dirt paths, and a complete absence of motorized land vehicles (though some locals have added motors to their hand-hewn canoes).

EXPLORING

Bordered to the north by the Río San Juan and the frontier with Nicaragua is the vast, 905-square-km (350-square-mi) **Barra del Colorado Wildlife Refuge** *(Refugio Nacional de Vida Silvestre Barra del Colorado)*, Costa Rica's largest reserve, and really the only local attraction for non-anglers. Most people arrange trips here through their lodge. Transportation once you get here is almost exclusively waterborne, as there are virtually no paths in this swampy terrain. The list of species that you're likely to see from your boat is almost the same as that for Tortuguero; the main difference here is the feeling of being farther off the beaten

> **NICARAGUA CANAL?**
>
> During the 1840s California Gold Rush, the San Juan River became an important crossroads allowing miners and gold to move between New York and San Francisco some 70 years before the Panama Canal opened. Cornelius Vanderbilt financed the dredging of the waterway to allow ships to pass up the river to Lake Nicaragua. From here a rail line connected to the Pacific Ocean. As the Panama Canal ages, there is again talk of resurrecting this "wet-dry" canal. So far, plans remain on the drawing board.

track. You can realistically get as far as the 640,000-acre **Río Indio-Maíz Biological Reserve** when crossing the border here. The reserve is a continuation of the Barra del Colorado Wildlife Refuge, but in Nicaraguan territory. ✛*30 km/18 mi north of Tortuguero* ☎*No phone* ✉*Free* ☙*24 hours.*

CROSSING INTO NICARAGUA VIA THE SAN JUAN RIVER

Crossing into Nicaragua here is both difficult and easy. A stay at the Río Indio Lodge offers the easiest (and most expensive) option, with guided transportation included in your package price. The lodge will handle the $10 immigration fee levied by Nicaraguan authorities. (The border remains a thorny issue between Costa Rica and its northern neighbor, but it need not concern you as a visitor.) Less formally, a 40-km (24-mile) boat trip from Puerto Viejo de Sarapiquí up the Río Sarapiquí takes you to the San Juan and lets you officially enter Nicaragua. Passports are required for the trip, but you won't acquire a Nicaraguan stamp as a souvenir if you remain on the river, as is the case for most excursions. Venturing any farther into Nicaragua on your own is impossible here; you run up against the largely forested eastern half of the country. It remains essentially roadless, much like Tortuguero and Barra del Colorado immediately to the south. The western immigration point at Peñas Blancas provides a much easier entry into Nicaragua *(➪Chapter 3).*

THE SOUTHERN CARIBBEAN COAST

The landscape along the Guápiles Highway changes from farmland to tropical as you approach the port city of Limón. Place names change, too. You'll see signs to towns called Bristol, Stratford, and Liverpool,

The Nicas

Immigration issues generate intense debate in the United States and Western Europe. Who would guess that it has become a contentious matter here in Costa Rica, too? Over the past four decades, war, poverty, dictatorship, revolution, earthquakes, and hurricanes have beset Nicaragua, Costa Rica's northern neighbor. Each new calamity has brought a wave of refugees fleeing south. Approximations vary—no one can know for sure—but high-end estimates guess that 20% of Costa Rica's population today is Nicaraguan. Speaking with a faster, more clipped accent than Costa Ricans, they do not fade into the scenery.

The refrain among Ticos is a familiar one: "They're taking our jobs!" Yet, truth be told, Nicaraguans are performing the low-end labor that Costa Ricans just won't do anymore: your hotel chambermaid may likely be Nicaraguan; the glitzy resort where you're staying was probably built with the sweat of many Nicaraguan construction workers; the beans that went into that delicious morning cup of Costa Rican java were likely harvested by Nicaraguan coffee pickers.

reflecting the region's British Caribbean heritage. European visitors long ago discovered tourist towns par excellence Cahuita and Puerto Viejo de Talamanca; until recently, both were little known in American circles.

LIMÓN

100 km (62 mi) southeast of Guápiles, 160 km (100 mi) north and east of San José.

The colorful Afro-Caribbean flavor of one of Costa Rica's most important ports (population 90,000) is the first sign of life for seafaring visitors to Costa Rica's east coast. Christopher Columbus was the first visitor: he dropped anchor here on his final voyage to the New World in 1502. Limón (sometimes called "Puerto Limón") is a lively, if shabby, town with a 24-hour street life. The wooden houses are brightly painted, but the grid-plan streets look rather worn, partly because of the damage caused by a 1991 earthquake. Street crime, including pickpocketing and nighttime mugging, is not uncommon here. Long charged with neglecting the city, the national government has now turned attention to Limón. New businesses are coming in, a positive sign of urban renewal, and the town has beefed up security with a more visible police presence.

Limón receives thousands of visitors every year, owing in large part to its newest incarnation as a port of call. Carnival, Celebrity, Holland America, Norwegian, Princess, and Royal Caribbean cruise ships all dock here on certain of their Panama Canal or Western Caribbean itineraries. The downtown Terminal de Cruceros hums with activity between October and August, with one or two boats each day December through March, but many fewer outside those peak months. This is the place to find telephones, Internet cafés, manicurists (they do quite a brisk business), a tourist-information booth, and tour-operator stands, too. Downtown shopkeepers have all learned how to convert their colón prices to dollars, and post the day's exchange rate. St. Thomas or Puerto Vallarta it is not—perhaps someday, residents hope—but Limón has a tourist vibe these days that the city has never before experienced. The terminal contains souvenir stands staffed by low-key vendors who invite you to look, but don't pester you if your answer is "*No, gracias.*"

> ### SHIP AHOY!
>
> If you arrive in Limón on a cruise ship, a day in the Caribbean is yours for the taking. The Tortuguero canals, the beaches at Puerto Viejo de Talamanca, or the sloth rescue center at Aviarios del Caribe near Cahuita are three popular excursions. A few hardy souls venture as far away as the Rain Forest Aerial Tram or San José. A legion of taxi drivers waits at the terminal exit if you have not arranged an organized shore excursion through your cruise company.

NAVIGATING LIMÓN *Avenidas* (avenues) run east and west, and *calles* (streets) north and south, but Limón's street-numbering system differs from that of other Costa Rican cities. "Number one" of each avenida and calle begins at the water and numbers increase sequentially as you move inland, unlike the evens-on-one-side, odds-on-the-other scheme used in San José. But the scarcity of street signs means everyone uses landmarks anyway. Official red taxis ply the streets, or wait at designated taxi stands near Parque Vargas, the Mercado Municipal, and the cruise-ship terminal.

GETTING HERE & AROUND

If you're coming to the Caribbean coast, you'll pass through Limón. The Guápiles Highway that began in San José ends here at the ocean, but bypasses the heart of downtown by a couple of blocks. Budget about three and a half hours for the ride. Just after the sign to SIXAOLA and the coastal highway south to Cahuita and Puerto Viejo de Talamanca is the city center. The main bus terminal lies at Avenida 2 and Calle 8, across from the soccer stadium, and serves routes from San José, Guápiles, and Siquirres, with buses arriving several times daily from each. Opt for the *directo* (express) service from San José rather than the *corriente* buses, which make many stops along the route. Buses to Cahuita and Puerto Viejo de Talamanca and all points on the south coast arrive and depart from a stop across from Radio Casino on Avenida 4 between Calles 3 and 4.

LIMÓN ESSENTIALS

Bank/ATM BAC San José (⊠ *Avda. 3, Cs. 2–3* ☎ *2798–0155*). **Banco Nacional** (⊠ *Avda. 2, Cs. 3–4* ☎ *2758–0094*). **Scotiabank** (⊠ *Avda. 3 and C. 2* ☎ *2798–0009*).

Hospital Hospital Dr. Tony Facio (⊠ *Highway to Portete* ☎ *2758–2222*).

Pharmacy Farmacia Buenos Aires (⊠ *25 m east of Mercado Municipal* ☎ *2798–4732*). **Farmacia Limonense** (⊠ *1st fl, Radio Casino* ☎ *2758–0654*).

Internet **Café Internet** (⊠ *Gran Terminal del Caribe, Avda. 2 and C. 8, across from the soccer stadium* ☎ *2798–0128*). **Internet Cinco Estrellas** (⊠ *50 m north of Terminal de Cruceros* ☎ *2758–5752*).

Post Office **Correos** (⊠ *Avda. 2 and C. 4*). **DHL** (⊠ *Across from Terminal de Cruceros* ☎ *2758–1256*). **UPS** (⊠ *West side of Parque Vargas* ☎ *2798–3637*).

Visitor Information **JAPDEVA** (*Atlantic Port Authority* ⊠ *Terminal de Cruceros* ☞ *Accessible to cruise-ship passengers only*).

EXPLORING

The aquamarine wooden port building faces the cruise terminal, and just to the east lies the city's palm-lined central park, **Parque Vargas.** From the promenade facing the ocean you can see the raised dead coral left stranded by the 1991 earthquake. Nine or so Hoffman's two-toed sloths live in the trees of Parque Vargas; ask a passerby to point them out, as spotting them requires a trained eye.

A couple of blocks west of the north side of Parque Vargas is the lively enclosed **Municipal Market** (*Mercado Municipal* ⊠ *Pedestrian mall, Avda. 2, Cs. 3–4*), where you can buy fruit for the road ahead and experience the sights, sounds, and smells of a Central American market.

On the left side of the highway as you enter Limón is a large **cemetery.** Notice the COLONIA CHINA ("Chinese colony") and corresponding sign in Chinese on the hill in the cemetery: Chinese workers made up a large part of the 1880s railroad-construction team that worked here. Thousands died of malaria and yellow fever.

A branch of Monteverde's **Original Canopy Tour** (⊠ *Veragua de Liverpool* ⊹ *15 km [9 mi] west of Limón* ☎ *2291–4465 in San José* ⊕ *www.canopytour.com*) lies about 30 minutes west of Limón and offers you the chance to zip from platform to platform—10 in all—through the rain-forest canopy. The $45 tour lasts 1½ hours.

OUTDOOR ACTIVITIES

Limón's growing crop of tour operators serves cruise-ship passengers almost exclusively. **Laura Tropical Tours** (⊠ *Terminal de Cruceros* ☎ *2758–1240*) has excursions to banana plantations, Tortuguero, and Cahuita National Park. **Mambo Tours** (⊠ *Terminal de Cruceros* ☎ *2798–1542*) can take you on three- to eight-hour excursions around the region, and even on an all-day trip to the Rain Forest Aerial Tram or San José.

WHERE TO STAY & EAT

$–$$ ✕ **Brisas del Caribe.** Here's a case study in what happens when cruise ships come to town. This old downtown standby, once charmingly as off-kilter as the crooked umbrellas on its front tables, got rid of its video poker machines (and the locals who always hoped to get lucky playing them), tiled the floors, and remodeled. The food is still good—seafood and surprisingly decent hamburgers, a real rarity in Costa Rica, are the fare here—but a bit of the local color has faded. ⊠ *North side of Parque Vargas* ☎ *2758–0138* ▤ *AE, D, DC, MC, V.*

CLOSE UP

Caribbean Carnaval

If you're here in early or mid-October, don't miss Limón's Carnaval, arguably Costa Rica's biggest blowout. The weeklong celebration is held around October 12 (Columbus Day in the U.S.), which is celebrated by the rest of Latin America as the Día de la Raza (Day of the Race), "race" referring to the mixed population resulting from the encounter of European and indigenous peoples, a day that tends to have decidedly leftist political overtones. But in Costa Rica the holiday is the Día de las Culturas (Day of the Cultures), a joyous multicultural celebration of the encounter of New and Old Worlds in the country's most multicultural city. Historians here debate whether or not Carnaval was ever intended to coincide with the Columbus Day holiday. Most agree that it was simply a revitalization of the October Sin Kitt harvest celebrations once held on the Caribbean island of St. Kitts, the native home of 19th-century Afro-Caribbeans who immigrated to Costa Rica to work on the Atlantic Railroad. Expect a week's worth of colorful parades and vibrant reggae and calypso music. Book lodging weeks in advance if you plan to be in Limón during that time.

$ 🏨 **Hotel Maribú Caribe.** Perched on a cliff overlooking the Caribbean Sea between Limón and Portete, these white conical thatch huts have great views, but you're a long way from the ocean itself. The lovely grounds have green lawns, shrubs, palm trees, and a large, kidney-shape pool. The poolside bar discourages exertion. The hotel is immensely popular on weekends, but during the week you'll likely have the place to yourself. **Pros:** Good moderate value, seclusion **Cons:** No access to beach, far from sights ✚4 km (2½ mi) north on road to Portete 🖃Apdo. 623–7300, ☎2795–2543 🖷 2795–3241 ✉maribu@racsa. co.cr 🛏50 rooms ♿In-room: Wi-Fi. In-hotel: restaurant, bar, laundry service ▤AE, D, DC, MC, V ⊙EP.

¢ 🏨 **Hotel Park.** The prices at this pastel-and-pink business-class hotel in central Limón can't be beat. All rooms have modern furnishings and private balconies, so opt for one fronting the ocean. The air-conditioned dining room is a pleasant respite from the heat of the port city. **Pros:** Good budget value, great ocean views **Con:** Small rooms. 🖃Avda. 3, Cs. 2–3 ☎2798–0555 🖷 2758–4363 ✉irlyxie@racsa. co.cr 🛏32 rooms ♿In-hotel: restaurant ▤AE, DC, MC, V ⊙EP.

SHOPPING

The cruise-ship terminal contains an orderly maze of souvenir stands. Vendors are friendly; there's no pressure to buy. Many shops populate the restored port building across the street as well. Spelling is not its forte, but the **Caribean Banana** (🖃50 m north Terminal de Cruceros, west side of Parque Vargas) stands out from the other shops in the cruise-terminal area with a terrific selection of wood carvings.

The Old Atlantic Railroad

Christopher Columbus became the Caribbean's (and the country's) first tourist when he landed at Uvita Island near Limón during his fourth voyage to the New World in 1502. But the region was already home to thriving, if small, communities of Kekoldi, Bribrí, and Cabécar indigenous peoples. If Costa Rica was an isolated backwater, its Caribbean coastal region remained even more remote from colonial times through most of the 19th century.

New York industrialist Minor Keith changed all that in 1871 with his plan to launch the British-funded Atlantic Railroad, a mode of transportation that would permit easier export of coffee and bananas to Europe. Such a project required a massive labor force, and thousands of West Indians, Asians, and Italians were brought to Costa Rica to construct the 522-km (335-mi) railroad from Limón to San José. Thousands are reputed to have died of yellow fever, malaria, and snakebite during construction of the project. Those who survived were paid relatively well, however, and by the 1930s many Afro-Caribbean residents owned their own small plots of land. When the price of cacao rose in the 1950s, they emerged as comfortable landowners. Not that they had much

choice about going elsewhere: until the Civil War of 1948, black Costa Ricans were forbidden from crossing into the Central Valley lest they upset the country's racial balance, and they were thus prevented from moving when United Fruit abandoned many of its blight-ridden northern Caribbean plantations in the 1930s for green-field sites on the Pacific plain.

Costly upkeep of rail service, construction of the Braulio Carrillo Highway to the coast, declining banana production, and an earthquake that rocked the region in 1991 all sounded the death knell for the railroad. The earthquake was also a wake-up call for many here. The long lag-time for aid to reach stricken areas symbolized the historic neglect of the region by the central government. Development has been slow to reach this part of the country. (Telephones and electricity are still newfangled inventions in some smaller communities here.) As elsewhere in the country, communities now look to tourism to put colones in the coffers. San José has resurrected commuter-rail service, and a few folks here hold out faint hopes that Caribbean train service will start up once again, but that's likely a long way off.

MOÍN

5 km (3 mi) north of Limón.

The docks at Moín are a logical next stop after visiting neighboring Limón, especially if you want to take a boat north to explore the Caribbean coast.

GETTING HERE
Moín is a quick taxi ride from the center of Limón.

You'll probably be able to negotiate a waterway and national-park tour with a local guide, and if you call in advance, you can arrange a tour with the man considered the best guide on the Caribbean coast:

★ **Modesto Watson** (☎2226–0986 ⊕*www.tortuguerocanals.com*), a local Miskito Indian guide. He's legendary for his bird- and animal-spotting skills as well as his howler monkey imitations. The family's *Riverboat Francesca* can take you up the canals for two-day–one-night excursions to Tortuguero for $175–$190 per person, depending on the lodge used.

CAHUITA

44 km (26 mi) southeast of Limón.

Dusty Cahuita, its main dirt street flanked by wooden-slat cabins, is a backpackers' vacation town—a hippie hangout with a dash of Afro-Caribbean spice tossed in. And after years of negative crime-related publicity, Cahuita has beefed up security—this is one of the few places in the country where you will be conscious of a visible and reassuring, though not oppressive, police presence—and is making a well-deserved comeback on the tourist circuit. Tucked in among the backpackers' digs are a few surprisingly nice get-away-from-it-all lodgings, and restaurants with some tasty cuisine at decent prices. No question that nearby Puerto Viejo de Talamanca has overtaken Cahuita and has become the hottest spot on the southern Caribbean coast. But as Puerto Viejo grows exponentially, Cahuita's appeal is that it remains small and manageable. It's well worth a look.

NAVIGATING CAHUITA Cahuita's tiny center is quite walkable, if dusty in the dry season and muddy in the wet season. It's about a 30-minute walk to the end of the Playa Negra road to Hotel La Diosa. Take a taxi to or from Playa Negra after dark. Cahuita has no officially licensed red taxis; transportation is provided informally by private individuals. To be on the safe side, have your hotel or restaurant call a driver for you.

Bicycles are a popular means of utilitarian transport in Cahuita. Seemingly everyone rents basic touring bikes for $4–$8 per day, but quality varies widely. **Cabinas Brigitte** (⊠*Playa Negra road* ⊠*1½ km [1 mi] from town* ☎2755–0053) rents good bikes for $6 per day. **Cahuita Tours**(⇨*below*) also has bike rentals.

GETTING HERE & AROUND

Autotransportes MEPE buses travel from San José four times a day, and hourly throughout the day from Limón and Puerto Viejo de Talamanca. Car travel is straightforward: watch for signs in Limón and head 45 minutes south on the coastal highway. Road conditions wax and wane with the severity of the previous year's rains, and with the speed at which highway crews patch the potholes. They're quite good at this writing, but *¿Quién sabe?* (Who knows?) next year. Cahuita has three entrances from the highway: the first takes you to the far north end of the Playa Negra road, near the Magellan Inn; the second, to the middle section of Playa Negra, near the Atlántida; and the third, to the tiny downtown.

The proximity of the Panamanian border means added police vigilance on the coastal highway. No matter what your mode of transport,

7

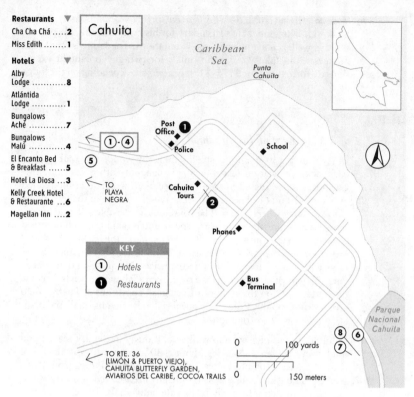

Cahuita

Caribbean Sea

Punta Cahuita

Post Office ❶
Police
School
TO PLAYA NEGRA
Cahuita Tours ❷
Phones
Bus Terminal
Parque Nacional Cahuita

TO RTE. 36
(LIMÓN & PUERTO VIEJO),
CAHUITA BUTTERFLY GARDEN,
AVIARIOS DEL CARIBE, COCOA TRAILS

0 — 100 yards
0 — 150 meters

KEY
① Hotels
❶ Restaurants

expect a passport inspection and cursory vehicle search at a police checkpoint just north of Cahuita. If you're on public transportation, you'll disembark from the bus while it is searched.

CAHUITA ESSENTIALS

Bank/ATM Banco de Costa Rica (⊠ *Entrance to town* ☎ *2755–0401* ▭ *Visa only*).

Internet Cabinas Palmer Internet (⊠ *50 m east of Coco's* ☎ *2755–0435*).

EXPLORING

A full-fledged nature center a few miles northwest of Cahuita and well worth a stop,

Fodor$Choice **Aviarios del Caribe** (Aviaries of the Caribbean) has dense gardens that
★ have attracted over 300 bird species. Proceeds go to goodhearted own-
☾ ers Judy and Luis Arroyo's sloth rescue center on the premises. Buttercup, the very first of their charges, holds court in the nature-focused
gift shop. ⊹ *9 km (5 mi) northwest of Cahuita, follow signs on Río*
Estrella delta ☎ *2750–0775* ⊕ *www.slothrescue.org* ✉ *$25 for tours*
☾ *Daily* 6 AM–*3:30* PM.

At most butterfly gardens around Costa Rica you get wet during the rainy season. (The mesh enclosures don't offer much protection from the moisture.) But that's not the case at the **Cahuita Butterfly Garden,** where a wood roof covers the perimeter of the 1,100-square-meter facility. The friendly owners conduct tours in English, French, and Spanish. There's a souvenir shop and small café that serves refreshments, as well as a lounge area outfitted with whimsical wooden chairs. (The owner is a sculptor.) ⊠ *Coastal highway, 200 m before main entrance to Cahuita* ☎ *2755–0361* ⊠ *$8* ⊙ *Daily 8:30–3:30.*

> ## RECYCLE!
>
> Unfortunately it's difficult to recycle in most places in Costa Rica, but Cahuita and Puerto Viejo de Talamanca have made it a breeze. Deposit your aluminum cans and glass and plastic beverage bottles in the *Recicaribe* barrels you'll see in either community.

The chocolate trade contributed substantially to this region's economy in the 19th century, and you can get a figurative and literal taste of that fact at **Cocoa Trails,** an outdoor museum devoted to the cultivation of cacao and its transformation into chocolate. There is also a museum documenting indigenous history on-site, with an emphasis on shaman-style healing. Finish off with a visit to the thatch-roof restaurant and a hearty Caribbean lunch. ⊠ *Coastal highway ✛ 5 km (3 mi) south of main entrance to Cahuita* ☎ *2756–8186* ⊠ *$15, $25 with guided tour* ⊙ *Mon. –Sat. 8–4.*

OUTDOOR ACTIVITIES

Cahuita is small enough that its tour operators don't focus simply on the town and nearby national park, but instead line up excursions around the region, even as far away as the Tortuguero canals to the north and Bocas del Toro, Panama, to the south. **Cahuita Tours** (⊠ *Main street, 180 m north of Coco's* ☎ *2755–0000 or 2755–0101* ⊕ *www.cahuitatours.com*) is the town's largest and most established tour operator. They can set you up with any of a variety of adventures, including river rafting and kayaking, tours of the Tortuguero canals and mountains, and of indigenous reserves (for a glimpse into traditional life). They can also reconfirm flights and make lodging reservations. We recommend them over their competitors.

WHERE TO EAT

$-$$ ✕ **Cha Cha Chá.** Québécois owner Bertrand Fleury's sign triumphantly

Fodor's Choice announces CUISINE OF THE WORLD at the entrance to his restaurant on

★ Cahuita's main street. (He counts French, Italian, Brazilian, and Canadian heritage in his family tree.) Thai shrimp salad and Tex-Mex fajitas are two of the typically eclectic dishes. The menu is small, but what's done is done impeccably well. A delectable specialty is *langosta cha cha chá,* lobster in a white-wine garlic sauce with fresh basil. Paintings by local and Cuban artists hang on the walls of the candlelit semi-outdoor dining area, separated from the street by miniature palm trees. The place is (deservedly) popular and has a scant 32 places. Make it a stop; it's one of the country's top restaurants. ⊠ *Main street, 200 m north of Coco's* ☎ *2755–0476 or 8394–4153* ⊛ *Reservations essential* ⊟ *MC, V* ⊙ *Closed Mon. No lunch.*

$ ✕**Miss Edith.** Miss Edith is revered for her flavorful Caribbean cooking, vegetarian meals, and herbal teas for whatever ails you. Back in the old days, she served on her own front porch; she's since moved to more ample surroundings on an easy-to-miss side street at the north end of town. A bit of the mystique disappeared with the move, but her made-to-order dishes—*rondón* (stew of vegetables and beef or fish) and spicy jerk chicken—are good

A TERM OF RESPECT
No one calls older, established women in Costa Rica's Afro-Caribbean communities Señora. Instead, everyone addresses them as Miss plus their first name, regardless of their marital status. Cahuita has Miss Edith; Tortuguero, Miss Junie; and Puerto Viejo, Miss Sam.

no matter where they are served. You can get breakfast (except Sunday), and with advance notice Miss Edith will even give you a half-day Caribbean cooking lesson. ⊠ *East of police station* ☎*2755–0248* ▤*No credit cards.*

WHERE TO STAY

$$ ▦ **Magellan Inn.** Arguably Cahuita's most elegant lodging, this group of
★ bungalows is graced with tile-floor terraces facing a pool and gardens growing on an ancient coral reef. Carpeted rooms have original paintings and custom-made wooden furniture. Feast on intensely flavored French and creole seafood specialties at the Casa Creole ($–$$), open for dinner each evening on the hotel's patio; don't miss the house pâté or the homemade ice cream. The open-air bar rocks to great blues and jazz recordings in the evening and mellows with classical music at breakfast. **Pros:** Seclusion, good value. **Cons:** Far from sights. ⊹*2 km (1 mi) north of town at end of Playa Negra road* ⌂*Apdo. 1132–7300, Limón* ☎*2755–0035* ⊕*www.magellaninn.com* ⇆*6 rooms* ⌂*In-room: no a/c (some), no phone, no TV, Wi-Fi. In-hotel: restaurant, bar, pool, laundry service* ▤*AE, D, DC, MC, V* ⏀*CP.*

$–$$ ▦ **Hotel La Diosa.** The owners' interest in Eastern religions is evidenced in the hotel's name (La Diosa means "goddess") and by the sign depicting a Hindu goddess. They have also opted for little touches such as the rounding of corners and cachá-wood rails to "enhance feminine energy." The place hosts occasional yoga workshops, too, but that's as New Age as it gets. Brightly painted stone or wood cabins—a few have air-conditioning, a rarity here—are scattered around the grounds. All have bright furnishings and art posters hang on the walls, and one room even comes with a whirlpool tub. A bridge leads from the pool to the beach. **Pro:** Seclusion. **Con:** Far from sights. ⊹*2 km (1 mi) north of town at end of Playa Negra road* ☎*2755–0055* ⊟ *2755–0321* ⊕*www.hotelladiosa.net* ⇆*13 cabins* ⌂*In-room: no a/c (some), no phone, no TV. In-hotel: restaurant, bar, pool, no elevator, public Wi-Fi* ▤*AE, D, DC, MC, V* ⏀*BP.*

$ ▦ **Atlántida Lodge.** Attractively landscaped grounds, the beach across the road, and a large pool are Atlántida's main assets. You're welcomed to your room by a lovely assortment of fresh and dried flowers; the rooms themselves are a little on the rustic side, but have tile floors and pretty terraces. Two rooms have hot tubs. All the coffee and bananas you can drink and eat are yours as well. **Pro:** Good value. **Con:** Dark rooms. ✉*Next to soccer field at Playa Negra* ☎*2755–0115* 🖷 *2755–0213* ✐*atlantis@racsa.co.cr* 🛏*32 rooms, 2 suites* 🔧*In-room: no a/c, no phone, no TV. In-hotel: restaurant, bar, pool, gym, laundry service* ▤*AE, D, DC, MC, V* ⍐*EP.*

$ 🖫**Bungalows Malú.** This is one of the rare places with air-conditioning on the coast, but it doesn't need it: the octagonal stone-and-wood bungalows spread out on the grounds here get plenty of cool breezes from the beach across the road. Each unit has shuttered screened windows, hardwood floors, and a private porch with a hammock. **Pros:** Good value, air-conditioning. **Con:** Far from sights. ✉*Playa Negra road* ✉*2 km (1 mi) north of Cahuita* ☎*2755–0114* 🖷 *2755–0006* ✐*bungalowmalu@gmail.com* 🛏*6 bungalows* 🔧*In-room: no phone, no TV. In-hotel: restaurant, bar, pool* ▤*MC, V* ⍐*BP.*

$ 🖫**El Encanto Bed & Breakfast Inn.** Zen Buddhist owners have cultivated a serene and beautiful environment here, ideal for physical and spiritual relaxation. Lodgings are in a garden with an extensive bromeliad collection and Buddha figures. Choose between comfortable rooms or bungalows, all decorated with art from around the globe; some rooms have a double vaulted ceiling with strategically placed screens that keep the place wonderfully ventilated. Amenities include queen-size beds, hot water, and secure parking. Breakfast comes complete with homemade breads and cakes. The beach is across the street, and massage and yoga classes are available on weekends. **Pros:** Friendly owners, good value, central location. **Con:** Not for young travelers looking for a scene. ✉*200 m west of police station on Playa Negra road* ✐*Apdo. 7-7302, Cahuita* ☎*2755–0113* 🖷 *2755–0432* ⊕*www.elencantobedandbreakfast.com* 🛏*3 rooms, 3 bungalows, 1 apartment* 🔧*In-room: no a/c, no phone, kitchen (some), no TV (some). In-hotel: pool, no elevator* ▤*AE, MC, V* ⍐*BP.*

FodorśChoice
★

7

¢–$ 🖫**Bungalows Aché.** Like Alby Lodge next door, Aché scatters wooden bungalows—three octagonal structures in this case—around wooded grounds that make the close-by town center seem far away. The buildings are new, and each comes with a rocking chair and porch hammock. The largest bungalow sleeps four. The Swiss owner accepts euros, dollars, and colónes. **Pro:** Central location. **Con:** Small rooms. ✉*180 m west of national park entrance* ✐*Apdo. 740-7300, Limón* ☎*2755–0119* ⊕*www.bungalowsache.com* 🛏*3 bungalows* 🔧*In-room: no a/c, no phone, refrigerator, no TV* ▤*No credit cards* ⍐*EP.*

¢ 🖫**Alby Lodge.** You're right in town, but you'd never know it at this friendly lodging. Cabins with hardwood floors are propped up on stilts and have hot-water baths, log tables, mosquito nets, and a hammock on the front porch. Make use of the shared kitchen facilities and outdoor barbecue. The forested grounds and high thatch roof keep the temperature pleasantly bearable in otherwise balmy Cahuita. It's next to the park, so the howler monkeys are your morning alarm clock. **Pro:** Central location. **Con:** Sometimes a bit noisy. ⊠*180 m west of national park entrance* ☎*2755–0031* ⊕*www.albylodge. com* ⇆*4 cabins* ⚭*In-room: no a/ c, no phone, no TV* ⊟*No credit cards* ❘⊚❘*EP.*

¢   🖼 **Kelly Creek Hotel & Restaurante.** Owners from Madrid have created a wonderful budget option in a handsome wooden hotel on the creek bank across a short pedestrian bridge from the park entrance. Each of the four hardwood-finished guest rooms is big enough to sleep a small army and has two double beds. Owner Andrés de Alcalá barbecues meat and fresh fish on an open-air grill and also cooks paella and other Spanish specialties. Stop by the restaurant ($–$$) for dinner, even if you're not staying here, but order the paella by 2 PM. Caimans come to the creek bank in search of snacks, and the monkeys and parrots who live in the national park are just yards away, as is the lively center of Cahuita. You'll get a small discount if you pay in cash. **Pros:** Good value, great Spanish restaurant. **Con:** Dark rooms. ⊠*Next to park entrance* ☎*2755–0007* ⊕*www.hotelkellycreek.com* ⇆*4 rooms* ⚭*In-room: no a/c, no phone, no TV. In-hotel: restaurant* ⊟*AE, D, DC, MC, V* ❘⊚❘*EP.*

> ### A TOWN THAT WON'T LET YOU DOWN
>
> Cahuita's first tourist of note was Costa Rican president Alfredo González, whose boat shipwrecked on this stretch of coast in 1915. The president was so grateful for the aid settlers gave him that he purchased a tract of land here and donated it to them to construct a town.

NIGHTLIFE

Aside from a local bar or two, Cahuita's nightlife centers on restaurants, all pleasant places to linger over dinner for the evening. Lively reggae, soca, and samba blast weekend evenings from the turquoise **Coco's Bar** (⊠*Main road*). The assemblage of dogs dozing on its veranda illustrates the rhythm of local life.

CAHUITA NATIONAL PARK

Just south of Cahuita.

The only Costa Rican park jointly administered by the National Parks Service and a community, Parque Nacional Cahuita starts at the southern edge of the town of Cahuita. The park's rain forest extends right to the edge of its curving, utterly undeveloped 3-km (2-mi) white-sand beach. Roughly parallel to the coastline, a 7-km (4-mi) trail passes through the forest to Cahuita Point, encircled by a 2½-square-km (1½-square-mi) coral reef. The hike takes only a few hours, but you have to ford several rivers on the way, so check conditions beforehand, as they can be impassible in the rainy season.

There's good snorkeling off Cahuita Point—watch for blue parrot fish and angelfish as they weave their way among equally colorful species of coral, sponges, and seaweeds. Sadly, the coral reef is slowly being killed by sediment, intensified by deforestation and the erosive effects

Reefs at Risk

One of the most complex organisms in the marine world, a coral reef is an extraordinary and extraordinarily delicate habitat. Coral reefs are the result of the symbiotic relationship between single-cell organisms called zooxanthellae and coral polyps. The zooxanthellae grow inside the cells of the polyps, producing oxygen and nutrients that are released into the coral tissues. Corals secrete calcium carbonate (limestone) that, over time, forms the vast coral reef "superstructure." Zooxanthellae require exposure to sunlight to thrive. The healthiest coral reefs are in clear, clean, tropical seawater at a temperature of 20°C to 25°C (70°F to 80°F). Healthy coral reefs are biologically rich gardens occupied by a diverse selection of life forms, from microscopic unicellular algae and phytoplankton to a wide range of fish.

Unfortunately, coral reefs in Costa Rica are in danger. Dirt and sediment from banana plantations and logging areas, as well as runoff from pesticide use, are killing them. The dirty runoff literally clogs the pores of the zooxanthellae and smothers them. In the Golfo Dulce, 98% of one of the oldest reefs in Costa Rica has been destroyed by this sedimentation. The once-enormous reefs of Cahuita are almost entirely gone.

Human visitors, including careless snorkelers, have also damaged reefs. Just touching a reef damages it. When exploring a coral reef, look but don't touch, and snorkel only on its outer side, preferably in calm weather. Can the reefs be saved? With commitment and time, yes. Coral is resilient, and will grow back—if the Costa Rican government makes it a priority.

7

of the 1991 earthquake. ■TIP→ **Use a local guide to find the best reefs (or if snorkeling independently, swim out from the beach on the Puerto Vargas side), and don't snorkel for a few days after it rains, as the water is sure to be murky.** You can take a ride in a glass-bottom boat from Cahuita; visibility is best in September and October. The road to the park headquarters at Puerto Vargas is 5 km (3 mi) south of Cahuita on the left. Here you find the ranger station as well as campsites that have been carved out of the jungle, scattered along the beachfront. ☎2755–0461 Cahuita entrance, 2755–0302 Puerto Vargas entrance ✉By donation at Cahuita entrance, $10 at Puerto Vargas entrance ☉Daily 6–5 Cahuita entrance, daily 7–4 Puerto Vargas entrance.

GETTING HERE & AROUND

Choose from two park entrances: one is at the southern end of the village of Cahuita; the other is at Puerto Vargas, just off the main road, 5 km (3 mi) south of town. If you don't have a car, you can get here easily via bike or taxi.

OUTDOOR ADVENTURES

Operators in Cahuita or Puerto Viejo de Talamanca can hook you up with excursions to and in the park, or you can go on your own, especially if you use the entrance at the south edge of the village.

BICYCLING   You can bike through Cahuita National Park, but the trail gets pretty muddy at times, and you run into logs, river estuaries, and other obstacles. Nevertheless, mountain bikes are a good way to get around on the dirt roads and trails surrounding Cahuita and Puerto Viejo de Talamanca. (The southern entrance to the park is close enough to Puerto Viejo that you could bike there just as easily as from Cahuita.) Cycling is easiest in the dry season, though many hardy souls are out during the long rainy season. Rent bikes in Cahuita or Puerto Viejo.

HIKING   A serious hiking trail extends as far as Puerto Vargas. If you're coming from Cahuita, you can take a bus or catch a ride into Puerto Vargas and hike back around the point in the course of a day. Be sure to bring plenty of water, food, and sunscreen. Along the trail you might spot howler and white-faced capuchin monkeys, coatis, armadillos, and raccoons.

SNORKELING   Cahuita's reefs are just one of several high-quality snorkeling spots in the region. Rent snorkeling gear in Cahuita or Puerto Viejo de Talamanca or through your hotel; most hotels also organize trips. It's wise to work with a guide, as the number of good snorkeling spots is limited and they're not always easily accessible. Cahuita established a community lifeguard team in 2002, unusual in Costa Rica. ■TIP➔**As elsewhere up and down the Caribbean coast, the undertow poses risks for even experienced swimmers. Use extreme caution and never swim alone.**

PUERTO VIEJO DE TALAMANCA

16 km (10 mi) south of Cahuita.

This muddy, colorful little town has become one of the hottest spots on the international budget-travel circuit, and swarms with surfers, New Age hippies, beaded and spangled punks, would-be Rastafarians of all colors and descriptions, and wheelers and dealers—both pleasant and otherwise. Time was when most kids came here with only one thing on their mind: surfing. Today many seem to be looking for a party, with or without the surf.

But if alternative lifestyles aren't your bag, there are plenty of more "grown-up" offerings on the road heading southeast and northwest out of town. At last count, some 45 nationalities were represented in this tiny community, and most are united in concern for the environment and orderly development of tourism. (Few want to see the place become just another Costa Rican resort community.) Some locals bemoan the loss of their town's innocence, as drugs and other evils have surfaced, but only in small doses: this is still a fun town to visit, with a great variety of hotels, cabinas, and restaurants in every price range. Unlike other parts of Costa Rica, no one has been priced out of the market here.

Locals use "Puerto Viejo" to refer to the village. They drop the "de Talamanca" part; we use the complete name to avoid confusion with the other Puerto Viejo: Puerto Viejo de Sarapiquí in the Northern Plains. You have access to the beach right in town, and the Salsa Brava, famed in surfers' circles for its pounding waves, is here off the coast, too. The best strands of Caribbean sand are outside the village: Playa Cocles, Playa Chiquita (technically a series of beaches), and Punta Uva, all dark-sand beaches, line the road heading southeast from town. Playa Negra—not the Playa Negra near Cahuita—is the black-sand beach northwest of town. Punta Uva, with fewer hotels and the farthest from the village, sees fewer crowds and more tranquillity. Playa Negra shares that distinction, too—for now—but developers have eyed the beach as the next area for expansion.

NAVIGATING
PUERTO
VIEJO DE
TALAMANCA You can manage the town center quite easily on foot, though it is dusty in the dry season and muddy when it rains. (The main street is, thankfully, paved.) Everyone gets around by bike here, and seemingly everyone has one for rent. Quality varies widely. Expect to pay a $4–$8 per day for a good bike. **Cabinas Grant** (⊠ *100 m south of bus stop* ☎*2750–0292*) has the best selection of quality bikes in town. Priority is given to guests at **Casa Verde Lodge** (⊠ *200 m south and 200 m east of bus stop* ☎*2750–0015*), but they usually have extra bikes you can rent for a half or full day even if you don't stay here. There are a couple of official red licensed cabs, but most taxi service here is informal, with private individuals providing rides. To be on the safe side, have your hotel or restaurant call one for you.

GETTING HERE & AROUND

The turnoff to Puerto Viejo de Talamanca is 10 km (6 mi) down the coastal highway south of Cahuita. (The highway itself continues south to Bribrí and Sixaola at the Panamanian border.) The village lies another 5 km (3 mi) beyond the turnoff. The paved road passes through town and continues to Playas Cocles and Chiquita and Punta Uva before the pavement peters out at the entrance to the village of Manzanillo. "Badly potholed" describes the condition of the road from the highway into town, and as far as Playa Cocles. The newer paved sections beyond Cocles haven't disintegrated . . . yet. Autotransportes MEPE buses travel from San José four times a day, and hourly through-out the day from Limón and Cahuita. All buses from San José go into Puerto Viejo de Talamanca; most, though not all, Limón-originating buses do as well, but a couple drop you off on the highway. Check if you board in Limón.

A scant three buses per day ply the 15-km (9-mi) paved road between Puerto Viejo and Manzanillo, so unless your schedule meshes exactly with theirs, you're better off biking or taking a taxi to and from the far-flung beaches along the way. Taxis charge $7 to Playas Cocles and Chiquita (as well as north to Playa Negra), $8 to Punta Uva, and $12 to Manzanillo.

PUERTO VIEJO DE TALAMANCA ESSENTIALS

Bank/ATM **Banco de Costa Rica** (⊠ *50 m south of bridge at entrance to town* ☎*2750–0707* ☞ *Visa only*).

Pharmacy **Farmacia Amiga** (⊠ *Next to Banco de Costa Rica* ☎*2750–0698*).

Internet **ATEC** (⊠ *Across from Restaurant Tamara* ☎*2750–0398*). **Café Internet**

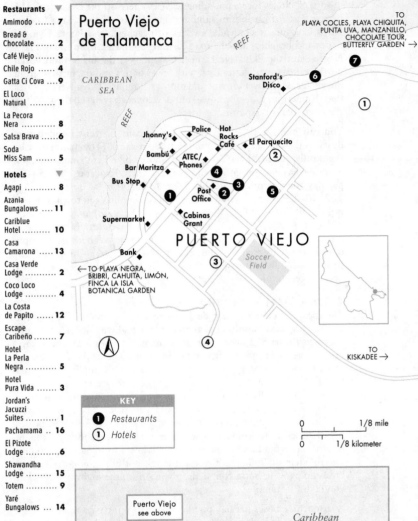

Restaurants ▼

Amimodo **7**

Bread &
Chocolate **2**

Café Viejo **3**

Chile Rojo **4**

Gatta Ci Cova **9**

El Loco
Natural **1**

La Pecora
Nera **8**

Salsa Brava **6**

Soda
Miss Sam **5**

Hotels ▼

Agapi **8**

Azania
Bungalows **11**

Cariblue
Hotel **10**

Casa
Camarona **13**

Casa Verde
Lodge **2**

Coco Loco
Lodge **4**

La Costa
de Papito **12**

Escape
Caribeño **7**

Hotel
La Perla
Negra **5**

Hotel
Pura Vida **3**

Jordan's
Jacuzzi
Suites **1**

Pachamama .. **16**

El Pizote
Lodge **6**

Shawandha
Lodge **15**

Totem **9**

Yaré
Bungalows ... **14**

Puerto Viejo de Talamanca

TO PLAYA COCLES, PLAYA CHIQUITA, PUNTA UVA, MANZANILLO, CHOCOLATE TOUR, BUTTERFLY GARDEN →

REEF

CARIBBEAN SEA

REEF

Stanford's Disco

Jhonny's
Police
Hot Rocks Café
El Parquecito

Bambú
ATEC/ Phones

Bar Maritza

Bus Stop

Post Office

Cabinas Grant

Supermarket

PUERTO VIEJO

Soccer Field

Bank

← TO PLAYA NEGRA, BRIBRI, CAHUITA, LIMÓN, FINCA LA ISLA BOTANICAL GARDEN

TO KISKADEE →

KEY

❶ *Restaurants*

① *Hotels*

| 0 | | 1/8 mile |
| 0 | | 1/8 kilometer |

Puerto Viejo
see above

Caribbean Sea

Playa Negra

Finca La Isla Botanical Garden

Playa Cocles

Chocolate Tour

Café Internet Río Negro

Playa Chiquita

Butterfly Garden

Punta Uva

Río Cocles

Río Cabo Negro

← TO LIMON

Gandaca-Manzanillo National Wildlife Refuge

TO MANZANILLO →

Afro-Caribbean Heritage

Costa Rica doesn't get more ethnically diverse than in its Caribbean region. Roughly a third of the people here are Afro-Caribbean, descendants of West Indians who arrived in the late 19th century to build the railroad and remained to work on banana and cacao plantations. Although Jamaicans brought some aspects of British colonial culture with them, such as cricket and the maypole dance, these habits have long since given way to reggae, salsa, and soccer, much to the chagrin of the older generation. The substantial East Asian population here also counts railroad workers as its ancestors, and small pockets of indigenous peoples have lived here since pre-Columbian times.

The Atlantic coast's long African-Caribbean heritage makes it the likeliest place in the country to find English-speakers, though residents will speak a Caribbean-accented English that may sound unfamiliar to you. "Okay" is a general all-purpose greeting heard on the coast, and is gradually replacing the older generation's traditional "Wha' happin!" (What's happening?) With Spanish now the language of instruction in all schools, young people here are less likely than their elders to speak English.

Río Negro (⊠ *Playa Cocles* ✢ *4 km (2½ mi) southeast of town* ☎ *2750–0801*).
El Tesoro (⊠ *Playa Cocles* ☎ **$$** *750–0128*).

Post Office **Correos** (⊠ *50 m west of ATEC*).

Visitor Information **ATEC** (⊠ *Across from Restaurant Tamara* ☎ *2750–0191* ⊕ *www.greencoast.com/atec.htm*).

EXPLORING

At the **Finca la Isla Botanical Garden** you can explore a working tropical fruit, spice, and ornamental plant farm. Sloths abound, and you might see a few poison dart frogs. A $10 guided tour includes admission and a glass of the farm's homemade fruit juice. You get the fruit juice if you wander around on your own, too—a $1 self-guided-tour book is available in English, Spanish, French, or German. Watch the demonstration showing how cacao beans are turned into chocolate, and sample some of the product at the end of the tour. ✢ *½ km (¼ mi) west of town at Playa Negra* ☎ *2750–0046* ⊕ *www.greencoast.com/garden.htm* ▨ *$5, guided tour $10* ☉ *Fri.–Mon. 10–4.*

🕭 Cacao once ruled the Talamanca region, but few plantations are left these days. One friendly Swiss couple continues the tradition and shows you the workings of their chocolate plantation on their **Chocorart** chocolate tour. Follow the little-known life cycle of this crop from cultivation to processing. There's sampling at the tour's conclusion. Call or e-mail to reserve a tour (you need a minimum of four people) and to be picked up from the Playa Chiquita School. Since these folks are Swiss, they can tailor the commentary in German, French, or Italian, in addition to English or Spanish. ✢ *6 km (4 mi) southeast of town at Playa Chiquita* ☎ *2750–0075* ✎ *chocorart@racsa.co.cr* ▨ *$15 per person* ☉ *By appointment.*

7

Unlike most such establishments in Costa Rica, which are for show only, the working **Butterfly Garden** cultivates 60 to 80 species of butterflies, three of which are unique to the area, for shipment to similar facilities around the world. The knowledgeable staff provides guided tours with bilingual commentary. *+7 km (4½ mi) southeast of town at Punta Uva* ☎2750–0086 *≤$5, free for kids under 6 ⊙Daily 8–4.*

OUTDOOR ACTIVITIES

As in Cahuita, tour operators and outfitters here can set up tours and activities anywhere on the south Caribbean coast.

Tours with **ATEC** *(Talamancan Association of Ecotourism and Conservation)* *⊠Across from Restaurant Tamara* ☎2750–0191 *⊕www. greencoast.com/atec.htm*) have an environmental or cultural bent, such as Afro-Caribbean or indigenous-culture walks—tours to the nearby Kekoldi indigenous reserve are especially popular—rain-forest hikes, coral-reef snorkeling trips, fishing trips, bird-watching tours, night walks, and adventure treks. Local organizations and wildlife refuges receive 15%–20% of ATEC's proceeds. Well-established operator **Terra Aventuras** (*⊠100 m south of bus stop* ☎2750–0750 *⊕www. terraventuras.com*) can lead you around Puerto Viejo de Talamanca and Cahuita, or take you on excursions to Tortuguero, the Gandoca-Manzanillo Wildlife Refuge, and Bocas del Toro in Panama. It also rents good-quality surfboards, bicycles, boogie boards, and snorkeling gear.

RAFTING ★ Rafting excursions lie about two hours away, but one San José–based outfitter has an office here. **Exploradores Outdoors** (*⊠Across from ATEC* ☎2750–0641, 2222–6262 in San José *⊕www.exploradoresoutdoors. com*) is highly regarded, and has day excursions on the Pacuare and Reventazón rivers, with a pickup point here or in San José, and the option to start in one place and be dropped off at the other.

SURFING Surfing is the name of the game in Puerto Viejo, for everyone from newbies to Kelly Slaters. The best conditions are late December through March, but there's action all year. Longtime surfers compare the south Caribbean to Hawaii, but without the "who-do-you-think-you-are?" attitude. There are a number of breaks here, most famously **Salsa Brava,** which translates to "wild sauce." It breaks fairly far offshore and requires maneuvering past some tricky currents and a shallow reef. Hollow and primarily right-breaking, Salsa Brava is one gnarly wave when it gets big. If it gets *too* big, or not big enough, check out the breaks at Punta Uva, Punta Cocles, or Playa Chiquita. Boogie-boarders and bodysurfers can also dig the beach-break waves at various points along this tantalizingly beautiful coast.

If you're, say, over 30, but have always wanted to try surfing, consider the friendly, three-hour $35 surf school at **Aventuras Bravas** (*⊠Across from Stanford's* ☎8849–7600). You start out with a small wave near the bus stop, and get a money-back guarantee that you'll be standing by the end of the lesson. You can also rent equipment here.

WHERE TO EAT

$$–$$$
Fodor'sChoice
★

✕**La Pecora Nera.** Though the name means "black sheep" in Italian, there's nothing shameful about this thatch-roof roadside restaurant. There's always a lot more to choose from than you'll see on the sparse-looking menu. Wait for owner/ chef Ilario Giannoni to come out of the kitchen and triumphantly announce—with flair worthy of an Italian opera—which additional light Tuscan entrées, appetizers,

and desserts they've concocted that day. Be prepared for a long, leisurely dining experience with attentive service. It's worth the wait; this is one of the country's top Italian restaurants. ✛ *3 km (2 mi) southeast of town at Playa Cocles* ☎*2750–0490* ▭*AE, D, DC, MC, V* ⊘*Closed Mon. No lunch.*

$$
★
✕**Amimodo.** The name translates to "my way," and the exuberant Italian owners really do it their way, combining the cuisine of their native northern Italy with Caribbean flavors. Your antipasto might be classic bruschetta or *jamón de tiburón* (shark ham with avocado dressing), and your ravioli might be stuffed with tropical shrimp, pineapple, and curry, with avocado sauce on the side. The tropical veranda with gingerbread trim spills over onto the beach with abundant greenery, and the restaurant is a popular gathering place for Puerto Viejo's Italian community. ⊠*200 m east of Stanford's* ☎*2750–0257* ▭*MC, V* ⊘*Closed Tues.*

$
✕**Café Viejo.** This has fast become the hot place to see and be seen on Puerto Viejo's main drag. The owners, four brothers who learned to cook at the knee of their Italian grandmother back in Rimini, have concocted a menu, several pages long, of pizzas and handmade pastas. Recorded reggae and mambo music bops in the background. ⊠*Across from ATEC* ☎*2750–0817* ▭*AE, D, DC, MC, V* ⊘*Closed Tues. No lunch.*

$
✕**Chile Rojo.** There's not a thing about the name or furnishings to reflect its Thai and Middle-Eastern offerings, and you might miss this hole-in-the-wall place when you drive by on Puerto Viejo's main street. Choose from Thai grilled tuna, falafel, hummus, and samosas. Sushi is available on Saturday. In deference to the town's European tourist trade, the restaurant accepts euros as payment, too. ⊠*Across from ATEC* ☎*2750–0025* ▭*No credit cards.*

$
✕**Gatta Ci Cova.** Chef-owner Ilario Giannoni strolls the 100 meters over from his La Pecora Nera restaurant to watch over his new baby these days. The restaurant, whose name comes from an Italian expression meaning "things kept secret," provides a less formal, less expensive alternative to the original, but still has all the flair and all the fun. Lunch offerings focus on the $10 plato del día, a bargain with appetizer, salad, a rotating selection of pastas, dessert, and a glass of wine.

7

✛*3 km (2 mi) southeast of town at Playa Cocles* ☎*2750–0730* ▭*AE, D, DC, MC, V* ⊘*Closed Mon.*

$ ✗**El Loco Natural.** El Loco Natural epitomizes Puerto Viejo: lively,
Fodor'sChoice organic, all the rage, but confident enough not to seek trendiness.
★ Ordering is by sauces: Thai peanut, Indonesian-Caribbean curry, Mexican chipotle, Jamaican jerk-style, or Malaysian-guayaba curry. Then select vegetables, chicken, shrimp, or fish (marlin or tuna). Bar stools on the balcony face the street and let you survey the goings-on below. You'll be better able to converse with your fellow diners if you sit at the tables inside. Live music gets going late on Thursday and Sunday evenings, and in high season (December–April) often on another weeknight, too. It's easy to miss its second-floor location above the Color Caribe souvenir shop; look up as you walk by. ⊠*100 m south of bus stop* ☎*2750–0263* ▭*No credit cards* ⊘*Closed Wed. No lunch.*

$ ✗**Salsa Brava.** The restaurant at Salsa Brava—with sublime surf vistas—has taken the name of this famed surfing spot. Opt for casual counter service or grab a seat at one of the colorful roadside tables. Lunch and dinner center on grilled fish and meat, with red snapper prepared in olive oil, garlic, and cayenne pepper a specialty. ⊠*100 m east of Stanford's* ☎*2750–0241* ▭*AE, D, DC, MC, V* ⊘*Closed Mon.*

¢   ✗**Bread & Chocolate.** The take-away line for brownies forms at the gate
★ before this place opens at 6:30 AM, but stick around and fortify yourself with a hearty breakfast of cinnamon-oatmeal pancakes, French toast, or creamy scrambled eggs, washed down with a cup of French-press coffee. Lunch brings jerk chicken, roasted red peppers, and chocolate truffles. Everything is homemade, right down to the mayonnaise. Make your dinner early; the place closes at 6 PM. This is one of several bakery-slash-breakfast-and-lunch cafés open in town; the friendly owner gives this place the edge. ⊠*50 m south of post office* ☎*2750–0051* ▭*No credit cards* ⊘*Closed Mon. and Tues. No dinner Sun.*

¢   ✗**Soda Miss Sam.** Longtime restaurateur Miss Sam still dishes up hearty Caribbean cuisine at this small restaurant, a Puerto Viejo institution—she prefers not to divulge how many years she's been doing so—and the front porch is still full of diners. Rice and beans are usually going, or you can get a *casado* with chicken, beef, pork, or fish and freshly squeezed fruit juices as accompaniment. It's open for breakfast, too. ⊠*300 m south, 200 m east of bus stop* ☎*2750–0108* ▭*No credit cards* ⊘*Closed Tues.*

WHERE TO STAY

$$ ▦**Azania Bungalows.** Eight thatch-roof, A-frame bungalows spread around Azania's ample gardens, and sleep four. The first floor contains a queen-size bed, and a ladder leads to the second floor with a pair of single beds. Much-appreciated mosquito netting covers all of them. You'll luxuriate in the semi-open shower in the blue-tile bathrooms. Meals are served in the rancho dining area next to the free-form pool. **Pro:** Good value. **Con:** Difficult to make reservations. ✛*1½ km (1 mi) southeast of town at Playa Cocles* ☎*2750–0540* 📠*2750–0371* ⊕*www.azania-costarica.com* ⟿*8 bungalows* ⌂*In-room: no a/c, no phone, refrigerator, no TV. In-hotel: restaurant, bar, pool, no elevator* ▭*AE, D, DC, MC, V* ⅟⊙*BP.*

$$ ⊡**Cariblue Hotel.** The youthful Italian owners who came here to surf
Fodor'sChoice years ago stayed on and built a lodging that combines refinement with
★ that hip Puerto Viejo vibe in exactly the right proportions. Cariblue's finely crafted all-wooden bungalows are spaciously arrayed on the edge of the jungle, across the road from the splendid white-sand beaches of Punta Cocles. Cabinas are linked to the main ranch-style building by paths that meander across a gently sloping lawn shaded by enormous trees. Expansive verandas and beautiful tile mosaics in the bathrooms add an air of refinement; hammocks add an air of relaxation. Breakfasts are huge. Italian cuisine dominates for lunch, and dinner is served at the lively Soleluna restaurant ($–$$) on-site. **Pros:** Friendly owners, good restaurant. **Con:** Need car to stay here. *⊕2 km (1 mi) southeast of town at Playa Cocles ⌂Apdo. 51–7304, Puerto Viejo de Talamanca* ☎*2750–0035 or 2750–0518* 🖷*2750–0057* ⊕*www.cariblue. com* ⬏*21 bungalows* ⌂*In-room: no a/c (some), no phone, safe, no TV (some). In-hotel: restaurant, bars, pool, laundry service public Wi-Fi* ⊟*AE, D, DC, MC, V* ¶◎¶*BP.*

$$ ⊡**Hotel La Perla Negra.** Fine design is evident in the construction of this handsome, two-story dark-wood structure across a tiny dirt road near the end of Playa Negra. All rooms have balconies, half with ocean views, half with jungle views. The three-meal restaurant features grilled meats and fish. Between the building and the beach is a spacious, inviting pool. Though the hotel does not accept credit cards, you can make your payment through Pay Pal. **Pro:** Secluded. **Con:** Far from sights. ⊠*Playa Negra* *⊕1 km (½ mi) north of Puerto Viejo* ☎*2750–0111* 🖷*2750–0114* ⊕*www.perlanegra-beachresort.com* ⬏*24 rooms, 7 houses* ⌂*In-room: no a/c (some), no phone, no TV. In-hotel: restaurant, bar, tennis court, pool, no elevator, laundry service* ⊟*No credit cards* ¶◎¶*BP.*

$$ ⊡**Shawandha Lodge.** The service is personalized and friendly at Shawandha, whose spacious, beautifully designed bungalows are well back
★ from the road at Playa Chiquita. The thatch-roof bungalows have elegant hardwoods, four-poster beds, and verandas with hammocks. Each bathroom has a unique and beautiful tile mosaic. The hearty breakfast starts off with an impressive fruit plate. A white-sand beach lies 180 meters away, across the road. Even if you don't stay here, stop by and enjoy a distinctive French-Caribbean dinner in the open-air restaurant. **Pros:** Elegant bungalows. **Cons:** Far from sights. *⊕6 km (4 mi) southeast of town at Playa Chiquita* ☎*2750–0018* 🖷*2750–0037* ⊕*www.shawandhalodge.com* ⬏*13 bungalows* ⌂*In-room: no a/c, no phone, safe, no TV. In-hotel: restaurant, bar, laundry service* ⊟*AE, MC, V* ¶◎¶*BP.*

$$ ⊡**Totem.** Each of the tropical-blue units here contains a living room and bedroom with bamboo furnishings, a queen bed, and bunks. We like the two rooms on the upper balcony with stupendous ocean views and overlooking the gurgling, fountain-fed pool. The restaurant serves Italian food. **Pro:** Good value. **Cons:** Need car to stay here. *⊕1½ km (1 mi) southeast of town at Playa Cocles* ☎*2750–0758* 🖷 *2750–0825* ⊕*www.totemsite.com* ⬏*6 cabinas, 1 suite* ⌂*In-room: no a/c (some),*

refrigerator. *In-hotel: restaurant, bar, pool, no elevator, public Internet, public Wi-Fi* ⊟*AE, D, DC, MC, V* ⓄⒾ*BP.*

$–$$ ⬚ **La Costa de Papito.** Papito's raised cabins are deep in the property's wooded grounds and are furnished with whimsical bright tropical-blue and zebra-stripe prints. Breakfast, with an extra cost of $6, is served at the table and chairs on your porch, which has a hammock or swing chair. You'll get a 15% discount if you pay in cash. **Pro:** Good value. **Con:** Need car to stay here. ✛*2 km (1 mi) southeast of town at Playa Cocles* ☎☎*2750–0080* ⊕*www.lacostadepapito.com* ✍*13 cabins* ⚄*In-room: no phone, no TV. In-hotel: restaurant, spa, bicycles, no elevator, public Internet* ⊟*AE, D, DC, MC, V* ⓄⒾ*EP.*

$–$$ ⬚ **Jordan's Jacuzzi Suites.** As befits the name of the place, each of the eight suites here contains its own whirlpool tub. What's atypical of Puerto Viejo is the use of Japanese styling in each large unit, with statuary, fabric, and local woods used throughout, as well a four-poster king-size bed and air-conditioning. (You'll find four well-apportioned rooms here, too.) The suites bear names such as "Shogun," "Samurai," and "Geisha." **Pro:** Central location. **Con:** Businesslike owner. ✉*200 m east of Stanford's* ☎*2750–0232* ⊕*www.thelotusgarden.net* ✍*4 rooms, 9 suites* ⚄*In-room: no a/c (some), no phone, kitchen, refrigerator (some), no TV (some). In-hotel: restaurant, pool* ⊟*AE, D, DC, MC, V* ⓄⒾ*EP.*

¢–$$ ⬚ **Agapi.** Agapi means "love" in Greek, and Costa Rican–Greek owners Cecilia and Tasso lovingly watch over their guests with some of the most attentive service around. Seven furnished apartments overlook the beach and come complete with fully equipped kitchen, hot-water bath, hammock, mosquito nets over the beds, and private balcony. An additional six rooms have two full-size beds each, and all have an ocean view. A common area in the back contains a beachside barbecue. **Pros:** Kitchens, central location. **Con:** Not for travelers who want anonymity ✛*1 km (½ mi) southeast of Stanford's* ☎*2750–0446* ☎*2750–0148* ⊕*www.agapisite.com* ✍*5 rooms, 12 apartments* ⚄*In-room: no a/c (some), no phone, kitchen (some), refrigerator. In-hotel: no elevator, laundry service* ⊟*AE, D, DC, MC, V* ⓄⒾ*EP.*

$ ⬚ **Casa Camarona.** Though half the rooms have air-conditioning at this secluded lodging, you hardly need it. The abundant shade and sea breezes keep the rooms delightfully cool. All the spacious, wooden, rustic rooms front the ocean—the second-story rooms have the best view—and have two double beds. Meals are served at the seaside Caribbean restaurant. **Pros:** Good value, air-conditioning. **Con:** Need a car to stay here. ✛*3 km (2 mi) south of town at Playa Cocles* ⓓ*Apdo. 2070–1002, San José* ☎*2750–0151 or 283–6711 in San José* ☎*750–0210* ⊕*www.casacamarona.co.cr* ✍*19 rooms* ⚄*In-room: no a/c (some), no phone, no TV. In-hotel: restaurant, bar, no elevator, laundry facilities, no-smoking rooms* ⊟*AE, DC, MC, V* ⓄⒾ*CP.*

$ ⬚ **Escape Caribeño.** Wonderfully friendly Italian owners Gloria and Mauro Marchiori are what make this place: they treat you like family. A dozen immaculate hardwood bungalows line a pleasant garden amply populated with hummingbirds, just outside of town. All cabins have hammocks, mosquito nets, double beds, and even a bunk bed or two for larger groups. Across the road lie two stucco cabins in a wooded spot on the beach. Breakfast is served in a thatch-roof dining area in the center of the garden. You'll receive a small discount if you pay with cash. **Pros:** Central location, friendly owners. **Con:** Some small rooms. ✉ *400 m southeast of Stanford's* ☎/📠 *2750–0103* 🌐 *www.escapecaribeno.com* *16 cabins* *In-room: no a/c (some), no phone, safe, refrigerator, no TV (some), Wi-Fi (some)* 💳 *AE, D, DC, MC, V* *EP.*

$ **El Pizote Lodge.** El Pizote observes local architectural mores while offering more than most in the way of amenities. All standard rooms have polished wood paneling, reading lamps, mirrors, and firm beds. Each of the two-room bungalows sleeps six. The restaurant serves breakfast, dinner, and drinks all day. Guanábana and papaya grow on the grounds, and hiking trails lead off into the jungle. Tranquil Playa Negra is just across the road. **Pro:** Good value. **Cons:** Small rooms, far from sights. ✉ *300 m before entrance to town at Playa Negra* *Apdo. 1371–1000, San José* ☎ *2750–0088 or 2750–0227* 📠 *2750–0226* 🌐 *www.pizotelodge.com* *8 rooms, 12 bungalows* *In-room: no a/c (some), no phone, no TV. In-hotel: restaurant, bar, pool, laundry service* 💳 *MC, V* *EP.*

$ **Yaré Bungalows.** The sound of the jungle is overpowering, especially at night, as you relax in your brightly pastel-painted Yaré cabina. All rooms have hot water and verandas with hammocks. The restaurant is open for breakfast, lunch, and dinner. **Pro:** Good value. **Con:** Sound travels far. ✣ *3½ km (2 mi) southeast of town at Playa Cocles* *Apdo. 117–1007, San José* ☎ *2750–0106* 📠 *2750–0420* 🌐 *www.bungalowsyare.com/swf/banner.swf* *22 rooms* *In-room: no phone, kitchen (some), refrigerator, no TV. In-hotel: restaurant, bar, no elevator, laundry service* 💳 *AE, D, DC, MC, V* *BP.*

¢–$ **Casa Verde Lodge.** If you've graduated from your backpacker days

Fodor's Choice ★

and are a bit more flush with cash but still want to be near the action, this old standby on a quiet street a couple of blocks from the center of town is ideal. The comfortable cabinas are decorated with an interesting variety of touches such as shell mobiles, watercolor frescoes, and indigenous tapestries. Overall, rooms have a neat-as-a-pin quality. Exotic birds flutter constantly through the lush plantings that screen the cabinas from the street. The place is immensely popular, since the price is low and it's clean and well run; reserve well in advance. You'll receive a small discount if you pay in cash. **Pro:** Good value. **Cons:** Difficult to find space, businesslike staff. ✉ *200 m south and 200 m east of bus stop* *Apdo. 37–7304, Puerto Viejo de Talamanca* ☎ *2750–0015* 📠 *2750–0047* 🌐 *www.cabinascasaverde.com* *17 rooms, 9 with bath; 2 apartments* *In-room: no phone, refrigerator, no TV. In-hotel: restaurant, pool, bicycles, laundry service* 💳 *AE, DC, MC, V* *EP.*

¢–$ **Coco Loco Lodge.** The cool, forested grounds here lie close to the center of town but seem so far away. The Austrian owners lavish you with lots of personal attention. The bungalows on stilts are simply furnished but contain hot-water baths, mosquito nets over the beds (you'll need them), and hammocks on the porch. There are also two fully furnished houses available for short- or long-term rental. Great coffee is included in the room rate; a huge buffet breakfast is extra. You'll receive a small discount if you pay with cash. **Pros:** Good budget value, central location. **Cons:** Rustic rooms, dark road at night. ✉ *180 m south of bridge at entrance to town* ☎ *2750–0281* ⊕ *www.cocolocolodge.com* ⇆ *8 cabins, 2 houses* ⚇ *In-room: no a/c, no phone, kitchen (some), refrigerator (some). In-hotel: public Internet, public Wi-Fi* ▤ *MC, V* ⏻ *EP.*

¢–$ ▦ **Pachamama.** So cool and shady is this place set within the confines of the Gandoca-Manzanillo Wildlife Refuge that the owners took out the ceiling fans. No one ever needed them. Though still within sight of the Puerto Viejo–Manzanillo road, Pachamama delivers a get-away-from-it-all nature experience at a fraction of the cost of other Costa Rican eco-lodges. Cozy wood cabins are simply furnished with two beds and mosquito netting and have colorful spreads and drapes. A house can be rented by the week or month. Personal touches such as breakfast (included in the rates of the bungalows, but not the kitchen-equipped house) brought to the porch of your cabin are standard. The bungalows are joined by a kitchen and are ideal for renting by a group or family. **Pro:** Seclusion. **Con:** Far from sights. ⊹ *9 km (5½ mi) southeast of town at Punta Uva* ☎ *2759–9196* ⊕ *www.pachamamacaribe. com* ⇆ *2 bungalows, 1 house* ⚇ *In-room: no a/c, no phone, no TV. In-hotel: bicycles, laundry service* ▤ *MC, V* ⏻ *EP, BP.*

¢ ▦ **Hotel Pura Vida.** The friendly owners help make this the nicest of the lowest-end budget lodgings in the center of town. Rooms are very basic, but clean, bright, and well ventilated and arranged around a center patio. Guests have use of the shared kitchen. **Pros:** Central location, good budget value. **Con:** Spartan rooms. ✉ *270 m south of bus stop* ☎ *2750–0002* ⇆ *10 rooms, 5 with bath* ⚇ *In-room: no a/c, no phone, no TV* ▤ *AE, D, DC, MC, V* ⏻ *EP.*

A BAD RAP

The Caribbean has a reputation among Costa Ricans for being crime-ridden, mainly because of a few high-profile cases here years ago, the nearness of the Panamanian border, and the fact that this is an impoverished region compared to other parts of the country. In actuality, the problem is no better or worse here than elsewhere. Just take the standard precautions you would when you travel anywhere and stick to well-traveled tourist paths.

NIGHTLIFE

The distinction between dining spot and nightspot blurs as the evening progresses, as many restaurants become pleasant places to linger over dinner. Bars each have their special nights for live music. The town's main drag between El Loco Natural and Salsa Brava is packed with pedestrians, bicycles, and a few cars most evenings, the block between Café Viejo and El Parquecito getting the most action. Wander around; something is bound to entice you in. ■ **TIP**➔ **When out after dark, ask a staff member at the restaurant, bar, or club to call you a taxi at the end of the night.**

BARS   Grab a beer, and chow down on pizza or sandwiches at **El Dorado** (✉*Across from ATEC*), a much quieter alternative to the noisier bars. **Hot Rocks Café** (✉*50 m east of ATEC*) isn't so much a building as an open-air canvas enclosure serving up drinks and big-screen movies many evenings. **Bar Maritza** (✉*50 m east of bus stop*) is frequented by locals, and has live music on Sunday night. Tex Mex appetizers and all types of cocktails are the draw at **Sunset Tapas Bar** (✉*On beach near bus stop*), a block off the main drag. You can watch U.S. football on television during the season.

DANCE CLUBS   Ticos come from miles around for the Friday and Monday reggae nights at **Bambú** (✉*Next to Jhonny's*), but the place is closed most other evenings. **Jhonny's Place** (✉*230 m east of bus stop*) has nights variously devoted to reggae, jazz, R&B, and hip-hop. **Stanford's Disco** (✉*100 m from the town center on the road to Manzanillo*) is the place to merengue or salsa the weekend nights away.

LIVE MUSIC   Caribbean and Italian restaurant **El Parquecito** (✉*50 m east of ATEC*) pulls live-music duty Tuesday, Friday, and Saturday evenings. You're bound to hear "No Woman No Cry" and all the other reggae anthems. Second-floor organic-food restaurant **El Loco Natural** (✉*150 m west of ATEC* ☎*2750–0263*) has live music Thursday and Saturday evenings, and some Sundays.

SHOPPING

Vendors set up stands at night on the beach road near El Parquecito, jewelry being the prime fare. But the town counts a few honest-to-goodness souvenir stores, too.

Buy your semiofficial Puerto Viejo T-shirt at **Color Caribe** (✉*100 m south of bus stop*), and also check out the huge selection of Rastafarian clothing, and the hammocks, wood carvings, and whimsical mobiles.

★ Puerto Viejo's best shop, **Luluberlu** (✉*200 m south and 50 m east of bus stop*), sells a wonderful selection of local indigenous carvings—balsa and *chonta* wood are especially popular—and jewelry, paintings, and ceramics by 30 artists from the region.

GANDOCA-MANZANILLO NATIONAL WILDLIFE REFUGE

15 km (9 mi) southeast of Puerto Viejo.

The Refugio Nacional de Vida Silvestre Gandoca-Manzanillo stretches along the southeastern coast from the town of Manzanillo to the Panamanian border. Because of weak laws governing the conservation of refuges and the rising value of coastal land in this area, Gandoca-Manzanillo is less pristine than Cahuita National Park and continues to be developed. However, the refuge still has plenty of rain forest, *orey* (a dark tropical wood) and jolillo (raffia palm) swamps, 10 km (6 mi) of beach where four species of turtles lay their eggs, and almost 3 square km (1 square mi) of *cativo* (a tropical hardwood) forest and coral reef. The Gandoca estuary is a nursery for tarpon and a wallowing spot for crocodiles and caimans.

GETTING HERE

The road from Puerto Viejo de Talamanca ends at the entrance to the village of Manzanillo. Just three buses each day—morning, midday, and late afternoon—connect the two. All taxi drivers in Puerto Viejo charge $10 for the trip here.

EXPLORING

The easiest way to explore the refuge is to hike along the coast south of Manzanillo. You can hike back out the way you came in or arrange (in Puerto Viejo de Talamanca) to have a boat pick you up at Punta Mono (Monkey Point), a three- to four-hour walk from Manzanillo, where you find secluded beaches hidden by tall cliffs of fossilized coral. The mangroves of Gandoca, with abundant caimans, iguanas, and waterfowl, lie six to eight hours away. Park administrators can tell you more and recommend a local guide; inquire when you enter Manzanillo village and the locals will point you toward them. ⊠ *15 km/9 mi southeast of Puerto Viejo de Talamanca* ☎*2750–0398 for ATEC* ⊙*Daily 7–4.*

The nearby village of **Manzanillo** maintains that "end of the world" feel. Tourism is still in its infancy this far down the coast, though with the road paved all the way here, the town is now a popular destination among people in Limón for weekend day trips. The rest of the week, you'll likely have the place to yourself.

OUTDOOR ACTIVITIES

A guide can help you get the most out of this relatively unexplored corner of the country. The **Association of Naturalist Guides of Manzanillo** (⊠*Main road* ☎*2759–9064 or 8843–9122* ✐*guiasmant@yahoo. com.mx*) is a consortium of quality, knowledgeable local guides who know the area well and lead a variety of half- and full-day tours. They can take you for a hike in the reserve or out to Monkey Point, with a return trip by boat. They also have horseback riding; bird-, dolphin-, and turtle-watching; and traditional fishing excursions.The friendly

DIVING & SNORKELING
staff at **Aquamor Talamanca Adventures** (⊠*Main road* ☎*2759–0612* ⊕*www.greencoast.com/aquamor.htm*) specializes in land- and ocean-focused tours of the Gandoca-Manzanillo Wildlife Refuge, and can tend to all your water-sporting needs in these parts, with guided kayaking, snorkeling, and scuba-diving tours, as well as equipment rental. They also offer the complete sequence of PADI-certified diving courses. Companies in Puerto Viejo de Talamanca *(⇨above)* can arrange boat trips to dive spots and beaches in the refuge as well.

DOLPHIN-WATCHING
The **Talamanca Dolphin Foundation** (⊠*Main road, Manzanillo* ☎*2759–9115* ⊕*www.dolphinlink.org*) has 2½-hour dolphin observation tours—excellent opportunities to see bottlenose, *tucuxi* (gray), and Atlantic spotted dolphins swimming this section of the coast.

WHERE TO STAY & EAT

$ ✕ **Restaurant Maxi's.** Cooled by sea breezes and shaded by tall, stately palms, this two-story, brightly painted wooden building offers weary travelers cold beer, potent cocktails, and great seafood at unbeatable prices after a day's hike in the refuge. Locals and expatriates alike—and even chefs from Puerto Viejo's fancier restaurants—come here for their lobster fix, and the fresh fish is wonderful, too. At one time, perhaps before tourism became big in this area, Costa Ricans made Maxi's into an entire day trip. Now that the road is paved all the way to Manzanillo, the weekend crowds are getting even larger. Locals tend to congregate in the rowdy but pleasant downstairs bar, where reggae beats into the wee hours. ⊠*Main road, Manzanillo* ☎*2759–9073* ⊟*No credit cards.*

$$$–$$$$ 🏕️**Almonds & Corals Tent Lodge Camp.** Buried in a dark, densely atmospheric beachfront jungle within the Gandoca-Manzanillo Wildlife Refuge, Almonds & Corals takes tent camping to a new level. The "campsites" are freestanding platforms raised on stilts and linked by boardwalks lighted by kerosene lamps. Each safari-style tent is protected by a peaked roof, enclosed in mosquito netting, and has beds, electric lamps, hammocks, and hot water. A fine three-meal restaurant is tucked into the greenery halfway down to the property's exquisite, secluded beach. Rustic camping this is not, but the locale does provide that close-to-nature experience. Your wake-up call is provided by howler monkeys and chatty parrots. These folks also offer multiday packages that include round-trip transportation from San José. **Pros:** Rustic comfort, lots of activities. **Con:** Far from sights. ⊠*Near end of road to Manzanillo* 🖃*Apdo. 681–2300, San José* ☎*2759–9056, 2272–2024 in San José* 📠*2272–2220* ⊕*www.almondsandcorals.com* 🛏️*24 tent-cabins* ⚒️*In-room: no a/c, no phone (some), refrigerator (some), no TV. In-hotel: restaurant, bar, laundry service, public Internet, airport shuttle* ⊟*AE, D, DC, MC, V* 🍽️*MAP.*

¢ 🏕️**Cabinas Something Different.** On a quiet street, these shiny, spic-and-span motel-style cabinas are the nicest option in the village of Manzanillo. Each bright tile-floor unit comes with a TV—quite a rarity in these parts—a table, and a small porch. Several sleep up to four people. **Pro:** Good budget value. **Con:** Small rooms. ⊠*180 m south of Aquamor, Manzanillo* ☎*2759–9014* 🛏️*18 cabinas* ⚒️*In-room: no a/c (some), no phone, refrigerator* ⊟*No credit cards* 🍽️*EP.*

CROSSING INTO PANAMA VIA SIXAOLA

Costa Rica's sleepy border post at Sixaola fronts Guabito, Panama's equally quiet border crossing, 44 km (26 mi) south of the turnoff to Puerto Viejo de Talamanca. Both are merely collections of banana-plantation stilt houses and a few stores and bars; neither has any lodging or dining options, but this is a much more low-key crossing into Panama than the busy border post at Paso Canoas on the Pan-American Highway near the Pacific coast. If you've come this far, you're likely headed to **Bocas del Toro,** the real attraction in the northwestern part of Panama. This archipelago of 68 islands continues the Afro-Caribbean and indigenous themes seen on Costa Rica's Atlantic coast, and offers diving, snorkeling, swimming, and wildlife-viewing. The larger islands are home to a growing selection of hotels and restaurants, everything from funky to fabulous. "Bocas" has acquired a cult following among long-term foreign visitors to Costa Rica, who find it a convenient place to travel when their permitted three-month status as a tourist has expired, since a quick 72-hour jaunt out of the country gets you another three months in Costa Rica.

ANOTHER GOOD BOOK

If you're headed to Panama, we'd be remiss in not recommending that you pick up a copy of *Fodor's Panama* for far more detail about Bocas del Toro and the rest of the country than we can provide here.

■ TIP→ **Whatever your destination in Panama, come armed with dollars.** Panama uses U.S. currency, but refers to the dollar as the *balboa.* (It does mint its own coins, all the same size as their U.S. counterparts.) No one anywhere will accept or exchange your Costa Rican colones.

Costa Rican rental vehicles may not leave the country, so crossing into Panama as a tourist is an option only via public transportation. The public bus route from San José to Cahuita and Puerto Viejo de Talamanca terminates here at the border approximately six hours after leaving the capital. Taxis in Puerto Viejo de Talamanca charge about $50 for the jaunt to the border, a much quicker and reasonable option if you can split the fare among a group. Disembark and head for the Costa Rican immigration office down a flight of stairs from the west end of a former railroad bridge. Officials place an exit stamp in your passport, after which you walk across the bridge and present your passport to Panamanian immigration. U.S., U.K., and Canadian visitors must also purchase a $5 tourist card for entry into the country; Australian and New Zealand citizens need only their passports.

The **Consulate of Panama** (☎ 2280–1570) in San José can provide more information. The border crossings are open 7 AM–5 PM (8 AM–6 PM Panamanian time) daily. Set your watch one hour ahead when you enter Panama.

Taxis wait on the Panamanian side to transport you to the small city of Changuinola, the first community of any size inside the country, from which there are bus and air connections for travel farther into Panama. Taxis can also take you to Almirante, where you'll find boat launches to Bocas del Toro.

CARIBBEAN ESSENTIALS

TRANSPORTATION

BY AIR

ARRIVING & DEPARTING You can fly daily from San José to the airstrip in either Tortuguero (TTQ) or Barra del Colorado (BCL) via Nature Air or SANSA. Flights to the small airport just south of Limón (LIO) remain in a state of flux at this writing, pending resolution of disputes between airlines and the government over fuel and immigration. On paper, SANSA and Nature Air fly here daily, and a shuttle van meets all SANSA flights for overland travel to Puerto Viejo de Talamanca. Reserve van space with the airline. Check the status of flights with either airline. Nature Air also serves the small airport in Bocas del Toro, Panama (BOC). *For more information about air travel between the Caribbean and San José, see By Air Travel in Costa Rica Essentials.*

BY BUS

ARRIVING &
DEPARTING

The transport companies serving this part of the country provide reliable service. London has retired its fabled double-decker buses, but you'll ride such vehicles on many of the runs to Limón and Guápiles. Autotransportes MEPE, which has a lock on bus service to the south Caribbean coast, has a reputation for being lackadaisical, but is really quite dependable. Drivers and ticket sellers are accustomed to dealing with foreigners; even if their English is limited, they'll figure out what you want. Bus fares to this region are reasonable. From San José, expect to pay $2 to Guápiles, $4 to Limón, $6 to Cahuita, $7 to Puerto Viejo de Talamanca, and $9 to Sixaola and the Panamanian border.

All bus service to this part of the country must take alternate routes when heavy rains and landslides close the highway through Braulio Carrillo National Park north of San José. The detour passes through Cartago, Paraíso, and Turrialba and rejoins the Caribbean highway at Siquirres. It can add anywhere from one to three hours to your journey. Check before you set out if you travel during the worst of the rainy season.

For more information about bus travel between the Caribbean and San José, see By Bus in Costa Rica Essentials.

GETTING
AROUND

Buses from San José stop first in Cahuita, then Puerto Viejo de Talamanca before heading to Sixaola. Many buses originate in Limón, traveling to points south. It's the most cost-efficient way to travel.

BY CAR

ARRIVING &
DEPARTING

You'll find a couple of rental agencies in this region, but most visitors rent a vehicle back in San José. There are few major highways in this region, making your choices limited. The paved two-lane Guápiles Highway continues from Santa Clara southeast to Guápiles, EARTH, Siquirres, and Limón, a total distance from San José to the coast of about 160 km (100 mi). South of Limón, a paved road covers the roughly 40 km (25 mi) to Cahuita, then passes the Cahuita turnoff and proceeds for roughly 16 km (10 mi) toward Puerto Viejo de Talamanca. It is paved as far as the village of Manzanillo. Four-wheel drive is always preferable, but the major roads in this region are generally passable by any car. Just watch for potholes and unpaved sections—they can appear on any road at any time, without marking or warning. The heavier the previous year's rainy season has been, the deeper the *huecos* (potholes, in Costa Rican vernacular), and some years sections are *very* slow going. One-lane bridges appear frequently south of Limón. If the triangular CEDA EL PASO sign faces you, yield to oncoming traffic.

Road travel to and from this part of the country occasionally becomes more complicated when heavy rains cause landslides blocking the highway near the Zurquí Tunnel in Braulio Carrillo National Park

7

just north of San José. The alternate route is a long, slow journey via Cartago, Paraíso, and Turrialba, rejoining the main route at Siquirres. Check before you set out when traveling during the heaviest of the rainy season.

You cannot drive to Tortuguero or Barra del Colorado; you must fly or take a boat.

■**TIP**➔Several gas stations flank the highway between Guápiles and Limón, many open 24 hours. South of Limón you'll find just one, at Penshurt, north of Cahuita. Fill the tank when you get the chance.

Local Rental Agencies **Poás rent a car** (⊠ *Suerre Hotel, Guápiles Hwy., Guápiles* ☎ *2710–4380* ⊠ *Between Cahuita and Puerto Viejo de Talamanca* ☎ *2750–0400* ⊕ *www.poasrentacar.com*).

BY SHUTTLE VAN

ARRIVING &
DEPARTING

If you prefer a more private form of travel, consider taking a shuttle. Gray Line Tourist Bus has daily service that departs from many San José hotels at 6:30 AM for Cahuita and Puerto Viejo de Talamanca. Tickets are $29 and must be reserved at least a day in advance. Comfortable air-conditioned Interbus vans depart from San José hotels daily at 7:50 AM for Guápiles, Siquirres, Limón, Cahuita, and Puerto Viejo de Talamanca. Reserve tickets ($29) a day in advance.

Shuttle Van Services **Gray Line Tourist Bus** (☎ *2220–2126* ⊕ *www.grayline costarica.com*). **Interbus** (☎ *2283–5573* ⊕ *www.interbusonline.com*).

CONTACTS & RESOURCES

Banks and emergency contacts are listed at the end of each town entry.

BANKS & EXCHANGING SERVICES

Most larger tourist establishments are prepared to handle credit cards. Banks are sparse in this region. Changing U.S. dollars or traveler's checks is possible at the few offices of Banco Nacional, but lines are long. The Scotiabank and BAC San José in downtown Limón have ATMs that accept Plus- and Cirrus-affiliated cards. The Banco de Costa Rica's ATM in Puerto Viejo de Talamanca accepts only Plus cards. You're best off getting cash with your ATM card back in San José before venturing here.

INTERNET

There are public computers for Internet use in Cahuita, Guápiles, Limón, Puerto Viejo de Talamanca, and Tortuguero. Expect to pay $2–$3 per hour. Connection times are slower in this part of the country than in San José, although a few now boast of their DSL connections.

MAIL & SHIPPING

The privatized Correos de Costa Rica provides reasonable postal service from this part of the country, but your best bet is to wait and mail letters and cards from San José. DHL and UPS have offices in Limón for express shipping of packages.

Ecotourism Costa Rica–Style

Baby Turtles

WORD OF MOUTH

"Monteverde is also unique in that it is 'developed' for eco-tourism. I don't mean condos and glitz. They have found some very creative ways to make nature accessible. The locals have taken a very active role in preserving the natural environment, and are extremely willing to share it with visitors. This area is a model for sustainable tourism."

—Pat_Hewitt

WITH MORE BIRD SPECIES THAN the United States and Canada packed into an area about half the size of Kentucky, and an array of landscapes that run the gamut from lowland rain forest to highland *páramo*, Costa Rica offers nature lovers more interesting stuff than could ever fit in one vacation. The Costa Rican government realized several decades ago that the country's greatest assets were its flora, fauna, and natural beauty, and they set on a course of conservation that has left about a quarter of the national territory in national parks and other protected areas today.

The tourism industry has capitalized on Costa Rica's natural assets and made it one of the easiest places in the world to experience the beauty and complexity of tropical nature. The country has become synonymous with ecotourism, but the term has many interpretations in Costa Rica—from travel that benefits conservation to an abundance of potted plants. Critics note that in Costa Rica not all that is green is eco. Clearly the importance of nature to the country's most lucrative industry has made Costa Ricans more inclined to protect their natural resources, but as tourism and infrastructure grow, conservationists warn that this kind of development can also be a destructive force. Some wonder just how many parking lots paradise can handle.

Conscientious travelers have plenty of options for ensuring that their Costa Rica vacation contributes to the preservation of the nature they travel so far to see. Nevertheless, the level of eco-hype is such that they could just as easily choose hotels and tour companies that do nothing for nature, or offer little exposure to the country's wild things. Any business can use photos of wildlife in its brochures and on its Web site; providing guests with a quality experience, and ensuring a positive impact on the local environment and culture, are more difficult challenges that not every entrepreneur is willing or able to meet. This section is meant to help concerned travelers do the right thing, and to make their Costa Rica trip as enjoyable, educational, and environmentally friendly as possible.

WHERE THE WILD THINGS ARE

Geography and biology have conspired to endow little Costa Rica with a disproportionate diversity of landscapes and wildlife. From its sultry, coastal mangrove swamps to its cool and precipitous cloud forests, the country holds a mosaic of natural landscapes that are packed with an amazing array of flora and fauna. An explanation of this extraordinary biodiversity is twofold. First is the interaction between its mountainous topography and global weather patterns, which result in an abundance of microclimates and provide the unique conditions for Costa Rica's varied ecosystems. Second is the country's tropical location in a landbridge between two continents—each of which has contributed many plant and animal species. The country is home to South American wildlife such as sloths and toucans, North American creatures such as coyotes and cottonmouths, and a significant number of endemic species such as the volcano junco and Central American squirrel monkey.

Eco- or Sustainable Tourism

Ecotourism, a relatively recent addition to the English language, has been defined as travel to natural areas to observe and learn about wildlife, tourism that refrains from damaging the environment, or tourism that strengthens conservation and improves the lives of local people. The latter two definitions could also apply to sustainable tourism, which has a wider scope than ecotourism and pushes for improvements in everything from city hotels to cruise ships. Whereas proponents of ecotourism believe it has the potential to conserve nature by providing economic opportunities for the rural poor, who are responsible for much of the deforestation in the tropics, sustainable tourism advocates note that all tourism has the potential for negative impacts, and they push for improvement across the entire industry.

If you define ecotourism as tourism that contributes to conservation and community development, then ecotourism is always sustainable tourism. However, not all sustainable tourism is ecotourism, since tourism businesses located far from natural areas can and should implement sustainable practices. The list of hotels certified by the Costa Rican Tourism Board's Sustainable Tourism Certification program, for example, ranges from award-winning eco-lodges to city hotels that have made improvements such as installing sewage treatment systems and switching to energy-saving light bulbs. For conscientious travelers who are looking for close contact with nature, sustainable may not be enough.

Add to this the fact that Costa Rica is the seasonal home for hundreds of migrating species—from ruby-throated hummingbirds to humpback whales—and you've got a whole lot of wild things out there.

What this means for visitors is that a short trip within the country can take them to very diverse landscapes that are home to whole new sets of plants and animals. Each of Costa Rica's regions has its own natural attractions, but 60 percent to 70 percent of the country has been urbanized or converted to agriculture, so if you want to see varied nature, you need to know where to go. The country's renowned national park system holds examples of all of its major ecosystems, and some of its most impressive sights—active volcanoes and flocks of scarlet macaws, for example. There are, however, a growing number of private reserves that protect a significant amount of wilderness. Some of these properties are even better places to see wildlife than the national parks. The government decentralized its national parks system more than a decade ago, grouping the parks and preserves into a series of "conservation areas." For travelers, contemplating the country's protected areas by region is the most practical way to decide what to see.

THE CENTRAL VALLEY

Home to more than half of Costa Rica's population, the Central Valley's forests were converted to towns and coffee farms generations ago, but the mountains that tower over it still retain some significant expanses of cloud forest, which can easily be explored on a day trip from San

Osa Peninsula—Eco Hot Spot

Though nature seems to work overtime all over the country, Costa Rica's wildest area is the Osa Peninsula, in the South Pacific, much of which is covered by Corcovado National Park. The peninsula's exuberant rain forest is dominated by massive ceiba, espavel, and mahogany trees draped with thick lianas. It is home to scarlet macaws, chestnut-mandibled toucans, spider monkeys, and iridescent blue morpho butterflies. It is no coincidence that Corcovado is surrounded by eco-lodges—many of which rank among the country's best—and is visited by dozens of nature cruises every year. Corcovado is an isolated area far from roads, but it can be easily visited via boat from nearby Drake Bay. The coast to the north and south of the park is also backed by thick jungle that holds much of the same wildlife as the park. Most travelers opt for spending a few nights in either the Cabo Matapalo area, near Puerto Jiménez, or Drake Bay.

José. Tapantí National Park, at the eastern end of the valley, is an excellent spot to experience the beauty of the cloud forest, whereas the rain forests of Guayabo National Monument and the private reserve of Rancho Naturalista are more like the protected areas of the Caribbean coast and Northern Plains.

THE NORTHERN PLAINS
Though much of the Northern Plains has been converted to farmland, this vast and verdant region holds some of Costa Rica's best ecological gems. The mountain ranges that define its western and southern borders are topped by lush cloud forest, and the rolling lowlands are dotted with protected rain forests and wetlands, which constitute important ecological oases. The region's principal national parks protect the impressive volcanoes of Poás and Arenal, and the vast wilderness of Braulio Carrillo. It also holds the country's most important private preserves—La Selva Biological Station and the Monteverde Cloud Forest Preserve—two of the best places in the country to see wildlife. Protected areas are complemented by a selection of nature lodges that offer excellent exposure to the region's varied tropical nature. Some of our favorites are Villablanca, Laguna del Lagarto Lodge, Hotel Bosques de Chachagua, Villa Decary, and Selva Verde Lodge.

THE NORTHERN PACIFIC
These sweeping plains bordered by dormant volcanoes hold some of the last remnants of Central America's extremely rare tropical dry forest, which changes from a relatively lush wilderness during the rainy season to a desertlike panorama in the dry months (this actually facilitates wildlife-watching). The national parks of Santa Rosa, Rincón de la Vieja, Palo Verde, and Barra Honda all offer exposure to the dry forest, as do the private reserves of Hacienda Guachipelín, Rincón de la Vieja Mountain Lodge, and Reserva Biológica Nosara. Rustic accommodations are available near the wetlands of Palo Verde at the Organization for Tropical Studies' biological station, but a more comfortable way to experience the tropical dry forest is by floating down

the Corobicí River on a rafting tour, or on a horseback tour at one of the eco-lodges above. This region also holds the important sea-turtle nesting beaches of Playa Grande, where the massive leatherback lays its eggs from October to March, and Ostional, where thousands of olive ridley turtles clamber ashore on certain nights from July to January.

THE CENTRAL PACIFIC

An ecological transition zone between the dry forests of the North Pacific and the rain forests of the South Pacific, the Central Pacific is home to plants and animals found in both regions. It is one of the few places in the country where you can see such rare animals as the Central American squirrel monkey and the scarlet macaw. It is also probably the easiest place to get a good look at the American crocodile, dozens of which sometimes gather near the bridge over the Tarcoles River, just north of Carara National Park. Carara protects the largest expanse of forest in the region, but the smaller protected areas, such as the Curú National Wildlife Reserve, Manuel Antonio National Park, and Cabo Blanco Absolute Nature Reserve are excellent places to see wildlife. The private Complejo Ecológico la Catarata, Punta Leona, and Rain-maker reserves protect some impressive scenery and complement the flora and fauna. This region may not have as many eco-lodges, but most of Manuel Antonio's hotels are set in the rain forest and offer exposure to nearly all the wildlife found in the nearby national park.

THE SOUTH PACIFIC

Costa Rica's wildest corner, and one of the last regions of the country to be settled, the South Pacific has vast expanses of wilderness ranging from the cloud forest and páramo of the Talamanca Mountain Range to the lowland rain forest of Corcovado National Park. This region offers some of the best opportunities to see quetzals and other birds in San Gerardo de Dota, and scarlet macaws and countless other critters that abound on the Osa Peninsula. It also has some of the country's most impressive, though least accessible national parks—Chirripó, La Amistad, and Corcovado—as well as the greatest concentration of eco-lodges and private preserves. Stunning marine wonders can be found at the Golfo Dulce, the dive spots around Caño Island Biological Reserve, and between that island and Ballena Marine National Park, where the seasonal whale migrations occur. The lodges around Drake Bay offer access to the island and, together with the lodges of Carate and Cabo Matapalo (to the east of Corcovado), provide some of the country's best exposure to tropical nature. This region also has the country's most impressive botanical gardens and more than a dozen private reserves, which means it would be quite feasible to spend several weeks exploring its diverse wilderness.

THE CARIBBEAN

The lush jungles, beaches, and canals of the Caribbean coast boast the kind of scenery that most people conjure up when they contemplate the tropics—curtains of dense foliage rising up from dark waters, golden sand shaded by tall coconut palms, and coral reefs set in turquoise waters. Better still, those settings are animated by nesting sea turtles, howling monkeys, chirping frogs, and the flitting colors of hundreds

RESPONSIBLE TRAVEL TIPS

The International Ecotourism Society has defined ecotourism as: "responsible travel to natural areas that conserves the environment and improves the well-being of local people." There are plenty of steps that responsible travelers can take to ensure that their trip into the wilderness, or to a rural community, contributes to its preservation. The following are some simple ways that travelers can ensure that their trip has a positive impact:

■ Stray from the beaten path—by visiting areas that few tourists go to, you can avoid adding to the stress on hot spots and enjoy a more authentic Costa Rican experience.

■ Use locally owned lodges, car-rental agencies, or tour companies. Eat in local restaurants, shop in local markets, and attend local events. Enrich your experience and support the local economy by hiring local guides.

■ Don't be overly aggressive if you bargain for souvenirs and don't shortchange local people on payments or tips for services.

■ Support conservation by paying entrance fees to parks and protected sites, contributing to local environmental groups.

■ Don't litter—pack up all your trash and try to pick up any trash you find.

■ Don't remove plants or animals from their natural environment and don't purchase handicrafts that are made from them, such as turtle-shell or black-coral jewelry.

■ Don't feed wildlife or engage in disruptive behavior—making loud noises to scare birds into flight, for example.

■ Make sure your tour company or hotel follows sustainable policies, including contributing to conservation, hiring and training locals for most jobs, educating visitors about the local ecology and culture, and taking steps to mitigate negative impacts on the environment.

of bird species. The region's premier natural destination is Tortuguero, where coastal canals and rain forest border a beach where thousands of sea turtles nest each year. Turtle-watching is a nocturnal affair that is best from July to October, but the surrounding forest and waterways offer excellent wildlife observation year-round, and all the area's large lodges provide guides and boats for exploring the wilderness. The region's other natural destination is Puerto Viejo de Talamanca, in the country's southeast corner. Here the beach town of Cahuita lies a short walk from the forest, beaches, and coral reef of Cahuita National Park. Some of the hotels south of Puerto Viejo lie in, or near, the tangled forest of the Gandoca-Manzanillo National Wildlife Refuge. Some recommendations include: La Costa de Papito, Shawandha Lodge, and the Almonds & Corals Tent Lodge Camp.

COMFORT VERSUS ADVENTURE

Though many nature lovers may rough it in Costa Rica, it is easy to enjoy close contact with the country's amazing wildlife without sacrificing any creature comforts. There are lodges that offer first-class accommodations and dining just a stone's throw from the nearest sloth. Some of them also make significant contributions to conservation and community development. Nevertheless, sacrificing a bit of comfort can have its rewards, such as waking up at a biological station as the daily bird chorus begins, or visiting a community tourism project and gaining insight into the local culture. Every traveler knows his or her limit, but if you push yourself beyond what you might normally be inclined to put up with now and then, your vacation can become more of an adventure.

The unique experiences to be had by trimming a bit on creature comforts include spending a night at La Selva Biological Station, where simple food and accommodations are compensated for by mind-boggling wildlife and one of the country's best nature walks. Opt for an overnight rafting trip on the Pacuare River and a hike through the surrounding jungle. Other rough and rewarding options are available at the dozens of community tourism projects throughout the country. They can be booked through the local organizations ACTUAR and COOPRENA. An overnight at one of the country's community lodges can add an interesting cultural aspect to a Costa Rica trip, and will probably make your next night in a nice hotel seem that much more luxurious.

WHO PROMOTES SUSTAINABLE TOURISM?

Various organizations are promoting sustainable tourism to businesses, communities, and travelers, though some are more active in Costa Rica than others. The Rainforest Alliance's sustainable tourism department is based in Costa Rica and has provided training in sustainable practices for dozens of lodges, tour operators, and communities. They have developed a convenient searchable database of sustainable lodges on a conservation portal called the EcoIndex. The International Ecotourism Society, based in Washington, D.C., also works in Costa Rica and its Web site has a database of tour companies, hotels, and other travel services that are committed to sustainable practices. Conservation International promotes sustainable practices to businesses and travelers alike. It has a Web site dedicated to ecotourism that includes a list of links to other eco-organizations. The U.S.-based World Wildlife Fund organizes nature tours to Costa Rica and other countries, the profits of which support conservation.

The Costa Rican Tourism Board has a rating system for hotels and lodges called the Certification for Sustainable Tourism (CST), which rates companies on a scale of one to five based on their interaction with the environment and local communities, their policies for sustainability, and the degree to which they encourage clients to support sustainability. However, some of the country's best eco-lodges aren't in the database. The program has certified many of the hotels in San

ON THE ROAD TO SUSTAINABILITY

The conservation nonprofit Rainforest Alliance has spent years promoting sustainable tourism in Costa Rica, and its efforts have included the publication of a guide to best practices for tourism, and the organization of dozens of workshops for hotel managers and owners. The following hotels have participated in that sustainable tourism training, and some of them have taken significant steps to improve their environmental and social impacts:

The Central Valley: Finca Rosa Blanca Country Inn (Heredia).

The Northern Plains: Villablanca (San Ramón); Hotel Bosques de Chachagua (La Fortuna); Fonda Vela, Sapo Dorado, and Trapp Family Lodge (Monteverde); Selva Verde Lodge (Puerto Viejo de Sarapiquí); and Caño Negro Natural Lodge (Caño Negro National Wildlife Refuge).

The North Pacific: Borinquen Mountain Resort Thermae & Spa, Rincón de la Vieja Mountain Lodge, and Hacienda Guachipelín (Rincón de la Vieja National Park); Villa Del Sueño Hotel (Playa Hermosa); Cala Luna (Playa Langosta); El Jardín del Edén (Tamarindo); El Sueño Tropical, Hotel Belvedere, and Hotel Giada (Samara).

The Central Pacific: Los Mangos Hotel (Montezuma); Hotel Villa Lapas and Villa Caletas (Tárcoles); Costa Verde, Hotel Casitas Eclipse, Hotel Playa Espadilla, and Cabinas Espadilla (Manuel Antonio).

The South Pacific: Savegre Hotel de Montaña (San Gerardo de Dota); Roca Verde, Hacienda Barú, Hotel Diuwak, and Villas Río Mar (Dominical); Villas Gaia (Ballena Marine National Park); Tiskita Jungle Lodge (Playa Pavones); Parrot Bay Village and Villa Corcovado (Puerto Jiménez); Bosque del Cabo and Hotel Lapa Ríos (Cabo Matapalo); Luna Lodge (Carate); Aguila de Osa Inn, Casa Corcovado, Drake Bay Wilderness Resort, Jinetes de Osa, Delfín Amor Eco Lodge, and Punta Mareco Lodge (Drake Bay).

The Caribbean: Evergreen Lodge, Laguna Lodge, Mawamba Lodge, Pachira Lodge (Tortuguero); Cariblue Bungalows, Cabinas Casa Verde, Casa Camarona, Escape Caribeño, La Costa de Papito (Puerto Viejo); and Almonds & Corals Tent Lodge Camp (Gandoca-Manzanillo).

José that have taken steps to becoming greener—recycling, installing energy-efficient light bulbs, and putting signs in rooms asking guests to reuse their towels. The CST Web site has a searchable database of certified hotels.

Resources **Certification for Sustainable Tourism** (*CST* ⊕ *www.turismo-sostenible. co.cr*). **The International Ecotourism Society** (⊕ *www.ecotourism.org*). **Conservation International** (⊕ *www.ecotour.org/xp/ecotour*). **Rainforest Alliance** (⊕ *www.rainforest-alliance.org/programs/tourism*). **World Wildlife Fund** (⊕ *www. worldwildlife.org/travel*).

THE BEST ECO-LODGES

The growth of ecotourism over the past decade has left Costa Rica with an overabundance of nature lodges, unevenly distributed through the country. Those lodges range from fairly rustic accommodations with plenty of wildlife, like La Selva Biological Station and the Corcovado

Community Ecotourism

The majority of Costa Rica's tourist lodges belong to foreigners who had the vision, or capital, that most of the locals lacked. Though the true eco-lodges take steps that benefit local communities, many people who live near wild and beautiful areas lack the knowledge and resources needed to get into tourism. Two Costa Rican nonprofit organizations, the Costa Rican Association for Community Rural Tourism (ACTUAR) and the National Ecotourism Network Consortium (COOPRENA), have consequently provided rural communities with the tools and knowledge that they need to run their own tourism businesses, and in the process become better stewards of their natural resources. These umbrella groups run networks that function like travel agencies, offering day trips, overnights, and tour packages to dozens of community lodges and restaurants.

ACTUAR helps more than 20 community-based eco-lodges and tour operations market their offerings. They can book anything from a day trip to a multiday package including meals and transportation. COOPRENA provides a similar service for about a dozen cooperative tourism businesses around the country. Not only do these organizations help rural communities sell their tourism offerings, but they also provide training in areas as granular as kitchen hygiene. Their tours head well off the beaten path, offer exposure to local culture, and serve as incentives for communities to protect their natural resources. They include hiking, horseback, or boat trips up jungle rivers to see waterfalls, rain forest, and much of the same wildlife found in the national parks. They are very inexpensive, but the low-budget pace of the multiday trips might be too slow for many travelers.

8

Lodge Tent Camp, to more luxurious accommodations like the Lapa Ríos and the Evergreen Lodge. All of them offer close contact with nature, and most have first-rate guides who can help you understand the complexity of tropical ecology and point out things that you might otherwise walk right past. Most of these lodges also protect significant patches of wilderness, benefit local communities, and take steps to decrease their environmental impacts.

THE BEST TOUR COMPANIES

The best thing about having a reputable nature-tour operator arrange your trip is that they can set you up with an educated, bilingual guide who will show and teach you about the country's wildlife and ecology. The Costa Rican company Horizontes is known for the quality of its guides (most are biologists) and its commitment to conservation and sustainability. Costa Rica Expeditions, the country's original natural-history tour operator, competes with Horizontes to recruit the best guides, but collaborates in contributing to local conservation efforts. Sun Tours, another of the country's original nature specialists, is a smaller company that offers good service and guides. Costa Rica Nature Adventures is a white-water rafting outfitter with its own lodge and nature reserve on the Pacuare River; they also run bike tours and offer multiday packages. "Soft adventure" travelers are well catered to aboard the 185-foot M.V. *Pacific Explorer,* run by Cruise West,

ECOTOURISM LODGING

LOCATION	LODGE	ATTRACTIONS
Central Valley		
Turrialba	Rancho Naturalista	Bird-watching
Northern Plains		
Ciudad Quesada	Laguna del Lagarto Lodge	Isolated wetlands and rain forests
Puerto Viejo de Sarapiquí	Selva Verde Lodge	Set in the rain forest, community projects
Puerto Viejo de Sarapiquí	La Selva Biological Station	Amazing wildlife, excellent guides
North Pacific		
Rincón de la Vieja National Park	Rincón de la Vieja Mountain Lodge	Forest hikes and horseback tours
Rincón de la Vieja National Park	Hacienda Guachipelín	Protected forest, horseback tours
South Pacific		
San Gerardo de Dota	Savegre Hotel de Montaña	Birding, hiking, protected forest
San Vito	Wilson Botanical Garden	Gardens, guides, protected forest
Dominical	Hacienda Barú	Rain-forest tours
Golfo Dulce	Playa Nicuesa Rainforest Lodge	Rain forest, hikes
Playa Pavones	Tiskita Jungle Lodge	Rain forest, hikes, bird-watching
Cabo Matapalo	Bosque del Cabo	Rain forest, wildlife, views, conservation
Cabo Matapalo	Lapa Ríos	Great wildlife, hikes, community projects
Carate	Corcovado Lodge Tent Camp	Deep in the forest, wildlife, hiking
Drake Bay	Delfín Amor Eco Lodge	Rain forest, dolphin- and whale-watching
Drake Bay	Casa Corcovado	Wildlife, hiking
Caribbean		
Tortuguero	Evergreen Lodge	Rain forest, wetlands
Tortuguero	Tortuga Lodge	Nature tours, turtles
Gandoca-Manzanillo	Almonds & Corals Tent Lodge Camp	Set in the rain forest, beach, wildlife

with multiday natural-history cruises that visit the rain forests of Costa Rica's South Pacific coast and Panama. Lindblad Expeditions runs nature cruises to the same area aboard the larger *Sea Voyager*.

The Costa Rican nonprofit organizations ACTUAR and COOPRENA can arrange day trips and overnights to dozens of community lodges and reserves scattered around the country. Those rustic, homespun adventures take travelers far from the beaten path to expose them to rural Costa Rican life and culture. The Talamanca Ecotourism and Conservation Association (ATEC), in the center of Puerto Viejo de Talamanca, offers many locally run day trips and overnights, from a visit to a Bribrí Indian village to dolphin-watching excursions.

Contacts **ACTUAR** (☎2248–9470 ⊕ www.actuarcostarica.com). **ATEC** (☎2750–0191 ⊕ www.greencoast.com/atec.htm). **COOPRENA** (☎2290–8646 ⊕ www.turismoruralcr.com). **Costa Rica Expeditions** (☎2257–0766 ⊕ www.costarica expeditions.com). **Costa Rica Nature Adventures** (☎2225–3939, 800/321–8410 in North America ⊕ www.toenjoynature.com). **Cruise West** (☎888/851–8133 ⊕ www.cruisewest.com). **Horizontes** (☎2222–2022 ⊕ www.horizontes.com). **Lindblad Expeditions** (☎800/397–3348 ⊕ www.expeditions.com). **Sun Tours** (☎2296–7757 ⊕ www.crsuntours.com).

VOLUNTEER & LEARNING VACATIONS

The Earthwatch Institute, of Massachusetts, runs expeditions to Costa Rica that allow travelers to participate in research and conservation of sea turtles, monkeys, and other creatures. Elderhostel runs excellent educational programs to Costa Rica, though younger travelers might feel a bit out of place on them. Globe Aware arranges volunteer vacations at a community conservation project near Carara National Park, in the Central Pacific. United Planet offers short-term volunteer programs all over Costa Rica, most of which involve supporting rural ecotourism and conservation efforts.

Contacts **Earthwatch** (☎800/776–0188 ⊕ www.earthwatch.org). **Elderhostel** (☎800/454-5768 ⊕ www.elderhostel.org). **Globe Aware** (☎877/588–4562 ⊕ www.globeaware.org). **United Planet** (☎800/292–2316 ⊕ www.unitedplanet.org).

8

UNDERSTANDING
COSTA RICA

COSTA RICA AT A GLANCE

FAST FACTS

Capital: San José
Type of government: Democratic republic
Independence: September 15, 1821 (from Spain)
Population: 4,248,508
Population density: 82 persons per square km (204 persons per square mi)
Literacy: 95%
Language: Spanish (official); English spoken by most in the tourism industry
Ethnic groups: White (including mestizo) 94%, black 3%, Amerindian 1%, Asian 1%, other 1%
Religion: Roman Catholic 76%, Evangelical Protestant 15%, other 6%, none 3%

GEOGRAPHY & ENVIRONMENT

Land area: 51,100 square km (19,730 square mi); slightly smaller than the U.S. state of West Virginia)
Coastline: 1,290 km (802 mi)
Terrain: Rugged central range with 112 volcanic craters that separates the eastern and western coastal plains
Natural resources: Hydroelectric power, forest products, fisheries products
Natural hazards: Droughts, flash floods, thunderstorms, earthquakes, hurricanes, active volcanoes, landslides
Flora: 9,000 species, including 1,200 orchid species and 800 fern species; tidal mangrove swamps, tropical rain forest, subalpine forest
Fauna: 36,518 species, including 34,000 species of insects and 2,000 species of butterflies
Environmental issues: Deforestation, rapid industrialization and urbanization, air and water pollution, soil degradation, plastic waste, fisheries protection

ECONOMY

Currency: Colón, *(pl.)* colones
GDP: $37.97 billion
Per capita income: $4,670
Unemployment: 6.6%
Major industries: Tourism, microprocessors, food processing, textiles and clothing, construction materials, fertilizer, plastic products
Agricultural products: Bananas, coffee, pineapples, sugarcane, corn, rice, beans, potatoes, beef
Exports: $6.2 billion
Major export products: Bananas, coffee, pineapples, electronic components, fertilizers, sugar, textiles, electricity
Export partners: (in order of volume) U.S., Hong Kong, Holland, Guatemala, Canada, Malaysia, Nicaragua, Germany
Imports: $7.84 billion
Major import products: Chemicals, consumer goods, electronic components, machinery, petroleum products, vehicles
Import partners: U.S. (41%), Japan (5.6%), Venezuela (4.8), Mexico (4.8%), Ireland (4.2%), China (4.2%), Brazil (4.2%)

DID YOU KNOW?

■ Tourism earns more foreign exchange than bananas and coffee combined.
■ Costa Rica did away with its military in 1949.
■ Five percent of the world's identified plant and animal species are found in this country.
■ Costa Rica is the home of five active volcanoes—including Volcán Arenal, the second-largest active volcano in the world.

A BRIEF HISTORY

First Encounters

In mid-September 1502, on his fourth and last voyage to the New World, Christopher Columbus was sailing along the Caribbean coast of Central America when his ships were caught in a violent tropical storm. He found sanctuary in a bay protected by a small island; ashore, he encountered native people wearing heavy gold disks who spoke of great amounts of gold in the area. Sailing farther south, Columbus encountered more natives wearing gold. He was convinced that he had discovered a land of great wealth.

The Spanish Colonial Era

The first few attempts by the Spanish to conquer Costa Rica, beginning in 1506, were unsuccessful owing to sickness and starvation among the Spanish troops, hearty resistance by the indigenous population, and rivalries between various expeditions. By 1560, almost 60 years after its discovery, no permanent Spanish settlement existed in Costa Rica, and early settlers were largely left to their own devices. But that all changed in 1563, when explorer Juan Vásquez de Coronado—a "good Coronado" as Ticos are fond of saying, to distinguish him from other pillaging conquistadors named Coronado—founded the colonial capital of Cartago.

Costa Rica remained the smallest and poorest of Spain's Central American colonies, producing little wealth for the empire. Unlike other mineral-rich colonies around it, Costa Rica was largely ignored. The population stayed at fewer than 20,000 for centuries, and was mainly confined to small, isolated farms in the highland Central Valley and the Pacific lowlands. By the end of the 18th century, however, Costa Rica began to emerge from isolation. Some trade with neighboring Spanish colonies was carried out and the population began to expand across the Central Valley.

When Napoléon defeated and removed King Charles IV in 1808 and installed his brother Joseph on the Spanish throne, Costa Rica pledged support to the old regime, even sending troops to Nicaragua in 1811 to help suppress a rebellion against Spain. By 1821, though, sentiment favoring independence from Spain was prevalent throughout Central America, and a declaration of independence for all of Central America was issued by Guatemala on September 15 of that year. Costa Rica then became part of the Mexican empire until 1826, when it became part of the United Provinces of Central America. Costa Rica declared its independence as a sovereign nation in 1838.

The only major threat to that sovereignty took place in 1856, when the mercenary army of U.S. adventurer William Walker invaded the country from Nicaragua, which it had conquered the year before. Walker's plan to turn the Central American nations into slave states was cut short by Costa Rican president Juan Rafael Mora, who raised a volunteer army and repelled the invaders, pursuing them into Nicaragua and joining troops from various Central American nations to defeat the mercenaries. This conflict produced national hero Juan Santamaría, a young drummer boy from a poor family (⇨ CloseUp "A National Hero" *in* Chapter 2).

Foundations of Democracy

For most of the 19th century the country was ruled by a succession of wealthy families. Coffee was introduced to the country in the 1820s and bananas in the 1870s, and these crops became the country's major sources of foreign exchange. The government spent profits from the coffee trade on improving roads and ports, and other civic projects that included San José's Teatro Nacional.

In 1889 the first free popular election was held, characterized by full freedom of the press, frank debates by rival candidates, an honest tabulation of the vote, and the first peaceful transition of power from a ruling group to the opposition. This provided the foundation of political stability that Costa Rica enjoys to this day.

Booming exports were cut short by the arrival of World War I, followed by the Great Depression and World War II. Poverty soared and a social revolution threatened in the late 1930s, as the popular Communist Party threatened strikes and violence. Costa Rica's version of the New Deal came in 1940, when conservative president Rafael Angel Calderón Guardia allied with the Catholic Church and implemented many of the Communist Party's demands, leading to a system of socialized medicine, minimum-wage laws, low-cost housing, and worker-protection laws.

The success of Calderón's social reforms was tainted by accusations of corruption, which resulted in a civil uprising in 1948, led by the still-revered José "Don Pepe" Figueres Ferrer, who had been exiled by Calderón as the political leader of the opposition. After a few months of armed conflict, a compromise was reached—Figueres would respect Calderón's social guarantees and preside over an interim government for 18 months. In 1949 Figueres abolished Costa Rica's military and created a national police force, nationalized the banking system and public utilities, and implemented health and education reforms. He stepped down after 18 months, only to be reelected twice in free elections.

The Modern Era

During the 1950s and 1960s, insurance, telecommunications, the railroad system (now defunct), ports, and other industries were nationalized. The state-led economic model, although increasingly inefficient, led to a rising standard of living until the early 1970s, when an economic crisis introduced Costa Ricans to hyperinflation. By the mid-1980s Costa Rica had

begun pulling out of its economic slump, in part thanks to efforts to diversify the economy. By the mid-1990s, tourism had surpassed bananas as the country's largest earner of foreign exchange, and high-tech companies such as Intel and Motorola opened plants and service centers in Costa Rica, providing well-paid jobs for educated professionals.

Recent years have seen the continued growth of the tourism industry, and the establishment of a thriving but controversial Internet-based gambling industry tied to U.S. sporting events. The economy continues to bedevil Costa Rica: inflation hovers around 10% annually and the country's currency continues to be devalued on a regular basis. Attempts to privatize state-owned industries have been unsuccessful, and the process of negotiating a Central American free-trade agreement with the United States (and its mandated opening of state enterprises to competition) continues to generate heated debate.

Today the challenge facing Costa Rica is how to conserve its natural resources while still permitting modern development. The government has been unable or unwilling to control illegal logging, an industry that threatens to destroy the country's old-growth forests. Urban sprawl in the Central Valley and the development of megaresorts along the Pacific coast threaten forests, wildlife, and the slow pace of life that makes Costa Rica so enjoyable for visitors. Although tourism provides a much-needed injection of foreign exchange into the economy, the government has not fully decided which direction it should take. The buzzwords now are "ecotourism" and "sustainable development," and it is hoped that Costa Rica will find it possible to continue down these roads.

WILDLIFE & PLANT GLOSSARY

Here is a rundown of some of the most common and attention-grabbing mammals, birds, reptiles, amphibians, plants, and even a few insects that you might encounter. We give the common Costa Rican names, so you can understand the local lingo, followed by the latest scientific terms.

Fauna

Agouti (*guatusa*; *Dasyprocta punctata*): A 20-inch, tail-less rodent with small ears and a large muzzle, the agouti is reddish brown on the Pacific side, more of a tawny orange on the Caribbean slope. It sits on its haunches to eat large seeds and fruit and resembles a large rabbit without the long ears.

Anteater (*oso hormiguero*): Three species of anteater inhabit Costa Rica—the very rare giant (*Myrmecophaga tridactyla*), the nocturnal silky (*Cyclopes didactylus*), and the Collared, or Vested (*Tamandua mexicana*). Only the last is commonly seen, and too often as roadkill. This medium-size anteater, 30 inches long with an 18-inch tail, laps up ants and termites with its long, sticky tongue and has long, sharp claws for ripping into insect nests.

Armadillo (*cusuco*; *Dasypus novemcinctus*): The nine-banded armadillo is widespread in Costa Rica and also found in the southern United States. This nocturnal and solitary edentate roots in soil with a long muzzle for a varied diet of insects, small animals, and plant material.

Baird's Tapir (*danta*; *Tapirus bairdii*): The largest land mammal in Costa Rica (to 6½ feet), Baird's Tapir is something like a small rhinoceros without armor. Adapted to a wide range of habitats, it's nocturnal, seldom seen, but said to defecate and sometimes sleep in water. Tapirs are herbivorous and use their prehensile snouts to harvest vegetation. The best opportunities for viewing wild tapirs are in Corcovado National Park.

Bat (*murciélogo*): With more than 100 species, Costa Rica's bats can be found eating fruit, insects, fish, small vertebrates, nectar, and even blood, in the case of the infamous vampire bat (*vampiro,Desmodus rotundus*), which far prefers cattle blood to that of any tourist. As a group, bats are extremely important ecologically, and are essential to seed dispersal, pollination, and controlling insect populations.

Butterfly (*mariposa*): Estimates of the number of butterfly species in Costa Rica vary, but all range in the thousands. The growing number of butterfly gardens popping up around the country is testament to their popularity among visitors. Three Costa Rican Morpho species—spectacular, large butterflies—have a brilliant-blue upper wing surface, giving them their local nickname of *pedazos de ciel* (pieces of sky). The blue morpho (*Morpho peleides*), arguably the most distinctive, is common in moister areas and has an intense ultraviolet upper surface. Adults feed on fermenting fruit; they never visit flowers.

Caiman (*caiman*): The spectacled caiman (*Caiman crocodilus*) is a small crocodilian (to 7 feet) inhabiting fresh water, subsisting mainly on fish. Most active at night (it has bright-red eye shine), it basks by day. It is distinguished from the American crocodile by a sloping brow and smooth back scales.

Coati (*pizote*; *Nasua narica*): This is a long-nose relative of the raccoon, its long tail often held straight up. Lone males or groups of females with young are active during the day, on the ground, or in trees. Omnivorous coatis feed on fruit, invertebrates, and small vertebrates. Unfortunately, many have learned to beg from tourists, especially in Monteverde and on the roads around Arenal.

Cougar (*puma*; *Felis concolor*): Mountain lions are the largest unspotted cats (to 8 feet, including the tail) in Costa Rica. Widespread but rare, they live in essentially all-wild habitats and feed on vertebrates ranging from snakes to deer.

Crocodile (*lagarto*; *Crocodylus acutus*): The American crocodile, up to 16 feet in length, is found in most major river systems, particularly the Tempisque and Tárcoles estuaries. It seldom attacks humans, preferring fish and birds. It's distinguished from the caiman by size, a flat head, narrow snout, and spiky scales.

Ctenosaur (*garrobo*; *Ctenosaura similis*): Also known as the black, or spiny-tailed, iguana, this is a large (up to 18 inches long with an 18-inch tail) tan lizard with four dark bands on its body and a tail ringed with sharp, curved spines, reminiscent of a dinosaur. Terrestrial and arboreal, it sleeps in burrows or tree hollows. It lives along the coast in the dry northwest and in wetter areas farther south. The fastest known reptile (clocked on land), the ctenosaur has been recorded moving at 21.7 mi per hour.

Dolphin (*delfín*): Several species, including bottlenose dolphins (*Tursiops truncatus*), frolic in Costa Rican waters. Often seen off Pacific shores are spotted dolphins (*Stenella attenuata*), which are small (up to 6 feet), with pale spots on the posterior half of the body; they commonly travel in groups of 20 or more and play around vessels and in bow wakes. Tucuxi dolphins (*Sotalia fluviatilis*) have also been spotted in small groups off the southern Caribbean coast, frequently with bottlenose dolphins.

Frog and Toad (*rana*, frog; *sapo*, toad): Some 120 species of frog exist in Costa Rica; many are nocturnal. The most colorful daytime amphibians are the tiny strawberry poison dart frog (*Dendrobates pumilio*) and green-and-black poison dart frog. The bright coloration of these two species, either red with blue or green hind legs or charcoal black with fluorescent green markings, warns

potential predators of their toxicity. The red-eyed leaf frog (*Agalychnis callidryas*) is among the showiest of nocturnal species. The large, brown marine toad (*Bufo marinus*), also called cane toad or giant toad, comes out at night.

Howler Monkey (*mono congo*; *Alouatta palliata*): These dark, chunky-bodied monkeys (to 22 inches long with a 24-inch tail) with black faces travel in troops of up to 20. Lethargic mammals, they eat leaves, fruits, and flowers. The males' deep, resounding howls sound like lions roaring, but actually serve as communication among and between troops.

Hummingbird (*Trochilidae*): Weighing just a fraction of an ounce, hummingbirds are nonetheless some of the most notable residents of tropical forests. At least 50 varieties can be found in Costa Rica, visiting typically red, tubular flowers in their seemingly endless search for energy-rich nectar. Because of their assortment of iridescent colors and bizarre bills and tail shapes, watching them can be a spectator sport. Best bets are hummingbird feeders and anywhere with great numbers of flowers.

Iguana (*iguana*): Mostly arboreal but good at swimming, the iguana is Costa Rica's largest lizard: males can grow to 10 feet, including tail. Only young green iguanas (*Iguana iguana*) are bright green; adults are much duller, females dark grayish, and males olive (with orangish heads in breeding season). All have round cheek scales and smooth tails.

Jaguar (*tigre*; *Panthera onca*): The largest New World feline (to 6 feet, with a 2-foot tail), this top-of-the-line predator is exceedingly rare but lives in a wide variety of habitats, from dry forest to cloud forest. It's most common in the vast Amistad Biosphere Reserve, but it is almost never seen in the wild.

Jesus Christ Lizard (*gallego*): Flaps of skin on long toes enable this spectacular lizard to run across water. Costa Rica has three species of this lizard, which is more properly called the basilisk: lineated (*Basiliscus basiliscus*) on the Pacific side is brown with pale lateral stripes; in the Caribbean, emerald (*Basiliscus plumifrons*) is marked with turquoise and black on a green body; and striped (*Basiliscus vittatus*), also on the Caribbean side, resembling the lineated basilisk. Adult males grow to 3 feet (mostly tail), with crests on the head, back, and base of the tail.

Leaf-Cutter Ant (*zompopas*; *Atta* spp.): Found in all lowland habitats, these are the most commonly noticed neotropical ants, and one of the country's most fascinating animal phenomena. Columns of ants carrying bits of leaves twice their size sometimes extend for several hundred yards from an underground nest to plants being harvested. The ants don't eat the leaves; their food is a fungus they cultivate on the leaves.

Macaw (*lapas*): Costa Rica's two species are the scarlet macaw (*Ara macao*), on the Pacific side (Osa Peninsula and Carara Biological Reserve), and the severely threatened great green macaw (*Ara ambigua*), on the Caribbean side. These are huge, raucous parrots with long tails; their immense bills are used to rip fruit apart to reach the seeds. They nest in hollow trees and are victimized by pet-trade poachers and deforestation.

Magnificent Frigatebird (*tijereta del mar*; *Fregata magnificens*): A large, black soaring bird with slender wings and forked tail, this is one of the most effortless and agile flyers in the avian world. More common on the Pacific coast, it doesn't dive or swim but swoops to pluck its food, often from the mouths of other birds.

Manatee (*manatí*; *Trichechus manatus*): Although endangered throughout its range, the West Indian manatee can be spotted in Tortuguero, meandering along in shallow water, browsing on submerged vegetation. The moniker "sea cow" is apt, as they spend nearly all their time resting or feeding. Their large, somewhat amorphous bodies won't win any beauty contests, but they do appear quite graceful.

Margay (*caucel*; *Felis wiedii*): Fairly small, this spotted nocturnal cat (22 inches long, with an 18-inch tail) is similar to the ocelot but has a longer tail and is far more arboreal: mobile ankle joints allow it to climb down trunks head first. It eats small vertebrates.

Motmot (*pájaro bobo*): These handsome, turquoise-and-rufous birds of the understory have racket-shape tails. Nesting in burrows, they sit patiently while scanning for large insect prey or small vertebrates. Costa Rica has six species.

Northern Jacana (*gallito de agua*; *Jacana spinosa*): These birds are sometimes called "lily trotters" because their long toes allow them to walk on floating vegetation. Feeding on aquatic organisms and plants, they're found in almost any body of water. They expose yellow wing feathers in flight. Sex roles are reversed; "liberated" females are larger and compete for mates (often more than one), whereas the males tend to the nest and care for the young.

Ocelot (*manigordo*; *Felis pardalis*): Mostly terrestrial, this medium-size spotted cat (33 inches long, with a 16-inch tail) is active night and day, and feeds on rodents and other vertebrates. Forepaws are rather large in relation to the body, hence the local name, *manigordo*, which means "fat hand."

Opossum (*zorro pelón*; *Didelphis marsupialis*): Like the kangaroo, the common opossum belongs to that rare breed of mammals known as marsupials, distinguished by their brief gestation period and completion of development and nourishment following birth in the mother's pouch. The Costa Rican incarnation does not "play possum," and will bite if cornered rather than pretend to be dead.

Oropendola (*oropéndola*; *Psarocolius* spp.): These crow-size birds in the oriole family have a bright-yellow tail and nest in colonies, in pendulous nests (up to 6 feet long) built by females in isolated trees. The Montezuma species has an orange beak and blue cheeks, the chestnut-headed has a yellow beak. Males make an unmistakable, loud, gurgling liquid call. The bird is far more numerous on the Caribbean side.

Parakeet and Parrot (*pericos*, parakeets; *loros*, parrots): There are 15 species in Costa Rica (plus two macaws), all clad in green, most with a splash of a primary color or two on the head or wings. They travel in boisterous flocks, prey on immature seeds, and nest in cavities.

Peccary Piglike animals with thin legs and thick necks, peccaries travel in small groups (larger where the population is still numerous); root in soil for fruit, seeds, and small creatures; and have a strong musk odor. You'll usually smell them before you see them. Costa Rica has two species: the collared peccary (*saíno,Tayassu tajacu*) and the white-lipped peccary (*chancho de monte,Tayassu pecari*). The latter is now nearly extinct.

Pelican (*pelícano*): Large size, a big bill, and a throat pouch make the brown pelican (*Pelecanus occidentalis*) unmistakable in coastal areas (it's far more abundant on the Pacific side). Pelicans often fly in V formations and dive for fish.

Quetzal One of the world's most exquisite birds, the resplendent quetzal (*Pharomachrus mocinno*) was revered by the Maya. Glittering green plumage and the male's long tail coverts draw thousands of people to highland cloud forests for sightings from February to April.

Roseate Spoonbill (*garza rosada*; *Ajaja ajaja*): Pink plumage and a spatulate bill set this wader apart from all other wetland birds; it feeds by swishing its bill back and forth in water while using its feet to stir up bottom-dwelling creatures. Spoonbills are most common around Palo Verde and Caño Negro.

Sloth (*perezoso*): Costa Rica is home to the brown-throated, three-toed sloth (*Bradypus variegatus*) and Hoffmann's two-toed sloth (*Choloepus hoffmanni*). Both grow to 2 feet, but two-toed (check forelegs) sloths often look bigger because of longer fur and are the only species in the highlands. Sloths are herbivorous, accustomed to a low-energy diet, and well camouflaged.

Snake (*culebra*): Costa Rica's serpents can be found in trees, above and below ground, and even in the sea on the Pacific coast. Most of the more than 125 species are harmless, but are best appreciated from a distance. Notable members of this group include Costa Rica's largest snake, the boa constrictor (*Boa constrictor*), reaching up to 15 feet, and the fer-de-lance (*terciopelo,Bothrops asper*), which is a much smaller (up to 6 feet) but far more dangerous viper.

Spider Monkey (*mono colorado, mono araña*): Lanky and long-tailed, the black-handed spider monkey (*Ateles geoffroyi*) is the largest monkey in Costa Rica (to 24 inches, with a 32-inch tail). Moving in groups of two to four, they eat ripe fruit, leaves, and flowers. Incredible aerialists, they can swing effortlessly through branches using long arms and legs and prehensile tails. They are quite aggressive and will challenge onlookers and often throw down branches. Caribbean and southern Pacific populations are dark reddish brown; northwesterners are blond.

Squirrel Monkey (*mono tití*): The smallest of four Costa Rican monkeys (11 inches, with a 15-inch tail), the red-backed squirrel monkey (*Saimiri oerstedii*) has a distinctive facial pattern (black cap and muzzle, white mask) and gold-orange coloration on its back. It is the only Costa Rican monkey without a prehensile tail. The species travels in noisy, active groups of 20 or more, feeding on fruit and insects. Numbers of this endangered species have been estimated between 2,000 and 4,000 individuals. Most squirrel monkeys in Costa Rica are found in Manuel Antonio National Park, in parts of the Osa Peninsula, and around the Golfo Dulce.

Three-Wattled Bellbird (*pájaro campana; Procnias tricarunculata*): Although endangered, the bellbird can be readily identified in cloud forests (around Monteverde, for example), where it breeds by its extraordinary call, a bold and aggressive "bonk," unlike any other creature in the forest. If you spot a male calling, look for the three pendulous wattles at the base of its beak.

Toucan (*tucán, tucancillo*): The keel-billed toucan (*Ramphastos sulfuratus*) with the rainbow-colored beak is familiar to anyone who's seen a box of Froot Loops cereal. Chestnut-mandibled toucans (*Ramphastos swainsonii*) are the largest (18 inches and 22 inches); as the name implies, their lower beaks are brown. The smaller, stouter emerald toucanet (*Aulacorhynchus prasinus*) and yellow-eared toucanet (*Selenidera spectabilis*) are aptly named. Aracaris (*Pteroglossus Spp.*) are similar to toucans, but colored orange-and-yellow with the trademark toucan bill.

Turtles (*tortuga*): Observing the nesting rituals of the five species of marine turtles here is one of those truly memorable Costa Rican experiences. Each species has its own nesting season and locale. The olive ridley (*lora; Lepidochelys olivacea*) is the smallest of the sea turtles (average carapace, or hardback shell, is 21–29 inches) and the least shy. Thousands engage in nighttime group nesting rituals on the North Pacific's Ostional. At the other extreme, but only slightly farther north on Playa Grande, nests the leatherback (*baula; Dermochelys coriacea*) with its five-foot-long shell. On the north Caribbean coast, Tortuguero hosts four of them: the leatherback, the hawksbill (*carey; Eretmochelys imbricata*), the loggerhead (*caguama; Caretta caretta*), and the green (*tortuga verde; Chelonia mydas*), with its long nesting season (June–October) that draws the most visitors and researchers.

Whales (*ballena*): Humpback whales (*Megaptera novaeanglia*) appear off the Pacific coast between November and February; they migrate from California and as far as Hawaii. You can also spot Sey whales, Bryde's whales, and farther out to sea, blue whales and sperm whales. On the Caribbean side, there are smaller (12 to 14 feet) Koiga whales.

White-Faced Capuchin Monkey (*mono cara blanca; Cebus capuchinus*): Medium-size and omnivorous, this monkey (to 18 inches, with a 20-inch tail) has black fur and a pink face surrounded by a whitish bib. Extremely active foragers, they move singly or in groups of up to 20, examining the environment closely and even coming to the ground. It's the most commonly seen monkey in Costa Rica. It's also the most often fed by visitors, to the point where some monkey populations now have elevated cholesterol levels.

White-Tailed Deer (*venado; Odocoileus virginianus*): Bambi would feel at home in Costa Rica, although his counterparts here are slightly smaller. As befits the name, these animals possess the distinctive white underside to their tail (and to their bellies). They are seen in drier parts of the country, especially in the northwest province of Guanacaste.

White-Throated Magpie-jay (*urraca; Calocitta formosa*): This southern relative of the blue jay, with a long tail and distinctive topknot (crest of forward-curved feathers), is found in the dry northwest. Bold and inquisitive, with amazingly varied vocalizations, these birds travel in noisy groups of four or more.

Flora

Ant-acacia (*acacia; Acacia* spp.): If you'll be in the tropical dry forest of Guanacaste, learn to avoid this plant. As if its sharp thorns weren't enough, acacias exhibit an intense symbiosis with various ant species (*Pseudomyrmex* spp.) that will attack anything—herbivores, other plants, and unaware human visitors that come in contact with the tree. The ants and the acacias have an intriguing relationship, though, so do look, but don't touch.

Bromeliad (*piña silvestre*): Members of the family Bromeliaceae are *epiphytes*, living on the trunk and branches of trees. They are not parasitic, however, and so have adapted to acquire all the necessary water and nutrients from what falls into the central "tank" formed by the leaf structure. Amphibians and insects also use the water held in bromeliads to reproduce, forming small aquatic communities perched atop tree branches. In especially wet areas, small bromeliads can even be found on power lines. Their spectacular, colorful efflorescences are popular—and expensive—houseplants in northern climes.

Heliconia (*helicónia; Heliconia* spp.): It's hard to miss these stunning plants, many of which have huge inflorescences of red, orange, and yellow, sometimes shaped like lobster claws, and leaves very much the size and shape of a banana plant. With luck, you'll catch a visiting hummingbird with a beak specially designed to delve into a heliconia flower—truly a visual treat.

Mangroves (*manglares*): Taken together, this handful of salt-tolerant trees with tangled, above-ground roots make up their own distinct ecosystem. Buttressing the land against the sea, they serve as nurseries for countless species of fish, crabs, and other marine animals and provide roosting habitat for marine birds. Mangroves are found on the coast in protected areas such as bays and estuaries.

Naked Indian Tree (*indio desnudo; Bursera simaruba*): This tree can be found in forests throughout Costa Rica, often forming living fences, and is instantly identifiable by its orange bark that continually sloughs off, giving rise to another common name, the sunburnt tourist tree. One theory suggests that the shedding of its bark aids in removing parasites from the tree's exterior.

Orchid (*orquídea*): The huge Orchidaceae family has more than 1,200 representatives in Costa Rica alone, with nearly 90% percent living as epiphytes on other plants. The great diversity of the group includes not only examples of great beauty but exquisite adaptations between flowers and their insect pollinators. With a combination of rewards (nectar) and trickery (visual and chemical cues), orchids exhibit myriad ways of enticing insects to cooperate.

Strangler Fig (*Matapalo; Ficus spp.*): Starting as seedlings high in the canopy, these aggressive plants grow both up toward the light, and down to the soil, slowly taking over the host tree. Eventually they encircle and appear to "strangle" the host, actually killing it by hogging all the available sunlight, leaving a ring of fig trunk around an empty interior. Figs with ripe fruit are excellent places for wildlife spotting, as they attract monkeys, birds, and an assortment of other creatures.

MENU GUIDE

Rice and beans are the heart of Costa Rica's *comida típica* (typical food). It's possible to order everything from sushi to crepes in and around San José, but most Ticos have a simple diet built around rice, beans, and the myriad fruits and vegetables that flourish here. Costa Rican food isn't spicy, and many dishes are seasoned with the same five ingredients—onion, salt, garlic, cilantro, and red bell pepper.

SPANISH	ENGLISH

GENERAL DINING

Spanish	English
Almuerzo	Lunch
Bocas	Appetizers or snacks (literally "mouthfuls") served with drinks in the tradition of Spanish tapas.
Casado	Heaping plate of rice, beans, fried plantains, cabbage salad, tomatoes, *macarrones* (noodles), and fish, chicken, or meat—or any variation thereof; *casado* and *plato del día* are often used interchangeably
Cena	Dinner
Desayuno	Breakfast
Plato del día	Plate of the day
Soda	An inexpensive café; casados are always found at sodas

ESPECIALIDADES (SPECIALTIES)

Spanish	English
Arreglados	Sandwiches or meat and vegetable puff pastry
Arroz con mariscos	Fried rice with fish, shrimp, octopus, and clams, or whatever's fresh that day
Arroz con pollo	Chicken with rice
Camarones	Shrimp
Ceviche	Chilled, raw seafood marinated in lime juice, served with chopped onion and garlic
Chilaquiles	Meat-stuffed tortillas
Chorreados	Corn pancakes, served with *natilla* (sour cream)
Corvina	Sea bass

Empanadas	Savory or sweet pastry turnover filled with fruit or meat and vegetables
Empanaditas	Small empanadas
Gallo pinto	Rice sautéed with black beans (literally, "spotted rooster"), often served for breakfast
Langosta	Lobster
Langostino	Prawns
Olla de carne	Soup of beef, chayote squash, corn, yuca (a tuber), and potatoes
Palmitos	Hearts of palm, served in salads or as a side dish
Pejibaye	A nutty, orange-colored palm fruit eaten in salads, soups, and as a snack
Pescado ahumado	Smoked marlin
Picadillo	Chayote squash, potatoes, carrots, or other vegetables chopped into small cubes and combined with onions, garlic, and ground beef
Pozol	Corn soup
Salsa caribeño	A combination of tomatoes, onions, and spices that accompanies most fish dishes on the Caribbean coast

POSTRES (DESSERTS) & DULCES (SWEETS)

Cajeta de coco	Fudge made with coconut and orange peel
Cajeta	Molasses-flavored fudge
Dulce de leche	Thick syrup of boiled milk and sugar
Flan	Caramel-topped egg custard
Mazamorra	Cornstarch pudding
Pan de maiz	Sweet corn bread
Torta chilena	Flaky, multilayered cake with dulce de leche filling
Tres leches cake	"Three milks" cake, made with condensed and evaporated milk and cream

FRUTAS (FRUITS)

Aguacate	Avocado

Anon	Sugar apple; sweet white flesh; resembles an artichoke with a thick rind
Banano	Banana
Bilimbi	Looks like a miniature cucumber crossed with a star fruit; ground into a savory relish
Fresa	Strawberry
Cas	A smaller guava
Granadilla	Passion fruit
Guanábana	Soursop; large, spiky yellow fruit with white flesh and a musky taste
Guayaba	Guava
Mamon chino	Rambutan; red spiky ball protecting a white fruit similar to a lychee
Mango	Many varieties, from sour green to succulently sweet Oro (golden); March is the height of mango season
Manzana de agua	Water apple, shaped like a pear; juicy but not very sweet
Marañon	Cashew fruit; used in juices
Melon	Cantaloupe
Mora	Blackberry
Palmito	Heart of palm
Piña	Pineapple
Papaya	One of the most popular and ubiquitous fruits
Pipa	Green coconut; sold at roadside stands with ends chopped off and straws stuck inside
Sandia	Watermelon
Carambola	Star fruit

BEBIDAS (BEVERAGES)

Agua dulce	Hot water sweetened with raw sugarcane
Batido	Fruit shake made with milk (con leche) or water (con agua)
Café con leche	Coffee with hot milk

Café negro	Black coffee
Fresco natural	Fresh-squeezed juice
Guaro	Harsh, clear spirit distilled from fermented sugarcane
Horchata	Cinnamon-flavored rice drink
Refrescos	Tropical fruit smoothie with ice and sugar

VOCABULARY

	ENGLISH	SPANISH	PRONUNCIATION
BASICS			
	Yes/no	Sí/no	see/no
	OK	De acuerdo	de a-**kwer**-doe
	Please	Por favor	pore fah-**vore**
	May I?	¿Me permite?	may pair-**mee**-tay
	Thank you (very much)	(Muchas) gracias	(**moo**-chas) **grah**-see-as
	You're welcome	Con mucho gusto	con **moo**-cho **goose**-toe
	Excuse me	Con permiso	con pair-**mee**-so
	Pardon me	¿Perdón?	pair-**dohn**
	Could you tell me?	¿Podría decirme?	po-dree-ah deh-**seer**-meh
	I'm sorry	Disculpe	Dee-**skool**-peh
	Good morning!	¡Buenos días!	**bway**-nohs **dee**-ahs
	Good afternoon!	¡Buenas tardes!	**bway**-nahs **tar**-dess
	Good evening!	¡Buenas noches!	**bway**-nahs **no**-chess
	Goodbye!	¡Adiós!/¡Hasta luego!	ah-dee-**ohss**/ah-stah-**lwe**-go
	Mr./Mrs.	Señor/Señora	sen-**yor**/sen-**yohr**-ah
	Miss	Señorita	sen-yo-**ree**-tah
	Pleased to meet you	Mucho gusto	**moo**-cho **goose**-toe
	How are you?	¿Cómo está usted?	**ko**-mo es-**tah** oo-**sted**
	Very well, thank you.	Muy bien, gracias.	**moo**-ee bee-**en**, **grah**-see-as
	And you?	¿Y usted?	ee oos-**ted**

DAYS OF THE WEEK

	Sunday	domingo	doe-**meen**-goh
	Monday	lunes	**loo**-ness
	Tuesday	martes	**mahr**-tess
	Wednesday	miércoles	me-**air**-koh-less

Thursday	jueves	hoo-**ev**-ess
Friday	viernes	vee-**air**-ness
Saturday	sábado	**sah**-bah-doh

MONTHS

January	enero	eh-**neh**-roh
February	febrero	feh-**breh**-roh
March	marzo	**mahr**-soh
April	abril	ah-**breel**
May	mayo	**my**-oh
June	junio	**hoo**-nee-oh
July	julio	**hoo**-lee-yoh
August	agosto	ah-**ghost**-toh
September	septiembre	sep-tee-**em**-breh
October	octubre	oak-**too**-breh
November	noviembre	no-vee-**em**-breh
December	diciembre	dee-see-**em**-breh

USEFUL PHRASES

Do you speak	¿Habla usted	**ah**-blah oos-**ted**
English?	inglés?	in-**glehs**
I don't speak Spanish	No hablo español	no **ah**-bloh es-pahn-**yol**
I don't understand (you)	No entiendo	no en-tee-en-doh
I understand (you)	Entiendo	en-tee-**en**-doh
I don't know	No sé	no seh
I am American/ British	Soy americano (americana)/ inglés(a)	soy ah-meh-ree-**kah**-no (ah-meh-ree-**kah**-nah)/ in-**glehs** (ah)
What's your name?	¿Cómo se llama usted?	koh-mo seh **yah**-mah oos-**ted**
My name is . . .	Me llamo . . .	may **yah**-moh
What time is it?	¿Qué hora es?	keh **o**-rah es
It is one, two, three . . . o'clock.	Es la una. . . . Son las dos, tres	es la **oo**-nah/sohn lahs dohs, tress

How?	¿Cómo?	**koh**-mo
When?	¿Cuándo?	**kwahn**-doh
This/Next week	Esta semana/ la semana que entra	**es**-teh seh-**mah**-nah/lah seh-**mah**-nah keh **en**-trah
This/Next month	Este mes/el próximo mes	**es**-teh mehs/el **proke**-see-mo mehs
This/Next year	Este año/el año que viene	**es**-teh **ahn**-yo/el ahn-yo keh vee-**yen**-ay
Yesterday/today/ tomorrow	Ayer/hoy/mañana	ah-**yehr**/oy/mahn-**yah**-nah
This morning/ afternoon	Esta mañana/ tarde	**es**-tah mahn-**yah**-nah/**tar**-deh
Tonight	Esta noche	**es**-tah **no**-cheh
What?	¿Qué?	keh
What is it?	¿Qué es esto?	keh es **es**-toh
Why?	¿Por qué?	pore **keh**
Who?	¿Quién?	kee-**yen**
Where is . . . ?	¿Dónde está . . . ?	**dohn**-deh es-**tah**
the bus stop?	la parada del autobus?	la pah-**rah**-dah del oh-toh-**boos**
the post office?	la oficina de correos?	la oh-fee-**see**-nah deh koh-**reh**-os
the museum?	el museo?	el moo-**seh**-oh
the hospital?	el hospital?	el ohss-pee-**tal**
the bathroom?	el baño?	el **bahn**-yoh
Here/there	Aquí/allá	ah-**key**/ah-**yah**
Open/closed	Abierto/cerrado	ah-bee-**er**-toh/ser-**ah**-doh
Left/right	Izquierda/derecha	iss-key-**er**-dah/dare-**eh**-chah
Straight ahead	Derecho	dare-**eh**-choh
Is it near/far?	¿Está cerca/lejos?	es-**tah sehr**-kah/**leh**-hoss
I'd like . . . a room	Quisiera . . . un cuarto/una habitación	kee-see-**ehr**-ah oon **kwahr**-toh/**oo**-nah ah-bee-

		tah-see-**on**
the key	la llave	lah **yah**-veh
a newspaper	un periódico	oon pehr-ee-**oh**-dee-koh
a stamp	la estampilla	lah es-stahm-**pee**-yah

I'd like to buy . . .	Quisiera comprar . . .	kee-see-**ehr**-ah kohm-**prahr**
a dictionary	un diccionario	oon deek-see-oh-**nah**-ree-oh
soap	jabón	hah-**bohn**
suntan lotion	loción bronceadora	loh-see-**ohn** brohn-seh-ah-**do**-rah
a map	un mapa	oon **mah**-pah
a magazine	una revista	oon-ah reh-**veess**-tah
a postcard	una tarjeta postal	**oon**-ah tar-**het**-ah post-**ahl**

How much is it?	¿Cuánto cuesta?	**kwahn**-toh **kwes**-tah

Telephone	Teléfono	tel-**ef**-oh-no

Help!	¡Auxilio! ¡Ayuda! ¡Socorro!	owk-**see**-lee-oh/ ah-**yoo**-dah/ soh-**kohr**-roh

Fire!	¡Incendio!	en-**sen**-dee-oo

Caution!/Look out!	¡Cuidado!	kwee-**dah**-doh

SALUD (HEALTH)

I am ill	Estoy enfermo(a)	es-**toy** en-**fehr**-moh(mah)
Please call a doctor	Por favor llame a un médico	pohr fah-**vor ya**-meh ah oon **med**-ee-koh
acetaminophen	acetaminofen	a-say-ta-**mee**-no-fen
ambulance	ambulancia	ahm-boo-**lahn**-see-a
antibiotic	antibiótico	ahn-tee-bee-**oh**-tee-co
aspirin	aspirina	ah-spi-**ree**-na
capsule	cápsula	**cahp**-soo-la
clinic	clínica	**clee**-nee-ca
cold	resfriado	rays-free-**ah**-do
cough	tos	toess
diarrhea	diarrea	dee-ah-ray-a

fever	fiebre	fee-**ay**-bray
flu	Gripe	**gree**-pay
headache	dolor de cabeza	doh-**lor** day cah-**bay**-sa
hospital	hospital	oh-spee-**tahl**
medication	medicamento	meh-dee-cah-**men**-to
pain	dolor	doh-**lor**
pharmacy	farmacia	fahr-**mah**-see-a
physician	médico	**meh**-dee-co
prescription	receta	ray-**say**-ta
stomach ache	dolor de estómago	doh-**lor** day eh-**sto**-mah-go

Costa Rica Essentials

PLANNING TOOLS, EXPERT INSIGHT,
GREAT CONTACTS

There are planners and there are those who,
excuse the pun, fly by the seat of their pants.
We happily place ourselves among the planners.
Our writers and editors try to anticipate all the
issues you may face before and during any journey, and then they do their research. This section
is the product of their efforts. Use it to get excited
about your trip to Costa Rica, to inform your travel
planning, or to guide you on the road should the
seat of your pants start to feel threadbare.

TRANSPORTATION

▌ BY AIR

If you are visiting several regions of the country, flying into San José's Juan Santamaría Airport, in the center of the country, is the best option. Flying into Liberia's Daniel Oduber Airport makes sense if you are planning to spend your vacation in Guanacaste. Bus travel time between the Liberia airport and most of the resorts is less than two hours.

Most travelers fly into the larger San José airport, the transportation hub to nearly every point in the country. Rarely does an international flight get into San José early enough to make a domestic connection, particularly in the rainy season, as the weather is typically unsuitable for flying in the afternoon. So you'll likely end up spending your first night in or near the city, and leave for your domestic destination the next morning out of the SANSA terminal next to the international airport or via Nature Air out of tiny Tobias Bolaños Airport.

Heavy rains in the afternoon and evening during the May to November rainy season sometimes cause flights coming into San José to be rerouted to Panama City, where you may be forced to spend the night. October tends to be the worst month for reroutes. ▌TIP→**In the rainy season, always book a flight with the earliest arrival time available.**

Once you're in Costa Rica, some airlines recommend that you call the San José office about three days before your return flight to reconfirm; others, such as TACA, explicitly say it's not necessary. It's always a good idea to call the local office the day before you are scheduled to return home to make sure your flight time hasn't changed.

The tiny, domestic passenger planes in Costa Rica require that you pack light. A luggage weight limit of 25 pounds (11.3 kilograms) is imposed by SANSA and Macaw; Nature Air allows 30 pounds (13.6 kilograms). Weight restrictions include carry-ons. On some flights extra luggage is allowed, but is charged about $0.55–$1 per pound. Heavy packers can leave their surplus for free in a locked area at Nature Air's terminal. SANSA does not store extra baggage.

If you arrive in Costa Rica and your baggage doesn't, the first thing you should do is go to the baggage claims counter and file an official report with your specific contact information. Then call your airline to find out if they can track it and how long you have to wait—generally bags are located within two days. Continue on your trip as you can; bags can be sent to you just about anywhere in the country. Don't expect too much from local officials; try to get updates from the airline directly.

If your bag has been searched and contents are missing or damaged, file a claim with the TSA Consumer Response Center as soon as possible. If your bags arrive damaged or fail to arrive at all, file a written report with the airline before leaving the airport.

When you fly out of Costa Rica, you'll have to pay a $26 airport departure tax in colones or with a Visa credit card. You can pay the tax upon arrival or departure at the Bancrédito counter in the airport, or at any Bancrédito or Banco de Costa Rica branch in Costa Rica during your trip. Lines can be long, so don't leave it until the last minute. The Four Seasons, Punta Islita, the Hotel Marriott in Belén, and Hotel Presidente in the capital allow you to pay for the tax on your hotel bill and give you the receipt for the airport. If you're staying at an upscale hotel, ask— the program is catching on fast.

Airlines & Airports **Airline and Airport Links.com** (www.airlineandairportlinks.com) has links to many of the world's airlines and airports.

Airline Security Issues **Transportation Security Administration** (www.tsa.gov) has answers for almost every question that might come up.

AIRPORTS

Costa Rica has two international airports. Juan Santamaría International Airport (SJO) is the country's main airport. It's about 17 km (10 mi), or 30 minutes by car, northwest of downtown San José, just outside the city of Alajuela. The SANSA terminal for domestic flights is here. The country's other international airport is Daniel Oduber International Airport (LIR), a small airport near Liberia, in the North Pacific, the hub for domestic charter airline Macaw Air. Six commercial airlines fly to Liberia: United Airlines, from Chicago (Dec.–Apr.); Northwest, from Minneapolis; American Airlines, from Dallas and Miami; Delta, from Atlanta and Los Angeles; Continental, from Houston and Newark; and US Airways from Charlotte, NC; regularly

scheduled charter flights from the United States are few. The tiny Tobías Bolaños airport, in the San José suburb of Pavas (west of the city), serves domestic airline Nature Air, domestic charter companies, and a handful of private planes.

Other places where planes land in Costa Rica aren't exactly airports. They're more like a carport with a landing strip, at which an airline representative arrives just minutes before a plane is due to land or take off.

Prepare yourself for long waits at immigration and customs, and for check-in and security checkpoints, especially at Juan Santamaría, where you need to get to the airport three hours before your flight. This is slowly improving—eight new gates were finished in December 2007—but infrastructure improvements and other issues still face a bumpy road. Most North American flights arrive at this airport in the evening and depart early in the morning, which are the busiest times.

Liberia is a tiny airport, so check-in times are usually shorter. However, infrastructure hasn't quite caught up to the exponential increase in flights, so we recommend that you arrive at least two hours before international departures.

Juan Santamaría is a full-service airport with many arrivals and departures each day, so if you miss your flight or have some other unexpected mishap, you're better off here. Fares are usually lower to San José than to Liberia.

Airport Information **Aeropuerto Internacional Daniel Oduber** (LIR ✛13 km [10 mi] west of Liberia ☎506/2668–1010 in Costa Rica). **Aeropuerto Internacional Juan Santamaría** (SJO ✛17 km [10 mi] northwest of downtown San José, just outside Alajuela ☎506/2440–1328, 506/2437–2626 in Costa Rica for departure and arrival info). **Aeropuerto Internacional Tobías Bolaños** (✛6 km [4 mi] west of San José, Pavas ☎506/232–2820 in Costa Rica).

GROUND TRANSPORTATION FROM JUAN SANTAMARÍA AIRPORT

You exit the airport into a fume-filled parking area flanked by hordes of taxis and tour vans. If you're with a tour, you need only look for a representative of your tour company with a sign that bears your name. If you need a taxi, first buy a voucher at a counter just to the left of the arrivals exit, then present it to the driver of one of the orange Taxis Unidos cabs (no other taxis are allowed in the arrivals area). Rates are standardized to the various parts of town; most areas of San José are $18–$20. Avoid the shuttle companies' *collectivos,* or minivans—they're almost the same price as a taxi (for two or fewer people), but the van is often crammed with other passengers, and you'll have to make stops at their hotels, making your transfer another journey in itself.

FLIGHTS

From the United States: Miami has the highest number of direct flights, but nonstop flights are also available from New York; Houston; Dallas; Atlanta; Phoenix; Washington, D.C.; Charlotte; Fort Lauderdale; and Los Angeles. Continental, American, America West, Delta, US Airways, and United are the major U.S. carriers with nonstop service to Costa Rica. Martinair has nonstop flights from Orlando and Miami. From New York, flights to San José are 5½ hours nonstop or 7 to 8 hours via Miami. From Los Angeles, flights are about 5½ hours nonstop or 8½ hours via Houston; from Houston, 3½ hours nonstop; from Miami, 3 hours; from Charlotte, 4 hours; and from Chicago, 7 hours, through Houston or Charlotte. In general, nonstop flights aren't that much more expensive. Median ticket prices from hubs such as New York, Los Angeles, and Seattle hover between $400 and $600, although the range can vary widely up or down.

Spirit Air, the first of the low-cost U.S. carriers to fly to Costa Rica, offers service to San José from Fort Lauderdale. Frontier Airlines followed suit in late 2007, with direct flights from Denver. Other than obvious considerations such as price and scheduling, a regional airline like Mexicana and TACA (a Central American airline) is a good choice if you're visiting more than one Central American country; major U.S. airlines don't serve routes such as Costa Rica–Honduras.

From elsewhere in Central America: international flights to Costa Rica tend to be cheaper than those to Nicaragua or Panama, so if you're doing two or three countries, it makes sense, budget-wise, to start in Costa Rica. Copa, TACA, and Lacsa fly between Panama City and San José and between Managua, Nicaragua, and San José. Nature Air flies between Bocas del Toro, Panama, and San José. SANSA makes the Bocas del Toro run as well. At this writing, Nature Air flights into Limón were still on offer, but the fate of the route was uncertain due to infrastructure problems.

Given Costa Rica's often difficult driving conditions, distances that appear short on a map can represent hours of driving on dirt roads pocked with craters; buses can be a slow and uncomfortable way to travel. Domestic flights are a desirable and practical option. And because 4WD rental rates can be steep, flying is often cheaper than driving. Most major destinations are served by daily domestic flights.

The informality of domestic air service—"airports" other than Liberia and San José usually consist of only an airstrip with no central building at which to buy tickets—means you might want to purchase your domestic airplane tickets in advance (by phone or online), although you can buy them at the San José or Liberia airports or at travel agencies once you're in the country. In theory, you can purchase tickets up to two hours before the flight is set to go. This is a potentially viable option in the May-through-October low season, but

Domestic Flights

we recommend grabbing a seat as soon as you know your itinerary.

There are two major domestic commercial airlines: SANSA and Nature Air. Most Nature Air and SANSA flights leave from the San José area (⇨Airports). Commercial planes are small—holding between 6 and 19 passengers. Charter company Macaw Air flies its five-passenger Cessna 206 out of Liberia, allowing you to bypass San José altogether. Domestic flights originating in San José are generally nonstop, with the exception of some flights to the far south, where you might stop in Drake Bay first, then continue on to Puerto Jiménez, for example. SANSA and Nature Air both have a few nonstop inter-destinational flights, such as Tamarindo–Liberia, and a number of flights with quick connections or stops. You can buy SANSA and Nature Air tick-

ets online, over the phone, and at most travel agencies in Costa Rica. Reserve Macaw Air tickets by e-mail or by phone.

■TIP➔During the low season, Nature Air's Adventure Pass offers unlimited domestic flights for one ($274) or two ($384) weeks.

Charter flights within Costa Rica are not as expensive as one might think, and can be an especially good deal if you are traveling in a group of five people. If a group this size charters a small plane, the price per person will be only slightly more than taking a regularly scheduled domestic flight, and you can set your own departure time. The country has dozens of airstrips that are accessible only by charter planes. Charter planes are most often booked through tour operators, travel agents, or remote lodges. Most charter planes are smaller than domestic commercial planes.

■TIP→ **Don't book a domestic flight for the day you arrive in or leave Costa Rica;** connections will be extremely tight, if possible at all, and you'll be at the mercy of temperamental weather and delays.

Airline Contacts **Air Canada** (☎888/247–2262 in North America, 506/2243–1860 in Costa Rica ⊕www.aircanada.com). **American Airlines** (☎800/433–7300, 506/2257–1266 in Costa Rica ⊕www.aa.com). **Continental Airlines** (☎800/231–0856 for international reservations, 0800/2044–0005 in Costa Rica ⊕www.continental.com). **Delta Airlines** (☎800/241–4141 for international reservations, 0800/2056–2002 in Costa Rica ⊕www.delta.com). **Frontier Airlines** (☎800/432–1359 for international reservations ⊕www.frontierairlines.com). **Iberia** (☎506/2232–3246 or 2431–5633 in Costa Rica ⊕www.iberia.com). **Martinair** (☎800/627–8462 in U.S., 506/2232–3246 in Costa Rica ⊕www.martinairusa.com).

Northwest (☎800/225–2525 in U.S. ⊕www.nwa.com). **Spirit Air** (☎800/772–7117 in the U.S., 0800/2011–1103 in Costa Rica ⊕www.spiritair.com). **United Airlines** (☎800/538–2929 for international reservations, 0800/2052–1243 in Costa Rica ⊕www.united.com). **US Airways** (☎800/622–1015 for international reservations, 0800/2011–0793 in Costa Rica ⊕www.usairways.com).

Domestic & Charter Airlines **Aerobell Air Charter** (☎506/2290–0000 in Costa Rica ⊕www.aerobell.com). **Macaw Air** (☎506/8364–1223 in Costa Rica ⊕www.macawair.com). **Nature Air** (☎800/235–9272 in North America, 506/2299–6000 in Costa Rica ⊕www.natureair.com). **SANSA** (☎506/2290–4100 or 2221–9414 in Costa Rica ⊕www.flysansa.com).

■ BY BUS

Tica Bus has daily runs between Costa Rica and Panama or Nicaragua; Transnica has daily service between Costa Rica and

Granada and Managua. We recommend choosing Tica Bus if at all possible, but Transnica is acceptable in a pinch. Both companies offer "executive" service on Managua–Costa Rica runs: for about $7–$12 more you'll get breakfast and a little more legroom (on Transnica), but also a 3 AM departure time (Tica Bus). Both companies have comfortable, air-conditioned coaches with videos and onboard toilets, and help with border procedures. *For border-crossing details, see Chapters 4 and 7.* All Costa Rican towns are connected by regular bus service. Bus service in Costa Rica is reliable, comprehensive, and inexpensive; fares for long-distance routes are usually $3–$8 one way. Buses between major cities are modern and air-conditioned, but once you get into the rural areas, you may get a converted school bus without air-conditioning. The kind of bus you get is the luck of the draw (no upgrades here). Bus travel in Costa Rica is formal, meaning no pigs or chickens inside and no people or luggage on the roof. On longer routes, buses stop midway at modest restaurants. Near the ends of their runs many non-express buses turn into large taxis, dropping passengers off one by one at their destinations; to save time, take a *directo* (express) bus. Be prepared for bus-company employees and bus drivers to speak Spanish only.

The main inconvenience of buses is that you usually have to return to San José to travel between outlying regions and that long-distance service is much slower than flying. For example, a bus from San José to the Osa Peninsula is nine hours or more, whereas the flight is one hour. Shorter distances reduce the difference—the bus to Quepos is 3½ hours and the flight 30 minutes—and in those cases the huge price difference might be worth the extra hours of travel. There is no main bus station in San José; buses leave from a variety of departure points depending on the region they serve.

TIP Don't put your belongings in the overhead bin unless you have to, and if you do, keep your eye on them. If anyone—even someone who looks like a bus employee—offers to put your luggage on the bus or in the luggage compartment underneath for you, politely decline. If you must put your luggage underneath the bus, get off quickly when you arrive to retrieve it.

Many visitors choose the more convenient (but more expensive) alternative of booking a private shuttle van (⇨ *Shuttle-Van Services, below*) or hiring a private driver (⇨ *By Car*). Both options are still cheaper than flying in most cases. Costa Rica Shuttle specializes in private transfers; for groups of five to six, the rates are comparable or even cheaper than scheduled buses.

Bus companies don't have printed bus schedules to give out, although departure times may be printed on a sign at the bus company's office and ticket window. Busline phones are usually busy or go unanswered. The schedules and prices we list are accurate at this writing, but change frequently. **TIP** For up-to-date information, go to the bus station a day before your departure. The ICT tourist office (⇨ *Visitor Information below*) hands out bus schedules and provides a PDF version on its Web site, but this should be used as only a rough guide, as it is updated infrequently. Hotel employees can usually give you the information you need.

Buses usually depart and arrive on time; they may even leave a few minutes before the scheduled departure time if full.

Tickets are sold at bus stations and on the buses themselves; reservations aren't accepted, and you must pay in person with cash. If you pay on the bus, be sure to have loose change and small bills handy; avoid paying with a 10,000 colón bill. Buses to popular beach and mountain destinations often sell out on weekends and the days before and after a holiday. It's also difficult to get tick-

ets back to San José on Sunday afternoon. Some companies won't sell you a return ticket from the departure point; especially during the peak season, make sure the first thing you do upon arrival is buy your ticket back. Sometimes tickets include seat numbers, which are usually printed on the tops of the chairs. Smoking is not permitted on buses.

Two private bus companies, Gray Line Tours Fantasy Bus and Interbus, travel to the most popular tourist destinations in modern, air-conditioned vans. Interbus vans usually seat seven people, and coaches can also be reserved for large groups; Gray Line vans seat 14 to 28 people. Be sure to double-check information that is listed on the Web site—published prices may not be accurate and routes are not always running. This service costs about $25–$45 one way, but can take hours off your trip. Gray Line has a Fantasy Bus Pass ($115) good for unlimited travel for one week, reservations need to be made 24 hours in advance. Interbus offers three- to seven-trip Flexipasses; prices range from $139 to $235 and the passes are good for one month. Hotel-to-hotel service is offered as long as your lodging is on the route; if you're heading off the beaten track, it's a hotel-to-nearest-hotel service.

Bus Information Tica Bus (✉ 200 m north and 100 m west of Torre Mercedes, Paseo Colón, San José ☎ 2221–0006 ⊕ www.ticabus. com). **Transnica** (✉ C. 22, Avdas. 3–5, San José ☎ 2223–4123 or 2223–4242 ✉ Restaurante El Rancho, Liberia ☎ 2665–6060 ⊕ www. transnica.com).

Shuttle-Van Services Costa Rica Shuttle (☎ 2289–9509 ⊕ www.costaricashuttle.com). **Gray Line Tourist Bus** (☎ 2232–3681 or 2220–2126 ⊕ www.graylinecostarica.com). **Interbus** (☎ 2283–5573 ⊕ www.interbus online.com).

BUS COMPANY	SERVES	COSTS	PHONE	WEB
Gray Line Tourist Bus	Domestic destinations, Granada, Managua	$33–$43, $10 per surfboard	2232–3681 or 2220–2126	www.grayline costarica.com
Interbus	Domestic destinations	$25–$45, $10 per surfboard	2283–5573	www.interbus online.com
Tica Bus	Major Central American hubs	$13 to Nicaragua, $20 for "executive" service	2221–0006	www.ticabus.com
Transnica	Managua, Granada	$13 to Nicaragua, $25 for "executive" service	2223–4123	www.transnica. com

▌ BY CAR

Hiring a car with a driver makes the most sense for sightseeing in and around San José. You can also usually hire a taxi driver to ferry you around; most will stick to the meter, which at this writing will tick at a rate of about $5 per hour for the time the driver is waiting for you. At $75–$120 per day plus the driver's food, hiring a driver for areas outside the San José area costs almost the same as renting a 4WD, but is more expensive for multi-day trips, when you'll also have to pay for the driver's room. Some drivers are also knowledgeable guides; others just drive. Unless they're driving large passenger vans for established companies, it's doubtful that drivers have any special training or licensing. Hotels can usually direct you to trusted drivers; you can also find recommendations on fodors.com. Alternatively, Alamo (⇨ below) provides professional car-and-driver services for minimum three-day rentals (available May–November only). You pay $75 on top of the rental fee, plus the driver's food and lodging. Costa Rica Shuttle (⇨ By Bus) provides drivers on similar terms for $130 per day.

Most rental companies have an office close to Juan Santamaría Airport where you can drop off your car (even if you picked up the car at another San José

branch) and provide transport to get you to your flight. Leave yourself a half hour for the return time and shuttle.

GASOLINE

There is no self-service gas in Costa Rica; 24-hour stations are generally available only in San José or on the Pan-American Highway. Most other stations are open from about 7 to 7, some until midnight. It is not customary to tip attendants.

Gas prices are fixed by Public Services Regulatory Authority (ARESEP), and gas stations around the country are legally bound to stick to the determined prices. Try to fill your tank in cities—gas is more expensive (and more likely to be dirty) at informal fill-up places in rural areas, where gas stations can be few and far between. Major credit cards are widely accepted. Ask the attendant if you want a *factura* (receipt). Regular unleaded gasoline is called *regular* and high-octane unleaded is called *super*. Gas is sold by the liter. The cost at this writing is 86¢ per liter ($3.27 per gallon) for regular and 92¢ per liter ($3.50 per gallon) for super.

PARKING

On-street parking is scarce in downtown San José; where you find it, you'll also find *guachimanes* (informal, usually self-appointed guards). They freely admit they don't get paid enough to actually get involved if someone tries something with your car, but it's best to give them a couple of hundred colones per hour anyway. In centers such as San José, Alajuela, and Heredia, you'll find several signs with a large E in a red circle, and the words con boleto (with a ticket). These tickets can be bought for ½ hour (190 colones), 1 hour (375 colones) or 2 hours (750 colones) at the respective municipal hall. Popular areas attract *guachimanes who hawk these tickets on-site; in other areas you're out of luck. It's a 3,700-colón fine (about $7) if you're caught in one of these spaces without a ticket.* Safer and ubiquitous are the public lots (*parqueos*), which average flat rates of approximately $1.25 per hour. Most are open late, especially near hopping nightspots or theaters, but check beforehand. Never leave anything inside the car. It is illegal to park in the zones marked by yellow curb paint, or in front of garage doors or driveways, usually marked with signs reading No Estacionar (No Parking). Downtown parking laws are strictly enforced; the fine for illegal parking is 5,000 colones (about $10). However, the city center's narrow throughways are often bottlenecked by "waiting" cars and taxis—double-parked with someone in the car. Despite the cacophonic honking, this is largely tolerated. Outside of the main hubs of the Central Valley, parking rules are far more lax, and *guachimanes,* private walled, and guarded hotel or restaurant parking are the rule, with few public lots.

RENTAL CARS

When you reserve a car, ask about cancellation penalties, taxes, drop-off charges (if you're planning to pick up the car in one city and leave it in another), and surcharges (for being under or over a certain age, for additional drivers, or for driving across state or country borders or beyond a specific distance from your point of rental). All these things can add substantially to your costs. Request car seats and extras such as a GPS when you book.

Rates are sometimes—but not always—better if you book in advance or reserve through a rental agency's Web site. There are other reasons to book ahead, though: for popular destinations, during busy times of the year, or to ensure that you get certain types of cars (vans, SUVs, exotic sports cars).

■TIP➜**If you're planning to go to only one or two major areas, taking a shuttle van or a domestic flight is usually a better and cheaper option than driving.** Renting is a good choice if you're destination hopping, staying at a hotel that's a trek to town, or going well off the beaten path. Car trips to northern Guanacaste from San José can take an entire day, so flying is probably better if you don't have long to spend in the country. Flying is definitely better than driving for visiting the South Pacific.

Many travelers shy away from renting a car in Costa Rica, if only for fear of the road conditions, acknowledged as a crisis by the government in 2005. Indeed, this is not an ideal place to drive: in San José traffic is bad and car theft is rampant (look for guarded parking lots or hotels with lots); in rural areas roads are often unpaved or potholed—and tires aren't usually covered by the basic insurance. And Ticos are reckless drivers—with one of the highest accident rates in the world. But though driving can be a challenge, it's a great way to explore certain regions, especially Guanacaste, the Northern Plains, and the Caribbean coast (apart from Tortuguero and Barra del Colorado). Keep in mind that mountains and poor road conditions make most trips longer than you'd normally expect.

A standard vehicle is fine for most destinations, but a *doble-tracción* (4WD) is often essential to reach the remoter parts of the country, especially during the rainy season. Even in the dry season, you must have a 4WD vehicle to reach Monteverde and some destinations in Guanacaste. The big 4WD vehicles, such as a Suzuki Grand

Vitara, can cost roughly twice as much as an economy car, but compact 4WDs, such as the Daihatsu Terios, are more reasonable, and should be booked well in advance. Agencies may try to bump you up a category—stay firm. Most cars in Costa Rica have manual transmissions. ■TIP➔**Specify when making the reservation if you want an automatic transmission; it usually costs about $5 more per day, but some companies such as Alamo and Hertz don't charge extra.** Larger, more expensive automatic Montero and Sorento models are also available. If you plan to rent any kind of vehicle between December 15 and January 3, or during Holy Week (the week leading up to Easter)—when most Costa Ricans are on vacation—reserve several months ahead of time.

Costa Rica has around 30 car-rental firms. Most local firms are affiliated with international car-rental chains and offer the same guarantees and services as their branches abroad; local company Tricolor gets high marks from travelers on our Fodor's Forum. At least a dozen rental offices line San José's Paseo Colón; most large hotels and Juan Santamaría Airport have representatives. Renting in or near San José is by far the easiest way to go. It's getting easier to rent outside of San José, particularly on the Pacific coast. Several rental companies have set up branches in Liberia, Quepos, Jacó, Tamarindo, and La Fortuna. In most other places across the country it's either impossible or very difficult and expensive to rent a car.

Car seats are compulsory for children under four years old, and can be rented for about $5 per day; reserve in advance. Rental cars may not be driven across borders to Nicaragua and Panama. For a $50 fee, National and Alamo will let you drop off a Costa Rican rental car at the Nicaragua border and provide you with a Nicaraguan rental on the other side. Seat-belt use is compulsory in the front seat. Fuel-efficiency measures restrict certain cars from San José's city center during rush

hours once a week, according to the final license-plate number (e.g., plates that end in 9 are restricted on Fridays). However, this does not apply to rental cars; if you are stopped, do not pay a bribe. To rent a car, you need a driver's license, a valid passport, and a credit card. The minimum renter age varies; agencies such as Economy, Budget, and Alamo rent to anyone over 21; Avis sets the limit at 23, Hertz at 25. Though it's rare, some agencies have a maximum age limit.

High-season rates in San José begin at $45 a day and $300 a week for an economy car with air-conditioning, manual transmission, unlimited mileage, plus obligatory insurance; but rates fluctuate considerably according to demand, season, and company. Rates for a 4WD vehicle during high season are $70–$90 a day and $450–$550 per week. Often companies will also require a $1,000 deposit, payable by credit card. It's getting easier to rent a vehicle with automatic transmission, but some companies still charge about $5 more per day; reserve well in advance and know that options are more limited.

Cars picked up at or returned to Juan Santamaría Airport incur a 12% surcharge. Arrangements can be made to pick up cars directly at the Liberia airport, but a range of firms have offices nearby and transport you from the airport free of charge—and with no surcharge for an airport pickup. Check cars thoroughly for damage before you sign the rental contract. Even tough-looking 4WD vehicles should be coddled. ■TIP➔**The charges levied by rental companies for damage—no matter how minor—are outrageous even by U.S. or European standards.**

One-way service surcharges are $50–$150, depending on the drop-off point; National allows travelers free car drop-off at any of its offices with a minimum three-day rental. To avoid a hefty refueling fee, fill the tank just before you turn in the car. It's almost never a deal to buy the tank of gas that's in the car when you rent it; the understanding is that you'll return it empty, but some fuel usually remains. Additional drivers are about $5–$10 per day if there is any charge at all. Almost all agencies, with the exception of Budget Rent-a-Car, have cell-phone rental; prices range between $2 and $6 per day, with national per-minute costs between 50¢ and $2.

International driving permits (IDPs), which are used only in conjunction with a valid driver's license and translate your license into 10 languages, are not necessary in Costa Rica. Your own driver's license is good for the length of your initial tourist visa. You must carry your passport, or a copy of it with the entry stamp, to prove when you entered the country.

Automobile Associations U.S.: **American Automobile Association** (AAA ☎315/797–5000 ⊕www.aaa.com); most contact with the organization is through state and regional members. **National Automobile Club** (☎650/294–7000 ⊕www.thenac.com); membership is open to California residents only.

Major Agencies Alamo (☎800/570–0671, 506/2233–7733 in Costa Rica ⊕www.alamocostarica.com). **Avis** (☎506/2293–2222 in Costa Rica ⊕www.avis.co.cr). **Budget** (☎800/244–6877, 506/2436–2000 in Costa Rica ⊕www.budget.co.cr). **Dollar** (☎866/746–7765 in North America, 506/2443–2950 in Costa Rica ⊕www.dollarcostarica.com). **Hertz** (☎800/850–7576 in North America, 506/2221–1818 in Costa Rica ⊕www.costaricarentacar.net). **National Car Rental** (☎778/227–7368 in North America, 506/2242–7878 in Costa Rica ⊕www.natcar.com).

Local Agencies Economy (☎877/326–7368 in North America, 506/2299–2000 in Costa Rica ⊕www.economyrentacar.com). **Tricolor** (☎800/949–0234 in North America, 506/2257–1158 in Costa Rica ⊕www.tricolorcarrental.com).

ROAD CONDITIONS

San José is terribly congested during weekday morning and afternoon rush hours (7–9 AM and 4–6 PM). Avoid returning to the city on Sunday evening, when traffic to San José from the Pacific coast beaches backs up for hours. The winding Pan-American Highway south of the capital is notorious for long snakes of traffic stuck behind slow-moving trucks. Look out for potholes, even in the smoothest sections of the best roads, whether you're in San José or in the countryside. Also watch for unmarked speed bumps where you'd least expect them, particularly on rural main thoroughfares. During the rainy season roads are in much worse shape. Check with your destination before setting out; roads, especially in Limón Province, are prone to washouts and landslides.

San José has many one-way streets and traffic circles. Streets in the capital are narrow. Pedestrians are supposed to have the right-of-way but do not in reality, so be alert when walking. The local driving style is erratic and aggressive but not fast, because road conditions don't permit too much speed. Frequent fender benders tie up traffic. Keep your windows rolled up in the center of the city, because thieves may reach into your car at stoplights and snatch your purse, jewelry, and so on.

Signage is notoriously bad, but improving. Watch carefully for *No Hay Paso* (Do Not Enter) signs; one-way streets are common, both in small towns as well as in San José, and it's not unusual for a street to transform from a two-way to a one-way, forcing a not-so-obvious turn. Streetlights are often out of service and key signs missing or knocked down because of accidents.

Outside of San José you'll run into long stretches of unpaved road. Frequent hazards in the countryside are potholes, landslides during the rainy season, and cattle on the roads. Drunk drivers are a hazard throughout the country on weekend nights. Driving at night is not recommended anyway, since roads are poorly lighted and many don't have painted center lines or shoulder lines.

ROADSIDE EMERGENCIES

Costa Rica has no highway emergency service organization. In Costa Rica 911 is the nationwide number for accidents. Traffic police are scattered around the country, but Costa Ricans are very good about stopping for people with car trouble. Whatever happens, don't move the car after an accident, even if a monstrous traffic jam ensues. Call 911 first if the accident is serious (nearly everyone has a cell phone here and it's almost a given that someone will offer to help). Also be sure to call the emergency number your car-rental agency has given you. For fender benders, contact the Traffic Police, who will try to locate a person to assist you in English—but don't count on it. If you don't speak Spanish, you may want to contact the rental agency before trying the police. If your own car is stolen, call the Judicial Investigative Police (OIJ, pronounced oh-ee-hota), which will find an English-speaking representative to assist you.

Emergency Services Ambulance and Police (☎911). Judicial Investigative Police (OIJ ☎2295–3318). Traffic Police (☎800/872–6748).

RULES OF THE ROAD

Driving is on the right side of the road in Costa Rica. The highway speed limit is usually 90 kph (54 mph), which drops to 60 kph (36 mph) in residential areas. In towns limits range from 30 to 50 kph (18 to 31 mph). Speed limits are enforced in all regions of the country. Seat belts are required, and an awareness campaign has increased enforcement. *Alto* means "stop" and *ceda* means "yield." Right turns on red are permitted except where signs indicate otherwise, but in San José this is usually not possible because of one-way streets and pedestrian crossings.

Local drunk driving laws are strict. You'll get nailed with a 10,000-colón fine if you're caught driving in a "pre-drunk" state (blood alcohol levels of 0.049%–0.099%). If your level is higher than that, you'll pay 20,000 colones, the car will be confiscated, and your license taken away. Policemen who stop drivers for speeding and drunk driving are often looking for payment on the spot—essentially a bribe. Whether you're guilty or not, you'll get a ticket if you don't give in. Asking for a ticket instead of paying the bribe discourages corruption and does not compromise your safety. You can generally pay the ticket at your car-rental company, which will remit it on your behalf.

The Óscar Arias administration has taken a hard line on Costa Rica's dreadful roadway safety record—one of the world's worst. At this writing, a bill to drastically hike penalties for traffic violations was still awaiting debate in the Legislative Assembly. If the proposal is approved, the fines for speeding and drunk driving would skyrocket from 20,000 colones ($50) to 280,000 colones ($560), among other increases. Car seats are required for children ages four and under, but car-seat laws are not rigorously enforced. Many Tico babies and children ride on their parents' laps. Children over 12 are allowed in the front seat. Drivers are prohibited from using handheld cell phones, but this is almost never enforced, and distracted chatters are the rule.

Fuel-efficiency measures restrict certain cars from the city center during rush hour once a week, according to the final license-plate number (e.g., plates that end in 9 are restricted on Fridays). This does not apply to rental cars; if you are stopped, don't pay a bribe. ■TIP➔**There are plenty of questionable drivers on Costa Rican highways; be prepared for harebrained passing on blind corners, tailgating, and failing to signal.** Watch, too, for two-lane roads that feed into one-lane bridges with specified rights-of-way.

There's not always a method to the driving madness, but locals use two tactics that are surprisingly effective. Stick your left hand out the window and wave slightly if you want to merge left (get your passenger to do it to maneuver to the right), and flick your lights if you want oncoming traffic to slow down so you can turn left. Hone your reflexes: drivers behind you will honk at you a millisecond before the light turns green. Green traffic lights flash just before turning to yellow; always look carefully, as drivers regularly speed through lights that have long since turned red.

BY CRUISE SHIP

The quality of shore excursions at Costa Rica's Pacific ports (Caldera, Quepos, Golfito) and Limón, on the Caribbean, has skyrocketed in past years, as operators scramble to serve the influx of cruisers that stop in, usually on their way to or from the Panama Canal. Most large cruises stop in the country only once, although some make stops on both coasts. Small-scale ships, such as Windjammer Barefoot Cruises (122 berths) offer more time in Costa Rica. Windstar Cruises (capacity for 145), Seabourn (60 guests), and highly recommended, conservation-minded Lindblad (60 guests) offer Costa Rica–focused cruises along the Pacific coast.

Cruise Lines **Lindblad** (☎800/397–3348 ⊕www.expeditions.com). **Seabourn Cruise Line** (☎305/463–3000 or 800/929–9391 ⊕www.seabourn.com). **Windjammer Barefoot Cruises** (☎305/672–6453 or 800/327–2601 ⊕www.windjammer.com). **Windstar Cruises** (☎206/2225–3198 or 800/258–7245 ⊕www.windstarcruises.com).

BY TAXI

Taxis are cheap and your best bet for getting around San José. Just about every driver is friendly and eager to use a few English words to tell you about a cousin or sister in New Jersey; however, cabbies truly conversant in English are scarce. Most are knowledgeable, but given the haphazard address system, may cheerfully engage passersby or other taxi drivers to find your destination. Tipping is not expected, but a good idea when you've had some extra help.

Cabs are red, usually with a yellow light on top. To hail one, extend your hand and wave it at about hip height. If it's available, the driver will often flick his headlights before pulling over. Cabs can be scarce when it's raining or during rush hour. The city is dotted with *paradas de taxi,* taxi lineups where you stand the best chance of grabbing one. Two of the most convenient are north of the *Parque Central* and at the east end of the central pedestrian walkway. Your hotel can usually call you a reputable taxi or private car service, and when you're out to dinner or on the town, the restaurant or disco can just as easily call you a cab—it's much easier than trying to hail one on the street in the wee hours, and safer, too.

■ TIP ➡ Taxi drivers are infamous for "not having change." If it's just a few hundred colones, you may as well round up. If it's a lot, ask them to drive to a store or gas station where you can make change. They'll often miraculously come up with the difference, or wait patiently while you get it. To avoid this situation, never use a 10,000-colón bill in a taxi, and avoid paying with 5,000-colón bills unless you've run up almost that much in fares.

At this writing, the meter starts at 405 colones for the first kilometer, ticking off 380 colones per additional kilometer. Technically this system applies throughout the country, but rural and unofficial cabs often use their odometers to creatively calculate fares. Manuel Antonio drivers are notorious for overcharging. It's illegal, but taxis charge up to double for hotel pickups or fares that take them out of the province (such as San José to Alajuela or vice versa). Ask the manager at your hotel about the going rate for the destination to which you're heading. Drivers have a fairly standard list of off-the-meter illegal fares.

In the capital there's usually no reason to take the risk with an unofficial taxi (*pirata*), but they are often the only option outside main hubs. See the regional chapters for recommended drivers, or check with your hotel or restaurant for reliable service.

It's always a good idea to make a note of the cab number (painted in a yellow triangle on the door), and sit in the backseat for safety.

▌ BY TRAIN

The earthquake in 1991 wreaked havoc on the country's century-old rail links, and service was completely suspended in 1995. Revived interest in commuter trains as a solution to the city's traffic snarls has been hit-and-miss. The only regular route crosses San José east to west and is of little use to travelers.

More popular is the Tico Train, a tourist day trip that leaves from the Pacific station in southern San José to the Pacific port of Caldera. Trains leave Saturday and Sunday at 7 AM, returning by 8:30 PM ($39 per passenger over 4 years old). Fueled as much by nostalgia as hydrocarbons, the scenic trip (4 hours each way) follows a historic route; passengers are serenaded by a strolling guitar player, given traditional snacks, and free to wander about on a five-hour beach stop.

Information **Tico Train Tour to Caldera** (☎ 506/2233–3300 in Costa Rica ⊕ www. ticotraintour.com).

ON THE GROUND

■ ACCOMMODATIONS

A number of Web sites help you through the lodging search. Some budget options can be found through Hostelling International *(⇨Hostels, below)*. Low-end alternatives are often referred to as *cabinas* whether they offer a cement cigar-box motel or free-standing rustic rooms. Most have private rooms, cold-water cement showers, fans instead of air-conditioning, limited—if any—secure parking or storage, and may share bathrooms. Owners tend to be Costa Rican. Often without Web sites, e-mail, or links to major agencies, these hotels tend to follow a first-come, first-served booking policy. They may have room during peak seasons when mid- or upper-end options are booked solid.

Mid-range options include boutique hotels, tasteful bungalows, bed-and-breakfasts, and downtown casino hotels. Those in the hotter beach areas may not have hot-water showers. Many have pools, Internet access, and meal options. They tend to be foreign-owned and, with the exception of the casinos, have personalized service. Because they're generally small, you may have to book one or two months ahead, and up to six months in the high season. Booking through an association or agency can significantly reduce the time you spend scanning the Internet, but you can often get a better deal and negotiate longer-stay or low-season discounts. The Costa Rican Hotel Association has online search and booking capabilities. ICT provides hotel lists searchable by star category. Costa Rica Travel Review lists and rates properties and provides a number of links.

High-end accommodations can be found almost everywhere. They range from luxury tents to exquisite hotels and villa rentals, and are often more secluded. You'll find all the amenities you expect at such areas, with one notable exception: the roads and routes to even five-star villas can be atrocious. This category is sometimes booked up to a year in advance for Christmas, and during this season you may only be able to book through agents or central reservations offices. Resorts are generally one of two kinds: luxurious privileged gateways to the best of the country (such as Punta Islita) or generic budget all-inclusives (such as the Barceló) that probably run counter to what you're coming to Costa Rica for. General local consensus is that the Four Seasons hotel is in a category unto itself, unmatched in pomp and price anywhere in the country.

Several chain hotels have franchises in Costa Rica, leaning toward the generic and all-inclusive. The upside is that they are rarely booked solid, so you can always fall back on one in a worst-case scenario, and they often have member discounts.

Nature lodges and hotels in the South Pacific (where restaurants aren't an option) may be less expensive than they initially appear, as the price of a room usually includes three hearty meals a day, and sometimes guided hikes. These, and other remote accommodations, may not have daily Internet access even though they have a Web site: be patient if you're attempting to book directly. Since many of the hotels are remote and have an eco-friendly approach (even to luxury), air-conditioning, in-room telephones, and TVs are exceptions to the rule. Consider how isolated you want to be; some rural and eco-lodges are miles from neighbors and other services and have few rainy-day diversions.

The ICT's voluntary "green leaf" rating system evaluates establishments in terms of sustainable-tourism criteria; a detailed description of the program and a search function to find lodging by sustainability level can be found at ⊕*www.turismo-sostenible.co.cr*.

■TIP➜Most hotels, especially those in San José, require that you reconfirm your reservation 24 to 48 hours before you arrive. If you don't reconfirm, you may find yourself without a room.

The lodgings we list are Costa Rica's cream of the crop in each price category. We always list the facilities that are available, but we don't specify whether they cost extra; when pricing accommodations, always ask what's included and what costs extra. Properties are assigned price categories based on the range from the least-expensive standard double room at high season (excluding holidays) to the most expensive. Keep in mind that hotel prices we list exclude 16.4% service and tax.

At Costa Rica's popular beach and mountain resorts reserve well in advance for the dry season (mid-December–April everywhere except the Caribbean, which has a short September–October "dry" season). During the rainy season (May–mid-December except on the Caribbean coast, where it's almost always rainy) most hotels drop their rates considerably, which sometimes sends them into a lower price category than the one we indicate.

■TIP➜If you're having trouble finding a hotel that isn't completely booked, consider contacting a tour operator who can arrange your entire trip. Since they reserve blocks of rooms far in advance, you might have better luck.

Most hotels and other lodgings require you to give your credit-card details before they will confirm your reservation. If you don't feel comfortable e-mailing this information, ask if you can fax it (some places even prefer faxes). However you book, get confirmation in writing and have a copy of it handy when you check in.

Be sure you understand the hotel's cancellation policy. Some places allow you to cancel without any kind of penalty—even if you prepaid to secure a discounted rate—if you cancel at least 24 hours in advance. Others require you to cancel a week in advance or penalize you the cost of one night. Small inns and B&Bs are most likely to require you to cancel far in advance. Most hotels allow children under a certain age to stay in their parents' room at no extra charge, but others charge for them as extra adults; find out the cutoff age for discounts.

■TIP➜Hotels operate on the European Plan (EP, no meals) unless we specify that they use the Breakfast Plan (BP, with full breakfast), Continental Plan (CP, continental breakfast), Full American Plan (FAP, all meals), or Modified American Plan (MAP, breakfast and dinner), or are all-inclusive (AI, all meals and most activities).

Lodging Resources **Costa Rica** Travel Review(⊕www.costaricatravelreview.com).

Costa Rican Hotel Association (☎506/2248–0990 in Costa Rica ⊕www.costaricanhotels.com). **Instituto Costarricense de Turismo** (ICT ☎866/267–8274 in North America, 506/2299–5800 in Costa Rica ⊕www.visitcostarica.com).

APARTMENT & HOUSE RENTALS

Rental houses are now common all over Costa Rica, and are particularly popular in the Pacific coast destinations of Manuel Antonio, Tamarindo, Ocotal, and Jacó. Furnished rentals accommodate a crowd or a family, often for less and at a higher comfort level. Generally properties are owned by individual owners or consortiums, most of them based in the United States with house managers in Costa Rica. Resort communities with villa-style lodgings are also growing. Nosara Home Page lists apartments and villas on the Nicoya Peninsula; Villas International has an extensive list of properties in Quepos and Tamarindo. For the southern Nicoya Peninsula check

Costa Rica Beach Rentals. The House of Rentals, a Century 21 affiliate, arranges houses and condos in the Flamingo and Potrero areas.

Contacts **Century 21/House of Rentals** (506/2654–5161 in Costa Rica, 877/661–2060 from the U.S. www.century 21costarica.net). **Costa Rica Beach Rentals** (506/2640–0065 www.costarica-beach rentals.com). **Nosara Home Page** (506/ 2682–0153 www.nosarabeachrentals.com).

Villas & Apartments Abroad (212/213–6435 in the U.S., 800/433–3020 www. vaanyc.com). **Villas Caribe** (800/645–7498 www.villascaribe.com).

Villas International (415/499–9490 in the U.S., 800/221–2260 www.villasintl.com).

BED & BREAKFASTS

A number of quintessential B&Bs—small and homey—are clustered in the Central Valley, generally offering hearty breakfasts and friendly inside information for $50 to $70 per night. You'll also find them scattered through the rest of the country, mixed in with other self-titled B&Bs that range from small cabins in the mountains to luxurious boutique hotel–style digs in northern Guanacaste.

Reservation Services **Bed & Breakfast.com** (512/322–2710 or 800/462–2632 www. bedandbreakfast.com) also sends out an online newsletter. **Bed & Breakfast Inns Online** (615/868–1946 or 800/215–7365 www. bbonline.com). **Pamela Lanier's Bed and Breakfasts, Inns and Guesthouses International** (www.lanierbb.com).

HOME EXCHANGES

With a direct home exchange you stay in someone else's home while they stay in yours. Some outfits also deal with vacation homes, so you're not actually staying in someone's full-time residence, just their vacant weekend place.

A handful of home exchanges are available; this involves an initial small registration fee and you'll have to plan ahead. It's an excellent way to immerse yourself in

the true Costa Rica, particularly if you've been here before and aren't relying so heavily on the tourism support that hotels can offer. Drawbacks include restricted options and dates. Many companies list home exchanges, but we've found HomeLink International, which lists a handful of jazzy houses in Costa Rica, and Intervac to be the most reliable.

Exchange Clubs **Home Exchange.com** (800/877–8723 www.homeexchange. com); $59.95 for a one-year online listing. **HomeLink International** (800/638–3841 www.homelink.org); $80 yearly for Web-only membership; $125 includes Web access and two catalogs. **Intervac U.S.** (800/756–4663 www.intervacus.com); $78.88 for Web-only membership; $126 includes Web access and a catalog.

HOSTELS

Hostels offer bare-bones lodging at low, low prices—often in shared dorm rooms with shared baths—to people of all ages, though the primary market is young travelers, especially students. Most hostels serve breakfast; dinner and/or shared cooking facilities may also be available. In some hostels you aren't allowed to be in your room during the day, and there may be a curfew at night. Nevertheless, hostels provide a sense of community, with public rooms where travelers often gather to share stories. Many hostels are affiliated with Hostelling International (HI), an umbrella group of hostel associations with some 4,500 member properties in more than 70 countries. Other hostels are completely independent and may be nothing more than a really cheap hotel.

Membership in any HI association, open to travelers of all ages, allows you to stay in HI-affiliated hostels at member rates. One-year membership is about $28 for adults; hostels charge about $10–$30 per night. Members have priority if the hostel is full; they're also eligible for discounts around the world, even on rail and bus travel in some countries.

Costa Rica has a sprinkling of youth hostels and hotels affiliated with Hostelling International; most are tantamount to inexpensive hotels, appropriate for families. Youth-oriented Hostal Toruma in San José, part of the Costarrican [sic] Hostel Network, is an exception, as is Hostel Playa Tamarindo; the former offers private rooms as well as dorms, and the latter has surf racks. Tranquilo Backpackers, Gaudy's Backpackers, and Hostel Costa Linda also lean toward boisterous, younger guests.

Information **Gaudy's Backpackers** (✉ Avda. 5, Cs. 36–38, Sabana Norte, San José ☎ 506/2258–2937 in Costa Rica ⊕ www.backpacker.co.cr). **Hostal Toruma** (✉ Avda. Central, Cs. 29–31, Barrio La California, San José ☎ 506/2234–8186 in Costa Rica). **Hostel Costa Linda** (✉ 100 m before traffic circle, Manuel Antonio ☎ 506/2777–0304 in Costa Rica ✎ costalindamicha@yahoo.de). **Hostelling International—USA** (☎ 301/495–1240 in the U.S. ⊕ www.hiusa.org).

Hostel Playa Tamarindo (✉ Next to Hotel Pasatiempo, Tamarindo ☎ 506/2653–0944 in Costa Rica ⊕ www.tamarindobeachhostel.com). **Tranquilo Backpackers** (✉ C. 7, Avdas. 9–11, Barrio Amón, San José ☎ 506/2223–3189 in Costa Rica ✉ Mal País ☎ 506/2640–0589 ⊕ www.tranquilobackpackers.com).

■ ADDRESSES

In Costa Rica addresses are usually given in terms of how many meters the place is from a landmark. Street names and building numbers are not commonly used. Churches, stores, even large trees that no longer exist—almost anything can be a landmark, as long as everyone knows where it is, or where it used to be. A typical address in San José is *100 metros este y 100 metros sur del Más X Menos* (100 meters east and 100 meters south from the Más X Menos supermarket). ■ TIP➔ **In towns and cities in Costa Rica, each block is assumed to be 100 meters, although some blocks may be much longer and some may be shorter. So if someone tells you to head down the road 500 meters, they mean five blocks.** Ticos, as Costa Ricans call themselves, are generally happy to help lost visitors, and they spend a lot of time describing where things are. But be warned—even if they don't know where something is, Ticos will often give uncertain or even wrong information rather than seem unhelpful; triangulated direction-asking is a must. Ask at least two, if not three, people in quick succession to avoid getting hopelessly lost. Key direction terms are: *lugar* (place), *calle* (street), *avenida* (avenue), *puente* (bridge), *piso* (floor), *edificio* (building), *cruce* (intersection), *semáforo* (traffic light), *rotonda* (traffic circle), and *cuadro* (block).

■ COMMUNICATIONS

INTERNET

Downtown San José is full of Internet cafés with high-speed connections; prices are usually less than $1 per hour. As you move away from the capital, prices rise to $2–$4 per hour and connections become slower and more unreliable. Wildly expensive satellite Internet is available at some remote, exclusive hotels. Cafés are generally good places to make international Internet calls, but expect echoes and a mediocre connection. Most major hotels have free wireless access or use of a guest Internet computer. Eateries such as Denny's, Bagelmen's, and a number of upscale cafés are also Wi-Fi friendly. Dial-up access is spotty and frustrating, but if you're desperate and have both a computer and access to a telephone line, you can buy one of RACSA's prepaid Internet cards in three amounts: 1,800 colones (5 hours), 3,550 colones (10 hours), and 5,300 colones (15 hours). Cards are sold at Kodak stores, Perimercado supermarkets, and some branches of the Banco Nacional. The cards come with the access numbers, and a help line with English-speaking operators.

Contacts Cybercafes (⊕ www.cybercafes. com) lists over 4,000 Internet cafés worldwide.

PHONES

The good news is that you can now make a direct-dial telephone call from virtually any point on earth. The bad news? You can't always do so cheaply. Calling from a hotel is almost always the most expensive option; hotels usually add huge surcharges to all calls, particularly international ones. In some countries you can phone from call centers or even the post office. Calling cards usually keep costs to a minimum, but only if you purchase them locally. And then there are mobile phones (⇨ below), which are sometimes more prevalent—particularly in the developing world—than landlines; as expensive as mobile phone calls can be, they are still usually a much cheaper option than calling from your hotel.

Domestic and international calls (aside from those to an operator) from almost all public phones require phone cards (⇨ below). Coin-operated phones exist, but are scarce.

When you are calling Costa Rica, the country code is 506.

CALLING WITHIN COSTA RICA

On March 20, 2008, all phone numbers in Costa Rica were assigned an extra number. A 2 was tacked on to the front

of all land-line numbers and an 8 was added to the front of all mobile phone numbers. In-country 800 numbers were not affected by the change.

The Costa Rican phone system is very good by the standards of other developing countries. However, phone numbers do change often. You can make local calls from any phone with a domestic calling card (⇨ Calling Cards, below). First dial 197, then the PIN on the back of your card (revealed after scratching off a protective coating), then the phone number. Some phones have a card reader on the right-hand side; swiping the card through once you've dialed 197 saves tedious keying, but the readers are hit-and-miss. There are no area codes in Costa Rica, so you only need dial a seven-digit number; without the 506 country code. Fewer and farther between are the gray coin-operated phones; posted on each are the coins accepted (it varies from phone to phone).

Dial 113 for domestic directory inquiries and 110 for domestic collect calls, usually your only option if you don't have a phone card. In both cases, cross as many fingers as you can to get an operator that speaks English; they're the exception.

CALLING OUTSIDE COSTA RICA

The country code for the United States is 1.

Internet telephony is by far the cheapest way to call home; it is a viable option in the Central Valley and major tourist hubs. For other regions or for more privacy, a pay phone using an international phone card (⇨ Calling Cards, below) is the next step up; you can also call from a pay phone using your own long-distance calling card. Dialing directly from a hotel room is very expensive, as is recruiting an international operator to connect you.

■ TIP➔ Watch out for pay phones marked CALL USA/CANADA WITH A CREDIT CARD. They are *wildly* expensive.

To call overseas directly, dial 00, then the country code (dial 1 for the U.S. and

Local Do's and Taboos

CUSTOMS OF THE COUNTRY

Ticos tend to use formal Spanish, preferring, for example, *con mucho gusto* (with much pleasure) instead of *de nada* for "you're welcome."

Ticos can be disarmingly direct; don't be surprised (or offended) if locals pick up on a physical trait and give you a nickname: *Chino* for anyone with the slightest slant to the eye, or *Gordita* if you have even an extra ounce around your hips. It's meant affectionately. In almost every other situation, a circumspect approach is advised; North American straightforwardness often comes across as abrupt here. Preceding requests with a bit of small talk (even if it's a hotel employee) goes a long way. Also, be very aware of body language and other cues—Costa Ricans don't like to say no, and will often avoid answering a question or simply say *gracias* when they really mean no.

A large number of Costa Rican men make a habit of ogling or making gratuitous comments when young women pass on the street. Women should wear a bra at all times. Family is very important in Costa Rica. It is considered polite to ask about your marital status and family—don't confuse this with prying.

The expression "Tico time" was coined for a reason. Transportation, theaters, government, and major businesses tend to stick to official schedules. Anything else is flexible, and best handled by building in a little buffer time and sliding into the tropical groove.

GREETINGS

Costa Ricans are extremely polite, quick to shake hands (light squeezes are the norm) and place a kiss on the right cheek (meaning you need to bear left when going in for the peck). The formal pronoun *usted* (you) is used almost exclusively; the slangier *vos* is thrown about in informal settings and among close or young friends and relatives.

SIGHTSEEING

As you would anywhere, dress and behave respectfully when visiting churches. In churches men and women should not wear shorts, sleeveless shirts, or sandals; women should wear skirts below the knee. Bathing suits, short shorts, and other skimpy attire are inappropriate city wear, but tend to be the uniform in beach towns; even here, however, cover up for all but the most informal restaurants. Locals tend to dress somewhat formally, with women favoring clothes that show off their curves. Beggars are not a major problem, but if you're in San José at all you'll come across a few. It's always better to give to an established organization, but the safety net for Costa Ricans with disabilities is riddled with holes, so even a couple of hundred colones will be appreciated. Simply keep walking past the addicts—they will almost always just move on to the next person. A couple of savvy panhandlers speak excellent English and will try to draw you into conversation with a sob story about a lost passport. Keep walking. Banks and other offices allow pregnant women and the elderly to move immediately to the front of the line, and this respect is carried over to other establishments and crowded buses. If you're in a crowd and need to step in front of them, murmur *con permiso* (excuse me).

OUT ON THE TOWN

To catch a waiter's attention, wave discreetly or say *"Disculpe, señor"* (or *señora* for women); best to leave the finger-snapping to the locals. For the bill, ask for *"La cuenta, por favor."* Pockets of no-smoking sections are growing, especially in the swankier restaurants, but smoking is still tolerated in many public spaces. It's prohibited in government buildings, cinemas, theaters, other public entertainment venues, and public transport. Excessive displays of affection draw frowns, clearly lost on the gaggles of lip-locked couples. Locals tend to dress up to go out, whatever the activity; a snazzy (but not too dressy) outfit will serve you well in San José. If invited to someone's home, bring a gift such as flowers or a bottle of wine or some trinket from your home country. If offered food at someone's home, accept it and eat it even if you aren't hungry. You will be offered coffee and should accept, although it's not necessary to finish the whole cup.

LANGUAGE

One of the best ways to avoid being an Ugly American is to learn a little of the local language. You need not strive for fluency; even just mastering a few basic words and terms is bound to make chatting with the locals more rewarding.

Spanish is the official language, although many tour guides and locals in heavily touristed areas speak English. You'll have a better time if you learn some basic Spanish before you go and if you bring a phrase book with you. At the very least, learn the rudiments of polite conversation—niceties such as *por favor* (please) and *gracias* (thank you) will be warmly appreciated. *For more words and*

phrases, see the Spanish glossary in the Understanding Costa Rica chapter. In the Caribbean province of Limón a creole English called Mekatelyu is widely spoken by older generations. English is understood by most everyone in these parts.

An open-ended *"Dónde está . . ."* ("Where is . . .") may result in a wall of rapid-fire Spanish. Better to avoid language as much as possible when asking for directions. You're going to have to stop often anyway, so it can be helpful to make the journey in segments: in the city, say the name of the place you want to go, and point (adding a questioning *izquierda* (left) *derecha* (right), or *directo* (straight); do this frequently, and you'll get there. On longer journeys, keep a good map handy, and use the same strategy, asking for a nearby town on your journey rather than the final destination—you're more likely to get accurate directions.

And of course, you can't go wrong with an amiable *Pura Vida*, which serves as "hello," "good-bye," "thanks," "cool," "how's it going," and all things amiable.

A phrase book and language-tape set can help get you started. *Fodor's Spanish for Travelers* (available at bookstores everywhere) is excellent.

Canada), the area code, and the number. You can make international calls from almost any phone with an international calling card purchased in Costa Rica. First dial 199, then the PIN on the back of your card (revealed after scratching off a protective coating), then dial the phone number as you would a direct long-distance call.

When requesting a calling card from your phone provider, ask specifically about calls from Costa Rica. Most 800-number cards don't work in Costa Rica. Callingcards.com is a great resource for pre-paid international calling cards. At this writing, it lists at least two calling-card companies with rates of 29¢ and 56¢ per minute for calls from Costa Rica to the United States.

You may find the local access number blocked in many hotel rooms. First ask the hotel operator to connect you. If the hotel operator balks, ask for an international operator, or dial the international operator yourself. For service in English, you'll have more luck dialing the international operator (☎175 or 116). One way to improve your odds of getting connected to your long-distance carrier is to sign up with more than one company: a hotel may block Sprint, for example, but not MCI. If all else fails, call from a pay phone.

AT&T, MCI, and Sprint access codes make calling long distance relatively convenient but can be very expensive.

To make a person-to-person direct-dial call from any phone, dial 09 (instead of 00 for a regular call), the country code for the country you're calling, and then the number. The operator will ask for the name of the person you're contacting, and billing at direct-dial rates begins only once that person comes to the phone.

Direct-dial calls to the United States and Canada are 27¢ per minute.

Access Codes **AT&T Direct** (☎0800/011–4114). **Canada Direct** (☎0800/015–1161). **MCI WorldPhone** (☎0800/012–2222). **Sprint International Access** (☎0800/013–0123).

Telephone Resources **Callingcards.com** (⊕www.callingcards.com). **International information** (☎124). **International operator** (☎175 or 116).

CALLING CARDS

Most public phones require phone cards (for local or international calls), but phone cards can also be used from any non-rotary telephone in Costa Rica, including residential phones, cell phones, and hotel phones. It's rare to be charged a per-minute rate for the mere use of the phone in a hotel.

Phone cards are sold in an array of shops, including Más X Menos supermarkets, post offices, offices of the Costa Rican Electricity Institute (ICE), and at any business displaying the gold-and-blue TARJETAS TELEFÓNICAS sign. International cards tend to be easier to find in downtown San José and in tourism areas.

Tarjetas para llamadas nacionales (domestic calling cards), are available in denominations of 500 colones and 1,000 colones. Phone-card rates are standard throughout the country, about 1¢ per minute, half that at night; a 500-colón card provides about 125 minutes of daytime landline calls. This decreases sharply if calling a cell phone; rates vary. *Tarjetas para llamadas internacionales* (international calling cards) are sold in $10, $20, 3,000-colón, and 10,000-colón amounts (denominations are inexplicably split between dollars and colones). It's harder to find the 10,000-colón cards; your best bet is to try a Fischel pharmacy or an ICE office. In busy spots, such as the Plaza de la Cultura, roaming card-hawkers abound; feel free to take advantage of the convenience—they're legit.

Some public phones accept *tarjetas chip* ("chip" cards), which record what you spend, though they're a dying breed.

■TIP→Avoid buying chip cards: they mal-function, you can use them only at the few-and-far-between chip phones, and they are sold in small denominations that are not sufficient for international calls.

MOBILE PHONES

If you have an unblocked multiband phone (some countries use different fre-quencies than what's used in the United States) and your service provider uses the world-standard GSM network (as do T-Mobile, Cingular, and Verizon), you can probably use your phone abroad. Roaming fees can be steep, however: 99¢ a minute is considered reasonable. And overseas you normally pay the toll charges for incoming calls. Most rental companies in Costa Rica do not charge for text messages.

■TIP→If you travel internationally fre-quently, save one of your old mobile phones or buy a cheap one on the Internet; ask your cell phone company to unlock it for you, and take it with you as a travel phone, buying a new SIM card with pay-as-you-go service in each destination.

If your cell phone or pager company has service to Costa Rica, you theoretically can use it here, but expect reception to be impossible in many areas of this moun-tainous country. Costa Rica works on a 1,800 MHz system—a tri-band phone is your best bet.

Most car-rental agencies have good deals on cell phones, often better than the com-panies that specialize in cell-phone rental. If you're not renting a car, a number of companies will rent TDMA or GSM phones; remember, coverage is spotty. While service is evening out, TDMA phones have tended to work best in the Central Valley and Guanacaste; GSM is better for remote areas such as Domini-cal, Sámara, and Tortuguero. Specify your destination when renting. Rates range from $5 to $15 per day, plus vary-ing rates for local or international cover-age and minimum usage charges. Local

calls average 70¢ per minute, interna-tional $1.25–$1.50. You'll need your ID, a credit card, and a deposit, which var-ies per phone and service but averages $300–$400; some rent only to those over 21. The deposit drops significantly with companies that can hook you up with a rented local chip for your own phone.

Friendly and professional, Cell Service Costa Rica will get you hooked up and provides door-to-door service; it doesn't rent SIM cards. Cellular Telephone Rent-als Costa Rica has higher daily rates but free local calls, and will set you up with a card for your phone.

Contacts **Cell Service Costa Rica** (☎506/2296–5553 in Costa Rica⊕www.cellservicecr.com). **Cellular Telephone Rent-als Costa Rica** (☎800/769–7137 in the U.S., 506/2290–7534 or 506/8845–4427 in Costa Rica⊕www.cellulartelephonerentals.com).

▌CUSTOMS & DUTIES

You're always allowed to bring goods of a certain value back home without having to pay any duty or import tax. But there's a limit on the amount of tobacco and liquor you can bring back duty free, and some countries have separate limits for perfumes; for exact figures, check with your customs department. The values of so-called duty-free goods are included in these amounts. When you shop abroad, save all your receipts, as customs inspec-tors may ask to see them as well as the items you purchased. If the total value of your goods is more than the duty-free limit, you'll have to pay a tax (most often a flat percentage) on the value of every-thing beyond that limit.

When shopping in Costa Rica, keep receipts for all purchases. Be ready to show customs (*aduanas*) officials what you've bought. Pack purchases together in an easily accessible place. The Patri-mony Protection Department recommends obtaining a letter (free) from its office in the National Museum attesting that high-quality replicas of pre-Columbian artifacts are in fact copies, to avoid customs hassles. In practice, few people request such a letter, and problems with such souvenirs are infrequent. The only orchids you can take home are packaged in a tube and come with an export permit.

If you think a duty is incorrect, appeal the assessment. If you object to the way your clearance was handled, note the inspector's badge number. In either case, first ask to see a supervisor. If the problem isn't resolved, write to the appropriate authorities, beginning with the port director at your point of entry. It usually takes about 10–30 minutes to clear customs when arriving in Costa Rica.

Visitors entering Costa Rica may bring in 500 grams of tobacco, 5 liters of wine or spirits, 2 kilograms of sweets and chocolates, and the equivalent of $500 worth of merchandise. One camera and one video camera, six rolls of film, binoculars, and electrical items for personal use only are also allowed. Make sure you have personalized prescriptions for any medication you are taking. Customs officials at San José's international airport rarely examine tourists' luggage, but if you enter by land, they'll probably look through your bags. Officers at the airport generally speak English and are usually your best (only, really) option for resolving any problem. You can try calling the Customs office, but if you get through and get results, let us know!

Pets (cats or dogs) with updated health and vaccination certificates are welcome in Costa Rica; no prior authorization is required if bringing a dog or cat that has up-to-date health and vaccination cards. The Servicio Nacional de Salud Animal can provide more info.

Information in Costa Rica Customs (☎506/2441–6069 in Costa Rica ⊕www. hacienda.go.cr). **Patrimony Protection Office** (☎506/2291–3517 in Costa Rica). **Servicio**

Nacional de Salud Animal (☎506/2260–8300 in Costa Rica ⊕www.senasa.go.cr).

U.S. Information U.S. Customs and Border Protection (⊕www.cbp.gov).

▌ EATING OUT

The cilantro-and-onion flavor pot of rice and beans known as *gallo pinto* is synonymous with all things Tico, as evidenced by the expression "As Tico as *gallo pinto*." Nonetheless, Nicaraguans fiercely beg to differ, claiming the dish as their own and spurring a back-and-forth competition for the world's largest batch of the dish.

Molded mounds of this hearty breakfast can be found at the quintessential Costa Rican informal eatery—the *soda*. For lunch the beans and rice are separate, served with meat and coleslaw and called *casados*. Increasingly common as you move away from San José are the thatched conical roofs of the round, open *rancho* restaurants that serve up a combination of traditional staples with simple international fare. Kitchens cooking up sophisticated cuisine from Thailand, India, Italy, Lebanon, and more dot the capital and popular tourist centers. Vegetarians sticking to lower-budget establishments won't go hungry, but may develop a love-hate relationship with rice, beans, and fried cheese. A simple *sin carne* (no meat) request is often interpreted as "no beef," and you may get a plate of pork, chicken, or fish, so don't be afraid to sound high-maintenance. Specify *solo vegetales* (only vegetables), and for good measure, *nada de cerdo, pollo o pescado* (no pork, chicken, or fish). More cosmopolitan restaurants are more conscious of vegetarians—upscale Asian restaurants, such as excellent Tin Jo in downtown San José, often have a vegetarian section on the menu. In a pinch, the vegetarian fast-food chain Vishnu is always good for a quick meal. If your kids balk at the choices on the menu, ask for plain grilled chicken, fish, or beef: *"Pollo/pescado/carne sencillo para niños"* ("Grilled chicken/fish/meat for children"). Most restaurants are willing to accommodate with options and portion size.

Natural juices, called *frescos,* come with teeth-shattering amounts of sugar. If you're watching your child's intake, request one with only a little sugar (*con poco azúcar*); chances are it will be sweet enough, but you can always top it off if need be. Water is generally safe to drink (especially around San José), but quality can vary; to be safe, give kids bottled water.

MEALS & MEALTIMES

In San José and surrounding cities, *sodas* (informal eateries) are usually open daily 7 AM to 7 or 9 PM, though some close on Sunday. Other restaurants are usually open 11 AM–9 PM. In rural areas restaurants are usually closed on Sunday, except around resorts. In resort areas some restaurants may be open late. Most all-night restaurants are in downtown San José casinos. However, Nuestra Tierra and Manolos are both good 24-hour options, and for late-night cravings the doors at Denny's at the Best Western Irazú just north of San José are always open. Normal dining hours in Costa Rica are noon–3 and 6–9. *Desayuno* (breakfast) is served at most sodas and hotels. The traditional breakfast is *gallo pinto,* eggs, plantains, and often fried cheese; hotel breakfasts vary widely and generally offer fruit and lighter international options in addition to the local stick-to-your-ribs plate. *Almuerzo* (lunch) is *casado* time and *cena* (supper) runs the gamut of just about anything you choose.

Except for those in hotels, most restaurants close between Christmas and New Year's Day and during Holy Week (Palm Sunday to Easter Sunday). Call before heading out. Those that do stay open may not sell alcohol between Holy Thursday and Easter Sunday. Even if you keep your base in San José, consider venturing to the Central Valley towns for a meal or two.

Unless otherwise noted, the restaurants listed in this guide are open daily for lunch and dinner.

PAYING
For guidelines on tipping, see Tipping below.

■TIP➔Credit cards are not accepted at most restaurants in rural areas. Always ask before you order to find out if your credit card will be accepted. Visa and Master-Card are the most commonly accepted cards; American Express and Diners Club are less widely accepted. ■TIP➔Remember that 23% is added to all menu prices: 13% for tax and 10% for service. Because a gratuity is included, there's no need to tip, but if your service is good, it's nice to add a little money to the obligatory 10%.

CATEGORY	COST
$$$$	over $25
$$$	$15–$25
$$	$10–$15
$	$5–$10
¢	under $5

All prices are per person in U.S. dollars for a main course at dinner excluding 13% tax and 10% service fee.

RESERVATIONS & DRESS
Regardless of where you are, it's a good idea to make a reservation if you can. In some places (Hong Kong, for example), it's expected. We only mention them specifically when reservations are essential (there's no other way you'll ever get a table) or when they are not accepted. For popular restaurants, book as far ahead as you can (often 30 days), and reconfirm as soon as you arrive. (Large parties should always call ahead to check the reservations policy.) We mention dress only when men are required to wear a jacket or a jacket and tie.

Costa Ricans generally dress more formally than North Americans. For dinner, long pants and closed-toe shoes are standard for men except for beach locations, and women tend to wear dressy clothes that show off their figures, with high heels. Shorts, flip-flops, and tank tops are not acceptable, except at inexpensive restaurants in beach towns.

WINES, BEER & SPIRITS

The ubiquitous sodas generally don't have liquor licenses, but getting a drink in any other eatery isn't usually a problem. Don't let Easter Thursday and Friday or a local election catch you off guard—the country's dry laws are strictly in effect. Bars close, and coolers and alcohol shelves in restaurants and stores are sealed off with plastic and police tape. In general, restaurant prices for imported alcohol—which includes just about everything except beer, rum, and *guaro,* the local sugarcane firewater—may be more than what you'd like to pay. House wines are typically a low-end Chilean choice (this simply isn't wine-drinking country), so unless you see a familiar wine on the list, you might want to take a pass. Our advice? Go tropical! The country's abundant tropical fruit juices mix refreshingly well with rum, and to a lesser extent, *guaro.* You may also want to make a trip to the local supermarket to pick up something for an aperitif in your room—the selection will often be larger, and the prices much lower. Costa Rica's brewery—run by Florida Ice and Farms—has a virtual monopoly on beer production, but produces some respectable lagers that pair well with beach lounging. Emblematic Imperial (known by the red, black, and yellow eagle logo that adorns bar signs and tourist T-shirts) is the favorite. The slightly more bitter Pilsen is a close runner up, followed by the gold, dark, and light variations of Bavaria. Rock Ice is a relatively new product marketed to the younger crowd, with a higher alcohol content. The brewery also produces Heineken, and distributes imported

brands such as Mexico's Corona. Those with exotic tastes (and deep pockets) can also find beers from as far away as Italy.

▮ ELECTRICITY

North American appliances are compatible with Costa Rica's electrical system (110 volts) and outlets (parallel two-prong). Australian and European appliances require a two-prong adapter and a 220-volt to 110-volt transformer. Never use an outlet that specifically warns against using higher-voltage appliances without a transformer. Dual-voltage appliances (i.e., they operate equally well on 110 and 220 volts) such as most laptops, phone chargers, and hair dryers need only a two-prong adapter, but you should bring a surge protector for your computer.

Consider making a small investment in a universal adapter, which has several types of plugs in one lightweight, compact unit. Always check labels and manufacturer instructions to be sure. Don't use 110-volt outlets marked FOR SHAVERS ONLY for high-wattage appliances such as hair dryers.

Contacts **Steve Kropla's Help for World Travelers** (⊕ www.kropla.com) has information on electrical and telephone plugs around the world. **Walkabout Travel Gear** (⊕ www. walkabouttravelgear.com) has a good coverage of electricity under "adapters."

▌EMERGENCIES

Dial 911 for an ambulance, the fire department, or the police. Costa Ricans are usually quick to respond to emergencies. In a hotel or restaurant, the staff will usually offer immediate assistance, and in a public area passersby can be counted on to stop and help.

For emergencies ranging from health problems to lost passports, contact your embassy.

U.S. Embassy **United States Embassy** (Embajada de los Estados Unidos ⊠C. 120 and Avda. 0, Pavas, San José ☎506/2519-2000, 506/2519-2280 in Costa Rica for after-hours emergencies ⊕www.usembassy.or.cr).

General Emergency Contacts **Ambulance (Cruz Roja), Fire, Police** (☎911). **Traffic Police** (☎2222-9330).

▌HEALTH

The most common types of illnesses are caused by contaminated food and water. Infectious diseases can be airborne or passed via mosquitoes and ticks and through direct or indirect physical contact with animals or people. Some, including Norwalk-like viruses that affect your digestive tract, can be passed along through contaminated food. If you are traveling in an area where malaria is prevalent, use a repellent containing DEET and take malaria-prevention medication before, during, and after your trip as directed by your physician. Condoms can help prevent most sexually transmitted diseases, but they aren't absolutely reliable and their quality varies from country to country. Speak with your physician and/or check the CDC or World Health Organization Web sites for health alerts, particularly if you're pregnant, traveling with children, or have a chronic illness.

SHOTS & MEDICATIONS

Most travelers to Costa Rica do not get any vaccinations or take any special medications. However, according to the U.S. Centers for Disease Control, travel to Costa Rica poses some risk of malaria, hepatitis A and B, dengue fever, typhoid fever, rabies, Chagas' disease, and *E. coli*. The CDC recommends getting vaccines for hepatitis A and typhoid fever, especially if you are going to be in remote areas or plan to stay for more than six weeks.

Check with the CDC for detailed health advisories and recommended vaccinations. In areas with malaria and dengue, both of which are carried by mosquitoes, bring mosquito nets, wear clothing that covers your whole body, and apply repellent containing DEET in living and sleeping areas. There are some pockets of malaria near the Nicaraguan border on the Caribbean coast. You probably won't need to take malaria pills before your trip unless you are staying for a prolonged period in the north, camping on northern coasts, or crossing the border into Nicaragua or Panama. You should discuss the option with your doctor. Children traveling to Central America should have current inoculations against measles, mumps, rubella, and polio.

SPECIFIC ISSUES IN COSTA RICA

Malaria is not a problem in Costa Rica except in some remote northern Caribbean areas near the Nicaraguan border. Poisonous snakes, scorpions, and other pests pose a small (often overrated) threat. The CDC marks Costa Rica as an area infested by the *Aedes aegypti* (dengue-carrier) mosquito, but not as an epidemic region. A few thousand cases in locals are recorded each year; the numbers had been dropping, but dramatic spikes in 2005 and 2007 have spurred major eradication efforts. Cases of fatal hemorrhagic dengue are rare. The highest-risk area is the Caribbean, and the rainy season is peak dengue season elsewhere. You're unlikely to be felled by this disease, but you can't take its prevention too seriously: *repelente* (insect repellent spray) and *espirales* (mosquito coils) are sold in supermarkets and small country stores. U.S. insect repellent brands with DEET are sold in pharmacies and supermarkets. Mosquito nets are available in some remote lodges; you can buy them in camping stores in San José. ■TIP→Mild **insect repellents, like the ones in some skin softeners, are no match for the intense mosquito activity in the hot, humid regions of the Caribbean, Osa Peninsula, and Southern Pacific. Repellants made with DEET or picaridin are the most effective.** Perfume, aftershave, and other lotions and potions can actually attract mosquitoes.

Although it's unlikely you will contract malaria or dengue, if you start suffering from high fever, the shakes, or joint pain, make sure you ask to be tested for these diseases when you go to the local clinic. On the off chance you do have them, it's more likely doctors here will be able to provide an accurate diagnosis and treatment. Your embassy can provide you with a list of recommended doctors and dentists.

Government facilities—the so-called Caja hospitals (short for Caja Costarricense de Seguro Social, or Costa Rican Social Security System)—and clinics are of acceptable quality, but notoriously overburdened, a common complaint in socialized-medicine systems anywhere. Private hospitals are more accustomed to serving foreigners. They include Hospital CIMA, Clínica Bíblica, and Clínica Católica, which all have 24-hour pharmacies. Outside of San José most major towns have pharmacies that are open until at least 8 or 9 PM, but usually the nearest hospital emergency room is the only after-hours option. The long-established and ubiquitous Fischel pharmacies are great places for your prescription needs, and usually staff a doctor who can help with minor ailments; some branches, such as the

Roosevelt, San Pedro location, are open until midnight. Antibiotics and psychotropic medications (for sleep, anxiety, or pain) require prescriptions in Costa Rica. Little else does. But plan ahead and bring an adequate supply with you from home; matches may not be exact.

For specific clinic, hospital, and pharmacy listings, see Chapters 1 through 7. Do not fly within 24 hours of scuba diving.

Most food and water is sanitary in Costa Rica. In rural areas you run a mild risk of encountering drinking water, fresh fruit, and vegetables contaminated by fecal matter, which in most cases causes a bit of *turista* (traveler's diarrhea) but can cause leptospirosis (which can be treated by antibiotics if detected early). Although it may not be necessary, you can stay on the safe side by avoiding uncooked food, unpasteurized milk (including milk products), and ice—ask for drinks *sin hielo* (without ice)—and by drinking bottled water. Mild cases of turista may respond to Imodium (known generically as loperamide) or Pepto-Bismol (not as strong), both of which can be purchased over the counter. Drink plenty of purified water or tea; chamomile (*manzanilla* in Spanish) is a good folk remedy. In severe cases, rehydrate yourself with a salt-sugar solution (½ teaspoon salt and 4 tablespoons sugar per quart of water).

Ceviche, raw fish cured in lemon juice—a favorite appetizer, especially at seaside resorts—is generally safe to eat. ■TIP→**Buy organic foods whenever possible; chemicals, many of which have been banned elsewhere, are sprayed freely here without regulation.**

Heat stroke and dehydration are real dangers, especially for hikers, so drink lots of water. Take at least 1 liter per person for every hour you plan to be on the trail. Sunburn is the most common traveler's health problem. Use sunscreen with SPF 30 or higher. Most pharmacies and supermarkets carry sunscreen in a wide range of SPFs, though it is relatively pricey.

The greatest danger to your person actually lies off Costa Rica's popular beaches—riptides are common wherever there are waves, and tourists run into serious difficulties in them every year. If you see waves, ask the locals where it's safe to swim; and if you're uncertain, don't go in deeper than your waist. If you get caught in a rip current, swim parallel to the beach until you're free of it, and then swim back to shore. ■TIP→**Avoid swimming where a town's main river opens up to the sea. Septic tanks aren't common.**

OVER-THE-COUNTER REMEDIES

Farmacia is Spanish for "pharmacy," and the names for common drugs *aspirina,* Tylenol, and *ibuprofen* are basically the same as they are in English. Pepto-Bismol is widely available. Many drugs for which you need a prescription back home are sold over the counter in Costa Rica. Pharmacies throughout the country are generally open from 8 to 8, though it's best to consult with your hotel's staff to be sure. Some pharmacies in San José affiliated with clinics stay open 24 hours.

▌HOURS OF OPERATION

Like the rest of the world, Costa Rica's business hours have been expanding. Megamalls are usually open seven days a week, opening around 10 AM and closing around 9 PM; tourism-based businesses and museums also usually keep a Monday to Sunday schedule but open an hour earlier. Many smaller or rural museums are open Monday to Friday. National parks often close one day for maintenance; for example, Manuel Antonio is closed Monday. Restaurants in the city often close on Sunday, and sometimes Monday. Eateries in beach towns and other tourism-oriented areas are more likely to open seven days a week. Bars and nightclubs are generally open until 1 or 2 AM, at which time night owls flock to places like the El Pueblo center in San José to keep partying until 4 AM. Last calls vary from place to place, but it's not hard to find bartenders happy to sell you a drink for the road at closing time.

Some government offices and smaller businesses close for lunch, but *jornada continua* (without the lunch break) is becoming more common, and most commercial establishments follow an 8 AM to 5 PM schedule.

Three public holidays (April 11, July 25, and Oct. 12) are bumped to the following Monday when they fall on a weekend or mid-week. Government offices and commercial establishments observe all the holidays. The only days the country truly shuts down are Easter Thursday and Friday; some buses still run, but no alcohol can be purchased, and most restaurants and all stores are closed.

HOLIDAYS

January 1: First day of the year

April 11: Juan Santamaría Day, a national hero

Easter Week: Thursday and Good Friday, religious activities

May 1: International Labor Day

July 25: Anniversary of the Annexation of Guanacaste Province

August 2: Day of the Virgin of Los Angeles (patron saint of Costa Rica)

August 15: Mother's Day

September 15: Independence Day

October 12: Culture Day (*Día de la Cultura,* or *Día de la Raza*)

December 25: Christmas Day

▌MAIL

The Spanish word for post office is *correos.* Mail from the United States can take up to two to three weeks to arrive in Costa Rica (occasionally it never arrives at all). Within the country, mail service is even less reliable. Outgoing mail is marginally quicker, with delivery to North America in 5 to 10 days, especially when sent from San José. It's worth registering mail; prices are only slightly higher. All overseas cards and letters will automatically be sent airmail. Mail theft is a chronic problem, so do not mail checks, cash, or anything else of value.

Minimum postage for postcards and letters from Costa Rica to the United States and Canada costs the equivalent of U.S. 30¢.

You can have mail sent poste restante (*lista de correos*) to any Costa Rican post office (specify Correo Central to make sure it goes to the main downtown office). In written addresses, *apartado*, abbreviated *apdo.*, indicates a post office box.

Post offices are generally open weekdays 8–5:30, and on Saturday 8–noon. Stamps can be purchased at post offices and some hotels and souvenir shops. These vendors will also accept the mail you wish to send; don't bother looking for a mailbox, as only a handful (usually in rural areas with no post office) have been authorized. Always check with your hotel, which may sell stamps and post your letters for you.

Main Branch Correo Central (✉ C. 2, Avdas. 1–3, San José ☎ 506/2223–9766 in Costa Rica ⊕ www.correos.go.cr ☞ See regional chapters for other branches).

SHIPPING PACKAGES

Shipping parcels through the post office is not for those in a hurry, because packages to the United States and Canada can take weeks. Also, packages may be pilfered. However, post-office shipping is the cheapest way to go, with rates at $6–$13 per kilogram.

Some stores offer shipping, but it is usually quite expensive. If you can, carry your packages home with you.

UPS has offices in San José, Tamarindo, Jacó, Manuel Antonio, Sarchí, Nuevo Arenal, La Fortuna, and Limón. DHL has drop-offs in San José (Rohrmoser, Paseo Colón), Curridabat, Escazú, Heredia, Liberia, Limón, Ciudad Quesada, Jacó, Quepos, and San Isidro. Both have central information numbers with English-speaking staff to direct you to the nearest office. FedEx has offices in San José; it offers package pick-up service in San José and other centers, such as Limón; call for availability. Prices are about 10 times what you'd pay at the post office, but packages arrive in a matter of days. ("Overnight" is usually a misnomer—shipments to most North American cities take two days.)

Express Services Main Offices DHL (✉ 600 m northwest of the Real Cariari Mall, La Aurora, Heredia ☎ 506/2209–6000 in Costa Rica ☞ Call for other locations). **Federal Express** (✉ Zona Franca Metropolitana, Ciudad Barreal de Heredia, Local 1B, Heredia ✉ Centro de Servicio Mundial, Paseo Colón, 100 m east of León Cortés statue, San José ☎ 800/463–3339). **United Parcel Service** (UPS ✉ 50 m east of Pizza Hut, Pavas, San José ☎ 506/2290–2828 in Costa Rica ☞ Call for other locations).

∎ MONEY

In general, Costa Rica is cheaper than North America or Europe, but travelers looking for dirt-cheap developing-nation deals may find it's more expensive than they bargained for—and prices are rising as more foreigners visit and relocate here.

Food in modest restaurants and public transportation are inexpensive. A one-mile taxi ride costs about $1. Here are some sample prices to give you an idea of the cost of living in Costa Rica: the local currency is the colón (plural: colones).

ITEM	AVERAGE COST
Cup of Coffee	$1
Glass of Wine	$2–$5
Bottle of Beer	$1.50–$2
Sandwich	$2–$5
One-Mile Taxi Ride in Capital City	$1
Museum Admission	$1–$7

Prices throughout this guide are given for adults. Substantially reduced fees are almost always available for children, students, and senior citizens.

■TIP→Banks never have every foreign currency on hand, and it may take as long as a week to order. If you're planning to exchange funds before leaving home, don't wait till the last minute.

ATMS & BANKS

Your own bank will probably charge a fee for using ATMs abroad; the foreign bank you use may also charge a fee. Nevertheless, you'll usually get a better rate of exchange at an ATM than you will at a currency-exchange office or even when changing money in a bank. And extracting funds as you need them is a safer option than carrying around a large amount of cash.

Lines at San José banks would try the patience of a saint; instead, get your spending money at a *cajero automático* (ATM). If you do use the bank, remember that Monday, Friday, and the first and last days of the month are the busiest days.

Although they are springing up at a healthy rate, don't count on using an ATM outside of San José. Though not exhaustive, the A Todas Horas (ATH) company Web site lists locations of its cash machines, and notes which ones offer colones (usually in increments of 1,000 colones), dollars (in increments of $20), or both; click

on *Cajeros* then *búsqueda de cajeros* to see the lists by region.

All ATMs are 24-hour; you'll find them in major grocery stores, some hotels, gas stations, and even a few McDonald's, in addition to banks. ATH, Red Total, and Scotiabank machines supposedly accept both Cirrus (a partner with MasterCard) and Plus (a partner with Visa) cards, but often don't. If you'll be spending time away from major tourist centers, particularly in the Caribbean, get most or all of the cash you need in San José and carry a few U.S. dollars in case you run out of colones. It's helpful to have both a Visa and a MasterCard—even in San José—as many machines accept only one or the other. Both companies have sites with fairly comprehensive lists of accessible ATMs around the world (⇨*below*).

ATMs are sometimes out of order and sometimes run out of cash on weekends. ■TIP→PIN codes with more than four digits are not recognized at some ATMs in Costa Rica, such as those at Banco Nacional or Banco de Costa Rica. If you have a five-digit PIN, change it with your bank before you travel, or use only cash machines marked ATH.

The Credomatic office, housed in the Banco de San José central offices on C. Central between Avdas. 3 and 5, is the local representative for most major credit cards; get cash advances here, or at any bank (Banco Nacional and Banco San José are good for both MasterCard and Visa; Banex, Banco Popular, and Banco Cuscatlan always accept Visa).

State banks have branches with slightly staggered hours; core times are weekdays 9–4, and some are open Saturday morning. Several branches of Banco Nacional are open until 6, or occasionally 7. Private banks—Scotiabank, Banco Banex, and Banco de San José—tend to keep longer hours and are usually the best places to change U.S. dollars and traveler's checks; rates may be marginally better in state banks, but the long waits usually cancel out any benefit. The Banco de San José in Juan Santamaría International Airport is open every day 5 AM–10 PM.

■TIP➔**Though it might seem counterintuitive, whenever possible use ATMs only during bank business hours.** ATMs here have been known to "eat" cards, and are frequently out of cash. When the bank is open, you can go in to retrieve your card or get cash from a teller. As a safety precaution, look for a machine in a bank with a guard nearby.

Resources A Todas Horas (ATH ⊕www.ath. fi.cr). **MasterCard** (⊕www.mastercard.com/ atmlocator/index.jsp). **Visa** (⊕www.visalatam. com/e_index.jsp).

CREDIT CARDS

Throughout this guide, the following abbreviations are used: **AE**, American Express; **DC**, Diners Club; **MC**, MasterCard; and **V**, Visa.

It's a good idea to inform your credit-card company before you travel, especially if you're going abroad and don't travel internationally very often. Otherwise, the credit-card company might put a hold on your card owing to unusual activity—not a good thing halfway through your trip. Record all your credit-card numbers—as well as the phone numbers to call if your cards are lost or stolen—in a safe place, so you're prepared should something go wrong. Both MasterCard and Visa have general numbers you can call (collect if you're abroad) if your card is lost, but you're better off calling the number of your issuing bank, since MasterCard and Visa usually just transfer you to your bank; your bank's number is generally printed on your card.

If you plan to use your credit card for cash advances, you'll need to apply for a PIN at least two weeks before your trip. Although it's usually cheaper (and safer) to use a credit card abroad for large purchases (so you can cancel payments or be reimbursed if there's a problem), note

that some credit-card companies *and* the banks that issue them add substantial percentages to all foreign transactions, whether they're in a foreign currency or not. Check on these fees before leaving home, so there won't be any surprises when you get the bill.

■TIP➔**Before you charge something, ask the merchant whether or not he or she plans to do a dynamic currency conversion (DCC). In such a transaction the credit-card** *processor* **(shop, restaurant, or hotel, not Visa or MasterCard) converts the currency and charges you in dollars. In most cases you'll pay the merchant a 3% fee for this service in addition to any credit-card company and issuing-bank foreign-transaction surcharges.**

Dynamic currency conversion programs are becoming increasingly widespread. Merchants who participate in them are supposed to ask whether you want to be charged in dollars or the local currency, but they don't always do so. And even if they do offer you a choice, they may well avoid mentioning the additional surcharges. The good news is that you *do* have a choice. And if this practice really gets your goat, you can avoid it entirely thanks to American Express; with its cards, DCC simply isn't an option.

All major credit cards are accepted at most major hotels and restaurants in this book; establishments affiliated with Credomatic now also accept the Discover card. As the phone system improves and expands, many budget hotels, restaurants, and other properties have begun to accept plastic; but plenty of properties still require payment in cash. Don't count on using your credit card outside of San José. ■TIP➔**Carry enough cash to patronize the many businesses without credit-card capability.** Note that some hotels, restaurants, tour companies, and other businesses add a surcharge (around 5%) to the bill if you pay with a credit card, or give you a 5%–10% discount if you pay in cash. It's always a good idea to pay for large purchases with a major credit card if possible, so you can cancel payment or get reimbursed if there's a problem.

Reporting Lost Cards American Express (✉Behind the Controlaría, Sabana Sur, Oficentro Ejecutivo La Sabana, Torre No. 1, 1st fl., San José ☎0800/012–3211 collect to the U.S., 506/2242–8585 in Costa Rica). **Diners Club** (☎702/797–5532 collect to the U.S., 506/2295–9393 in Costa Rica). **MasterCard** (☎0800/011–0184 toll-free to the U.S.). **Visa** (☎0800/011–0030 toll-free to the U.S.)..

CURRENCY & EXCHANGE

Most non-U.S. currencies must be exchanged in banks. It is possible to change euros at exchange counters such as Global Exchange, but with such bad rates you probably won't want to.

In late 2006, after years of controlled, small devaluations, Costa Rica switched to a banded exchange rate that fluctuates between a floor and a ceiling. Check the Central Bank site ⊕*www.bccr.fi.cr/flat/bccr_flat.htm* for daily rates offered by institutions that deal with exchange; this *Tipo de cambio* chart is also published in the business pages of the daily Spanish-language *La Nación* newspaper. At this writing, the colón is 494 to the U.S. dollar and 707 to the euro.

Coins come in denominations of 5, 10, 20, 25, 50, 100 and 500 colones and a range of styles, as new coins mingle with the older ones. For example, a 10-colón coin can be small, heavy, and bronze; large, heavy, and silver-color (currently being phased out); or small and extremely light (feels almost like plasticky play money)—and all are legal tender. Be careful not to mix up the very similar 100- and 500-colón coins. Bills are more standardized, and come in denominations of 1,000; 2,000; 5,000; and 10,000 colones. Avoid using the two larger denomination bills in taxis or small stores. U.S. dollars are widely accepted.

Although ATM transaction fees may be higher here than at home, ATM rates are

WORST-CASE SCENARIO

All your money and credit cards have just been stolen. In these days of real-time transactions, this isn't a predicament that should destroy your vacation. First, report the theft of the credit cards. Then get any traveler's checks you were carrying replaced. This can usually be done almost immediately, provided that you kept a record of the serial numbers separate from the checks themselves. If you bank at a large international bank like Citibank or HSBC, go to the closest branch; if you know your account number, chances are you can get a new ATM card and withdraw money right away. **Western Union** (☎*800/325–6000*⊕*www.westernunion.com*) sends money almost anywhere. Have someone back home order a transfer online, over the phone, or at one of the company's offices, which is the cheapest option. The U.S. State Department's **Overseas Citizens Services** (☎*202/647–5225*) can wire money to any U.S. consulate or embassy abroad for a fee of $30. Just have someone back home wire money or send a money order or cashier's check to the State Department, which will then disburse the funds as soon as the next working day after it receives them.

excellent because they're based on wholesale rates offered only by major banks. You won't do as well at exchange booths in airports, in hotels, in restaurants, or in stores.

Costa Rican colones are sold abroad at terrible rates, so you should wait until you arrive in Costa Rica to get local currency. U.S. dollars are still the easiest to exchange, but euros can be exchanged for colones at just about any Banco Nacional branch and San José and Escazú branches of other banks, such as BAC San José. Private banks—Scotiabank, Banco Banex, and Banco de San José—are the best places to change U.S. dollars and traveler's checks. There is a branch of the Banco de San José in the airport (open daily 5 AM–10 PM) where you can exchange money when you arrive—it's a much better deal than the Global Exchange counter. Taxi and van drivers who pick up at the airport accept U.S. dollars.

Outdoor money changers are rarely seen on the street, but avoid them if they approach; you will most certainly get a bad deal.

■TIP➜Even if a currency-exchange booth has a sign promising no commission, rest assured that there's some kind of huge, hidden fee. (Oh . . . that's right. The sign didn't say no *fee*.) And as for rates, you're almost always better off getting foreign currency at an ATM or exchanging money at a bank.

TRAVELER'S CHECKS & CARDS

Some consider this the currency of the caveman, and it's true that fewer establishments accept traveler's checks these days. Nevertheless, they're a cheap and secure way to carry extra money, particularly on trips to urban areas. Both Citibank (under the Visa brand) and American Express issue traveler's checks in the United States, but Amex is better known and more widely accepted; you can also avoid hefty surcharges by cashing Amex checks at Amex offices. Whatever you do, keep track of all the serial numbers in case the checks are lost or stolen.

If you have an American Express card and can draw on a U.S. checking account, you can buy U.S.-dollar traveler's checks at the American Express office in San José for a 1% service charge.

Contacts American Express (☎800/528-4800 in the U.S., 336/393-1111 collect outside of the U.S. ⊕www.americanexpress.com).

▮ PACKING

Travel light, and make sure you can carry your luggage without assistance. Even if you're planning to stay only in luxury resorts, odds are at least once you'll have to haul your stuff a distance from bus stops, the shuttle drop-off, or the airport. Another incentive to pack light: domestic airlines have tight weight restrictions (at this writing 25–30 pounds [11.3–13 kilograms]) and not all buses have luggage compartments.

■TIP➜It's a good idea to pack essentials in one bag and extras in another, so you can leave one bag at your hotel in San José (most hotels allow this if you are staying with them again before your departure flight) or with Nature Air *(⇨ By Air above)*, if you exceed weight restrictions. Frameless backpacks and duffel bags can be squeezed into tight spaces and are less conspicuous than fancier luggage.

Bring comfortable, hand-washable clothing. T-shirts and shorts are acceptable near the beach and in tourist areas; long-sleeve shirts and pants protect your skin from ferocious sun and, in some regions, mosquitoes. Leave your jeans behind—they take forever to dry. Pack a waterproof, lightweight jacket and a light sweater for cool nights, early mornings, and trips up volcanoes; you'll need even warmer clothes for trips to Chirripó National Park or Cerro de la Muerte and overnight stays in San Gerardo de Dota or on the slopes of Poás Volcano. Bring at least one good (and wrinkle-free) outfit for going out at night.

Women might have a tough time finding tampons, so bring your own. For almost all toiletries, including contact lens supplies, a pharmacy is your best bet. Don't forget sunblock, and expect to sweat it off and reapply regularly in the high humidity. Definitely bring sufficient film and batteries, since they're expensive here.

Snorkelers staying at budget hotels should consider bringing their own equipment;

otherwise, you can rent gear at most beach resorts.

You have to get down and dirty—well, more like wet and muddy—to see many of the country's natural wonders. This following packing list is not comprehensive; it's a guide to some of the things you might not think to bring. For your main piece of luggage, a sturdy internal-frame backpack is great, but a duffel bag works, too. You can get by with a rolling suitcase, but then bring a smaller backpack as well.

PASSPORTS

U.S. citizens need only a passport to enter Costa Rica for stays of up to 90 days. Make sure it's up-to-date—you'll be refused entry if the passport is due to expire in less than one month. To be on the safe side, make sure it is valid for at least six months. The only way to extend your stay is to spend 72 hours in Nicaragua or Panama—but don't expect to do that undetected more than a couple of times. New customs forms ask how many visits you've made to Costa Rica in the past year.

Due to high rates of passport theft, travelers in Costa Rica are not required to carry their original documents with them at all times, although you must have easy access to them. Photocopies of the data page and your entry stamp are sufficient.

■TIP→For easy retrieval in the event of a lost or stolen passport, before you leave home scan your passport into a portable storage device (like an iPod) that you're carrying with you or e-mail the scanned image to yourself.

If your passport is lost or stolen, first call the police—having the police report can make replacement easier—and then call your embassy (⇨Emergencies, below). You'll get a temporary Emergency Travel Document that will need to be replaced once you return home. Fees vary according to how fast you [...] in some cases the fee cov[...] nent replacement as well. Th[...] ment will not have your entry [...] ask if your embassy takes care of this [...] whether it's your responsibility to get the necessary immigration authorization.

GENERAL REQUIREMENTS FOR COSTA RICA	
Passport	Must be valid for 1 month after date of arrival.
Visa	Required for Americans (free upon entry)
Vaccinations	None required
Driving	International driver's license not required; CDW is optional on car rentals
Departure Tax	US$26

RESTROOMS

Toilet paper is not discarded into the toilet in Costa Rica, but rather in a trash bin beside it. Septic systems are delicate and the paper will clog the toilet. At some public restrooms you might have to pay 50¢ or so for a few sheets of toilet paper. At others, there may not be any toilet paper at all. It's always a good idea to have some tissues at the ready. Gas stations generally have facilities, but you may decide not to be a slave to your bladder once you get a look at them. On long trips, watch for parked buses; generally this indicates some sort of better-kept public facilities.

Find a Loo The Bathroom Diaries (⊕www.thebathroomdiaries.com) is flush with unsanitized info on rest rooms the world over—each one located, reviewed, and rated.

SAFETY

Violent crime is not a serious problem in Costa Rica, but thieves can easily prey on tourists, so be alert. The government has been shamed into creating a Tourism

...ts and

...an get muddy

... (especially in the
... t transportation is
by boat, ... are no docks)

■ Knee-high socks ... the rubber boots that
are supplied at many lodges

■ A pair of lightweight pants (fire ants, mosquitoes, and other pests make covering yourself a necessity on deep-forest hikes)

■ Pants for horseback riding (if that's on
your itinerary)

■ Waterproof, lightweight jacket, wind-
breaker, or poncho

■ Day pack for hikes

■ Sweater for cool nights and early
mornings

■ Swimsuit

■ Insect repellent (with DEET, for forested
areas and especially on the Northern Caribbean coast, where there are pockets of
malaria)

■ Flashlight or headlamp with spare batteries (for occasional power outages or inad-
equately lighted walkways at lodges)

■ Sunscreen with a minimum of SPF 30
(waterproof sunscreens are best; even if
you're not swimming, you might be swimming in perspiration)

■ Large, portable water bottle

■ Hat and/or bandannas (not only do they
provide shade, but they prevent perspiration
from dripping down your face)

■ Binoculars (with carrying strap)

■ Camera (waterproof, or with a waterproof
case or dry bag, sold in outdoor-equipment
stores)

■ Film (film in Costa Rica can be expired and
is expensive)

■ Imodium and Pepto-Bismol (tablet form
is best)

■ Swiss Army knife (and remember to pack
it in your checked luggage, never your carry-
on—even on domestic flights in Costa Rica)

■ Ziplock bags (they always come in handy)

■ Travel alarm clock or watch with an alarm
(don't count on wake-up calls)

■ Nonelectric shaving utensils

■ Toilet paper (rarely provided in public
bathrooms)

Police unit, which in 2006 graduated its
first group of officers trained specifically
in assisting tourists and dealing with
tourism-specific crime. The force's 228
officers can be seen on bikes or motorcycles patrolling areas in Guanacaste,
San José, and the Arenal area. Only a
small fraction speak English well, but
language training is being beefed up.
Crimes against property are rife in San
José. In rural areas theft is on the rise.
For many English-speaking tourists,
standing out like a sore thumb can't be

avoided. But there are some precautions
you can take:

■ Don't bring anything you can't stand to
lose.

■ Don't wear expensive jewelry or watches.

■ In cities, don't carry expensive cameras or
lots of cash.

■ Carry backpacks on your front; thieves can
slit your backpack and run away with its contents before you notice.

■ Don't wear a waist pack, because thieves can cut the strap.

■ Distribute your cash and any valuables (including credit cards and passport) between a deep front pocket, an inside jacket or vest pocket, and a hidden money belt. (If you use a money belt, carry some cash in your purse or wallet so you don't have to reach for the hidden pouch in public.)

■ Keep your hand on your wallet if you are in a crowd or on a crowded bus.

■ Don't let your purse just dangle from your shoulder; always hold on to it with your hand for added security. If you cross the strap over your body, you run the risk of being dragged with your bag if you're mugged.

■ Keep car windows rolled up and car doors locked at all times in cities; elsewhere, roll up windows and lock doors whenever you leave your car.

■ Park in designated parking lots, or if that's not possible, accept the offer of the guachimán (a term adopted from English, pronounced "watchie man")—men or boys who watch your car while you're gone. Give them the equivalent of a dollar per hour when you return.

■ Never leave valuables visible in a car, even in an attended parking lot: take them inside with you whenever possible, or lock them in the trunk.

■ Padlock your luggage.

■ Talk with locals or your hotel staff about crime in the area. They will be able to tell you if it's safe to walk around after dark and what to avoid.

■ Never walk in a narrow space between a building and a car parked on the street close to it; a prime hiding spot for thieves.

■ Do not walk in parks at night.

■ Men should be suspicious of overly friendly or sexually aggressive females. At best they are probably prostitutes; at worst they have targeted you for a scam.

■ Never leave a drink unattended in a club or bar: scams involving date-rape drugs have been reported in the past few years, targeting both men and women.

■ Never leave your belongings unattended anywhere, including at the beach or in a tent.

■ If your hotel room has a safe, use it, even if it's an extra charge. If your room doesn't have one, ask the manager to put your valuables in the hotel safe and ask him or her to sign a list of what you are storing there.

■ If you are involved in an altercation with a mugger, immediately surrender your possessions and walk away quickly.

If the worst happens, at the risk of sounding cynical, we wouldn't recommend making a police report, unless your passport was stolen. You'll wait hours for an English-speaking officer, hours to give your statement, and probably the rest of your life to ever see justice done. Call your credit-card company using the numbers we provide (⇨ *Credit Cards in Money, above*).

Scams are common in San José, where a drug addict may tell tales of having recently been robbed, then ask you for donations; a distraction artist might squirt you with something, or spill something on you, then try to clean you off while his partner steals your backpack; pickpockets and bag slashers work buses and crowds. To top it all off, car theft is rampant. Beware of anyone who seems overly friendly, aggressively helpful, or disrespectful of your personal space. Be particularly vigilant around the Coca-Cola bus terminal, one of the rougher areas but a central tourism hub.

Don't believe taxi drivers when they say the hotel is closed, unless you've personally gotten out and checked it yourself. Many want to take you somewhere else to earn a commission. If a taxi driver says he does not have change and the amount is substantial, ask him to drive to a store or gas station where you can get change. This might be enough to prompt him to suddenly "find" the difference to give you. Avoid paying with large bills to prevent this.

A number of tourists have been hit with the slashed-tire scam: someone punctures the tires of your rental car (often right at the airport, when you arrive) and then comes to your "aid" when you pull off to the side of the road and robs you blind. Forget about the rims: always drive to the nearest open gas station or service center if you get a flat.

Lone women travelers will get a fair amount of attention from men, but in general should be safe. No one, let alone women traveling alone or in pairs, should hitchhike. Blondes and redheads will get more grief than brunettes. To avoid hassles, avoid wearing short shorts or skirts. On the bus, try to take a seat next to a woman. Women should not walk alone in San José at night or venture into dangerous areas of the city at all. Ask at your hotel which neighborhoods to avoid. Ignore unwanted comments. If you are being harassed on a bus, at a restaurant, or in some other public place, tell the manager. In taxis, sit in the backseat. If you want to fend off an earnest but decent admirer in a bar, you can politely say *"Por favor, necesito un tiempo a solas"* (I'd like some time on my own, please). Stronger is *"Por favor, no moleste"* (Please, stop bothering me), and for real pests the simple *"Váyase!"* (Go away!) is usually effective. Costa Rican men often fancy themselves Latin lovers and profess adoration before the first drink has even arrived; they lean toward machismo and can be persistent, even overaggressive.

Info **Transportation Security Administration** (TSA; ⊕www.tsa.gov).

▌TAXES

The airport departure tax for tourists is $26, payable in cash or with Visa. All Costa Rican businesses charge a 13% sales tax. Hotels charge a 16.4% fee covering service and tax. Restaurants add 13% tax and 10% service fee to meals. Tourists are not refunded for taxes paid in Costa Rica.

▌TIME

Costa Rica does not observe daylight saving time, so from November to April it's six hours behind GMT, the equivalent of Central Time in the United States (1 hour behind New York). The rest of the year, it is seven hours behind GMT, the equivalent of Mountain Time in the United States (2 hours behind New York).

Time Zones **Timeanddate.com** (⊕www.time anddate.com/worldclock).

▌TIPPING

TIPPING	
Bartender	$1–$5 per round of drinks, depending on the number of drinks
Bellhop	$1–$5 per bag, depending on the level of the hotel
Hotel Concierge	$5 or more, if he or she performs a service for you
Hotel Doorman	$1–$2 if he helps you get a cab
Hotel Maid	$1–$3 a day (either daily or at the end of your stay, in cash)
Hotel Room-Service Waiter	$1–$2 per delivery, even if a service charge has been added
Tour Guide	$10 per day
Waiter	10%–15%, with 15% being the norm at high-end restaurants; nothing additional if a service charge is added to the bill

Restroom attendants in more expensive restaurants expect some small change or $1. Tip coat-check personnel at least $1–$2 per item checked unless there is a fee, then nothing.

Costa Rica doesn't have a tipping culture, but positive reinforcement goes a long way to fostering a culture of good service, which is hit-and-miss. Tip only for good service. Taxi drivers aren't tipped, but it's common courtesy to leave an extra 200–300 colones if they've helped you navigate a complicated set of directions. ■TIP→**Do not use U.S. coins to tip, because there is no way for locals to exchange them.**

Chambermaids get 1,000–1,500 colones per day; for great service try to leave up to 10% of your room bill. Concierges are usually not tipped. Room-service waiters should be tipped about 500 colones, as should bellhops (more in the most expensive hotels).

Restaurant bills include a 13% tax and 10% service charge—sometimes these amounts are included in prices on the menu, and sometimes they aren't. If the menu doesn't indicate whether service is included, ask. An additional gratuity is not expected, especially in cheap restaurants, but people often leave something extra when service is good. Leave a tip of about 200 colones per drink for bartenders, too.

At some point on a trip, most visitors to Costa Rica are in the care of a naturalist guide, who can show them the sloths and special hiking trails they'd never find on their own. Give $10 (or 5,000 colones) per day per person to guides if they've transported and guided you individually or in small groups, and about 10% of the rental to a hired driver of a small car. Give less to guides or drivers on bigger tours. For tour guides, it's okay to pay with U.S. dollars.

▌ TOURS

BIKING

Costa Rica is mountainous and rough around the edges. It's a rare bird that attempts a road-biking tour here. But the payoff for the ungroomed, tire-munching terrain is uncrowded, wildly beautiful off-road routes. Most bike-tour operators want to make sure you're in moderately good shape and do some biking at home. Others, such as Coast to Coast Adventures, have easier two-day jaunts. Lava Tours offers great expert- and intermediate-level riding, as well as "gravity-assisted" (cruising down the paved road from Poás Volcano, for example) trips. Bike Arenal has mountain- and road-biking packages in the Arenal area for all skill levels, with short and long ride options for each day. Operators generally provide top-notch equipment, including bikes, helmets, water bottles, and so forth, but welcome serious bikers who bring their own ride. Leave the hybrids at home—this is mountain-biking territory. Operators usually meet you at the airport and take care of all logistics. All companies can design custom tours for extreme cyclists if requested.

The trails around Lake Arenal in the Northern Zone are a popular draw for tour groups, but become impassable rivers of mud when it rains. The rolling hills, valley views, and proximity to San José make the Orosí Valley a favorite for more Sunday-style riders. If you're hard-core, look into the Jungle Man Adventures' Pacific-to-Caribbean journey that takes about a week, following the infamous Ruta de los Conquistadores (Route of the Conquistadors), along which a grueling four-day race takes place each year.

Topographical maps (not biking maps per se) are generally provided as part of the tour, and include unpaved roads that are often perfect for mountain biking. If you're striking out on your own, these maps can usually be found at San José's Lehmann bookstore for about $3. Some basic Spanish is highly recommended if you're going to do it yourself—your chances of finding an English speaker on the jungle trail are limited.

Airlines do have policies on bikes, but veterans say it really comes down to who you talk to—call twice, get names and details, and have them handy when you check in. ■TIP→Check with individual airlines about packing requirements and blackouts—more than one eager tour participant has been turned away because of high-season bike bans. Cardboard bike boxes can be found at bike shops for about $15; more secure options start at $40. International travelers often can substitute a bike for a piece of checked luggage at no charge (if the box conforms to regular baggage dimensions); but, U.S. and Canadian airlines will sometimes charge a $100–$200 handling fee each way.

■TIP→Most airlines accommodate bikes as luggage, provided they're dismantled and boxed.

Bike Maps Lehmann (✉Avda. Central, Cs. 1–3, San José ☎2223–1212).

Contacts Bike Arenal (☎506/2479–9454, 866/465–4114 in North America ⊕www. bikearenal.com). **Coast to Coast Adventures** (☎506/2280–8054 in Costa Rica ⊕www. ctocadventures.com). **Jungle Man Adventures** (☎506/2225–7306 ⊕www.adventure race.com). **Lava Tours** (☎506/281–2458, 888/862–2424 in North America ⊕www. lava-tours.com).

BIRD-WATCHING

You will almost definitely get more out of your time in Costa Rica by taking a tour rather than trying to find birds on your own. Bring your own binoculars but don't worry about a spotting scope; if you go with a tour company that specializes in birding tours, your guide will have one. Expect to see about 300 species during a weeklong tour. Many U.S. travel companies that offer bird-watching tours subcontract with the Costa Rican tour operators listed below. By arranging your tour directly with the Costa Rican companies, you avoid the middleman and save money. Selva Mar, a tour agency specializing in the Southern Zone, runs comprehensive tours through Birding Escapes Costa Rica.

Contacts Birding Escapes Costa Rica (☎506/2771–4582 in Costa Rica ⊕www. birdwatchingcostarica.com). **Costa Rica Expeditions** (☎506/2257–0766 in Costa Rica ⊕www.costaricaexpeditions.com). **Horizontes** (☎506/2222–2022 in Costa Rica ⊕www.horizontes.com).

DIVING

Costa Rica's Cocos Island—one of the best dive spots in the world—can be visited only on a 10-day scuba safari with *Aggressor* or *Undersea Hunter*. But Guanacaste, the South Pacific, and to a lesser extent, the Caribbean, offer some respectable underwater adventures. Bill Beard's Costa Rica in the Gulf of Papagayo, Guanacaste, is a diving-tour pioneer and has countrywide options. Diving Safaris, in Playa Hermosa, has trips to dive sites in Guanacaste. In the South Pacific, Costa Rica Adventure Divers in Drake Bay arranges five-night trips. In this same area, Caño Island is a good alternative if you can't afford the money or time for Cocos Island, particularly in the rainy season, when dive sites closer to shore are clouded by river runoff.

Contacts Aggressor (☎506/2289–2261, 800/348–2628 in North America ⊕www. aggressor.com). **Bill Beard's Costa Rica** (☎877/853–0538 in the U.S. ⊕www.billbeard costarica.com). **Costa Rica Adventure Divers** (☎506/2236–5637, 866/466–5090 in the U.S. ⊕www.costaricadiving.com). **Diving Safaris** (☎506/2672–1259 in Costa Rica ⊕www. costaricadiving.net). Undersea Hunter (☎506/2228–6613,800/203–2120 in North America ⊕www.underseahunter.com).

ECOTOURS

If nature is the backbone of Costa Rica's tourism industry, ecotourism is what fleshes it out and gives it the signature profile everyone recognizes. *See the Ecotourism Costa Rica–Style chapter.* The following companies are well-known for excellent tours organized according to conservationist and community-friendly business practices.

Contacts **ACTUAR** (☎506/2248–9470 in Costa Rica, 877/922–8827 ⊕www.actuar costarica.com). **Costa Rica Expeditions** (☎506/2257–0766 in Costa Rica ⊕www. costaricaexpeditions.com). **Costa Rica Sun Tours** (☎506/2296–7757 in Costa Rica ⊕www.crsuntours.com). **Horizontes** (☎506/2222–2022 in Costa Rica ⊕www. horizontes.com). **Simbiosis Tours** (☎506/ 2290–8646 in Costa Rica ⊕www.turismoruralcr. com).

FISHING

If fishing is your primary objective in Costa Rica, you are better off booking a package. During peak season you may not even be able to find a hotel room in the hot fishing spots, let alone one of the top boats and skippers. If you're less of a planner, some Fodor's readers say they've had good luck hanging out at "fish bars" in popular areas and asking around for recommendations. The major fish populations move along the Pacific coast through the year, and tarpon and snook fishing on the Caribbean is subject to the vagaries of seasonal wind and weather, but viable year-round. San José–based Costa Rica Outdoors has been in business since 1995, arranging fishing packages; it is one of the best bets for full service and honest advice about where to go, and works with the widest range of operators around the country. More than 100 outfits have high-quality, regionally based services. Anglers in the know recommend Kingfisher Sportfishing in Playa Carrillo, Guanacaste; Blue Fin Sportfishing and J.P. Sportfishing Tours in Quepos; The Zancudo Lodge near Golfito; and Río Colorado Lodge on the northern Caribbean coast. While fishing is hit-or-miss, when booking a holiday, get it on record from your tour operator that it's the traditional season for the type of fishing you'd like to do. The Tico Times "Fishing Forum" (⊕*www.ticotimes.net/fishingforum*) *is also a good resource.*

Contacts **Blue Fin Sport Fishing** (☎506/2777–1676 in Costa Rica ⊕www. bluefinsportfishing.com). **Costa Rica Outdoors** (☎506/2231–0306,800/308–3394 in the U.S. ⊕www.costaricaoutdoors.com). **J.P. Sportfishing Tours** (☎506/2244–6361, 866/620–4188 in the U.S. ⊕www.jpsportfishing.com). **Kingfisher Sportfishing** (☎506/2656–0091 in Costa Rica ⊕www.costaricabillfishing.com). **Río Colorado Lodge** (☎506/2232–4063, 800/243–9777 in North America ⊕www. riocoloradolodge.com). **The Zancudo Lodge** (☎506/2776–0008, 800/854–8791 in the U.S. ⊕www.thezancudolodge.com).

FLIGHTSEEING

San José–based AeroTour will take you anywhere in Costa Rica for flightseeing and picture taking. The rate is $375 (for up to 3 people) per hour. Ultralight Tours, based in Bahía Ballena on the South Pacific, gives bird's-eye ultralight tours of the area's mangroves and national park, as well as in Sámara and Tambor; only one passenger per trip. Rides cost $75–$90 for 20 minutes. Liberia-based Macaw Air sends people into the North Pacific sunset for $400 (maximum 4 passengers), and has picture-taking trips on the Pacific coast.

Contacts **AeroTour** (☎506/2232–0660 in Costa Rica ⊕www.aerotourcr.com). **Macaw Air** (☎506/8364–1223 in Costa Rica ⊕www.macawair.com). **Ultralight Tours** (☎506/2743–8037 in Costa Rica ⊕www. flyultralight.com).

GOLF

Putting on a green against a dramatic Pacific backdrop isn't the first image that springs to mind for Costa Rican vacations, but the increase in luxury resorts and upscale tourism has created a respectable, albeit small, golfing circuit in the Central Valley and along the Pacific coast. Most packages maximize links time with side excursions to explore the country's natural riches. Costa Rica Golf Adventures Ltd. organizes multiday tours at four- and five-star lodgings. Costa Rican–run Golfing Costa Rica sets up packages around the country, largely in its own or affiliated accommodations.

Contacts **Costa Rica Golf Adventures** (☎506/2239–5176, 877/258–2688 in the U.S. ⊕ www.golfcr.com). **Golfing Costa Rica** (☎506/2233–2681 ⊕ www.costaricagolfing. com).

HIKING

Most nature-tour companies include hiking as part of their itineraries, but these hikes may be short and not strenuous enough for serious hikers. Let the tour operator know what you expect from a hike. Ask a lot of questions about hike lengths and difficulty levels before booking the tour or you may be disappointed with the amount of time you get to spend on the trails. The following companies cater to both moderate and serious hikers.

Contacts **Gap Adventures** (☎800/708–7761 in North America ⊕ www.gapadventures.com). **Serendipity Adventures** (☎877/507–1358 in North America, 506/2558–1000 in Costa Rica ⊕ www.serendipityadventures.com). **The Walking Connection** (☎602/978–1887 or 800/295–9255 in North America ⊕ www. walkingconnection.com).

SURFING

Most Costa Rican travel agencies and tour companies have packages that ferry both veteran and would-be cowboys (and cowgirls) of the ocean to and between the country's famed bi-coastal breaks. Local experts at Alacran Surf (which works with Surf Costa Rica) really know their stuff, and offer standard or custom packages. Del Mar Surf Camp on the Pacific specializes in women-only surf lessons and packages. Learn how to surf, camp on the beach, and delve into personal development on the Costa Rican Rainforest Outward Bound School's weeklong adult surf journeys.

Contacts **Costa Rican Rainforest Outward Bound School** (☎800/676–2018 in North America, 506/2278–6058 in Costa Rica ⊕ www. crrobs.org). **Del Mar Surf Camp** (☎506/2643–3197 in Costa Rica ⊕ www.costaricasurfing chicas.com). **Alacran Surf** (☎506/2280–7328 in Costa Rica, 619/955–7171 in North America ⊕ www.surf-costarica.com).

SPANISH-LANGUAGE PROGRAMS

Thousands of people travel to Costa Rica every year to study Spanish. Dozens of schools in and around San José offer professional instruction and homestays, and there are several smaller schools outside the capital. Conversa has schools off Paseo Colón, and in Santa Ana, west of the capital, offering hourly classes as well as a "Super Intense" program (5½ hours per day). On the east side of town, ILISA provides cultural immersion in San Pedro. Mesoamérica is a low-cost language school that is part of a nonprofit organization devoted to peace and social justice. La Escuela D'Amore is in beautiful Manuel Antonio. Language programs at the Institute for Central American Development Studies include optional academic seminars in English about Central America's political, social, and economic conditions.

Contacts **Conversa** (☎506/2221–7649, 888/669–1664 in North America ⊕ www. conversa.net). **ILISA** (☎506/2280–0700, 800/464–7248 in the U.S. ⊕ www.ilisa.com). **Institute for Central American Development Studies** (ICADS ☎506/2225–0508 in Costa Rica ⊕ www.icads.org). **La Escuela D'Amore** (☎506/2777–1143, 800/261–3203 in North America ⊕ www.edcostarica.com). **Mesoamérica** (☎506/2253–3195 in Costa Rica ⊕ www.mesoamericaonline.net).

VOLUNTEER AND EDUCATIONAL PROGRAMS

In recent years more and more Costa Ricans have realized the need to preserve their country's precious biodiversity. Both Ticos and far-flung environmentalists have founded volunteer and educational concerns to this end.

Volunteer opportunities span a range of diverse interests. You can tag sea turtles as part of a research project, build trails in a national park, or volunteer at an orphanage. Many of the organizations require at least rudimentary Spanish.

Most of the programs for volunteers who don't speak Spanish charge a daily fee for room and board. The Caribbean Conservation Corporation (CCC) is devoted to the preservation of sea turtles. Earthwatch Institute leads science-based trips studying monkeys, turtles, or the rain forest. The Talamancan Association of Ecotourism and Conservation (ATEC), as well as designing short group and individual outings centered on Costa Rican wildlife and indigenous culture, keeps an updated list of up to 30 local organizations that welcome volunteers. Beach cleanups, recycling, and some wildlife projects don't require proficiency in Spanish. The Costa Rican Humanitarian Foundation has volunteer opportunities with indigenous communities, women, community-based clinics, and education centers. They also organize homestays.

The Institute for Central American Development Studies (ICADS) is a nonprofit social justice institute that runs a language school and arranges internships and field study (college credit is available); some programs are available only to college students. ICADS can also place students with local social service organizations, environmental groups, and other organizations, depending on interests. The Costa Rica Rainforest Outward Bound School offers two adult programs that combine self-exploration with a truly rural learning experience.

Contacts **Costa Rica Rainforest Outward Bound School** (☎506/2278–6058, 800/676–2018 in the U.S.⊕www.crrobs.org). **Costa Rican Humanitarian Foundation** (☎506/8390–4192 in Costa Rica⊕www.crhf.org). **Institute for Central American Development Studies** (ICADS ☎506/2225–0508 in Costa Rica ⊕www.icads.org).

Caribbean Conservation Corporation (☎506/2297–5510 in Costa Rica, 352/373–6441 in the U.S.⊕www.cccturtle.org). **Earthwatch Institute** (☎978/461–0081 or 800/776–0188 in North America⊕www.earthwatch.org). **Talamancan Association**

of Ecotourism and Conservation (ATEC) (☎506/2750–0398 in Costa Rica ⊕www.greencoast.com/atec.htm).

VISITOR INFORMATION

The official tourism board, the Instituto Costarricense de Turismo (ICT), has free maps, bus schedules, and brochures. These folks could do better with the information they provide, but their Web site is comprehensive. Arrive armed with specific questions and know that they will not recommend hotels. At this writing, the Juan Santamaría airport desk had reopened. Visitor information is provided by the Costa Rica Tourist Board in Canada and in the United States.

Contacts **Instituto Costarricense de Turismo** (ICT ☎506/2299–5800, 866/267–8274 in North America ⊕www.visitcostarica.com ✉Juan Santamaría International Airport☎506/2443–1535 ⊗Closed Wed. and Sun. ✉Plaza de la Cultura, C. 5, Avdas. Central–2 ☎506/2222–1090).

ONLINE TRAVEL TOOLS

Info Costa Rica has a Web site with good cultural info, and chat rooms. For real estate, travel information, and traditional recipes, **Costa Rica.com** is a good bet. Horizontes is a tour operator that offers nature vacations but also has extensive information on Costa Rica and sustainable tourism on its Web site. The **U.S. Embassy's comprehensive site** has health information, travel warnings, lists of doctors and dentists, and much more. **The REAL Costa Rica** slips in a bit of attitude with its information, and is a bit lax on updating, but scores high marks for overall accuracy. Scope out detailed maps, driving distances, and pictorial guides to the locations of hotels and businesses in some communities at **Cos-**

taRicaMap.com. The **Association of Residents of Costa Rica** online forums are some of the region's most active and informed, with topics ranging from business and pleasure trips to the real-estate market. For current events, check out the English-language newspaper **the Tico Times**.

Contacts All About Costa Rica **Association of Residents of Costa Rica** online forums (⊕www.arcr.net). **The REAL Costa Rica** (⊕www.therealcostarica.com). **InfoCostaRica** (⊕www.infocostarica.com). **Costa Rica.com** (⊕www.costarica.com). **Horizontes** (⊕www.horizontes.com). **U.S. Embassy's Costa Rica** (⊕www.usembassy.or.cr). **The Tico Times** (⊕www.ticotimes.net).

INDEX

Photo Credits

5, *Ken Welsh/age fotostock.* 7, *Michael Javorka/viestiphoto.com.* 9 (left), 9 (left), *Jenny K. Frost.* 9 (right), *Juan Amighetti/Costa Rica Tourist Board (ICT).* 12 and 13, *Ken Ross/viestiphoto.com.* 14, *Philip Coblentz/Brand X Pictures.* 17 (left), *Jenny K. Frost.* 17 (right), *Ken Ross/viestiphoto.com.* 18, *Jenny K. Frost.* **Chapter 1: San José:** 23, *Costa Rica Tourist Board (ICT).* 24 (top), *Ken Ross/viestiphoto.com.* 24 (bottom), *José Fuste Raga/age fotostock.* 25 (top), *Ken Ross/viestiphoto.com.* 25 (bottom), *CostaRicaPhotos.com.* 26, *Ken Ross/viestiphoto.com.* 27, *Dan Peha/viestiphoto.com.* **Chapter 2: Central Valley:** 67, *Juan Amighetti/Costa Rica Tourist Board (ICT).* 68 (top), *Ken Ross/viestiphoto. com.* 68 (bottom), *Costa Rica Tourist Board (ICT).* 69 (top left), *Costa Rica Consulate.* 69 (top right), *Rios Tropicales.* 69 (bottom), *G. Cozzi /age fotostock.* 71, *Rancho Naturalista.* 99 (top), *Ken Ross/ viestiphoto.com.* 99 (bottom), *Philip Coblentz/Brand X Pictures.* 101, *Costa Rica Tourist Board (ICT).* 102, *Kevin Schafer/age fotostock.* 103, *Ken Ross/viestiphoto.com.* **Chapter 3: The Northern Plains:** 115, *Ken Ross/viestiphoto.com.* 116-18 (all), *Ken Ross/viestiphoto.com.* 132, *Ken Welsh/age fotostock.* 133, *Ken Ross/viestiphoto.com.* 144 (top), *Ken Ross/viestiphoto.com.* 144 (bottom) and 145 (top), *Sky Walk, Monteverde.* 145 (bottom), *Jenny K. Frost.* 146, *Ken Ross/viestiphoto.com.* **Chapter 4: The North Pacific:** 179, *Costa Rica Tourist Board (ICT).* 180 (top), *CostaRicaPhotos.com.* 180 (bottom), *Juan Amighetti/Costa Rica Tourist Board (ICT).* 181 (top left), *Ken Ross/viestiphoto.com.* 181 (top right), *Costa Rica Tourist Board (ICT).* 181 (bottom), *Alvaro Leiva/age fotostock.* 183, *Ken Ross/ viestiphoto.com.* 201 (top), *Ken Ross/viestiphoto.com.* 201 (bottom), *Joe Viesti/viestiphoto.com.* 202, *Ken Ross/viestiphoto.com.* 203 (top), *age fotostock.* 203 (center), *Hotel Luna Azul.* 203 (bottom), *Punta Islita Ocean Resort.* 204 (top), *Ken Ross/viestiphoto.com.* 204 (bottom), *Ken Ross/viestiphoto.com.* **Chapter 5: The Central Pacific:** 267, *Scott West/viestiphoto.com.* 268 (top), *CostaRicaPhotos.com.* 268 (center), *Juan Amighetti/Costa Rica Tourist Board (ICT).* 268 (bottom) and 269 (top), *Ken Ross/viestiphoto.com.* 269 (bottom), *Jenny K. Frost.* 270, *CostaRicaPhotos.com.* 315, *Philip Coblentz/Brand X Pictures.* 316, *Alvaro Leiva/age fotostock.* 317, *SuperStock/age fotostock.* 318, *Alison Skrabek.* 319, *Ken Ross/viestiphoto.com.* **Chapter 6: South Pacific:** 335 and 336, *Ken Ross/viestiphoto.com.* 337 (top left), *Costa Rica Tourist Board (ICT).* 337 (top right, center, and bottom) and 338, *Ken Ross/viestiphoto.com.* 393, *Ken Ross/viestiphoto.com.* 395 (first row left), *Ken Ross/viestiphoto.com.* 395 (first row center), *Philip Coblentz/Brand X Pictures.* 395 (first row right), *SuperStock/age fotostock.* 395 (second row left), *Robert Winslow/viestiphoto.com.* 395 (second row center), *Bill Terry/viestiphoto.com.* 395 (second row right), *Bill Terry/viestiphoto.com.* 395 (third row left), *Ken Ross/viestiphoto.com.* 395 (third row center), *Mary Clay/viestiphoto.com.* 395 (third row right), *Bill Terry/viestiphoto.com.* 395 (fourth row left), *Eric Horan/age fotostock.* 395 (fourth row center), *Kevin Schafer/age fotostock.* 395 (fourth row right), *Morales/age fotostock.* 395 (bottom), *Kevin Schafer/age fotostock.* **Chapter 7: The Caribbean Coast:** 403, *Alfredo Maiquez/age fotostock.* 404 (top), *Costa Rica Tourist Board (ICT).* 404 (bottom), *Alison Skrabek.* 405 (top left), *Costa Rica Tourist Board (ICT).* 405 (top right), *Ken Ross/ viestiphoto.com.* 405 (bottom), *Costa Rica Tourist Board (ICT).* 416, *Joe Viesti/viestiphoto.com.* 417, *Ken Ross/viestiphoto.com.* 418 (top), *Ken Ross/viestiphoto.com.* 418 (bottom), *Caribbean Conservation Corporation.* **Chapter 8: Ecotourism Costa Rica-Style:** 455, *Andoni Canela/age fotostock.* **Color Section:** View of Arenal Volcano on a clear day: *Ken Ross/viestiphoto.com.* Manuel Antonio National Park coastline: *Robert Winslow/viestiphoto.com.* Tica dancer performs at a cultural festival in San José: *Ken Ross/viestiphoto.com.* White-faced capuchin: *Philip Coblentz/Brand X Pictures.* Digging into Class-IV rapids on the Pacuáre River: *Dan Peha/viestiphoto.com.* Sky Walk's hanging-bridge hike in Monteverde Cloud Forest: *Ken Ross/viestiphoto.com.* A scarlet macaw and blue-and-gold macaw: *Kurt Ramseyer/viestiphoto.com.* Sun-seekers at Espadilla Beach, in Manuel Antonio National Park: *Alvaro Leiva/age fotostock.* Black river turtles hang out in Tortuguero: *Ken Ross/viestiphoto.com.* Coffee beans: *Michael Javorka/viestiphoto.com.* Painted oxcart: *Brand X Pictures.* The clear-blue crater lake at Poás Volcano: *Ken Ross/viestiphoto.com.* San José's Pre-Columbian Gold Museum: *Costa Rica Tourist Board.* Heliconia: *S. Murphy-Larronde/age fotostock.*

NOTES

NOTES

NOTES

NOTES